D0848347

WITHDRAWN

TOURO COLLEGE LIBRARY
*Bay Shore Campus*

# Multicultural Projects Index

# Multicultural Projects Index

TOURO COLLEGE LIBRARY
*Bay Shore Campus*

## Things to Make and Do to Celebrate Festivals, Cultures, and Holidays Around the World

**Fourth Edition**

*Mary Anne Pilger*

A Member of the Greenwood Publishing Group

Westport, Connecticut • London

BS

**Library of Congress Cataloging-in-Publication Data**

Pilger, Mary Anne.
    Multicultural projects index : things to make and do to celebrate festivals, cultures, and holidays around the world / Mary Anne Pilger.— 4th ed.
        p. cm.
    Includes bibliographical references and index.
    ISBN 1-59158-236-9 (alk. paper)
    1. Multicultural education—Bibliography. 2. Multicultural education—Activity programs—Indexes. 3. Festivals—Indexes. 4. Handicraft—Indexes. 5. Games—Indexes. I. Title.
    Z5814.M86P55 2005
    [LC1099]
    016.370117—dc22            2005011425

British Library Cataloguing in Publication Data is available.

Copyright © 2005 Mary Anne Pilger

All rights reserved. No portion of this book may be reproduced, by any process or technique, without the express written consent of the publisher.

Library of Congress Catalog Card Number: 2005011425
ISBN: 1-59158-236-9

First published in 2005

Libraries Unlimited, Inc., 88 Post Road West, Westport, CT 06881
A Member of Greenwood Publishing, Inc.
www.lu.com

Printed in the United States of America

The paper used in this book complies with the Permanent Paper Standard issued by the National Information Standards Organization (Z39.48–1984).

10 9 8 7 6 5 4 3 2 1

10 / 11 / 06

# Contents

Acknowledgments . . . . . . . . . . . . . . . . . . . . . . . . . . . ix

Introduction . . . . . . . . . . . . . . . . . . . . . . . . . . . . . xi

Subject Headings . . . . . . . . . . . . . . . . . . . . . . . . . . xiii

Key to Index . . . . . . . . . . . . . . . . . . . . . . . . . . . . . il

**ALPHABETICAL INDEX OF ENTRIES** . . . . . . . . . . . . . . . . . . 1

Books Indexed by Number . . . . . . . . . . . . . . . . . . . 183

Books Indexed by Author . . . . . . . . . . . . . . . . . . . . 207

 # Dedication

I dedicate this book to my son, Charles D. Pilger, who remains the lovely miracle of my life.

# Acknowledgments

I thank Mary Ann Still, Nancy Snickars, Mary and Ernie Franklin, and Jessica Macumber for all they have given me and for this book. And I thank them for the love they give my beagle Bonnie.

# Introduction

Crafts or handicrafts, those things we create in our minds and make with our hands, have been the visible proof of humankind's existence on our Earth; the visible demonstrations of cultures, now and in the past; the visible proof of humankind's struggle to find its very reason for being; the visible proof that humans and their cultures are different and unique.

The drive to create, to make, is inherent to human interpretation of the world. Human creations, crafts, or handicrafts give us a window to observe lives we cannot live or know. Our fragile existence on this Earth is measured by what we create, what we do with what we have; these creations leave a historical record for all to observe and interpret.

People, in their uniqueness, in their differences, and in their similarities, are what make the world's peoples so special. Before people can live in peace, there must be understanding, understanding the geography determines how they live and that their culture—their ethnic being—evolves from their need for survival and their need for self-expression. Adaptation to one's environment means providing food, clothing, and shelter. Adaptation to one's personal environment means providing customs for personal growth and creativity. Spiritual and family customs, language and speaking customs, music and dance customs, festival and holiday customs, folklore and games customs—these customs, from the most primitive tribes to our most sophisticated nations, are what makes us the same—and different.

We are now a country of many cultures, and our schools and classrooms are evidence of this. Almost every teacher today faces classrooms made up of children from many cultural backgrounds. Festivals, holidays, and family celebrations are no longer from only our older traditional American celebrations. Today educators need to know the importance and significance of cultural traditions from many countries, and they also need to know how to have all students understand the similarities and differences of these celebrations.

Books in this index represent a vast storehouse of knowledge and information about world cultures and their handicrafts. Each author is an artist bringing to his or her book an intensity and view based on his or her own personal inspiration to write a book about a particular handicraft from a particular culture or cultures.

Educators need the information that this multicultural projects index provides for crafts, clothing, and special activities for holiday celebrations and religious observances, such as the Mexican Cinco de Mayo, the Indian Holi Festival, the Japanese Boys Day Carp Festival, and the Fourth of July. Children's literature provides what is needed for classroom teachers to have meaningful programs; this index is a key to open the door to such information in children's books.

Multicultural was, is, and always will be a part of our lives. We live in a global village today, especially here in the United States with so many diverse cultures living here today. It is my dream and hope that this book will lead many interested teachers and students into the cultures of many countries through this index to festivals, handicrafts, foods, games, and more.

# Subject Headings

This listing contains all the used in the text. Consult the text for cross-references between headings.

ABORIGINES—BARK
    PAINTING
ABORIGINES—FOLKLORE
ABORIGINES—MUSICAL
    INSTRUMENTS
ACADIANS—COOKERY
ACOMA INDIANS—
    POTTERY
ADAMS, ABIGAIL (FIRST
    LADY)—COOKERY
ADAMS, JOHN
    (PRESIDENT)
ADAMS, JOHN QUINCY
    (PRESIDENT)
ADVENT—DECORATIONS
ADVENT—PUPPETS
AESOP'S FABLES
AESOP'S FABLES—
    PUPPETS
AFGHANISTAN—COOKERY
AFGHANISTAN—GAMES
AFGHANISTAN—JEWELRY
AFGHANISTAN—
    LANGUAGE
AFRICA—ANIMALS
AFRICA—COOKERY
AFRICA—COSTUMES
AFRICA—FOLKLORE
AFRICA—GAMES
AFRICA—HOUSES
AFRICA—JEWELRY
AFRICA—MASKS
AFRICA—MUSICAL
    INSTRUMENTS
AFRICA—PAPER CHAINS
AFRICA, CENTRAL—
    JEWELRY

AFRICA, CENTRAL—
    SCULPTURES
AFRICA, EAST—COOKERY
AFRICA, EAST—
    FESTIVALS—
    COOKERY
AFRICA, EAST—JEWELRY
AFRICA, EAST—
    SCULPTURES
AFRICA, NORTH—
    COOKERY
AFRICA, NORTH—
    PASSOVER—
    COOKERY
AFRICA, SOUTH—
    ANCIENT ART
AFRICA, SOUTH—
    ANIMALS
AFRICA, SOUTH—
    BIRTHDAYS—
    FACE PAINT
AFRICA, SOUTH—DOLLS
AFRICA, SOUTH—TOYS
AFRICA, WEST—ADINKRA
    CLOTH
AFRICA, WEST—CHARMS
AFRICA, WEST—
    CHRISTMAS—
    COOKERY
AFRICA, WEST—COOKERY
AFRICA, WEST—DOLLS
AFRICA, WEST—
    FESTIVALS—
    COOKERY
AFRICA, WEST—FLAGS
AFRICA, WEST—
    HANDICRAFTS
AFRICA, WEST—MASKS

AFRICA, WEST—MIDDLE
    AGES—GAMES
AFRICA, WEST—MIDDLE
    AGES—TIMBUKTU
AFRICA, WEST—MIDDLE
    AGES—TIMBUKTU—
    KINGS
AFRICA, WEST—MUD
    CLOTH
AFRICA, WEST—
    PAINTINGS
AFRICAN AMERICAN
    MONTH
AFRO-AMERICANS
AFRO-AMERICANS—
    CIVIL RIGHTS—
    HISTORY
AFRO-AMERICANS—
    CIVIL RIGHTS—
    HISTORY— COOKERY
AFRO-AMERICANS—
    COLONIAL AMERICA—
    SLAVE TRADE
AFRO-AMERICANS—
    COOKERY
AFRO-AMERICANS—
    DANCES
AFRO-AMERICANS—
    FICTION
AFRO-AMERICANS—
    FOLKLORE
AFRO-AMERICANS—
    GAMES
AFRO-AMERICANS—HAIR
AFRO-AMERICANS—
    HANDICRAFTS
AFRO-AMERICANS—
    HISTORY

AFRO-AMERICANS—
   HISTORY—CIVIL WAR
AFRO-AMERICANS—
   HISTORY—CIVIL
   WAR—FUNDRAISERS
AFRO-AMERICANS—
   HISTORY—CIVIL
   WAR— QUILTING
AFRO-AMERICANS—
   HISTORY—COLONIAL
   PERIOD—COOKERY
AFRO-AMERICANS—
   HISTORY—COOKERY
AFRO-AMERICANS—
   HISTORY—COWBOYS
AFRO-AMERICANS—
   HISTORY—
   EMANCIPATION—
   COOKERY
AFRO-AMERICANS—
   HISTORY—FESTIVALS
AFRO-AMERICANS—
   HISTORY—
   PLANTATION LIFE—
   COOKERY
AFRO-AMERICANS—
   HISTORY—
   PLANTATION LIFE—
   DOLLS
AFRO-AMERICANS—
   HISTORY—
   PLANTATION LIFE—
   GAMES
AFRO-AMERICANS—
   HISTORY—
   PLANTATION LIFE—
   MUSIC
AFRO-AMERICANS—
   HISTORY—
   PLANTATION LIFE—
   TOYS
AFRO-AMERICANS—
   HISTORY—
   REVOLUTIONARY
   WAR—GAMES
AFRO-AMERICANS—
   HISTORY—

REVOLUTIONARY
   WAR—SHIPS
AFRO-AMERICANS—
   HISTORY—SLAVERY
AFRO-AMERICANS—
   HISTORY—
   UNDERGROUND
   RAILROAD
AFRO-AMERICANS—
   HISTORY—UNDERGRO
   UND RAILROAD—
   FREEDOM TRAIL
AFRO-AMERICANS—
   HISTORY—
   UNDERGROUND
   RAILROAD—INDIANS
AFRO-AMERICANS—MASKS
AFRO-AMERICANS—
   MUSICAL
   INSTRUMENTS
AFRO-AMERICANS—
   PUPPETS
AFRO-AMERICANS—
   QUILTING
AFRO-AMERICANS—
   SLAVERY
ALABAMA—COOKERY
ALAMO—COOKERY
ALASKA—COOKERY
ALASKA—FOLKLORE—
   COOKERY
ALASKA—LANGUAGE
ALBANIAN-AMERICANS—
   COOKERY
ALEUTS—COOKERY
ALGERIA—COOKERY
ALGONQUIN INDIANS
ALGONQUIN INDIANS—
   MUSICAL INSTRUMENTS
ALICE IN
   WONDERLAND—TEA
   PARTIES—COOKERY
AMISH—COOKERY
AMISH—QUILTS
ANASAZI INDIANS—
   COOKERY
ANGELICO, FRA
   GIOVANNI

ANGLO-AMERICANS—
   COOKERY
ANTARCTICA
ANTARCTICA—ICEBERGS
ANTARCTICA—PENGUINS
ANTARCTICA—WHALES
ANTHONY, SUSAN B.
ANTHONY, SUSAN B.—
   BIRTHDAY
APACHE INDIANS—
   BASKETS
APACHE INDIANS—
   COOKERY
APACHE INDIANS—FACE
   PAINTS
APACHE INDIANS—
   GAMES
APACHE INDIANS—
   LANGUAGE
APPALACHIA—FOLKLORE
APPLES
APRIL FOOL'S DAY
APRIL FOOL'S DAY—
   COOKERY
APRIL FOOL'S DAY—
   DECORATIONS
APRIL FOOL'S DAY—
   FICTION
APRIL FOOL'S DAY—SOAP
APRIL THEMES
ARAB-AMERICANS—
   COOKERY
ARAPAHO INDIANS—
   GAMES
ARAPAHO INDIANS—
   POUCHES
ARBOR DAY
ARBOR DAY—
   DECORATIONS
ARCHITECTURE
ARCHITECTURE—GOTHIC
   STYLE
ARCTIC ANIMALS
ARCTIC INDIANS—DOLLS
ARCTIC INDIANS—
   KAYAKS
ARCTIC INDIANS—MASKS

BARBADOS—HANDICRAFTS
BARRIE, J. M.
BASQUE-AMERICANS—
    COOKERY
BASQUE PEOPLE—
    COOKERY
BAULE (AFRICAN
    PEOPLES)—MASKS
BAUM, FRANK L.
BEARS
BELGIAN-AMERICANS—
    COOKERY
BELGIUM—CHRISTMAS—
    COOKERY
BELGIUM—CHRISTMAS—
    HANDICRAFTS
BELGIUM—COOKERY
BELGIUM—FOLKLORE
BELGIUM—GAMES
BELGIUM—NEW YEAR—
    HANDICRAFTS
BELIZE—COOKERY
BELORUSSIAN-AMERICANS—
    COOKERY
BENTLEY, WILSON A.
BIBLE
BIBLE—AUTUMN CRAFTS
BIBLE—DESERT—CLOTHES
BIBLE—DESERT—COOKERY
BIBLE—DESERT—GAMES
BIBLE—DESERT—HOUSES
BIBLE—DESERT—JEWELRY
BIBLE—DESERT—RELIGION
BIBLE—DESERT—WEAVING
BIBLE—EGYPT,
    ANCIENT—BRICKS
BIBLE—EGYPT,
    ANCIENT—COOKERY
BIBLE—EGYPT,
    ANCIENT—DOLLS
BIBLE—EGYPT,
    ANCIENT—GAMES
BIBLE—EGYPT,
    ANCIENT—MUSICAL
    INSTRUMENTS
BIBLE—EGYPT,
    ANCIENT—WEAPONS
BIBLE—GAMES

BIBLE—GOOD FRIDAY
BIBLE—HANDICRAFTS
BIBLE—HANDICRAFTS—
    ADVENT
BIBLE—HANDICRAFTS—
    ANGELS
BIBLE—HANDICRAFTS—
    CHRISTMAS
BIBLE—HANDICRAFTS—
    CREATION MOBILE
BIBLE—HANDICRAFTS—
    CROSSES
BIBLE—HANDICRAFTS—
    EASTER
BIBLE—HANDICRAFTS—
    FATHER'S DAY
BIBLE—HANDICRAFTS—
    JONAH AND THE
    WHALE
BIBLE—HANDICRAFTS—
    MOSES
BIBLE—HANDICRAFTS—
    MOTHER'S DAY
BIBLE—HANDICRAFTS—
    NATIVITY AND
    EPIPHANY
BIBLE—HANDICRAFTS—
    NOAH'S ARK
BIBLE—HANDICRAFTS—
    PALM SUNDAY—
    DECORATIONS
BIBLE—HANDICRAFTS—
    PENTECOST
BIBLE—HANDICRAFTS—
    PUPPETS
BIBLE—HANDICRAFTS—
    VACATION BIBLE
    SCHOOL
BIBLE—ISRAELITES—
    ARMOR
BIBLE—ISRAELITES—
    CALENDAR
BIBLE—ISRAELITES—
    CANAAN—MAP
BIBLE—ISRAELITES—
    HOUSES
BIBLE—ISRAELITES—
    LAMPS

BIBLE—ISRAELITES—
    MEASUREMENT
BIBLE—ISRAELITES—
    MUSICAL
    INSTRUMENTS
BIBLE—ISRAELITES—
    NAMES
BIBLE—ISRAELITES—
    RELIGION
BIBLE—ISRAELITES—
    SCROLLS
BIBLE—ISRAELITES—
    SPICES
BIBLE—ISRAELITES—
    TITHES
BIBLE—NEW TESTAMENT
BIBLE—OLD TESTAMENT
BIBLE—PALM SUNDAY
BIBLE—PLAYS
BIBLE—PUPPETS
BIBLE—SPECIAL DAYS
BIBLE—SPRING CRAFTS
BIBLE—SUMMER CRAFTS
BIBLE—TEN
    COMMANDMENTS
BIBLE—TWELVE TRIBES—
    MAP
BIBLE—WEAPONS
BIBLE—WINTER CRAFTS
BIBLE STORIES—
    COOKERY
BIRDS
BIRTHDAYS
BIRTHDAYS—FICTION
BLACK MUSLIMS—
    COOKERY
BLACKFEET INDIANS—
    COOKERY
BLACKFEET INDIANS—
    LANGUAGE
BLAKE, WILLIAM
BOATS
BOBO (AFRICAN
    PEOPLES)—MASKS
BOLIVIA—CHRISTMAS—
    DECORATIONS
BOLIVIA—COOKERY
BOLIVIA—GAMES

BOLIVIA—GOD'S EYE
BOLIVIA—LANGUAGE
BOSNIA—GAMES
BOSTON TEA PARTY—
    COOKERY
BOSTON TEA
    PARTY—GAMES
BOTSWANA—GAMES
BOTTICELLI, SANDRO
BOURKE-WHITE,
    MARGARET
BRAQUE, GEORGES
BRAZIL—BIRTHDAYS—
    COOKERY
BRAZIL—BIRTHDAYS—
    GAMES
BRAZIL—CHRISTMAS—
    COOKERY
BRAZIL—COOKERY
BRAZIL—FESTIVALS—
    COOKERY
BRAZIL—FESTIVALS—
    FLAGS
BRAZIL—FESTIVALS—
    HANDICRAFTS
BRAZIL—FESTIVALS—
    HEADDRESSES
BRAZIL—FESTIVALS—
    JEWELRY
BRAZIL—FESTIVALS—
    MASKS
BRAZIL—FESTIVALS—
    SONGS
BRAZIL—FLAGS
BRAZIL—FOLKLORE
BRAZIL—GAMES
BRAZIL—LANGUAGE
BRAZIL—MUSICAL
    INSTRUMENTS
BRAZIL—NEW YEAR—
    COOKERY
BRAZIL—RAIN STICKS
BRAZILIAN-AMERICANS—
    COOKERY
BRITISH-AMERICANS—
    COOKERY
BUCHANAN, JAMES
    (PRESIDENT)

BUFFALO
BULGARIA—GAMES
BULGARIAN-AMERICANS
    — COOKERY
BUNTING, EVE
BUNYAN, PAUL
BURKINA FASO—
    CHRISTMAS—COOKERY
BURMA—COOKERY
BURMA—FOLKLORE
BURMA—PASSOVER—
    COOKERY
BURNETT, FRANCES
    HODGSON
BURTON, VIRGINIA LEE
BUSH, GEORGE H. W.
    (PRESIDENT)
BUSINESS

CAJUNS—COOKERY
CALDER, ALEXANDER
CALIFORNIA—COOKERY
CALIFORNIA INDIANS—
    FOLKLORE
CAMBODIA—GAMES
CAMBODIAN-AMERICANS—
    COOKERY
CAMEROON—BEADWORK
CAMEROON—CLAY TILES
CAMEROON—COOKERY
CAMEROON—GAMES
CAMEROON—LANGUAGE
CANADA—CHRISTMAS—
    COOKERY
CANADA—CHRISTMAS—
    DECORATIONS
CANADA—COOKERY
CANADA—FESTIVALS
CANADA—GAMES
CANADA—HANDICRAFTS
CANADA—LANGUAGE
CANADA—NEW YEAR—
    COOKERY
CANADA—NEW YEAR—
    MUSICAL
    INSTRUMENTS
CANADA—TOTEM POLES
CANALS

CANDLES
CANDY
CANDY—COOKERY
CAPE VERDEAN-
    AMERICANS—
    COOKERY
CAREERS
CARIBBEAN ISLANDS—
    CARS
CARIBBEAN ISLANDS—
    COOKERY
CARIBBEAN ISLANDS—
    EASTER—COOKERY
CARIBBEAN ISLANDS—
    FESTIVALS—COOKERY
CARIBBEAN ISLANDS—
    GAMES
CARIBBEAN ISLANDS—
    MUSICAL
    INSTRUMENTS
CARNIVAL
CARPATHO-RUSYN
    AMERICANS—
    COOKERY
CARTER, JAMES EARL
    (PRESIDENT)
CARVER, GEORGE
    WASHINGTON
CARVER, GEORGE
    WASHINGTON—
    HANDICRAFTS
CASSATT, MARY
CASTLES—COOKERY
CATAWBA INDIANS—
    COOKERY
CATS
CELTS—ARMOR
CELTS—BOOKS
CELTS—COOKERY
CELTS—GAMES
CELTS—HANDICRAFTS
CELTS—HOUSEHOLD
    ITEMS
CELTS—HOUSES
CELTS—JEWELRY
CELTS—METALWORK
CELTS—MUSICAL
    INSTRUMENTS

CELTS—RELIGION
CELTS—SYMBOLS
CELTS—TRANSPORTATION
CELTS—WRITINGS IN
	STONE
CENTRAL AMERICA—
	MUSICAL
	INSTRUMENTS
CENTRAL AMERICA—
	WEAVER
CEZANNE, PAUL
CHAGALL, MARC
CHALDEAN AMERICANS—
	COOKERY
CHALK
CHAMBERLAIN, JOHN
CHEERLEADING
CHEROKEE INDIANS—
	BASKETS
CHEROKEE INDIANS—
	COOKERY
CHEROKEE INDIANS—
	FOLKLORE
CHEROKEE INDIANS—
	LANGUAGE
CHEYENNE INDIANS—
	COOKERY
CHEYENNE INDIANS—
	GAMES
CHEYENNE INDIANS—
	HOUSES
CHEYENNE INDIANS—
	JEWELRY
CHEYENNE INDIANS—
	LANGUAGE
CHEYENNE INDIANS—
	MUSICAL
	INSTRUMENTS
CHEYENNE INDIANS—
	SHIELDS
CHICKASAW INDIANS—
	COOKERY
CHICKASAW INDIANS—
	DANCES
CHICKASAW INDIANS—
	FOLKLORE
CHILDREN'S BOOK WEEK

CHILE—CHRISTMAS—
	COOKERY
CHILE—COOKERY
CHILE—FESTIVALS—
	COOKERY
CHILE—FLAGS
CHILE—GAMES
CHILE—NEW YEAR—
	HANDICRAFTS
CHILE—STATUES
CHINA—BIRTH
	CUSTOMS—COOKERY
CHINA—BIRTHDAYS—
	COOKERY
CHINA—BOATS
CHINA—CHOPSTICKS
CHINA—CLOTHING
CHINA—COOKERY
CHINA—DRAGONS
CHINA—EMBROIDERY
CHINA—FANS
CHINA—FESTIVALS—
	COOKERY
CHINA—FESTIVALS—
	DECORATIONS
CHINA—FESTIVALS—
	DRAGONS
CHINA—FESTIVALS—
	GAMES
CHINA—FESTIVALS—
	HANDICRAFTS
CHINA—FESTIVALS—
	KITES
CHINA—FESTIVALS—
	LANTERNS
CHINA—FESTIVALS—
	PRINTS
CHINA—FESTIVALS—
	PUPPETS
CHINA—FESTIVALS—
	ZODIAC
CHINA—FICTION
CHINA—FOLKLORE
CHINA—GAMES
CHINA—HANDICRAFTS
CHINA—KITES
CHINA—LANGUAGE
CHINA—LANTERNS

CHINA—NEW YEAR—
	PUPPETS
CHINA—NEW YEAR'S
	DAY—COOKERY
CHINA—NUMBERS
CHINA—OPERA—MASKS
CHINA—PAPER CUTTING
CHINA—PAPERMAKING
CHINA—PUPPETS
CHINA—SCROLLS
CHINA—TANGRAMS
CHINA—TEA
	PARTIES—COOKERY
CHINA—TEA PARTIES—
	HANDICRAFTS
CHINA—TOYS
CHINA, ANCIENT—
	ABACUS
CHINA, ANCIENT—ARMOR
CHINA, ANCIENT—
	COOKERY
CHINA, ANCIENT—FANS
CHINA, ANCIENT—
	FESTIVALS—
	LANTERNS
CHINA, ANCIENT—
	HOUSES
CHINA, ANCIENT—
	INVENTIONS
CHINA, ANCIENT—
	JEWELRY
CHINA, ANCIENT—KITES
CHINA, ANCIENT—MASKS
CHINA, ANCIENT—
	MUSICAL
	INSTRUMENTS
CHINA, ANCIENT—
	PAGODAS
CHINA, ANCIENT—PAPER
	CUTTING
CHINA, ANCIENT—
	PRINTING
CHINA, ANCIENT—
	SAMPANS
CHINESE-AMERICANS—
	BRUSH PAINTINGS
CHINESE-AMERICANS—
	CHINESE NEW
	YEAR—COOKERY

COWBOYS—GAMES
COWBOYS—HATS
COWBOYS—PUPPETS
COWBOYS—ROPES
COWBOYS—TOYS
CRAYONS
CREE INDIANS—
    FOOTWEAR
CREE INDIANS—GAMES
CREEK INDIANS—
    COOKERY
CREOLES—CANE RIVER
    CREOLES—COOKERY
CREOLES—COOKERY
CROATIA—GAMES
CROATIA—LANGUAGE
CROATIAN-AMERICANS—
    COOKERY
CROW INDIANS—GAMES
CUBA—COOKERY
CUBA—DOLLS
CUBA—FESTIVALS—
    COOKERY
CUBA—GAMES
CUBAN-AMERICANS—
    COOKERY
CUSHMAN, KAREN
CZECH-AMERICANS—
    COOKERY
CZECH REPUBLIC—
    CHRISTMAS—
    COOKERY
CZECH REPUBLIC—
    CHRISTMAS—
    DECORATIONS
CZECH REPUBLIC—
    COOKERY
CZECH REPUBLIC—DOLLS
CZECH REPUBLIC—
    GAMES
CZECH REPUBLIC—
    HANDICRAFTS
CZECH REPUBLIC—
    LANGUAGE
CZECHOSLOVAKIA—
    GAMES

DA VINCI, LEONARDO

DA VINCI, LEONARDO—
    BIOGRAPHY
DA VINCI, LEONARDO—
    COOKERY
DA VINCI, LEONARDO—
    HERBS
DA VINCI, LEONARDO—
    MEASUREMENTS
DA VINCI, LEONARDO—
    MUSICAL
    INSTRUMENTS
DAHOMEY—GAMES
DAKOTA INDIANS—
    COOKERY
DAKOTA INDIANS—
    LANGUAGE
DAKOTA INDIANS—
    MOCCASINS
DAKOTA INDIANS—
    SONGS
DAKOTA INDIANS—
    WINTER COUNT
DAKOTA INDIANS. *See also*
    SIOUX INDIANS
DALI, SALVADORE
DALMATIANS. *See*
    CROATIAN
    AMERICANS
DANCING
DANCING—TEA PARTIES—
    COOKERY
DANISH-AMERICANS—
    COOKERY
DAVIS, JIM
DE REGNIERS, BEATRICE
    SCHENK
DEBRUNHOFF, JEAN
DECEMBER THEMES
DEGAS, EDGAR
DELAWARE—COOKERY
DELAWARE—FESTIVALS
    —COOKERY
DELAWARE INDIANS—
    DECORATIONS
DELAWARE
    INDIANS—MUSICAL
    INSTRUMENTS

DENMARK—CHRISTMAS
    —COOKERY
DENMARK—CHRISTMAS
    —DECORATIONS
DENMARK—COOKERY
DENMARK—FOLKLORE
DENMARK—GAMES
DENMARK—LANGUAGE
DEPAOLA, TOMIE
DESERTS—FICTION
DEWEY, MELVILLE—
    BIRTHDAY
DINEH INDIANS. *See*
    NAVAHO INDIANS
DINOSAURS
DOGON (AFRICAN
    PEOPLES)—MASKS
DOGS
DOLLS
DOMINICAN-AMERICANS—
    COOKERY
DOMINICAN REPUBLIC—
    COOKERY
DOUGHS
DRAGONS
DRAGONS—PUPPETS
DRAWING
DUCHAMP, MARCEL
DÜRER, ALBRECHT
DUTCH-AMERICANS—
    COOKERY
DYES

EAGLES
EARHART, AMELIA
EARTH DAY
EARTH DAY—
    DECORATIONS
EARTH DAY—FICTION
EARTH DAY—RECYCLING
EASTER
EASTER—COOKERY
EASTER—DECORATIONS
EASTER—FICTION
EASTER—HANDICRAFTS
EASTER—MASKS
EASTER—PUPPETS
EASTER—SOAP

FOURTH OF JULY—
COOKERY
FOURTH OF JULY—
DECORATIONS
FOURTH OF JULY—
FICTION
FOURTH OF JULY—MASKS
FOURTH OF JULY—
PUPPETS
FOURTH OF JULY—TOYS
FOX INDIANS—JEWELRY
FRANCE—BUILDINGS
FRANCE—CHRISTMAS—
COOKERY
FRANCE—COOKERY
FRANCE—COOKERY—
FRILLS
FRANCE—EASTER—
COOKERY
FRANCE—FESTIVALS—
COOKERY
FRANCE—FESTIVALS—
HANDICRAFTS
FRANCE—FICTION
FRANCE—FOLKLORE
FRANCE—GAMES
FRANCE—LANGUAGE
FRANCE—SILHOUETTES
FRANCE—TOYS
FRENCH-AMERICANS—
COOKERY
FRENCH-AMERICANS—
FESTIVALS—COOKERY
FRENCH-AMERICANS—
HERBS
FRENCH-CANADIAN
AMERICANS—COOKERY
FROG PRINCE
FRONTIER AND PIONEER
LIFE—CANALS
FRONTIER AND PIONEER
LIFE—CHRISTMAS—
DECORATIONS
FRONTIER AND PIONEER
LIFE—CLOTHING
FRONTIER AND PIONEER
LIFE—COOKERY

FRONTIER AND PIONEER
LIFE—DIARIES
FRONTIER AND PIONEER
LIFE—DOLLS
FRONTIER AND PIONEER
LIFE—FICTION
FRONTIER AND PIONEER
LIFE—FOOD
FRONTIER AND PIONEER
LIFE—FOOTWEAR
FRONTIER AND PIONEER
LIFE—GAMES
FRONTIER AND PIONEER
LIFE—HANDICRAFTS
FRONTIER AND PIONEER
LIFE—HOUSES
FRONTIER AND PIONEER
LIFE—JOURNALS
FRONTIER AND PIONEER
LIFE—LANTERNS
FRONTIER AND PIONEER
LIFE—LOG CABINS
FRONTIER AND PIONEER
LIFE—MUSICAL
INSTRUMENTS
FRONTIER AND PIONEER
LIFE—PADDLEBOATS
FRONTIER AND PIONEER
LIFE—QUILTING
FRONTIER AND PIONEER
LIFE—RAILROADS
FRONTIER AND PIONEER
LIFE—SCHOOLS
FRONTIER AND PIONEER
LIFE—TOOLS
FRONTIER AND PIONEER
LIFE—TOYS
FRONTIER AND PIONEER
LIFE—
TRANSPORTATION
FRONTIER AND PIONEER
LIFE—TRUNKS

GABON—STATUES
GAINSBOROUGH, THOMAS
GALAPAGOS ISLANDS
GAMBIA (AFRICAN
PEOPLES)—JEWELRY

GARFIELD, JAMES ABRAM
(PRESIDENT)
GARGOYLES—MASKS
GARIFUNA-AMERICANS—
COOKERY
GAUGUIN, PAUL
GEECHEE. *See* GULLAH
GEORGIA—COOKERY
GERMAN-AMERICANS—
COOKERY
GERMANS FROM
RUSSIA—COOKERY
GERMANY—BIRTHDAYS
—CANDLES
GERMANY—BIRTHDAYS
—COOKERY
GERMANY—CASTLES
GERMANY—CHRISTMAS
—COOKERY
GERMANY—CHRISTMAS
—DECORATIONS
GERMANY—CHRISTMAS
—HANDICRAFTS
GERMANY—COOKERY
GERMANY—EASTER—
COOKERY
GERMANY—EPIPHANY—
COOKERY
GERMANY—FESTIVALS—
COOKERY
GERMANY—FESTIVALS—
DECORATIONS
GERMANY—FESTIVALS—
LANTERNS
GERMANY—FOLKLORE
GERMANY—GAMES
GERMANY—LANGUAGE
GERMANY—NEW YEAR'S
DAY—COOKERY
GERMANY—NEW YEAR'S
DAY—GAMES
GERMANY—
PAPERCUTTING
GHANA—CHRISTMAS—
DECORATIONS
GHANA—CLOTHING
GHANA—COOKERY
GHANA—GAMES

GRENADA—HANDICRAFTS
GRIMM TALES
GROUNDHOG DAY
GROUNDHOG DAY—
    COOKERY
GROUNDHOG DAY—
    FICTION
GROUNDHOG DAY—
    PUPPETS
GRUELLE, JOHNNY
GRUELLE, JOHNNY—
    COOKERY
GRUELLE, JOHNNY—
    FICTION
GRUELLE, JOHNNY—
    GAMES
GUAMIANS (CHAMOROS)—
    COOKERY
GUATEMALA—COAT OF
    ARMS
GUATEMALA—COOKERY
GUATEMALA—
    DECORATIONS
GUATEMALA—DOLLS
GUATEMALA—FLAGS
GUATEMALA—GAMES
GUATEMALA—
    HANDICRAFTS
GUATEMALA—WEAVING
GUATEMALAN-
    AMERICANS—
    COOKERY
GUINEA—GAMES
GULLAH (GEECHEE AND
    SEA ISLANDERS)—
    COOKERY
GUYANA—GAMES
GUYANESE-AMERICANS
    (AND INDO-
    CARIBBEANS)—
    COOKERY
GYPSIES—HANDICRAFTS
GYPSY-AMERICANS
    (ROMANICHALS,
    TRAVELLERS, AND
    ROMA)—COOKERY

HAIDA INDIANS

HAIDA INDIANS—
    BASKETS
HAIDA INDIANS—
    COOKERY
HAIDA INDIANS—
    JEWELRY
HAIDA INDIANS—
    LANGUAGE
HAIDA INDIANS—
    MUSICAL
    INSTRUMENTS
HAITI—COOKERY
HAITI—FESTIVALS—
    HEADDRESSES
HAITI—GAMES
HAITI—HANDICRAFTS
HAITI—LANGUAGE
HAITI—NEW YEAR—
    FLAGS
HAITIAN-AMERICANS—
    COOKERY
HALL, DONALD
HALLOWEEN
HALLOWEEN—COOKERY
HALLOWEEN—COSTUMES
HALLOWEEN—
    DECORATIONS
HALLOWEEN—FACE
    PAINT
HALLOWEEN—FICTION
HALLOWEEN—GAMES
HALLOWEEN—JEWELRY
HALLOWEEN—MASKS
HALLOWEEN—PUPPETS
HALLOWEEN—SOAP
HAMBURGERS—HISTORY
HANUKKAH
HANUKKAH—BLESSINGS
HANUKKAH—COOKERY
HANUKKAH—DECORATIONS
HANUKKAH—DOLLS
HANUKKAH—FICTION
HANUKKAH—GAMES
HANUKKAH—HANDICRAFTS
HANUKKAH—PUPPETS
HARDING, WILLIAM
    (PRESIDENT)

HARRISON, BENJAMIN
    (PRESIDENT)
HARRISON, WILLIAM
    HENRY (PRESIDENT)
HARVEST
HARVEST—DECORATIONS
HAWAII
HAWAII—CLOTHING
HAWAII—COOKERY
HAWAII—COSTUMES
HAWAII—FESTIVALS
HAWAII—FOLKLORE
HAWAII—GAMES
HAWAII—LEIS
HAWAII—LUAU
HAWAII—QUILTING
HAYES, RUTHERFORD B.
    (PRESIDENT)
HEBREW LANGUAGE
HENNY PENNY
HIDATSA INDIANS—
    BOATS
HIDATSA INDIANS—
    COOKERY
HIDATSA INDIANS—
    GAMES
HIDATSA INDIANS—
    GARDENS
HINDUS—FESTIVALS—
    COOKERY
HINDUS—FESTIVALS—
    PLAYS
HINDUS—GAMES
HINDUS—YOGA
HIPPIES
HISPANIC AMERICANS—
    COOKERY
HISPANIC
    AMERICANS—DOLLS
HISPANIC HERITAGE
    MONTH—HEADBANDS
HISPANIC HERITAGE
    MONTH—
    HEADDRESSES
HMONG-AMERICANS—
    COOKERY
HOH INDIANS—COOKERY
HOKUSAI, KATSUSHIKA

HOLY WEEK—
    DECORATIONS
HOMER, WINSLOW
HONDURAN-AMERICANS—
    COOKERY
HONDURAS—FLAGS
HONG KONG—GAMES
HOOVER, HERBERT
    (PRESIDENT)
HOPI INDIANS—COOKERY
HOPI INDIANS—HOUSES
HOPI INDIANS—KACHINA
    DOLLS
HOPI INDIANS—POTTERY
HOPI INDIANS—TOYS
HORSES
HOUSES—FICTION
HOUSES—PUPPETS
HUICHOL INDIANS—
    FESTIVALS—SHIELDS
HUICHOL
    INDIANS—GOD'S EYE
HUNGARIAN-AMERICANS
    —COOKERY
HUNGARY—CHRISTMAS—
    COOKERY
HUNGARY—COOKERY
HUNGARY—DECORATIONS
HUNGARY—GAMES
HURON INDIANS—
    LANGUAGE

ICE CREAM CONE—
    HISTORY
ICELAND—CHRISTMAS—
    DECORATIONS
ICELAND—GAMES
ICELANDIC AMERICANS—
    COOKERY
IDAHO—COOKERY
IDAHO—FESTIVALS—
    COOKERY
ILLINOIS—COOKERY
IMMIGRANTS—FICTION
INCAS—BOATS
INCAS—CLOTHING
INCAS—COOKERY
INCAS—EMPERORS

INCAS—FUNERALS
INCAS—GODS
INCAS—GRANERIES
INCAS—HEADBANDS
INCAS—HEADDRESSES
INCAS—JEWELRY
INCAS—MATHEMATICS
INCAS—MEDICINE
INCAS—MUSICAL
    INSTRUMENTS
INCAS—POTTERY
INCAS—WARRIORS
INDIA—BATIK
INDIA—BIRTHDAYS—
    PUPPETS
INDIA—CHRISTMAS—
    DECORATIONS
INDIA—COOKERY
INDIA—DANCES
INDIA—ELEPHANTS
INDIA—FESTIVALS
INDIA—FESTIVALS—
    COOKERY
INDIA—FESTIVALS—
    DECORATIONS
INDIA—FESTIVALS—
    ELEPHANTS
INDIA—FESTIVALS—
    GAMES
INDIA—FESTIVALS—
    HANDICRAFTS
INDIA—FESTIVALS—
    LAMPS
INDIA—FESTIVALS—PETS
INDIA—FOLKLORE
INDIA—GAMES
INDIA—HANDICRAFTS
INDIA—LANGUAGE
INDIA—TEA PARTIES—
    COOKERY
INDIA—TEA PARTIES—
    HANDICRAFTS
INDIA—YOGA
INDIANA—COOKERY
INDIANS OF NORTH
    AMERICA
INDIANS OF NORTH
    AMERICA—BASKETS

INDIANS OF NORTH
    AMERICA—
    BULLROARER
INDIANS OF NORTH
    AMERICA—CANOES
INDIANS OF NORTH
    AMERICA—CLOTHING
INDIANS OF NORTH
    AMERICA—COOKERY
INDIANS OF NORTH
    AMERICA—COSTUMES
INDIANS OF NORTH
    AMERICA—DANCES
INDIANS OF NORTH
    AMERICA—DOLLS
INDIANS OF NORTH
    AMERICA—
    DREAMCATCHERS
INDIANS OF NORTH
    AMERICA—FICTION
INDIANS OF NORTH
    AMERICA—FOLKLORE
INDIANS OF NORTH
    AMERICA—
    FOOTWEAR
INDIANS OF NORTH
    AMERICA—GAMES
INDIANS OF NORTH
    AMERICA—GREAT
    PLAINS—COOKERY
INDIANS OF NORTH
    AMERICA—GREAT
    PLAINS—FOLKLORE
INDIANS OF NORTH
    AMERICA—GREAT
    PLAINS—HOUSES
INDIANS OF NORTH
    AMERICA—GREAT
    PLAINS—TEPEES
INDIANS OF NORTH
    AMERICA—
    HEADDRESSES
INDIANS OF NORTH
    AMERICA—JEWELRY
INDIANS OF NORTH
    AMERICA—MUSICAL
    INSTRUMENTS

INDIANS OF NORTH
AMERICA—NORTHEAST
—COOKERY
INDIANS OF NORTH
AMERICA—POTTERY
INDIANS OF NORTH
AMERICA—POUCHES
INDIANS OF NORTH
AMERICA—SHIELDS
INDIANS OF NORTH
AMERICA—SOUTH—
COOKERY
INDIANS OF NORTH
AMERICA—
SOUTHWEST—
COOKERY
INDIANS OF NORTH
AMERICA—
SOUTHWEST—
FICTION
INDIANS OF NORTH
AMERICA—
SOUTHWEST. *See also*
SOUTHWEST COAST
INDIANS
INDIANS OF NORTH
AMERICA—SYMBOLS
INDIANS OF NORTH
AMERICA—TEA
PARTIES—COOKERY
INDIANS OF NORTH
AMERICA—TEA
PARTIES—TEPEES
INDIANS OF NORTH
AMERICA—WAMPUM
INDIANS OF NORTH
AMERICA—WINTER
COUNT
INDIANS OF THE
NORTHWEST
COAST—BASKETS
INDIANS OF THE
NORTHWEST
COAST—CLOTHING
INDIANS OF THE
NORTHWEST COAST—
HOUSEHOLD ITEMS

INDIANS OF THE
NORTHWEST COAST—
SYMBOLS
INDIANS OF THE
NORTHWEST COAST—
TOTEM POLES
INDIANS OF THE
NORTHWEST COAST—
*See also* NORTHWEST
COAST INDIANS
INDIANS OF THE PLAINS—
FOLKLORE
INDIANS OF THE PLAINS—
HOUSES
INDO-CARIBBEANS—
COOKERY
INDONESIA—COOKERY
INDONESIA—DANCES
INDONESIA—FESTIVALS—
COOKERY
INDONESIA—GAMES
INDONESIA—LANGUAGE
INDONESIA—SHADOW
PUPPETS
INDONESIA—SONGS
INGALIK PEOPLES
INKS
INSECTS
INUIT INDIANS—
CARVINGS
INUIT INDIANS—
COOKERY
INUIT INDIANS—GAMES
INUIT INDIANS—HOUSES
INUIT INDIANS—
LANGUAGE
INUIT INDIANS—MASKS
INUIT INDIAN. *See also*
YUOIK INDIANS
INUKSUK
INUPIAK. *See* INUIT
INDIANS
INUPIAT
INDIANS—GAMES
IOWA—COOKERY
IRAN—COOKERY
IRAN—GAMES
IRAN—HANDICRAFTS

IRAN—NEW YEAR—
PLANTS
IRANIAN-AMERICANS—
COOKERY. *See*
PERSIAN-AMERICANS
(IRANIANS)—
COOKERY
IRAQ—COOKERY
IRAQ—GAMES
IRELAND—COOKERY
IRELAND—COSTUMES
IRELAND—DANCES
IRELAND—FOLKLORE
IRELAND—GAMES
IRELAND—HANDICRAFTS
IRELAND—LANGUAGE
IRELAND—LEPRECHAUNS
IRELAND—TEA PARTIES—
COOKERY
IRELAND—TEA PARTIES—
HANDICRAFTS
IRISH-AMERICANS—
COOKERY
IROQUOIS INDIANS—
BASKETS
IROQUOIS INDIANS—
COOKERY
IROQUOIS INDIANS—
DREAMCATCHERS
IROQUOIS INDIANS—
FOLKLORE
IROQUOIS INDIANS—
GAMES
IROQUOIS INDIANS—
HATS
IROQUOIS INDIANS—
HOUSES
IROQUOIS INDIANS—
LANGUAGE
IROQUOIS INDIANS—
MASKS
IROQUOIS INDIANS—
MUSICAL
INSTRUMENTS
IROQUOIS
INDIANS—POUCHES
IROQUOIS INDIANS—TREE
OF PEACE

JAPAN—TOYS
JAPAN, ANCIENT—
CALLIGRAPHY
JAPAN, ANCIENT—
COOKERY
JAPAN, ANCIENT—FANS
JAPAN, ANCIENT—
FESTIVALS
JAPAN, ANCIENT—
FESTIVALS—DOLLS
JAPAN,
ANCIENT—FLOWER
ARRANGEMENTS
JAPAN, ANCIENT—
HANDICRAFTS
JAPAN, ANCIENT—KITES
JAPAN, ANCIENT—
ORIGAMI
JAPAN, ANCIENT—PAPER
JAPAN, ANCIENT—
SAMURAI—HELMETS
JAPAN, ANCIENT—
SCREENS
JAPAN, ANCIENT—TEA
CEREMONY
JAPAN, ANCIENT—
THEATER MASKS
JAPANESE-AMERICANS—
COOKERY
JAPANESE-AMERICANS—
FICTION
JEFFERSON, THOMAS
(PRESIDENT)
JEFFERSON, THOMAS
(PRESIDENT)—
COOKERY
JESTERS—MASKS
JESUS—HANDICRAFTS
JEWELRY
JEWISH-AMERICANS—
COOKERY
JEWISH-AMERICANS—
HANUKKAH—GAMES
JEWS—ARK
JEWS—COOKERY
JEWS—FICTION
JEWS—FOLKLORE
JEWS—FOOTWEAR

JEWS—GAMES
JEWS—HANDICRAFTS
JEWS—JEWELRY
JEWS—LAMPS
JEWS—LANGUAGE
JEWS—NEW YORK
(STATE)—COOKERY
JEWS—NEW YORK
(STATE)—SONGS
JEWS—SCROLLS
JEWS—TEMPLES
JICARILLA APACHE
INDIANS—GAMES
JOHNNY APPLESEED
JOHNSON, ANDREW
(PRESIDENT)
JOHNSON, LYNDON B.
(PRESIDENT)
JORDAN—GAMES
JUNE THEMES

KAHLO, FRIDA
KANDINSKY, WASSILY
KANSAS—COOKERY
KANSAS—FESTIVALS—
COOKERY
KELLER, HELEN
KENNEDY, JOHN F.
(PRESIDENT)
KENTUCKY—COOKERY
KENYA—COOKERY
KENYA—FESTIVALS—
COOKERY
KENYA—FLY WHISKS
KENYA—GAMES
KENYA—LANGUAGE
KENYA—SHIELDS
KENYA—STAFFS
KIENHOLZ, EDWARD
KIKUYU (AFRICAN
PEOPLES)—SHIELDS
KING, MARTIN LUTHER,
JR. DAY
KING, MARTIN LUTHER,
JR. DAY—
DECORATIONS
KING, MARTIN LUTHER,
JR. DAY—FICTION

KING, MARTIN LUTHER,
JR. DAY—GAMES
KINGS—CROWNS
KITES
KLEE, PAUL
KNIGHTS—CODE OF
HONOR
KNIGHTS—GAMES
KNIGHTS—HELMETS
KNIGHTS—PUPPETS
KNIGHTS—SHIELDS
KNIGHTS—SWORDS
KNIGHTS—TOURNAMENTS
KNIGHTS—WEAPONS
KONIGSBURG, E. L.
KOREA—COOKERY
KOREA—FESTIVALS—
COOKERY
KOREA—FOLKLORE
KOREA—GAMES
KOREA—LANGUAGE
KOREA—MUSICAL
INSTRUMENTS
KOREA—NEW YEAR—
COOKERY
KOREAN-AMERICANS—
COOKERY
KOREAN-AMERICANS—
FICTION
KUBA (AFRICAN
PEOPLES)—MASKS
KUBLAI KHAN. See POLO,
MARCO—KUBLAI
KHAN
KWAKIUTL INDIANS—
GAMES
KWANZAA
KWANZAA—CLOTHING
KWANZAA—COOKERY
KWANZAA—DECORATIONS
KWANZAA—DOLLS
KWANZAA—FICTION
KWANZAA—FLAGS
KWANZAA—GAMES
KWANZAA—HANDICRAFTS
KWANZAA—HATS
KWANZAA—JEWELRY
KWANZAA—MASKS

LABOR DAY
LABOR DAY—COOKERY
LABOR DAY—GAMES
LAKOTA INDIANS—
    BEADED WORK
LAKOTA INDIANS—
    COOKERY
LAKOTA INDIANS—
    FOLKLORE
LAKOTA INDIANS—
    POUCHES
LAKOTA INDIANS—
    SHIELDS
LAKOTA INDIANS—
    TRAVOIS
LAKOTA-SIOUX
    INDIANS—COOKERY
LANGE, DORTHEA
LANTERNS
LAOS—GAMES
LAOTIAN-AMERICANS—
    COOKERY
LATIN AMERICA—
    CHRISTMAS—COOKERY
LATIN AMERICA—
    CHRISTMAS—
    DECORATIONS
LATIN AMERICA—
    CHRISTMAS—GOD'S
    EYE
LATIN AMERICA—
    CHRISTMAS—
    LANTERNS
LATIN AMERICA—
    COOKERY
LATIN AMERICA—
    FESTIVALS
LATIN AMERICA—NEW
    YEAR'S DAY—
    COOKERY
LATIN AMERICA—
    PIÑATAS
LATVIA—GAMES
LATVIAN-AMERICANS—
    COOKERY
LAWRENCE, JACOB
LEBANON—CHRISTMAS—
    DECORATIONS

LEBANON—COOKERY
LEBANON—EASTER—
    COOKERY
LEBANON—FESTIVALS—
    COOKERY
LEBANON—GAMES
LENAPE INDIANS—
    COOKERY
LENT—COOKERY
LESOTHO—FOLKLORE
LEWIS AND CLARK
LEWIS AND CLARK—
    ARTIFACTS
LEWIS AND CLARK—
    COOKERY
LEWIS AND CLARK—
    JOURNALS
LEWIS AND CLARK
    EXPEDITION
LEWIS AND CLARK
    EXPEDITION—BOATS
LEWIS AND CLARK
    EXPEDITION—
    CANOES
LEWIS AND CLARK
    EXPEDITION—
    COOKERY
LEWIS AND CLARK
    EXPEDITION—
    DANCES
LEWIS AND CLARK
    EXPEDITION—
    FOOTWEAR
LEWIS AND CLARK
    EXPEDITION—
    INDIANS
LEWIS AND CLARK
    EXPEDITION—LAND
    SURVEYS
LEWIS AND CLARK
    EXPEDITION—MASKS
LEWIS AND CLARK
    EXPEDITION—PLANTS
LEWIS AND CLARK
    EXPEDITION—SUPPLIES
LEWIS AND CLARK
    EXPEDITION—

SURVEY
    INSTRUMENTS
LIBERIA—GAMES
LIBERTY BELL
LIBYA—COOKERY
LIBYA—GAMES
LICHTENSTEIN, ROY
LIGHTHOUSES
LIGHTHOUSES—PUPPETS
LIMBOURG BROTHERS
LINCOLN, ABRAHAM
    (PRESIDENT)
LINCOLN, ABRAHAM
    (PRESIDENT)—
    BIRTHDAY
LINCOLN, ABRAHAM
    (PRESIDENT)—
    BIRTHDAY—GAMES
LINCOLN, ABRAHAM
    (PRESIDENT)—
    BIRTHDAY—PUPPETS
LINCOLN, ABRAHAM
    (PRESIDENT)—
    COOKERY
LINCOLN, ABRAHAM
    (PRESIDENT)— FICTION
LINCOLN, ABRAHAM
    (PRESIDENT)—
    HANDICRAFTS
LINCOLN, ABRAHAM
    (PRESIDENT)— HATS
LINCOLN, ABRAHAM
    (PRESIDENT)—
    PUPPETS
LINCOLN, ABRAHAM
    (PRESIDENT)— SIZE
LINCOLN, MARY TODD
    (FIRST LADY)—
    COOKERY
LINDBERGH, CHARLES
LINDBERGH, CHARLES—
    COOKERY
LINNAEUS, CARL
LITHUANIAN-AMERICANS—
    COOKERY
LITTLE RED HEN
LITTLE RED RIDING HOOD
LOBEL, ARNOLD
LOUISIANA—COOKERY

LOUISIANA, NEW ORLEANS—CARNAVAL
LUMBEE INDIANS OF NORTH CAROLINA—COOKERY
LUXEMBOURG—GAMES

MACEDONIAN-AMERICANS—COOKERY
MADAGASCAR—CLOTHING
MADAGASCAR—COOKERY
MADAGASCAR—HANDICRAFTS
MADAGASCAR—LANGUAGE
MADISON, DOLLEY (FIRST LADY)—COOKERY
MADISON, JAMES (PRESIDENT)
MAGRITTE, RENE
MAINE—COOKERY
MAINE—FICTION
MAKAH INDIANS—GAMES
MALAGASY. See MADAGASCAR
MALAWI—COOKERY
MALAWI—GAMES
MALAWI—TOYS
MALAYSIA—BIRTHDAY CUSTOMS
MALAYSIA—COOKERY
MALAYSIA—GAMES
MALAYSIA—LANGUAGE
MALAYSIA—SKY SCRAPERS
MALI (AFRICAN PEOPLES)—FESTIVALS—HATS
MALI (AFRICAN PEOPLES)—GAMES
MALI (AFRICAN PEOPLES)—MUD CLOTH
MALTA—EASTER—COOKERY

MALTA—GAMES
MANDAN INDIANS—BOATS
MANDAN INDIANS—COOKERY
MANDAN INDIANS—GAMES
MANDAN INDIANS—HOUSES
MANDAN INDIANS—LANGUAGE
MANET, EDOUARD
MAORIS—CLOTHING
MAORIS—FOLKLORE
MAORIS—GAMES
MAORIS—HAKA
MAORIS—HOUSES
MAORIS—TATTOOS
MAPS
MARCH THEMES
MARDI GRAS—COOKERY
MARDI GRAS—DECORATIONS
MARDI GRAS—MASKS
MARDI GRAS—MUSICAL INSTRUMENTS
MARTIN, JAQUELINE BRIGGS
MARYLAND—COOKERY
MASACCIO, TOMMASSO
MASAI (AFRICAN PEOPLES)—JEWELRY
MASKS
MASSACHUSETTS—COOKERY
MATISSE, HENRI
MAY DAY
MAY DAY—DECORATIONS
MAY DAY—MUSICAL INSTRUMENTS
MAY THEMES
MAYANS
MAYANS—BATIK
MAYANS—CODEX
MAYANS—COOKERY
MAYANS—GAMES
MAYANS—HOUSES

MAYANS—LANGUAGE
MAYANS—MATHEMATICS
MAYANS—POTTERY
MAYANS—PRAYERS
MAYANS—PYRAMIDS
MAYANS—TEMPLES
MAYANS—WEAVING
MAYFLOWER
MCCLOSKEY, ROBERT
MCCULLY, EMILY ARNOLD
MCDERMOTT, GERALD
MCKINLEY, WILLIAM (PRESIDENT)
MELUNGEONS—COOKERY
MEMORIAL DAY
MEMORIAL DAY—COOKERY
MEMORIAL DAY—DECORATIONS
MENOMINEE INDIANS—COOKERY
MERMAIDS
MESOPOTAMIA—ARMIES
MESOPOTAMIA—BOATS
MESOPOTAMIA—BURIALS
MESOPOTAMIA—COOKERY
MESOPOTAMIA—HOUSEHOLD ITEMS
MESOPOTAMIA—JEWELRY
MESOPOTAMIA—KINGS—CLOTHING
MESOPOTAMIA—KINGS—FLY WHISKS
MESOPOTAMIA—KINGS—PARASOLS
MESOPOTAMIA—MUSICAL INSTRUMENTS
MESOPOTAMIA—SEALS
MESOPOTAMIA—TEMPLES
MESOPOTAMIA—WEIGHTS
MESOPOTAMIA—WRITING TABLETS
MEXICAN-AMERICANS (CHICANOS)—COOKERY
MEXICAN-AMERICANS (CHICANOS)—FICTION

MEXICAN-AMERICANS (CHICANOS)—HANDICRAFTS
MEXICAN-AMERICANS (CHICANOS)—PIÑATAS
MEXICO
MEXICO—BIRTHDAY CUSTOMS
MEXICO—BIRTHDAYS—GAMES
MEXICO—CHRISTMAS—COOKERY
MEXICO—CHRISTMAS—DECORATIONS
MEXICO—CHRISTMAS—GOD'S EYE
MEXICO—CHRISTMAS—HANDICRAFTS
MEXICO—CHRISTMAS—LANTERNS
MEXICO—CLOTHING
MEXICO—COAT OF ARMS
MEXICO—COOKERY
MEXICO—COSTUMES
MEXICO—DOLLS
MEXICO—FESTIVALS
MEXICO—FESTIVALS—COOKERY
MEXICO—FESTIVALS—DANCERS
MEXICO—FESTIVALS—DECORATIONS
MEXICO—FESTIVALS—FLAGS
MEXICO—FESTIVALS—HANDICRAFTS
MEXICO—FESTIVALS—PIÑATAS
MEXICO—FESTIVALS—PUPPETS
MEXICO—FICTION
MEXICO—FLAGS
MEXICO—FOLKLORE
MEXICO—GAMES
MEXICO—GOD'S EYE
MEXICO—HANDICRAFTS
MEXICO—HANDICRAFTS —PAPEL PICADO

MEXICO—LANGUAGE
MEXICO—MARKETPLACE
MEXICO—MASKS
MEXICO—NEW YEAR
MEXICO—NUMBERS
MEXICO—PIÑATAS
MEXICO—POTTERY
MEXICO—SONGS
MICHELANGELO
MICHIGAN—COOKERY
MICMAC INDIANS—CLOTHING
MICMAC INDIANS—CRADLEBOARD
MIDDLE AGES—ARMOR
MIDDLE AGES—BOOKS
MIDDLE AGES—BOXES
MIDDLE AGES—CANDLEMAKING
MIDDLE AGES—CASTLES
MIDDLE AGES—CATAPULTS
MIDDLE AGES—CHRISTMAS—COOKERY
MIDDLE AGES—CLOTHING
MIDDLE AGES—COAT OF ARMS
MIDDLE AGES—COINS
MIDDLE AGES—COMPASS
MIDDLE AGES—COOKERY
MIDDLE AGES—CROCHETING
MIDDLE AGES—CROWNS
MIDDLE AGES—DOLLS
MIDDLE AGES—DRAWING
MIDDLE AGES—EMBROIDERY
MIDDLE AGES—FALCONRY
MIDDLE AGES—FESTIVALS
MIDDLE AGES—FESTIVALS—COOKERY
MIDDLE AGES—FICTION
MIDDLE AGES—FOOTWEAR
MIDDLE AGES—GAMES

MIDDLE AGES—GUILD SIGNS
MIDDLE AGES—HAIRSTYLES
MIDDLE AGES—HANDICRAFTS
MIDDLE AGES—HERALDRY
MIDDLE AGES—HERBS
MIDDLE AGES—HOUSEHOLD ITEMS
MIDDLE AGES—HOUSES
MIDDLE AGES—JEWELRY
MIDDLE AGES—KNIGHTS
MIDDLE AGES—KNITTING
MIDDLE AGES—MACE
MIDDLE AGES—MAGIC TRICKS
MIDDLE AGES—MANUSCRIPTS
MIDDLE AGES—MAPS
MIDDLE AGES—MASKS
MIDDLE AGES—MATHEMATICS
MIDDLE AGES—MURALS
MIDDLE AGES—MUSICAL INSTRUMENTS
MIDDLE AGES—PAINTS
MIDDLE AGES—PAPER
MIDDLE AGES—PARCHMENT
MIDDLE AGES—PERFUMES
MIDDLE AGES—PICTURES
MIDDLE AGES—PRINTING
MIDDLE AGES—PROVERBS
MIDDLE AGES—PUPPETS
MIDDLE AGES—RELIGION
MIDDLE AGES—SCULPTURES
MIDDLE AGES—SECRET MESSAGES
MIDDLE AGES—SOAP
MIDDLE AGES—STAINED GLASS
MIDDLE AGES—TIME
MIDDLE AGES—TOYS

MIDDLE AGES—WEAPONS
MIDDLE AGES—WEAVING
MIDDLE AGES—WEIGHTS
    AND MEASURES
MIDDLE AGES—WRITING
MIDDLE EAST—
    CLOTHING
MIDDLE EAST—COOKERY
MIDDLE EAST—DESERT—
    CLOTHING
MIDDLE EAST—DESERT—
    COOKERY
MIDDLE EAST—DESERT—
    GAMES
MIDDLE EAST—DESERT—
    HOUSES
MIDDLE EAST—DESERT—
    JEWELRY
MIDDLE EAST—DESERT—
    RELIGION
MIDDLE EAST—DESERT—
    WEAVING
MIDDLE EAST—
    FESTIVALS—COOKERY
MIDDLE EAST—NUMBERS
MIMBRENOS INDIANS
MINNESOTA—COOKERY
MINOANS—SEALS
MISSISSIPPI—COOKERY
MISSOURI—COOKERY
MODELL, FRANK
MOLAS—HANDICRAFTS
MONDRIAN, PIET
MONET, CLAUDE
MONGOLIA—COOKERY
MONGOLIA—GAMES
MONGOLIA—HOUSES
MONROE, JAMES
    (PRESIDENT)
MONTANA—COOKERY
MONTENEGRIN-
    AMERICANS—
    COOKERY. *See* SERBIAN
    AMERICANS—
    COOKERY
MOORE, HENRY
MORAVIANS—COOKERY
MORISOT, BERTHE

MORMONS—COOKERY
MOROCCO—COOKERY
MOROCCO—GAMES
MOROCCO—PASSOVER—
    COOKERY
MOTHER'S DAY
MOTHER'S DAY—
    COOKERY
MOTHER'S DAY—
    DECORATIONS
MOTHER'S DAY—FICTION
MOTHER'S DAY—TEA
    PARTIES
MOTHER'S DAY—TEA
    PARTIES—COOKERY
MOZAMBIQUE—GAMES
MUD
MUNCH, EDVARD
MUSIC
MUSICAL INSTRUMENTS
MUSLIMS—FESTIVALS—
    COOKERY
MYANMAR—GAMES

NARRAGANSETT
    INDIANS—COOKERY
NATIONAL CHILDREN'S
    BOOK WEEK—
    FICTION
NATIONAL LIBRARY
    WEEK
NAVAHO INDIANS—
    BLANKETS
NAVAHO INDIANS—
    COOKERY
NAVAHO INDIANS—
    FICTION
NAVAHO INDIANS—
    HOUSES
NAVAHO INDIANS—
    JEWELRY
NAVAHO INDIANS—
    LANGUAGE
NAVAHO INDIANS—
    MEDICINE MAN
NAVAHO INDIANS—SAND
    PAINTING

NAVAHO INDIANS—
    SECRET CODES
NAVAHO INDIANS—
    TRADING POSTS
NAVAHO INDIANS—
    WEAVING
NDEBELE (AFRICAN
    PEOPLES)—DOLLS
NDEBELE (AFRICAN
    PEOPLES)—HOUSES
NEBRASKA—COOKERY
NEPAL—GAMES
NESS, EVALINE
NETHERLANDS—
    BIRTHDAY CUSTOMS
NETHERLANDS—
    CHRISTMAS—
    COOKERY
NETHERLANDS—
    CHRISTMAS—
    DECORATIONS
NETHERLANDS—
    COOKERY
NETHERLANDS—
    COSTUMES
NETHERLANDS—EASTER
    —HANDICRAFTS
NETHERLANDS—
    FOLKLORE
NETHERLANDS—GAMES
NETHERLANDS—NEW
    YEAR'S DAY—
    COOKERY
NETHERLANDS—
    WINDMILLS
NEVADA—COOKERY
NEVELSON, LOUISE
NEW CALEDONIA—
    GAMES
NEW HAMPSHIRE—
    COOKERY
NEW JERSEY—COOKERY
NEW MEXICO—COOKERY
NEW MEXICO HISPANICS—
    COOKERY
NEW YEAR'S DAY
NEW YEAR'S DAY—
    COOKERY

NEW YEAR'S DAY—
    FICTION
NEW YEAR'S DAY—
    HANDICRAFTS
NEW YEAR'S DAY—SOAP
NEW YEAR'S EVE—
    DECORATIONS
NEW YORK CITY—
    COOKERY
NEW YORK CITY—
    FICTION
NEW ZEALAND—BIRDS
NEW ZEALAND—
    BIRTHDAY CUSTOMS
NEW ZEALAND—
    COOKERY
NEW ZEALAND—GAMES
NEW ZEALAND—HAKA
NEW ZEALAND—HOUSES
NEW ZEALAND—
    TATTOOS
NEW ZEALANDER-
    AMERICANS—
    COOKERY
NEZ PERCE INDIANS—
    CARRYING CASE
NEZ PERCE INDIANS—
    COOKERY
NEZ PERCE INDIANS—
    LANGUAGE
NICARAGUA—COAT OF
    ARMS
NICARAGUA—COOKERY
NICARAGUA—FLAGS
NICARAGUA—FOLKLORE
NICARAGUA—GAMES
NICARAGUA—LANGUAGE
NICARAGUA—MURALS
NICARAGUAN-
    AMERICANS—
    COOKERY
NIGER—LANGUAGE
NIGERIA—CHRISTMAS—
    DECORATIONS
NIGERIA—COOKERY
NIGERIA—FESTIVALS—
    COOKERY

NIGERIA—FESTIVALS—
    MUSICAL
    INSTRUMENTS
NIGERIA—FOLKLORE
NIGERIA—GAMES
NIGERIA—LANGUAGE
NIGERIA—NEW YEAR—
    MASKS
NIGERIAN-AMERICANS—
    COOKERY
NINETIES—COOKERY
NIXON, RICHARD
    (PRESIDENT)
NOOTKA INDIANS—
    GAMES
NORTH CAROLINA—
    COOKERY
NORTH CAROLINA—
    PASSOVER—COOKERY
NORTH DAKOTA—
    COOKERY
NORTHWEST COAST
    INDIANS—BLANKETS
NORTHWEST COAST
    INDIANS—FESTIVALS
NORTHWEST COAST
    INDIANS—GAMES
NORTHWEST COAST
    INDIANS—HEADBANDS
NORTHWEST COAST
    INDIANS—HOUSES
NORTHWEST COAST
    INDIANS—SYMBOLS
NORTHWEST COAST
    INDIANS—TOTEM
    POLES
NORTHWEST COAST
    INDIANS. See also
    INDIANS OF THE
    NORTHWEST COAST
NORWAY—CHRISTMAS—
    COOKERY
NORWAY—CHRISTMAS—
    DECORATIONS
NORWAY—COOKERY
NORWAY—FESTIVALS—
    COOKERY
NORWAY—FOLKLORE

NORWAY—GAMES
NORWAY—LANGUAGE
NORWEGIAN-
    AMERICANS—
    COOKERY
NOVEMBER THEMES
NURSERY RHYMES
NURSERY RHYMES—
    HANDICRAFTS
NURSERY RHYMES—
    PUPPETS

O'KEEFFE, GEORGIA
OAXACA—CHRISTMAS—
    COOKERY
OCCUPATIONS
OCTOBER THEMES
OHIO—COOKERY
OJIBWA INDIANS—
    COOKERY
OJIBWA INDIANS—
    DREAMCATCHERS
OJIBWA INDIANS—GAMES
OJIBWA INDIANS—
    LANGUAGE
OJIBWA INDIANS—
    PRAYERS
OKINAWAN-
    AMERICANS—
    COOKERY
OKLAHOMA—COOKERY
OLYMPICS
OLYMPICS—GAMES
OLYMPICS—PATTERNS
OMAHA INDIANS—GAMES
ONEIDA INDIANS—
    COOKERY
ONEIDA INDIANS—
    CREATION STORY
ONEIDA INDIANS—
    FOLKLORE
ONEIDA INDIANS—
    PRAYERS
OPPENHEIM, MERET
OREGON—COOKERY
OREGON TRAIL—
    COOKERY
OREGON TRAIL—GAMES

ORIENT—HANDICRAFTS
OSAGE INDIANS—FICTION
OSAGE INDIANS—GAMES
OSAGE INDIANS—
    WEAVING

PACIFIC ISLANDS—
    GAMES
PAIK, NAM JUNE
PAINTING
PAINTS
PAKISTAN—COOKERY
PAKISTAN—FESTIVALS—
    KITES
PAKISTAN—GAMES
PAKISTAN—LANGUAGE
PAKISTANI-AMERICANS—
    COOKERY
PAMUNKEY INDIANS—
    GAMES
PANAMA—COOKERY
PANAMA—GAMES
PANAMANIAN-
    AMERICANS—
    COOKERY
PAPER
PAPUA NEW GUINEA—
    GAMES
PARAGUAY—CHRISTMAS
    —COOKERY
PARAGUAY—COOKERY
PARAGUAY—FESTIVALS
    —COOKERY
PARAGUAY—GAMES
PARKS, ROSA
PARKS, ROSA—BIRTHDAY
PASSAMAQUODDY
    INDIANS—ART
PASSOVER
PASSOVER—COOKERY
PASSOVER—DECORATIONS
PASSOVER—GAMES
PASSOVER—HANDICRAFTS
PASSOVER—MUSICAL
    INSTRUMENTS
PASSOVER—PUPPETS
PASSOVER—SONGS
PASTES

PENDE (AFRICAN
    PEOPLES)—MASKS
PENDE (AFRICAN
    PEOPLES)—PUPPETS
PENNSYLVANIA—
    COOKERY
PENNSYLVANIA DUTCH—
    COOKERY
PENNSYLVANIA DUTCH—
    HANDICRAFTS
PENNSYLVANIA DUTCH—
    VALENTINE'S DAY—
    HANDICRAFTS
PENOBSCOT INDIANS—
    JEWELRY
PENS
PENTECOST—
    DECORATIONS
PEQUOT INDIANS—
    JEWELRY
PERSIA—COOKERY
PERSIAN-AMERICANS
    (IRANIANS)—
    COOKERY
PERU—COOKERY
PERU—GAMES
PERU—HANDICRAFTS
PERU—JEWELRY
PERU—KNITTING
PERU—LANGUAGE
PERU—NAZCA DRAWINGS
PERUVIAN-AMERICANS—
    COOKERY
PETER PAN
PETS
PHILIPPINES—BIRTHDAY
    CUSTOMS
PHILIPPINES—CHRISTMAS
    —DECORATIONS
PHILIPPINES—CHRISTMAS
    —LANTERNS
PHILIPPINES—COOKERY
PHILIPPINES—DANCES
PHILIPPINES—GAMES
PHILIPPINES—LANGUAGE
PHILIPPINES—WEAVING
PHILISTINES—
    ARCHITECTURE

PHILISTINES—BOWLS
PHILISTINES—CLOTHING
PHILISTINES—COOKERY
PHILISTINES—RELIGION
PHILISTINES—SCALES
PHILISTINES—WRITING
PHOENICIANS—
    ARCHITECTURE
PHOENICIANS—BOATS
PHOENICIANS—BOWLS
PHOENICIANS—CLOTHING
PHOENICIANS—COOKERY
PHOENICIANS—RELIGION
PHOENICIANS—SHIPS
PHOENICIANS. *See also*
    MESOPOTAMIA
PHOENIX BIRD—MASKS
PICASSO, PABLO
PICASSO, PABLO—
    BIOGRAPHY
PICTS—WRITINGS IN
    STONE
PIERCE, FRANKLIN
    (PRESIDENT)
PILGRIMS
PILGRIMS—COOKERY
PILGRIMS—COSTUMES
PILGRIMS—DOLLS
PILGRIMS—FICTION
PILGRIMS—HATS
PILGRIMS—ORNAMENTS
PILGRIMS—PUPPETS
PILGRIMS—THANKSGIVING
    —COOKERY
PILGRIMS—THANSKGIVING
    —DECORATIONS
PIMA AND PAPAGO
    (TOHONO O'ODHAM)
    INDIANS—COOKERY
PIMA INDIANS—GAMES
PIÑATAS
PINOCCHIO—PUPPETS
PIONEERS
PIONEERS—COOKERY
PIONEERS—COWS
PIONEERS—FICTION
PIONEERS—GAMES
PIONEERS—PARTIES

PIONEERS—QUILTING
PIONEERS—TOYS
PIONEERS—
    TRANSPORTATION
PIONEERS—WRITING
    SLATES
PIPER, WATTY
PIRATES—COSTUMES
PIRATES—FACE PAINT
PIRATES—GAMES
PIRATES—HANDICRAFTS
PIRATES—TREASURE
    CHESTS
PLAINS INDIANS
PLAINS INDIANS—
    ALPHABET
PLAINS INDIANS—
    BUFFALO
PLAINS INDIANS—
    COOKERY
PLAINS INDIANS—DOLLS
PLAINS INDIANS—
    FOLKLORE
PLAINS INDIANS—GAMES
PLAINS INDIANS—
    HEADBANDS
PLAINS INDIANS—
    HOUSES
PLAINS INDIANS—
    PARFLECHE
PLAINS INDIANS—SIGN
    LANGUAGE
PLAINS INDIANS—
    SYMBOLS
PLAINS INDIANS—
    WRITINGS
PLANTATION LIFE—
    COOKERY
PLANTATION LIFE—
    SOUTHERN STATES—
    HISTORY—19TH
    CENTURY—CALLING
    CARDS
PLANTATION LIFE—
    SOUTHERN STATES—
    HISTORY—19TH
    CENTURY— COOKERY

PLANTATION LIFE—
    SOUTHERN STATES—
    HISTORY—19TH
    CENTURY—COTTON
PLANTATION LIFE—
    SOUTHERN STATES—
    HISTORY—19TH
    CENTURY—GAMES
PLANTATION LIFE—
    SOUTHERN STATES—
    HISTORY—19TH
    CENTURY—
    HANDICRAFTS
PLANTATION LIFE—
    SOUTHERN STATES—
    HISTORY—19TH
    CENTURY—MEDICINE
PLANTATION LIFE—
    SOUTHERN STATES—
    HISTORY—19TH
    CENTURY—
    NOTEBOOKS
PLANTATION LIFE—
    SOUTHERN STATES—
    HISTORY—19TH
    CENTURY—SLAVES
PLASTIC
POCAHONTAS
POLAND—CHRISTMAS—
    COOKERY
POLAND—CHRISTMAS—
    DECORATIONS
POLAND—COOKERY
POLAND—EASTER—
    COOKERY
POLAND—GAMES
POLAND—LANGUAGE
POLAND—PAPERCUTTING
POLISH-AMERICANS—
    COOKERY
POLISH-AMERICANS—
    PISANKI EGGS
POLK, JAMES KNOX
    (PRESIDENT)
POLLACK, JACKSON
POLO, MARCO
POLO, MARCO— KUBLAI
    KHAN

POLO, MARCO—LANTERN
    FESTIVAL
POLO, MARCO—MONGOLS
POLO, MARCO—TIBET
POLO, MARCO—TIBET—
    COOKERY
POLO, MARCO—TIBET—
    GAMES
POMO INDIANS—
    BASKETRY
PONY EXPRESS
PONY EXPRESS—MAP
PONY EXPRESS—PUPPETS
PONY EXPRESS—RIDERS
POPCORN
POPCORN—COOKERY
PORTUGAL—GAMES
PORTUGAL—
    HANDICRAFTS
PORTUGAL—PASSOVER—
    HANDICRAFTS
PRTUGEAL—PASSOVER—
    HANDICRAFTS
PORTUGESE-AMERICANS—
    COOKERY
POTATOES
POTATOES—FICTION
POTAWATOMI INDIANS—
    COOKERY
POTAWATOMI INDIANS—
    GAMES
POTTER, BEATRIX—
    PUPPETS
POTTERY
POWHATAN INDIANS—
    COOKERY
POWHATAN INDIANS—
    LANGUAGE
PREHISTORIC MAN—
    ROCK CARVINGS
PREHISTORIC MAN—
    ROCK PAINTINGS
PRESIDENTS
PRESIDENTS—NAMES
PRESIDENTS' DAY
PRINCESSES—FACE PAINT
PRINCESSES—MASKS
PRINCESSES—TEA
    PARTIES

PRINCESSES—TEA
PARTIES—COOKERY
PRINCESSES—TEA
PARTIES—DECORATIONS
PRINCESSES—TEA
PARTIES—GAMES
PRINTING
PROVENSEN, ALICE
PUEBLO INDIANS
PUEBLO INDIANS—
COOKERY
PUEBLO INDIANS—
FICTION
PUEBLO INDIANS—
FOLKLORE
PUEBLO INDIANS—
HOUSES
PUEBLO INDIANS—
LANGUAGE
PUEBLO INDIANS—
POTTERY
PUEBLO INDIANS—ROCK
PAINTINGS
PUEBLO INDIANS—
STORYTELLERS
PUERTO RICAN
AMERICANS—
COOKERY
PUERTO RICAN-
AMERICANS—FICTION
PUERTO RICO—
CHRISTMAS—
COOKERY
PUERTO RICO—
CHRISTMAS—
DECORATIONS
PUERTO RICO—
CHRISTMAS—
MUSICAL
INSTRUMENTS
PUERTO RICO—COOKERY
PUERTO RICO—
EPIPHANY—COOKERY
PUERTO RICO—
FESTIVALS—COOKERY
PUERTO RICO—
FESTIVALS—MASKS
PUERTO RICO—FICTION

PUERTO RICO—
FOLKLORE
PUERTO RICO—GAMES
PUERTO RICO—
LANGUAGE
PUERTO RICO—MASKS
PUERTO RICO—MUSICAL
INSTRUMENTS
PUMPKINS
PUMPKINS—FICTION
PUPPETS
PURIM—COOKERY
PURIM—DECORATIONS

QUILTING
QUILTING—FICTION

RAGGEDY ANN—
COOKERY
RAGGEDY ANN—GAMES
RAILROADS
RAILROADS—FICTION
RAIN FOREST—BIRDS
RAIN FOREST—GAMES
RAIN FOREST—PRAYERS
RAMADAN—COOKERY
RANSOME, ARTHUR
RAPHAEL
RAUSCHENBERG, ROBERT
REAGAN, RONALD
(PRESIDENT)
REMBRANDT
RENAISSANCE—PAPER
MUSEUMS
RENAISSANCE—
PORTRAITS
RENOIR, PIERRE AUGUSTE
RHODE ISLAND—
COOKERY
RHODE ISLAND RED
CHICKENS—HISTORY
RINGGOLD, FAITH
RIVERA, DIEGO
ROARING TWENTIES—
COOKERY
ROBIN HOOD—CLOTHING
ROCKS
ROCKWELL, NORMAN

RODIN, AUGUSTE
ROMANIA—COOKERY
ROMANIA—EASTER—
EGGS
ROMANIA—GAMES
ROMANIA—NEW YEAR'S
DAY—DECORATIONS
ROMANIAN-AMERICANS—
COOKERY
ROME, ANCIENT—
AMPHORA
ROME, ANCIENT—
AQUEDUCTS
ROME, ANCIENT—
ARCHITECTURE
ROME, ANCIENT—ARMOR
ROME, ANCIENT—ARMY
ROME, ANCIENT—
ATHLETES
ROME, ANCIENT—
BASKETS
ROME, ANCIENT—BATHS
ROME, ANCIENT—
BRIDGES
ROME, ANCIENT—
BUILDINGS
ROME, ANCIENT—
CHARIOT RACES
ROME, ANCIENT—CLOCKS
ROME, ANCIENT—
CLOTHING
ROME, ANCIENT—COINS
ROME, ANCIENT—
COOKERY
ROME, ANCIENT—
EMPERORS
ROME, ANCIENT—
FESTIVALS
ROME, ANCIENT—
FOOTWEAR
ROME, ANCIENT—GAMES
ROME, ANCIENT—
GARDENS
ROME, ANCIENT—
GLADIATORS
ROME, ANCIENT—GODS
ROME, ANCIENT—HOUSES

ROME, ANCIENT—
JEWELRY
ROME, ANCIENT—LAMPS
ROME, ANCIENT—
LANGUAGE
ROME, ANCIENT—MASKS
ROME, ANCIENT—
MATHEMATICS
ROME, ANCIENT—
MOSAICS
ROME, ANCIENT—NAMES
ROME, ANCIENT—
NUMERALS
ROME, ANCIENT—
PAINTING
ROME, ANCIENT—
POTTERY
ROME, ANCIENT—ROADS
ROME, ANCIENT—RUINS
ROME, ANCIENT—
SCROLLS
ROME, ANCIENT—
SCULPTURES
ROME, ANCIENT—SHIPS
ROME, ANCIENT—SIGNS
ROME, ANCIENT—SOAP
ROME, ANCIENT—
SOLDIERS
ROME, ANCIENT—
SUNDIALS
ROME, ANCIENT—
TEMPLES
ROME, ANCIENT—
THEATER
ROME, ANCIENT—
TRIUMPHAL ARCH
ROME, ANCIENT—
TRIUMPHAL COLUMN
ROME, ANCIENT—
VOLCANOES
ROME, ANCIENT—
WEAPONS
ROME, ANCIENT—
WREATHS
ROME, ANCIENT—
WRITING
ROOSEVELT, EDITH (FIRST
LADY)—COOKERY

ROOSEVELT, ELEANOR
(FIRST LADY)
ROOSEVELT, FRANKLIN
DELANO (PRESIDENT)
ROOSEVELT, THEODORE
(PRESIDENT)
ROSH HASHANAH—
COOKERY
ROSS, BETSY—BIRTHDAY
ROSS, BETSY—HATS
ROUSSEAU, HENRI
RUBBER
RUBENS, PETER PAUL
RUDOLPH, WILMA
RUSSELL, C. M.
RUSSIA—BIRTHDAYS—
DECORATIONS
RUSSIA—CHRISTMAS—
COOKERY
RUSSIA—COOKERY
RUSSIA—DOLLS
RUSSIA—EASTER—
COOKERY
RUSSIA—EASTER—
DECORATIONS
RUSSIA—EPIPHANY—
COOKERY
RUSSIA—FESTIVALS
RUSSIA—FESTIVALS—
COOKERY
RUSSIA—FICTION
RUSSIA—FOLKLORE
RUSSIA—GAMES
RUSSIA—LANGUAGE
RUSSIA—LANTERNS
RUSSIA—PYSANKY EGGS
RUSSIA—TEA PARTIES—
COOKERY
RUSSIA—TEA PARTIES—
DANCES
RUSSIA—TOYS
RUSSIAN-AMERICANS—
COOKERY
RUSSIAN-AMERICANS—
EASTER—EGGS
RWANDA—GAMES

SAAMI PEOPLES—
CLOTHING
SABBATH—COOKERY
SABBATH—DECORATIONS
SACAJAWEA
SAILING SHIPS
SAILORS
SAILORS—CARGO
SAILORS—CARVING
SAILORS—COOKERY
SAILORS—DANCES
SAILORS—GAMES
SAILORS—HANDICRAFTS
SAILORS—MUSICAL
INSTRUMENTS
SAILORS—PLAYS
SAILORS—SAILS
SAILORS—VALENTINE'S
DAY
SALTEN, FELIX—PUPPETS
SALVADORIAN-
AMERICANS—
COOKERY
SAMOAN-AMERICANS—
COOKERY
SANDWICH DAY—
FICTION
SAUDI ARABIA—
FESTIVALS—COOKERY
SAUDI ARABIA—
FESTIVALS—
GREETING CARDS
SAUDI ARABIA—GAMES
SAUDI ARABIA—
WEDDINGS
SAY, ALLEN
SCANDINAVIA—
COOKERY
SCANDINAVIA—FAMILY
TREE
SCANDINAVIA—FLAGS
SCANDINAVIA—
HANDICRAFTS
SCARECROWS
SCHOOLS—FICTION
SCOTCH-IRISH
AMERICANS—
COOKERY

SCOTLAND—CHRISTMAS
—COOKERY
SCOTLAND—CHRISTMAS
—DECORATIONS
SCOTLAND—COOKERY
SCOTLAND—FAMILY
CREST
SCOTLAND—GAMES
SCOTLAND—LOCH NESS
MONSTER
SCOTLAND—NEW
YEAR—COOKERY
SCOTLAND—NEW
YEAR—SONGS
SCOTLAND—NEW YEAR'S
DAY—COOKERY
SCOTLAND—TARTANS
SCOTTISH-AMERICANS—
COOKERY
SCRAPBOOKS
SCRIMSHAW
SEA
SECRET CODES
SECRET GARDEN—
GARDENS
SECRET GARDEN—
HANDICRAFTS
SEDER—COOKERY
SEDER—DECORATIONS
SEMINOLE AND
MICCOSUKEE
INDIANS—CLOTHING
SEMINOLE AND
MICCOSUKEE
INDIANS—COOKERY
SEMINOLE INDIANS—
COOKERY
SEMINOLE INDIANS—
DOLLS
SEMINOLE INDIANS—
PATCHWORK
SENEGAL—COOKERY
SENEGAL—FESTIVALS—
COOKERY
SENEGAL—GAMES
SENSES
SENUFO (AFRICAN
PEOPLES)—PAINTINGS

SEPTEMBER THEMES
SERBIA—CHRISTMAS—
COOKERY
SERBIA—GAMES
SERBIAN-AMERICANS—
COOKERY
SEURAT, GEORGES
SHAKESPEARE, WILLIAM
SHAKESPEARE, WILLIAM—
BIRDFEEDERS
SHAKESPEARE, WILLIAM—
COAT OF ARMS
SHAKESPEARE, WILLIAM—
COOKERY
SHAKESPEARE,
WILLIAM—
COSTUMES
SHAKESPEARE,
WILLIAM—FAMILY
TREE
SHAKESPEARE,
WILLIAM—GAMES
SHAKESPEARE,
WILLIAM—
HANDICRAFTS
SHAKESPEARE,
WILLIAM—
HORNBOOK
SHAKESPEARE,
WILLIAM—PENS
SHAKESPEARE,
WILLIAM—PLAYS
SHAKESPEARE,
WILLIAM—SONGS
SHAKESPEARE,
WILLIAM—SWORD
FIGHT
SHAKESPEARE,
WILLIAM—WEAPONS
SHAVUOT—COOKERY
SHAVUOT—DECORATIONS
SHAWNEE INDIANS—
COOKERY
SHAWNEE INDIANS—
GAMES
SHAWNEE INDIANS—
JEWELRY

SHOSHONE INDIANS—
BASKETS
SHOSHONE INDIANS—
COOKERY
SHOSHONE INDIANS—
GOD'S EYE
SHOSHONE INDIANS—
LANGUAGE
SHROVE TUESDAY—
COOKERY
SIERRA LEONE—
COOKERY
SIHASAPA INDIANS. See
BLACKFEET INDIANS
SIKSIKA INDIANS—
COOKERY
SIKSIKA INDIANS—
LANGUAGE
SIKSIKA INDIANS. See also
BLACKFEET INDIANS
SIMCHAT TORAH—
COOKERY
SIMCHAT TORAH—FLAGS
SINGAPORE—COOKERY
SINGAPORE—GAMES
SINGAPORE—PASSOVER—
COOKERY
SIOUX INDIANS—
COOKERY
SIOUX INDIANS—OWNER
STICKS
SIXTIES—COOKERY
SLOPPY JOES—COOKERY—
HISTORY
SLOVAK-AMERICANS—
COOKERY
SLOVAK REPUBLIC—
GAMES
SLOVAKIA—DOLLS
SLOVENE-AMERICANS—
COOKERY
SLOVENIA—FOLKLORE
SMITH, DAVID
SNOW GLOBES
SNOWFLAKES
SNOWMEN
SOAP

STONE AGE PEOPLES— PAINTINGS
STONE AGE PEOPLES—POTTERY
STONE AGE PEOPLES— SCULPTURES
STONE AGE PEOPLES— TOOLS
STONE AGE PEOPLES— WEAPONS
STORYTELLING
SUDAN—GAMES
SUDAN—MUSICAL INSTRUMENTS
SUKBOT—DECORATIONS
SUMERIANS—BURIALS
SUMERIANS. *See also* MESOPOTAMIA
SURINAME—COOKERY
SURVEY INSTRUMENTS
SUTTER, JOHN AUGUSTUS
SWEDEN—BIRTHDAY CUSTOMS
SWEDEN—CHRISTMAS— COOKERY
SWEDEN—CHRISTMAS— DECORATIONS
SWEDEN—CHRISTMAS— HANDICRAFTS
SWEDEN—COOKERY
SWEDEN—COSTUMES
SWEDEN—EASTER— COOKERY
SWEDEN—FESTIVALS— CANDLES
SWEDEN—FESTIVALS— COOKERY
SWEDEN—GAMES
SWEDEN—LANGUAGE
SWEDISH-AMERICANS— COOKERY
SWISS-AMERICANS— COOKERY
SWITZERLAND—COAT OF ARMS
SWITZERLAND—COOKERY
SWITZERLAND— COWBELLS

SWITZERLAND—FESTIVALS —HANDICRAFTS
SWITZERLAND—GAMES
SWITZERLAND— HANDICRAFTS
SWITZERLAND—HATS
SWITZERLAND— LANGUAGE
SYMMETRY
SYRIA—COOKERY
SYRIA—GAMES

TAFT, WILLIAM HOWARD (PRESIDENT)
TANGRAMS—GAMES
TANZANIA—COOKERY
TANZANIA—FESTIVALS— COOKERY
TANZANIA—GAMES
TANZANIA—JEWELRY
TANZANIA—LANGUAGE
TARASCAN INDIANS— GAMES
TAXICABS—PUPPETS
TAYLOR, ZACHARY (PRESIDENT)
TEA
TEA—FICTION
TEA PARTIES
TEA PARTIES—COOKERY
TEA PARTIES— HANDICRAFTS
TEDDY BEAR DAY— FICTION
TEDDY BEARS
TEDDY BEARS—TEA PARTIES
TEDDY BEARS—TEA PARTIES—COOKERY
TEDDY BEARS—TEA PARTIES—HANDICRAFTS
TENNESSEE—COOKERY
TESSELLATION ART
TETON SIOUX INDIANS— GAMES
TEXAS—COOKERY
TEXAS—FOLKLORE

TEXAS WENDS— COOKERY
THAI-AMERICANS— COOKERY
THAILAND—FESTIVALS— DECORATIONS
THAILAND—FLOWERS
THAILAND—GAMES
THAILAND—LANGUAGE
THAILAND—NEW YEAR'S EVE—COOKERY
THANKSGIVING
THANKSGIVING— BIRDFEEDERS
THANKSGIVING—COOKERY
THANKSGIVING— DECORATIONS
THANKSGIVING—DOLLS
THANKSGIVING—FICTION
THREE BEARS
THREE KINGS DAY— COOKERY
TIBET—GAMES
TIBET—MANDALAS
TIBET—MASKS
TIE-DYE
TIME CAPSULES
TISHA-B'AV— HANDICRAFTS
*TITANIC*
TLINGIT INDIANS— BASKETS
TLINGIT INDIANS— BLANKETS
TLINGIT INDIANS— COOKERY
TLINGIT INDIANS— LANGUAGE
TLINGIT INDIANS— MOCCASINS
TLINGIT INDIANS— TOTEM POLES
TOBAGO—COOKERY
TOBAGO—FESTIVALS— COOKERY
TOBAGO—GAMES

VALENTINE'S DAY—
    FICTION
VALENTINE'S DAY—
    GAMES
VALENTINE'S DAY—
    HANDICRAFTS
VALENTINE'S DAY—
    JEWELRY
VALENTINE'S DAY—
    LANGUAGE
VALENTINE'S DAY—SOAP
VAN ALLSBURG, CHRIS
VAN BUREN, MARTIN
    (PRESIDENT)
VAN EYCK, JAN
VAN GOGH, VINCENT
VANILLA
VASARELY, VICTOR
VENEZUELA—COOKERY
VENEZUELA—GAMES
VENEZUELA—MUSICAL
    INSTRUMENTS
VERMONT—COOKERY
VERMONT—SNOWFLAKES
VETERAN'S DAY—
    DECORATIONS
VICTORIAN AGE—
    COOKERY
VIETNAM—COOKERY
VIETNAM—FESTIVALS—
    COOKERY
VIETNAM—FESTIVALS—
    LANTERNS
VIETNAM—FESTIVALS—
    MASKS
VIETNAM—FOLKLORE
VIETNAM—GAMES
VIETNAM—HATS
VIETNAM—LANGUAGE
VIETNAM—NEW YEAR—
    COOKERY
VIETNAM—NEW YEAR—
    DECORATIONS
VIETNAM—NEW YEAR'S
    DAY—COOKERY
VIETNAMESE-AMERICANS
    —COOKERY

VIETNAMESE-AMERICANS
    —FICTION
VIKINGS—AMULETS
VIKINGS—ART
VIKINGS—BURIALS
VIKINGS—CHIEFTAINS
VIKINGS—COINS
VIKINGS—COOKERY
VIKINGS—FOSSILS
VIKINGS—GAMES
VIKINGS—GODS
VIKINGS—HELMETS
VIKINGS—HOUSEHOLD
    ITEMS
VIKINGS—HOUSES
VIKINGS—JEWELRY
VIKINGS—LONGSHIPS
VIKINGS—NAVIGATORS
VIKINGS—RELIGION
VIKINGS—RUNESTONES
VIKINGS—SHIELDS
VIKINGS—SHIPS
VIKINGS—SLEDS
VIKINGS—TRADE
VIKINGS—WEATHER
    VANES
VIRGINIA—COOKERY
VLACH (ARUMANIAN)-
    AMERICANS—
    COOKERY
VUILLARD, EDOUARD

WAITRESSES
WALES—COOKERY
WALES—GAMES
WALES—LANGUAGE
WAMPANOAG INDIANS—
    COOKERY
WAMPANOAG INDIANS—
    JEWELRY
WAMPANOAG INDIANS—
    WIGWAMS
WARHOL, ANDY
WASHINGTON, D.C.—
    COOKERY
WASHINGTON, GEORGE
    (PRESIDENT)

WASHINGTON, GEORGE
    (PRESIDENT)—
    BIRTHDAY
WASHINGTON, GEORGE
    (PRESIDENT)—
    BIRTHDAY—
    COOKERY
WASHINGTON, GEORGE
    (PRESIDENT)—
    BIRTHDAY—GAMES
WASHINGTON, GEORGE
    (PRESIDENT)—
    FICTION
WASHINGTON, GEORGE
    (PRESIDENT)—HATS
WASHINGTON, GEORGE
    (PRESIDENT)—
    PUPPETS
WASHINGTON, GEORGE
    (PRESIDENT)—
    SILHOUETTES
WASHINGTON, MARTHA
    (FIRST LADY)—
    COOKERY
WASHINGTON (STATE)—
    COOKERY
WEAVING
WELSH AMERICANS—
    COOKERY
WEST INDIES—FESTIVALS
WEST NIGERIA—
    HANDICRAFTS
WEST (U.S.)—HISTORY—
    BOATS
WEST (U.S.)—HISTORY—
    CANALS
WEST (U.S.)—HISTORY—
    CANOES
WEST (U.S.)—HISTORY—
    DISCOVERY AND
    EXPLORATION. *See also*
    LEWIS AND CLARK
WEST (U.S.)—HISTORY—
    FICTION
WEST (U.S.)—HISTORY—
    FOOTWEAR
WEST (U.S.)—HISTORY—
    FORTS

WEST (U.S.)—HISTORY—
HOUSES
WEST (U.S.)—HISTORY—
INDIANS—HOUSES
WEST (U.S.)—HISTORY—
JOURNALS
WEST (U.S.)—HISTORY—
LAND SURVEYS
WEST (U.S.)—HISTORY—
LANTERNS
WEST (U.S.)—HISTORY—
MUSICAL
INSTRUMENTS
WEST (U.S.)—HISTORY—
SCHOONERS
WEST (U.S.)—HISTORY—
TOOLS
WEST (U.S.)—HISTORY—
WAGONS
WEST VIRGINIA—
COOKERY
WHALING SHIPS
WHALING SHIPS—
COOKERY
WHITE HOUSE
WILDER, LAURA INGALLS—
CHRISTMAS—
DECORATIONS
WILDER, LAURA
INGALLS—
CHRISTMAS—
HANDICRAFTS
WILDER, LAURA
INGALLS—COOKERY
WILSON, WOODROW
(PRESIDENT)
WINNEBAGO INDIANS—
GAMES
WINNEBAGO INDIANS—
SHOULDER BAGS
WINTER—FESTIVALS
WINTER SOLSTICE
WISCONSIN—COOKERY
*WIZARD OF OZ*
WOMEN'S SUFFRAGE. *See*
ANTHONY, SUSAN B.
WOODLAND INDIANS—ART

WOODLAND INDIANS—
BAGS
WOODLAND INDIANS—
CANOES
WOODLAND INDIANS—
CLOTHING
WOODLAND INDIANS—
COOKERY
WOODLAND INDIANS—
DESIGNS
WOODLAND INDIANS—
FLOWERS
WOODLAND INDIANS—
GAMES
WOODLAND INDIANS—
HAIRSTYLES
WOODLAND INDIANS—
HATS
WOODLAND INDIANS—
HOUSEHOLD ITEMS
WOODLAND INDIANS—
JEWELRY
WOODLAND INDIANS—
MASKS
WOODLAND INDIANS—
MUSICAL
INSTRUMENTS
WOODLAND INDIANS—
POTTERY
WOODLAND INDIANS—
POUCHES
WOODLAND INDIANS—
QUILLWORK
WOODLAND INDIANS—
WAMPUM
WOODLAND INDIANS—
WIGWAMS
WOODLAND INDIANS—
WRITINGS
WORLD CULTURES
WORLD WAR II—
AIRPLANES
WORLD WAR II—ALLIED
SHIPS—GAMES
WORLD WAR II—BIRDS
WORLD WAR II—
CHRISTMAS—
COOKERY

WORLD WAR II—
CHRISTMAS—
DECORATIONS
WORLD WAR II—
CLOTHING
WORLD WAR II—
COASTAL DEFENSES
WORLD WAR II—CODES
WORLD WAR II—
COOKERY
WORLD WAR II—
FLASHLIGHTS
WORLD WAR II—FOOD
RATIONING
WORLD WAR II—GAMES
WORLD WAR II—
HANDICRAFTS
WORLD WAR II—
LANGUAGES
WORLD WAR II—
MILITARY LINGO
WORLD WAR II—MOBILES
WORLD WAR II—RADIO
WORLD WAR II—SCRAP
METAL COLLECTION
WORLD WAR II—
SOLDIERS—RATION
KITS
WORLD WAR II—
SUBMARINES
WORLD WAR II—VICTORY
GARDENS
WORLD WAR II—V-MAIL
WORLD WAR II—
WEATHER
WORLD WAR II—
WEATHER VANES
WRIGHT, FRANK LLOYD
WYANDOT INDIANS—
COOKERY
WYETH, ANDREW
WYOMING—COOKERY

YEMEN—GAMES
YOLEN, JANE
YOM HA'AZTMA'UT—
COOKERY

# Key to Index

The index is arranged in the following order:

Subject

**DAKOTA INDIANS—WINTER COUNT**
Winter count for yourself, paper bag, making
2391:42

Cross-reference

**DAKOTA INDIANS.** *See also* **SIOUX INDIANS**

**DALI, SALVADORE**

Project
description

Dream photographs, making   2529:78

**DALMATIANS.** *See* **CROATIAN-AMERICANS**

**DANCING**
Language arts, poetry, hobby craft activities
2511:17-20

**DANCING—TEA PARTIES—COOKERY**
Chocolate covered fruit, recipe   2643:42 ——— Page number
Have a ball tea party, how to plan and set the
table   2643:40-41
Tea punch, recipe   2643:42

Book number
(refer to "Books
Indexed by Number")

After finding an activity of interest, check the book number in the back of the index to discover the author, title, and publication data for the book in which the activity is printed.

# A

**ABORIGINES—BARK PAINTING**
  Aboriginal bark painting, paper, paints, making
    2686:35-36
**ABORIGINES—FOLKLORE**
  *Why the Thunder Man Hurls Thunderbolts,* story
    and activities   2423:52-63
**ABORIGINES—MUSICAL INSTRUMENTS**
  Didgeridoo, paper tube, paints, making
    2686:37-38
  Didgeridoo wind instrument, long cardboard
    tube, poster paints, making   2784:18-19
**ACADIANS—COOKERY**
  Catfish court bouillon, recipe   2879:3
  Plogue, buckwheat flatbreads, recipe   2879:4
  Shrimp jambalaya, recipe   2879:2-3
  Smothered potatoes, recipe   2879:4-5
**ACOMA INDIANS—POTTERY**
  Painted Acoma bowl, clay, paints, making
    2523:23-25
**ADAMS, ABIGAIL (FIRST LADY)—COOKERY**
  Cream of corn soup, recipe   2549:9
  Flummery, recipe   2549:19
  Indian pudding, recipe   2549:11
  Raspberry shrub, recipe   2549:21
**ADAMS, JOHN (PRESIDENT)**
  Create a flag, making   2263:13
  Diary and quill pen, making   2263:11
  Reading club, old English initials, making
    2263:12
  Wildlife watcher's journal, making   2263:13
**ADAMS, JOHN QUINCY (PRESIDENT)**
  Adams family village, patterns, birthplace home,
    making   2263:28-31
  Tricorn hat, pattern, making   2263:31
**ADVENT—DECORATIONS**
  Advent candles, pattern, making   2798:7
  Advent wreath, pattern, making   2798:5-6
  Angel advent calendar, gummed note pad, yarn,
    making   2721:10-11
  Road to Bethlehem hand stamping, making
    2798:13
  Song of Mary, making   2798:8
  Zechariah's song wall plaque, making   2798:11

**ADVENT—PUPPETS**
  Donkey's story sock puppet, making   2798:12
  Paper bag puppets, patterns, making   2798:9-10
**AESOP'S FABLES**
  *Fables* by Arnold Lobel, activities, literature, art,
    science, poetry, social studies, webbing
    2435:1-24
  Racing tortoise and hare, toy cars, pom-pom,
    making   2729:40-41
  *Town Mouse and the Country Mouse;* soft sculp-
    ture town and country mice, paper, yarn,
    making   2729:20-22
**AESOP'S FABLES—PUPPETS**
  *Crow and the Pitcher,* smart crow puppet, black
    sock, making   2729:46-47
**AFGHANISTAN—COOKERY**
  Khatai cookies (pistachios), recipe   2397:53
  Raisin drink, recipe   2927:21
**AFGHANISTAN—GAMES**
  Bojol baazi (anklebone game), how to play
    2927:15
  Khana, Baudakan game, how to play
    2767:44-45
  Melon game, how to play   2767:45
**AFGHANISTAN—JEWELRY**
  Necklace; melon seed necklace, dental floss,
    seeds, making   2927:25
**AFGHANISTAN—LANGUAGE**
  Pashto language, learn to speak a few words
    2397:51
**AFRICA—ANIMALS**
  Striped zebra model, envelopes, black paper,
    making   2686:65-66
**AFRICA—COOKERY**
  Coconut ice cream, recipe   2962:13
  Groundnut stew, recipe   2962:10
  Lemon squash, recipe   2962:9
  Rice balls, recipe   2962:11
  Sautéed spinach, recipe   2962:12
**AFRICA—COSTUMES**
  Boy and girl costumes, patterns, making
    2753:130

1

**AFRICA—FOLKLORE**

*A Story, A Story: An African Tale*, by Gail E.
Haley, activities, projects, patterns, art,
crafts 2822:136-139

Activities, crafts, finger plays, games, songs, patterns 2829:14-15

*Shadow* by Marcia Brown, activities, projects,
patterns, art, crafts 2822:50-51

*Simba the Lion and the Clever Trap*, story and
activities 2423:15-30

*Superman vs. the Forest Giant*, story and activities 2423:50-63

*Who Can You Believe?*, story and activities
2423:35-45

*Why Spiders Have Tiny Waists*, folktales, puppets, patterns, songs, food 2591:67-70

*Why the Sun and the Moon Live in the Sky* by
Elphinstone Dayrell; activities, art, poetry,
maps, crafts, foods, patterns 2642:116-117

**AFRICA—GAMES**

Mancala game, how to build and play 2579:17

Mancala game, how to make and play
2779:18-19

Mancala game, how to make and play
2882:34-35

Mancala game, how to play 2926:30-33

**AFRICA—HOUSES**

Making an African home 2620:75

**AFRICA—JEWELRY**

Bead necklaces, beads, strings, making
2852:112-113

**AFRICA—MASKS**

African mask, foam, colored pens, patterns,
making 2683:10-11

African masks, foam sheets, lacing, patterns,
making 2884:18-21

Animal mask, paper, pattern, making
2642:116-117

Design a mask, black and white poster board,
string, pattern for mask given, making
2745:5-7

Lion mask, paper plate, markers, making
2686:71-72

**AFRICA—MUSICAL INSTRUMENTS**

Drum shape pencil pot, papier-mâché, paints,
making 2259:28-29

**AFRICA—PAPER CHAINS**

African paper chains, paper, paints, patterns,
making 2620:72-73

**AFRICA, CENTRAL—JEWELRY**

Collar necklace (Yoruba), cardboard, pastas, salt
dough (recipe given), paints, making
2620:36-37

Faux amber necklace, cardboard, pasta, salt
dough (recipe given), paints, making
2620:36-37

Funky paper rolls necklace, paper, vegetables,
making 2620:36-37

**AFRICA, CENTRAL—SCULPTURES**

Sculpted hyena, Benin leopard and wildebeest,
boxes, paper tubes, paints, patterns,
making 2620:30-31

**AFRICA, EAST—COOKERY**

Avocado and papaya salad, recipe 2627:40

Banana and meat stew, recipe 2627:49

Boiled fried plantains, and grilled plantains, recipe
2627:42

Chapatis, recipe 2627:33

Choroko sauce, recipe 2627:46

East African menu 2627:28-29

East African table, how to set 2627:27

Ethiopian flat bread, recipe 2627:64

Fresh steamed fish, recipe 2627:54

Greens with coconut milk, recipe 2627:41

Groundnut sauce, recipe 2271:42

Groundnut sauce, recipe 2627:48

Kashata, sweet treats, recipe 2627:61

Lamb and rice, recipe 2627:66

Lentil salad, recipe 2627:68

Luku, chicken dish, recipe 2627:52

Meat curry, recipe 2627:53

Meat on a stick, recipe 2627:34

Pilau, recipe 2627:57

Plantain and vegetable salad, recipe 2265:15

Plantain soup, recipe 2627:69

Rice pancakes, recipe 2627:33

Rice with fish, recipe 2627:65

Samusas, recipe 2627:36-37

Vegetable casserole, recipe 2627:56

Vermicelli and raisins, recipe 2627:60

**AFRICA, EAST—FESTIVALS—COOKERY**

Eid al-Fitr; lamb and rice, recipe 2627:66

Eid al-Fitr; rice with fish, recipe 2627:65

**AFRICA, EAST—JEWELRY**

Collar necklace (Yoruba), cardboard, pastas, salt
dough (recipe given), paints, making
2620:36-37

Faux amber necklace, cardboard, pasta, salt
dough (recipe given), paints, making
2620:36-37

Funky paper rolls necklace, paper, vegetables, making 2620:36-37

**AFRICA, EAST—SCULPTURES**

Sculpted hyena, Benin leopard and wildebeest, boxes, paper tubes, paints, patterns, making 2620:30-31

**AFRICA, NORTH—COOKERY**

Algerian eggplant salad, recipe 2871:42

Baked fish, recipe 2871:52

Brown lentils and rice, recipe 2871:32

Chicken tagine with couscous, recipe 2871:48-49

Chickpea and carrot stew, recipe 2871:50

Coconut and semolina cake, recipe 2871:58-59

Egyptian green herb soup, recipe 2871:38

Falafel with pita and tahini sauce, recipe 2871:33

Falafel, recipe 2439:12

Fruit and nut drops, recipe 2871:68-69

Harira with lamb and chicken, recipe 2871:66

Lamb stew with dates and apricots, recipe 2871:64-65

Libyan fish soup, recipe 2871:39

Libyan potatoes with bzar, recipe 2871:53

Mashed zucchini salad, recipe 2871:34

Meatballs in tomato sauce, recipe 2871:46-47

Milk and pastry pudding, recipe 2871:56

Moroccan couscous, recipe 2265:19

Moroccan orange and radish salad, recipe 2871:41

North African menu 2871:28

Tunisian cucumber salad, recipe 2871:43

**AFRICA, NORTH—PASSOVER—COOKERY**

North African chicken soup, recipe 2481:36-37

**AFRICA, SOUTH—ANCIENT ART**

Kalahari ostrich eggs, plastic eggs, paints, designs from ancient eggs given, making 2620:56-57

**AFRICA, SOUTH—ANIMALS**

Slotted African animals, cardboard, paints, patterns, making 2620:62-63

**AFRICA, SOUTH—BIRTHDAYS—FACE PAINT**

Xhosa tribe animal face painting, how to do 2957:40-41

**AFRICA, SOUTH—DOLLS**

Beaded cloth doll, fabric, beads, buttons, making 2620:66-67

**AFRICA, SOUTH—TOYS**

Galimoto wire toy, wire, wooden blocks, making 2620:54-55

**AFRICA, WEST—ADINKRA CLOTH**

Adinkra cloth, fabric, paints, embroidery floss, patterns, making 2620:22-23

Adire eleko cloth, fabric, paints, embroidery floss, patterns, making 2620:22-23

**AFRICA, WEST—CHARMS**

Good-luck charms; gris gris, fabric, beads, buttons, yarn, ribbon, making 2620:18-19

**AFRICA, WEST—CHRISTMAS—COOKERY**

Couscous, recipe 2677:20-21

Groundnut cookies, recipe 2628:69

**AFRICA, WEST—COOKERY**

African fruit salad, recipe 2396:30

Akara, snack, recipe 2628:36

Boiled corn and beans, recipe 2628:43

Boiled, fried, grilled and baked plantains, recipes 2628:43-46

Casamance fish stew, recipe 2628:60

Chicken yassa, recipe 2628:64-65

Coconut crisps, recipe 2628:39

Coconut soup, recipe 2265:13

Curry chicken dish, recipe 2628:61

Dovi, West African peanut butter stew, recipe 2265:11

Egusi soup, recipe 2628:50

Fresh fish pepper soup, recipe 2628:51

Fruit salad, recipe 2628:42

Fufu, recipe 2628:32

Ginger-fried fish, recipe 2628:66

Groundnut balls, recipe 2628:38

Groundnut sauce, recipe 2271:42

Groundnut sauce, recipe 2628:35

Jollof rice, recipe 2628:56

Okra soup, recipe 2628:52

Spinach stew, recipe 2628:57

Sweet balls, recipe 2628:39

Sweet potato fritters, recipe 2628:33

Vegetables in peanut sauce, recipe 2628:58

West African menu 2628:28-29

West African table, how to set 2628:27

Yams and squash, recipe 2628:68

**AFRICA, WEST—DOLLS**

Akuba doll, heavy cardboard, paints, fabric, gold cord, making 2620:20-21

**AFRICA, WEST—FESTIVALS—COOKERY**

Eid al-Fitr; chickpea salad, recipe 2628:69

Yoruba Naming Ceremony; ginger-fried fish, recipe 2481:52

**AFRICA, WEST—FLAGS**

Asafo warrior people of Fante flags, fabric, felt, patterns, making 2620:26-27

3

**AFRICA, WEST—HANDICRAFTS**

Tuareg containers, paper, yarn, colored markers, making  2620:14-15

**AFRICA, WEST—MASKS**

Dogon animals mask, railroad board, paints, pattern, making  2620:12-13

Lion mask, yellow cardboard, red raffia, crepe paper, pipe cleaners, making  2784:10-11

Tall Bobo dance mask, large cardboard, paints, patterns, making  2620:24-25

**AFRICA, WEST—MIDDLE AGES—GAMES**

Call-and-response game, how to play  2745:16

**AFRICA, WEST—MIDDLE AGES— TIMBUKTU**

Potato stamp painting of city of Timbuktu, making  2745:11-12

**AFRICA, WEST—MIDDLE AGES— TIMBUKTU—KINGS**

King's scepter, paper bowls, cardboard tube, gold paint, making  2745:13-14

**AFRICA, WEST—MUD CLOTH**

Mud cloth, fabric, paints, embroidery floss, patterns, making 2620:22-23

Mud paints, how to make and paint on cloth 2331:12-13

**AFRICA, WEST—PAINTINGS**

Senufo figures prints, paper, fabric, paints, patterns, making  2620:16-17

**AFRICAN AMERICAN MONTH**

Activities, patterns, making  2754:99-108

**AFRO-AMERICANS**

Philip Randolph brotherhood of sleeping car porters' puzzle, making  2731:34-35

Benjamin Banneker model, paper, making 2731:4-5

Benjamin Banneker; make a star-watching chart, how to do  2745:48-49

Carter G. Woodson timeline of black American heroes, making  2731:32-33

George Washington Carver peanut magnet, making  2731:20-21

George Washington Carver; conduct a scientific experiment, how to do  2745:176-177

George Washington Carver; grow a sweet potato vine, how to do  2745:175

George Washington Carver; make peanut butter, how to do  2745:173

Granville T. Woods invention puzzle, making 2731:16-17

Harriet Tubman's route to freedom maze, box, straws, making  2731:12-13

Ida B. Wells-Barnett "all kinds of people" pin, yarn, beads, eyes, making  2731:18-19

James Weldon Johnson collection game, making  2731:27-29

Jesse Owens running model, making 2731:44-45

Jesse Owens; 100-meter race, how to do 2745:191-192

Jesse Owens; 400-meter relay, how to do 2745:193-194

Jesses Owens; long jump, how to do  2745:195

Jesse Owens; medals, metal lids, paints, making 2745:196

Louis Armstrong; play the cornet, make from vinyl tubing  2745:186

Martin Luther King Jr. all one family necklace, making  2731:46-47

Mary McLeod Bethune school that grew model, making  2731:30-31

Matthew A. Henson on the North Pole display, making  2731:22-24

Paul Laurence Dunbar paper and pencil magnet, making  2731:14-15

Ralph Johnson Bunche bookmark, making 2731:42-43

W.E.B. DuBois file box of black American heroes, making  2731:25-26

Write an almanac, how to do  2745:45-47

**AFRO-AMERICANS—CIVIL RIGHTS— HISTORY**

Carry a card supporting nonviolence, how to do 2745:202-203

Demonstrate your commitment activity 2956:101-102

Dressing to express activity  2956:86-87

Express yourself, make a political button 2956:145-146

Food drive activity  2956:131

Freedom feast activity  2956:133-135

Freedom film festival activity  2956:84-85

Freedom school activities  2956:53-55

Freedom singers activity  2956:114-119

Hand fan, craft stick, paper, pattern for fan, making  2745:209-210

Letter writing campaign for prisoners of conscience activity  2956:132

Love beads, clay, paints, string, making 2956:120

Lunch counter play: *What Is This World Coming To?*, how to do  2956:47-56

March on Washington, carry a sign, poster board, stick, making  2745:212-213

Musical drama: *From the Back of the Bus,* how
   to do   2956:69-72
Plan a civil rights event, how to do   2956:17-19
Recital day activities   2956:98-100
Record oral histories activity   2956:112-113
Tie-dye clothing, how to do   2956:147-148
Walk for justice, how to do   2956:34
Workshop on nonviolence, covering principles of
   nonviolence, how to do   2956:32-33
Write a freedom ride journal, how to do
   2956:68

**AFRO-AMERICANS—CIVIL RIGHTS—
   HISTORY—COOKERY**
Corn bread, recipe   2956:134-135
Gumbo, recipe   2956:133-134

**AFRO-AMERICANS—COLONIAL
   AMERICA—SLAVE TRADE**
Slave trade bead necklace, clay, wire, making
   2745:28-29

**AFRO-AMERICANS—COOKERY**
Baked grits, recipe   2879:6
Benné cookies, recipe   2975:9
Collard greens and pot likker, recipe   2879:7
Cornbread and biscuits, recipe   2520:104-106
Cornbread, recipe   2478:96
Fried plantain, recipe   2520:107-108
Marinated pork chops, recipe   2879:6-7
Neck bones and rice, recipe   2879:8
Potato salad, recipe   2478:96
Sweet potato pie, recipe   2633:unp
Sweet potato pie, recipe   2879:7-8
White potato pie, recipe   2879:8

**AFRO-AMERICANS—DANCES**
Tap shoes, sneakers, pennies, making
   2520:93-94

**AFRO-AMERICANS—FICTION**
*Cornrows* by Camille Yarbrough; activities, art,
   poetry, maps, crafts, foods, patterns
   2642:84-86
*Honey, I Love* by Eloise Greenfield; activities,
   art, poetry, maps, crafts, foods, patterns
   2642:20-23
*Wagon Wheels* by Barbara Brenner, activities for
   art, music, food, clothing and history
   2478:73-104
*Wagon Wheels* by Barbara Brenner; activities,
   art, poetry, maps, crafts, foods, patterns
   2642:39-43

**AFRO-AMERICANS—FOLKLORE**
*Brer Possum and Brer Snake,* story and activities
   2423:22-30

**AFRO-AMERICANS—GAMES**
Chigoro Danda, how to play   2520:69-71
Little Sally Walker, how to play   2520:64-65
Mancala, how to make and play   2975:23
Mancala, how to make game board and play
   2520:61-63
Muraburaba, how to make game board and play
   2520:66-68

**AFRO-AMERICANS—HAIR**
Hair braiding, cornrows, how to do   2520:31-34

**AFRO-AMERICANS—HANDICRAFTS**
Adire (tie-dyeing), T-shirt, string, dyes, making
   2520:46-49
Calabash model, papier-mâché, making
   2520:43-45

**AFRO-AMERICANS—HISTORY**
Election Day parade, how to do   2745:105-106

**AFRO-AMERICANS—HISTORY—CIVIL WAR**
Make a Congressional Medal of Honor ribbon,
   making   2745:138-139
U.S. colored troops, patterns given, how to do
   2745:140-145

**AFRO-AMERICANS—HISTORY—CIVIL
   WAR—FUNDRAISERS**
Have a taffy-pull, how to do, recipe for taffy
   given   2745:153-154
Hold an egg-cracking party, how to do
   2745:151-152

**AFRO-AMERICANS—HISTORY—CIVIL
   WAR—QUILTING**
Bible quilt, fabric, batting, making
   2745:148-150

**AFRO-AMERICANS—HISTORY—COLONIAL
   PERIOD—COOKERY**
Peanut soup, recipe   2516:31

**AFRO-AMERICANS—HISTORY—COOKERY**
Election Day cakes, recipe   2745:107-108

**AFRO-AMERICANS—HISTORY—COWBOYS**
Design a brand, paper bowl, cardboard tube,
   making   2745:165-166

**AFRO-AMERICANS—HISTORY—
   EMANCIPATION—COOKERY**
Juneteenth Day; favorite drink, recipe
   2745:160-161

**AFRO-AMERICANS—HISTORY—FESTIVALS**
Juneteenth picnic basket, paper strips, making
   2520:16-17
Pinkster Day; dance on a shingle, how to do
   2745:117

Pinkster Day; hold a high-jump contest, how to do   2745:118-119

Pinkster Day; King Charles red coat, red and black paper, gold lace, making 2745:111-112

Pinkster Day; King Charles silver buckles, cardboard, foil, making   2745:114

Pinkster Day; King Charles tricornered hat, black paper, gold fabric, making   2745:113

Pinkster Day; wear a chain of blummies, tissue paper, pipe cleaners, making 2745:115-116

**AFRO-AMERICANS—HISTORY— PLANTATION LIFE—COOKERY**

Fried mush, recipe   2745:58-59

Greens, recipe   2745:59

Grits, recipe   2745:58

**AFRO-AMERICANS—HISTORY— PLANTATION LIFE—DOLLS**

Sew a doll, fabric, sock, cotton balls, making 2745:77-79

**AFRO-AMERICANS—HISTORY— PLANTATION LIFE—GAMES**

Old grey horse game, how to play   2745:76

Skip to the barbershop game, how to play 2745:72-73

William, William, Trembletoe game, how to play   2745:74-75

**AFRO-AMERICANS—HISTORY— PLANTATION LIFE—MUSIC**

Jingle a tambourine, how to make and play 2745:85-87

Patting, how to do   2745:83

Playing the bones, how to do   2745:84

Washtub bass, washtub, clothesline, broom handle, how to make and play   2745:88-89

**AFRO-AMERICANS—HISTORY— PLANTATION LIFE—TOYS**

Hoop and stick, how to play   2745:80

**AFRO-AMERICANS—HISTORY— REVOLUTIONARY WAR—GAMES**

Marbles, clay, how to make and play 2745:41-42

**AFRO-AMERICANS—HISTORY— REVOLUTIONARY WAR—SHIPS**

Merchant ships, 3-D picture of sailing ship, making   2745:36-38

**AFRO-AMERICANS—HISTORY— UNDERGROUND RAILROAD**

Carry a candle, how to make and do 2745:123-124

Carry a stick, how to make and do   2745:125

Follow the North star, how to do   2745:128-129

Wear armbands, red felt, beads, making 2745:132-134

Wear cuffs, brown paper, pattern, making 2745:130-131

**AFRO-AMERICANS—HISTORY— UNDERGROUND RAILROAD— FREEDOM TRAIL**

Uncode a spiritual, decide what messages were in codes to direct slaves to underground railway   2745:94-97

**AFRO-AMERICANS—HISTORY— UNDERGROUND RAILROAD— INDIANS**

Make a Native American apron, brown bag, ribbon, pattern, making   2745:130-131

**AFRO-AMERICANS—MASKS**

Mask making, tribal mask, papier-mâché, making 2520:50-53

**AFRO-AMERICANS—MUSICAL INSTRUMENTS**

Talking drum, plastic flowerpots, rubber inner tubing, making   2520:54-57

Tambourine, aluminum pie pan, small noise objects, making   2520:79-80

Wind instrument, tube of bamboo, making 2520:83

**AFRO-AMERICANS—PUPPETS**

Frederick A. Douglass talking puppet, cardboard, paper, making   2731:10-11

Louis "Satchmo" Armstrong puppet, making 2731:36-38

Marian Anderson singing puppet, making 2731:39-41

Sojourner Truth puppet, sock, felt, Styrofoam ball, making   2731:7-9

**AFRO-AMERICANS—QUILTING**

Miniature quilt, fabric, fiber fill, making 2520:35-40

**AFRO-AMERICANS—SLAVERY**

Kneeling slave medallion, how to do 2745:50-52

**ALABAMA—COOKERY**

'Bama butter, recipe   2534:13

Carmel pecan turtles, recipe   2405:61

**ALAMO—COOKERY**

Hot and spicy Texas ribs, recipe   2359:54-55

Meatless chili, recipe   2359:56-57

Tacos, recipe   2359:52-53

**ALASKA—COOKERY**

Northwest salmon sandwiches, recipe    2534:14
Pollock fish dish, recipe    2775:55

**ALASKA—FOLKLORE—COOKERY**

Akutaq, fish and berry dish, recipe    2979:last
    page

**ALASKA—LANGUAGE**

Commonly used Alaska expressions    2775:51

**ALBANIAN-AMERICANS—COOKERY**

Boat (meat-stuffed pie), recipe    2879:9-10
Hamburger with potato (moussaka), recipe
    2879:9

**ALEUTS—COOKERY**

Cranberries, recipe    2879:102
Salmon chowder, recipe    2879:102
White fish soup, recipe    2879:102

**ALGERIA—COOKERY**

Algerian eggplant salad, recipe    2871:42
Fruit and nut drops, recipe    2871:68-69

**ALGONQUIN INDIANS**

*Little Burnt Face,* story and activities
    2423:143-166

**ALGONQUIN INDIANS—MUSICAL
    INSTRUMENTS**

Birch bark rattle, cardboard, felt strips, yarn,
    beads, patterns, making    2621:47
Dew claw ankle rattle, scrunchy, paper, patterns,
    making    2621:47
Gourd rattle, papier-mâché, stickers, feathers,
    beans, paints, patterns, making    2621:47

**ALICE IN WONDERLAND—TEA PARTIES—
    COOKERY**

Blackberry tea, recipe    2643:30
Cheshire cat smiles, recipe    2386:30
Peanut butter and chocolate swirls, recipe
    2643:30
Queen's stolen tarts, recipe    2386:32-33
Tea lemonade, recipe    2386:29
White rabbit's nibble platter, recipe    2386:31
Mad Hatter's tea party; invitations, decorations,
    foods, crafts, games, how to do
    2386:26-35

**AMISH—COOKERY**

Apple fritters, recipe    2880:61
Back-to-basics brunch, recipe    2534:30
Chicken in a pot, recipe    2880:63
Fried tomatoes, recipe    2880:61
Hamburger meal, recipe    2880:62
Peach or apple strudel, recipe    2880:62
Peanut butter spread, recipe    2879:11

Pumpkin bread, recipe    2880:63
Split pea soup with ham, recipe    2880:63
Sweet potato patties, recipe    2880:61
Vegetable soup, recipe    2880:62
Yummasetti (spaghetti dish), recipe
    2879:11-12

**AMISH—QUILTS—FICTION**

*Plain Girl* by Virginia Sorensen; activities, story
    quilt, feast and quilting bee    2880:17-37

**ANASAZI INDIANS—COOKERY**

Anasazi bean dip and corny tortillas, recipe
    2534:19

**ANGELICO, FRA GIOVANNI**

Painting with silver leaf, how to do    2529:16

**ANGLO-AMERICANS—COOKERY**

Connecticut Kedgeree rice and lentil dish, recipe
    2879:14
Custard Johnny cake, recipe    2879:13-14
Rhode Island Johnny cake, recipe    2879:13
Sally Lunn cake, recipe    2879:14
Yorkshire pudding, recipe    2879:15

**ANTARCTICA**

Antarctic animals, activities, patterns
    2755:113-124

**ANTARCTICA—ICEBERGS**

Iceberg model, Styrofoam plates, blue paper,
    making    2686:122-123

**ANTARCTICA—PENGUINS**

Adelie penguin model, paper tube, paints, mak-
    ing    2686:120-121

**ANTARCTICA—WHALES**

Blue whale model, blue paper, Styrofoam tray,
    making    2686:124-125

**ANTHONY, SUSAN B.**

Susan B. Anthony portrait, pattern    2758:80

**ANTHONY, SUSAN B.—BIRTHDAY**

February 15, 1820, stories, music, games, activi-
    ties, projects, patterns    2377:46-52

**APACHE INDIANS—BASKETS**

Lightweight basket, twine, raffia, making
    2644:13

**APACHE INDIANS—COOKERY**

Acorn bread, recipe    2879:16
Acorn stew, recipe    2278:53
Acorn stew, recipe    2879:15-16
Black walnut cornbread, recipe    2879:16-17
Fry bread, recipe    2278:52

**APACHE INDIANS—FACE PAINTS**

Apache face paint, recipe    2349:27

7

**APACHE INDIANS—GAMES**

Jackstones, how to play 2767:163-164

Marbles, how to play 2767:164-165

Raven Goes to His Child, how to play 2767:168

**APACHE INDIANS—LANGUAGE**

Everyday words in Apache language 2278:91

**APPALACHIA—FOLKLORE**

*Ashpet,* story and activities 2423:147-166

*Catskins,* story and activities 2423:149-166

**APPLES**

History of apples 2717:38-39

Teaching themes, activities, games, crafts, patterns, recipes 2410:15-29

**APRIL FOOL'S DAY**

April Fool's Day activities 2752:34-35

History of April Fool's Day 2877:28

**APRIL FOOL'S DAY—COOKERY**

Lemon poppy pound cake, recipe 2877:31

Oatmeal raisin "ant" cookies, recipe 2877:30

**APRIL FOOL'S DAY—DECORATIONS**

Foolish face, pattern, making 2752:36

Jack in the box, pattern, making 2752:40-41

Jumping jack, straws, ribbon, rubber bands, making 2778:20-21

**APRIL FOOL'S DAY—FICTION**

*Arthur's April Fool* by Marc Brown, activities, crafts, patterns, games, masks, puppets, making 2329:101-103

**APRIL FOOL'S DAY—SOAP**

April Fool's soap, making 2936:43

**APRIL THEMES**

Thematic units, lessons, activities, art, poetry, crafts, patterns, recipes 2320:220-248

**ARAB-AMERICANS—COOKERY**

Kibbee (wheat and meat), recipe 2879:18

Kibbee balls (wheat and ground lamb), recipe 2879:18

Tabouli salad, recipe 2879:18-19

**ARAPAHO INDIANS—COOKERY**

Buffalo jerky, recipe 2429:13

**ARAPAHO INDIANS—GAMES**

Ring and Pin, how to play 2767:165-166

**ARAPAHO INDIANS—POUCHES**

Beaded pouch, felt or cloth, large beads, making 2555:22

**ARBOR DAY**

Arbor Day activities 2752:44-45

**ARBOR DAY—DECORATIONS**

Arbor Day invitation, pattern, making 2752:49

Arbor Day name tag, pattern, making 2752:49

Arbor Day vine, pattern, making 2752:46

Crown of leaves, pattern, making 2752:50

My Arbor Day book, pattern, making 2752:47

Reading tree, pattern, making 2752:48

**ARCHITECTURE**

Castle, how to build 2511:2

Language arts, poetry, hobby craft activities 2511:1-6

**ARCHITECTURE—GOTHIC STYLE**

Gothic mirror, papier-mâché, paints, making 2259:20-21

**ARCTIC ANIMALS**

Arctic animals, activities, patterns 2755:113-124

**ARCTIC INDIANS—DOLLS**

Arctic and subarctic figures, felt, cardboard, patterns, making 2351:32-33

**ARCTIC INDIANS—KAYAKS**

Inuit kayak, clay, paints, string, patterns, making 2351:38-39

**ARCTIC INDIANS—MASKS**

Yup'ik spirit mask, paper plate, feathers, markers, patterns, making 2351:27-28

**ARCTIC PEOPLES—CARVING**

Inuit carving, soap, felt, making 2456:48-49

**ARCTIC PEOPLES—CLOTHING**

Drawstring purse, chamois leather, felt, shoelace, beads, making 2456:20-21

Mittens, chamois leather, felt, making 2456:44-45

Saami hat, felt, ribbons, cardstock, making 2456:46-47

**ARCTIC PEOPLES—DWELLINGS**

Nenet tent, blankets, bamboo sticks, string, making 2456:14-15

**ARCTIC PEOPLES—GAMES**

Hole and pin game, cardstock, paints, chopstick, making 2456:24-25

**ARCTIC PEOPLES—HUNTING**

Hunting blind, felt, bamboo sticks, leaves, making 2456:32-33

**ARCTIC PEOPLES—JEWELRY**

Brooch, cardstock, foil, button, making 2456:52-53

**ARCTIC PEOPLES—LAMPS**

Oil lamp, clay, paints, making 2456:18-19

**ARCTIC PEOPLES—RELIGION**

Shaman's drum, cardstock, chamois leather, paints, making   2456:50-51

**ARCTIC PEOPLES—SLEDS**

Model sled, cardstock, balsa wood, chamois leather, paints, making   2456:26-27

**ARCTIC PEOPLES—SNOW GOGGLES**

Snow goggles, chamois leather, cardstock, making   2456:34-35

**ARCTIC PEOPLES—TOYS**

Feeding birds toy, clay, paints, making   2456:22-23

**ARCTIC PEOPLES—TRANSPORTATION**

Umiak model, chamois leather, cardstock, dowel, paints, making   2456:28-31

**ARGENTINA—CAVES—PAINTINGS**

Cave painting of hands, paper, poster paints, making   2373:15

**ARGENTINA—CLOTHING**

Poncho, old blanket, yarn, making   2647:16

**ARGENTINA—COOKERY**

Alfajores, wafer cookies, recipe   2647:19

Breaded beef cutlets, recipe   2670:40

Chimichurri sauce, recipe   2922:50

Dulce de leche, recipe   2358:105

Finger sandwiches, recipe   2670:56

Flan (milk pudding), recipe   2670:55

Mate tea, how to make   2358:106

Peach licuado drink, recipe   2419:30-31

Peas, recipe   2670:49

Turnovers, recipe   2670:62-63

**ARGENTINA—GAMES**

Blind horseman game, how to play   2525:170

Captain's ride game, how to play   2525:181

El Caracol (The Snail), how to play   2767:46-47

Geometry class game, how to play   2525:193

Headband tag game, how to play   2525:134

Pillma, how to play   2767:47

Polo game, how to play   2525:161

Sea serpent game, how to play   2373:29

Stolen ball game, how to play   2525:142

**ARGENTINA—GAUCHOS**

Gaucho belt, cardboard, foil, yarn, making   2686:113-114

**ARGENTINA—LANGUAGE**

Phrases, numbers and days of the week in Spanish   2358:112

Spanish words for family members   2373:21

Spanish words and phrases   2373:19

**ARGENTINA—ORNAMENTS**

Cockade badge-like ornament, cardboard, button, making   2419:28-29

**ARGENTINA—SPORTS**

Soccer ball, how to make from old newspapers and old sock   2419:27

**ARIZONA—COOKERY**

Cactus candy, recipe   2786:62

Powwow wow bread (fry bread), recipe   2534:15

**ARKANSAS—COOKERY**

Watermelon frappe, recipe   2534:16

**ARMENIA—GAMES**

Egg jousting, how to play   2767:48

**ARMENIAN-AMERICANS—COOKERY**

Bean salad, recipe   2879:20

Lemon yogurt cake, recipe   2879:20

Nutmeg cake, recipe   2879:21

Prinzov pilaf, recipe   2879:21-22

Tan (yogurt drink), recipe   2879:21

**ARP, HANS**

*Muse of Chance* collage, making   2529:74

**ARTHUR, CHESTER ALAN (PRESIDENT)**

Circle of roses, making   2263:73

Stained glass roses, pattern, making   2263:73

**ARTISTS**

Angelico; painting with silver leaf, how to do   2529:16

Arp; *Muse of Chance* collage, making   2529:74

Audubon; nature notebook, making   2529:35

Blake; hand colored prints, making   2529:32

Botticelli; art in the round, making   2529:18

Bourke-White; ABC photography, how to do   2529:89

Braque; Cubist collage, making   2529:68

Calder; standing mobile, making   2529:66

Cassatt; tempera monoprint, making   2529:44

Cezanne; Seeing shapes still life, making   2529:48

Chagall; scenery mural, making   2529:76

Chamberlain; big junk, making   2529:97

Christo; transformations, making   2529:99

Constable; cloudscape, making   2529:33

Cornell; portrait box collage, making   2529:94

Courbet; palette knife painting, how to do   2529:36

Da Vinci; drawing things apart, how to do   2529:19

Da Vinci; inventions, how to do   2529:20-21

Dali; dream photographs, making   2529:78

Davis; comic creatures, making   2529:105

Degas; chalk on cloth, making   2529:41

Degas; resist in motion, making   2529:40

Duchamp; happy accident string drop, making
2529:73

Dürer; wood block print, making   2529:22

El Greco; drawing tall figures, how to do
2529:26

Escher; tessellation design, how to do   2529:65

Gainsborough; portrait on landscape, making
2529:31

Gauguin; surprising colors, making   2529:51

Ghiberti; Florentine relief, making   2529:14

Giacometti; sticks 'n straws, making   2529:79

Giotto di Bondone; egg paint, making   2529:12

Grandma Moses; busy folk art scene, making
2529:84

Hokusai; Surimono greeting, making   2529:34

Homer; wilderness watercolor, making
2529:43

Kahlo; special self-portrait, making   2529:80-81

Kandinsky; painting music, how to do   2529:60

Kienholz; walk through sculpture, making
2529:98

Klee; one line designs, making   2529:62-63

Lange; photo story collage, making   2529:88

Lawrence; series drawing, how to do   2529:90

Lichtenstein; comic dots, making   2529:102

Limbourg Brothers; book of days, making
2529:13

Linnaeus; botanical illustrations, making
2529:30

Magritte; giant tennis shoes, making   2529:77

Manet; still-life in melted crayon, making
2529:38

Masaccio; profile portrait, making   2529:17

Matisse; story color collage, making   2529:58

Michelangelo; fresco plaque, making   2529:24

Michelangelo; lie-down painting, making
2529:25

Mondrian; straight line design, making   2529:61

Monet; dabble in paint, how to do   2529:39

Moore; carving stone, how to do   2529:67

Morisot; texture paints, making   2529:42

Munch; clay facial expressions, making
2529:59

Nevelson; scrap box art, making   2529:95

O'Keeffe; close-up flower painting, making
2529:86

Oppenheim; wacky work of Dada, making
2529:75

Paik; robot people, making   2529:100-101

Picasso; fractured friend, making   2529:70-71

Picasso; one color painting, how to do   2529:69

Pollack; action splatter, how to do   2529:93

Raphael; mother and baby, making   2529:23

Rauschenberg; combines, making   2529:96

Rembrandt; making faces, how to do   2529:28

Rembrandt; shadowy faces, how to do   2529:29

Renoir; mixed media still-life, making   2529:45

Ringgold; quilted work, making   2529:104

Rivera; giant projector mural, making   2529:72

Rockwell; tell-a-story illustration, making
2529:85

Rodin; carving clay, how to do   2529:50

Rousseau; jungle prints, making   2529:49

Rubens; chalk light face, making   2529:27

Russell; western sunset, making   2529:56

Seurat; pointillist color cards, making   2529:54

Smith; cubi structure, making   2529:91

Stella; mixed media lines, making   2529:64

Toulouse-Lautrec; event poster, making
2529:52-53

Van Allsburg; glowing house, making
2529:106

Van Eyck; triptych panel, making   2529:15

Van Gogh; impasto, making   2529:46

Van Gogh; starry night, making   2529:47

Vasarely; dizzy op art, making   2529:92

Vuillard; artist's studio; making   2529:55

Warhol; lots of me, making   2529:103

Wright; box house architect, making   2529:82

Wyeth; first snow, making   2529:87

**ASANTE (AFRICAN PEOPLES)—MUSICAL
INSTRUMENTS**

Sanza or thumb piano, box, paints, craft sticks,
pattern, making   2620:60-61

**ASCENSION—DECORATIONS**

He will come again spiral mobile, making
2798:48

Lord is with me action picture, pattern, making
2798:49-50

Witness to the Lord shrink necklace, making
2798:51

**ASHANTI (AFRICAN PEOPLES)—CLOTH**

Ashanti Kente cloth, colored paper, making
2686:77-78

**ASHANTI (AFRICAN PEOPLES)—DOLLS**

Akuba doll, heavy cardboard, paints, fabric, gold
cord, making   2620:20-21

**ASHANTI (AFRICAN PEOPLES)—STAFFS**

Elephant staff carved by the Ashanti Peoples,
cardboard, paints, making   2620:44-45

**ASIA—BIRDS**

Flamingo model, pink paper, pipe cleaners, making   2686:58-59

**ASIA—CAMELS**

Bactrian camel model, egg carton, paints, making 2686:46-48

**ASIA—COOKERY**

Zaru soba noodle dish, recipe   2381:unp

**ASIAN INDIAN AMERICANS—COOKERY**

Baked yogurt, recipe   2879:24

Nuked rice, recipe   2879:24-25

Peanut potatoes, recipe   2879:23-24

Sheera (candy), recipe   2879:23

Stuffed green peppers, recipe   2879:22-23

**ASSYRIAN-AMERICANS—COOKERY**

Booshala soup, recipe   2879:26-27

Flat egg and fresh herb pancakes, recipe 2879:26

Lettuce leaves with honey, vinegar and mint, recipe   2879:25

Zazich dip, recipe   2879:26

**ASSYRIANS.** *See* **MESOPOTAMIA**

**AUDUBON, JOHN JAMES**

Nature notebook, making   2529:35

**AUSTRALIA—ANIMALS**

Kangaroo model, paper tube, paints, making 2686:39-40

**AUSTRALIA—BIRTHDAYS—COOKERY**

Fairy bread, recipe   2957:8

**AUSTRALIA—BIRTHDAYS—PUPPETS**

Puppet, lunch bag, markers, pattern, making 2957:8-9

**AUSTRALIA—BOOMERANG**

Boomerang, cardboard, markers, making 2847:8-9

**AUSTRALIA—CHRISTMAS—COOKERY**

Acorn squash, stuffed, recipe   2898:76

Anzac biscuits (cookies), recipe   2898:79

Cheese and sage damper (bread), recipe 2898:77

Crabmeat and spinach roulade, recipe   2898:75

Damper (bread), recipe   2898:76

Frozen Christmas pudding, recipe   2898:79

Grilled grapefruit, recipe   2898:75

Kangaroo and mushrooms, recipe   2898:74

Lamingtons cake, recipe   2403:8-9

Meat pie, recipe   2898:73

Pavlova dessert, recipe   2898:78

Pumpkin scones, recipe   2898:78

Shrimp on the Barbie, recipe   2898:74

Spiced pears, recipe   2898:77

Sunshine salad, recipe   2898:73

**AUSTRALIA—CHRISTMAS—DECORATIONS**

Christmas cracker, tissue paper, confetti, ribbons, candies, making   2898:64-65

Festive pillowcase, fabric, ribbon, making 2740:22-23

**AUSTRALIA—CHRISTMAS—HANDICRAFTS**

Bay leaf tree centerpiece, green Styrofoam cone, bay leaves, beads, sequins, making 2898:70

Glitter ornaments, waxed paper, glitter, making 2898:68-69

Kookaburra bird in a eucalyptus wreath, eucalyptus branches, twig wreath, Styrofoam eggs, feathers, making   2898:66-67

**AUSTRALIA—COOKERY**

Anzac biscuits, recipe   2360:108

Anzac biscuits, recipe   2427:41

Anzac biscuits, recipe   2845:8

Australian menu   2427:28-29

Beef curry, recipe   2427:48-49

Bread and butter custard, recipe   2427:57

Creamy pumpkin soup, recipe   2271:39

Creamy pumpkin soup, recipe   2427:44

Crunchy fish fillets, recipe   2427:46-47

Damper biscuits, recipe   2427:64

Egg and bacon pie, recipe   2427:32

Fresh fruit salad, recipe   2427:33

Glazed kiwi tart, recipe   2427:54

Grub tucker, recipe   2845:9

Lamingtons, cake dessert, recipe   2300:49

Lamingtons, recipe   2396:40

Lamingtons, recipe   2427:55

Macadamia nut bread, recipe   2427:69

Mint sauce, recipe   2427:63

Pavlova dessert, recipe   2427:66-67

Pineapple fruit cup, recipe   2427:34

Rich gravy, recipe   2427:62

Roast leg of lamb, recipe   2427:60

Roast vegetables, recipe   2427:61

Sunshine salad with vinaigrette dressing, recipe 2427:51

Tea, recipe   2427:38

Tomato and mint sandwiches, recipe   2427:39

**AUSTRALIA—FESTIVALS—COOKERY**

Nuts and raisin candy, recipe   2846:8

Pavlova dessert, recipe   2983:43

**AUSTRALIA—FOLKLORE**

Activities, finger plays, songs, rhymes, crafts, patterns   2829:22-23

*Why the Thunder Man Hurls Thunderbolts,* story and activities   2423:52-63

**AUSTRALIA—GAMES**

Back-pass beanbag game, how to play   2525:98

Broomball game, broom, ball, how to play   2328:134-135

Change the spot game, how to play   2525:144

Charge game, how to play   2525:132

Hoop soccer game, how to play   2525:169

Hoop tag game, how to play   2525:47

Humpy, bumpy caterpillar game, how to play   2525:187

I looked high game, how to play   2385:13

Jackstones, how to play   2767:48-50

Kickball game, how to play   2525:45

Leap ball game, how to play   2525:162

Nucks marbles, how to play   2495:22-23

Sardines game, how to play   2385:32

Seesaw game, how to play   2525:172

Snow White game, how to play   2525:8

Super-duper hoop game, how to play   2525:88

With my hands game, how to play   2385:18

**AUSTRALIA—LANGUAGE**

Learn to speak Strine   2300:47

Phrases in Australian English   2360:112

Strine words and their meanings   2600:25

**AUSTRALIAN-AMERICANS—COOKERY**

Anzacs (cookies), recipe   2879:28

New Zealand bacon and egg pie, recipe   2879:28

Pikelets (grill cakes), recipe   2879:28-29

**AUSTRIA—CHRISTMAS—COOKERY**

Fried carp, recipe   2485:67

Red cabbage with apples, recipe   2485:68

**AUSTRIA—COOKERY**

Austrian menu   2485:26-27

Breaded veal, recipe   2485:38

Broccoli salad with bacon, recipe   2485:45

Cinnamon and almond snails, rolls, recipe   2485:32-33

Cooked potato salad, recipe   2485:43

Cucumber salad, recipe   2485:46

Egg custard soup, recipe   2485:36

Gram's goulash soup, recipe   2879:30

Herb-stuffed eggs, recipe   2485:61

Jelly rolls, recipe   2485:30-31

Linzer cake, recipe   2485:50

Linzer torte, recipe   2879:31-32

Mixed green salad, recipe   2485:46

Oatmeal soup, recipe   2879:30-31

Paprika chicken, recipe   2485:37

Pork stew, recipe   2485:58

Potato noodles, recipe   2485:42

Sacher cake, recipe   2485:54-55

Sacher torte, recipe   2396:48-49

Salami cones, recipe   2485:60

Salzburger bread, recipe   2879:29-30

Salzburger sweet soufflé, recipe   2485:53

Smoked salmon-stuffed eggs, recipe   2485:61

Tomato baskets, recipe   2485:60

Trout Vienna style, recipe   2485:41

**AUSTRIA—GAMES**

Blind hen game, how to play   2525:115

Blind snake game, how to play   2525:76

Detective game, how to play   2525:127

Halli Hallo game, how to play   2525:120

Neckball pass game, how to play   2525:183

Numbers tag, how to play   2767:50

Robot game, how to play   2525:192

Sculptor game, how to play   2525:189

Shoelace catch game, how to play   2525:132

Weird wheel game, how to play   2525:183

**AUSTRIA—NEW YEAR'S DAY—COOKERY**

Bacon bread, recipe   2485:64-65

Holiday fruit bread, recipe   2485:66

**AUSTRIAN-AMERICANS—COOKERY**

Gram's goulash soup, recipe   2879:30

Linzer torte, recipe   2879:31-32

Oatmeal soup, recipe   2879:30-31

Salzburger bread, recipe   2879:29-30

**AUTHORS, AMERICAN—19TH CENTURY—BIOGRAPHY**

Twain, Mark; match fingerprints, how to do   2935:119

Twain, Mark; scrapbook keeping, how to do   2935:99

Twain, Mark; superstitions, how to collect   2935:97

Twain, Mark; write maxims, how to do   2935:136

**AUTUMN—COOKERY**

Candy corn wreath, recipe   2576:33-36

Turkey, wobble gobble cookies, recipe   2576:41-44

**AZTECS**

Activities, hair designs, food, temples, Aztec math, statues, patterns   2421:36-42

Ancient people of Mexico, history, activities   2759:72-75

**AZTECS—CALENDAR**

Aztec calendar, pattern   2759:75

**AZTECS—CODEX**

Codex, cardboard, paints, making   2581:46-47

**AZTECS—CODICES**

Codice, paper, ribbon, making    2671:7

**AZTECS—COOKERY**

Chocolate drink, recipe    2928:31

Tortillas, recipe    2581:28-29

**AZTECS—FANS**

Feather fan, cardboard, feathers, felt, paints, making    2581:12-13

**AZTECS—FESTIVALS—HANDICRAFTS**

Festival of Our Lady of Guadalupe; dancers Aztec shield, gold foil paper, yarn, paints, making    2276:28-29

**AZTECS—GAMES**

Patolli board game, how to make and play    2581:56-57

**AZTECS—GODS**

Statue of a God, clay, plaster of Paris, paints, making    2581:50-51

**AZTECS—HEADDRESSES**

Feather headdress; feathers from paper, ribbon, jewelry, making    2928:30

**AZTECS—HELMETS**

Eagle helmet, clay, felt, ribbon, paints, making    2581:40-41

**AZTECS—JEWELRY**

Bat brooch, cardboard, paints, making    2581:32-33

Beaded jewelry, magazine pages, glue, making    2508:38-39

Necklace, papier-mâché, paints, making    2259:24-25

**AZTECS—MASKS**

Mosaic mask, clay, papier-mâché, paints, making    2508:18-19

Mosaic mask, papier-mâché, clay, paints, making    2581:34-35

**AZTECS—MOSAICS**

Aztec book cover, foam, paints, pattern, making    2683:26-27

**AZTECS—MUSICAL INSTRUMENTS**

Flute, cardboard, paints, making    2508:42-43

Rattle, clay, bamboo cane, paints, making    2581:54-55

**AZTECS—POTTERY**

Aztec bowl, papier-mâché, paints, making    2508:34-35

**AZTECS—SCULPTURES**

Chacmool statue, sawdust clay, foil, making    2508:22-23

**AZTECS—SUN STONE**

Sun stone, clays, paints, making    2581:48-49

**AZTECS—TEMPLES**

Great Temple model, sand clay (recipe given), making    2508:30-31

**AZTECS—TOYS**

Wheeled dog, clay, dowel, paint, making    2581:38-39

**AZTECS—WARRIORS**

Warrior helmet, T-shirt, felt, feathers, paint, making    2508:14-15

**AZTECS—WEAVING**

Backstrap loom, dowels, cardboard, yarn, paints, making    2581:16-17

**AZTECS—WRITING**

Codex, paper tubes, yarn, paint, making    2508:26-27

# B

**BABE RUTH—COOKERY**

Baby Ruth homerun bars, recipe   2359:103-104

**BABYLONIANS.** *See* **MESOPOTAMIA**

**BAHAMAS—COOKERY**

Crab and rice dish, recipe   2879:33

Old sour hot sauce, recipe   2879:33

**BAHAMAS—FESTIVALS—COOKERY**

Junkanoo Festival; potato salad, recipe   2925:68

**BAHAMIAN-AMERICANS—COOKERY**

Crab and rice dish, recipe   2879:33

Old sour hot sauce, recipe   2879:33

**BAHRAIN—GAMES**

Loabat A-Haloo game, how to play   2525:28

**BAKOTA (AFRICAN PEOPLES)—STATUES**

Bronze Bakot statue, railroad board, aluminum baking sheet, patterns, making   2620:40-41

**BALLET—FICTION**

*Angelina Ballerina* by Katherine Holabird, activities, projects, patterns, art, crafts   2822:118-120

**BALLET—PUPPETS**

Ballerina finger puppets, gloves, patterns, making   2675:61-63

**BAMBARA (AFRICAN PEOPLES)—FESTIVALS—HATS**

Chi Wara Festival; hats, cardboard, paints, raffia, patterns, making   2620:58-59

**BANGLADESH—GAMES**

Gul Tara (Tossing to the Stars), how to play   2767:50-51

**BANNEKER, BENJAMIN**

Benjamin Banneker model, paper, making   2731:4-5

**BARBADIAN-AMERICANS—COOKERY**

Codfish cakes, recipe   2879:34-35

Cou cou or turn corn, recipe   2879:34

**BARBADOS—CHRISTMAS—COOKERY**

Jug-jug (beef and cornmeal stew), recipe   2925:46-47

Sweet potato pone, recipe   2925:63

**BARBADOS—COOKERY**

Bajan rice and stew, recipe   2932:53

Coconut ice, recipe   2925:56

Coconut sugar cakes, recipe   2932:52

Codfish cakes, recipe   2879:34-35

Corn pie, recipe   2932:52

Cou cou or turn corn, recipe   2879:34

Lime sweet bread, recipe   2932:52

Oxtail soup, recipe   2380:unp

Peanut punch, recipe   2932:53

**BARBADOS—FESTIVALS—COOKERY**

Crop-Over Sugarcane Festival; ginger beer, recipe   2504:83

**BARBADOS—FESTIVALS—POTTERY**

Crop-Over Sugarcane Festival; clay pot, clay, paints, making   2504:80-81

**BARBADOS—GAMES**

Cat and rat game, how to play   2525:14

Dog and bone game, how to play   2525:10

Four squares game, how to play   2525:138

Through the obstacle game, how to play   2525:99

**BARBADOS—HANDICRAFTS**

Barbadian shell crafts, decorate box with shells, making   2817:12-15

**BARRIE, J. M.**

*Peter Pan;* flying Peter Pan, paper, paints, making   2729:30-31

**BASQUE-AMERICANS—COOKERY**

Basque beans or Sheepherder beans, recipe   2879:36

Basque soup, recipe   2879:36

Walnut pudding, recipe   2879:37

Wyoming Basque potatoes, recipe   2879:37

**BASQUE PEOPLE—COOKERY**

Gold nugget flan, recipe   2534:48-49

**BAULE (AFRICAN PEOPLES)—MASKS**

Goli dance simple masks, cardboard, paints, buttons, making   2620:44-45

**BAUM, FRANK L.**

*Wizard of Oz;* spinning house, milk carton, paper, making   2729:26-27

**BEARS**

Thematic units, lessons, activities, art, poetry, crafts, patterns, recipes   2320:279-304

**BELGIAN-AMERICANS—COOKERY**

Belgian pies (rice and prune tarts), recipe
2879:39-40

Chicken booyah soup, recipe   2879:38-39

Flemish beef and beef stew, recipe   2879:40-41

**BELGIUM—CHRISTMAS—COOKERY**

Buche de Noel, Christmas log cake, recipe
2899:74-75

Chestnut-cranberry stuffing, recipe   2899:76

Flemish beef stew, recipe   2899:73

Piquant beet salad, recipe   2899:72

Smitane sauce, recipe   2899:76

Speculoos cookies, recipe   2899:75

Waffles, recipe   2899:71

White asparagus soup, recipe   2899:72

**BELGIUM—CHRISTMAS—HANDICRAFTS**

Lace medallion, cotton lace doily, spray starch,
ribbon, making   2899:65

Lacy snowflakes, white paper, tree branch, patterns, how to cut   2899:68

Potpourri bag, dried flowers and leaves, spices,
making   2899:67

Snow globe, clear glass jar, plastic figurine, glitter, making   2899:66

**BELGIUM—COOKERY**

Belgian pies (rice and prune tarts), recipe
2879:39-40

Chicken booyah soup, recipe   2879:38-39

Flemish beef and beef stew, recipe   2879:40-41

**BELGIUM—FOLKLORE**

*Mr. Louse and Mrs. Louse,* story and activities
2423:36-45

**BELGIUM—GAMES**

Blindball game, how to play   2525:163

Chenille-assis (Caterpillar Sitting Down), how to
play   2767:51

Five-and-ten ball game, how to play   2525:27

Foot searching game, how to play   2525:101

Grandmother, what do you want game, how to
play   2385:22

Klinkslagen game, how to play   2525:64

Lemon, lemon game, how to play   2525:20

Olika bolika game, how to play   2385:14

Pina-one game, how to play   2385:37

Skittleball game, how to play   2525:91

Telegram game, how to play   2525:57

Tunnel race, how to play   2767:52

**BELGIUM—NEW YEAR—HANDICRAFTS**

Saint Sylvester Day letter to parents, paper, glitter, pens, making   2402:8-9

**BELIZE—COOKERY**

Avocado eggnog, recipe   2941:53

Carrot coconut bread, recipe   2941:52

Conch escabeche fish dish, recipe   2496:119

Honey candy, recipe   2941:53

Orange eggnog, recipe   2941:52

Rice and beans, recipe   2941:53

Sweet potato pudding, recipe   2941:52

**BELORUSSIAN-AMERICANS—COOKERY**

Apples baked with honey, recipe   2879:41-42

Milk soup, recipe   2879:41

Sauerkraut soup, recipe   2879:42

**BENTLEY, WILSON A.**

*Snowflake Bentley* by Jaqueline Briggs Martin,
activities, literature, science, poetry, social
studies, webbing   2435:151-170

**BIBLE**

Angel's arms, pattern, making   2793:55

Christmas star, pattern, making   2793:55

Fish and loaf of bread, pattern, making   2793:56

Palm branch, pattern, making   2793:56

Saw and hammer, pattern, making   2793:56

Shepherd's head covering, staff, crown, patterns,
making   2793:54

**BIBLE—AUTUMN CRAFTS**

Face mask, patterns, making   2354:16

Owl, patterns, making   2354:17-20

Parrot, patterns, making   2354:11-14

Pilgrim children, patterns, making   2354:9

Pilgrim hat, patterns, making   2354:6

Pumpkin, patterns, making   2354:5

Turkey, patterns, making   2354:7-8

World, patterns, making   2354:10

**BIBLE—DESERT—CLOTHES**

Boy's outfit, fabric, making   2746:27-28

Girl's outfit, fabric, making   2746:24-26

**BIBLE—DESERT—COOKERY**

Lentil stew, recipe   2746:17-18

**BIBLE—DESERT—GAMES**

Sheep, goats, lions and bears game, how to play
2746:21-22

**BIBLE—DESERT—HOUSES**

Sleeping mat, towels, fiberfill, making   2746:14

**BIBLE—DESERT—JEWELRY**

Anklet; decorate an anklet, pipe cleaners, buttons, making   2746:33

Necklace; design a necklace, pennies, index card,
making   2746:34

Ring; make a ring, pipe cleaners, buttons,
making   2746:33

**BIBLE—DESERT—RELIGION**

Memories display bowl, papier-mâché, making 2746:41-42

**BIBLE—DESERT—WEAVING**

Weaving with a loom, how to do    2746:29-31

**BIBLE—EGYPT, ANCIENT—BRICKS**

Baking bricks, clay, straw, making    2746:49-50

**BIBLE—EGYPT, ANCIENT—COOKERY**

Unleavened bread, recipe    2746:57-58

**BIBLE—EGYPT, ANCIENT—DOLLS**

Egyptian paddle doll, cardboard, paints, beads, making    2746:52-53

**BIBLE—EGYPT, ANCIENT—GAMES**

No yeast game, how to play    2746:59

**BIBLE—EGYPT, ANCIENT—MUSICAL INSTRUMENTS**

Trumpet, poster board, making    2746:67-68

**BIBLE—EGYPT, ANCIENT—WEAPONS**

Serpent-headed throwing stick, wooden spoon, paints, making    2746:54-55

**BIBLE—GAMES**

Penny toss game, making    2751:58

Pick a number game, making    2751:59

**BIBLE—GOOD FRIDAY**

He died for me Good Friday cross, paper, making    2800:57

**BIBLE—HANDICRAFTS**

Accomplishment pencil can, colored paper, ribbons, making    2725:16-17

Adam and Eve; sewing on a stocking, yarn, making    2803:14

Alive in Christ shell butterfly, making    2801:51

All about you, construction paper, pattern, making    2622:21

All God's creatures potato creations, making    2801:11

Angel advent calendar, gummed note pad, yarn, making    2721:10-11

Angel decoration, paper bags, patterns, making    2308:23-24

Angel of God, patterns, making    2616:7

Angel to-do list, roll adding machine tape, gold ribbon, Styrofoam ball, making    2721:12-13

Angel's message glory in the highest, tissue wind sock, patterns, making    2802:37-38

Animals, paper plates, patterns, making    2766:23-57

Apples, making    2616:60

Baby cradle, paper bags, patterns, making    2308:57

Baby in a basket, paper, yarn, patterns, making    2803:20-21

Baseball player, construction paper, pattern, making    2622:38

Beaded candleholder, cardboard, foil, colored beads, making    2721:24-25

Bear, paper plate, pattern, making    2766:5

Beasts, patterns, making    2616:13-16

Bible bookmark, white envelope, gold sequin, making    2721:48-49

Bible character masks, paper bags, patterns, making    2308:13

Bible characters plaster of Paris eggs, making    2801:17

Bible favorites bookmark, paper, ribbon, making    2725:38-39

Bible headdress, paper bags, patterns, making    2308:38

Bible memory place cards, paper bags, patterns, making    2308:18

Bible ornament, small matchbox, black felt, making    2721:18-19

Bible verse piñata, paper bags, patterns, making    2308:46

Bible verse wreath, making    2277:36

Big-fish tale, cardboard tube, pattern, making    2799:21-22

Bird's nest, patterns, making    2616:29-30

Blessed are the peacemakers pressed-flower bookmark, making    2801:38

Bloom for the Lord, cardboard tube, making    2799:6

Blow for the Lord, cardboard tube, making    2799:20

Book cover, paper bags, patterns, making    2308:14

Book for all time cornhusk scroll, making    2801:23

Born in Bethlehem straw drawing, making    2801:30

Boy Jesus in the temple, patterns, making    2616:43-44

Break an egg, making    2751:57

A "bright" nativity, paper bags, patterns, making    2308:10

Bright star reads "A star to follow," tissue egg, making    2802:40

Bunny cup, construction paper, pattern, making    2622:58

Burning bush tissue on a twig, tissue paper, making    2802:16

Bush that kept burning, colored tissue paper, yarn, making 2803:24

Bush that kept burning stick sculpture, making 2801:16

Butterfly, paper plate, pattern, making 2766:6

Butterfly, patterns, making 2616:20-21

Camel gift bag, padded mailing envelope, two shoulder pads, jingle bell, making 2721:36-37

Camel, paper plate, pattern, making 2766:7

Candle flame, making 2616:10

Carrots, patterns, making 2616:56-57

Cat, paper plate, pattern, making 2766:8

Caterpillar, patterns, making 2616:11-12

Celebrate his birth shape ornaments, paper, patterns, making 2800:39-40

Cheerful cookie box, plastic container, photos, making 2725:44-45

Chick cup, construction paper, pattern, making 2622:60

Christ the Savior is born pinecone manger scene, making 2801:31-32

Christmas angel, tissue and lace tree topper, patterns, making 2802:31-32

Christmas is coming advent garland, making 2801:28

Christmas memory book, brown paper grocery bags, old envelopes, making 2721:58-59

Church attendance stabile, clay, pipe cleaners, bells, beads, making 2725:33

Church designs, paper bags, patterns, making 2308:9

Church, patterns, making 2616:17-19

Circle of angels, construction paper, pattern, making 2622:47

Circle of love, construction paper, pattern, making 2622:61

Classy mural, paper bags, patterns, making 2308:51

Coat of many colors cardboard tube puppet, yarn, making 2803:20

Come, Holy Spirit paper-sculpture poster, paper, patterns, making 2800:59-60

Cone angel, construction paper, pattern, making 2622:14

Cone bunny, construction paper, pattern, making 2622:29

Cone cat, construction paper, pattern, making 2622:15

Cooperation garland, sequins, glitter, ribbons, making 2721:56-57

Cooperation tulips, paper, paints, making 2725:62-63

Cornucopia, paper bags, patterns, making 2308:45

Cow, paper plate, pattern, making 2766:9

Craft stick figures, paper bags, patterns, making 2308:47-50

Create your own stationery, paper bags, patterns, making 2308:31-32

Creation container, yarn-decorated vase, making 2803:10

Creatures that creep and fly walnut shell animals, making 2801:10

Critter bag, paper bags, patterns, making 2308:29-30

Cross bookmark, construction paper, pattern, making 2622:54

Cross for the King, cardboard tube, patterns, making 2799:53-54

Cross, patterns, making 2616:27-28

Crown bookmark, construction paper, pattern, making 2622:22

Crown of life paper sculpture, paper, patterns, making 2800:63-64

Daily journal, construction paper, pattern, making 2622:27

Daisy spinner, construction paper, pattern, making 2622:23

Daniel and the lions paper bag puppets, patterns, making 2803:31-32

Daniel and the lions, cardboard tube, making 2799:26

Daniel and the lions stand-up puppet, patterns, making 2802:23-24

Deborah saves the day, cardboard tube, making 2799:23

Decorated pot, flowerpot, old sock, buttons, making 2725:50-51

Desk paper organizer, priority mailboxes, pretty paper, making 2725:28-29

Dog, construction paper, pattern, making 2622:43

Dog, paper plate, pattern, making 2766:10

Donkey, construction paper, pattern, making 2622:10

Donkey, paper plate, pattern, making 2766:11

Dove and the rainbow mobile, tag board, yarn, patterns, making 2803:17-18

Dove came down, tin-can printing, making 2803:35

Dove, patterns, making 2616:37-38

Earth shows His handiwork layered-sand paperweight, making 2801:5

Elephant, paper plate, pattern, making 2766:12

Elephant puppet, construction paper, pattern, making 2622:32

Elijah fed by ravens, crushed tissue paper food, making 2802:22

Embroidered cards, making 2616:45

Empty tomb rock sculpture, making 2801:58

Esther crown for the queen, crushed tissue paper crown, patterns, making 2802:26-27

Ezra's scroll, cardboard tube, making 2799:27

Fall booklet, construction paper, pattern, making 2622:16

Fan bird, construction paper, pattern, making 2622:9

Fancy gift bag, paper bags, patterns, making 2308:5

Feel God's world texture collage, making 2801:8

Fish mobile, construction paper, pattern, making 2622:42

Fish puppet, paper bags, patterns, making 2308:25-26

Fish stitchery, yarn on vegetable netting, making 2803:36

Fish symbol, yarn, paper, patterns, making 2803:44-45

Fish, paper plate, pattern, making 2766:13

Fish, patterns, making 2616:31-32

Fish, tissue fish, construction paper, pattern, making 2622:57

Fish, wooden-spoon fish necklace, making 2277:37

Flower message, construction paper, pattern, making 2622:52

Flower, patterns, making 2616:33-34

Flowers of the field pleated flowers, paper, making 2800:53-54

Flowers, paper bags, patterns, making 2308:57

Flutter bird, construction paper, pattern, making 2622:33

Follow that star, star tree, making 2801:34

Forgiveness bracelet, plastic bottle, trim, yarn, making 2725:56-57

Friendship belt, patterns, making 2616:50-51

Friendship hearts, construction paper, pattern, making 2622:26

From a tiny seed, seeds in a bottle, making 2801:49

From Saul to Paul, cardboard tube, patterns, making 2799:61-62

Full heart ornament, matchbox, gold glitter, red paper, making 2721:46-47

Furry creature basket, paper bags, patterns, making 2308:15-17

Get ready for Jesus advent tree, paper, making 2800:31-32

Get ready for Jesus pinecone advent wreath, making 2801:27

Giraffe, paper plate, pattern, making 2766:14

Give thanks dried-bean plaque, making 2801:45-46

Give us this day cornhusk basket, making 2801:41

Given for you seed mosaic, cup and bread pattern, making 2801:53-54

Glow-in-the-dark prayer reminder, yarn, glow-in-the-dark paint, gold glitter, making 2721:28-29

Go tell it on the mountain pinecone bell, making 2801:33

God cares for the birds mobile, paper, making 2800:49-52

God cares for you pressed-flower picture, making 2801:40

God cares for you tissue flowers, making 2802:47-49

God helps me move peanut puppet, making 2801:44

God leads me, yarn pathfinder, making 2803:16

God made land and sea paper sculpture, paper, making 2800:6-8

God made our beautiful world torn tissue plaque, tissue paper, making 2802:5

God made seas, sky and land, tissue paper, making 2802:6

God sends the seasons, pressed-leaf sun catcher, making 2801:63

God watches over me feather collage, making 2801:39

God's colorful creation waxed-leaf collage, making 2801:7

God's creeping creation, cardboard tube, making 2799:9

God's four-footed friends crushed tissue animals, tissue paper, making 2802:10

God's gift, jewelry gift box, Christmas paper, nativity picture, making 2721:30-31

God's happy hopper folder rabbit, paper, making 2800:14-16

God's marvelous creation, weaving on poster board, yarn, making 2803:9

God's night owl, cardboard tube, making 2799:8

God's plant creation pressed leaf picture, tissue paper, making 2802:9

God's special star starfish ornament, making 2801:35

God's tiny creations dried-flower bouquet, making 2801:9

God's under the sea water animals tissue-cord picture, patterns, making 2802:11-12

God's world book, paper, Styrofoam ball, making 2725:60-61

Good grapes from Canaan, cardboard tube, making 2799:19

Good King Josiah paper crown, paper, making 2800:25-27

Good-news rabbit, cardboard tube, patterns, making 2799:57-58

Grapes, patterns, making 2616:49

Gratitude jar, plastic jar, old sock, red paper, making 2725:26-27

Grow in God's Word, cardboard tube, making 2799:24

Hand bird, construction paper, pattern, making 2622:48

Hand booklet, construction paper, pattern, making 2622:40

Hang a banner, construction paper, pattern, making 2622:49

Hanging hearts, construction paper, pattern, making 2622:53

Happy Birthday baby Jesus tag board and tissue hat, patterns, making 2802:28

Happy Birthday Jesus party hat, paper, making 2800:33-34

Happy Birthday Jesus, roll adding machine tape, doily, making 2721:60-61

Happy heart basket, paper bags, patterns, making 2308:53-54

Happy to be me, cardboard tube, making 2799:7

Harvest is ready paper plate plaque, tissue paper, making 2802:53

He died for you bark cross, making 2801:57

He is risen, cardboard tube, making 2799:56

Heart baskets, construction paper, pattern, making 2622:19

Heart bookmark, construction paper, pattern, making 2622:41

Heart butterfly, construction paper, pattern, making 2622:35

Heart mobile, construction paper, pattern, making 2622:17

Heart mouse, construction paper, pattern, making 2622:5

Heart pockets, construction paper, pattern, making 2622:11

Hearts to share, yarn printing, patterns, making 2803:38-39

Heavens declare His glory creation mobile, paper, making 2800:9-10

Helpful hand magnet, paper, magnet, making 2725:24-25

Hinged locket, metal hinge, sequins, making 2721:26-27

Horse, paper plate, pattern, making 2766:15

Hosanna to the King leaf mobile, making 2801:52

House of the Lord, cardboard tube, making 2799:25

I am God's creation, paper silhouette, yarn, making 2803:15

I become God's child seashell plaque, making 2801:36

I shall not be moved pinecone tree, making 2801:24

Ice candles, plastic container, candle, making 2725:52-53

In the beginning yarn board, making 2803:8

Jacob's dream ladder to heaven tissue paper chain, making 2802:15

Jacob's ladder, weaving on a Styrofoam tray, yarn, making 2803:19

Jacob's tent, paper bags, patterns, making 2308:42

Jesus calls Peter to fish, hanging fish, tissue paper, making 2802:45

Jesus is alive butterfly collage, paper, making 2800:58

Jesus is alive painted eggs, egg patterns, making 2801:59-60

Jesus is the reason fluffed tissue wreath, tissue paper, patterns, making 2802:29-30

Jesus is with me, yarn, paper, patterns, making 2803:42-43

Jesus lives, tissue covered balloon, making 2802:57

Jesus loves me rock brooch, making 2801:43

Jesus loves you pop-up card, paper, patterns, making 2800:47-48

Jesus' ascension, He will come again "leaded" tissue window, patterns, making 2802:63-64

Jesus' birth; nativity mobile, tissue and construction paper, patterns, making 2802:33-34

Jesus' death, Calvary's cross, stained glass window, tissue paper, patterns, making 2802:55-56

Jesus' little lamb pinecone figures, making 2801:50

Jesus' resurrection Easter butterfly, tissue paper, patterns, making 2802:59-30

Jesus' resurrection Easter garden, tissue flowers, making 2802:54

Jesus' resurrection Easter joy, marbled egg, tissue paper, making 2802:58

Jonah and the big fish, patterns, making 2616:35-36

Joseph's coat of many colors, patterns, making 2616:41-42

Joseph's robe, paper bags, patterns, making 2308:39

Joy to the World magnet, colored pasta letters, gold ribbon, foil, making 2721:20-21

Joy to the world pop-up Christmas card, paper, pattern, making 2800:35-37

Joy to the world tissue Christmas tree, patterns, making 2802:35-36

Joyful card holder, plastic berry basket, red plaid ribbon, jingle bells, making 2721:16-17

Joyful noise hat, party hat, party blower, making 2725:12-13

Key chain, making 2616:46

King for God's people, construction paper crown, patterns, making 2803:33-34

Kingly crown, paper bags, patterns, making 2308:20

Lamb mission bank, black glove, fiberfill, making 2725:10-11

Land of milk and honey cornhusk collage, making 2801:20

Let down your net leaf collage, making 2801:37

Light in the sky hanging star, paper, making 2800:45-46

Light to shine in the darkness, pleated star, tissue paper, making 2802:42

Lights in the sky yarn and tissue mobile, tissue paper, patterns, making 2802:7-8

Lilies of the field, paper, pipe cleaners, making 2725:58-59

Lion puppet, construction paper, pattern, making 2622:24

Lion, paper plate, pattern, making 2766:16

Lionhearted, construction paper, pattern, making 2622:45

Little quacker, paper bags, patterns, making 2308:52

Loaves and fishes pin, wooden spoon, markers, making 2725:48-49

Loopy bunny, construction paper, pattern, making 2622:12

Loopy cat, construction paper, pattern, making 2622:28

Loopy caterpillar, construction paper, pattern, making 2622:20

Loopy frog, construction paper, pattern, making 2622:6

Loopy ladybug, construction paper, pattern, making 2622:7

Loopy mouse, construction paper, pattern, making 2622:34

Loopy owl, construction paper, pattern, making 2622:63

Lord is my shepherd sheep, tissue paper, patterns, making 2802:19-20

The Lord's Prayer paper sun catcher, tissue paper, making 2802:46

Love necklace, making 2616:26

Love notes, sticky magnet strip, clamp, clothespin, making 2721:54-55

Love one another painted-rock paperweight, making 2801:48

Love one another paper banner, tissue paper, patterns, making 2802:51-52

Loving heart beanbag, red sock, yarn, making 2725:8-9

Magi recipe holder, felt, ribbon, yarn, clay, making 2721:14-15

Making music with Miriam, cardboard tube, making 2799:17

Manna in the wilderness folded basket, paper, making 2800:22

Manna in the wilderness woven basket, making 2801:18-19

Measuring fish, construction paper, pattern, making 2622:30

Message pinwheel, paper bags, patterns, making 2308:37

Money bag, paper bags, patterns, making 2308:41

Mother's Day card, construction paper, pattern, making 2622:50

Mother's Day present, paper bags, patterns, making 2308:21

Moved by the Spirit, cardboard tube, patterns, making 2799:63-64

Mustard seed necklace, wiggle eyes, mustard seeds, making 2725:54-55

Mustard seed, from a tiny seed, tube and tissue tree, patterns, making 2802:43-44

My book of gifts to give back to God, adding machine tape, foil, making 2721:50-51

My family bookmark, paper, photos, ribbon, making 2725:22-23

My helping hand, stitchery on burlap, yarn, making 2803:28

Native hut, paper bags, patterns, making 2308:19

Nativity panels, cardboard, old jewelry, Christmas cards with Christmas story scenes, making 2721:8-9

Noah's ark, patterns, making 2616:5-6

Note pad, construction paper, pattern, making 2622:13

Oh holy night triangle-fold manger scene, paper, patterns, making 2800:41-44

Old rugged cross, cardboard tube, making 2799:55

Ostrich, paper plate, pattern, making 2766:17

Our food comes from the Lord, cardboard tube, making 2799:18

Owl, paper plate, pattern, making 2766:18

Party popper, paper bags, patterns, making 2308:58

Peaceful dove ornament, felt, glitter, Christmas card with word "Peace," making 2721:44-45

People puppets, paper bags, patterns, making 2308:59-63

Photo frame, construction paper, pattern, making 2622:39

Photo frames, bottle caps, photos, making 2725:20-21

Pig, paper plate, pattern, making 2766:19

Pot of tulips, construction paper, pattern, making 2622:44

Potpourri wreath, paper plate, potpourri, paint, making 2721:22-23

Praise God for plants dried weed collage, paper, making 2800:11-13

Praise the God of all creation nature brush, making 2801:25

Prayer journal, construction paper, pattern, making 2622:46

Prayer necklace, red and white paper, ribbon, making 2721:52-53

Prayer place mat, construction paper, pattern, making 2622:18

Praying hands, patterns, making 2616:24-25

Print it, paper bags, patterns, making 2308:22

Proclaim God's word necklace, pipe cleaner, plastic lid, yarn, making 2725:42-43

Put your trust in the Lord tissue paper bookmark, making 2802:50

Rabbit, paper plate, pattern, making 2766:20

Rainbow, patterns, making 2616:8-9

Raindrops, patterns, making 2616:47-48

Reason for the season cross ornament, paper, making 2800:38

Recycled crayons, foil cupcake papers, crayons, making 2725:46-47

Ribbon angel; ribbon, wooden bead, yarn, making 2721:34-35

Ring the bell, paper bags, patterns, making 2308:6

Safe with God shell collage, ark pattern, making 2801:12-13

Sailing for the Lord boat in a bottle, making 2801:62

Sailing for the Lord folded boat, paper, making 2800:61-62

Samson and his hair, paper bag puppets, patterns, making 2802:17-18

Sandals, paper bags, patterns, making 2308:40

Saved from the lions shell puppets, making 2801:26

Scripture card, patterns, making 2616:39-40

Scripture holder, construction paper, pattern, making 2622:64

Seashells wall mural, patterns, making 2616:63-64

See what God made branch weaving, yarn, making 2803:13

See what God made, cardboard tube, making 2799:5

Sharing basket, yarn-woven basket, making 2803:37

Sheep of His pasture, coiled yarn on paper, patterns, making 2803:40-41

Sheep, paper plate, pattern, making 2766:21

Shepherd, patterns, making 2616:22-23

Sing Hosanna, cardboard tube, making 2799:52

Sing to the Lord, Styrofoam tray harp, yarn, patterns, making 2803:25-27

Sleep, baby, sleep nutshell ornament, making 2801:29

Snake, cardboard tube, making 2799:11

Soap surprise, soap chips, small surprises, making 2725:14-15

Sower of seeds, making 2277:38

Spiritual heart, construction paper, pattern, making 2622:59

Spread the good news tissue and yarn ornament, making 2802:39

Spread the good word, cardboard tube, making 2799:59

Spring tulips, construction paper, pattern, making 2622:36

Stable, paper plate, pattern, making 2766:62-63

Stand-up Bible men and boys, paper bags, patterns, making 2308:35-36

Stand-up Bible women and girls, paper bags, patterns, making 2308:33-34

Stand-up story bag, paper bags, patterns, making 2308:27

Stars for Abram, cardboard tube, making 2799:15

Stars, spiral of stars, construction paper, pattern, making 2622:51

Stars, swirling stars, construction paper, pattern, making 2622:55

Stars, toothpick star ornament, toothpicks, gold glitter, making 2721:40-41

Sun, patterns, making 2616:54-55

Sunshine and starlight seed collage, making 2801:6

Take up His cross, patterns, making 2616:61-62

Talking face, paper bags, patterns, making 2308:55-56

Tennis girl, construction paper, pattern, making 2622:25

"Thankful for my food" book, paper plates, yarn, making 2725:30-32

Thank-you card, construction paper, pattern, making 2622:62

Thank-you note to God, paper, envelope, glitter, making 2721:62-63

Thoughts box, box, photo, making 2725:18-19

Three days in a fish, yarn-laced puppets, patterns, making 2803:29-30

Three Kings banner, felt, old neckties, yarn, gold glitter, making 2721:42-43

Three men saved from the flames spoon puppets, making 2802:25

Thy will be done shadow box, pattern, making 2801:55-56

Tissue box, trims, making 2725:37

To a new land cornhusk people, making 2801:14-15

Town; tabletop town, making 2751:60-62

Tree bookmark, construction paper, pattern, making 2622:8

Tree by the water, papier-mâché tree, tissue paper, making 2802:21

Tree craft, construction paper, pattern, making 2622:56

Tree, patterns, making 2616:52-53

Trust in God straw cross, making 2801:22

Tunic, woven tunic, paper bags, patterns, making 2308:43-44

Turtle, paper plate, pattern, making 2766:22

Twelve Apostles, patterns, making 2616:58-59

Twelve on a mission rock painting, making 2801:42

Two disciples scripture eggs, tissue stencils, making 2802:61-62

Victory plaque, construction paper, pattern, making 2622:37

We are His handiwork, cardboard tube, making 2799:10

We will serve the Lord paper house, paper, making 2800:23-24

We will serve the Lord rock house, making 2801:21

Where to find it, paper bags, patterns, making 2308:64

Wise men's gifts wrapped with love, stamped wrapping paper, making 2802:41

Witness bracelet, cardboard tube, making 2799:60

Witness for the Lord pumpkin seed necklace, making 2801:61

Woolly sheep ornament, fleece fabric, black felt, ribbon, making 2721:38-39

Woven basket, paper bags, patterns, making 2308:28

Yea for yaks and other fuzzy friends, stand-up animals, yarn, patterns, making 2803:11-12

Your world, construction paper, pattern, making 2622:31

Zacchaeus, come down pressed-leaf picture, making 2801:47

**BIBLE—HANDICRAFTS—ADVENT**
Foam Advent wreath, making 2277:15

**BIBLE—HANDICRAFTS—ANGELS**
5 x 5 tiny angels, making 2277:35

Angel; foam plate angel, making 2277:22

Angel; lacy spoon angel, making 2277:23

Angel; wallpaper angel, making 2277:22

Paper roll angel tree topper, making 2277:34

Wooden angel ornament, making 2277:35

**BIBLE—HANDICRAFTS—CHRISTMAS**
Bell decorations, cream cups, paints, trims, making 2277:17

Bell ornament, plastic bottle, ribbon, cord, making 2277:17

Stars, craft sticks, making 2277:18

**BIBLE—HANDICRAFTS—CREATION MOBILE**
Fifth Day paper-bag fish, making 2277:4

First Day sunburst, making 2277:2

Fourth Day heavenly lights, paper, glitter, ribbon, craft stick, making   2277:4

Pop bottle mobile, making   2277:2-3

Second Day rainbow over the ocean, paper, making   2277:3

Seventh Day God's bed, purple and white paper, making   2277:4

Sixth Day Adam-and-Eve spoon dolls, plastic spoons, yarn, felt, making   2277:4

Third Day traced-hands tree, paper, making 2277:3-4

## BIBLE—HANDICRAFTS—CROSSES

Burnt-match cross, making   2277:40

## BIBLE—HANDICRAFTS—EASTER

Butterfly Easter plaque, making   2277:26

Folded paper Easter baskets, making   2277:27

Pom-pom Easter chicks, making   2277:26

## BIBLE—HANDICRAFTS—FATHER'S DAY

Shoe-polish desk set, making   2277:32

## BIBLE—HANDICRAFTS—JONAH AND THE WHALE

God hears Jonah folded fish, paper, making 2800:28-30

## BIBLE—HANDICRAFTS—MOSES

God cares for Moses, cardboard tube, making 2799:16

## BIBLE—HANDICRAFTS—MOTHER'S DAY

Pop-bottle flower frame, making   2277:32

## BIBLE—HANDICRAFTS—NATIVITY AND EPIPHANY

Epiphany figures, clothespins, making 2277:19-20

Stable, pinecones, making   2277:21

## BIBLE—HANDICRAFTS—NOAH'S ARK

Ark, paper plate, pattern, making   2766:60-61

Noah and his friends, cardboard tubes, patterns, making   2799:12-14

Noah's ark, animals, doves, Mr. and Mrs. Noah, patterns, making   2277:5

Noah's dove folded bird, paper, making 2800:19-21

Noah's rainbow tissue mosaic, tissue paper, patterns, making   2802:13-14

## BIBLE—HANDICRAFTS—PALM SUNDAY—DECORATIONS

Newspaper palm tree, making   2277:24-25

## BIBLE—HANDICRAFTS—PENTECOST

Tongues of fire, tissue paper, making 2277:30-31

## BIBLE—HANDICRAFTS—PUPPETS

Papier-mâché puppets, making   2277:11-13

Stick puppets, making   2277:10-13

## BIBLE—HANDICRAFTS—VACATION BIBLE SCHOOL

Prayer journals, making   2277:33

## BIBLE—ISRAELITES—ARMOR

Armored vest, fabric, plastic jugs, pattern, making   2746:86-88

## BIBLE—ISRAELITES—CALENDAR

Calendar, paper plate calendar, making 2746:76-78

## BIBLE—ISRAELITES—CANAAN—MAP

Salt-dough map, salt dough, paints, pattern, making   2746:83-84

## BIBLE—ISRAELITES—HOUSES

Basket; design a bee basket, plastic bottle, burlap, making   2746:108-109

Build with headers and stretchers, how to do 2746:98

Foot washing, how to do   2746:105

Keeping clean, how to do   2746:103

Washing clothes, how to do   2746:106

## BIBLE—ISRAELITES—LAMPS

Lamp; oil lamp, clay, making   2746:101-102

## BIBLE—ISRAELITES—MEASUREMENT

Measuring tape, fabric, ribbon   2746:132-133

Scale, stick, string, cups   2746:134-135

## BIBLE—ISRAELITES—MUSICAL INSTRUMENTS

Cymbals; make cymbals, metal lids   2746:118

Lyre; make a lyre, plastic hanger, rubber bands 2746:113

Sistrum; make a sistrum, milk carton, dowel, wire   2746:114-115

Timbrel; make a timbrel, wooden embroidery hoops, ribbon, bells   2746:116-117

## BIBLE—ISRAELITES—NAMES

Choosing a new name, list of names and meanings   2746:139

## BIBLE—ISRAELITES—RELIGION

High Priest's breastplate, poster board, gold wrap, buttons, ribbon, making   2746:73

High Priest's outfit and turban, paper, plastic bag, gold wrap, making   2746:72

## BIBLE—ISRAELITES—SCROLLS

Cyrus cylinder, cardboard tube, making 2746:146-147

Seal, create your own seal, clay, making 2746:148-149

**BIBLE—ISRAELITES—SPICES**

Make a spice chart, poster board, markers 2746:161-162

**BIBLE—ISRAELITES—TITHES**

Calculate tithes, how to do 2746:158-159

**BIBLE—NEW TESTAMENT**

Five loaves and two fishes, making 2751:38

Great catch, making 2751:32

Heavenly dove, making 2751:31

John the Baptist's meal, patterns, making 2751:29-30

Parable of the sower, making 2751:35

Peter's rooster, patterns, making 2751:39-40

Prodigal son feeds the pigs, patterns, making 2751:36-37

Sailing with Paul, patterns, making 2751:41-42

This little light, making 2751:34

Twelve Disciples, making 2751:33

**BIBLE—OLD TESTAMENT**

Daniel's lion, making 2751:27

David's sheep, making 2751:26

God's rainbow, patterns, making 2751:13-14

Jacob's ladder, making 2751:16

Jonah's big fish, making 2751:28

Joseph's coat of many colors, patterns, making 2751:17-19

Moses in a basket, making 2751:20

Noah's big boat, patterns, making 2751:10-12

Pharaoh's chariots, making 2751:22

Plague of frogs, making 2751:21

Promised Land, making 2751:24

Serpent in the garden, making 2751:9

Ten Commandments, making 2751:23

Tower of Babel, making 2751:15

**BIBLE—PALM SUNDAY**

Hosanna Palm Sunday poster, paper, patterns, making 2800:55-56

**BIBLE—PLAYS**

Prophesy of Isaiah, play, costumes, masks, script, making 2277:6-8

**BIBLE—PUPPETS**

All creatures great and small finger puppets, paper, making 2800:17-18

Baby puppet, paper bag, pattern, making 2793:5-6

Bear puppet, paper bag, pattern, making 2793:41-42

Boy puppet, paper bag, pattern, making 2793:9-10

Camel puppet, paper bag, pattern, making 2793:27-28

Cat puppet, paper bag, pattern, making 2793:35-36

Cow puppet, paper bag, pattern, making 2793:29-30

Dog puppet, paper bag, pattern, making 2793:37-38

Donkey puppet, paper bag, pattern, making 2793:25-26

Duck puppet, paper bag, pattern, making 2793:39-40

Elephant puppet, paper bag, pattern, making 2793:49-50

Girl puppet, paper bag, pattern, making 2793:7-8

Goat puppet, paper bag, pattern, making 2793:31-32

Goliath, the Giant puppet, paper bag, pattern, making 2793:19-22

Good manners puppet, pudding box, yarn, making 2725:40-41

Lamb puppet, paper bag, pattern, making 2793:23-24

Lion puppet, paper bag, pattern, making 2793:47-48

Middle-aged or older man or Jesus puppet, paper bag, pattern, making 2793:17-18

Middle-aged or older woman puppet, paper bag, pattern, making 2793:16-17

Monkey puppet, paper bag, pattern, making 2793:43-44

Pig puppet, paper bag, pattern, making 2793:33-34

Prayer puppet, paper plates, yarn, paints, making 2725:34-36

Spoon puppets, plastic spoons, yarn, making 2721:32-33

Teenage boy or young man puppet, paper bag, pattern, making 2793:13-14

Teenage girl or young woman puppet, paper bag, pattern, making 2793:11-12

Tiger puppet, paper bag, pattern, making 2793:45-46

Zebra puppet, paper bag, pattern, making 2793:50-51

**BIBLE—SPECIAL DAYS**

Babe is born, patterns, making 2751:43-44

Christmas wreath, patterns, making 2751:49-50

Cross of Jesus, patterns, making 2751:51-52

Easter card, making 2751:53

God's messenger, making 2751:45

May Day basket, making 2751:54

Shepherd diorama, making 2751:46

Thank-you turkey, making 2751:55

Valentine bells, making    2751:56
Wise men and their camels, patterns, making
    2751:47-48

**BIBLE—SPRING CRAFTS**
Butterfly, patterns, making    2354:40
Easter crosses, patterns, making    2354:41-42
Easter cutout, patterns, making    2354:35
Easter lily, patterns, making    2354:37-39
Ladybug, patterns, making    2354:46
Lion-lamb, patterns, making    2354:45
Rainbow, patterns, making    2354:44
Sparrow, patterns, making    2354:43
Swan, patterns, making    2354:47-48
Umbrella, patterns, making    2354:36

**BIBLE—SUMMER CRAFTS**
Balloon, patterns, making    2354:52
Blooming for Jesus, patterns, making
    2354:61-62
Children of the World, patterns, making
    2354:53
Fan, patterns, making    2354:50
Fish, patterns, making    2354:59-60
Mother's Day Basket, patterns, making
    2354:54
Shield, patterns, making    2354:63
Sun, patterns, making    2354:49
Turtle, patterns, making    2354:55-56
Watch for the Lord, patterns, making
    2354:57-58
Watermelon slice, patterns, making    2354:51

**BIBLE—TEN COMMANDMENTS**
Ten Commandments, clay, making    2746:62

**BIBLE—TWELVE TRIBES—MAP**
Puzzle map, styrofoam trays, pattern, making
    2746:93-95

**BIBLE—WEAPONS**
Bow and quiver of arrows, stick, string, making
    2746:123-125
Sling and stones, making    2746:121-122

**BIBLE—WINTER CRAFTS**
Angel, patterns, making    2354:22
Christmas wreath, patterns, making    2354:23-24
Clock, patterns, making    2354:25-26
Mouse, patterns, making    2354:32
Snowflake, patterns, making    2354:31
Snowman, patterns, making    2354:27-30
Valentine holder, patterns, making    2354:33-34

**BIBLE STORIES—COOKERY**
Adam and Eve baked apples ala mode, recipe
    2566:11

Adam and Eve fresh figs and sour cream, recipe
    2566:11
Bitya's eggplant omelet, recipe    2566:31
Bitya's fatoosh bread salad, recipe    2566:31
Bitya's mayonnaise, recipe    2566:30
Children of Israel honey-sweet carrots, recipe
    2566:47
Children of Israel open-toasted tofu sandwich,
    recipe    2566:39
Children of Israel pulpy grape juice, recipe
    2566:47
Children of Israel scrambled tofu, recipe
    2566:35
Children of Israel spicy cucumbers and garlic
    salad, recipe    2566:43
Children of Israel tuna spread, recipe    2566:43
Children of Israel yogurt-topped watermelon,
    recipe    2566:43
David's meatballs in soy sauce, recipe    2566:59
David's mock chopped liver, recipe    2566:58
David's rice and chickpeas, recipe    2566:59
Jacob's lentil stew, recipe    2566:23
Jacob's spicy lentil dip, recipe    2566:23
Joseph's pasta salad, recipe    2566:27
Joseph's tabouleh, recipe    2566:27
Noah's 3-bean olive salad, recipe    2566:15
Noah's grapefruit salad, recipe    2566:15
Passover charoset, recipe    2566:35
Passover cold egg soup, recipe    2566:35
Passover matzah brie, recipe    2566:35
Promised Land goat cheese sandwich spread,
    recipe    2566:51
Promised Land hot milk with cinnamon, recipe
    2566:51
Queen Esther's fresh herb mezze, recipe
    2566:63
Queen Esther's Persian kebab, recipe    2566:63
Queen Esther's Persian rice, recipe    2566:63
Ruth's barley and onions, recipe    2566:55
Ruth's caraway seed cabbage salad, recipe
    2566:55
Sarah's filled pita pockets, recipe    2566:19
Sarah's homemade hummus, recipe    2566:19

**BIRDS**
Bird feeder, how to build    2511:8
Language arts, poetry, hobby craft activities
    2511:7-12

**BIRTHDAYS**
Around the world birthday party, making
    2547:27-29
Birthday superstitions 2547:24-25

**BIRTHDAYS—FICTION**

*Happy Birthday!* by Gail Gibbons, activities, crafts, patterns, games, masks, puppets, making 2329:132-135

**BLACK MUSLIMS—COOKERY**

Bean pie, recipe 2879:43
Muhammad supreme bean soup, recipe 2879:43-44

**BLACKFEET INDIANS—COOKERY**

Buffalo pot roast, recipe 2279:57
Pemmican patties, recipe 2430:13

**BLACKFEET INDIANS—LANGUAGE**

Everyday words in Blackfeet Indian language 2279:88-89

**BLAKE, WILLIAM**

Hand colored prints, making 2529:32

**BOATS**

Lead line to measure depth of water for boats (called "Mark Twain"), making 2935:62-63
Paddlewheel boat (from Mark Twain's books), foam board, pattern, making 2935:34-35

**BOBO (AFRICAN PEOPLES)—MASKS**

Tall Bobo dance mask, large cardboard, paints, patterns, making 2620:24-25

**BOLIVIA—CHRISTMAS—DECORATIONS**

Clay model of gifts children want, clay, making 2403:10-11

**BOLIVIA—COOKERY**

Breakfast pastries, recipe 2913:53
Corn packages, recipe 2670:50
Peanut soup, recipe 2913:52
Peanut soup, recipe 2922:51
Picante sauce, recipe 2913:53
Spicy chicken, recipe 2913:52

**BOLIVIA—GAMES**

La Polleria, how to play 2767:53-54
Marbles, how to play 2310:43-46
Marbles, how to play 2767:52-53

**BOLIVIA—GOD'S EYE**

Spider web Ojo de Dios, wool, yarn, beads, wire, making 2779:28-29

**BOLIVIA—LANGUAGE**

Quechua riddles 2255:90
Quechua, Aymara and Spanish words for colors 2255:91

**BOSNIA—GAMES**

Skola (School), how to play 2767:54-55

**BOSTON TEA PARTY—COOKERY**

Boston cream pie, recipe 2643:46
Darjeeling tea, recipe 2643:46
How to plan and set the table 2643:44-45

**BOSTON TEA PARTY—GAMES**

Revolutionary tea-bag toss, how to play 2643:47

**BOTSWANA—GAMES**

Bucket ball game, how to play 2525:88
Cattle stockade game, how to play 2882:46-47
Hidden object game, how to play 2525:96
Jump ball game, how to play 2525:173
Kitchen ball game, how to play 2525:43
Piggyback polo game, how to play 2525:141
Step on my shadow game, how to play 2525:23
Three boys game, how to play 2525:166
Three sticks game, how to play 2525:128
Underball game, how to play 2525:158
We are from Tlhahana game, how to play 2525:58

**BOTTICELLI, SANDRO**

Art in the round, making 2529:18

**BOURKE-WHITE, MARGARET**

ABC photography, how to do 2529:89

**BRAQUE, GEORGES**

Cubist collage, making 2529:68

**BRAZIL—BIRTHDAYS—COOKERY**

Bolo de laranja cake, recipe 2957:12

**BRAZIL—BIRTHDAYS—GAMES**

Peteca, how to play 2957:13

**BRAZIL—CHRISTMAS—COOKERY**

Codfish bites, recipe 2885:66-67
Salted codfish stew, recipe 2670:67-68

**BRAZIL—COOKERY**

Avocado cream, recipe 2885:57
Avocado cream, recipe 2942:53
Beef and bean soup, recipe 2922:50
Black bean casserole, recipe 2670:41
Black bean feijoada, recipe 2942:53
Black-eyed pea fritters, recipe 2885:44
Brazilian menu 2885:28-29
Brazilian pork chops, recipe 2885:49
Brazilian-style rice, recipe 2942:52
Cheese balls, recipe 2845:12
Cheese rolls, recipe 2885:40
Chicken and potato salad, recipe 2885:42-43
Chicken rice soup, recipe 2670:32
Chicken, shrimp and peanut stew, recipe 2885:50

Cocada Branca, sweet dessert, recipe
2609:30-31
Coconut candies, recipe 2885:54
Coffee cake, recipe 2885:58
Collard greens, recipe 2885:39
Cornmeal mash, recipe 2885:34
Cornstarch cookies, recipe 2885:59
Cream of palm heart soup, recipe 2942:52
Deep-fried filled pastry, recipe 2942:53
Fish stew, recipe 2885:48
Flan (milk pudding), recipe 2670:55
Fried bananas with cinnamon sugar, recipe
2396:55
Fruit punch, recipe 2942:52
Fruit salad, recipe 2855:39
Kale, recipe 2670:49
Lemonade, recipe 2885:55
Mashed beans, recipe 2885:38
Negrinho, dessert, recipe 2301:51
Pumpkin soup, recipe 2885:51
Sauteed white rice, recipe 2670:48
Shrimp and peanut sauce, recipe 2885:35
Toasted manioc flour, recipe 2885:32
Turnovers, recipe 2670:62-63
White rice, recipe 2885:33

**BRAZIL—FESTIVALS—COOKERY**
Black bean stew, recipe 2885:64
Carnaval coconut cooler, recipe 2504:40-41
Carnaval; cinnamon doughnuts, recipe 2885:69
Turnovers, recipe 2885:62-63

**BRAZIL—FESTIVALS—FLAGS**
Samba school flag, fabric, dowel, paints, making
2504:38-39

**BRAZIL—FESTIVALS—HANDICRAFTS**
Carnival; cascarones, eggs, confetti, colored
paper, making 2609:26

**BRAZIL—FESTIVALS—HEADDRESSES**
Carnival; cap, paper, feathers, sequins, glitters,
paints, making 2609:28-29

**BRAZIL—FESTIVALS—JEWELRY**
Bonfim Festival; bracelet, ribbons, making
2855:30

**BRAZIL—FESTIVALS—MASKS**
Carnival; Carnival mask, cardboard, dowel, glitter, feathers, patterns, making 2846:12-13
Carnaval; mystery masks, poster board, paints,
decorations, making 2852:108-109

**BRAZIL—FESTIVALS—SONGS**
Carnival; song 2609:27

**BRAZIL—FLAGS**
Brazilian flag, paper, markers, pattern, making
2671:22-23

**BRAZIL—FOLKLORE**
*Princess and the Sea Serpent,* story and activities
2423:130-166

**BRAZIL—GAMES**
Hit it off game, how to make and play 2882:16
Hoop game, how to make and play 2882:17
Jogo game, how to play 2525:104
Luta de Galho (Cockfight), how to play
2767:55-56
Number relay game, how to play 2525:27
Peteca, how to play 2767:56
Quei mada (forest fire) game, how to play
2847:12-13
Tampa game, how to play 2525:77

**BRAZIL—LANGUAGE**
Learn to speak Portugese 2301:48
Numbers in Spanish and Portugese 2855:20
Portugese words for family members 2855:41

**BRAZIL—MUSICAL INSTRUMENTS**
Maraca, plastic egg or small box, dried beans,
markers, making 2855:27
Reco-reco instrument, corrugated cardboard,
making 2686:115-116

**BRAZIL—NEW YEAR—COOKERY**
Ano novo, rbanada, French toast, recipe
2402:10-11

**BRAZIL—RAIN STICKS**
Rain stick, cardboard tube, nails, paints, making
2845:13

**BRAZILIAN-AMERICANS—COOKERY**
Canja (chicken soup), recipe 2879:45
Couve a mineira (collard dish), recipe 2879:45
Quindim custard dessert, recipe 2879:44

**BRITISH-AMERICANS—COOKERY**
Blueberry pie, recipe 2635:25

**BUCHANAN, JAMES (PRESIDENT)**
Colossal banquet menu, patterns, making
2263:55
Tree collage, patterns, making 2263:55

**BUFFALO**
Buffalo pattern 2475:12

**BULGARIA—GAMES**
Gaping, how to play 2767:56-57

**BULGARIAN-AMERICANS—COOKERY**
Bulgarian cucumber soup, recipe 2879:48
Bulgarian meatball soup, recipe 2879:48-49

Macedonian-style peppers, recipe    2879:46-47
Vlach cheese corn bread, recipe    2879:47

**BUNTING, EVE**

*Mother's Day Mice*, activities, crafts, patterns
2637:unp
*A Perfect Father's Day* literature unit    2404:unp
*Valentine Bears*, activities, language arts, foods
(recipes given), science, arts and music
2446:7-17

**BUNYAN, PAUL**

Grease Paul Bunyan's griddle, paper plate, foil,
making    2729:14-15

**BURKINA FASO—CHRISTMAS—COOKERY**

Groundnut cookies, recipe    2628:69

**BURMA—COOKERY**

Burmese prawn curry, recipe    2874:130
Htamane rice and nut dish, recipe    2874:131
Sago dessert, recipe    2874:127

**BURMA—FOLKLORE**

*Kho and the Tiger*, story and activities
2423:17-30

**BURMA—PASSOVER—COOKERY**

Rangoon charoset, recipe    2737:79-80

**BURNETT, FRANCES HODGSON**

Mary's skipping rope, making, English skipping
rhymes included    2342:108-112

**BURTON, VIRGINIA LEE**

*The Little House*, literature, activities, art,
curriculum    2436:75-86

**BUSH, GEORGE H. W. (PRESIDENT)**

52 great books to read, making    2263:127
Celebrate the presidency fan, pattern, making
2263:127
Starfish pasta collage, pattern, making
2263:127

**BUSINESS**

Language arts, poetry, hobby craft activities
2511:119-125

# C

**CAJUNS—COOKERY**

Bread pudding with fruit, recipe   2359:41-42
Catfish court bouillon, recipe   2879:3
Down-on-the-bayou gumbo, recipe   2534:34-35
King cake, recipe   2359:43-45
Plogue, buckwheat flatbreads, recipe   2879:4
Shrimp and ham jambalaya, recipe   2359:39-40
Shrimp jambalaya, recipe   2879:2-3
Smothered potatoes, recipe   2879:4-5

**CALDER, ALEXANDER**

Standing mobile, making   2529:66

**CALIFORNIA—COOKERY**

Chinatown dragon cakes, recipe   2534:17

**CALIFORNIA INDIANS—FOLKLORE**

Thunder and Fire, story and activities
2423:53-63

**CAMBODIA—GAMES**

Angkunh game, how to play   2649:22
Handkerchief game, how to play   2767:57
Leak Pong Kaek (hiding mother crow's eggs),
how to play   2767:57-58
Muoy, pi, bey game, how to play   2385:21

**CAMBODIAN-AMERICANS—COOKERY**

B'baw poat (corn pudding), recipe   2879:50
Ngiom (coleslaw), recipe   2879:49-50

**CAMEROON—BEADWORK**

Beaded hat band, cardboard, markers, making
2620:46-47
Hat with a crown, cardboard, markers, making
2620:46-47
Hat with face or dangling creature, cardboard,
markers, making   2620:46-47
Lizard from Cameroon, cardboard, markers, patterns, making   2620:46-47

**CAMEROON—CLAY TILES**

Patterned tiles, clay, objects for impressions,
making   2331:14-15

**CAMEROON—COOKERY**

Egussi stew, recipe   2969:122

**CAMEROON—GAMES**

Carry it game, how to play   2969:127
Clap, clap, clap ball game, how to play
2385:28

**CAMEROON—LANGUAGE**

Common words and phrases in Bamileke,
Ervondo and Fulfulde languages   2969:87

**CANADA—CHRISTMAS—COOKERY**

Barley toys candy, recipe   2403:12-13

**CANADA—CHRISTMAS—DECORATIONS**

Tree skirt, felt, ribbons, making   2740:14-15

**CANADA—COOKERY**

French toast, recipe   2460:27
Maple ice cream, recipe   2302:55
Pancakes with maple syrup, recipe   2261:30-31

**CANADA—FESTIVALS**

Canada Day; maple leaf sponge art, patterns,
making   2262:94-95

**CANADA—GAMES**

Acka backa boo game, how to play   2385:14
Beanbag pass game, how to play   2525:54
Borden ball game, how to play   2525:38
Broomball game, broom, ball, how to play
2328:134-135
Catch a falling star game, how to play   2525:90
Changing positions game, how to play
2525:165
Drop the handkerchief, how to play   2767:59
Emergency game, how to play   2525:22
Empire strikes back game, how to play
2525:143
Firefighter rescue game, how to play   2525:170
Hoopscotch game, how to play   2525:162
I looked high game, how to play   2385:13
Ice floe game, how to play   2328:68-69
Jumping the hoop game, how to play   2525:175
Kick the can game, how to play   2525:6
Moving musical hoops game, how to play
2525:193
Pattywhack game, how to play   2525:102
Pin'an, how to play   2767:171
Sardines game, how to play   2385:32
Scoops game, how to play   2525:117
Stick tag game, how to play   2525:135
Tcoskumina-a (sliding game), how to play
2767:59-60
Tihitpintowan (rolling game), how to play
2767:60

Two-person catch game, how to play   2525:93

**CANADA—HANDICRAFTS**

Leaf cuts, paper, paste, making   2407:24

**CANADA—LANGUAGE**

Few basic words in French   2302:50

**CANADA—NEW YEAR—COOKERY**

Butter tarts, recipe   2888:24-25

**CANADA—NEW YEAR—MUSICAL INSTRUMENTS**

Make music with spoons, metal or
  wooden   2402:12-13

**CANADA—TOTEM POLES**

Totem pole, cardboard tube, markers, making
  2460:39

Totem pole, paper tube, cardboard, markers,
  making   2686:26-27

**CANALS**

Build a canal lock, milk cartons, tape, making
  2497:28-29

**CANDLES**

Dipped candles, wax, making   2440:51

Eggshell candles, wax, making   2440:49

Flowery candles, wax, making   2440:48

Iced candles, wax, making   2440:50

Molded candles and layered candles, wax,
  making   2440:45-47

Seashell candles, wax, making   2440:48

Water balloon candle, wax, making   2440:52

**CANDY**

History of candy   2815:unp

**CANDY—COOKERY**

"Belly-guts" taffy, recipe   2815:unp

Sugar paste, 16th to 17th century recipe
  2815:unp

Vassar fudge, recipe   2815:unp

**CAPE VERDEAN-AMERICANS—COOKERY**

Cachupa stew, recipe   2879:54-55

Canja (chicken rice soup), recipe   2879:56

Jag (rice and beans dish), recipe   2879:55-56

**CAREERS**

Anthropologist; interview, projects, stories, recipes, activities   2823:1-4

Architect; interview, projects, stories, activities   2823:9-11

Art Teacher; interview, projects, stories, recipes,
  activities   2823:13-15

Baker; interview, projects, stories, recipes,
  activities   2823:17-19

Beautician; interview, projects, stories, recipes,
  activities   2823:25-27

Biomedical Equipment Technician; interview,
  projects, stories, recipes, activities
  2823:29-30

Candy Store Clerk; interview, projects, stories,
  recipes, activities   2823:31-33

Car Factory Worker; interview, projects, stories,
  recipes, activities   2823:35-40

Carpenter; interview, projects, stories, recipes,
  activities   2823:41-43

Child-Care Director; interview, projects, stories,
  recipes, activities   2823:45-47

Children's Book Author; interview, projects, stories, recipes, activities   2823:49-51

Computer Expert; interview, projects, stories,
  recipes, activities   2823:53-54

Creature Effects Technician; interview, projects,
  stories, recipes, activities   2823:55-59

Dancer; interview, projects, stories, recipes,
  activities   2823:61-62

Doctor; interview, projects, stories, recipes,
  activities   2823:63-65

Elementary School Teacher; interview, projects,
  stories, recipes, activities   2823:67-69

Fashion Designer; interview, projects, stories,
  recipes, activities   2823:71-73

Firefighter; interview, projects, stories, recipes,
  activities   2823:75-76

Folk Artist; interview, projects, stories, recipes,
  activities   2823:77-78

Geologist; interview, projects, stories, recipes,
  activities   2823:79-82

Historical Building Window Restorer; interview,
  projects, stories, recipes, activities
  2823:83-85

Historical Village Actor; interview, projects, stories, recipes, activities   2823:87-90

Illustrator; interview, projects, stories, recipes,
  activities   2823:91-93

Librarian; interview, projects, stories, recipes,
  activities   2823:95-97

Lobster Fisherman; interview, projects, stories,
  recipes, activities   2823:99-102

Maple Syrup and Cheese Business Owner; interview, projects, stories, recipes, activities
  2823:103-108

Mural Painter; interview, projects, stories, recipes,
  activities   2823:109-110

Park Ranger; interview, projects, stories, recipes,
  activities   2823:113-114

Peace Corps Worker; interview, projects, stories,
  recipes, activities   2823:115-117

Piano Teacher; interview, projects, stories, recipes, activities   2823:119-121

Postal Worker; interview, projects, stories, recipes, activities 2823:123-125

Prison Teacher and Director; interview, projects, stories, recipes, activities 2823:127-128

River Trip Guide; interview, projects, stories, recipes, activities 2823:129-132

Secretary; interview, projects, stories, recipes, activities 2823:133-134

Sheepherder; interview, projects, stories, recipes, activities 2823:135-138

Superintendent of Schools; interview, projects, stories, recipes, activities 2823:143-145

Train Engineer; interview, projects, stories, recipes, activities 2823:35-40

Truck Driver; interview, projects, stories, recipes, activities 2823:147-149

Weaver; interview, projects, stories, recipes, activities 2823:151-153

**CARIBBEAN ISLANDS—CARS**

Tap-tap trucks, clay, cardboard, paints, making 2817:26-33

**CARIBBEAN ISLANDS—COOKERY**

Baked fish with lime and orange juice, recipe 2603:20-21

Baked ground provisions (vegetables), recipe 2603:22-23

Banana bread, recipe 2603:34-35

Banana curry, recipe 2603:24-25

Banana fritters, recipe 2925:58

Banana soup, recipe 2603:12-13

Bean and egg salad, recipe 2603:26-27

Caribbean menu 2925:26-27

Caribbean sorbet, recipe 2396:54

Caribbean-style rice, recipe 2925:50

Chicken and banana skewers, recipe 2603:14-15

Chicken in coconut sauce, recipe 2603:16-17

Coconut custard, recipe 2603:30-31

Coconut milkshake, recipe 2603:42-43

Fish and shrimp bake, recipe 2603:18-19

Foo-foo plantain dish, recipe 2925:53

Fried plantains, recipe 2270:9

Ginger beer, recipe 2603:40-41

Mango ice cream, recipe 2603:38-39

Pancakes with mangoes, recipe 2603:36-37

Pumpkin soup, recipe 2603:10-11

Red, yellow, and green salad, recipe 2603:28-29

Rice and peas, recipe 2925:51

Sweet potato and pumpkin pudding, recipe 2603:32-33

**CARIBBEAN ISLANDS—EASTER—COOKERY**

Easter buns, recipe 2925:66-67

**CARIBBEAN ISLANDS—FESTIVALS— COOKERY**

Carnival; baked bananas, recipe 2962:19

Carnival; baked plantains, recipe 2962:15

Carnival; Island sugar cakes, recipe 2270:21

Carnival; Jamaican jerk chicken, recipe 2962:17

Carnival; rice and beans, recipe 2962:18

Carnival; sautéed greens, recipe 2962:16

**CARIBBEAN ISLANDS—GAMES**

Limbo game, how to make and play 2882:20-21

Mosquito one game, how to play 2385:34

Tootsie in the moonlight singing game, how to play 2385:38

**CARIBBEAN ISLANDS—MUSICAL INSTRUMENTS**

Caribbean drums, coffee can, fabric, string, making 2817:46-51

**CARNIVAL**

Carnival headdress, papier-mâché, beads, feathers, paints, making 2259:16-17

**CARPATHO-RUSYN-AMERICANS—COOKERY**

Pagach (meatless meat pies), recipe 2879:58

Pierogy (easy bake turnovers), recipe 2879:57-58

Tomato gravy, recipe 2879:57

**CARTER, JAMES EARL (PRESIDENT)**

Mount St. Helens, a rainbow eruption, making 2263:122

Peanut picnic, making 2263:122

**CARVER, GEORGE WASHINGTON**

Conduct a scientific experiment, how to do 2745:176-177

Grow a sweet potato vine, how to do 2745:175

Make peanut butter, how to do 2745:173

**CARVER, GEORGE WASHINGTON— HANDICRAFTS**

George Washington Carver peanut magnet, making 2731:20-21

**CASSATT, MARY**

Every picture tells a story game, how to do 2738:76

Tempera monoprint, making 2529:44

**CASTLES—COOKERY**

Haunted castle decorated cake, recipe 2583:16-17

**CATAWBA INDIANS—COOKERY**
 Roasted corn, recipe  2311:26-28

**CATS**
 Language arts, poetry, hobby craft activities
  2511:13-16

**CELTS—ARMOR**
 Helmet, papier-mâché, gold and bronze paints,
  making  2582:16-17
 Shield, cardboard, leather strips, plasticine,
  paints, making  2582:22-23

**CELTS—BOOKS**
 Celtic border, cardstock, paints, making
  2582:60-61

**CELTS—COOKERY**
 Oat cakes, recipe  2582:38-39

**CELTS—GAMES**
 Board game, how to make and play  2582:40-41

**CELTS—HANDICRAFTS**
 Stained glass window, cardboard, colored cellophane, pattern, making  2784:8-9

**CELTS—HOUSEHOLD ITEMS**
 Mirror, gold mirrored cardboard, clay, gold
  paint, making  2582:46-47
 Pot, papier-mâché, paints, making  2582:36-37

**CELTS—HOUSES**
 Round house, brown cardboard, dowels,
  plasticine, making  2582:28-31

**CELTS—JEWELRY**
 Brooch, clay, paints, making  2582:44-45
 Torc (neck jewelry), clay, gold or bronze paint,
  making  2582:48-49

**CELTS—METALWORK**
 Celtic goblet, papier-mâché, plastic bottle, cardboard, beads, paints, making  2259:12-13

**CELTS—MUSICAL INSTRUMENTS**
 Harp, cardboard, colored string, paints, making
  2582:52-53

**CELTS—RELIGION**
 Gundestrup bowl, plastic bowl, foil, making
  2582:54-55

**CELTS—SYMBOLS**
 Pig, clay, balsa wood, metallic paint, making
  2582:56-57

**CELTS—TRANSPORTATION**
 Wagon, cardstock, balsa wood, leather strip,
  paints, making  2582:32-33

**CELTS—WRITINGS IN STONE**
 Ogham stone, clay, cardstock, white paint, making
  2582:50-51

**CENTRAL AMERICA—MUSICAL
  INSTRUMENTS**
 Bird whistle, clay, making  2331:19

**CENTRAL AMERICA—WEAVER**
 Weaver; interview, projects, stories, recipes,
  activities  2823:151-153

**CEZANNE, PAUL**
 How to paint still life like Cezanne  2738:90
 Seeing shapes still life, making  2529:48
 Stenciling Cezanne with colorful rectangles, how
  to do  2738:97

**CHAGALL, MARC**
 Scenery mural, making  2529:76

**CHALDEAN-AMERICANS—COOKERY**
 Booshala soup, recipe  2879:26-27
 Flat egg and fresh herb pancakes, recipe
  2879:26
 Lettuce leaves with honey, vinegar and mint,
  recipe  2879:25
 Zazich dip, recipe  2879:26

**CHALK**
 Bright stick, recipe  2918:57
 Clay chalk, recipe  2918:60
 Rainbow chalk, recipe  2918:58-59
 Sidewalk chalk, easy, recipe  2918:55
 Sidewalk chalk, recipe  2918:53-54
 Squeeze 'n' paint chalk, recipe  2918:56
 Window chalk, recipe  2918:61

**CHAMBERLAIN, JOHN**
 Big junk, making  2529:97

**CHEERLEADING**
 Pompoms, paper, making  2407:56

**CHEROKEE INDIANS—BASKETS**
 Cherokee and Iroquois stenciled baskets, baskets,
  paints, making  2350:14-15

**CHEROKEE INDIANS—COOKERY**
 Berry cobbler, recipe  2480:82
 Blue dumplings, recipe  2879:59-60
 Cherokee or Brunswick stew, recipe  2480:82
 Corn and beans, recipe  2280:45
 Huckleberry bread, recipe  2879:60-61
 Succotash, recipe  2879:60
 Wild onions and eggs, recipe  2879:61

**CHEROKEE INDIANS—FOLKLORE**
 *How the People Got Fire*, story and activities  2423:68-78

Water spider legend, water spider on rock, paints, patterns, making  2350:37-38

**CHEROKEE INDIANS—LANGUAGE**

Cherokee alphabet  2280:79

Cherokee moon; Cherokee words for  2280:81

Cherokee word book, paper, yarn, making  2311:29-32

Everyday words in Cherokee language  2280:76-81

**CHEYENNE INDIANS—COOKERY**

Buffalo burger, recipe  2281:58

Wild chokeberry pudding, recipe  2569:42

**CHEYENNE INDIANS—GAMES**

Basket game, how to make and play  2882:6-7

Hand or stick game, how to play  2569:43

Moccasin game, how to make and play  2894:18

**CHEYENNE INDIANS—HOUSES**

Play tipi, manila folder, markers or paints, making  2894:12-13

**CHEYENNE INDIANS—JEWELRY**

Bear claw necklace, clay, beads, cord, paints, making  2840:10-11

**CHEYENNE INDIANS—LANGUAGE**

Everyday words in Cheyenne language  2281:94-95

Parts of the body in Cheyenne language  2281:95

**CHEYENNE INDIANS—MUSICAL INSTRUMENTS**

Namshim drum, coffee can, paints, plastic, making  2557:22

**CHEYENNE INDIANS—SHIELDS**

Cheyenne shield, wire, chamois, making  2523:61-63

**CHICKASAW INDIANS—COOKERY**

Pashofa (pork and hominy dish), recipe  2879:62

Pumpkin cookies, recipe  2879:62-63

**CHICKASAW INDIANS—DANCES**

Stomp dance wear; shell shakers for girls, gorget for boys, making  2431:22

**CHICKASAW INDIANS—FOLKLORE**

*Baby Rattlesnake* by Te Ata; activities, art, poetry, maps, crafts, foods, patterns  2642:112-115

**CHILDREN'S BOOK WEEK**

Activities, crafts, patterns  2760:47-58

Activities, projects, programs  2378:27-35

**CHILE—CHRISTMAS—COOKERY**

Christmas bread, recipe  2396:64

Christmas fruitcake, recipe  2670:60-61

**CHILE—COOKERY**

Avocado and zucchini soup, recipe  2943:52

Beans with vegetables, recipe  2670:45

Corn packages, recipe  2670:50

Grape zucchini quick bread, recipe  2943:53

Marinated chicken, recipe  2670:42

Salad platter and dressing, recipe  2670:37

Seafood salad, recipe  2670:36

Stew, recipe  2943:52

Sweet corn wraps, recipe  2943:53

Turnovers, recipe  2670:62-63

**CHILE—FESTIVALS—COOKERY**

La Fiesta de la Virgen de la Tirana; Chilean quinoa salad, recipe  2670:64

**CHILE—FLAGS**

Chilean flag, paper, markers, pattern, making  2671:23

**CHILE—GAMES**

Cielo, Luna, Mar (Sky, Moon, Ocean), how to play  2767:60-61

La Gallina Que Se Va (The Running Hen), how to play  2767:61

Uno, dos, tres game, how to play  2385:21

**CHILE—NEW YEAR—HANDICRAFTS**

Ano Nuevo, gold bracelets, macaroni, gold paint, making  2402:14-15

**CHILE—STATUES**

Carved stone statue model, paper bag, paints, making  2686:111-112

**CHINA—BIRTH CUSTOMS—COOKERY**

Long-life noodles with egg, recipe  2963:13

**CHINA—BIRTHDAYS—COOKERY**

Birthday noodles, recipe  2658:21

Long life noodles, recipe  2796:33

Long-life noodles, recipe  2565:30-31

**CHINA—BOATS**

Dragon boat, paper bag, patterns, making  2934:153-156

Junk boat, paper bag, dowel, making  2934:151-152

**CHINA—CHOPSTICKS**

How to use chopsticks  2344:unp

**CHINA—CLOTHING**

Man and woman traditional clothing, patterns  2642:55

## CHINA—COOKERY

Almond cookies, recipe   2572:62
Almond cookies, recipe   2873:57
Almond fruit float, recipe   2873:56
Almond sesame cookies, recipe   2743:51
Baat Bo Fon (rice pudding), recipe   2266:21
Bean sprouts with scallions, recipe   2873:53
Beggar's chicken, recipe   2572:57-59
Boiled dumplings, recipe   2873:62
Braised mushrooms, recipe   2565:20-21
Cantonese sweet and sour pork, recipe   2266:17
Cantonese sweet and sour pork, recipe   2585:15
Carrots with honey, recipe   2604:30-31
Celery and shrimp salad, recipe   2604:32-33
Chicken porridge, recipe   2565:32-33
Chicken stir-fry, recipe   2684:72
Chilled cucumber and sesame salad, recipe
    2572:37
Chinese cabbage, recipe   2873:52
Chinese fish cakes, recipe   2604:16-17
Chinese fried rice, recipe   2864:48-49
Chinese menu   2873:28-29
Chinese noodles in peanut sauce, recipe
    2585:17
Chinese omelet, recipe   2565:26-27
Chinese scrambled eggs, recipe   2604:12-13
Chinese tea, recipe   2934:110
Chinese white rice, recipe   2572:23
Chocolate litchies, recipe   2604:40-41
Chow Fon (fried rice), recipe   2266:13
Cold sesame noodles, recipe   2572:33
Congee or jook rice porridge, recipe   2873:32
Don Far Tong (chicken egg-drop soup with scal-
    lions), recipe   2266:9
Egg rolls, recipe   2572:34-35
Egg tarts, recipe   2565:36-37
Egg-drop soup, recipe   2585:11
Egg-flower soup, recipe   2873:38
Five-spice popcorn, recipe   2700:67
Fortune cookies, recipe   2873:58
Four-color soup, recipe   2565:14-15
Fried rice, recipe   2565:28-29
Fried rice, recipe   2572:30-31
Fried rice, recipe   2585:9
Fried rice, recipe   2873:42
Ginger and green onion noodles, recipe
    2604:34-35
Ginger beef with green beans, recipe
    2572:50-51
Homemade chicken stock, recipe   2572:18-19
Homemade vegetable stock, recipe   2572:20
Honey chicken, recipe   2604:22-23
Hot and sour soup, recipe   2572:28-29

Lemon chicken stir-fry, recipe   2604:20-21
Lemon chicken, recipe   2924:22-23
Long life noodles, recipe   2345:unp
Long-life noodles, recipe   2565:30-31
Moon cakes, recipe   2572:64-65
Mushroom and water chestnut soup, recipe
    2604:10-11
Noodles with ground pork, recipe   2604:24-25
Orange tea, recipe   2604:42-43
Pork with green pepper and pineapple, recipe
    2873:48
Red bean soup, recipe   2565:34-35
Rice pudding, recipe   2585:21
Rice, how to cook, recipe   2873:32
Shrimp and pork dim sum, recipe   2565:10-11
Shrimp with ginger sauce, recipe   2604:14-15
Shrimp with hoisin sauce, recipe   2873:49
Spiced roast chicken, recipe   2873:46
Spring rolls, recipe   2565:8-9
Stir-fried beef with sugar peas, recipe   2873:45
Stir-fried beef wraps with smoked tofu, recipe
    2572:52-53
Stir-fried fish with mushrooms and cucumber,
    recipe   2604:18-19
Stir-fried green beans and green onions, recipe
    2572:41
Stir-fried orange chicken, recipe   2572:47-49
Stir-fried shrimp and red peppers, recipe
    2572:54-55
Sweet and sour prawns, recipe   2565:16-17
Sweet and sour tofu stir-fry, recipe   2572:42-43
Sweet bird's nest, recipe   2934:111
Sweet chestnut balls, recipe   2604:38-39
Sweet corn soup, recipe   2565:12-13
Sweet eight treasures rice pudding, recipe
    2344:unp
Sweet red bean paste, recipe   2873:69
Tea, how to make, recipe   2873:33
Three rice dishes, recipe   2604:36-37
Tofu stir-fry, recipe   2604:28-29
Tofu with pork, recipe   2565:18-19
Vegetable chow mein, recipe   2604:26-27
Vegetables with oyster sauce, recipe
    2565:24-25
Velvet corn soup, recipe   2572:27
Watercress soup, recipe   2873:39
Wonton, recipe   2873:36
Yellow sesame noodles, recipe   2381:unp

## CHINA—DRAGONS

Chinese dragon, black poster board, paints, tem-
    plate given, making   2978:31
Egg carton dragons, pattern, making
    2642:135-136

**CHINA—EMBROIDERY**

Needlework purse, plastic canvas, yarn, making 2818:36-45

**CHINA—FANS**

Paper fan, paper, making 2686:49-51

**CHINA—FESTIVALS—COOKERY**

Clear Brightness Festival; almond and sesame cookies, recipe 2796:27

Cold Foods Festival; barbecued chicken drumsticks, recipe 2769:42

Cold Foods Festival; fresh spring rolls, recipe 2769:40-41

Cold Foods Festival; tea eggs, recipe 2769:39

Dragon Boat Festival; charsiu roast pork, recipe 2824:18-19

Dragon Boat Festival; dragon boat dumplings, recipe 2796:39

Dragon Boat Festival; mung bean soup, recipe 2824:20

Dragon Boat Festival; sticky rice, recipe 2824:16-17

Dragon Boat Festival; sweet rice packages, recipe 2769:56-57

Harvest Moon Festival; moon cookies, recipe 2514:23

Lantern Festival; crisp-cooked vegetarian noodles, recipe 2769:16-17

Lantern Festival; New Year dumplings, recipe 2769:14-15

Lantern Festival; sweet rice balls, recipe 2769:27

Lantern Festival; vegetable sticks with peanut dip, recipe 2769:13

Mid-Autumn Festival; moon cakes, recipe 2824:24-25

Mid-Autumn Festival; red hard-boiled eggs, recipe 2824:26-27

Mid-Autumn Festival; sweet rice balls, recipe 2824:28

Mid-Autumn Moon Festival; five-treasure moon cakes, recipe 2769:66-67

Mid-Autumn Moon Festival; rabbit-in-the-moon cookies, recipe 2769:68-69

Moon Festival; moon cakes, recipe 2478:135

Moon Festival; moon cakes, recipe 2659:11

Moon Festival; moon cakes, recipe 2873:68-69

Moon Festival; sweet and sour soup, recipe 2478:135

Qing Ming Festival; barbecued chicken drumsticks, recipe 2769:42

Qing Ming Festival; fresh spring rolls, recipe 2769:40-41

Qing Ming Festival; tea eggs, recipe 2769:39

Winter Solstice Festival; tang yuan sweet dessert, recipe 2334:30-31

**CHINA—FESTIVALS—DECORATIONS**

Cold Foods Festival; pinwheels, making 2769:43

Dragon Boat Festival; bamboo clackers, wood, tape, making 2769:53

Dragon Boat Festival; dragon boats, paper, making 2769:54

Honeycomb paper crafts, making 2407:65

Moon Festival; candle holder, flour and salt dough, making 2586:35

Qing Ming Festival; pinwheels, making 2769:43

**CHINA—FESTIVALS—DRAGONS**

Giant dancing dragon, paper, beads, feathers, making 2478:137

**CHINA—FESTIVALS—GAMES**

Lantern Festival; Chinese shuttlecock, how to make and play 2769:18

**CHINA—FESTIVALS—HANDICRAFTS**

Dragon Boat Festival; charms, fragrant bag, fabric, dried flowers, making 2769:55

Lantern Festival; Good luck characters, red paper, paint, making 2769:11

**CHINA—FESTIVALS—KITES**

Cold Foods Festival; kites, fabric, tissue paper, dowels, making 2769:44-45

Qing Ming Day Festival; kite, crepe paper, tissue paper, paints, making 2334:28-29

Qing Ming Festival; kites, fabric, tissue paper, dowels, making 2769:44-45

**CHINA—FESTIVALS—LANTERNS**

Lantern Festival; lantern riddles, making 2769:29-31

Lantern Festival; paper lantern, making 2769:28

Moon Festival; moon and stars lantern, fruit cans, silver cord, candles, patterns, making 2883:78-79

Yuan Hsiao Lantern Festival; lantern, making 2407:54

**CHINA—FESTIVALS—PRINTS**

Lantern Festival; New Year Prints, red or white paper, inks, making 2769:10-11

**CHINA—FESTIVALS—PUPPETS**

Mid-Autumn Moon Festival; shadow puppets and theater, oak tag, bamboo skewers, making 2769:70-71

**CHINA—FESTIVALS—ZODIAC**

Lantern Festival; Chinese zodiac    2769:19-22

**CHINA—FICTION**

*Chinese Mother Goose Rhymes* by Robert
Windham; activities, art, poetry, maps,
crafts, foods, patterns    2642:110-111

**CHINA—FOLKLORE**

Activities, finger plays, songs, rhymes, crafts,
patterns    2829:38-39

*Eyes of the Dragon* by Margaret Leaf; activities,
art, poetry, maps, crafts, foods, patterns
2642:133-136

*Lon Po Po: A Red-Riding Hood Story from
China* by Ed Young; activities, art, poetry,
maps, crafts, foods, patterns    2642:137-139

*Lon Po Po: A Red-Riding Hood Story from
China* by Ed Young, activities, literature,
art, science, poetry, social studies, webbing
2435:35-45

**CHINA—GAMES**

Calling the chickens, how to play    2767:61-62

Chase me game, how to play    2525:143

Chopstick race, how to play    2658:15

Dragon game, how to play    2659:25

Drop the hanky game, how to play    2525:18

Electric gate game, how to play    2525:26

Go game, how to play    2926:20-23

Juggling, spinning plates, how to do
2494:21-25

Nine connected rings tangram game, how to
play    2382:21-23

Seven Clever Pieces, tangram game from China,
how to play    2310:9-13

Shuttlecock, how to play    2767:62-63

Spillikins game, how to make and play
2882:10-11

Sz'kwa, how to play    2767:63-64

Three pin tag game, how to play    2525:129

Tui-u, dominoes game, how to play
2310:26-30

Under the leg game, how to play    2525:166

Zhua San Jacks game, how to play
2330:126-128

**CHINA—HANDICRAFTS**

Huang-hua window flowers, making    2407:12

Pinpricking lamp shade, wrapping paper, making
2407:11

Wheat straw pictures, paper, toothpicks, paints,
making    2818:46-49

**CHINA—KITES**

Six-sided kite, paper, dowels, string, making
2818:22-27

**CHINA—LANGUAGE**

Chinese words for family members    2701:13

Learn to speak Chinese    2743:46

Writing the numbers and counting in Chinese,
words and characters given    2478:136

**CHINA—LANTERNS**

Glow lamp, paper, glass jar, candle, making
2407:21

**CHINA—NEW YEAR—PUPPETS**

Sun Nin, dragon puppet, red paper, making
2402:16-17

**CHINA—NEW YEAR'S DAY—COOKERY**

Boiled dumplings, recipe    2481:30

**CHINA—NUMBERS**

*Count Your Way through China* by Jim Haskins;
activities, art, poetry, maps, crafts, foods,
patterns    2642:98-109

**CHINA—OPERA—MASKS**

Create an opera mask for your face, making
2586:26

**CHINA—PAPER CUTTING**

Cobweb cut paper garlands, making    2407:53

Paper cutouts, paper, patterns, making
2818:12-15

**CHINA—PAPERMAKING**

Deckle and mold for making paper, how to do
2441:121

Making paper, how to do    2441:122-123

**CHINA—PUPPETS**

String puppets, cardboard, thread, paints, making
2818:28-31

**CHINA—SCROLLS**

Painted scroll, paper, paint, making
2441:124-125

Picture scrolls, colored paper, dowel, paints,
making    2818:50-55

**CHINA—TANGRAMS**

Tangrams, how to play    2934:143-145

Tangrams, paper, making    2407:10

Tangrams, paper, patterns, making    2818:32-35

**CHINA—TEA PARTIES—COOKERY**

Fortune cookies, recipe    2643:26

How to plan and set the table    2643:24-25

Oolong tea, recipe    2643:26

**CHINA—TEA PARTIES—HANDICRAFTS**

Fortunes writing for fortune cookies, how to
do    2643:27

**CHINA—TOYS**

Dough clay figures, clay, making    2818:16-21

**CHINA, ANCIENT—ABACUS**

Abacus, cardboard, clay, brown paint, dowels, making   2789:30-31

**CHINA, ANCIENT—ARMOR**

Armor, felt, silver card stock, silver paint, making   2789:58-59

**CHINA, ANCIENT—COOKERY**

Red bean soup, recipe   2789:26-27

**CHINA, ANCIENT—FANS**

Fan, cardboard, tissue paper, balsa strips, wooden skewers, making   2789:44-45

**CHINA, ANCIENT—FESTIVALS—LANTERNS**

Lantern, cardboard, red tissue paper, blue and yellow cardstock, bamboo stick, making   2789:60-61

**CHINA, ANCIENT—HOUSES**

House, thick cardboard, dowel, paints, making   2789:18-19

**CHINA, ANCIENT—INVENTIONS**

Wheelbarrow, cardboard, balsa wood, dowel, making   2789:34-35

**CHINA, ANCIENT—JEWELRY**

Necklace, wire, foil, making   2789:38-39

**CHINA, ANCIENT—KITES**

Kite, wooden skewers, paper, dowel, paints, making   2789:52-53

**CHINA, ANCIENT—MASKS**

Dancing dragon mask, cardboard, tissue, making   2750:29-31

Mask, clay, beads, paints, making   2789:50-51

**CHINA, ANCIENT—MUSICAL INSTRUMENTS**

Pellet drum, cardboard, bamboo stick, paints, making   2789:28-29

**CHINA, ANCIENT—PAGODAS**

Pagoda, thick cardboard, dowel, paints, making   2789:16-17

**CHINA, ANCIENT—PAPER CUTTING**

Colored paper, making   2789:46-47

**CHINA, ANCIENT—PRINTING**

Printing blocks, paper, clay, ink, making   2789:48-49

**CHINA, ANCIENT—SAMPANS**

Sampan, cardboard, wooden skewers, paints, making   2789:56-57

**CHINESE-AMERICANS—BRUSH PAINTINGS**

Brush painting, step by step, how to do   2795:49

**CHINESE-AMERICANS—CHINESE NEW YEAR—COOKERY**

Potstickers, meat pastry dish, recipe   2795:39

**CHINESE-AMERICANS—CHINESE NEW YEAR—DANCES**

Lion dance, how to do   2795:33

**CHINESE-AMERICANS—COOKERY**

"Bow" Chinese buns, recipe   2632:26

Chinatown dragon cakes, recipe   2534:17

Chop suey, recipe   2359:83-84

Corn and egg dish, recipe   2879:65

Cucumber salad, recipe   2879:66

Fried rice, recipe   2795:9

Hot chicken bu soup, recipe   2795:17

Iceberg lettuce egg drop soup, recipe   2879:64-65

Shoyu chicken, recipe   2879:66-67

Turkey bones and rice chowder, recipe   2879:66

**CHINESE-AMERICANS—DOLLS**

Chinese dolls, sticks, clay, yarn, fabric, making   2632:21

**CHINESE-AMERICANS—FICTION**

*In the Year of the Boar and Jackie Robinson* by Bette Bao Lord, activities for art, music, food, clothing and history   2478:106-138

*Lion Dancer: Ernie Wan's Chinese New Year* by Kate Waters; activities, art, poetry, maps, crafts, foods, patterns   2642:81-83

**CHINESE-AMERICANS—GAMES**

Chinese chess, how to play   2795:28-30

Pebble game, jacks, how to play   2632:22

Tangram puzzle, how to make and play   2478:130-132

**CHINESE NEW YEAR**

Activities, finger plays, songs, rhymes, crafts, patterns   2828:50-51

Activities, patterns   2755:71-90

Chinese boy and girl, patterns   2755:84-85

**CHINESE NEW YEAR—BANNERS**

Red paper banners, paper, paints, making   2504:10-11

**CHINESE NEW YEAR—CHARACTERS**

Good luck characters, red paper, paint, making   2769:11

**CHINESE NEW YEAR—COOKERY**

Almond cookies, recipe   2888:55

Candied walnuts, recipe   2888:56

Chiao-tzu dumpling, filling and wrappers, recipes   2504:7-9

Chicken with cashews, recipe   2962:24

Cold sesame noodles, recipe   2962:22

Crisp-cooked vegetarian noodles, recipe
2769:16-17

Egg drop soup, recipe   2962:21

Eight-treasure sweet rice, recipe   2888:54

Festive sweet turnovers, recipe   2796:19

Fortune cookies, recipe   2642:82

Fortune cookies, recipe   2755:79

Fried rice, recipe   2962:25

Fruit salad, recipe   2888:59

New Year dumplings, recipe   2769:14-15

New Year's cake, recipe   2396:60-61

New Year's cake, recipe   2565:22-23

New Year's cake, recipe   2873:64

New Year's noodles, recipe   2271:66

New Year's noodles, recipe   2873:67

Nian-gao cake, baked recipe   2343:unp

Nian-gao cake, steamed recipe   2343:unp

Orange slices with brown sugar, recipe
2888:58

Poached tangerines, recipe   2888:57

Rice cakes, recipe   2888:53

Spare ribs, recipe   2962:23

Spring rolls, recipe   2824:8-9

Steamed dumplings, recipe   2824:10-12

Sweet rice balls, recipe   2769:27

Vegetable sticks with peanut dip, recipe
2769:13

## CHINESE NEW YEAR—DECORATIONS

Banger, corrugated cardboard, beads, making
2407:77

Chinese zodiac, how to make   2755:74-77

Dragon display, paper, patterns, making
2755:88-89

Dragon shaker, paper, plates, rice, dragon pattern, making   2262:84-86

Happy New Year envelope, bright red paper, pattern, making   2755:82

New Year banner and lantern, red paper, yarn, making   2755:83

Yuan tan red envelope, making   2407:44

## CHINESE NEW YEAR—DRAGONS

Chinese dragon, red and gold paper, gold ribbon, pattern, making   2784:22-23

Dancing dragon, egg carton, crepe paper, felt, paints, making   2778:8-9

New Year's dragon, paper, ribbon, making
2407:87

Toy dragon, egg carton, paints, making   2658:29

## CHINESE NEW YEAR—FICTION

*Gung Hay Fat Chow* by June Behrens, activities, crafts, patterns, games, masks, puppets, making   2329:72-75

## CHINESE NEW YEAR—GAMES

Chinese dragon activities, how to play   2755:87

Chinese shuttlecock, how to make and play
2769:18

Dragon game, how to make and play
2755:80-81

Tangram, how to make and play   2755:86

## CHINESE NEW YEAR—HANDICRAFTS

New Year dragon, cardboard box, paper, making
2755:73

## CHINESE NEW YEAR—KITES

Fish kite, pattern, making   2755:78

## CHINESE NEW YEAR—LANTERNS

Lantern riddles, making   2769:29-31

Paper lantern, making   2769:28

Paper lanterns, red paper, paints, making   2328:121-123

## CHINESE NEW YEAR—MONEY

Red envelopes for money, red paper, making
2708:44

## CHINESE NEW YEAR—PRINTS

New Year prints, red or white paper, inks, making   2769:10-11

## CHINESE NEW YEAR—ZODIAC

Chinese zodiac   2769:19-22

## CHIPPEWA INDIANS—GAMES

Moccasin games, how to play   2767:166

## CHITIMACHA INDIANS—COOKERY

Baked duck, recipe   2879:68

Corn soup, recipe   2879:68

Macque choux (corn dish), recipe   2879:67-68

## CHOCTAW INDIANS—COOKERY

Banaha (corn shuck bread), recipe   2558:22

Banaha (corn shuck bread), recipe   2879:69-70

Banaha (cornmeal dish), recipe   2282:48

Tonshla bona (hominy and pork dish), recipe
2879:69

## CHOCTAW INDIANS—LANGUAGE

Everyday words in Choctaw language and how to pronounce them   2282:89-93

## CHRISTMAS

Activities and patterns   2753:21-36

Candles and bells; activities, finger plays, songs, rhymes, crafts, patterns   2828:42-43

Gifts; activities, finger plays, songs, rhymes, crafts, patterns   2828:44-45

History of Christmas   2877:98

Santa; activities, finger plays, songs, rhymes, crafts, patterns   2828:40-41

Story times, activities, angel tubey pattern, craft instructions   2636:78-80

Story times, activities, elf tubey pattern, craft instructions   2636:71-73

Story times, activities, Santa tubey pattern, craft instructions   2636:74-77

Thematic units, lessons, activities, art, poetry, crafts, patterns, recipes   2320:97-128

## CHRISTMAS—BIRD FEEDERS

Milk carton, twine, making   2335:56-57

Pinecone bird feeder, making   2923:32-33

## CHRISTMAS—COOKERY

Angel cookies, recipe   2318:34-35

Brown bread, recipe   2888:243

Candy cane hot chocolate, recipe   2877:102

Chocolate sandwich rounds, recipe   2888:242

Christmas tree cookie ornament, recipe   2888:236

Christmas tree decorated cake, recipe   2583:18

Christmas wreath cookies, recipe   2335:47

Cookie dough for cutout cookies, recipe   2888:233-234

Cornish game hens, recipe   2692:17

Cranberry-apple tea loaf, recipe   2877:105

Eggless eggnog, recipe   2877:100

Gingerbread people, recipe   2692:11

Graham cracker holiday house, recipe   2335:49

Meringue hands, recipe   2783:20-21

Mrs. Claus's favorite fudge, recipe   2335:48

Mulled apple cider, recipe   2877:101

Mulled cranberry cider, recipe   2692:15

Peppermint candy cane cookies, recipe   2888:237-238

Plum pudding, recipe   2877:106-107

Rainbow salad, recipe   2692:21

Santa's cookie factory truffles, recipe   2318:36-37

Spiced and iced gingerbread animals, recipe   2877:103

Stained-glass cookies, recipe   2335:46

Stained-glass cookies, recipe   2888:239-240

Stollen, recipe   2888:244-245

Sugar cookies made with colored dough, recipe   2857:18-19

Toffee crinkles cookies, recipe   2888:241

Truffles, recipe   2318:36

Truffles, recipe   2783:14-15

Yuletide date logs and snowballs, recipe   2877:104

## CHRISTMAS—DECORATIONS

3-D greeting cards, making   2318:10-11

3-D table tree, cardboard, paper, sequins, patterns, making   2937:24-25

Advent box, little boxes, cardboard, gold paint, small gifts, making   2318:6-7

Advent calendar, poster board, felt, making   2335:54-55

Advent ornaments, stitchery on felt, patterns, making   2803:46-48

Angel ornament, pattern, making   2753:52

Angel, foil, yarn, paper, making   2722:36-37

Angel, paper folds angel, catalog, gold glitter, ribbon, making   2724:58-60

Angel, snack bag angel, snack bags, gold garland, blue plastic wrap, making   2722:56-57

Angel, tissue box angel, tissue box, foil, metallic trim, yarn, making   2724:40-42

Angel; tissue paper angel, making   2335:8-9

Away in a manger paper ornament, pattern, making   2798:15-16

Berry-basket snowflakes, yarn, glitter, making   2335:11

Bible sewing cards, yarn on Styrofoam tray, making   2803:56

Born in a stable, cardboard tube, patterns, making   2799:31-32

Candy canes, pipe cleaners, ribbon, making   2937:22-23

Candy tree, cardboard, tinsel, ribbons, silver paint, candies, making   2783:10-11

Candy-cane ornament, making   2335:10

Celebrate His birthday, yarn balloon, making   2803:54

Christmas candles, cardboard tubes, paper, making   2335:14-15

Christmas mouse magnet, felt, walnut, making   2335:35

Christmas stitchery, burlap banners, yarn, patterns, making   2803:50-53

Christmas stocking, felt, yarn, making   2335:26-27

Christmas tree card, paper, pattern, making   2335:52-53

Christmas tree centerpiece, paper towel tube, paints, making   2335:13

Come, let us adore Him, cardboard tube, patterns, making   2799:33-36

Cranberry and popcorn garlands, making   2740:6-7

Deer knob, felt, making   2335:34

Dove of peace, pattern, making   2753:79

Egg-carton jingle bells, making   2335:12

Eggshell Santa ornament, making   2335:5

Elves; jiggling elves, felt, pom-poms, making 2937:14-15

Elves; pinecones, glitter, paints, felt, making 2335:16-17

Felt ornaments, making   2740:6-7

Gift-wrap gift box, paper, making   2335:60-61

Gingerbread house, clay, milk carton, making 2884:62-65

Gingerbread man, pattern, making   2753:67

Glory to God pop-out card, making   2798:20

Glory to God, cardboard tube, patterns, making 2799:29-30

Good news angel tree ornament, making 2798:19

Holiday cards, patterns, making   2753:66

Ice candles, decorations, candle, making 2318:38-41

International Christmas tree, pattern, making 2753:73

International greetings word search, making 2753:72

Jesus is born, cardboard tube, making   2799:28

Jesus tree, Christmas tree, making   2798:14

Light for those in darkness, yarn-wrapped cardboard tube, making   2803:49

Manger, table manger, sticks, felt, yarn, making   2722:16-18

Mobiles, cardboard, glitter, making   2318:22-23

Mouse topper, pattern, making   2753:61

Moveable gingerbread man, pattern, making 2753:70

Moveable reindeer, pattern, making   2753:56

Moveable Santa, pattern, making   2753:57

Nativity scene, milk cartons, yarn, paints, making 2335:18-19

Nativity scene, stand-up picture, pattern, making 2798:17-18

Paper bag tree ornaments, making   2748:54-57

Penguin gift box with penguin suit, making 2318:30-33

Peppermint candy in cookie cutter shapes, making   2857:23

Peppermint wreath, making   2857:22

Photo frame, poster board, wrapping paper, ribbons, making   2937:12-13

Pomander, orange, spices, making   2335:58-59

Pompoms and baubles, making   2318:14-17

Pop-up Christmas card, yarn, tissue paper, making   2335:50-51

Radical reindeer, pattern, making   2753:60

Reindeer antlers, pattern, making   2753:64

Reindeer headband, making   2778:40-41

Reindeer ornament, craft sticks, yarn, pom-pom, making   2400:41

Rudolph and the gang, pipe cleaners, pom-poms, making   2937:20-21

Santa Claus chalet and sleigh, cardboard, milk carton, cookies, candy canes, making 2318:28-29

Santa Claus face mobile, paper plates, fiberfill, making   2923:28-30

Santa Claus's cottage, foil, cardboard, sugar cubes, gumdrops, making   2335:20-21

Santa ornament, pattern, making   2753:53

Santa sneeze box, box of tissues, felt, patterns, making   2937:18-19

Santa tissue box, tissue box, paper, cotton balls, making   2722:20-21

Santa, cone table Santa, cone hat, trims, paper, paint, making   2722:30-31

Santa, jumbo triangle Santa, jumbo size poster board, fiberfill, making   2722:58-59

Santa, tall cardboard tube, making   2778:44-45

Santa's helper, felt, peanut, cotton balls, making 2335:4

Shining stars, waxed paper, glitter, making 2335:6-7

Smile wreath, paper, photos, making 2335:28-29

Snowflakes, paper, how to cut   2318:12-13

Snowstorm in a jelly jar, glitter, small toys, making   2318:24-27

Sock snowman, sock, yarn, fabric, making 2937:10-11

Spread the word bell ornament, making 2798:21

St. Nick sitting, felt, pom-poms, making 2335:24-25

Stained glass pictures, pattern, making   2753:62

Stained-glass shepherd, tissue paper, cellophane, making   2335:32-33

Stained-glass window, paints, making   2937:8-9

Stained-glass window, tissue paper, making 2335:30-31

Stars; puffy felt stars, felt, batting, patterns, making   2883:38-40

Stockings, felt, how to make and decorate 2318:46-47

Story of the gingerbread man   2753:68

Tabletop tree, green crepe paper, paints, stars, making   2335:22-23

Three Kings, plastic cups, tissue paper, yarn, clip on earrings, small bottle, making 2722:42-44

Tidings of great joy, cardboard tube, patterns, making 2799:37-38

Tree baubles, cardboard, tissue paper, sequins, making 2778:42-43

Tree, bow tree, bows, felt, trims, making 2722:6-7

Tree bows, bows, glitter, making 2724:62-63

Tree, catalog Christmas tree, catalog, sequins, glitter, making 2724:48-49

Tree, cone Christmas tree, party hat, sparkle stems, sequins, making 2722:19

Tree, countdown to Christmas tree, metal cookie tin, ribbon, yarn, making 2724:6-7

Tree, rag Christmas tree, berry basket, fabric, gold trim, making 2724:52-53

Village; Christmas village, colored paper, silver glitter, patterns, making 2937:16-17

Visitors from the East, cardboard tubes, patterns, making 2799:39-41

We have Seen His star, sewing on paper, yarn, making 2803:55

Wreath of candy, making 2778:38-39

Wreath, Christmas wreath hanger, wire hanger, ribbons, pipe cleaners, making 2724:8-9

Wreath, stick wreath, sticks, paint, trims, making 2722:8-9

## CHRISTMAS—FICTION

*Littlest Angel* by Charles Tazewell, activities, art, games, songs, crafts, patterns 2812:28-33

*Nine Days to Christmas* by Marie Hall Ets, literature, activities, art, curriculum 2436:105-114

*The Polar Express* by Chris Van Allsburg, activities and patterns 2325:36-48

*The Polar Express* by Chris Van Allsburg, activities, crafts, patterns, games, masks, puppets, making 2329:51-56

*The Polar Express* by Chris Van Allsburg, activities, literature, art, science, poetry, social studies, webbing 2435:103-114

*Polar Express* by Chris Van Allsburg, activities, projects, patterns, art, crafts 2822:114-115

*'Twas the Night before Christmas* by Clement C. Moore, activities, art, games, songs, crafts, patterns 2812:34-40

## CHRISTMAS—GAMES

Knucklebones, how to make and play 2335:40-41

## CHRISTMAS—HANDICRAFTS

Decoupage frame, wrapping paper, frame, making 2748:51-53

Decoupage plates, paper, paints, making 2748:48-50

Jolly Santa toy, tissue tube, crepe paper, making 2335:42-43

Photobox, box with lid, scrapbook papers, making 2748:58-60

## CHRISTMAS—ORNAMENTS

Angel head, making 2318:21

Angel ornament, coffee filters, craft bead, wiggly eyes, making 2723:62-63

Angel; hands and foot angel ornament, sequins, yarn, pipe cleaner, making 2723:46-47

Bead and bell ornament, beads, bell, pipe cleaner, making 2723:27

Candy cups, making 2318:21

Christmas bell ornament, Styrofoam ball, paper napkin, ribbon, making 2723:42-43

Christmas stocking ornament, old glove, wiggle eyes, rickrack, making 2723:52-53

Circle garland ornament, old Christmas cards, rickrack, making 2723:36-37

Crisscross ornament, corrugated cardboard, felt, yarn, making 2723:14-15

Dog biscuit doggie ornament, dog biscuit, felt, wiggle eyes, making 2723:22-23

Feed the birds ornament, pipe cleaners, bird pictures, making 2723:20-21

Foil ring ornament, tissue tube, foil, yarn, making 2723:34-35

Gingerbread cookie ornament, gingerbread cookie cutter, ribbon, making 2723:40-41

Glitter card dangles, making 2318:21

Handprint reindeer ornament, paints, yarn, wiggle eyes, making 2723:28-29

Napkin-covered balls ornament, Christmas napkins, Styrofoam ball, making 2723:18-19

Paper filled ornaments, clear glass ball, fancy paper, making 2978:50

Peaceful dove ornament, coffee filters, pipe cleaner, ribbon, making 2723:32-33

Photo locket ornament, jar lids, photo, rickrack, making 2723:60-61

Plate ornament, Christmas paper plates, wiggle eyes, trims, making 2723:12-13

Poinsettia ornament, egg carton, sequins, paints, making 2723:58-59

Reindeer ornament, old necktie, wiggle eyes, ribbon, making 2723:56-57

Reindeer ornament, pipe cleaners, felt, wiggle eyes, making 2723:16-17

Reindeer ornament, tissue tube, yarn, bell, making 2723:48-49

Reindeer treat holder ornament, party hat, wiggle eyes, felt, making 2723:24-25

Salt dough dangles, making 2318:20

Santa-down-the-chimney ornament, match boxes, felt, fiberfill, making 2723:8-9

Snowflakes ornament, plastic basket, glitter, making 2723:54-55

Snowman ornament, ice cream spoon, felt, making 2723:44-45

Tinsel garland tree ornament, Christmas tree garland, sequins, making 2723:50-51

Tray of cookies ornament, cardboard, foil, felt, ribbon, making 2723:32-33

Twinkle star ornament, ice cream spoons, felt, glitter, making 2723:10-11

Wreath ornament, shank buttons, pipe cleaner, making 2723:26-27

Wreath ornament, spaghetti, food coloring, making 2723:38-39

### CHRISTMAS—PUPPETS

Angel puppet, cup, foil, pipe cleaner, making 2335:44-45

Christmas tree puppet, pattern, making 2753:65

Holiday finger puppets, patterns, making 2753:48

Rudolph puppet, pantyhose, paper, making 2335:36-37

Santa puppet, pattern, making 2753:558

Snowman, cotton balls, sock, felt, fabric yarn, making 2335:38-39

### CHRISTMAS EVE—FICTION

*Christmas Tree Memories* by Aliki, activities, crafts, patterns, games, masks, puppets, making 2329:47-50

### CHRISTO, JAVACHEFF

Transformations, making 2529:99

### CHUMASH INDIANS—COOKERY

Acorn pancakes, recipe 2915:17

### CHUMASH INDIANS—GAMES

Ring-and-stick game 2311:77-79

### CINCO DE MAYO

Activities, crafts, cookery, puppets, patterns 2759:67-78

Ojo de dios, sticks, dowels, yarn, making 2759:70

Story times, activities, Mexican boy and girl tubey patterns, craft instructions 2636:34-39

### CINCO DE MAYO—COOKERY

Biscochitos, aniseed cookies, recipe 2888:136

Bread pudding, recipe 2888:135

Cornmeal crunchies, recipe 2888:130-131

Gorditas, thick tortillas, recipe 2671:19

Mango strawberry sauce, recipe 2888:133

Pecan cinnamon cookies, recipe 2888:134

Sopaipillas, pastries, recipe 2888:132

### CINCO DE MAYO—DECORATIONS

Chiles on a string, paper, string, making 2671:13

Oaxacan sun, dough, food coloring, yarn, making 2671:18

Tin art, patterns given, foil squares, making 2671:14-17

### CINCO DE MAYO—FICTION

*Fiesta!* By June Behrens, activities, art, poetry, maps, crafts, foods, patterns 2642:90-93

*Fiesta!* By June Behrens, activities, crafts, patterns, games, masks, puppets, making 2329:111-113

### CINCO DE MAYO—FLAGS

Mexican flag, tissue papers, glue, making 2437:42-43

### CIRCUS

Activities, crafts, puppets, patterns 2759:101-122

### CIRCUS—FICTION

*Thumbprint Circus* by Rodney Peppe, activities, projects, patterns, art, crafts 2822:87-89

### CIRCUS—PUPPETS

Clown finger puppets, gloves, clown hat and shoes, patterns, making 2675:16-18

### CITIZENSHIP DAY

History of Citizenship Day, projects to do 2813:6-9

### CIVIL RIGHTS MOVEMENT—SCHOOLS

Globe, papier-mâché covered Styrofoam ball, making 2528:19

### CLAY

Beadwork clay, recipe 2918:45-46

Bread clay, recipe 2918:44

Carving clay, recipe 2918:43

Flour and salt clay, recipe 2350:47

Flour and salt clay, recipe 2351:47

Plasticine dough, recipe 2918:41

Play clay, recipe 2684:129

Play clay, recipe 2918:39-40

Quick clay, recipe 2918:42

Salt clay recipe 2507:38

Sand sculpting clay, recipe 2918:49-50

Snow clay, recipe 2918:51-52

Soap carving clay, recipe 2918:47-48

**CLEVELAND, GROVER (PRESIDENT)**

    Angler's planning calendar, making  2263:75

    Lady Liberty foil sculpture, making  2263:75

    Lady Liberty storage tube, patterns, making
    2263:75

**CLINTON, WILLIAM JEFFERSON
(PRESIDENT)**

    Make your own crossword puzzles  2263:130

    Peanut butter and banana party, making
    2263:130

    Poem for a President, making  2263:130

**CLOWNS**

    Clown face, big patterns, making
    2759:114-115

    Clown mask, papier-mché, making  2407:95

    Parachuting clown, felt, fabric, string,
    clothespins, wooden beads, patterns,
    making  2884:84-87

**CLOWNS—FACE PAINT**

    Clown face paint, recipe  2918:116

    Hobo face painting, how to do  2952:10-11

    Mime face painting, how to do  2952:8-9

    Peeper, near white face painting, how to do
    2952:12-13

**COLLODI, CARLO—PUPPETS**

    *Pinocchio*; growing nose Pinocchio puppet, Sty-
    rofoam ball, paints, making  2729:32-33

**COLOMBIA—COOKERY**

    Chicken soup, recipe  2914:52

    Colombian feast, recipes  2924:30-31

    Cornmeal pancakes, recipe  2914:52

    Fried green plantains, recipe  2922:51

    Fried plantains, recipe  2303:51

    Fried plantains, recipe  2914:53

    Ground beef sauce, recipe  2914:53

**COLOMBIA—GAMES**

    Los Listones (The Ribbons), how to play
    2767:64-65

**COLOMBIA—LANGUAGE**

    Learn to speak Spanish  2303:49

**COLOMBIA—MASKS**

    Gold mask, paper, foil, yarn, making
    2686:105-106

**COLOMBIA—NEW YEAR—HANDICRAFTS**

    Año Nuevo, globos, papier-mâché balloon with
    printed wishes inside, making  2402:18-19

**COLOMBIAN-AMERICANS—COOKERY**

    Arepas (white corn cakes), recipe  2879:70-71

    Arequipe (custard dish), recipe  2879:71

    Coconut rice, recipe  2879:71-72

**COLORADO—COOKERY**

    Anasazi bean dip and corny tortillas, recipe
    2534:19

    Beef jerky, recipe  2466:44

    Cherries in the snow, recipe  2624:57

**COLUMBUS DAY**

    Activities, play, props, patterns, making
    2388:4-9

    Activities, puppets, patterns  2761:83-90

    History of Christopher Columbus Day
    2813:10-13

**COLUMBUS DAY—BOATS**

    Christopher Columbus's ship picture, paper,
    crayons, patterns, making  2811:11-13

    Niña, Pinta and Santa Maria, patterns
    2761:86-87

**COLUMBUS DAY—DECORATIONS**

    Sailboat, paper, clay, walnut shell, making
    2539:44

**COLUMBUS DAY—FICTION**

    *Follow the Dream: the Story of Christopher Co-
    lumbus* by Peter Sis, activities, crafts, pat-
    terns, games, masks, puppets, making
    2329:15-18

**COLUMBUS DAY—GAMES**

    Columbus Day search game  2813:13

    Columbus Day secret message game  2813:14

**COLUMBUS DAY—HATS**

    Columbus hat, pattern, making  2761:88

**COLUMBUS DAY—PUPPETS**

    Columbus puppet, pattern, making  2761:89

**COMANCHE INDIANS—COOKERY**

    Pemmican, recipe  2283:67

    Plum bars, recipe  2909:15

**COMANCHE INDIANS—FOLKLORE**

    *Legend of the Bluebonnet* by Tomie dePaola;
    activities, art, poetry, maps, crafts, foods,
    patterns  2642:129-132

**COMANCHE INDIANS—GAMES**

    Grizzly Bear, how to play  2767:166-167

**COMANCHE INDIANS—LANGUAGE**

    Everyday words in Comanche language
    2283:100-101

**COMANCHE INDIANS—PARFLECHE**

    Comanche parfleche, oak tag, paints, designs
    given, making  2352:32

**COMANCHE INDIANS—RAIN DANCE**

    Rain dance, how to do  2642:130

**COMMUNITIES—FICTION**

*The Little House* by Virginia Lee Burton, literature, activities, art, curriculum   2436:75-86

**COMMUNITIES—UNITED STATES**

Airport; activities, crafts, projects, songs, finger plays   2685:93-97

Animal Shelter; activities, crafts, projects, songs, finger plays   2685:46-51

Construction site; activities, crafts, projects, songs, finger plays   2685:57-62

Fire station; activities, crafts, projects, songs, finger plays   2685:28-33

Garden center; activities, crafts, projects, songs, finger plays   2685:68-74

Gas station; activities, crafts, projects, songs, finger plays   2685:108-117

Grocery store; activities, crafts, projects, songs, finger plays   2685:86-92

Hospital; activities, crafts, projects, songs, finger plays   2685:40-45

Ice-cream shop; activities, crafts, projects, songs, finger plays   2685:103-107

Library; activities, crafts, projects, songs, finger plays   2685:23-27

My home; activities, crafts, projects, songs, finger plays   2685:6-10

Park; activities, crafts, projects, songs, finger plays   2685:34-39

Police station; activities, crafts, projects, songs, finger plays   2685:17-22

Post Office; activities, crafts, projects, songs, finger plays   2685:52-56

Railroad station; activities, crafts, projects, songs, finger plays   2685:63-67

Restaurant; activities, crafts, projects, songs, finger plays   2685:118-123

School; activities, crafts, projects, songs, finger plays   2685:11-16

Senior Citizens' center; activities, crafts, projects, songs, finger plays   2685:75-80

Theater; activities, crafts, projects, songs, finger plays   2685:98-102

Town Hall; activities, crafts, projects, songs, finger plays   2685:81-85

**CONNECTICUT—COOKERY**

Dreamy creamy clam chowder, recipe   2534:20

Lollipops, recipe   2425:63

**CONSTABLE, JOHN**

Cloudscape, making   2529:33

**CONSTRUCTION SITES**

Theme unit on construction sites; activities for math, social studies and art   2972:1-32

**COOLIDGE, CALVIN (PRESIDENT)**

Holiday gifts collage, making   2263:96

Popcorn balls, recipe   2263:96

Shoulder pets, making   2263:96

**CORNELL, JOSEPH**

Portrait box collage, making   2529:94

**CORNISH-AMERICANS—COOKERY**

Cornish pastries, recipe   2879:72-74

Saffron bread, recipe   2879:74

**COSTA RICA—CHRISTMAS—COOKERY**

Tamales, recipe   2677:22-23

**COSTA RICA—COAT OF ARMS**

Costa Rican coat of arms, paper, markers, pattern, making   2671:24

**COSTA RICA—COOKERY**

Black beans, hearts of palm and corn salad, recipe   2944:52

Cartago corn cake, recipe   2944:52

Ensalada de fruitas (fruit salad), recipe   2408:30-31

Mega maca muffins, recipe   2944:53

Salsa, recipe   2944:52

Tortillas and eggs, recipe   2944:53

**COSTA RICA—FLAGS**

Costa Rican flag, paper, markers, pattern, making   2671:24

**COSTA RICA—OXCARTS**

Oxcart, shoe box, dowels, paints, making   2408:28-29

**COSTA RICA—SCULPTURES**

Pre-Columbian clay figure, clay, beads, making   2408:26-27

**COTTON**

Cotton boll pattern   2475:9

**COURBET, GUSTAVE**

Palette knife painting, how to do   2529:36

**COWBOYS**

Activities, crafts, patterns   2756:67-80

Cowboy mobile, poster board, dowel, string, cowboy shapes, making   2523:9-11

Finding direction, how to do   2523:33

Measuring distance, how to do   2523:34-37

Poke pouch, chamois, felt, rawhide lacing, making   2523:12-14

**COWBOYS—BRANDS**

Designing a brand stamp, block of wood, felt, making   2523:7-9

**COWBOYS—COOKERY**

Beef jerky, recipe   2523:20-21

Chuck wagon beans, recipe   2488:57
Cowboy bean bake, recipe   2864:62-63
Frijoles refritos, recipe   2523:68-69
Fruit leather, recipe   2523:38-40
Ranch scrambled eggs, recipe   2523:93-94
Ranch-style fruit punch, recipe   2523:19
Sourdough flapjacks, recipe   2523:17-18
Sourdough starter, recipe   2523:16-17
Vinegar pie, recipe   2488:50

**COWBOYS—GAMES**

Mustang and cowboys board game, how to make
and play   2523:85-86

**COWBOYS—HATS**

Big hat, fabric, string, making   2441:105-107
Cowboy and cowgirl hat pattern   2756:74

**COWBOYS—PUPPETS**

Cowboy finger puppets, gloves, cowboy hat, patterns, making   2675:64-67

**COWBOYS—ROPES**

Knot know-how, how to do a half hitch, hitching
post, clove hitch and neckerchief knot
2523:77-80
Making a lariat, yarn, making   2523:75-76

**COWBOYS—TOYS**

Cork horse, corks, yarn, making   2441:108-109

**CRAYONS**

Chunky crayon, recipe   2918:2-3
Fabric crayon, recipe   2918:6-7
Popsicle crayon, recipe   2918:4-5
Sculpt 'n' color crayon, recipe   2918:9-10
Soap doodler crayon, recipe   2918:11-12
Super-slick pastel crayon, recipe   2918:8

**CREE INDIANS—FOOTWEAR**

Moccasins, felt, thread, embroidery floss,
making   2311:99-105

**CREE INDIANS—GAMES**

Sliding game, how to play   2702:22
Tcoskumina-a (sliding game), how to play
2767:59-60
Tihitpintowan (rolling game), how to play
2767:60

**CREEK INDIANS—COOKERY**

Corn pudding, recipe   2879:75-76
Grape dumplings, recipe   2559:22
Muskogean shuck bread, recipe   2890:15
Osafkee (hot cereal drink), recipe   2879:75

**CREOLES—CANE RIVER**
          **CREOLES—COOKERY**

Cinnamon praline pecans, recipe   2879:54
Creole meat pies, recipe   2879:52

Creole tea cakes, recipe   2879:52-53
Okra gumbo, recipe   2879:53

**CREOLES—COOKERY**

Bread pudding with fruit, recipe   2359:41-42
Coush-coush (cornmeal dish), recipe   2879:78
Gumbo Z'Herbes, recipe   2879:77
King cake, recipe   2359:43-45
Red beans, recipe   2879:78
Shrimp and ham jambalaya, recipe   2359:39-40
Turnips and pork ribs, recipe   2879:78-79

**CROATIA—GAMES**

Jack, where are you?, how to play   2767:65-66
Toothpaste game, how to play   2968:122

**CROATIA—LANGUAGE**

Common Croatian words and phrases   2968:81

**CROATIAN-AMERICANS—COOKERY**

Ajvar spread, recipe   2879:81
Dalmation baked fish, recipe 2879:80
Spinach pie, recipe   2879:80-81
Zgance (Depression dish, cornmeal mush dish),
recipe   2879:81-82

**CROW INDIANS—GAMES**

Icbirikyu, how to play   2767:167

**CUBA—COOKERY**

Avocado salad, recipe   2886:34
Baked custard, recipe   2886:60-61
Baked eggs, recipe   2886:55
Beef hash, recipe   2886:54
Black beans, recipe   2886:44-45
Black beans, recipe   2911:51
Caribbean rice, recipe   2270:19
Creole chicken, recipe   2886:51
Creole sauce, recipe   2886:40
Cuban meatloaf, recipe   2886:52
Cuban menu   2886:28-29
Cuban white rice, recipe   2886:41
Fried plantains, recipe   2886:46-47
Garbanzo bean salad, recipe   2886:32
Garlic soup, recipe   2886:35
Garlicky shrimp, recipe   2886:50
Mango and papaya milk shake, recipe   2886:59
Meat and potato stew, recipe   2886:36
Moors and Christians rice and black bean dish,
recipe   2966:25
Rice pudding, recipe   2886:58
Yellow rice, recipe   2886:42

**CUBA—DOLLS**

Cuban yarn dolls, cardboard, yarn, felt, making
2817:16-21

**CUBA—FESTIVALS—COOKERY**

Cuban cookies, recipe   2886:68

Fried yucca with garlic sauce, recipe   2886:65
Red beans and rice, recipe   2886:66-67
Roast pork, recipe   2886:64

**CUBA—GAMES**

Color tag game, how to play   2525:140
Cuban dominoes, how to play   2548:12
El Cenconmigo (come with me), how to play   2767:66-67
La tabla de mani picao game, how to play   2525:74
Name the animal game, how to play   2525:109

**CUBAN-AMERICANS—COOKERY**

Black bean soup, recipe   2879:82-83
Picadillo meat mixture, recipe   2879:83
Puffed wheat batido drink, recipe   2879:83

**CUSHMAN, KAREN**

*Catherine, Called Birdy* by Karen Cushman; activities, projects, reading, writing, science, social studies, food and art   2849:5-16

**CZECH-AMERICANS—COOKERY**

Kolaches (pastries), recipe   2879:85-86
Molasses cookies, recipe   2879:87
Poppy seed cake, recipe   2879:87
Varmuza pancake potato dish, recipe   2879:85

**CZECH REPUBLIC—CHRISTMAS— COOKERY**

Vanilla crescents, recipe   2973:126

**CZECH REPUBLIC—CHRISTMAS— DECORATIONS**

Paper chain for a Christmas tree, paper, paste, making   2653:28-29

**CZECH REPUBLIC—COOKERY**

Bramorak, potato pancake, recipe   2653:30-31

**CZECH REPUBLIC—DOLLS**

Gourd dolls, gourd, paints, making   2407:84

**CZECH REPUBLIC—GAMES**

Continuous motion game, how to play   2525:189
Czech jacks game, how to play   2330:56-57
Double the fun game, how to play   2525:106
Fastest and mostest game, how to play   2525:117
Friendly knockout game, how to play   2525:129
Gates game, how to play   2525:146
Golden Gate, how to play   2767:67
Shoot the duck game, how to play   2525:49

**CZECH REPUBLIC—HANDICRAFTS**

Animals from fruits and vegetables, making   2653:26-27

**CZECH REPUBLIC—LANGUAGE**

Common Czech terms and phrases   2973:86

**CZECHOSLOVAKIA—GAMES**

Golden gate game, how to play   2882:26-27

# D

**DA VINCI, LEONARDO**

Activities, games, crafts, patterns to celebrate the life of Leonardo da Vinci   2501:3-47

Banner, create a banner, how to do   2472:25

Discovery notebook, making   2472:33

Drawing things apart, how to do   2529:19

Inventions, how to do   2529:20-21

Kitchen clay, making   2472:15

Proportions of Leonardo, how to observe   2472:35

**DA VINCI, LEONARDO—BIOGRAPHY**

*Da Vinci* by Mike Venezia, activities, projects, patterns, art, crafts   2822:15-17

**DA VINCI, LEONARDO—COOKERY**

Leonardo's lunch, recipe   2472:46

Salai's aniseed sweets, recipe   2472:49

**DA VINCI, LEONARDO—HERBS**

Renaissance herb garden, making   2472:77

**DA VINCI, LEONARDO—MEASUREMENTS**

How tall is that tree, how to measure   2472:66

**DA VINCI, LEONARDO—MUSICAL INSTRUMENTS**

Leonardo's lute, making   2472:31

**DAHOMEY—GAMES**

Godo, how to play   2767:67-68

**DAKOTA INDIANS—COOKERY**

Beans and bacon, recipe   2879:255-256

Boiled meat, recipe   2879:254

Corn balls, recipe   2879:255

Fry bread, recipe   2827:21

Fry bread, recipe   2879:253

Popovers, recipe   2879:254

Stuffed pumpkin, recipe   2879:254-255

Wojapi (fruit pudding), recipe   2296:58

Wojapi pudding, recipe   2879:253

Wojapi, berry pudding, recipe   2391:44

**DAKOTA INDIANS—LANGUAGE**

Everyday words in Dakota language   2296:98-100

**DAKOTA INDIANS—MOCCASINS**

Western Dakota moccasins, leather or felt fabric, yarn, rawhide, beads, pattern, making   2440:75-77

**DAKOTA INDIANS—SONGS**

Dakota Sioux song   2391:43

**DAKOTA INDIANS—WINTER COUNT**

Winter count for yourself, paper bag, making   2391:42

**DAKOTA INDIANS.** *See also* **SIOUX INDIANS**

**DALI, SALVADORE**

Dream photographs, making   2529:78

**DALMATIANS.** *See* **CROATIAN-AMERICANS**

**DANCING**

Language arts, poetry, hobby craft activities   2511:17-20

**DANCING—TEA PARTIES—COOKERY**

Chocolate covered fruit, recipe   2643:42

Have a ball tea party, how to plan and set the table   2643:40-41

Tea punch, recipe   2643:42

**DANISH-AMERICANS—COOKERY**

Kringle dessert, recipe   2879:89

Ris a la mande (rice porridge), recipe   2879:88-89

**DAVIS, JIM**

Comic creatures, making   2529:105

**DE REGNIERS, BEATRICE SCHENK**

*May I Bring a Friend?* By Beatrice Schenk de Regniers, literature, activities, act, curriculum   2436:87-103

**DEBRUNHOFF, JEAN**

*Babar* by Jean DeBrunhoff, elephant treasure keeper, detergent bottle, paper, glitter, making   2729:8-9

**DECEMBER THEMES**

Thematic units, lessons, activities, art, poetry, crafts, patterns, recipes   2320:97-128

**DEGAS, EDGAR**

Camera capers, how to take Kodak picture of scenes like Degas did   2738:68

Chalk on cloth, making   2529:41

Resist in motion, making   2529:40

**DELAWARE—COOKERY**

Ginger peachy chicken, recipe   2315:63

**DELAWARE—FESTIVALS—COOKERY**

World Championship Punkin' Chunkin' Festival; punkin' chunkin' cheesecake, recipe 2534:22

**DELAWARE INDIANS—DECORATIONS**

Leaf designs, making 2560:22

**DELAWARE INDIANS—MUSICAL INSTRUMENTS**

Turkey rattle, cardboard, paints, felt, dowel, feathers, making 2621:31

**DENMARK—CHRISTMAS—COOKERY**

Rice pudding, recipe 2481:62

**DENMARK—CHRISTMAS—DECORATIONS**

Star mobile, plastic straws, paper, paste, string, making 2407:91

Woven hearts, heavy paper, shiny Christmas wrap, making 2740:16-17

Woven hearts, paper, making 2407:58

**DENMARK—COOKERY**

Smorrebrod, lunch dish, recipe 2640:22

**DENMARK—FOLKLORE**

Little Mermaid statue, paper cup, popsicle stick, making 2686:92-93

**DENMARK—GAMES**

Ocean is stormy, how to play 2767:68

Open the window game, how to play 2525:29

Pinball game, how to play 2525:105

**DENMARK—LANGUAGE**

Few words in Danish 2640:23

**DEPAOLA, TOMIE**

*Lady of Guadalupe* by Tomie dePaola, activities, art, poetry, maps, crafts, foods, patterns 2642:127-128

*Legend of the Bluebonnet* by Tomie dePaola, activities, art, poetry, maps, crafts, foods, patterns 2642:129-132

*Legend of the Indian Paintbrush* by Tomie dePaola, activities, patterns 2644:40-45

*Nana Upstairs & Nana Downstairs* by Tomie dePaola, activities, crafts, patterns, games, masks, puppets 2329:11-14

*Now One Foot, Now the Other* by Tomie dePaola, activities, crafts, patterns, games, masks, puppets, making 2329:11-14

*Popcorn Book* by Tomie dePaola, activities 2298:22-23

**DESERTS—FICTION**

*I'm in Charge of Celebrations* by Byrd Baylor; activities, art, poetry, maps, crafts, foods, patterns 2642:12-16

**DEWEY, MELVILLE—BIRTHDAY**

Activities, projects, programs to celebrate Melville Dewey's birthday (December 10, 1851) 2378:36-44

**DINEH INDIANS. *See* NAVAHO INDIANS**

**DINOSAURS**

Thematic units, lessons, activities, art, poetry, crafts, patterns, recipes 2320:185-219

**DOGON (AFRICAN PEOPLES)—MASKS**

Dogon animals mask, railroad board, paints, pattern, making 2620:12-13

**DOGS**

Fidough biscuits, recipe 2511:22

Language arts, poetry, hobby craft activities 2511:21-25

**DOLLS**

Pilgrim corn dolly, corn husks, pipe cleaners, yarn, making 2504:89-90

Scarecrow, cornhusk dolls, making 2445:59

**DOMINICAN-AMERICANS—COOKERY**

Coconut fish stew, recipe 2879:91

Fried pork rinds of chicken, recipe 2879:90-91

**DOMINICAN REPUBLIC—COOKERY**

Black bean soup, recipe 2954:52

Corn pudding, recipe 2954:53

Mangu, plantain dish, recipe 2954:52

Sancocho, chicken, yucca and vegetable dish, recipe 2911:51

Vanilla cake, recipe 2954:53

**DOUGHS**

Apple-cinnamon dough, recipe 2918:30-31

Confetti dough, recipe 2918:35

Dirt dough, recipe 2918:38

Fizzy fun dough, recipe 2918:34

Greatest dough on earth, recipe 2918:28

No-cook play dough, recipe 2918:32

Play dough, recipe 2684:128

Salt dough, recipe 2918:33

Scented play dough, recipe 2918:29

Shampoo dough, recipe 2918:37

Soft soap dough, recipe 2918:36

**DRAGONS**

Dragon helmet, foam sheets, patterns, making 2883:19-21

**DRAGONS—PUPPETS**

Dragon finger puppets, gloves, patterns, making 2675:72-75

**DRAWING**

Language arts, poetry, hobby craft activities 2511:27-30

**DUCHAMP, MARCEL**

Happy accident string drop, making    2529:73

**DÜRER, ALBRECHT**

Wood block print, making    2529:22

**DUTCH-AMERICANS—COOKERY**

Anise milk, recipe    2879:93

Coleslaw, recipe    2879:94

Dutch apple koek (bread), recipe    2879:95

Dutch carrots, recipe    2879:96

Krullers, recipe    2879:94

St. Nickolas koekjes (cookies), recipe
    2879:95-96

**DYES**

Coffee dye, recipe    2918:81

Eggshell dye, recipe    2918:73

Flower power dye, recipe    2918:77

Funky fabric dye, recipe    2918:69-70

Magical color dye, recipe    2918:78-79

Natural dyes, how to make and use    2331:22-23

Veggie dye, recipe    2918:75-76

# E

**EAGLES**

U.S. eagle symbols, three eagle patterns   2475:77-78

**EARHART, AMELIA**

Amelia Earhart portrait, pattern   2758:92

**EARTH DAY**

April 22, activities, projects, literature   2390:unp

Earth First! Booklet, patterns   2752:59

Earth First! visor, pattern   2752:57

Environmental acts of kindness pledge   2752:54

Environmental kindness parent letter   2752:56

Family's recycling report, pattern   2752:58

My Garbage Can story, patterns   2752:60

Random acts of environmental kindness record sheet   2752:55

Save the Earth activities   2752:52-53

**EARTH DAY—DECORATIONS**

Stone paperweight, stone, paints, making   2540:42-43

**EARTH DAY—FICTION**

*Just a Dream* by Chris Van Allsburg, activities, crafts, patterns, games, masks, puppets, making   2329:104-106

**EARTH DAY—RECYCLING**

Recycle your lunch to make compost in plastic bottle   2714:unp

**EASTER**

Easter activities   2752:63

History of Easter   2877:32

Story times, activities, Easter bunny tubey pattern, craft instructions   2636:24-26

Thematic units, lessons, activities, art, poetry, crafts, patterns, recipes   2320:220-248

**EASTER—COOKERY**

Almond-topped creamy lemon pie, recipe   2888:119

Candy Easter egg nests, recipe   2693:17

Carrot-walnut bunny bread, recipe   2888:120-121

Chopped egg salad, recipe   2877:35

Decorating Easter eggs, recipe   2877:34

Deviled eggs, recipe   2693:15

Easter basket cupcakes, recipe   2888:124-125

Easter bunny cake, recipe   2888:116

Easter bunny decorated cake, recipe   2583:21

Ham and cheese pie, recipe   2693:19

Hot cross breakfast buns, recipe   2877:36

Hot cross buns, recipe   2677:8-9

Hot cross buns, recipe   2888:114-115

Roast lamb, recipe   2877:37

Strawberry bread, recipe   2888:122-123

Strawberry-rhubarb crisp, recipe   2888:127

**EASTER—DECORATIONS**

Basket egg holder, yarn, ribbon, making   2726:22-23

Basket full of Easter friends, old gloves, felt, making   2726:20-21

Basket; giant bunny basket, carton, paper plates, fiberfill, making   2726:14-15

Bunny basket, paper, cotton balls, patterns, making   2811:37-38

Bunny friend, old glove, fiberfill, yarn, making   2726:8-9

Bunny wheel, patterns   2752:72-73

Bunny, cut and paste bunny, paper, patterns, making   2811:39-41

Bunny, pattern   2752:65

Carrot booklet, pattern   2752:81

Chick and egg, patterns   2752:68

Chick; Easter chick, envelopes, making   2726:30-31

Chick; fluffy pinecone chick, pinecone, fiberfill, making   2726:32-33

Chick; hanging Easter basket chick, paper plates, wallpaper, making   2726:34-35

Chicken or the egg, patterns, making   2752:70-71

Chicks-in-a-nest, cotton balls, pipe cleaners, making   2778:18-19

Daffodils and Easter lilies, patterns   2752:74-75

Easter basket party hat, paper, ribbons, making   2726:18-19

Easter basket, yarn, making   2726:16-17

Easter bonnet wall hanging, paper plates, pipe cleaners, making   2726:42-43

Easter butterfly, cardboard weaving, yarn, patterns, making   2803:62-63

Easter crafts   2752:64

Easter egg matching card, paper, yarn, making
2726:26-27
Easter egg memory game, wallpaper, making
2726:24-25
Easter place card, patterns  2752:78
Egg; giant foil egg, foil, pipe cleaners, making
2726:28-29
Eggs; patchwork Easter eggs, making
2748:31-33
Hatching chicks, patterns  2752:66-67
He died for you yarn rubbing, making  2803:61
He is risen, laced paper plate, yarn, making
2803:64
Hopping bunny, pattern  2752:76
Joy, a wrapping-paper banner, patterns, making
2803:58-60
Lamb; handprint lamb Easter card, making
2726:40-41
Lamb; spring lamb, Styrofoam trays, paper,
making  2726:38-39
Mr. Bunny, pattern  2752:82
Mr. Rabbit figure, paper, crayons, beads, pat-
terns, making  2811:42-43
My Easter book, pattern  2752:80
Papier-mâché Easter egg, making  2923:14-15
Pop-up rabbit, patterns  2752:79
Rabbit necklace, yarn, nail polish, making
2726:10-11
Woven cross, yarn, burlap, making  2803:57
Wreath; puzzle pieces Easter wreath, paper
plates, yarn, flowers, making  2726:46-47

**EASTER—FICTION**

*Country Bunny and the Little Gold Shoes* by Du
Bose Heyward, activities, art, games, songs,
crafts, patterns  2812:87-96
*Rechenka's Eggs* by Patricia Polacco, activities,
crafts, patterns, games, masks, puppets,
making  2329:94-96
*The Tale of Peter Rabbit* by Beatrix Potter, activities, crafts, patterns, games, masks, puppets, making  2329:97-100

**EASTER—HANDICRAFTS**

Easter flowerpots, making  2748:28-30
Patchwork Easter eggs, making  2748:31-33

**EASTER—MASKS**

Bunny mask, pattern, making  2752:77

**EASTER—PUPPETS**

Bunny puppet, neckties, paper, making
2726:12-13
Bunny puppet, pattern, making  2752:69
Chick; tennis ball chick puppet, paper, feathers,
making  2726:36-37

**EASTER—SOAP**

Easter eggs soap, making  2936:42

**EASTER ISLAND**

Carved stone statue model, paper bag, paints,
making  2686:111-112

**ECUADOR—ANIMALS**

Giant tortoise model, paper bag, markers,
making  2686:107-108

**ECUADOR—COOKERY**

Corn packages, recipe  2670:50
Garden salad with mushrooms, recipe  2959:52
Lettuce and potato salad with dressing, recipe
2959:52
Locro soup, recipe  2959:53
Red pepper and garbanzo bean salad, recipe
2959:52
Tomato soup with bananas, recipe  2959:53
Turnovers, recipe  2670:62-63

**ECUADOR—DECORATIONS**

Windspinners, paper, making  2407:76

**ECUADOR—GAMES**

El Siete Loco (crazy seven), how to play
2767:68-69

**ECUADOR—NEW YEAR—COOKERY**

Año Viejo fruit salad, recipe  2504:24-25

**ECUADOR—NEW YEAR—PUPPETS**

Año Viejo, old clothes and newspapers puppet,
making  2504:22-24

**ECUADORIAN-AMERICANS—COOKERY**

Llapingachos (stuffed potato tortillas), recipe
2879:96-97
Locro (soupy potato or vegetable stew), recipe
2879:97

**EGGS**

Egg tree, how to make  2511:32
History of eggs  2717:14-15
Language arts, poetry, hobby craft activities
2511:31-34
Thematic units, lessons, activities, art, poetry,
crafts, patterns, recipes  2320:220-248

**EGYPT—BIRTHDAYS—DECORATIONS**

Zeena garland, paper, making  2957:16-17

**EGYPT—COOKERY**

Baked almond-stuffed apricots, recipe
2830:42-43
Baked fish with nut sauce, recipe  2830:28-29
Broad bean rissoles, recipe  2830:10-11
Brown fava beans, recipe  2271:54
Cheese and egg pastries, recipe  2830:16-17
Chicken kebabs, recipe  2830:30-31

Coconut and semolina cake, recipe   2871:58-59
Date and nut pastries, recipe   2830:34-35
Date cake, recipe   2830:38-39
Eggplant dip, recipe   2830:12-13
Egyptian bread, recipe   2830:18-19
Fattosh (crunchy salad), recipe   2830:22-23
Fava bean stew, recipe   2830:26-27
Goat's cheese and mint salad, recipe
     2830:24-25
Green herb soup, recipe   2871:38
Hummus, recipe   2805:33
Hummus, recipe   2845:16
Koshaf, sweet fruit dish, recipe   2304:53
Mediterranean meatballs, recipe   2924:12-13
Melon fruit salad with rose water and mint,
     recipe   2830:40-41
Milk and pastry pudding, recipe   2871:56
Onion omelette, recipe   2830:20-21
Rice with vermicelli, recipe   2830:32-33
Semit (sesame rings), recipe   2830:14-15
Um'ali (pastry pudding), recipe   2830:36-37

**EGYPT—CROCODILES**
Nile crocodile model, paper, paints, making
     2686:69-70

**EGYPT—FESTIVALS—COOKERY**
Eid-el-Fitr; grandma's nut cake, recipe
     2272:30-31

**EGYPT—FICTION**
*Bill and Pete Go Down the Nile* by Tomie
     dePaola, activities, projects, patterns, art,
     crafts   2822:133-135
*Day of Ahmed's Secret* by Florence Parry Heide;
     activities, art, poetry, maps, crafts, foods,
     patterns   2642:68-70

**EGYPT—GAMES**
Pyramid bowling game, how to make and
     play   2847:17
Seega, how to play   2767:69-70
Snake game, how to make and play   2371:22
Taia ya taia game, how to play   2385:24

**EGYPT—LANGUAGE**
Family member words in Arabic   2805:15
Learn to speak Arabic   2304:50
Numbers in Arabic   2805:20
Six Arabic words   2371:23

**EGYPT, ANCIENT—BOATS**
Reed boat, straw, balsa sticks, string, making
     2788:58-59

**EGYPT, ANCIENT—BRICKS**
Baking bricks, clay, straw, making   2746:49-50

**EGYPT, ANCIENT—BURIALS**
Canopic jars, clay, paints, making   2788:28-29
Udjat eye amulet, clay, paints, making
     2788:30-31

**EGYPT, ANCIENT—CLOCKS**
Water clock, clay, flowerpot, paints, making
     2788:48-49

**EGYPT, ANCIENT—COOKERY**
Bean stew, ful medames, recipe   2363:89
Cake, recipe   2788:38-39
Eggplant omelet, recipe   2566:31
Fatoosh (bread salad), recipe   2566:31
Fuul bean dish, recipe   2869:109
Mayonnaise, recipe   2566:30
Pasta salad, recipe   2566:27
Spicy cucumbers and garlic salad, recipe
     2566:43
Tabouleh, recipe   2566:27
Tuna spread, recipe   2566:43
Unleavened bread, recipe   2746:57-58
Yogurt-topped watermelon, recipe   2566:43

**EGYPT, ANCIENT—DOLLS**
Egyptian paddle doll, cardboard, paints, beads,
     making   2746:52-53

**EGYPT, ANCIENT—FOLKLORE**
Phoenix bird clip, gold paper, felt, flexible straw,
     glitter pens, feathers, pattern, making
     2781:20-21

**EGYPT, ANCIENT—GAMES**
Mehen snake game board, clay, counters, making
     2788:52-53
No yeast game, how to play   2746:59
Seega game, how to play   2847:16
Senet, racing board, how to make and play
     2310:87-92
Snake game, how to make and play   2505:42-43

**EGYPT, ANCIENT—GODS**
Egyptian god, cardboard, gold trim, beads, mak-
     ing   2257:22-23
List of Egyptian Gods   2363:42

**EGYPT, ANCIENT—HIEROGLYPHICS**
Hieroglyph necklace, leather, clay, leather cord,
     patterns, making   2884:104-107
Hieroglyphic alphabet   2642:69
How to write with hieroglyphs   2846:16-17
Reading and writing hieroglyphs, how to do
     2379:40-44
Scarab amulet, clay, plaster of Paris, making
     2505:18-19

**EGYPT, ANCIENT—HOUSEHOLD ITEMS**
Mirror, mirror card, clay, gold paint, making 2788:42-43

**EGYPT, ANCIENT—HOUSES**
House model, cardboard, paints, pattern, making 2788:16-17

**EGYPT, ANCIENT—JEWELRY**
Egyptian bracelet and necklace, pasta noodles, string, paints, making 2505:34-35
Necklace, pasta shells, metallic paints, pattern, making 2683:16-17

**EGYPT, ANCIENT—KNITTING**
Cat's-tail finger-knitting, yarn, making 2440:97-98

**EGYPT, ANCIENT—LANGUAGE**
Names from Ancient Egypt, list to choose from 2363:19
Phrase and numbers in Egyptian Colloquial Arabic 2869:111

**EGYPT, ANCIENT—MASKS**
Falcon mask, felt, baseball cap, feathers, paints, fabric, making 2750:21-23

**EGYPT, ANCIENT—MEASUREMENT**
One-cubit measuring tool, how to make 2363:88

**EGYPT, ANCIENT—MUMMIES**
Canopic jars for internal organs, papier-mâché, paints, making 2505:26-27
Mummified cat doll, tube socks, tea bags, paints, making 2505:22-23

**EGYPT, ANCIENT—MUSICAL INSTRUMENTS**
Rattle, clay, balsa wood, paints, making 2788:50-51
Trumpet, poster board, making 2746:67-68

**EGYPT, ANCIENT—PAINTINGS**
Painting rules of the Egyptian canon 2869:98

**EGYPT, ANCIENT—PHARAOHS**
Beaded collar, Velcro, braid, colored beads, felt, making 2272:28-29
Royal headdress, T-shirt, foil, papier-mâché, paints, making 2505:30-31

**EGYPT, ANCIENT—POTTERY**
Faience plate, blue glazed earthenware, salt, clay, paints, making 2505:38-39

**EGYPT, ANCIENT—PYRAMIDS**
Great pyramid model, cereal box, making 2686:63-64
Pyramid model, cardboard, paints, patterns, making 2788:24-25

Pyramid model, sand clay, recipe given 2505:14-15

**EGYPT, ANCIENT—RELIGION**
Cat goddess figure, papier-mâché, paints, making 2259:22-23

**EGYPT, ANCIENT—SHADUF**
Shaduf model, cardboard, string, making 2788:36-37

**EGYPT, ANCIENT—SHOPPING**
Price of common goods in debens chart 2363:27

**EGYPT, ANCIENT—SOLDIERS**
Golden fly badge, reward for soldiers, clay, cardboard, paints, making 2788:56-57

**EGYPT, ANCIENT—TILES**
Lotus tile, clay, paints, making 2788:20-21

**EGYPT, ANCIENT—TOMBS**
Tomb poem 2869:103

**EGYPT, ANCIENT—TOYS**
Lion that roars toy, clay, balsa wood, paints, making 2788:54-55

**EGYPT, ANCIENT—WEAPONS**
Serpent-headed throwing stick, wooden spoon, paints, making 2746:54-55

**EGYPTIAN-AMERICANS—COOKERY**
Eggplant and zucchini salad, recipe 2879:99
Falafel, fried bean cakes, recipe 2879:98

**EIGHTIES—COOKERY**
Fettuccine with porcini mushrooms and parmesan cheese, recipe 2359:159-160
Lemon blueberry muffins, recipe 2359:157-158
Roasted veggie pita rounds, recipe 2359:161-162

**EISENHOWER, DWIGHT DAVID (PRESIDENT)**
Accordion book, making 2263:108
Create a campaign paperweight, making 2263:108
Design a campaign button, making 2263:108
Holidays in the White House, making 2263:108
Purple mountains majesty, making 2263:107
Vegetable soup for two, recipe 2263:107
What's your favorite color, making 2263:107

**EL GRECO**
Drawing tall figures, how to do 2529:26

**EL SALVADOR—COAT OF ARMS**
El Salvadorian coat of arms, paper, markers, pattern, making 2671:25

**EL SALVADOR—COOKERY**

Arroz con leche, rice pudding, recipe    2945:52
Pickled cabbage, recipe    2945:53
Pupusas, cornmeal cake and chopped meat dish, recipe    2945:52
Quesadilla, cake dessert, recipe    2945:52-53
Red kidney bean soup, recipe    2945:53

**EL SALVADOR—FESTIVALS—MASKS**

Carnaval Festival; donkey mask, papier-mâché, making    2407:95

**EL SALVADOR—FLAGS**

El Salvadorian flag, paper, markers, pattern, making    2671:25

**EL SALVADOR—GAMES**

El Siete Loco (crazy seven), how to play    2767:68-69
El Venconmigo (come with me), how to play    2767:66-67
La Gallina Ciega (the blind hen), how to play    2767:70

**ELECTION DAY**

Activities, crafts, patterns    2760:59-76

**ELECTION DAY—DECORATIONS**

Wreath; pinwheel wreath, paper plate, red, white and blue paper, making    2735:30-31

**ELVES**

Elves and fairies clay pins, colored clay, pin backs, making    2883:98-104

**ENGLAND—16TH CENTURY**

Julius Caesar; produce a scene from *Julius Caesar*, how to do    2251:102-105

**ENGLAND—16TH CENTURY—BIRD FEEDERS**

Build a bird feeder or nesting shelf, plastic jug, wire, making    2251:27
Feed the birds, suet recipe and hummingbird nectar recipe    2251:28

**ENGLAND—16TH CENTURY—COAT OF ARMS**

Design a Coat of Arms, poster board, making    2251:76-78

**ENGLAND—16TH CENTURY—COOKERY**

Apple moye, sweet apple dish, recipe    2251:34

**ENGLAND—16TH CENTURY—COSTUMES**

Slashed-shirt costume, T-shirt, colored tights, making    2251:95-96

**ENGLAND—16TH CENTURY—FAMILY TREE**

Your own family tree, how to do    2251:21

**ENGLAND—16TH CENTURY—GAMES**

Juggling; learn how to juggle    2251:17-19
Nine Men's Morris, how to make and play    2251:49-50
Teetotum game, how to make and play    2251:48-49

**ENGLAND—16TH CENTURY—HANDICRAFTS**

Folio; bind your own folio, paper, yarn, ribbons, making    2251:122-123
Gloves; decorate a pair of gloves, leather gloves, lace, making    2251:12-13
Pomander ball, orange, cloves, spices, ribbons, making    2251:8-9

**ENGLAND—16TH CENTURY—HORNBOOK**

Hornbook, cardboard, paper, clear plastic, making    2251:31-32

**ENGLAND—16TH CENTURY—PENS**

Quill pen, feather, ink, making    2251:67-68

**ENGLAND—16TH CENTURY—PLAYS**

Goblet for a prop, foil, plastic cup, making    2251:87-89
Sound effects, how to make    2251:84

**ENGLAND—16TH CENTURY—SONGS**

Compose a sonnet, how to do    2251:69-70

**ENGLAND—16TH CENTURY—SWORD FIGHT**

Stage a sword fight, how to do    2251:99-100

**ENGLAND—16TH CENTURY—WEAPONS**

Sword, cardboard tube, crepe paper, making    2251:97-98

**ENGLAND—CHRISTMAS—COOKERY**

Wassail punch, recipe    2477:69

**ENGLAND—CHRISTMAS—DECORATIONS**

Christmas cracker, paper roll, crepe paper, ribbons, making    2660:25
Christmas fairy, felt, lace, yarn, craft netting, making    2740:24-27
Crown, paper, making    2403:22-23

**ENGLAND—CHRISTMAS—GREETING CARDS**

Christmas cards, paper, making    2394:22

**ENGLAND—COOKERY**

Browned roast potatoes, recipe    2477:39
Connecticut Kedgeree rice and lentil dish, recipe    2879:14
Cream tea, scones and tea recipes    2490:112
Custard Johnny cake, recipe    2879:13-14
Derbyshire oatcakes, recipe    2477:34

English menu    2477:28-29
Fried bread, recipe    2477:32
Hasty pudding, recipe    2660:15
Mushrooms on toast recipe    2477:33
Poached fish, recipe    2477:58
Rhode Island Johnny cake, recipe    2879:13
Roast beef, recipe    2477:38
Sally Lunn cake, recipe    2879:14
Scones, recipe    2477:48
Scones, recipe    2861:30-31
Shepherd's pie, recipe    2477:54
Shortbread, recipe    2477:47
Summer pudding, recipe    2477:42
Tea, recipe    2477:46
Vegetable Cornish pasties, recipe    2838:34-35
Vegetarian Shepherd's pie, recipe    2477:56-57
Victorian sandwich, recipe    2477:50-51
Yorkshire pudding, recipe    2477:42
Yorkshire pudding, recipe    2879:15

## ENGLAND—DOLLS

English peddlar doll, doll, felt, making
2934:137-139

## ENGLAND—EASTER—COOKERY

Easter biscuits, recipe    2477:65

## ENGLAND—FESTIVALS—COOKERY

Guy Fawkes Night; gingerbread, recipe
2477:68
Harvest Festival; hearty autumn hot pot, recipe
2477:66-67

## ENGLAND—FESTIVALS—DECORATIONS

Guy Fawkes Day; make your own Guy, old
clothes, pillow case, straw, newspapers,
making    2983:23

## ENGLAND—FESTIVALS—HANDICRAFTS

Guy Fawkes Day; guy, old clothes, newspaper,
string, making    2861:28-29
Harvest Festival; corn dollies, cornhusks, cotton
balls, string, making    2982:27
May Day; basket of flowers, making    2861:27

## ENGLAND—FOLKLORE

*Gingerbread Boy* running, ribbon spool, pipe
cleaner, making    2729:38-39
*Henny Penny;* hand wings Henny Penny, feathers, paper, making    2729:34-35
*Three Bears* family, poster board, making
2729:28-29
*Three Pigs,* folktales, puppets, patterns, songs,
food    2591:53-58

## ENGLAND—FOLKLORE—HANDICRAFTS

Pixie pen tops, clay, poster paints, making
2781:16-17

## ENGLAND—FOLKLORE—PUPPETS

*Three Little Pigs*; huff-and-puff wolf puppet, oatmeal box, sock, fiberfill, making
2729:16-17

## ENGLAND—GAMES

ABC dribble game, how to play    2525:169
Acka backa boo game, how to play    2385:14
Albert Adams ate an alligator, how to play
2767:148
Andy Mandy, sugar candy game, how to play
2385:37
Ball in the basket game, how to play    2525:93
Beat the ball game, how to play    2525:44
Beats me game, how to play    2525:114
Beetle game, how to make and play
2882:42-43
Bluebells, cockle shells game, how to play
2385:37
Bomb in the box game, how to play    2525:179
Bounce eye marble game, how to play    2882:18
Butterflies game, how to play    2525:87
Catch a caterpillar game, how to play    2525:95
Cold winds game, how to play    2525:137
Cribbage game, how to play    2926:46-49
Dusty bluebells game, how to play    2385:41
Gold game, how to play    2525:110
Higher and higher game, how to play    2385:37
Hopscotch, how to play    2767:145-146
Hot potato game, how to play    2385:26
How many fingers? how to play    2767:148
Hum a dum dum game, how to play    2385:13
Hundreds marble game, how to play    2882:19
I looked high game, how to play    2385:13
Jack, Jack shine your light game, how to play
2385:30
Jump hoop game, how to play    2525:158
Marble pyramid game, how to play    2882:18
Monday, Tuesday, how to play    2767:146-147
My father went to sea game, how to play
2385:34
Nine Men's Morris, how to play    2926:10-11
North, east, south, west game, how to play
2525:73
Olika bolika game, how to play    2385:14
One, two three a-leerie ball game, how to play
2385:28
One, two, three, whoops game, how to play
2385:32
Picking plums marble game, how to play
2882:19
Pig in the middle ball game, how to play
2385:28
Pina-one game, how to play    2385:37

Prisoner's base game, how to play  2525:21

Queenie I.O. game, how to play  2525:59

Queenie, Queenie ball game, how to play
2385:26

Rock, scissor, paper game, how to play  2525:70

Sardines game, how to play  2385:32

Snip, snap, snorem, how to play  2660:19

Stroke the baby game, how to play  2385:13

Stuck in the mud game, how to play  2525:12

Tag bag game, how to play  2525:126

Three Men's Morris, how to play
2767:147-148

Tickum-tackum game, how to play  2385:17

Tiddly winks game, how to make and play
2372:22

Un, deux, trois, quatre game, how to play
2385:24

Wall catch game, how to play  2525:165

With my hands game, how to play  2385:18

ENGLAND—HANDICRAFTS

Corn figures and a scarecrow, straw, raffia,
making  2331:28-29

Portrait case, folded paper, making  2407:38

Treasure box for holding tea, cardboard carton,
quilling pen, glass nuggets, beads, stickers,
making  2784:26-27

Window pictures, tissue paper, making
2407:20

ENGLAND—JEWELRY

Paper beads, paper, paste, making  2407:68

ENGLAND—KINGS

Royal crown model, foil, cardboard, making
2686:96-97

ENGLAND—LANGUAGE

British names for common things  2372:23

ENGLAND—LENT—COOKERY

Carlings, dried pea dish, recipe  2477:62

ENGLAND—PASSOVER—COOKERY

Charoses, recipe  2737:78

ENGLAND—TEA PARTIES—COOKERY

English breakfast teas, recipe  2643:14

How to plan and set the table  2643:12-13

Scones, recipe  2643:14

ENGLAND—TEA PARTIES—HANDICRAFTS

Painting umbrellas, how to do  2643:15

ENGLAND—YORKSHIRE—COOKERY

Apple crumble, recipe  2342:59-60

Clotted cream, recipe  2342:49

Cottage loaf, recipe  2342:58

Crumpets, recipe  2342:62-63

Currant buns, recipe  2342:74-75

Doughcakes, recipe  2342:56-57

Homemade bread, recipe  2342:43-45

Muffins, recipe  2342:50-51

Oatcakes, recipe  2342:54-55

Oatcakes, recipe  2342:72-73

Orange marmalade, recipe  2342:40-41

Porridge, recipe  2342:37-38

Raspberry jam, recipe  2342:47-48

Roasted eggs, recipe  2342:68-69

Roasted potatoes, recipe  2342:70-71

Robin cake, recipe  2342:64-65

Sizzling ham, recipe  2342:52

Snow-white eggs, recipe  2342:46

Treachle syrup, recipe  2342:39

ENGLISH CANADIAN–AMERICANS—
COOKERY

Lemon cookies, recipe  2879:101

Nanaimo bars (chocolate squares), recipe
2879:100-101

EPIPHANY—DECORATIONS

Dove mobile, pattern, making  2798:27-28

Remember your baptism banner, making
2798:25-26

Star of wonder tree ornament, making  2798:24

Star over Bethlehem silhouette picture, making
2798:22

We have Seen his star tree topper, making
2798:23

ERITREAN-AMERICANS—COOKERY

Atakelte (vegetable dish), recipe  2879:105

Azifa (lentil salad), recipe  2879:105-106

Injera (pancakes), recipe  2879:104-105

ESCHER, M. C.

Tessellation design, how to do  2529:65

ESKIMOS

Activities, animals, homes, inventions, boats,
masks, games, patterns  2421:1-14

Activities, patterns  2755:103-112

ESKIMOS—CARVING

Inuit carving, soap, felt, making  2456:48-49

Miniature Inuit carvings, soap, patterns, making
2351:23-25

ESKIMOS—COOKERY

Aleut ices, recipe  2351:41

Cranberries, recipe  2879:102

Salmon chowder, recipe  2879:102

White fish soup, recipe  2879:102

ESKIMOS—COSTUMES

Inuit, Eskimo boy and girl, patterns
2755:110-111

56

**ESKIMOS—FOLKLORE**

*How Fire and Water Came to the Far North,* story and activities  2423:69-78

**ESKIMOS—FOLKLORE—COOKERY**

Akutaq, fish and berry dish, recipe  2979:last page

**ESKIMOS—GAMES**

Canadian Inuit game, Alaqaq, cup, string, making  2351:40

Holes and pin game, how to make and play  2421:14

Inupaq yo-yo, fur or fabric, rope, thread spool, wood, shell, pattern, making  2440:71-74

Tug-of-war game, how to make and play  2882:26-27

**ESKIMOS—HANDICRAFTS**

Scrimshaw medallions, plaster of Paris, making  2755:106

Snow glasses, poster board, paints, making  2755:106

Totem pole, pattern, making  2755:112

**ESKIMOS—IGLOOS**

Model igloo, clay, card stock, paint, making  2456:16-17

**ESKIMOS—JEWELRY**

Sealskin bracelet, felt, chamois cloth, yarn, patterns, making  2351:25

**ESKIMOS—KAYAKS**

Inuit kayak, clay, paints, string, patterns, making  2351:38-39

**ESKIMOS—MASKS**

Eskimo mask, pattern, making  2421:13

Finger mask, paper, pattern, making  2761:76

Inuit mask, plaster cloth, patterns, paint, making  2934:140-142

**ESKIMOS—PAINTINGS**

Inuit stone paintings, stones, markers, patterns, making  2351:29-31

**ESKIMOS—RECORD STICKS**

Inuit record stick, cardboard, wood, markers, making  2351:26

**ESKIMOS—SNOW SCENE**

Igloo snow scene, clay, paints, patterns, making  2351:36-37

**ESKIMOS—WRITINGS**

Native American writings, how to copy and display  2351:42-45

**ESKIMOS.** *See also* **INUIT INDIANS**

**ESTONIA—GAMES**

Chick chickabiddy game, how to play  2525:29

**ESTONIAN-AMERICANS—COOKERY**

Pancakes, recipe  2879:104

Rosolje (beef and potato salad), recipe  2879:103

**ETHIOPIA—CHRISTMAS—DECORATIONS**

Timkat umbrella, gold paper, craft sticks, making  2403:14-15

**ETHIOPIA—COOKERY**

Black-eyed bean cakes, recipe  2838:14-15

Dabo kolo bread dish, recipe  2561:51

Dabo kolo, fried snacks or treats, recipe  2907:21

Dabo kolo (spicy cookie), recipe  2273:30-31

Lentil salad, recipe  2627:68

Luku, chicken dish, recipe  2627:52

Meat on a stick, recipe  2627:34

**ETHIOPIA—FESTIVALS**

Buhe Children's Christian Holiday, how to celebrate  2273:26-27

**ETHIOPIA—FESTIVALS—COOKERY**

Maskal Festival; flat bread, recipe  2627:64

**ETHIOPIA—FOLKLORE**

*Lion's Whiskers,* folktales, puppets, patterns, songs, food  2591:34-35

**ETHIOPIA—GAMES**

Keliblibosh jacks game, how to play  2384:22

Mancha (hopscotch) game, how to play  2907:15

Spear the hoop, how to play  2767:70-71

**ETHIOPIA—JEWELRY**

Lucky charm necklace, clay, paints, twine, making  2273:28-29

Necklace; lucky charm necklace, clay, pony beads, cord, making  2907:25

**ETHIOPIA—LANGUAGE**

Amharic language, learn to speak a few words  2561:48

Amharic words  2384:23

**ETHIOPIA—NEW YEAR—DECORATIONS**

Enqutatash, rose, red tissue paper, green pipe cleaners, making  2402:20-21

**ETHIOPIA—PASSOVER—HANDICRAFTS**

Ethiopian clay figures, making  2737:167

**ETHIOPIA—TEMPLES**

Sandstone column, sand, cornstarch, making  2745:3-4

**ETHIOPIAN-AMERICANS—COOKERY**
Atakelte (vegetable dish), recipe    2879:105
Azifa (lentil salad), recipe    2879:105-106
Injera (pancakes), recipe    2879:104-105

**ETS, MARIE HALL**
*Nine Days to Christmas*, literature, activities, art,
curriculum    2436:105-114

**EUROPE—ARCHITECTURE**
Gothic mirror, papier-mâché, paints, making
2259:20-21

**EUROPE—FESTIVALS**
Martinmas; how to celebrate    2328:131-132

**EUROPE—HANDICRAFTS**
Peek-in sugar eggs, plastic egg, sugar, making
2440:82-85

**EUROPE—PASSOVER—COOKERY**
Charoses, recipe    2737:77

# F

## FACE PAINT

Butterfly face painting, how to do  2952:22
Cat face painting, how to do  2952:14-15
Dalmatian dog face painting, how to do
2952:16-17
Face paint, recipe  2684:130
Face painting, how to do  2511:36
Language arts, poetry, hobby craft activities
2511:35-38
Lion face painting, how to do  2952:20-21
Rabbit face painting, how to do  2952:18-19

## FAIRIES

Elves and fairies clay pins, colored clay, pin
backs, making  2883:98-104

## FAIRIES—BASKETS

Fairy basket, basket, branch, flowers, feathered
birds, making  2309:26-29

## FAIRIES—COSTUMES

Fairy costume, wand, skirt, wings, shoes, rose,
halo, headband, choker, making
2309:38-50

## FAIRIES—DOLLS

Fairy dolls, floral wire, flowers, beads, paints,
making  2309:16-19

## FAIRIES—FACE PAINT

Fairy face painting, how to do  2952:36-37

## FAIRIES—HANDICRAFTS

Bookmarks, plastic sheet, ribbons, flowers, patterns, making  2309:80-81
Flower necklace, beads, cord, making
2309:76-78
Flower sachets, fabric, cord, flowers, making
2309:79
Flying fairies, kitchen scourer, wool, beads,
golden wire, dried moss, fabric, flowers,
making  2781:28-29
Note cards, tissue paper, stickers, making
2309:82-85
Petal purse, fabric, flowers, ribbons, making
2309:74-75

## FAIRIES—PARTIES

Fairy party, invitations, lanterns, bracelets, table-
ware, making  2309:55-69

## FAIRIES—PLAYGROUND

Fairy playground, floral foam disks, fabric, dowels, floral wire, making  2309:20-25

## FAIRY TALES

Fairy card, cardboard, fabric, beads, sequins,
making  2257:18-19

## FALL

Teaching themes, activities, games, crafts, patterns, recipes  2410:7-48

## FALL—DECORATIONS

Harvest basket, fabrics, basket, making
2748:43-44
Tablecloth and napkins, fabric, paints, making
2748:45-47

## FALL—FICTION

*Biggest Pumpkin Ever* by Steven Kroll, activities, art, games, songs, crafts, patterns  2812:3-10

## FAMILY TREE

Family crest, clay, paints, making  2578:18-19
Family tree batik banner, making  2700:70-72
Family tree pedigree chart, how to do
2578:12-16
Family tree, how to make  2977:27

## FANG (AFRICAN PEOPLES)—STATUES

Bronze Bakot statue, railroad board, aluminum
baking sheet, patterns, making  2620:40-41

## FANTE (AFRICAN PEOPLES)—FLAGS

Asafo warrior people of Fante flags, fabric, felt,
patterns, making  2620:26-27

## FARM

Activities, food, songs, poetry, literature
2298:5-80

## FARM—COOKERY

Butter, recipe  2298:70
Haystacks, peanuts, chow mein noodles, butter-
scotch pieces, recipe  2298:70
Pudding dirt, recipe  2298:70

## FARM—FICTION

*Big Red Barn* by Margaret Wise Brown, activities
2298:14-15
*Cloudy with a Chance of Meatballs* by Judi
Barrett, activities  2298:26-27

*Day Jimmy's Boa Ate the Wash* by Trinka Noble,
  activities   2298:16-17
*Eating the Alphabet* by Lois Ehlert, activities
  2298:24-25
*Little Red Hen* by Paul Galdone, activities
  2298:30-31
*Popcorn Book* by Tomie dePaola, activities
  2298:22-23
*Rosie's Walk* by Pat Hutchins, activities
  2298:18-19
*Three Little Pigs* by James Marshall, activities
  2298:32-33
*Town Mouse and the Country Mouse* by Lorinda
  Cauley, activities   2298:28-29

**FARM—GAMES**

Back to the barn game, patterns, how to make
  and play   2298:74-75
Barnyard animal concentration game, patterns,
  how to make and play   2298:76-78
Barnyard bingo game, patterns, how to make and
  play   2298:71-73

**FARM—HANDICRAFTS**

Farm sewing cards, shoelaces, patterns, making
  2298:68-69
Scarecrows for class crops, oak tag, craft sticks,
  making   2298:64

**FARM—NURSERY RHYMES**

Farm nursery rhymes   2298:37

**FARM—POETRY**

Farm poems and activities   2298:35

**FARM—PUPPETS**

Farm animal stick puppet, paper, paints, making
  2298:66

**FARM—SONGS**

Farm songs   2298:63

**FARMER, FANNIE MERRITT—COOKERY**

Griddle cakes, recipe   2483: last

**FATHER'S DAY**

Activities, patterns   2757:59-68
Activities, patterns, crafts   2404:all
Daddy and me; activities, finger plays, songs,
  rhymes, crafts, patterns   2828:88-89
History of Father's Day   2877:56

**FATHER'S DAY—COOKERY**

Belgian waffles and blueberry pancakes, recipe
  2877:58
Chocolate chip cookies, recipe   2877:59
Papa's lemonade, recipe   2877:59

**FATHER'S DAY—DECORATIONS**

Father's Day pencil holder, paper, crayons, soup
  can, patterns, making   2811:47-48
Planter, foam cups, soil, seeds, making
  2923:20-21
We will serve the Lord Father's Day decoration,
  making   2798:60

**FATHER'S DAY—FICTION**

*A Perfect Father's Day* by Eve Bunting, activities, crafts, patterns, games, masks, puppets,
  making   2329:119-121
*A Perfect Father's Day* by Eve Bunting, literature unit   2404:unp
Activities, finger plays, songs, rhymes, crafts,
  patterns   2829:48-49

**FEBRUARY THEMES**

Thematic units, lessons, activities, art, poetry,
  crafts, patterns, recipes   2320:158-184

**FIBERS**

Natural fibers and their use, making   2331:26-27

**FIBONACCI NUMBERS**

Fibonacci numbers and their importance in
  nature   2571:14-15
Fibonacci numbers pattern stamped on T-shirt,
  making   2571:16-17

**FIFTIES—COOKERY**

Coco-nutty pecan frosting, recipe   2359:139
German chocolate mini-cakes, recipe
  2359:137-138
Make-your-own TV dinners, recipe
  2359:135-136
Vegetable platter with sour cream and onion dip,
  recipe   2359:133-134

**FILIPINO-AMERICANS—COOKERY**

Adobo monok (chicken dish), recipe   2879:107
Bibinka royale (coconut sweet dish), recipe
  2879:108
Pork adobo, recipe   2879:107-108

**FILLMORE, MILLARD (PRESIDENT)**

Keep your memories in letters, making
  2263:49
Organize a book fair, patterns, making   2263:49

**FINGER PAINTS**

Basic finger paint, recipe   2918:13
Finger paint, recipe   2684:131

**FINLAND—BIRTHDAY CUSTOMS**

Finland birthday customs   2547:10-11

**FINLAND—CHRISTMAS—COOKERY**

Cinnamon buns, recipe   2337:76
Donuts, recipe   2337:77
Ginger cookies, recipe   2337:76
Glogg drink, recipe   2337:75
Liver casserole, recipe   2337:74
Pasty, recipe   2337:73
Potato casserole, recipe   2337:74
Salted salmon, recipe   2337:73
Strawberry snow dessert, recipe   2337:77
Tarts, recipe   2337:75

**FINLAND—CHRISTMAS—DECORATIONS**

Himmeli straw decoration, straws, thread, making
   2337:68-69
Ice lantern, bowl, plastic container, stones,
   candle, making   2337:70-71
St. Lucia's crown, poster board, markers, making
   2337:66-67
Star boy hat, poster board, glitter, string, making
   2337:65
Straw ornaments, straw, red thread, making
   2740:28-29

**FINLAND—GAMES**

Steak, how to play   2767:71

**FINNISH-AMERICANS—COOKERY**

Air pudding (cranberry dish), recipe
   2879:108-109
Moijakka (beef stew), recipe   2879:109-110
Pulla (coffee bread), recipe   2879:110-111

**FIRST NATIONS—DREAMCATCHERS**

Dreamcatcher, embroidery hoop, yarn, beads,
   feathers, paints, making   2261:28-29

**FIRST NATIONS—GAMES**

Snow snake game, how to make snow snake
   from tree branch   2261:27

**FISHING**

Language arts, poetry, hobby craft activities
   2511:39-41

**FLACK, MARJORIE—FICTION—PUPPETS**

*Ask Mister Bear* bear hug puppet, paper cups,
   yarn, making   2729:12-13

**FLAG DAY**

Activities, patterns   2757:49-58
Betsy Ross, colored picture, pattern   2813:44
Coat-of-Arms of the United States, pattern
   2813:45-47
Flag Day puzzle   2813:43
History of Flag Day, June 14   2813:42

**FLAG DAY—DECORATIONS**

Flag mosaic, red paper, ribbon, making
   2735:10-11

**FLAG DAY—GAMES**

Celebrating Independence, game   2813:48

**FLORIDA—COOKERY**

Citrus smoothie, recipe   2776:53
Sunshine juice, recipe   2534:23

**FOLKLORE—AMULETS**

Magic amulet, white plastic bottle, round candle
   base, purple and gold tinsel, purple foil,
   candy wrappers, silver paint, making
   2781:6-7

**FOLKLORE—HANDICRAFTS**

Pot of gold, cardboard, round yogurt container,
   felt, gold paper, paints, pattern, making
   2781:18-19

**FORD, GERALD (PRESIDENT)**

Bells across America, a Bicentennial mobile,
   making   2263:119
Garland of bells, making   2263:119
Parade of tall ships poster, making   2263:120

**FORTS**

Fort Laramie model, popsicle sticks, dowels,
   making   2497:78-79

**FOURTH OF JULY**

Activities, crafts, puppets, patterns   2756:55-66
Activities, finger plays, songs, rhymes, crafts,
   patterns   2828:96-97
Story times, activities, Uncle Sam tubey pattern,
   craft instructions   2636:45-47

**FOURTH OF JULY—COOKERY**

All-American fruit salad, recipe   2877:65
American flag cake, recipe and activities
   2576:165-168
Barbecue sauce, recipe   2984:33
Blueberry cake, recipe   2888:154-155
Chocolate chip blondies, recipe   2888:158
Firecracker potato salad, recipe   2877:62
Ice cream sundae, red, white and blue, recipe
   2541:43
Lemon flag bars, recipe   2888:159-160
Lemon ice box dessert, recipe   2888:151
Maine blueberry sauce, recipe   2888:162
Patriotic cheesecake, recipe   2877:64
Patriotic pancakes, oatmeal blueberry pancakes,
   recipe   2684:10
Patriotic parfait, recipe and activities
   2576:169-172

Pound cake with three berries, recipe
2888:152-153
Stars and stripes fusilli, recipe 2877:63
Strawberry shortcake, recipe 2888:156-157
Sweet sparkler cookies, recipe and activities
2576:161-164

**FOURTH OF JULY—DECORATIONS**

Antennae tassel, patriotic colors, Styrofoam ball,
map pins, making 2735:12-13
Betsy Ross's colonial hat, tissue paper, ribbon,
making 2735:8-9
Fire works picture, making 2923:22-23
Firecracker lapel pin, marker cap, sparkle stems,
making 2735:5
Fireworks trinket box, plastic cap, sparkle stems,
Styrofoam ball, making 2735:20-21
Flag mosaic, red paper, ribbon, making
2735:10-11
God Bless our native land Fourth of July mobile,
making 2798:61
Heart flag necklace, plastic plates, ribbons,
making 2735:42-43
Independence Day word poster, patterns,
making 2262:94-96
Name pin; red, white and blue name pin, ruler,
string, macaroni letters, making
2735:46-47
Patriotic flying disc, red plates, sequins, glitter,
making 2735:24-25
Patriotic headband, foil, cardboard, pony beads,
bells, making 2735:26-27
Ribbon flag magnet, cardboard, magnet, ribbons,
making 2735:6-7
Sparkler, ribbon, cardboard tube, glitter, making
2541:42
Uncle Sam; newspaper Uncle Sam, paints, ribbons, making 2735:38-40

**FOURTH OF JULY—FICTION**

*Fourth of July Bears* by Kathryn Lasky, activities, crafts, patterns, games, masks, puppets,
making 2329:122-125

**FOURTH OF JULY—MASKS**

Uncle Sam mask, paper plates, fiberfill, colored
paper, making 2733:18-19

**FOURTH OF JULY—PUPPETS**

Firecracker finger puppets, coin wrappers, bubble wrap, pom-pom, wiggle eyes, making
2733:20-21
Patriotic puppets, plastic lids, pipe cleaners,
pom-poms, making 2735:18-19
Popping firecracker puppet, red paper, pom-pom,
bubble wrap, making 2735:22-23

**FOURTH OF JULY—TOYS**

Popper, folded paper, making 2407:46

**FOX INDIANS—JEWELRY**

Bear claw necklace, clay, beads, cord, paints,
making 2840:10-11

**FRANCE—BUILDINGS**

Eiffel Tower model, paper, markers, making
2686:82-85

**FRANCE—CHRISTMAS—COOKERY**

Buche de Noel or Yule log cake, recipe
2610:30-31
Yule log miniatures, recipe 2403:16-17
Yule log, recipe 2481:64-65
Yule log, recipe 2843:66-67

**FRANCE—COOKERY**

Apple tart, recipe 2831:34-35
Asparagus with aioli, recipe 2843:62
Bacon and egg custard tart, recipe 2573:40-41
Basic crepe batter, recipe 2843:37
Beef stew with tomatoes and olives, recipe
2573:55-57
Cheese soufflé, recipe 2573:36-39
Cherry cake, recipe 2573:66
Chicken stock, recipe 2573:20-21
Chicken with apples and cream, recipe
2573:50-51
Chocolate mousse, recipe 2843:56
Chocolate pastry, recipe 2843:42
Chocolate sauce, recipe 2573:70
Chocolate truffles, recipe 2831:42-43
Clafoutis, cherry tarts, recipe 2433:28-29
Combination salad, recipe 2573:28-29
Cream puffs with ice cream and chocolate sauce,
recipe 2573:68-69
CrPme brulee (dessert), recipe 2831:36-37
CrPme brulee, vanilla custard, recipe
2433:36-37
Crepe au fromage, cheese crepes, recipe
2433:10-11
Crepe cones, recipe 2717:43
Crepe purses, recipe 2717:44
Crepe rolls, recipe 2717:44
Crepes with strawberries, recipe 2271:62-63
Crepes with strawberries, recipe 2843:52
Crepes, gift wrapped, recipe 2717:41-42
Crepes, history of crepes 2717:46-47
Crepes, recipe 2864:114-115
Crepes, recipe 2958:unp
Croque monsieur (grilled cheese sandwich),
recipe 2831:24-25
Croque monsieur, recipe 2843:43

Croque-monsieur, toasted cheese and ham sand-
wich, recipe   2433:8-9
Dessert crepe batter, recipe   2843:51
Fish goujons with aioli, recipe   2831:16-17
French bread, recipe   2573:30-31
French menu   2843:26-27
French onion soup, recipe   2573:23-25
Glazed carrots, recipe   2573:63
Glazed carrots, recipe   2843:50
Gratin dauphinois (potato and cheese dish),
recipe   2831:28-29
Gratin de macaroni, baked macaroni, recipe
2433:12-13
Green salad, recipe   2843:36
Hachis parmentier, minced meat and potato pie,
recipe   2433:24-25
Ham and broccoli crepes with mornay sauce,
recipe   2843:38-39
Ham and cheese crunches, recipe   2573:33
Leg of lamb with white beans, recipe
2843:60-61
Mousse au chocolat, chocolate mousse, recipe
2433:32-33
Mushroom omelette, recipe   2831:30-31
Nicoise salad, recipe   2831:22-23
Nicoise salad, recipe   2843:34
Omelette aux tomates, tomato omelette, recipe
2433:14-15
Onion soup, recipe   2831:10-11
Pain au chocolat (bread and chocolate), recipe
2700:67
Pate de fruit, recipe   2527:51
Pears Helen, recipe   2806:25
Pears Helen, recipe   2843:55
Peas French style, recipe   2843:50
Pissaladiere (bread dough with onion top),
recipe   2831:20-21
Pork chops Normandy style, recipe   2843:48
Potato and leek soup, recipe   2271:41
Potato and leek soup, recipe   2573:26-27
Potato and leek soup, recipe   2843:30
Potato cake, recipe   2843:49
Poulet en brochettes, chicken skewers, recipe
2433:20-21
Profiteroles (cream puffs), recipe   2831:38-39
Profiteroles, chocolate cream puffs, recipe
2433:34-35
Quiche Lorraine, quiche with bacon, recipe
2433:16-17
Quiche Lorraine, recipe   2831:18-19
Quiche Lorraine, recipe   2843:33
Ratatouille (vegetable dish), recipe   2831:32-33
Roast chicken, recipe   2573:48-49

Roast pork with dried plums, rec-
ipe   2573:52-53
Salade nicose, tuna, egg and tomato salad, recipe
2433:18-19
Sauteed chicken, recipe   2843:46
Scalloped potatoes, recipe   2573:62
Scallops in cream sauce, recipe   2573:44-45
Sole meuniere, butter, lemon sole, recipe
2433:26-27
Spinach quiche, recipe   2924:20-21
Steak with herb butter, recipe   2831:26-27
Strawberry tartlets, recipe   2843:65
Tarte aux fraises, strawberry tarts, recipe
2433:30-31
Tarte tatin, recipe   2489:107
Tomato salad and green salad, recipe
2831:14-15
Tuiles (cookies), recipe   2831:40-41
Turbot with fresh vegetables, recipe
2573:46-47
Vegetable casserole, recipe   2573:59-61
Vichyssoise (potato and leek soup), recipe
2831:12-13
Whipped cream, recipe   2573:71

**FRANCE—COOKERY—FRILLS**
Paper frills to decorate food, making   2407:56

**FRANCE—EASTER—COOKERY**
Strawberry tartlets, recipe   2481:69

**FRANCE—FESTIVALS—COOKERY**
Bastille Day; cheese and fruit plate, recipe
2962:27
Bastille Day; crepes, recipe   2888:161
Bastille Day; French silk pie, recipe   2962:31
Bastille Day; onion tarte, recipe   2962:29
Bastille Day; salade nicoise, recipe   2962:30
Bastille Day; smoked salmon mousse, recipe
2962:28
Feast of the Kings; la fete des rois cake, recipe
2433:22-23
King's cake, recipe   2843:68
Twelfth Night cake, recipe   2738:57

**FRANCE—FESTIVALS—HANDICRAFTS**
April Fools' Day or April Fish Day; fish mobile,
cardboard, string, paints, making
2610:28-29

**FRANCE—FICTION**
*Glorious Flight: Across the Channel with Louis
Bleriot* by Alice Provensen, literature, activities, art, curriculum   2436:29-43
*Linnea in Monet's Garden* by Christina Bjork,
activities, projects, patterns, art,
crafts   2822:5-11

*Madeline* by Ludwig Bemelmans, activities, crafts, patterns, games, masks, puppets, making 2329:126-131

**FRANCE—FOLKLORE**

Activities, finger plays, songs, rhymes, crafts, patterns 2829:52-53

**FRANCE—GAMES**

Ball thrower game, how to play 2525:161
Escargot hopscotch, how to play 2492:20-22
Fly game, how to play 2525:43
Flying goalie game, how to play 2525:90
French draw dominoes game, how to play 2548:14
Le Grelots (bell tag), how to play 2767:71-72
Mic Mac relay game, how to play 2525:24
Petanque game, how to play 2355:22
Pipopipette, how to play 2767:45
Prince of Paris, how to play 2767:72-73
Un, deux, trois, quatre game, how to play 2385:24
Uno, due, tre, stella game, how to play 2385:24
Wolf, wolf, where are you game, how to play 2385:10

**FRANCE—LANGUAGE**

Everyday phrases in French 2355:23
French words for family members 2806:23
Learn to speak French 2527:48
Phrases, numbers and days of the week in French 2489:110

**FRANCE—SILHOUETTES**

Paper silhouettes, making 2407:8

**FRANCE—TOYS**

Bilboquet, cup, ball and string toy, making 2310:106-108

**FRENCH-AMERICANS—COOKERY**

Hugenot torte, recipe 2879:112
Pecan pralines, recipe 2879:113
Shrimp B la creolo, recipe 2879:112-113

**FRENCH AMERICANS— FESTIVALS—COOKERY**

Mardi Gras; King cake, recipe 2976:25

**FRENCH-AMERICANS—HERBS**

Grow fresh herbs, how to do 2976:11

**FRENCH CANADIAN-AMERICANS— COOKERY**

Pork pie, recipe 2879:115
Ragout (meatballs in gravy), recipe 2879:115
Soup aux pois (yellow pea soup), recipe 2879:114

**FROG PRINCE**

*Frog Prince* magnet, felt, sequins, magnet, making 2729:36-37

**FRONTIER AND PIONEER LIFE—CANALS**

Build a canal lock, milk cartons, tape, making 2497:28-29

**FRONTIER AND PIONEER LIFE— CHRISTMAS—DECORATIONS**

Straw star, straw, red thread, making 2523:105-106

**FRONTIER AND PIONEER LIFE—CLOTHING**

Pioneer cap, fabric, ribbon, making 2523:47-48

**FRONTIER AND PIONEER LIFE—COOKERY**

African American cooked greens, recipe 2518:18
African American fried green tomatoes, recipe 2518:19
African American sweet potato pie, recipe 2518:21
Asian fish soup, recipe 2518:25
Bacon cornbread, recipe 2488:15
Blueberry jam, recipe 2518:12
Cowboy Spanish omelet, recipe 2518:24
Dried apple pie, recipe 2488:26-27
English beef stew, recipe 2518:26
English flapjacks, recipe 2518:14
English scotch broth, recipe 2518:19
English shepherd's pie, recipe 2518:27
English Welsh rarebit fajita, recipe 2518:31
Fish cakes, recipe 2518:25
French parsnip soup, recipe 2518:20
Fruit and nut porridge, recipe 2518:17
German baked apples, recipe 2518:29
German rainbow coleslaw, recipe 2518:19
Gingerbread, recipe 2518:10
Homemade butter, recipe 2518:7
Hot apple cider punch, recipe 2518:30
Irish soda bread, recipe 2518:10
Italian dandelion and spinach salad, recipe 2518:18
Jewish smoked salmon spread, recipe 2518:13
Johnnycake, recipe 2868:13
Johnnycake, recipe 2895:16-17
Mexican style potato skins, recipe 2518:21
Muffins, recipe 2518:11
Native American fry bread, recipe 2518:11
Native American Johnnycake, recipe 2518:22
Native American maple syrup lemonade, recipe 2518:30
Native American pudding, recipe 2518:28

Native American wild rice with cranberries, recipe   2518:23

Oven fried chicken, recipe   2518:27

Overnight oats, recipe   2518:17

Popcorn balls, recipe   2497:88

Popcorn trail mix, recipe   2518:23

Potato skins, recipe   2518:21

Skillet bread, recipe   2488:24

Strawberry butter, recipe   2518:12

Strawberry shortcake, recipe   2518:29

Swedish rice cream, recipe   2518:17

## FRONTIER AND PIONEER LIFE—DIARIES

Pioneer diary, fabric, notebook, making 2523:42-44

## FRONTIER AND PIONEER LIFE—DOLLS

Stump doll, stump, paint, natural materials, making   2823:89-90

## FRONTIER AND PIONEER LIFE—FICTION

*Bear That Heard Crying* by Natalie Kinsey Warnock; readers theater booktalks with literature, poetry, music and creative writing activities   2681:15

*Daniel Boone* by James Daugherty; readers theater booktalks with literature, poetry, music and creative writing activities   2681:17

*Davy Crockett* by Justine Korman; readers theater booktalks with literature, poetry, music and creative writing activities   2681:22

*A Dog Came, Too* by Ainslie Manson; readers theater booktalks with literature, poetry, music and creative writing activities 2681:19

*Johnny Appleseed* by Gina Ingoglia; readers theater booktalks with literature, poetry, music and creative writing activities   2681:20

## FRONTIER AND PIONEER LIFE—FOOD

Growing beans, how to do   2895:44-45

## FRONTIER AND PIONEER LIFE—FOOTWEAR

Moccasins, felt, laces, making   2895:25-31

## FRONTIER AND PIONEER LIFE—GAMES

Ball games; nine holes, dodge ball, how to play 2519:15

Buttonhole puzzle, how to make and play 2523:83-84

Cat's cradle string games, how to play   2519:18

Cheyenne throwing sticks game, how to play 2868:13

Clap your hands games; Miss Mary Mac, how to play   2519:30

Hide and seek, how to play   2519:8

Hiding games; home free, whoop hide and seek, sardine, kick the can, how to play   2519:9

Hoop games; hoop and stick, through the hoop, grace hoops, how to play   2519:21

Hopping games; leap frog, keep the kettle boiling, hopscotch, let's get hopping, watch your step, how to play   2519:10-11

Marble games; ring taw, boss-out, how to play 2519:23

School Field Day games; push the potato, three-legged race, egg-in-the-spoon, how to play   2519:28-29

School games; hot buttered beans, I spy, how to play   2519:26

Skipping games, how to play   2519:12-13

Tag games; tiger in the corner, red lion, how to play   2519:7

Tops games; peg-in-the ring, conqueror, how to play   2519:20

Winter games; fox and geese, ice shinny, how to play   2519:25

## FRONTIER AND PIONEER LIFE— HANDICRAFTS

Berry basket, yogurt container, ribbons, making 2895:8-10

Pot holders, woven, cardboard loom, scraps of cloth, making   2852:114-115

## FRONTIER AND PIONEER LIFE—HOUSES

Flatboat house model, cardboard, felt, paints, making   2688:8-9

Paper windows, brown paper bag, salad oil, making   2497:86

Sod house, brownies decorated with icing, making   2895:37-41

## FRONTIER AND PIONEER LIFE—JOURNALS

Twine trail journal, cardboard, paper, twine, making   2688:10-11

## FRONTIER AND PIONEER LIFE—LANTERNS

Tin can lantern, tin can, paints, wire handle, making   2688:18-19

## FRONTIER AND PIONEER LIFE—LOG CABINS

Log cabin model, snap-on building sticks, brown paper, making   2688:12-13

## FRONTIER AND PIONEER LIFE—MUSICAL INSTRUMENTS

Fiddle, cardboard model, twine, making 2688:20-21

**FRONTIER AND PIONEER LIFE—
PADDLEBOATS**

Paddleboat model, milk cartons, making
2497:37-39

**FRONTIER AND PIONEER LIFE—QUILTING**

Quilt, fabric, batting, making   2895:13-15

*The Quilt-Block History of Pioneer Days* by
Mary Cobb; activities   2880:5-16

**FRONTIER AND PIONEER LIFE—
RAILROADS**

Laying the tracks model, making   2497:32-33

**FRONTIER AND PIONEER LIFE—SCHOOLS**

Slate, cardboard, paints, making   2895:42-43

**FRONTIER AND PIONEER LIFE—TOOLS**

Ax; wooden pioneer ax, cardboard, balsa wood,
foil, making   2688:14-15

**FRONTIER AND PIONEER LIFE—TOYS**

Balancing acrobat, cardboard, paints, dowels,
making   2523:50-52

Buzz saw toy, making   2497:35

Chromatrope toy, poster board, string, making
2523:102-104

Circus cutouts, paper toy, making   2523:53-56

Pinwheel, stiff paper, making   2523:45-46

**FRONTIER AND PIONEER LIFE—
TRANSPORTATION**

Covered wagon model, cardboard, yarn, plastic
horses, making   2688:6-7

Covered wagon pattern   2475:5

Covered wagon, shoebox, plastic lids, cardboard,
dowels, fabric, making   2895:20-23

Prairie schooner model, box, balsa wood, fabric,
paints, making   2497:44-45

**FRONTIER AND PIONEER LIFE—TRUNKS**

Trunk model, shoebox, fabric, making   2497:52

# G

**GABON—STATUES**
Bronze Bakot statue, railroad board, aluminum baking sheet, patterns, making 2620:40-41

**GAINSBOROUGH, THOMAS**
Portrait on landscape, making 2529:31

**GALAPAGOS ISLANDS**
Giant tortoise model, paper bag, markers, making 2686:107-108

**GAMBIA (AFRICAN PEOPLES)—JEWELRY**
Woven bracelets with Gambian design, plastic bottle, crochet thread, pattern, making 2784:14-15

**GARFIELD, JAMES ABRAM (PRESIDENT)**
Ocean life mobile, making 2263:70
Ship in a bottle, making 2263:70

**GARGOYLES—MASKS**
Grumpy green gargoyle mask, papier-mâché, foil, paints, making 2750:38-40

**GARIFUNA-AMERICANS—COOKERY**
Cabbage salad, recipe 2879:140
Chicken with rice, recipe 2879:141
Rice and beans, recipe 2879:140

**GAUGUIN, PAUL**
Cup of Gauguin, decorate in Gauguin style, making 2738:107
Surprising colors, making 2529:51

**GEECHEE.** *See* **GULLAH**

**GEORGIA—COOKERY**
Georgia peach pie, recipe 2535:63
Peach cobbler, recipe 2787:61
Peaches, sunny-side up, recipe 2534:24

**GERMAN-AMERICANS—COOKERY**
Hoppel-poppel (egg dish) recipe 2879:117-118
Lebkuchen (spice cake), recipe 2879:117
Sauerbraten, recipe 2879:116
Schman (egg dish), recipe 2879:118
Steam buns, recipe 2879:118-119
Stewed red cabbage, recipe 2879:116-117

**GERMANS FROM RUSSIA—COOKERY**
Dill pickles, recipe 2879:121
Kraut beerucks or cabbage busters, recipe 2879:120-121
Shtirum (pancakes), recipe 2879:121

**GERMANY—BIRTHDAYS—CANDLES**
Life candle, beeswax, cookie cutter, making 2957:21

**GERMANY—BIRTHDAYS—COOKERY**
Butter kuchen rolls, recipe 2957:20

**GERMANY—CASTLES**
Castle model, cardboard tubes, making 2686:90-91

**GERMANY—CHRISTMAS—COOKERY**
Christmas sweet bread, recipe 2669:67
Gingerbread house, recipe 2677:24-25
Kinderluwein drink, recipe 2577:30-31
Marzipan, recipe 2669:68-69
Peppernut cookies, recipe 2669:63
Spritz cookies, recipe 2888:232

**GERMANY—CHRISTMAS—DECORATIONS**
Advent calendar, cardboard, magazine pictures, making 2577:27
Advent calendar, cardboard, markers, ribbon, making 2846:20-21
Advent calendar, fabric, ribbon, treats, making 2740:30-31
Advent calendar, paper, decorations, candy, toys, making 2403:18-19
Cornucopias, paper, paste, making 2407:73
Interlocking bells, paper, making 2407:57

**GERMANY—CHRISTMAS—HANDICRAFTS**
Weihnacht angel folded paper ornament, making 2407:37

**GERMANY—COOKERY**
Apple cake, recipe 2669:56
Asparagus, recipe 2669:39
Baked cheesecake, recipe 2832:36-37
Baked eggs with cheese, recipe 2669:48
Beef rolls in cream sauce, recipe 2669:32-33
Black Forest cake, recipe 2832:38-39
Black Forest torte, recipe 2669:54-55
Butter cookies, recipe 2669:58-59
Cabbage rolls, recipe 2832:26-27
Clear beef broth, recipe 2669:37
Cold meat platter, recipe 2832:14-15
Cooked red cabbage, recipe 2832:30-31
Fish with mustard sauce, recipe 2669:34
German menu 2669:26-27

Gingerbread house, recipe    2648:112

Heaven and earth (meatless main course), recipe    2669:51

Herring in sour cream, recipe    2832:16-17

Hot potato salad, recipe    2669:50

Lebkuchen (cookies), recipe    2832:42-43

Marzipan critters, recipe    2845:21

One-pot meal with chicken, recipe    2669:40

Open-faced sandwiches, recipe    2669:46

Pancake soup, recipe    2832:10-11

Pfeffernuesse cookies, recipe    2418:25

Pork and apple casserole, recipe    2832:18-19

Pork and beef rissoles, recipe    2832:20-21

Pork roast, recipe    2669:30

Potato dumplings, recipe    2669:38

Potato dumplings, recipe    2832:28-29

Potato pancakes with stewed fruit, recipe    2832:24-25

Potato salad recipe    2832:32-33

Potato soup, recipe    2669:47

Raspberry gelatin, recipe    2832:40-41

Red cabbage, recipe    2669:43

Rye bread, recipe    2832:12-13

Spaetzle, recipe    2669:31

Spicy stars cookies, recipe    2845:20

Stewed apples, recipe    2832:34-35

Vienna-style escalopes (meat dish), recipe    2832:22-23

**GERMANY—EASTER—COOKERY**

Easter manikins, recipe    2669:64

Marzipan, recipe    2669:68-69

**GERMANY—EPIPHANY—COOKERY**

Pepper nuts, cookies, recipe    2888:33

**GERMANY—FESTIVALS—COOKERY**

Oktoberfest; apple strudel, recipe    2962:37

Oktoberfest; Bavarian bratwurst, recipe    2962:33

Oktoberfest; German potato salad, recipe    2962:35

Oktoberfest; green beans with spaetzle, recipe    2962:36

Oktoberfest; red cabbage, recipe    2962:34

**GERMANY—FESTIVALS—DECORATIONS**

First-day school cones, paper, paste, ribbons, goodies, making    2407:72

**GERMANY—FESTIVALS—LANTERNS**

St. Martin's Day; lantern, cardboard, transparent paper, wire, candle, dowel, making    2577:28-29

**GERMANY—FOLKLORE**

Activities, finger plays, songs, rhymes, crafts, patterns    2829:56-57

Baskets, making    2423:3

*Brementown Musicians,* story and activities    2423:101-119

Day the sky fell, story and activities    2423:37-45

*Frog Prince* magnet, felt, sequins, magnet, making    2729:36-37

Little Red pop-up, making    2423:7

Map to grandmother's house, making    2423:4

Pop-up wolf, making    2423:5-6

*Rapunzel* by Paul O. Zelinsky, activities, literature, art, science, poetry, social studies, webbing    2435:115-135

*Rumpelstiltskin,* story and activities    2423:81-95

Wolf's envelope, making    2423:9

Wolf's letter, making    2423:8

**GERMANY—GAMES**

Alle Vogel Vliegen (all birds fly), how to play    2767:73

Black cat game, how to play    2525:8

Blind horse game, how to play    2525:163

Brunt game, how to play    2525:38

Fingertips game, how to play    2525:159

Gummi twist game, how to play    2525:55

Hinkspiel (hopscotch), how to play    2767:73-75

Hunter and wolf game, how to play    2525:125

Kegelin game, how to make and play    2356:22

Merry-go-round game, how to play    2525:103

Muhle, tic-tac-toe game, how to play    2310:82-86

Olika bolika game, how to play    2385:14

Pirates game, how to play    2525:190

Plumpsack game, how to play    2847:20-21

Robots game, how to play    2525:186

Spacehopper flight game, how to play    2525:94

**GERMANY—LANGUAGE**

Everyday phrases in German    2356:23

Phrases, numbers and days of the week in German    2648:111

**GERMANY—NEW YEAR'S DAY—COOKERY**

New Year's pork and kraut, recipe    2669:62

**GERMANY—NEW YEAR'S DAY—GAMES**

Saint Sylvester Day fortune telling game, how to make and play    2402:22-23

**GERMANY—PAPER CUTTING**

Papierschnitt chain of people or animals, making    2418:17

Scherenschnitte, colored paper, making
2407:27

**GHANA—CHRISTMAS—DECORATIONS**

Crepe paper garlands, making  2403:20-21

**GHANA—CLOTHING**

Adinkra cloth, Adinkra symbols given, cloth,
making  2478:101-102

Adinkra cloth, fabric, paints, embroidery floss,
patterns, making  2620:22-23

**GHANA—COOKERY**

Boiled corn and beans, recipe  2628:43

Sweet balls, recipe  2628:39

Sweet potato fritters, recipe  2628:33

**GHANA—GAMES**

Achi, how to play  2767:75-76

Big snake tag game, how to play  2361:22

Che-che-koo-lay game, how to play  2385:41

Snake Tag, how to play  2767:76

Sugar and honey game, how to play  2525:31

Swing ball, how to make and play  2882:24-25

**GHANA—LANGUAGE**

Twi words, everyday words  2361:23

**GHANA—NAMES**

What your name would be in Ghana  2439:33

**GHANA—NEW YEAR—MUSICAL
INSTRUMENTS**

Homowo, balloon shaker, papier-mâché, dried
beans or rice, making  2402:24-25

**GHIBERTI, LORENZO**

Florentine relief, making  2529:14

**GIACOMETTI, ALBERTO**

Sticks 'n straws, making  2529:79

**GINGERBREAD HOUSES**

Gingerbread house, clay, milk carton, making
2884:62-65

**GINGERBREAD MAN**

Gingerbread boy running, ribbon spool, pipe
cleaner, making  2729:38-39

Story times, activities, gingerbread man tubey
pattern, craft instructions  2636:69-70

**GINGERBREAD MAN—PUPPETS**

Gingerbread men finger puppets, gloves, patterns, making  2675:25-28

**GIOTTO DI BONDONE**

Egg paint, making  2529:12

**GLUES**

Homemade glue, recipe  2918:62

Homemade glues, recipes  2684:140-141

Peel 'n' stick window glue, recipe  2918:64

Rainbow glue, recipe  2918:63

**GOBLE, PAUL**

*Girl Who Loved Wild Horses* by Paul Goble, literature, activities, art, curriculum
2436:15-28

**GOD—EARTH**

Animals; button animals, buttons, pipe cleaners,
making  2732:46-47

Bird; flying bird, feathers, paper, straw, making
2732:36-37

Bunnies; spoons bunny magnet, magnet, yarn,
making  2732:48-49

Caterpillar on a leaf, tissue paper, felt, making
2732:44-45

Cross pin, safety pins, seed beads, making
2732:58-59

Earth; glue and tissue Earth, tissue, string,
making  2732:8-9

Garden; handprints garden, poster paints, old
seed catalog, making  2732:34-35

Grass hat, paper, making  2732:24-25

Heart frame mask, red paper, stickers, paper
plate, making  2732:60-61

Label necklace, corrugated cardboard, electrical
tape, ribbon, making  2732:56-57

Land; dry land appearing, tissue paper, making
2732:22-23

Moon; changing moon, tissue paper, round lid,
making  2732:16-17

Night to day wheel, paper plates, paints, making
2732:10-11

People; different people envelopes puzzle,
making  2732:54-55

People; row of people, egg carton, paints, yarn,
buttons, making  2732:52-53

Plants; growing plants, old glove, trims, making
2732:30-31

Sea; bottom of the sea diorama, plastic container,
glitter, making  2732:40-41

Star hair snaps, snaps, stars, tinsel, making
2732:18-19

Tree; spaghetti tree pin, green glitter, making
2732:28-29

Water covering the Earth, paper, stars, glitter,
yarn, making  2732:20-21

Worms; wiggle worm apple house, old CD disc,
paper, making  2732:42-43

**GOD—EARTH—PUPPETS**

Bird finger puppet, necktie, feathers, felt, making
2732:38-39

Dogs; glove dog puppet, old glove, pom-poms,
making  2732:50-51

Flowers; growing flower puppet, old sock, fiberfill, yarn, making 2732:32-33

Praise puppet, flip-top can, red paper, pom-pom, making 2732:62-63

Sky puppet, brown bag, fiberfill, making 2732:12

Sunrise cup puppet, cup, coffee filter, paints, making 2732:14-15

Tree with squirrel puppet, tissue tube, tissue paper, making 2732:26-27

**GOLD RUSH**

Gold Rush poster, poster board, making 2689:8-9

John Sutter mask, poster board, yarn, making 2689:6-7

**GOLD RUSH—BANKS**

Banking house model, shoe box, felt, paints, clothespins, making 2689:20-21

**GOLD RUSH—COOKERY**

Cornish pasties, recipe 2488:42
Root beer, recipe 2441:84-85
Sourdough flapjacks, recipe 2488:37
Sourdough pancakes, recipe 2441:79-80
Sourdough starter, recipe 2488:36

**GOLD RUSH—FICTION**

*Wild Bill Hickock* by Maryann Weidt; readers theater booktalks with literature, poetry, music and creative writing activities 2681:39

**GOLD RUSH—GAMES**

Gold Rush playing cards, poster board, making 2689:16-17

**GOLD RUSH—HANDICRAFTS**

Old jeans backpack, making 2441:76-78
Pouch for precious things, laced or sewn pouch, making 2441:73-75

**GOLD RUSH—PANNING**

Gold rush pan and pieces of gold, aluminum pie dish, paints, making 2689:12-13

**GOLD RUSH—SCALES**

Scale for weighing gold, box, balsa wood, stick, paints, making 2689:18-19

**GOLD RUSH—TOWNS**

Gold Rush town, felt, popsicle sticks, gold paint, making 2689:14-15

**GOLF—TEA PARTIES—COOKERY**

Sun tea, recipe 2643:22
Tee-cakes with green frosting, recipe 2643:22

**GOLF—TEA PARTIES—HANDICRAFTS**

Miniature golf course, making 2643:23

**GRANDMA MOSES (ANNA MAY ROBERTSON)**

Busy folk art scene, making 2529:84

**GRANDPARENTS**

Activities, finger plays, songs, rhymes, crafts, patterns 2828:36-37

**GRANDPARENTS' DAY**

Activities, crafts, games, food and memories 2578:1-157

Activities, crafts, puppets, games, patterns 2762:117-124

Family crest, clay, paints, making 2578:18-19

Family patchwork quilt, fabric, batting, making 2578:30-33

Family tree, pedigree chart, how to do 2578:12-16

**GRANDPARENTS' DAY—COOKERY**

Applesauce, recipe 2578:149
Cookie surprise, recipe 2578:140-141
Dilled bean sticks, recipe 2578:148
Family birthday cake, recipe 2578:142-143
Ginger cookies, recipe 2578:138-139
Sweet-tooth fudge, recipe 2578:136-137

**GRANDPARENTS' DAY—FICTION**

*Nana Upstairs & Nana Downstairs* by Tomie dePaola, activities, crafts, patterns, games, masks, puppets, making 2329:11-14

*Now One Foot, Now the Other* by Tomie dePaola, activities, crafts, patterns, games, masks, puppets, making 2329:11-14

*Thanksgiving at the Tappletons'* by Eileen Spinelli, activities, crafts, patterns, mathematics, art, music and science 2445:31-41

**GRANDPARENTS' DAY—GAMES**

Categories game, how to play 2578:48-49
Concentration game, how to play 2578:52
Cribbage for two, how to play 2578:68-71
Jacks, how to play 2578:78-79
Marbles, how to play 2578:72-75
Tangrams, how to make and play 2578:56-57
Toothpick teasers, how to play 2578:54
Vanishing saltshaker and coin, how to play 2578:58-59
Yo-yo game, how to play 2578:80-81

**GRANDPARENTS' DAY—HANDICRAFTS**

Beading, how to do 2578:92-93
Cone puppet, fabric, cup, dowel, making 2578:104-105
Family stamp, eraser, ink pad, making 2578:94-95

Mix 'n' match books, cardboard, making
2578:128-129

Pinball board, wood, nails, rubber bands, making
2578:96-97

Potpourri, recipe, making    2578:120-121

**GRANT, JULIA DENT (FIRST LADY)—COOKERY**

Apple pancakes and ham, recipe    2552:13

Baked cheese hominy grits, recipe    2552:17

Petits fours and butter glaze frosting, recipe
2552:19

**GRANT, ULYSSES SIMPSON (PRESIDENT)**

Bean bag horse race, making    2263:64

Equine collage, horse patterns, making    2263:64

Memoir storyboard mural, making    2263:64

**GREAT DEPRESSION—COOKERY**

Baked macaroni and cheese, recipe
2359:115-116

Depression cake, recipe    2359:117

Speedy vegetable and barley soup, recipe
2359:113-114

**GREAT DEPRESSION. *See also* U.S. HISTORY— THE GREAT DEPRESSION, 1929— COOKERY**

**GREECE—CHRISTMAS—COOKERY**

Butter cookies, recipe    2481:58

Chocolate bells, recipe    2842:66

**GREECE—CHRISTMAS—DECORATIONS**

Triangle musical instrument, coat hanger, bells,
making    2403:24-25

**GREECE—COOKERY**

Almond cake, recipe    2833:36-37

Avgolemono (egg-lemon soup), recipe    2267:19

Baked fish, recipe    2842:48

Baklava, recipe    2833:40-41

Beef and onion stew, recipe    2842:50

Burekakia (pastries), recipe    2833:20-21

Butter cookies, recipe    2271:61

Butter cookies, recipe    2842:56

Chicken soup with lemon, recipe    2380:unp

Chicken with lemons and olives, recipe
2833:34-35

Cucumber and yogurt dip, recipe    2842:45

Egg and lemon soup, recipe    2842:42

Eggplant and lentil soup, recipe    2833:10-11

Fish with red pepper and tomato sauce, recipe
2833:28-29

Greek menu    2842:28-29

Greek salad, recipe    2267:9

Greek salad, recipe    2650:53

Greek salad, recipe    2842:36

Greek salad, recipe    2924:14

Honey cheese pie, recipe    2842:59

Horiatiki salata (Greek salad), recipe
2833:16-17

Koulourakia (Greek cookies), recipe    2267:21

Lamb kebabs, recipe    2833:26-27

Lemonade, recipe    2833:42-43

Lentil soup, recipe    2842:44

Mediterranean meatballs, recipe    2924:12-13

Moussaka (meat and vegetables), recipe
2833:18-19

Orzo salad, recipe    2381:unp

Orzo with browned butter sauce, recipe
2842:51

Pita bread, recipe    2833:12-13

Pita toppers, recipe    2924:10-11

Popolettes (potato patties), recipe    2833:22-23

Skewered lamb, recipe    2842:33

Spiced rice and lentils, recipe    2833:32-33

Spinach pie, recipe    2842:34-35

Stuffed grape leaves, recipe    2833:30-31

Stuffed grape leaves, recipe    2842:40-41

Stuffed peppers and tomatoes, recipe
2833:24-25

Stuffed tomatoes with feta cheese, recipe
2271:36

Stuffed tomatoes with feta cheese, recipe
2842:52

Tzatziki (cucumber-yogurt sauce), recipe
2267:11

Tzatziki sauce with grilled vegetables, recipe
2833:14-15

Tzatziki, yogurt, herbs and vegetable dip, recipe
2905:21

Walnut-honey pastry, recipe    2842:60-61

Yogurt pie, recipe    2396:44

Yogurt with honey and fruit, recipe    2833:38-39

**GREECE—EASTER—COOKERY**

Easter eggs, recipe    2842:66

Holiday meat pie, recipe    2842:64-65

Roast lamb, recipe    2677:10-11

**GREECE—EASTER—EGGS**

Greek Easter eggs, how to dye    2905:25

**GREECE—EASTER—GAMES**

Egg-cracking contest, how to play    2703:22

**GREECE—FESTIVALS—COOKERY**

Athenian Feast, baklava, recipe    2962:43

Athenian Feast; Greek salad, recipe    2962:39

Athenian Feast; moussaka, recipe    2962:41

Athenian Feast; spanikopita, recipe    2962:40

Athenian Feast; vasilopita bread, recipe
2962:42

**GREECE—FOLKLORE**

*Ant and the Grasshopper* an Aesop's Fable, folktales, puppets, patterns, songs, food 2591:7-10

**GREECE—GAMES**

Backside throw game, how to play    2525:174
Balls and funnels game, how to play    2525:51
Carriage and driver game, how to play    2525:30
Flees game, how to play    2905:17
Kukla, how to play    2767:76-77
Marbles game, how to play    2525:60
Nose to nose game, how to play    2525:121
Olympic snowball game, how to play    2328:137
Pair tag game, how to play    2525:140
Somersault game, how to play    2525:14
Statue game, how to play    2525:125
Tallia game, how to play    2525:178
Worm game, how to play    2525:188

**GREECE—LANGUAGE**

Few Greek words    2703:23
Learn to speak a few words in Greek    2650:48

**GREECE—LENT—DECORATIONS**

Lenten calendar, folded paper, making    2407:48

**GREECE—NEW YEAR'S DAY—COOKERY**

Feast of Saint Basil; vasilopita, bread with coin inside, recipe    2402:26-27
St. Basil's cake, recipe    2984:33

**GREECE—NEW YEAR'S DAY—DECORATIONS**

Kalanda star, folded paper, making    2407:49

**GREECE—NEW YEAR'S EVE—COOKERY**

New Year's bread, recipe    2842:68-69

**GREECE, ANCIENT—ABACUS**

Greek abacus, shoebox lid, string, beads, paints, making    2506:22-23

**GREECE, ANCIENT—CLOCKS**

Water clock; plastic containers, straw, making 2929:30

**GREECE, ANCIENT—CLOTHING**

Boys chiton, fabric, buttons, cord, making 2816:32-33
Chiton for men, cloth, pattern, making 2323:12-13

**GREECE, ANCIENT—COOKERY**

Asparagus, recipe    2323:23
Baked fish in grape leaves, recipe    2323:28
Mini pizzas, recipe    2323:26
Pancakes with honey and sesame seeds, recipe 2816:26-27

Roasted chicken, recipe    2323:29
Sesame circles, recipe    2323:30-31
Spinach triangles, recipe    2323:24-25

**GREECE, ANCIENT—FRESCOES**

Dolphin fresco, paper, clay, paints, making 2816:22-23

**GREECE, ANCIENT—GAMES**

Brazen fly, how to play    2767:76
Knucklebones game, how to make and play 2816:28-29

**GREECE, ANCIENT—GEOMETRY**

Platonic bodies, patterns, making    2323:60-66

**GREECE, ANCIENT—JEWELRY**

Charm and necklace, clay, paints, making 2506:34-35
Stone pendant, stone, wire, making    2323:20

**GREECE, ANCIENT—MASKS**

Bird mask, papier-mâché over balloon, red poster board, making    2816:44-45
Comedy, tragedy and slave masks, making 2323:40

**GREECE, ANCIENT—MATHEMATICS**

Sieve of Eratosthenes, making    2323:58

**GREECE, ANCIENT—MEDICINE**

Leg offering to the Gods, clay, paints, making 2816:54-55

**GREECE, ANCIENT—MOSAICS**

Construction paper mosaic, how to make 2364:86
Paper mosaic, colored papers, making 2323:46-47
seed and bean mosaic coaster, beans, seeds, making    2323:48

**GREECE, ANCIENT—MUSICAL INSTRUMENTS**

Lyre, paper plates, skewer, dowel, beads, making 2781:10-11
Timpanon, corrugated cardboard, poster board, ribbons, making    2816:46-47
Tortoise lyre, cardboard, sticks, string, paints, making    2506:26-27

**GREECE, ANCIENT—MYTHOLOGY**

Cyclops eye, egg crate, PVA glue, paints, making 2781:22-23
Medusa head model, clay, paints, making 2816:40-41
Pandora's box, paper, box, pattern, making 2323:41-42

**GREECE, ANCIENT—MYTHOLOGY—
    WEAPONS**
Glinting dagger, cardboard, foil, glitter pens, patterns, making    2781:14-15
**GREECE, ANCIENT—PAINTING**
Paint back-to-front Greek style    2929:31
**GREECE, ANCIENT—PARTHENON**
Parthenon model, box, plastic straws, paints, making    2506:30-31
**GREECE, ANCIENT—POTTERY**
Black and red pottery, papier-mâché, foil, paints, making    2506:42-43
Clay pot, red clay, paints, making    2323:49-50
Panathenaic vase, papier-mâché over balloon, paints, making    2816:48-49
**GREECE, ANCIENT—RELIEFS**
Relief, clay, plaster of Paris, making    2323:44-45
**GREECE, ANCIENT—RELIGION**
Votives, foil tray, string, making    2506:38-39
**GREECE, ANCIENT—SCIENCE**
Archimedes screw model, plastic bottle, clay, making    2816:52-53
**GREECE, ANCIENT—SCROLLS**
Scroll, paper, balsa wood, door knobs, wooden rod, making    2816:30-31
**GREECE, ANCIENT—SCULPTURES**
Sculpt a statue, wire, clay, making    2323:43
**GREECE, ANCIENT—SEALS**
Minoan seal, clay, glue, varnish, making    2816:10-11
**GREECE, ANCIENT—SHOPPING**
Price of several common goods    2364:21
**GREECE, ANCIENT—TABLETS**
Clay tablet, cookie dough, making    2323:54-55
**GREECE, ANCIENT—TEMPLES**
Parthenon model, poster board, shoebox, corrugated cardboard, making    2816:34-37
**GREECE, ANCIENT—THEATER**
Comedy and tragedy masks, papier-mâché, paints, yarn, fur, beads, making    2506:18-19
**GREECE, ANCIENT—TROJAN HORSE**
Trojan horse model, boxes, paints, making    2506:14-15
Trojan horse, large box, felt, tissue paper tubes, cork, wooden skewers, pattern, making    2781:26-27

**GREECE, ANCIENT—VOTING**
Voting tokens, balsa wood, clay, paints, making    2816:14-15
**GREECE, ANCIENT—WARRIORS**
Greaves leg protectors, plaster, bandages, gold paint, making    2816:58-59
**GREECE, ANCIENT—WEAVING**
Drop spindle; make and use a drop spindle, how to do    2323:81-83
Round mat; weave a round mat, cardboard, yarn, making    2323:84-85
String art, string a circle, cardboard, embroidery thread, making    2323:88-89
String art, string an angle, cardboard, embroidery thread, making    2323:86-87
**GREEK-AMERICANS—COOKERY**
Loukoumathes, honey dough balls, recipe    2980:25
Pecan crescents, recipe    2879:124
Stuffed grape leaves, recipe    2879:122-123
Tourlou (roasted vegetable dish), recipe    2879:124
**GREEK-AMERICANS—JEWELRY**
Worry beads, pictures from magazines, glue, yarn, making    2980:13
**GRENADA—HANDICRAFTS**
Grenadian spice hangers, fabric, ribbon, spices, making    2817:22-25
**GRIMM TALES**
Baskets, making    2423:3
Little Red pop-up, making    2423:7
Map to grandmother's house, making    2423:4
Pop-up wolf, making    2423:5-6
Wolf's envelope, making    2423:9
Wolf's letter, making    2423:8
**GROUNDHOG DAY**
Activities, puppets, patterns, making    2754:33-42
Groundhog, pattern    2754:36
**GROUNDHOG DAY—COOKERY**
Gumdrop groundhog, recipe and activities    2576:81-84
**GROUNDHOG DAY—FICTION**
*A Garden for a Groundhog* by Lorna Balian, activities, crafts, patterns, games, masks, puppets, making    2329:76-78
**GROUNDHOG DAY—PUPPETS**
Groundhog paper bag puppet, paper, pattern, making    2754:35

Groundhog pop-up puppet, paper cup, paper, pattern, making   2754:37

**GRUELLE, JOHNNY**

Raggedy Ann invitations, making   2951:unp
Raggedy Ann tea party, how to do   2951:unp

**GRUELLE, JOHNNY—COOKERY**

Raggedy Ann's and Marcella's lemonade, recipe   2951:unp
Raggedy Ann's and Uncle Clem's scotch shortbread, recipe   2951:unp
Raggedy Ann's candy heart cookies, recipe   2951:unp
Raggedy Ann's easy chocolate cake with creamy pink and white icing, recipe   2951:unp
Raggedy Ann's tiny sandwiches, recipe   2951:unp
Super-special stripey cake, recipe   2768:unp

**GRUELLE, JOHNNY—FICTION**

Raggedy Ann pin, pompoms, beads, making   2729:6-7

**GRUELLE, JOHNNY—GAMES**

Pin the tail on the donkey, how to play   2768:unp
Spider web game, how to play   2768:unp

**GUAMIANS (CHAMOROS)—COOKERY**

Chicken salad from Guam, recipe   2879:125
Hot sauce, recipe   2879:125-126

**GUATEMALA—COAT OF ARMS**

Guatemalan coat of arms, paper, markers, pattern, making   2671:26

**GUATEMALA—COOKERY**

Baked plantains, recipe   2946:52
Fried black bean paste, recipe   2946:53
Guatemalan-style rice, recipe   2946:53
Pickled vegetables, recipe   2946:52
Radish salad, recipe   2946:52

**GUATEMALA—DECORATIONS**

Dulce señorita, poster board, pipe cleaners, markers, candy, making   2407:88

**GUATEMALA—DOLLS**

Worry doll, paper, pipe cleaners, fabric, making   2686:101-102

**GUATEMALA—FLAGS**

Guatemalan flag, paper, markers, pattern, making   2671:26

**GUATEMALA—GAMES**

Wall Bounce, how to play   2767:77-78

**GUATEMALA—HANDICRAFTS**

Friendship bracelets, embroidery thread, acrylic yarn, making   2440:86-90

**GUATEMALA—WEAVING**

Belt and headband, loom and yarn, making   2440:94-96
Homemade loom, popsicle sticks, making   2440:93

**GUATEMALAN-AMERICANS—COOKERY**

Polo guisado (chicken stew), recipe   2879:127
Radish salad, recipe   2879:126

**GUINEA—GAMES**

Sand game, how to play   2767:78-79

**GULLAH (GEECHEE AND SEA ISLANDERS)—COOKERY**

Hoppin' John, recipe   2879:129
Proper Geechee rice (hoppin' John dish), recipe   2879:128-129
Red rice, recipe   2879:128

**GUYANA—GAMES**

Ring on a string, how to play   2767:79-80

**GUYANESE-AMERICAN (AND INDO-CARIBBEANS)—COOKERY**

Garlic pork, recipe   2879:130-131
Sea trout salad, recipe   2879:130

**GYPSIES—HANDICRAFTS**

Anklet; gypsy anklet, black hemp, elastic cord, silver beads, silver bells, making   2883:105-110

**GYPSY-AMERICANS (ROMANICHALS, TRAVELLERS, AND ROMA)—COOKERY**

Irish scones, recipe   2879:133-134
Pirogo, Gypsy cake or pudding, recipe   2879:133
Sax suklo (stew dish), recipe   2879:132-133

# H

## HAIDA INDIANS
Haida Creation story designs, patterns, paints, making 2351:21

## HAIDA INDIANS—BASKETS
Tlinglit and Haida baskets for a potlatch, straw basket, paints, patterns, making 2351:18-19

## HAIDA INDIANS—COOKERY
Fish chowder, recipe 2879:273
Fish perok pie, recipe 2879:274
Salmon patties, recipe 2284:63

## HAIDA INDIANS—JEWELRY
Sealskin bracelet, felt, chamois cloth, yarn, patterns, making 2351:25

## HAIDA INDIANS—LANGUAGE
Everyday words in Haida language 2284:99-100

## HAIDA INDIANS—MUSICAL INSTRUMENTS
Haida drum, coffee can, paints, patterns, making 2351:22

## HAITI—COOKERY
Beans and rice, recipe 2451:49
Blancmange, sweet dessert, recipe 2645:30-31
Chicken in sauce, recipe 2955:53
Fried plantain, recipe 2955:53
Griot (fried pork), recipe 2955:52
Griot, pork loin dish, recipe 2911:51
Soup de Haiti, recipe 2955:52

## HAITI—FESTIVALS—HEADDRESSES
Carnival; headdress, large hat, crepe paper, colorful cloth, making 2645:28-29

## HAITI—GAMES
Marelle (hopscotch), how to play 2767:80-81
Osselets game, how to make and play 2374:22
Osselets, jacks game, how to play 2330:88-89
Osselets, jacks, how to play 2493:24-25

## HAITI—HANDICRAFTS
Haitian metal cutouts, aluminum pan, patterns, making 2817:34-39

## HAITI—LANGUAGE
Learn to speak French and Creole 2451:47
Words in Creole, how to speak 2374:23

## HAITI—NEW YEAR—FLAGS
Joudlan, Haitian flag, paper, craft sticks, making 2402:28-29

## HAITIAN-AMERICANS—COOKERY
Griots (pork dish), recipe 2879:135
Haitian cake, recipe 2879:136
Hot sauce, recipe 2879:135-136
Red beans and rice, recipe 2879:134-135

## HALL, DONALD
*Ox-Cart Man*, literature, activities, art, curriculum 2436:121-132

## HALLOWEEN
Activities, puppets, patterns 2761:101-128
Activities, recipes, songs, games 2863:131-140
Dressing up; activities, finger plays, songs, rhymes, crafts, patterns 2828:26-27
History of Halloween 2877:72
Spooky stories; activities, finger plays, songs, rhymes, crafts, patterns 2828:28-29
Thematic units, lessons, activities, art, poetry, crafts, patterns, recipes 2320:41-68

## HALLOWEEN—COOKERY
Acorn squash soup, recipe 2877:74
Apples with gummy worms, recipe 2888:187
Beastly buffet, how to make 2319:32-35
Black and orange pasta, recipe 2877:75
Cauldron cocktail punches, recipe 2319:40-43
Chocolate chip pizza, recipe 2888:183
Dirt pudding pie, recipe 2888:188
Dracula's blood milkshake, recipe 2888:190
Frozen chocolate jack-o-lanterns, recipe 2888:189
Ghoulish orange popcorn balls, recipe 2888:182
Halloween haunted house party foods, recipes 2877:73
Hanging horrors cookies, recipe 2319:38-39
Haystacks, cookies, recipe 2888:180
Jack-o-lantern decorated cake, recipe 2583:24
Monster cupcakes, recipe 2888:191-192
Monster muffins, recipe 2877:76
Pumpkin cookies, recipe 2877:77
Pumpkin ice cream, recipe 2863:133
Pumpkin muffins, recipe 2863:132

Pumpkin-oatmeal cookies, recipe 2888:184
Sweet treats, how to make 2319:36-37
Witches' brew punch, recipe 2888:181

**HALLOWEEN—COSTUMES**

Creepy costumes, making 2319:16-19
Face paint fearsome features, making 2319:20-23
Paper plate faces, making 2319:24-27

**HALLOWEEN—DECORATIONS**

Bats on a branch, black paper, wiggle eyes, black yarn, patterns, making 2938:22-23
Batty ear dangles, black felt, black yarn, making 2719:16-17
Big Foot's feet, shoeboxes, yarn, making 2734:14-15
Brain; giant brain, panty hose, fiberfill, making 2734:26-27
Can pumpkin favor, round can, cardboard tube, making 2719:6-7
Card; Halloween pop-up card, paper, envelope, making 2938:18-19
Changing face magnets, metal lids, magnet, making 2719:20-21
Changing face pumpkin bag, paper plate, old gift bag, paints, making 2719:42-43
Coffin; trick-or-treat coffin, shoebox, liquid soap, black paint, making 2938:14-15
Creep from the deep hat, pantyhose, poster paint, making 2734:36-37
Creeping metal hand, foil, pipe cleaner, beads, making 2734:6-7
Doll clothes scarecrow, doll clothes, felt, foil, making 2719:8-9
Dracula soap dispenser pump bottles, red food coloring, making 2734:24-25
"Eggs"ellent Halloween favors, eggshells, felt, paint, making 2719:38-39
Flickering pumpkin face, pumpkins, making 2319:4-7
Floating ghost candy cups, ruler, tissue paper, soda bottle, making 2719:18-19
Frankenstein paper keeper, cereal box, colored paper, making 2734:30-31
Frankenstein treasure keeper, old black sock, foil, ribbon, making 2719:34-35
Ghost zipper pull, plastic milk container, yarn, black paper, making 2719:22-23
Ghost; tissue ghost, spray starch, tissue paper, making 2734:28-29
Ghostly guest, balloon, old sheet or pillowcase, patterns, making 2938:16-17
Ghostly tissue box, box tissues, pom-poms, making 2719:31

Ghosts in the graveyard, foam trays, craft sticks, pattern, making 2938:20-21
Ghoulish helping hand, plastic glove, green paper, cotton balls, making 2938:12-13
Ghouls, felt scraps, making 2748:34-36
Glow-in-the-dark haunted photograph, paints, photograph framed under glass, making 2719:40-41
Great spider race, plastic lids, plastic straw, string, making 2719:36-37
Hairy tarantula, black pipe cleaners, wiggle eyes, making 2938:6-7
Hand, plaster of Paris, rubber glove, food colors, making 2734:32-33
Haunted house, black, yellow and orange paper, patterns, making 2938:10-11
Jack-o-lantern antenna marker, balloon, Styrofoam ball, ballpoint pen, making 2719:12-13
Jeering jars, glass jars, tissue paper, flashlights, making 2319:10-13
Juggling apples and pumpkins, balloons, dough, making 2883:31-33
Lantern; paper, yarn, crepe paper, making 2923:24-25
Mini-ghosts, tissue paper, making 2709:43
Monster in a box, detergent box, sock, fiberfill, making 2734:44-45
Monster lanterns, red and orange paper, making 2783:16-17
Mummy pin, wooden spoons, sneaker laces, wiggle eyes, making 2734:10-11
Nessie the sea monster, paper plates, plastic tub, paints, wiggle eyes, making 2734:42-43
Paper chains, ghosts, pumpkins, black cats, making 2319:14-15
Peeking eyes, glow in the dark paints, making 2734:20-21
Puzzle pieces ghost pin, puzzle pieces, paint, making 2719:4-5
Reptile; giant reptile, paper plates, poster paints, making 2734:34-35
Safety owl treat bag, compact discs, fiberfill, making 2719:44-45
Skeleton scatter pin, white cotton swabs, yarn, dried lima bean, making 2719:28-30
Slinky, slithery snakes, necktie, felt scraps, making 2748:37-39
Something weird in a jar, large jar with lid, fiberfill, old pantyhose, making 2719:46-47
Spooky shades, plastic bottle, paints, making 2778:28-29

Swooping bats and petrified pumpkins silhouette
    window decorations, making    2319:8-9
Treat buckets, how to make    2319:28-31
Trick-or-treat bucket, fabric, foil, paints, making
    2748:40-42
Wanda witch figure, paper, crayons, patterns,
    making    2811:3-4
Washboard cat, folded paper, making    2407:40
Witchy pen, felt, yarn, ruler, making
    2719:10-11
Yarn-wrapped black cat, felt, black pipe cleaner,
    black yarn, making    2719:32-33

**HALLOWEEN—FACE PAINT**

Alien face painting, how to do    2952:34-35
Count Dracula face painting, how to do
    2952:30-31
Creepy skin, recipe    2918:123
Dr. Frankenstein's monster face painting, how to
    do    2952:28-29
Fake blood, recipe    2918:122
Halloween face putty, recipe    2918:113-114
Mummy paste, recipe    2918:126-127
Scars, scabs, burns and wrinkles, recipe
    2918:124-125
Skeleton face painting, how to do    2952:26-27
Witch face painting, how to do    2952:24-25

**HALLOWEEN—FICTION**

Activities, finger plays, songs, rhymes, crafts,
    patterns    2829:58-59
*Funny Bones* by Janet and Allan Ahlberg, activi-
    ties, crafts, patterns, games, masks, puppets,
    making    2329:22-24
*Little Witch's Big Night* by Deborah Hautzig, ac-
    tivities, art, games, songs, crafts, patterns
    2812:11-16
*The Biggest Pumpkin Ever* by Steven Kroll, ac-
    tivities, crafts, patterns, games, masks, pup-
    pets, making    2329:19-21

**HALLOWEEN—GAMES**

Ghost train, plunge in grunge, shadow theater,
    slimy funny feelings, how to play
    2319:44-45

**HALLOWEEN—JEWELRY**

Alien necklace, wooden spoons, green yarn,
    making    2734:40-41
Blob in a bottle necklace, corn syrup, plastic vial,
    wiggle eyes, making    2734:16-17
Bracelet; candy corn bracelet, elastic cord, clay,
    wooden skewers, making    2883:74-77
Necklace; creepy Halloween necklace, card-
    board, craft stick, black yarn, making
    2938:24-25

**HALLOWEEN—MASKS**

Doll masks, making    2719:26
Howling Banshee mask, paper plates, party horn,
    paints, pipe cleaners, making    2734:8-9
Monster mask, papier-mâché, foil, paints, making
    2978:94-97

**HALLOWEEN—PUPPETS**

Bat puppet, felt, sock, yarn, patterns, making
    2938:8-9
Brain; throbbing brain puppet, soda bottle, sock,
    detergent bottle, making    2734:38-39
Count Dracula puppet, old shirt, tennis ball, egg
    carton, making    2719:14-15
Dragon; fire-breathing dragon puppet, oatmeal
    box, green sock, pom-poms, making
    2734:18-19
Haunted house puppet, shoe box, old knit glove,
    felt, making    2734:22-23
Peering mummy puppet, cardboard tube, white
    toilet paper, making    2719:24-25
Slimy monster mitt puppet, Zip lock bags, craft
    foam, hair gel, making    2734:12-13

**HALLOWEEN—SOAP**

Gross eyeballs soap, making    2936:48-49
Halloween treat's soap, making    2936:44

**HAMBURGERS—HISTORY**

Cornhusker burger, recipe    2534:46-47

**HANUKKAH**

History of Hanukkah    2877:86

**HANUKKAH—BLESSINGS**

Three blessings    2875:5

**HANUKKAH—COOKERY**

Applesauce, recipe    2657:54
Applesauce, recipe    2875:15
Baked apples, recipe    2877:89
Bimuelos/Ponchiks doughnuts, recipe
    2521:64-65
Carrot pancakes, recipe    2888:221
Cinnamon applesauce, recipe    2888:226
Cinnamon-stick applesauce, recipe    2877:89
Doughnuts with honey syrup, recipe
    2888:223-224
Dreidel, munch menorahs, recipe    2919:38
Fudgy gelt, recipe    2888:222
Gelt mix, recipe    2521:68
Hanukkah cookies, recipe    2521:69
Jelly nuggets, recipe    2875:16
Judah Maccabee's secret applesauce, recipe
    2521:60
Judith's recipe for applesauce    2521:61
Latke platter, recipe    2919:37

Latkes, recipe    2642:71
Latkes, recipe    2657:52
Latkes, recipe    2919:36
Maple-baked apples, recipe    2888:227
Non-potato latkes, recipe    2657:53
Potato latkes, baked recipe    2346:42
Potato latkes, recipe    2346:41-42
Potato latkes, recipe    2504:110-111
Potato latkes, recipe    2875:14
Potato latkes, recipe    2877:88
Potato latkes, recipe    2888:219
Potato pancakes, recipe`    2256:59
Rugelach cookies, recipe    2888:225
Sufganiyot (jelly donuts), recipe    2877:90-91
Sugar syrup, recipe    2521:66-67
Sweet potato latkes, recipe    2657:53
Sweet potato latkes, recipe    2888:220

## HANUKKAH—DECORATIONS

Applesauce jar, jar, fabric, yarn, making
    2727:18-19
Baskets for gifts, paper bag, bows, ribbons,
    making    2857:21
Can menorah, foil, cans, sand, making    2657:16
Candle candy holder, toilet paper tubes, tissue
    paper, candy, making    2889:24-25
Candle Hanukkiah, ceramic tile, plated nuts, mo-
    saic square, making    2919:26-27
Cards; holiday cards, making    2919:42
Clay dreidel, clay, paints, making    2778:34-35
Collage bookmark, tissue paper, silver ribbon,
    making    2889:20-21
Dreidel braided key chain, cord or lacing, pony
    beads, making    2889:22-23
Dreidel candy holder, milk carton, straw, ribbon,
    making    2919:40-41
Dreidel card, envelopes, metallic trim, making
    2727:20-21
Dreidel chain, gift wrap, making    2657:38
Dreidel mobile, cardboard, paint, string, patterns,
    making    2889:6-7
Dreidel notepad, making    2657:49
Dreidel pin, old tie, foil, making    2727:26-27
Dreidel; giant dreidel, large carton, yarn, making
    2727:22-23
Dreydl, pattern, making    2753:118
Embossed place cards, paper, foil, making
    2889:10-11
Flameless menorah, cardboard, felt, yarn,
    making    2657:17
Flameless menorah, egg carton, construction pa-
    per, making    2657:14
Gelt holder, brown, bag, blue paper trim, making
    2727:14-15
Gelt holder, detergent bottle, yarn, making
    2657:48
Glitter menorah card, making    2657:43
Glitter mobile, making    2657:37
Hand-to-hand menorah, handprints, foil, glitter,
    making    2657:15
Hanukkah chain, paper, making    2657:42
Hanukkah gift bags, shoebox, gift wrap, making
    2727:44-45
Hanukkah jigsaw puzzle, making    2657:49
Hanukkah magnets, craft foam, glitter, magnets,
    making    2889:14-15
Hanukkah match holder, pill bottle, yarn, felt,
    making    2727:10-11
Hanukkah memory book, paper, yarn, making
    2727:46-47
Hanukkah symbol stamps, blocks of woods, craft
    foam, ink pad, making    2889:12-13
Holiday cards, paper, glitter, stickers, making
    2889:16-17
Kiddush cup door hanging, making    2727:32-33
Kiddush cup necklace, pipe cleaners, gold cord,
    making    2727:30-31
Kiddush cup, making    2727:28-29
Maccabee soldier, fabric, fabric trims, making
    2727:42-43
Menorah candleholder, round cardboard con-
    tainer, clay, permanent pens, making
    2440:53-54
Menorah from egg carton and foil, making
    2657:13
Menorah from jar lids, making    2262:84
Menorah from salt dough (recipe given), making
    2657:12
Menorah from spools, making    2875:6
Menorah matchbox, foil, felt, making    2657:16
Menorah stabile, thread spool, pipe cleaners,
    gold garland, making    2727:12-13
Menorah, foil, cardboard, candles, making
    2727:8-9
Menorah; helping hands menorah, felt, card-
    board, envelopes, glitter, making    2889:8-9
Menorah, pattern, making    2753:117
Menorah, wire hanger, clay, paints, making
    2507:26-27
Oil Hanukkah, baby food jars, oil, wicks, making
    2919:28
Paper punch cards, making    2657:43
Potato print stamps, making    2875:31
Pull out menorah card, making    2657:47
Rebus cards, making    2657:44
Shamash holder, plastic clothespin, paint stirrer,
    making    2919:29

Spinning stars, paper, making 2657:39
Spiral mobile, making 2657:36
Sponge design cards, making 2657:43
Sponge print wrapping paper, making 2875:31
Stand up menorah card, making 2657:45
Star of David candleholder, pie tins, glitter, making 2727:38-39
Star of David mobile, fabric, trims, yarn, making 2727:40-41
Star of David mobile, pipe cleaners, making 2657:41
Star of David ornament, black paper, tissue paper, pattern, making 2889:18-19
Star of David pendant, cardboard, foil, making 2657:38
Star of David window ornaments, silver or gold pipe cleaners, making 2857:20
Star of David, ice cream sticks, paint, making 2778:36-37
Star of David; patchwork Star of David, old neckties, trim, making 2727:36-37
Straw Star of David card, making 2657:46
Window light ups, making 2657:40
Wrapping paper, paper, potato, paints, making 2919:39
Yarn menorah card, making 2657:46

## HANUKKAH—DOLLS

Doll yarmulke, felt, metallic trim, making 2727:34-35

## HANUKKAH—FICTION

*Hanukkah!*, by Roni Schotter, activities, crafts, patterns, games, masks, puppets, making 2329:44-46

*Hershel and the Hanukkah Goblins* by Eric A. Kimmel; activities, art, poetry, maps, crafts, foods, patterns 2642:71-73

## HANUKKAH—GAMES

Dreidel from paper, making 2657:21
Dreidel from pencil and cardboard, making 2657:20
Dreidel from salt dough (recipe given), making 2657:19
Dreidel game, how to make and play 2346:43
Dreidel game, how to make and play 2401:38-39
Dreidel game, how to make and play 2504:111-113
Dreidel game, how to make and play 2642:72
Dreidel game, how to make and play 2727:24-25
Dreidel game, how to play 2521:77-78
Dreidel game, how to play 2857:20-21

Dreidel game, how to play 2875:25
Dreidel, how to make 2875:26-27
Dreidl game, foam dreidel, craft foam, making 2919:32-33
Dreidl game, how to play dreidel 2919:31
Dreidl game, paper dreidel, making 2919:34
Drop in the bucket game, how to make and play 2657:27
Eight candles match-up game, how to play 2657:25
Flip the latke game, how to make and play 2657:26
Gelt; charity gelt toss, making 2919:35
Gelt; make your own gelt 2919:35
Latke toss, how to make and play 2657:27
Latkes in the pan game, how to make and play 2727:16-17
Maccabee bowling game, how to make and play 2657:24
Maccabee checkers, how to make and play 2657:29
Maccabee dreidel game, how to play 2657:23
Pin the candle on the Menorah game, how to make and play 2657:28
To the temple board game, how to make and play 2657:30-31
Variations on dreidel game, how to play 2521:82-83

## HANUKKAH—HANDICRAFTS

Hanukkah place mats, fabric, making 2657:51
Star of David picture frame, ice cream sticks, making 2657:50

## HANUKKAH—PUPPETS

Judah, Mattathias and King Antiochus puppets, tongue depressors, yarn, glitter, pipe cleaners, making 2875:34-35
Shadow puppets of Greek soldier and Maccabee, patterns, making 2919:44-45

## HARDING, WILLIAM (PRESIDENT)

Cubing a still life, making 2263:93
Our family gazette, making 2263:93

## HARRISON, BENJAMIN (PRESIDENT)

China cabinet, patterns, making 2263:78
Race to Oklahoma, making 2263:78

## HARRISON, WILLIAM HENRY (PRESIDENT)

Inaugural parade floats, patterns, making 2263:38
Pockets full of petitions, making 2263:38

## HARVEST

Teaching themes, activities, games, crafts, patterns, recipes 2410:7-14

Teaching themes, activities, games, crafts, patterns, recipes   2410:41-48

**HARVEST—DECORATIONS**

Harvest basket, fabrics, basket, making 2748:43-44

Tablecloth and napkins, fabric, paints, making 2748:45-47

**HAWAII**

Activities, maps, volcanoes, hula dance, plants, lei necklace, patterns   2421:25-35

**HAWAII—CLOTHING**

Feather cape, paper bag, feathers, making 2934:161-162

Hula skirts, grocery bags, yarn, making 2757:124

**HAWAII—COOKERY**

Aloha-bobs, fruit kabobs, recipe   2534:25

Bananas baked, recipe   2934:157

Haupia (coconut pudding), recipe 2879:136-137

Lomi salmon, recipe   2879:137

**HAWAII—COSTUMES**

Happy hula outfit, paper, tissue paper, making 2676:18-19

**HAWAII—FESTIVALS**

Lei Day; story times, activities, Hawaiian boy and girl tubey patterns, craft instructions 2636:30-33

**HAWAII—FOLKLORE**

*Maui and the Secret Fire,* story and activities 2423:71-78

**HAWAII—GAMES**

Kimo, picking up stones game, how to play   2934:160

Kimokimo, how to play   2767:179

No'a, Hawaiian game, how to play   2934:159

Puhenehene game, how to play   2328:108

**HAWAII—LEIS**

Beautiful lei, paper, yarn, pasta, making 2686:31-32

Flower lei, flowers, thread, making 2441:117-118

Leis, tissue paper, pattern, making   2757:124

String a flower garland, making   2934:158

**HAWAII—LUAU**

Luau flower leis, how to make   2328:106-107

**HAWAII—QUILTING**

Pineapple quilt, paper, making   2407:29

**HAYES, RUTHERFORD B. (PRESIDENT)**

Concentration eggs, patterns, making   2263:67

Egg forest for the President, patterns, making 2263:67

Lemonade and mulled cider, recipe   2263:67

**HEBREW LANGUAGE**

How to count in Hebrew   2940:41

**HENNY PENNY**

Hand wings Henny Penny, feathers, paper, making 2729:34-35

**HIDATSA INDIANS—BOATS**

Bull-boat model, cardboard, pipe cleaners, making   2894:36-37

**HIDATSA INDIANS—COOKERY**

Drying squash, how to do   2894:38-39

**HIDATSA INDIANS—GAMES**

Hoop and pole game, how to play   2473:56

**HIDATSA INDIANS—GARDENS**

Sunflowers, how to plant, grow and roast the seeds   2894:41-43

**HINDUS—FESTIVALS—COOKERY**

Divali; coconut barfi, recipe   2588:20

Divali; mattar paneer, recipe   2588:16-17

Divali; pulao rice with peas and nuts, recipe 2588:18-19

Ganesh Chaturthi; kheer, recipe   2588:24-25

Ganesh Chaturthi; ladoos, recipe   2588:26-27

Ganesh Chaturthi; scented almond drink, recipe 2588:28

Holi Festival; pakoras, vegetables fried in batter, recipe   2985:19

Holi; garam doodh, recipe   2588:12

Holi; onion bhajis, recipe   2588:10-11

Holi; samosas, recipe   2588:8-9

Rasksha Bandhan; sohan halva sweets, recipe 2589:9

**HINDUS—FESTIVALS—PLAYS**

Ramayana epic poem play   2589:16-22

**HINDUS—GAMES**

Andar Bahar game, how to play   2385:10

**HINDUS—YOGA**

Three Hatha yoga poses, how to do 2774:102-103

**HIPPIES**

Way-out hippie hair, metallic paper, tissue paper, glitter, sequins, making   2676:22-23

**HISPANIC AMERICANS—COOKERY**

Aqua de Jamaica (hibiscus flower-flavored water), recipe   2671:64

Cascarones, recipe   2671:6
Salsa, recipe   2671:65-66
Sweet tamales, recipe   2671:65
Vegetable stew, recipe   2631:27

**HISPANIC AMERICANS—DOLLS**

Sock doll, old socks, buttons, making   2631:21

**HISPANIC HERITAGE MONTH—DOLLS**

Corn husk doll, making   2671:30-31

**HISPANIC HERITAGE MONTH—
HEADBANDS**

Incan headband, tissue paper, glue, making
2671:34-35

**HISPANIC HERITAGE MONTH—
HEADDRESSES**

Incan headdress, papier-mâché, feathers,
making   2671:32-33

**HMONG-AMERICANS—COOKERY**

Hmong salad, recipe   2879:138
Watercress and beef, recipe   2879:138-139

**HOH INDIANS—COOKERY**

Fry bread, recipe   2311:88-91

**HOKUSAI, KATSUSHIKA**

Surimono greeting, making   2529:34

**HOLY WEEK—DECORATIONS**

Easter bouquet paper collage, pattern, making
2798:43-44
Easter joy tissue flower, making   2798:45
Easter lily pop-up puppet, making   2798:42
Empty tomb box lid collage, pattern, making
2798:39-40
Flower cross wall plaque, making   2798:41
Good Friday cross wall plaque, pattern, making
2798:37-38
Hosanna stamped picture, making   2798:29-30
In the garden diorama, pattern, making
2798:33-34
Lord is risen butterfly mobile, making   2798:47
My Savior lives plastic lid sun catcher, making
2798:46
Praying hands crayon window, pattern, making
2798:35-36
Sing Hosanna palm leaves, making   2798:31
Thy will be done stand-up heart, making
2798:32

**HOMER, WINSLOW**

Wilderness watercolor, making   2529:43

**HONDURAN-AMERICANS—COOKERY**

Cabbage salad, recipe   2879:140
Chicken with rice, recipe   2879:141

Rice and beans, recipe   2879:140

**HONDURAS—FLAGS**

Honduran flag, paper, markers, pattern, making
2671:27

**HONDURAS—GAMES**

La Rayuela, how to play   2767:81-82

**HONG KONG—GAMES**

Crosscut beancurd game, how to play   2525:32

**HOOVER, HERBERT (PRESIDENT)**

Grocery bag medicine ball, making   2263:99
Papier-mâché fish, making   2263:99
Rock collector's box, making   2263:99

**HOPI INDIANS—COOKERY**

Pinto beans, recipe   2879:142
Whole wheat stew, recipe   2879:141-142

**HOPI INDIANS—HOUSES**

Model pueblo, cardboard boxes, paints, cornmeal
or sand, making   2523:29-30

**HOPI INDIANS—KACHINA DOLLS**

Kachina doll, cardboard tube, paints, making
2804:22-23

**HOPI INDIANS—POTTERY**

Hopi coiled pot, clay, paints, making
2891:32-34

**HOPI INDIANS—TOYS**

Hopi toy, button and string, how to make and
play   2891:36-37

**HORSES**

Language arts, poetry, hobby craft activities
2511:43-46

**HOUSES—FICTION**

*The Little House* by Virginia Lee Burton, literature, activities, art, curriculum   2436:75-86

**HOUSES—PUPPETS**

House finger puppets, gloves, patterns, making
2675:68-71

**HUICHOL INDIANS—FESTIVALS—SHIELDS**

Festival of Our Lady of Guadalupe; dancers Aztec shield, gold foil paper, yarn, paints,
making   2276:28-29

**HUICHOL INDIANS—GOD'S EYE**

God's eye, popsicle sticks, yarn, making
2440:107

**HUNGARIAN-AMERICANS—COOKERY**

Chicken paprika, recipe   2879:144
Paprika potatoes, recipe   2879:144
Pogachels (butter cookies), recipe   2879:144

**HUNGARY—CHRISTMAS—COOKERY**

    Pancakes with walnut filling and chocolate
        sauce, recipe    2461:66-69

    Walnut filled roll, recipe    2461:65

**HUNGARY—COOKERY**

    Apple strudel, recipe    2479:unp

    Apple strudel, recipe    2710:123

    Bean soup with smoked sausage, recipe
        2461:40

    Cold cherry soup, recipe    2461:41

    Creamed spinach with fried rolls, recipe
        2461:57

    Cucumber salad, recipe    2461:47

    Goulash, recipe    2461:42

    Hungarian cold plate, recipe    2461:34

    Hungarian menu    2461:30-31

    Hungarian salad dressing, recipe    2461:45

    Hungarian scrambled eggs, recipe    2461:36

    Noodles with cottage cheese, recipe    2461:58

    Paprika cheese spread, recipe    2461:35

    Paprika chicken, recipe    2461:48

    Pinched noodles, recipe    2461:43

    Small dumplings, recipe    2461:44

    Strudel with cottage cheese or cherry filling,
        recipe    2461:62-63

    Stuffed green peppers with potatoes, recipe
        2461:54-55

    Tomato salad, recipe    2461:45

    Ujhazi chicken soup, recipe    2461:52-53

    Winter vegetable goulash, recipe    2838:30-31

**HUNGARY—DECORATIONS**

    Peasant staffs, making    2407:66

**HUNGARY—GAMES**

    Dobi-dobi, how to play    2767:82

    Grab the rag game, how to play    2525:121

    Hungarian dominoes, how to play    2491:25-26

**HURON INDIANS—LANGUAGE**

    Words and phrases about daily life
        2285:103-105

# I

**ICE CREAM CONE—HISTORY**

Show-me cream 'n' homemade cones, recipe
2534:43-44

**ICELAND—CHRISTMAS—DECORATIONS**

Christmas pockets, paper, yarn, making
2403:26-27

**ICELAND—GAMES**

Fox and Geese, how to play    2767:82-83

**ICELANDIC-AMERICANS—COOKERY**

Creamed potatoes, recipe    2879:147
Stack cake, recipe    2879:146-147

**IDAHO—COOKERY**

Potato nachos, recipe    2672:63

**IDAHO—FESTIVALS—COOKERY**

Idaho Spud Day Festival; cheesy spuds, recipe
2534:27

**ILLINOIS—COOKERY**

Deep-dish pizza pie, recipe    2534:28-29
Pumpkin cookery, recipe    2777:55

**IMMIGRANTS—FICTION**

*Klara's New World* by Jeanette Winter; readers
theater booktalks with literature, poetry,
music and creative writing activities
2681:40
*Mike Fink* by Steven Kellog; readers theater
booktalks with literature, poetry, music and
creative writing activities    2681:25
*True Confessions of Charlotte Doyle* by Avi;
readers theater booktalks with literature, poetry, music and creative writing activities
2681:23

**INCAS—BOATS**

Reed boat model, straw or hay, plastic lid,
making    2790:26-27

**INCAS—CLOTHING**

Tunic, felt, yarn, paints, making    2790:32-33

**INCAS—COOKERY**

Bean stew, recipe    2790:30-31

**INCAS—EMPERORS**

Feather fans for the emperor, feathers, paints,
making    2790:10-11

**INCAS—FUNERALS**

Grave doll, fabric, yarn, paints, red pipe cleaners,
making    2790:56-57

**INCAS—GODS**

Gold sun God mask, cardboard, gold and black
paint, making    2790:40-41
Tumi ceremonial knife model, cardboard, clay,
paints, making    2790:38-39

**INCAS—GRANARIES**

Granary model building, cardboard, paints, hay
or straw, making    2790:18-19

**INCAS—HEADBANDS**

Incan headband, tissue paper, glue, making
2671:34-35

**INCAS—HEADDRESSES**

Incan headdress, papier-mâché, feathers, making
2671:32-33

**INCAS—JEWELRY**

Gold and silver necklace, clay, paints, making
2790:34-35

**INCAS—MATHEMATICS**

Quipu string, rope or string, paint, making
2790:50-51

**INCAS—MEDICINE**

Medicine bag, fabric, yarn, paints, making
2790:48-49

**INCAS—MUSICAL INSTRUMENTS**

Hand-drum, cardboard, fabric, paints, dowel,
yarn, making    2790:46-47

**INCAS—POTTERY**

Jaguar model, papier-mâché, making
2790:36-37
Water jar, clay, paints, making    2790:14-15

**INCAS—WARRIORS**

Helmet, fabric, papier-mâché, paints, making
2790:58-59

**INDIA—BATIK**

Batik, dyed cloth, making    2474:92-93

**INDIA—BIRTHDAYS—PUPPETS**

Shadow puppets, poster board, patterns, making
2957:24-25

**INDIA—CHRISTMAS—DECORATIONS**

Garlands, paper, tape, making   2403:28-29

**INDIA—COOKERY**

Apple chutney, recipe   2584:61

Baked yogurt, recipe   2879:24

Banana curry, recipe   2605:20-21

Banana fritters, recipe   2605:38-39

Banana yogurt, recipe   2584:58

Burfi sweet treat, recipe   2512:30-31

Carrots with grated coconut, recipe   2584:51

Chapati, whole wheat flatbread, recipe   2807:31

Chapatis, recipe   2605:32-33

Chapatis, unleavened whole wheat bread, recipe
    2271:28-29

Chicken bhuna, recipe   2605:16-17

Corn and coconut salad, recipe   2605:34-35

Cucumber yogurt, recipe   2584:59

Curried chickpeas, recipe   2271:53

Curried chickpeas, recipe   2584:48

Fish and coconut soup, recipe   2605: 12-13

Fresh coriander chutney, recipe   2584:60

Garam masala, recipe   2584:35

Gobi paratha (bread stuffed with vegetables),
    recipe   2838:16-17

Ground lamb kebabs, recipe   2584:40

Ice cream, recipe   2587:10

Indian menu   2584:26

Kulfi (Indian cream), recipe   2605:40-41

Lamb and cashew nut curry, recipe   2785:127

Lassi (yogurt dish), recipe   2605:42-43

Lassi, recipe   2584:36

Lentil patties, recipe   2605:28-29

Lentils with garlic and onion, recipe   2584:50

Lima beans with raisins, recipe   2605:10-11

Mango dessert, recipe   2486:47

Mango lassie, recipe   2845:25

Naan bread, recipe   2785:130

Nuked rice, recipe   2879:24-25

Peanut potatoes, recipe   2879:23-24

Pilau rice with fruit and nuts, recipe
    2605:30-31

Potatoes and peas, recipe   2584:32

Pumpkin curry, recipe   2584:46-47

Raita (yogurt and vegetable dish), recipe
    2594:53

Raita (yogurt dish), recipe   2605:36-37

Raita, recipe   2845:24

Rasqulla, cream cheese balls in syrup, recipe
    2785:131

Rice pudding, recipe   2396:36

Sheera (candy), recipe   2879:23

Shrimp patia, recipe   2605:18-19

Spiced ground meat, recipe   2584:33

Spiced rice, recipe   2584:56

Spiced tea, recipe   2474:100

Spiced tea, recipe   2584:36

Spicy chickpeas, recipe   2605:22-23

Spicy fried fish, recipe   2584:42

Spicy okra, recipe   2605:26-27

Spicy scrambled eggs, recipe   2605:14-15

Stuffed green peppers, recipe   2879:22-23

Stuffed pastries, recipe   2584:30-31

Unleavened whole wheat bread, recipe
    2584:54-55

Vegetable Biryani rice dish, recipe   2605:24-25

Vegetable curry, recipe   2924:8-9

Yogurt and bananas, recipe   2271:42

Yogurt chicken, recipe   2584:41

**INDIA—DANCES**

Ankle bracelets for dancing, making   2587:25

**INDIA—ELEPHANTS**

Indian elephant model, paper, markers, making
    2686:56-57

**INDIA—FESTIVALS—COOKERY**

Apricot fool dessert, recipe   2888:213

Couscous, recipe   2962:46

Cucumbers in yogurt, recipe   2962:45

Divali rice pudding, recipe   2888:208

Divali sweet yogurt with saffron, recipe
    2888:209

Diwali Rice Festival; Indian toffee, recipe
    2584:65

Diwali Rice Festival; sweetened rice, recipe
    2584:65

Holi; nutty milk shake, recipe   2584:68

Holi; stuffed sweet bread, recipe   2584:66

Lemon cardamom cookies, recipe   2888:215

Mango pudding, recipe   2962:49

Pistachio fudge, recipe   2888:212

Ramadan; vermicelli pudding, recipe   2584:69

Semolina pudding, recipe   2888:211

Shrimp curry, recipe   2962:48

Surya Pongal Feast; Pongal sweet rice dish,
    recipe   2504:67-68

Tandoori chicken, recipe   2962:47

Vermicelli rice pudding, recipe   2888:210

Yogurt cheese dessert with saffron, recipe
    2888:214

**INDIA—FESTIVALS—DECORATIONS**

Diwali; rangoli patterns, rice, food coloring,
    making   2984:21

Mehndi hand painting, how to do   2587:20

Mehndi hand painting, stamp pad, inks, making
    2846:24-25

**INDIA—FESTIVALS—ELEPHANTS**

Indian elephant shoe bag, fabric, felt, feathers, sequins, pattern, making   2683:14-15

**INDIA—FESTIVALS—GAMES**

Diwali Festival; light the flame or Diya, how to make and play   2933:40-41

**INDIA—FESTIVALS—HANDICRAFTS**

Diwali; divas lamp, clay, paints, candle, making   2402:30-31

Raksha Bandhan Rakhi Festival; good luck bracelet, making   2587:32

**INDIA—FESTIVALS—LAMPS**

Divali lamp, clay, paints, making   2512:28-29

Diwali Dipa lamps, tissue paper, patterns, making   2262:84

**INDIA—FESTIVALS—PETS**

Mattu Pongal; pet garland, soutache yarn, colored bells, making   2504:69

**INDIA—FOLKLORE**

*Hare and the Rumor,* story and activities   2423:39-45

*Horse Egg,* folktales, puppets, patterns, songs, food   2591:22-24

**INDIA—GAMES**

Andar Bahar game, how to play   2385:10

Chilly hopscotch, how to play   2492:23-25

Drop the hankie game, how to play   2882:32-33

Gulam Chor, card game, how to play   2310:21-25

Guli danda game, how to play   2484:42-43

Kabaddi game, how to play   2847:24-25

KHO game, how to play   2525:26

Kokla-chau pakee game, how to play   2587:41

Lagoria game, how to play   2484:40-41

Magic tag, how to play   2767:84

Marbles, how to play   2484:37-38

Nirali batel game, how to play   2525:45

Pachisi, how to play   2512:26-27

Sota-pani, how to play   2767:84

Spinning tops games, how to play   2484:38-40

Tripple dribble game, how to play   2525:172

Vultures and crows, how to play   2767:85-86

**INDIA—HANDICRAFTS**

Indian mirror, mirror tile, pink cardboard, gold paper, shiny stickers, pattern, making   2784:12-13

**INDIA—LANGUAGE**

Hindi language, learn to speak a few words   2594:51

Hindi words for family members   2807:29

Hindi, say a few Hindi words   2474:97

**INDIA—TEA PARTIES—COOKERY**

Chai tea, recipe   2643:34

Curry and sweet mango sandwiches, recipe   2643:34

How to plan and set the table   2643:32-33

**INDIA—TEA PARTIES—HANDICRAFTS**

Henna tattooing, how to do   2643:36

**INDIA—YOGA**

How to do yoga   2484:18-19

**INDIANA—COOKERY**

Back-to-basics brunch, recipe   2534:30

Three-corn casserole, recipe   2814:63

**INDIANS OF NORTH AMERICA**

Activities, crafts, puppets, games, patterns   2762:109-116

Thematic units, lessons, activities, art, poetry, crafts, patterns, recipes   2320:69-96

**INDIANS OF NORTH AMERICA—BASKETS**

Woven basket, poster papers, marking pens, making   2523:64-66

**INDIANS OF NORTH AMERICA—BULLROARER**

Bullroarer, wood paint stirrer, heavy cord, paints, making   2840:32-33

**INDIANS OF NORTH AMERICA—CANOES**

Canoe model, cardboard, paint, making   2804:12-13

**INDIANS OF NORTH AMERICA—CLOTHING**

Skin robe, sheet, felt, thread, making   2804:26-27

**INDIANS OF NORTH AMERICA—COOKERY**

Corn cakes, recipe   2804:24-25

Corn chowder, recipe   2523:91-92

Cranberry corn bread, recipe   2629:19

Indian ice cream, recipe   2629:21

**INDIANS OF NORTH AMERICA—COSTUMES**

Native American shirt and headdress, crepe paper, ribbon, making   2676:24-25

**INDIANS OF NORTH AMERICA—DANCES**

Dance wand, balsa stick, paper, paints, making   2804:56-57

**INDIANS OF NORTH AMERICA—DOLLS**

Clay doll, clay, fabric, paints, making   2840:30-31

Cloth doll, fabric, pattern, making   2480:121-130

Corncob doll, cornhusks, fabric, paints, making   2840:29

Cornhusk doll, cornhusk, fabric, paints, making
2840:26-28

## INDIANS OF NORTH AMERICA—DREAMCATCHERS

Dreamcatcher, making   2644:32-33
Dreamcatcher, metal ring, ribbons, gold thread,
beads, feathers, making   2784:16-17
Dreamcatcher, rings (metal, craft hoops), basket
(reeds, vines), yarn, string, feathers, beads,
making   2440:68-70
Snow and ice dream catcher, embroidery hoop,
silver cord, feathers, felt, making
2884:38-41

## INDIANS OF NORTH AMERICA—FICTION

Activities, finger plays, songs, rhymes, crafts,
patterns   2829:80-81
*Girl Who Loved Wild Horses* by Paul Goble, activities, projects, patterns, art, crafts
2822:46-49
*Legend of the Paint Brush* retold and illustrated
by Tomie dePaola, activities, projects, patterns, art, crafts   2822:28-30

## INDIANS OF NORTH AMERICA—FOLKLORE

*Girl Who Loved Wild Horses* by Paul Goble, literature, activities, art, curriculum
2436:15-28
*Rainbows Here on Earth,* folktales, puppets, patterns, songs, food   2591:43-44
Storytelling hand, heavy paper, pattern, making
2350:38

## INDIANS OF NORTH AMERICA—FOOTWEAR

Moccasins, felt, paint, thread, making
2840:22-25
Native American moccasins, sock, felt, fabric,
making   2349:29

## INDIANS OF NORTH AMERICA—GAMES

Ball races, how to play   2896:27-28
Batball game, how to play   2896:24-25
Blanketball game, how to play   2896:22
Blindfold game, how to play   2445:70
Bowl game, how to play   2445:70
Doubleball game, how to play   2896:20-22
Firewood awareness game, how to play
2896:78-80
Hoop and dart, how to make and play
2882:14-15
Hoop and pole game, how to play   2440:70
Hoop and pole hoop game, how to play
2896:63-67
Hubbub game of chance, how to play
2896:42-46

Lacrosse stick, cardboard, bamboo sticks, paints,
making   2804:38-39
Moccasin game of chance, how to play
2896:46-49
Ring and pin hoop game, how to play
2896:59-63
Ring game, how to make and play   2690:18-19
Rock awareness game, how to play   2896:80-82
Snow snake game, how to play   2328:38-39
Stalking awareness game, how to play
2896:76-77
Stalking the drum awareness game, how to play
2896:77-78
Stickball game, how to play   .2896:26-27
Toss and catch, how to make and play
2523:72-73

## INDIANS OF NORTH AMERICA—GREAT PLAINS—COOKERY

Snow food, recipe   2629:11

## INDIANS OF NORTH AMERICA—GREAT PLAINS—HOUSES

Paper tepee model, twigs, paper, yarn, making
2688:16-17
Tipi model, fabric, paints, making   2252:28-29
Wickiup model, making   2626:28-29

## INDIANS OF NORTH AMERICA—GREAT PLAINS—TEPEES

Paper copy of tepee, pattern, making   2644:19

## INDIANS OF NORTH AMERICA—HEADRESSES

Headdress, paper, feathers, making   2690:10-11
Headdress, ribbons, balsa dowels, feathers, felt,
making   2804:14-17

## INDIANS OF NORTH AMERICA—JEWELRY

Bead necklace, macaroni, string, food coloring,
making   2523:87-89
Beaded bracelet, seed beads, thread, making
2840:14-15
Leather bracelet, leather scraps, pony beads,
making   2883:22-23
Necklace, clay, beads from paper tubes, paints,
making   2804:18-19
Rosette necklace, seed beads, felt, thread, making   2840:12-13
Seed and bead jewelry, seeds, thread, making
2840:8-9

## INDIANS OF NORTH AMERICA—MUSICAL INSTRUMENTS

Ankle bells, felt, small bells, making
2804:50-51

Drum beater, stick, leather, leather lace, making 2840:40-41

Hoop drum, cookie tin, leather, leather lace, making 2840:38-39

Native American rattle, tin can, paper, pennies, pebbles, making 2690:14-15

Rasp, wood, dowel, paints, making 2840:34-35

Rattle, cardboard, balsa wood strips, clay, paints, making 2804:52-53

Snake dance rattle, toilet paper tubes, felt, string, pony beads, making 2884:26-30

Turtle rattle, stick, paper plates, beans, making 2840:36-37

## INDIANS OF NORTH AMERICA—NORTHEAST—COOKERY

Pumpkin-corn sauce, recipe 2629:15

Three sisters; squash, beans and corn dish, recipe 2629:13

## INDIANS OF NORTH AMERICA—POTTERY

Clay pinch pot, clay, paints, making 2840:16-17

Tankard (cup), clay, paints, making 2804:36-37

## INDIANS OF NORTH AMERICA—POUCHES

Fabric pouch, felt, muslin, paints, making 2480:130-136

Painted pouch, felt, yarn, paints, making 2840:18-19

## INDIANS OF NORTH AMERICA—SHIELDS

Shield, cardboard, paints, making 2804:48-49

## INDIANS OF NORTH AMERICA—SOUTH—COOKERY

Baked sweet potatoes, recipe 2629:17

## INDIANS OF NORTH AMERICA—SOUTHWEST—COOKERY

Indian fry bread, recipe 2629:7

## INDIANS OF NORTH AMERICA—SOUTHWEST—FICTION

*When Clay Sings* by Byrd Baylor; activities, art, poetry, maps, crafts, foods, patterns 2642:87-89

## INDIANS OF NORTH AMERICA—SYMBOLS

Beaded rosette, heavy fabric or felt, seed beads, patterns, making 2350:32-33

## INDIANS OF NORTH AMERICA—TEA PARTIES—COOKERY

Corn muffins, recipe 2643:50

How to plan and set the table 2643:48-49

Smoky tea, recipe 2643:50

## INDIANS OF NORTH AMERICA—TEA PARTIES—TEPEES

Broom tepee, how to build 2643:51

## INDIANS OF NORTH AMERICA—WAMPUM

Macaroni and food dye wampum, making 2644:34

## INDIANS OF NORTH AMERICA—WINTER COUNT

Winter count, fabric, paints, making 2804:30-31

## INDIANS OF THE NORTHWEST COAST—BASKETS

Tlinglit and Haida baskets for a potlatch, straw basket, paints, patterns, making 2351:18-19

## INDIANS OF THE NORTHWEST COAST—CLOTHING

Whale blanket, felt, fabric, buttons, patterns, making 2351:34-35

## INDIANS OF THE NORTHWEST COAST—HOUSEHOLD ITEMS

Treasure box, wooden or cardboard box, paints, patterns, making 2351:14-15

## INDIANS OF THE NORTHWEST COAST—SYMBOLS

Northwest Coast designs and symbols, patterns, making 2351:10-13

## INDIANS OF THE NORTHWEST COAST—TOTEM POLES

Northwest Coast totem poles, cardboard tubes, paints, patterns, making 2351:16-17

## INDIANS OF THE NORTHWEST COAST—TOTEM POLES. *See also* NORTHWEST COAST INDIANS

## INDIANS OF THE PLAINS—FOLKLORE

*Legend of the Indian Paintbrush* by Tomie dePaola; activities, patterns 2644:40-45

## INDIANS OF THE PLAINS—HOUSES

Earth lodge model, paper bowl, dried grass, paints, making 2644:19

## INDO-CARIBBEANS—COOKERY

Curried chicken, recipe 2879:275

Potato bread, recipe 2879:275-276

## INDONESIA—COOKERY

Aromatic chicken, recipe 2834:24-25

Balinese vegetable soup, recipe 2903:32

Carrot and apple salad, recipe 2903:44

Carrot and mooli salad, recipe 2834:30-31

Chicken in coconut cream sauce, recipe 2903:52

Chicken satay, recipe 2834:22-23

Coconut pancakes, recipe 2834:40-41

Corn fritters, recipe 2903:33

Crab and baby sweet corn soup, recipe
2834:16-17

Es teller drink and dessert, recipe   2625:122

Fermented soybean and green beans in coconut
milk, recipe   2625:130

Festive rice cone, recipe   2834:38-39

Fried bananas, recipe   2903:56

Fruit salad, recipe   2834:42-43

Gado-gado (vegetables and rice dish), recipe
2568:41

Gado-gado salad, recipe   2903:40-41

Indonesian menu   2903:28-29

Mixed vegetable salad with peanut sauce, recipe
2625:131

Nasi goreng (fried rice, chicken, beef, prawns),
recipe   2834:20-21

Peanut fritters, recipe   2834:10-11

Peanut sauce, recipe   2834:12-13

Potato snowball cookies, recipe   2903:59

Prawn and rice noodle soup, recipe   2834:18-19

Soy sauce fish, recipe   2903:48

Spiced beef and coconut stew, recipe
2834:26-27

Spicy fruit salad, recipe   2903:42

Spicy scrambled eggs, recipe   2834:32-33

Steamed cabbage with coconut, recipe
2834:28-29

Steamed coconut custard, recipe   2903:60

Stir-fried noodles with shrimp, recipe   2903:50

Sumatran-style lamb chops, recipe   2834:34-35

Sweet and sour beef sate with peanut sauce,
recipe   2903:36-37

Tempeh (soybean dish), recipe   2274:30-31

Thai fragrant (Jasmine) rice, recipe   2903:44

Tofu omelettes, recipe   2834:36-37

Tomato, cucumber and onion salad, recipe
2903:45

Vanilla gelatin pudding, recipe   2903:57

Vegetable gado-gado, recipe   2834:14-15

Vegetable sauté, recipe   2903:51

Vegetable sour soup, recipe   2903:34

**INDONESIA—DANCES**

Topeng, the Masked Dance, how to do
2274:26-27

**INDONESIA—FESTIVALS—COOKERY**

Festive rice, recipe   2903:64

Indonesian ice drink, recipe   2903:69

Pork sate, recipe   2903:66

Ramadan; curried java soup, recipe   2903:67

**INDONESIA—GAMES**

Kelereng marbles, how to play   2495:24-25

Man, ant, elephant, how to play   2767:86

Ram, ram, rip game, how to play   2385:17

Sorok-sorok, how to play   2767:86-87

**INDONESIA—LANGUAGE**

Bahasa Indonesia greetings   2568:25

Bahasa Indonesia words for family members
2568:19

Learn a few words in Bahasa, Indonesia
language   2704:23

**INDONESIA—SHADOW PUPPETS**

Shadow puppet, cardboard, paints, dowels,
making   2274:28-29

Shadow puppets, poster board, markers, straws,
making   2407:82

Wayang kulit, flat shadow puppet, making
2704:22

Wayang-kulit, shadow puppet play, how to do
2474:101

**INDONESIA—SONGS**

Indonesian children's song   2568:37

**INGALIK PEOPLES**

Igloo snow scene, clay, paints, patterns, making
2351:36-37

**INKS**

Berry good ink, recipe   2918:80

Fabric ink, recipe   2918:71-72

Stamp pad ink, recipe   2918:74

**INSECTS**

Language arts, poetry, hobby craft activities
2511:47-51

**INUIT INDIANS—CARVINGS**

Soapstone sculptures, soap, making
2328:72-73

Miniature Inuit carvings, soap, patterns, making   2351:23-25

**INUIT INDIANS—COOKERY**

Seafood chowder, recipe   2286:64

**INUIT INDIANS—GAMES**

Ball and stick (Jacks), how to play   2480:86

Duck and ptarmigans, how to play
2767:167-168

Eskimo yo-yo, how to make and play
2328:78-79

Inuit clay bird game, how to make and play
2328:74-75

Knee jump, how to play   2480:85

Knuckle hopping, how to play   2480:85

Stick pull, how to play   2480:85

**INUIT INDIANS—HOUSES**

Igloo model, flour, salt, water, dough model,
making   2347:28-29

**INUIT INDIANS—LANGUAGE**

Everyday words in Inuit language   2286:98-101

**INUIT INDIANS—MASKS**

Spirit mask, paper plates, decorations, making   2328:82-83

**INUIT INDIANS.** *See also* **YUPIK INDIANS**

**INUKSUK**

Inuksuk stones, adhesives, how to build   2844:6-9

**INUPIAK.** *See* **INUIT INDIANS**

**INUPIAT INDIANS—GAMES**

Inupiat Maq and Inupiat Aakuu games, how to play   2311:109-111

**IOWA—COOKERY**

Caramel apples, recipe   2536:63
Popzacorn balls, recipe   2534:31

**IRAN—COOKERY**

Pita toppers, recipe   2924:10-11
Walnut, fenugreek and yogurt soup, recipe   2838:12-13

**IRAN—GAMES**

Anou game, how to play   2525:137
Kick the hat, how to play   2767:87
Omlar game, how to play   2525:31
Tickum-tackum game, how to play   2385:17
Who was it, how to play   2767:87-88

**IRAN—HANDICRAFTS**

Marblizing paper, paints, making   2407:13

**IRAN—NEW YEAR—PLANTS**

Nouruz, sabzeh, pot of wheat or lentil seeds, making   2402:32-33

**IRANIAN-AMERICANS—COOKERY.** *See* **PERSIAN-AMERICANS (IRANIANS)—COOKERY**

**IRAQ—COOKERY**

Pita toppers, recipe   2924:10-11

**IRAQ—GAMES**

Knucklebones, how to play   2767:88-89

**IRELAND—COOKERY**

Apple and barley pudding, recipe   2595:51
Colcannon, recipe   2838:22-23
Irish soda bread, recipe   2656:17
Tea bread, recipe   2931:19

**IRELAND—COSTUMES**

Boy and girl costumes, patterns   2758:48-49

**IRELAND—DANCES**

Irish jig, how to do   2758:37

**IRELAND—FOLKLORE**

Activities, finger plays, songs, rhymes, crafts, patterns   2829:64-65
*Clever Leprechaun,* folktales, puppets, patterns, songs, food   2591:14-16
*Eileen and the Three Hags,* story and activities   2423:83-95
*Jack and the Traveling Animals,* story and activities   2423:104-119
*Trembling,* story and activities   2423:133-166

**IRELAND—GAMES**

Dead fox game, how to play   2931:23
Hot potato game, how to play   2385:26
Pass the Brogue, how to play   2767:89
Pig in the middle ball game, how to play   2385:28

**IRELAND—HANDICRAFTS**

St. Bridget's cross, paper, making   2407:60

**IRELAND—LANGUAGE**

Gaelic language, learn to speak a few words   2595:47

**IRELAND—LEPRECHAUNS**

Plant leprechaun; plastic cup, potting soil, wiggle eyes, grass seed, making   2931:29

**IRELAND—TEA PARTIES—COOKERY**

Green clover cookies, recipe   2643:54
How to plan and set the table   2643:52-53
Irish breakfast tea, recipe   2643:54

**IRELAND—TEA PARTIES—HANDICRAFTS**

Painting pots and planting shamrocks, how to do   2643:55

**IRISH-AMERICANS—COOKERY**

Colcannon, recipe   2879:149
Corned beef and cabbage, recipe   2879:150
Irish bread, recipe   2879:148-149
Potato-chive pancakes, recipe   2879:149-150

**IROQUOIS INDIANS—BASKETS**

Cherokee and Iroquois stenciled baskets, baskets, paints, making   2350:14-15

**IROQUOIS INDIANS—COOKERY**

Corn soup, recipe   2287:62
Onondaga ghost bread, recipe   2879:152
Roast corn soup, recipe   2879:151
Strawberry juice, recipe   2398:15
Yellow squash soup, recipe   2879:153

**IROQUOIS INDIANS—DREAMCATCHERS**

Dreamcatcher, embroidery hoop, yarn, beads, feathers, paints, making   2261:28-29

**IROQUOIS INDIANS—FOLKLORE**

Great turtle sculpture, clay, paints, yarn, beads, making   2350:20-21

## IROQUOIS INDIANS—GAMES

Snow snake game, how to make snow snake from tree branch 2261:27

## IROQUOIS INDIANS—HATS

Feathers-in-front hat, quills, paper, paints, making 2621:53

Iroquois gestowah hat with draping feathers, paper, feathers, patterns, making 2621:53

## IROQUOIS INDIANS—HOUSES

Model longhouse, shoebox, twigs, felt, paints, making 2887:28-29

## IROQUOIS INDIANS—LANGUAGE

Everyday words in Mohawk language 2287:96-99

## IROQUOIS INDIANS—MASKS

False face mask, clay, paints, pattern, making 2350:24-25

Iroquois cornhusk mask, cardboard, cornhusks, making 2350:18-19

Iroquois false face masks, paper, raffia, yarn, patterns, making 2621:41

Spirit mask, papier-mâché, paints, making 2804:34-35

## IROQUOIS INDIANS—MUSICAL INSTRUMENTS

Birch bark rattle, cardboard, felt strips, yarn, beads, patterns, making 2621:47

Dew claw ankle rattle, scrunchy, paper, patterns, making 2621:47

Gourd rattle, papier-mâché, stickers, feathers, beans, paints, patterns, making 2621:47

## IROQUOIS INDIANS—POUCHES

Iroquois thunderbird pouch, paper, ribbons, beads, yarn, making 2621:33

## IROQUOIS INDIANS—TREE OF PEACE

Iroquois tree of peace, pine tree branch, coffee can, making 2311:13-16

## ISLAM—BIRTH CUSTOMS—COOKERY

Lentil soup, recipe 2963:13

## ISLANDS—FICTION

*Hey, Al* by Arthur Yorinks, literature, activities, art, curriculum 2436:53-64

## ISRAEL—COOKERY

Baked fish, recipe 2256:48

Bean soup, recipe 2256:46

Carrot salad, recipe 2457:32

Cheese blintzes, recipe 2256:42-43

Egg and tomato scramble, recipe 2256:32

Falafel in pita, recipe 2256:37

Falafel patties, recipe 2453:108

Falafel, recipe 2940:23

Ground meat with sesame sauce, recipe 2256:47

Haman's ears, recipe 2396:62-63

Hummus, recipe 2256:38

Israeli doughnuts, recipe 2256:36

Israeli salad, recipe 2256:33

Melon dessert, recipe 2256:44

Pita toppers, recipe 2924:10-11

Poppy seed cake, recipe 2256:50-51

## ISRAEL—COSTUMES

Boy and girl costumes, patterns, making 2753:112

## ISRAEL—DANCES

Hora dance, how to do 2940:39

Hora, how to dance; Sukkot, song words and music given 2414:26-27

## ISRAEL—FESTIVALS—COOKERY

Chicken stuffed with oranges, recipe 2256:63

Haman's ears, recipe 2256:60

Independence Day; honey roasted chicken, recipe 2962:54

Independence Day; hummus, recipe 2962:51

Independence Day; Israeli salad, recipe 2962:52

Independence Day; Mandelbrot, recipe 2962:55

Independence Day; tabbouleh, recipe 2962:53

Noodle pudding, recipe 2256:65

Passover popovers, recipe 2256:66

Passover; haroset balls, recipe 2305:53

Sabbath stew, recipe 2256:69

Sukkot stew, recipe 2256:56

Teyglakh, recipe 2256:54-55

Tu B'Shevat salad, recipe 2256:64

## ISRAEL—GAMES

Adras, tic-tac-toe game, how to play 2940:33

Circle balance game, how to play 2525:52

Country and city game, how to play 2525:75

Five stone jacks game, how to make and play 2882:8-9

Hamesh Avanim jacks game, how to play 2330:122-123

Hat race, how to play 2767:90

Passing in the square game, how to play 2525:173

Shooball game, how to play 2525:105

Shoot the top game, how to play 2525:108

## ISRAEL—LANGUAGE

Few basic words in Hebrew and Arabic 2305:51

Hebrew words for family members 2457:19

Phrases in Hebrew, how to say numbers, days of the week   2453:113

**ISRAEL—MOSAICS**

Mosaic, paper, glue, making   2457:37

**ISRAEL—NEW YEAR—COOKERY**

Rosh Hashanah, apples dipped in honey, recipe 2402:34-35

**ISRAEL—PASSOVER—COOKERY**

Spicy eggplant, recipe   2737:134-135
Sweet Israel chicken, recipe   2737:135-136

**ISRAEL—PASSOVER—HANDICRAFTS**

Jerusalem puzzle, a paper cut Mizrach, making 2737:180-187

**ISRAEL—PURIM—COOKERY**

Hamantashen cookies, recipe   2414:30-31

**ISRAEL—SCROLLS**

Tora Megillah scroll, cardboard tubes, paper, paints, making   2414:28-29

**ISRAEL—TREES**

Orange tree model, paper tube, paper, making 2686:60-61

**ISRAELITES—ARMOR**

Armored vest, fabric, plastic jugs, pattern, making   2746:86-88

**ISRAELITES—BRICKS**

Baking bricks, clay, straw, making   2746:49-50

**ISRAELITES—CALENDAR**

Calendar, paper plate calendar, making   2746:76-78

**ISRAELITES—CANAAN—MAP**

Build a salt-dough map, salt dough, paints, pattern, making   2746:83-84

**ISRAELITES—CLOTHING**

Armbands or ankle bracelets, pipe cleaners, making   2313:22
Boy's tunic, kilt and belt; t-shirt, fabric, making 2313:19
Boy's turban, bed sheets, making   2313:20
Girls headscarf, fabric, making   2313:22

**ISRAELITES—COOKERY**

Ancient Israelite meal, how to serve and eat 2313:41
Stomping grapes into juice, how to do   2313:40
Unleavened bread, recipe   2746:57-58

**ISRAELITES—DOLLS**

Egyptian paddle doll, cardboard, paints, beads, making   2746:52-53

**ISRAELITES—FAMILY TREE**

Family tree, how to make   2746:90

**ISRAELITES—FARMS**

Terrace farm model, plastic dishpan, cardboard, dirt, making   2313:32
Water; balancing act, carrying water, how to do 2313:34

**ISRAELITES—GAMES**

No yeast game, how to play   2746:59

**ISRAELITES—HOUSES**

Basket; design a bee basket, plastic bottle, burlap, making   2746:108-109
Build with headers and stretchers, how to do 2746:98
Foot washing, how to do   2746:105
Furniture making, clay, twine, felt, making 2313:13
Keeping clean, how to do   2746:103
Pillared house model, cardboard box, pebbles, paints, making   2313:9-12
Washing clothes, how to do   2746:106

**ISRAELITES—LAMPS**

Lamp; oil lamp, clay, making   2746:101-102

**ISRAELITES—MEASUREMENT**

Measuring tape, fabric, ribbon, making   2746:132-133
Scale, stick, string, cups, making   2746:134-135

**ISRAELITES—MUSICAL INSTRUMENTS**

Cymbals; make cymbals, metal lids   2746:118
Lyre; make a lyre, plastic hanger, rubber bands   2746:113
Sistrum; make a sistrum, milk carton, dowel, wire   2746:114-115
Timbrel; make a timbrel, wooden embroidery hoops, ribbon, bells   2746:116-117
Trumpet, poster board, making   2746:67-68

**ISRAELITES—NAMES**

Choosing a new name, list of names and meanings   2746:139

**ISRAELITES—RELIGION**

Blessing scroll, foil, string, making   2313:46
High Priest's breastplate, poster board, gold wrap, buttons, ribbon, making   2746:73
High Priest's outfit and turban, paper, plastic bag, gold wrap, making   2746:72

**ISRAELITES—SCROLLS**

Create your own seal, clay, making   2746:148-149
Cyrus cylinder, cardboard tube, making 2746:146-147

**ISRAELITES—SPICES**

Spice chart, poster board, markers, making 2746:161-162

**ISRAELITES—TITHES**

Calculate tithes, how to do    2746:158-159

**ISRAELITES—TWELVE TRIBES—MAP**

Puzzle map, Styrofoam trays, pattern, making 2746:93-95

**ISRAELITES—WEAPONS**

Bow and quiver of arrows, stick, string, making 2746:123-125

Sling and some stones, making    2746:121-122

Serpent-headed throwing stick, wooden spoon, paints, making    2746:54-55

**ISRAELITES—WRITING**

Stamp seal, clay, string, making    2313:28-29

Writing Ancient Israelite style, how to do 2313:25

Writing on a smashed pot, clay flower pot, artist's charcoal, making    2313:25

**ITALIAN-AMERICANS—COOKERY**

Chicken cacciatore, recipe    2879:153-154

Greens and beans, recipe    2879:154

Meatballs and spaghetti, recipe    2879:155-156

Pasta and bean soup, recipe    2879:154-155

Red and white herb roasted potatoes, recipe 2879:157

Risotto, recipe    2879:156-157

**ITALY—CHRISTMAS—DECORATIONS**

La Befana witch, pattern, making    2753:91

Nativity scene, felt, wooden beads, yarn, fancy trims, making    2740:32-35

Wreath, pattern, making    2753:94

**ITALY—CHRISTMAS—PUPPETS**

La Befana puppet, pattern, making    2753:95

**ITALY—COOKERY**

Antipasto, recipe    2962:57

Appetizer, recipe    2299:32

Asparagus with parmesan and butter, recipe 2574:56-57

Baked fish and potatoes, recipe    2606:28-29

Biscuit tortoni, recipe    2299:56

Bisignano spinach, recipe    2299:49

Bocconcini salad, recipe    2924:15

Bruschetta (bread and tomato dish), recipe 2299:60

Bruschetta (garlic bread), recipe    2606:34-35

Bruschetta, tomato and basil topping on toast, recipe    2434:8-9

Bruschetta, tomato mixture on bread, recipe 2271:68

Butterfly pizza, recipe    2717:17-18

Butternut squash soup, recipe    2606:12-13

Cheese and tomato pizza, recipe    2606:22-23

Chicken, hunter's style, recipe    2299:47

Chicken, hunter's style, recipe    2574:52-54

Chinese pasta, recipe    2299:36-37

Chocolate and walnut cake, recipe    2574:62-63

Chocolate risotto, recipe    2606:38-39

Cotolette alla Milanese, Milanese-style veal scallops, recipe    2434:28-29

Country-style pork, recipe    2574:54-55

Crostini, chicken liver toasts, recipe 2434:10-11

Double chocolate walnut biscotti, recipe 2396:47

Eggplant and mozzarella towers, recipe 2606:30-31

Fava bean pate with ciabatta toast, recipe 2838:10-11

Fresh fruit with strawberry glaze, recipe 2574:64

Gelato di crema con salsa al cioccolato, ice cream with chocolate sauce, recipe 2434:36-37

Gnocchi al ragu, potato gnocchi with meat sauce, recipe    2434:20-21

Green beans with tomatoes, Roman style, recipe 2574:59

Hot cross buns, recipe    2299:63

Instant polenta, recipe    2574:47

Italian pasta bar, recipe    2924:16-17

Italian salad dressing, recipe    2299:33

Italian-style cauliflower, recipe    2299:50

Italian-style pork chops, recipe    2299:44

Lasagne, recipe    2606:20-21

Lemon granita, recipe    2606:42-43

Lentil soup, recipe    2380:unp

Linguine with pesto, recipe    2299:61

Margherita pizza, recipe    2717:22-23

Minestrone soup, recipe    2299:35

Minestrone soup, recipe    2606:10-11

Mini-pizzas, recipe    2717:20-21

Mixed salad, recipe    2574:26-27

Pasta al pesto, pasta with basil sauce, recipe 2434:18-19

Pasta Carbonara, recipe    2606:18-19

Pasta sauce from Bologna, recipe    2574:38-39

Pasta with spring vegetables, recipe 2574:32-33

Penne al pomodoro, pasta with tomato and basil sauce, recipe    2434:14-15

Pesce finto, false fish, potatoes and tuna dish, recipe    2434:30-31

Pesto pasta, recipe    2381:unp
Pesto, recipe    2606:36-37
Pizza buns, recipe    2852:122-123
Pizza dough, recipe    2574:42-43
Pizza from Naples, recipe    2574:44-45
Pizza, recipe    2271:48-49
Pizza, recipe    2275:30-31
Pizza, recipe    2299:54-55
Pizza, recipe    2434:12-13
Polenta and goat cheese salad, recipe
    2606:14-15
Polenta pie with sausage and cheese, recipe
    2574:48-49
Polpette al pomodoro, meatballs with tomato
    sauce, recipe    2434:26-27
Potato and blue cheese calzone, recipe
    2606:24-25
Rice and pea risotto, recipe    2299:64
Rich meat broth, recipe    2574:20
Risotto (rice dish), recipe    2299:40
Risotto, parmesan and saffron risotto, recipe
    2434:24-25
Shrimp and mushroom risotto, recipe
    2606:26-27
Spaghetti and meatballs, recipe    2574:35-36
Spaghetti Bolognese, recipe    2606:16-17
Spaghetti with meat sauce, recipe    2299:43
Straw and hay creamy noodles, recipe    2299:39
Stuffed pasta in broth, recipe    2299:67
Sun pizza, recipe    2717:19
Swordfish pasta, Sicilian style, recipe
    2574:40-41
Tagliatelle, fresh pasta with tomato sauce,
    recipe    2434:16-17
Tiramisu, creamy chocolate surprise dessert,
    recipe    2434:34-35
Tomato salad, recipe    2574:25
Tomato sauce, recipe    2574:37
Torta al cioccolato, chocolate cake, recipe
    2434:32-33
Vanilla ice cream, recipe    2606:40-41
Vegetable frittata, recipe    2606:32-33
Vegetable soup, recipe    2574:23-24

## ITALY—COSTUMES

Boy and girl costumes, patterns, making
    2753:92

## ITALY—EASTER—COOKERY

Cassata (ice cream dessert), recipe    2677:16
Colomba, bread, recipe    2677:12-13
Easter pie, recipe    2888:117

## ITALY—FESTIVALS—COOKERY

All Soul's Day; dead bone cookies, recipe
    2299:68
All Soul's Day; dead bone cookies, recipe
    2481:66
Bruschetta, recipe    2962:58
Carnavale; tramezzini sandwiches, recipe
    2504:52-53
Carnival; carnevale, cenci treats, recipe
    2434:22-23
Independence Day; garlic bread, recipe
    2962:58
Independence Day; tomato sauce, recipe
    2962:59
Sagra del Basiclico (Basil Festival); linguine
    with pesto, recipe    2481:42
St. Joseph's Day; bread, recipe    2888:77-78
St. Joseph's Day; chocolate biscotti, recipe
    2888:81-82
St. Joseph's Day; cornmeal butter cookies, recipe
    2888:83
St. Joseph's Day; doughnuts, recipe    2888:76
St. Joseph's Day; pastries, recipe    2888:79-80
Tiramisu (dessert), recipe    2962:61
Veal marsala, recipe    2962:60

## ITALY—FESTIVALS—DECORATIONS

Corpus Christi pictures out of flowers celebra-
    tion, how to do    2275:26-27

## ITALY—FESTIVALS—MASKS

Carnevale; masks, papier-mâché, balloon, paints,
    making    2504:50-52
Carnival mask, paper, feathers, sequins, making
    2275:28-29

## ITALY—FOLKLORE

*Cenerentola,* story and activities    2423:135-166
*Grandfather's Rock,* folktales, puppets, patterns,
    songs, food    2591:19-21

## ITALY—GAMES

Angels and demons, how to play    2767:90-91
Bocce game, how to play    2465:54-55
Bocce, how to play    2825:18
Claudia Berni game, how to play    2525:168
Crab soccer game, how to play    2525:42
Le Lotto, bingo game, how to play    2310:31-36
Morra, how to play    2767:91
Palo Berni game, how to play    2525:98
Scout ball game, how to play    2525:133
Uno, due, tre, stella game, how to play    2385:24
Wolf and lamb, how to play    2767:91-92

**ITALY—HANDICRAFTS**

Confetti, colored papers, magazine photographs, making   2407:22

Quilling, paper, glue, making   2407:69

**ITALY—LANGUAGE**

Days of the week in Italian   2327:107

Learn a little Italian   2472:52

Numbers in Italian   2327:107

**ITALY—LANTERNS**

Copper luminaries, copper sheet, brass brads, candles, patterns, making   2884:77-79

**ITALY—MASKS**

Venetian masks, paper, straws, glitter, sequins, making   2407:79

**ITALY—PASSOVER—COOKERY**

Sephardic Italian rice soup, recipe 2737:131-132

**ITALY—WEDDINGS—COOKERY**

Wedding cookies, recipe   2825:23

**IVORY COAST—GAMES**

Awele, how to play   2767:92-93

**IVORY COAST—MASKS**

Goli dance simple masks, cardboard, paints, buttons, making   2620:44-45

**IVORY COAST—STAFFS**

Akuba figure from the Akamba Peoples in Kenya, cardboard, paints, making 2620:44-45

Elephant staff carved by the Ashanti Peoples, cardboard, paints, making   2620:44-45

Horned staff made for a Zulu chief, cardboard, paints, making   2620:44-45

Human figure with Tsongan helmet and leg and neck rings, cardboard, paints, making 2620:44-45

# J

**JACKSON, ANDREW (PRESIDENT)**
  Bubble pipe collage, patterns, making   2263:32
  Football classic checkers game board, making
    2263:34
  Miniature portraits, patterns, making   2263:33
  Pretzel log cabin, patterns, making   2263:32

**JAMAICA—CHRISTMAS—COOKERY**
  Sorrel drink, recipe   2925:64
  Sweet potato pone, recipe   2925:63

**JAMAICA—CHRISTMAS—DECORATIONS**
  Tassel, yarn, making   2403:30-31

**JAMAICA—COOKERY**
  Akkra (black-eyed peas and chick peas), recipe
    2925:52
  Banana fritters, recipe   2960:52
  Banana porridge, recipe   2960:52
  Beef soup, recipe   2960:53
  Curried lamb, recipe   2925:44
  Curry chicken, recipe   2960:52
  Duckunoo, recipe   2925:57
  Escovitch fish, recipe   2925:41
  Jamaican patties, recipe   2925:42-43
  Jerk chicken, recipe   2911:50
  Pepperpot soup, recipe   2925:30
  Stamp and go, recipe   2925:40
  Vegetable callaloo, recipe   2960:53

**JAMAICA—GAMES**
  Because, yes, and no, how to play   2767:93
  Circle goal game, how to play   2525:167
  Copy us game, how to play   2525:180

**JAMAICA—LANGUAGE**
  Patois words and expressions   2322:23

**JAMAICA—WEAVING**
  Jamaican woven fish, paper, making
    2817:52-57

**JAMAICAN-AMERICANS—COOKERY**
  Curry goat/chicken, recipe   2879:158
  Oxtail stew with vegetables, recipe   2879:158

**JANUARY THEMES**
  Thematic units, lessons, activities, art, poetry,
    crafts, patterns, recipes   2320:129-157

**JAPAN—ABACUS**
  Abacus from box lid and beads, making
    2758:105

**JAPAN—BIRTHDAYS—GAMES**
  Hanetsuki game, how to play   2957:26

**JAPAN—BIRTHDAYS—SAMURAI HELMET**
  Origami samurai helmet, paper, making
    2957:28-29

**JAPAN—BOWING**
  How to bow correctly   2454:103

**JAPAN—CATS**
  Welcoming store cats, clay, paints, making
    2819:30-33

**JAPAN—CHOPSTICKS**
  Hashi (chopsticks), how to use   2845:28

**JAPAN—CHRISTMAS—DECORATIONS**
  Gold fans, gold paper, yarn, making
    2403:32-33

**JAPAN—CLOTHING**
  Furoshiki, square cloth carryall, cloth, paints,
    making   2441:127-129

**JAPAN—COOKERY**
  Basic clear soup, recipe   2856:42
  Bean paste soup, recipe   2856:43
  Beef sukiyaki, recipe   2268:19
  Beef tataki, recipe   2607:26-27
  Boiled spinach, recipe   2856:49
  Broiled chicken, recipe   2856:58
  Broiled shrimp and vegetables, recipe   2856:59
  Chicken in a pot, recipe   2856:54-55
  Chicken soup, recipe   2607:18-19
  Chilled noodles, recipe   2607:22-23
  Clear soup, recipe   2607:10-11
  Cold noodles, recipe   2531:33
  Cucumber with crab, recipe   2856:48
  Eggdrop soup, recipe   2856:42
  Green beans with sesame seeds, recipe
    2607:38-39
  Green tea, how to make   2454:106
  Grilled chicken, recipe   2607:16-17
  Grilled tofu, recipe   2607:14-15

Grilled veggies with Japanese marinade on skewers, recipe   2271:46-47
Grilled zucchini with ginger, recipe   2607:34-35
Japanese lunch box, recipe   2607:42-43
Japanese menu   2856:30-31
Miso shiru seaweed and soybean soup, recipe   2380:unp
Miso soup, recipe   2765:130
Musubi rice snacks, recipe   2531:11
Noodles, recipe   2856:36-37
Nori sushi roll, recipe   2845:29
Onigiri rice snack, recipe   2611:30-31
Onigiri rice snacks, recipe   2531:11
Oyako-Domburi (chicken, mushrooms, and egg on rice), recipe   2268:11
Rice balls, recipe   2607:32-33
Rice, recipe   2271:32
Rice, recipe   2856:34
Salmon teriyaki, recipe   2607:24-25
Salt-broiled fish, recipe   2856:60
Savory custard, recipe   2607:12-13
Sesame seed dressing with broccoli, recipe   2856:46
Shrimp and vegetable stir-fry, recipe   2607:20-21
Simmered beef and vegetables, recipe   2856:52
Steamed chicken with broccoli, recipe   2607:28-29
Suimono egg and pea soup, recipe   2268:9
Sushi rice, recipe   2845:29
Sweet potatoes with soy sauce, recipe   2607:36-37
Tea, recipe   2856:38
Teriyaki chicken bowl, recipe   2765:131
Toffee sweet potatoes, recipe   2607:40-41
Toffee sweet potatoes, recipe   2906:15
Tofu steaks, recipe   2924:26-27
Tuna and egg rice bowl, recipe   2607:30-31

## JAPAN—COSTUMES
Boy's costume, pattern   2758:98
Girl's costume, pattern   2758:99

## JAPAN—DECORATIONS
Mizuhiki paper strings, making   2407:64

## JAPAN—DOLLS
Daruma doll, papier-mâché, balloon, paints, making   2611:28-29
Daruma dolls, egg, tissue paper, glue, paints, making   2819:12-17
Daruma dolls, foam balls, rock, glue, paper cup, paints, making   2407:86
Japanese doll, cardboard, plastic bottle, making   2686:42-43

Ningyo doll, folded paper, making   2407:47

## JAPAN—FAMILY CRESTS
Ka-mon family crest, paper, making   2819:18-23

## JAPAN—FANS
Fan, paper, chalk, crayons, making   2758:105
Japanese fan, red cardboard, black paint, red thread, making   2784:28-29

## JAPAN—FESTIVALS—COOKERY
Beef negimaki, recipe   2962:65
Chicken yakitori, recipe   2962:66
Girl's Day; scattered sushi rice, recipe   2856:66-67
Green tea ice cream, recipe   2962:67
Japanese salad, recipe   2962:63
Miso soup, recipe   2962:64
Obon Festival of the Dead; soba noodle soup, recipe   2504:104
Snow Festival; noodle soup with chicken and bean paste, recipe   2856:68-69

## JAPAN—FESTIVALS—DECORATIONS
Children's Day; koi nobori, carp wind sock, fabric, paints, making   2819:24-29
Kamakura Festival; snow cottages, making   2328:4-5
Koi-Nobori, Boy's Festival; carp, paper, paints, wooden dowel, making   2407:78
Kor Nobori (Children's Day); carp streamers, paper, tissue, paints, string, making   2531:23
Tanabata Matsuri Festival; paper chains, making   2407:63
Tanabata Matsuri Star Festival; tassels, folded paper, making   2407:42
Tanabata paper netting, tissue paper, making   2819:48-51

## JAPAN—FESTIVALS—DOLLS
Hini Matsuri Festival dolls, paper, markers, paste, making   2407:74

## JAPAN—FESTIVALS—FICTION
Children's Day; *A Family in Japan* by Judith Elkin, activities, crafts, patterns, games, masks, puppets, making   2329:107-110

## JAPAN—FESTIVALS—KITES
Boys Day; carp streamers, paper, crepe paper, string, making   2846:28-29
Boy's Kite Festival; kite pattern, making   2758:101
Children's Day Festival; kite, paper, patterns, making   2642:67

**JAPAN—FESTIVALS—LANTERNS**

Obon Festival of the Dead; paper lantern, paper, string, making 2504:101-102

**JAPAN—FESTIVALS—ORIGAMI**

Cherry Blossom Festival; origami blossoms, making 2611:26

**JAPAN—FESTIVALS—PUPPETS**

Koi fish puppet, pattern, making 2758:103

**JAPAN—FICTION**

*Crow Boy* by Taro Yashima; activities, art, poetry, maps, crafts, foods, patterns 2642:47-49

*Funny Little Woman* by Blair Lent, activities, projects, patterns, art, crafts 2822:97-100

*How My Parents Learned to Eat* by Ina R. Friedman; activities, art, poetry, maps, crafts, foods, patterns 2642:66-67

*Kenju's Forest* by Junko Morimoto; activities, art, poetry, maps, crafts, foods, patterns 2642:78-80

*Sachiko Means Happiness* by Kimiko Sakai; activities, art, poetry, maps, crafts, foods, patterns 2642:24-29

**JAPAN—FOLKLORE**

*Inch Boy* by Junko Morimoto; activities, art, poetry, maps, crafts, foods, patterns 2642:118-121

**JAPAN—GAMES**

Alley tag game, how to play 2525:23

Bubble game, how to play 2525:77

Daruma staring game, how to play 2531:19

Fuku Wari, how to play 2767:94-95

Go game, how to play 2926:20-23

Hit the ball game, how to play 2525:87

Ichi, ni, san game, how to play 2385:18

Ishikeri (hopscotch) game, how to play 2847:28-29

Ishikeri, hopscotch game, how to play 2310:64-68

Jan Ken Po, how to play 2767:21, 95

Mat pull game, how to play 2525:191

Menko game, how to make and play 2531:35

Nine-person skip game, how to play 2525:183

One, two, three tag game, how to play 2525:141

Otedama jacks game, how to play 2330:72-73

Otedama, how to play 2767:95-96

Paper, scissors, rock game, how to play 2882:12-13

Quick number game, how to play 2525:97

Rocky boat game, how to play 2525:58

Stick exchange game, how to play 2525:160

Surround tag game, how to play 2525:134

**JAPAN—HAIKU**

How to write haiku 2848:9

**JAPAN—HANDICRAFTS**

Birds; folded paper birds, handmade paper, wire, gold cord, making 2883:80-85

Friendship bracelets, embroidery thread, acrylic yarn, making 2440:86-90

Hoshoshi, fold and dye paper, making 2407:50

Moni Kiri crests, paper, crayons, making 2407:17

Paste-resist stenciled fabrics, fabric, dye, making 2819:42-47

**JAPAN—KIRIGAMI**

Kirigami gift tags, paper, making 2978:34

**JAPAN—LANGUAGE**

Counting from 1 to 10 in Japanese 2808:22

Japanese words for family members 2808:20

Phrases and numbers in Japanese 2454:102

**JAPAN—LANTERNS**

Japanese lantern, pattern, making 2758:104

**JAPAN—NEW YEAR'S DAY—COOKERY**

Kuri Kinton dessert, recipe 2848:25

Rice cake soup with shrimp, recipe 2481:38-39

Rice cake soup with shrimp, recipe 2856:64-65

**JAPAN—NEW YEAR'S DAY—GAMES**

Fuku Wari game, how to play 2906:19

Oshogatsu Fuki Wari game, how to make and play 2402:36-37

**JAPAN—NUMBERS**

*Count Your Way through Japan* by Jim Haskins; activities, art, poetry, maps, crafts, foods, patterns 2642:98-109

**JAPAN—ORIGAMI**

Origami box, making 2407:43

Origami butterflies, colored papers, making 2852:118-119

Origami crane, paper, making 2819:34-41

Peace crane, origami paper, making 2978:70-74

Treat cup, origami paper, making 2906:25

**JAPAN—PEARLS**

Pearl and oyster, patterns, making 2758:106

**JAPAN—POETRY**

Haiku booklets, how to make 2758:86

**JAPAN—SHRINES**

Torii gate, pattern 2758:100

**JAPAN—SONGS**

Cherry Blossom song 2611:27

**JAPAN—TEA PARTIES—COOKERY**

Green tea, recipe 2643:70

How to plan and set the table 2643:68-69

Vegetable sushi, recipe 2643:70

**JAPAN—TEA PARTIES—HANDICRAFTS**

Origami swans, making 2643:71

**JAPAN—TOYS**

Den-den daiko play drum, corrugated cardboard, yarn, paints, making 2819:52-57

**JAPAN, ANCIENT—CALLIGRAPHY**

Calligraphy, how to do 2580:44-45

**JAPAN, ANCIENT—COOKERY**

Onigiri, rice balls, recipe 2580:24-25

**JAPAN, ANCIENT—FANS**

Fan, cardstock, red paper, paints, making 2580:36-37

**JAPAN, ANCIENT—FESTIVALS**

Boy's Day; carp streamer, paper, paints, long stick, string, making 2580:26-27

**JAPAN, ANCIENT—FESTIVALS—DOLLS**

Girl's Day (Hinamatsuri); dolls, clay, balsa wood, red and gold paper, paints, making 2580:54-55

**JAPAN, ANCIENT—FLOWER ARRANGEMENTS**

Ikebana arrangement, vase, twigs, string, flowers, leaves, making 2580:58-59

**JAPAN, ANCIENT—HANDICRAFTS**

Netsuke fox inro, clay, balsa wood, small box, paints, making 2580:40-41

**JAPAN, ANCIENT—KITES**

Kite, dowels, cardstock, bamboo stick, paints, string, making 2580:14-15

**JAPAN, ANCIENT—ORIGAMI**

Origami box, origami paper, making 2580:42-43

**JAPAN, ANCIENT—PAPER**

Paper, wood, nails, muslin for screen, flower petals, making 2580:46-47

**JAPAN, ANCIENT—SAMURAI—HELMETS**

Samurai helmet, cardstock, papier-mâché, paints, making 2580:16-19

**JAPAN, ANCIENT—SCREENS**

Screen, gold paper, cardstock, paint, making 2580:28-29

**JAPAN, ANCIENT—TEA CEREMONY**

Tea bowl, clay, plastic bottle, paints, making 2580:60-61

**JAPAN, ANCIENT—THEATER MASKS**

Noh theater mask, papier-mâché, paints, cord, making 2580:48-49

**JAPANESE-AMERICANS—COOKERY**

Chicken hekka, recipe 2879:161

Pan sushi, recipe 2879:160-161

Teriyaki sauce, recipe 2879:159-160

**JAPANESE-AMERICANS—FICTION**

*Grandfather's Journey* by Allen Say, literature, activities, art, curriculum 2436:45-52

**JEFFERSON, THOMAS (PRESIDENT)**

Book collector book plates, patterns given, making 2263:15

Monticello house, picture 2263:16

Monticello weather calendar, patterns given, making 2263:15

Respectfully yours, Lewis and Clark letter, making 2263:19

**JEFFERSON, THOMAS (PRESIDENT)—COOKERY**

Thomas Jefferson's lunchbox menu 2667:29

**JESTERS—MASKS**

Jester mask, cardboard, gold bells, pipe cleaners, ribbons, making 2750:14-15

**JESUS—HANDICRAFTS**

A dove appeared, cardboard tube, making 2799:42

God cares for you, cardboard tube, making 2799:48

Jesus helps a little girl, cardboard tube, making 2799:46

Jesus loves me, cardboard tube, patterns, making 2799:43-44

Jesus' little lamb, cardboard tube, making 2799:45

Light of the world, cardboard tube, making 2799:47

Safe with Jesus, cardboard tube, patterns, making 2799:49-50

Woman at the well, cardboard tube, making 2799:51

**JEWELRY**

Language arts, poetry, hobby craft activities 2511:53-57

Zipper pull, making 2511:54

**JEWISH-AMERICANS—COOKERY**

Bagels and lox, lox roll-ups, recipe 2924:18-19

Carrot-sweet potato tzimmes, recipe 2879:164

Huevos haminadoes (egg dish), recipe 2879:163-164

Matza brie omelet, recipe    2879:163
Matzo balls, recipe    2879:162-163
Poppy seed cookies, recipe    2967:15

**JEWISH-AMERICANS—HANUKKAH—GAMES**

Dreidel game, dowel, Styrofoam, how to make and play    2967:25

**JEWS—ARK**

Ark of the covenant, decorated box, box, clay, paints, making    2507:18-19

**JEWS—COOKERY**

Apple strudel, recipe    2710:123
Fruit and avocado salad, recipe    2478:67
Kompot (Russian punch), recipe    2478:67
Kugel pudding, recipe    2381:unp
No-flour cookies, recipe    2478:67
Noodle kugel, recipe    2359:96-97
Sephardic nut cookies, recipe    2679:9

**JEWS—FICTION**

*Molly's Pilgrim* by Barbara Cohen, activities for art, music, food, clothing and history    2478:38-72
*Molly's Pilgrim* by Barbara Cohen; activities, art, poetry, maps, crafts, foods, patterns    2642:53-57

**JEWS—FOLKLORE**

*Too Noisy,* folktales, puppets, patterns, songs, food    2591:59-62

**JEWS—FOOTWEAR**

Hebrew sandals, cardboard, string, paints, making    2507:30-31

**JEWS—GAMES**

Ancient Canaanite game board, box, paper clips, clay, paints, making    2507:42-43

**JEWS—HANDICRAFTS**

Star of David, wheat or wild grass stalks, making    2440:111

**JEWS—JEWELRY**

Beaded necklace, clay, string, paints, making (recipe for salt clay given)    2507:38-39

**JEWS—LAMPS**

Oil lamp, clay, making    2507:34-35

**JEWS—LANGUAGE**

Phrases in Yiddish    2478:68

**JEWS—NEW YORK (STATE)—COOKERY**

Tzimmes, recipe    2630:25

**JEWS—NEW YORK (STATE)—SONGS**

Yiddish lullaby, words    2630:21

**JEWS—SCROLLS**

Ancient scroll, paper tubes, brown paper, paints, making    2507:22-23

**JEWS—TEMPLES**

Solomon's temple model, box, paints, making    2507:14-15

**JICARILLA APACHE INDIANS—GAMES**

Raven goes to his child, how to play    2767:168

**JOHNNY APPLESEED**

Activities, crafts, puppets, games, patterns    2762:93-100
Activities, history, poetry, songs, games, recipes    2673:7-13
*Johnny Appleseed* by Gina Ingoglia; readers theater booktalks with literature, poetry, music and creative writing activities    2681:20
Story times, activities, Johnny Appleseed tubey pattern, craft instructions    2636:56-58
Thematic units, lessons, activities, art, poetry, crafts, patterns, recipes    2320:11-40

**JOHNSON, ANDREW (PRESIDENT)**

Circus checkers, patterns, making    2263:61
Presidential history quilt, patterns, making    2263:61

**JOHNSON, LYNDON B. (PRESIDENT)**

Breath of fresh air poster, making    2263:114
Texas dominoes game, making    2263:113
Winter holiday in outer space, making    2263:114

**JORDAN—GAMES**

Tied-up monkey, how to play    2767:96-97

**JUNE THEMES**

Thematic units, lessons, activities, art, poetry, crafts, patterns, recipes    2320:279-304

TOURO COLLEGE LIBRARY

# K

**KAHLO, FRIDA**

Special self-portrait, making   2529:80-81

**KANDINSKY, WASSILY**

Painting music, how to do   2529:60

**KANSAS—COOKERY**

Crunchy sunflower cereal, recipe   2534:32

Hemetschwenger (turnovers), recipe   2415:63

**KANSAS—FESTIVALS—COOKERY**

International Pancake Derby; pancakes, recipe
2593:77

**KELLER, HELEN**

Helen Keller portrait, pattern   2758:78

**KENNEDY, JOHN F. (PRESIDENT)**

Camelot in America, castle pattern, making
2263:111-112

If I could sail to the moon, making   2263:110

Quality of life medal, making   2263:110

**KENTUCKY—COOKERY**

Corn pudding, recipe   2866:67

Finger-lickin' chicken, recipe   2534:33

Popcorn marshmallow balls, recipe   2316:63

**KENYA—COOKERY**

Avocado and papaya salad, recipe   2627:40

Baked plantain on the shell, recipe   2601:31

Chapatis, recipe   2627:33

Greens with coconut milk, recipe   2627:41

Rice pancakes, recipe   2627:33

Ugali, maize dish, recipe   2741:53

Vermicelli and raisins, recipe   2627:60

**KENYA—FESTIVALS—COOKERY**

Maulidi al Nebi; rice pancakes, recipe
2513:30-31

**KENYA—FLY WHISKS**

Fly whisk, raffia, fringe, foil, making
2513:28-29

**KENYA—GAMES**

Bottle cap checkers, how to make and
play   2310:77-81

Jackstones, how to play   2310:39-42

Jackstones jacks game, how to play   2330:66-67

Jackstones, how to play   2767:97

Kigogo board game, how to make and play
2601:37

Kigogo game, how to make and play
2513:26-27

**KENYA—LANGUAGE**

Kiswahili words for family members   2601:22

Learn to speak Kiswahili   2741:50

**KENYA—SHIELDS**

Kikuyu initiation shields, large cardboard, paints,
patterns, making   2620:34-35

**KENYA—STAFFS**

Akuba figure from the Akamba Peoples in
Kenya, cardboard, paints, making
2620:44-45

**KIENHOLZ, EDWARD**

Walk through sculpture, making   2529:98

**KIKUYU (AFRICAN PEOPLES)—SHIELDS**

Kikuyu initiation shields, large cardboard, paints,
patterns, making   2620:34-35

**KING, MARTIN LUTHER, JR. DAY**

Activities, patterns   2755:91-102

Activities, timeline, making   2592:all

Color Dr. Martin Luther King, Jr., pattern
2813:22

Dr. King portrait, pattern, making   2755:95

History of Martin Luther King Jr. Day
2813:20-21

Martin Luther King Jr. portrait pattern   2475:58

Stories, music, games, activities, projects,
patterns   2377:21-29

Whole language thematic unit of activities in language, science, math, music and life skills
2797:6-18

**KING, MARTIN LUTHER, JR.
DAY—DECORATIONS**

Black History Month banner, paper, making
2520:12-13

Circle of friendship project, paper, markers,
making   2438:42-43

"Dream" mobile, paper, yarn, patterns, making
2755:99-101

Martin Luther King, Jr. Day scroll, paper, yarn,
making   2520:8-9

**KING, MARTIN LUTHER, JR. DAY—FICTION**

*What is Martin Luther King, Jr. Day?* by Margot Parker, activities, crafts, patterns, games, masks, puppets, making 2329:67-71

**KING, MARTIN LUTHER, JR. DAY—GAMES**

Dr. Martin Luther King, Jr. missing letters game 2813:24

Dr. Martin Luther King, Jr. picture crossword game 2813:23

Words to tell about Dr. Martin Luther King, Jr. game 2813:26

**KING, MARTIN LUTHER, JR.— HANDICRAFTS**

All one family necklace, making 2731:46-47

**KINGS—CROWNS**

Royal crowns, poster board, gold paper, ribbon, making 2676:6-7

**KITES**

Garbage bag kites, making 2511:60-61

Language arts, poetry, hobby craft activities 2511:59-64

**KLEE, PAUL**

One line designs, making 2529:62-63

**KNIGHTS—CODE OF HONOR**

List of knightly code of honor 2452:26

**KNIGHTS—GAMES**

Checkerboard and pieces, how to make and play 2452:19

**KNIGHTS—HELMETS**

Helmet, foilboard, making 2452:4

**KNIGHTS—PUPPETS**

Knights in shining armor finger puppets, gloves, patterns, making 2675:72-75

**KNIGHTS—SHIELDS**

Shield of arms, cardboard, paints, making 2452:11

**KNIGHTS—SWORDS**

Sword, cardboard, foil, making 2452:9

**KNIGHTS—TOURNAMENTS**

Jousting knights, how to make and have a tournament 2452:22

**KNIGHTS—WEAPONS**

Siege catapult, shoebox, plastic spoon, rubber band, paints, making 2452:28

**KONIGSBURG, E. L.**

*Proud Taste for Scarlet and Miniver* by E. L. Konigsburg; activities, projects, reading, writing, science, social studies, food and art 2849:17-29

**KOREA—COOKERY**

Barbequed beef, recipe 2340:54

Bean sprout salad, recipe 2340:40

Bulgogi barbequed meat dish, recipe 2970:122

Cold cucumber soup, recipe 2340:42

Dipping sauces, recipes 2340:36-37

Egg pancake, recipe 2340:32

Fish patties, recipe 2340:49

Glazed chicken wings, recipe 2340:48

Grilled beef and vegetable skewers, recipe 2340:62-63

Kimchi (green cabbage dish), recipe 2340:33

Korean dumplings, recipe 2340:56-57

Korean menu 2340:28-29

Mixed vegetables with noodles, recipe 2340:46

Noodles, recipe 2340:35

Potato soup, recipe 2340:43

Seaweed rice rolls, recipe 2340:66-67

Simmered beef short ribs, recipe 2340:55

Soy-sesame tofu, recipe 2340:50

Spinach salad, recipe 2340:41

Toasted sesame seeds, recipe 2340:36

White rice, recipe 2340:34

**KOREA—FESTIVALS—COOKERY**

Harvest Moon Festival; zucchini pancakes, recipe 2340:68

Tae-Bo-Rum; five-grain dish, recipe 2340:65

**KOREA—FOLKLORE**

Activities, finger plays, songs, rhymes, crafts, patterns 2829:66-67

*Chinese Mirror* by Mirra Ginsberg; activities, art, poetry, maps, crafts, foods, patterns 2642:122-124

*Kongjee,* story and activities 2423:137-166

**KOREA—GAMES**

Eyeglasses game, how to play 2525:28

Kick the bird, how to make and play 2882:22-23

Kong Keui jacks, how to play 2493:20-23

Marbles, how to play 2767:97-98

Mek Konk, how to play 2767:98-99

Seesaw game, how to play 2970:126

**KOREA—LANGUAGE**

Common Korean words and phrases 2970:84

**KOREA—MUSICAL INSTRUMENTS**

Drum, round carton, paper, decorations, making 2686:44-45

**KOREA—NEW YEAR—COOKERY**

New Year's beef-rice cake soup, recipe 2340:60

Barbecue, recipe 2879:165-166

Marinated chicken wings, recipe    2879:165
Spinach salad, recipe    2879:166

## KOREAN-AMERICANS—FICTION

*Aekyung's Dream* by Min Paek; activities, art, poetry, maps, crafts, foods, patterns 2642:58-59

## KUBA (AFRICAN PEOPLES)—MASKS

Kuba beaded mask, railroad board, paints, puffed cereal, patterns, making    2620:32-33

## KUBLAI KHAN. *See* POLO, MARCO—KUBLAI KHAN

## KWAKIUTL INDIANS—GAMES

Quaquatsewa-iu (stick drop), how to play 2767:168-169

## KWANZAA

History of Kwanzaa    2877:92

## KWANZAA—CLOTHING

African clothes, sheet, fabric paints, making 2916:20-21

## KWANZAA—COOKERY

Baked chicken nuggets, recipe    2877:96
Banana cake, recipe    2888:254
Benne cakes, recipe    2694:7
Benne cakes, recipe    2888:252
Black-eyed pea cutlets and collard greens, recipe    2877:97
Buttermilk corn bread, recipe    2877:94
Chocolate-peanut cookie pizza, recipe 2888:248-249
Coconut custard pie, recipe    2888:253
Cornbread, recipe    2504:119-120
Cornbread, recipe    2694:11
Karamu (coconut chicken chews), recipe 2694:19
Sweet potato and coconut pudding, recipe 2888:250
Sweet potato fritters, recipe    2694:15
Sweet potato pie, recipe    2888:251
Sweet potato pudding, recipe    2877:95

## KWANZAA—DECORATIONS

Basket centerpiece, berry basket, yarn, fruits and vegetables, making    2916:18-19
Beads, colored beads, paper, making 2778:46-47

Kinara candleholder, cardboard, clay, candles, making    2440:55-56
Kinara candleholder, pattern, making    2753:127
Kinaras, paper towel tubes, colored paper, making    2262:85
Kwanzaa Day celebration candelabra, clay, candles, making    2620:70-71
Mkeke mat, red, black and green paper, making 2504:116-118
Muhindi booklet cover, pattern, making 2753:129
Strip-quilt mkeka, fabric scraps, contact paper, making    2916:22-23
Symbols of Kwanzaa, patterns, making 2753:132-133

## KWANZAA—DOLLS

People dolls, wooden doll pins, paints, making 2916:8-9

## KWANZAA—FICTION

*Kwanzaa* by A. P. Porter, activities, crafts, patterns, games, masks, puppets, making 2329:57-60

## KWANZAA—FLAGS

Bendera ya taifa cards, red and green paper, making    2916:24-25

## KWANZAA—GAMES

Mancala counting game, how to make and play    2917:40-42
Seven candles games, how to make and play 2916:6-7

## KWANZAA—HANDICRAFTS

Home bank, milk carton, markers, decorations, making    2916:16-17
Storytelling stick, foil, crepe paper, yarn, making    2916:12-13

## KWANZAA—HATS

Kufi, felt, making    2745:226-227

## KWANZAA—JEWELRY

Necklace, macaroni, paints, making 2520:20-21
Rolled paper beads, colored paper, glue, making    2916:14-15

## KWANZAA—MASKS

Two-sides-of-me flip mask, paper plates, craft sticks, making    2916:10-11

# L

**LABOR DAY**

History of Labor Day    2813:3
History of Labor Day    2877:66

**LABOR DAY—COOKERY**

Easy chicken salad, recipe    2877:69
Laid-back banana bread, recipe    2877:68
Old-fashioned peach cobbler, recipe    2877:71
September s'mores, recipe    2877:71
Virtual burgers, recipe    2877:70

**LABOR DAY—GAMES**

Labor Day card game, how to make and
    play    2813:4-5

**LAKOTA INDIANS—BEADED WORK**

Beaded wristband, denim fabric, seed beads,
    making    2311:43-48

**LAKOTA INDIANS—COOKERY**

Pemmican, recipe    2894:27-28

**LAKOTA INDIANS—FOLKLORE**

*Lodge of the Bear,* story and activities
    2423:55-63

**LAKOTA INDIANS—POUCHES**

Pouch, felt, yarn, pony beads, making
    2894:29-31

**LAKOTA INDIANS—SHIELDS**

Model shield, paper plate, feathers, embroidery
    thread, making    2894:25-26

**LAKOTA INDIANS—TRAVOIS**

Model travois, dowels, pipe cleaners, cardboard,
    making    2894:22-24

**LAKOTA-SIOUX INDIANS—COOKERY**

Beans and bacon, recipe    2879:255-256
Boiled meat, recipe    2879:254
Corn balls, recipe    2879:255
Fry bread, recipe    2879:253
Indian popovers, recipe    2879:254
Stuffed pumpkin, recipe    2879:254-255
Wojapi pudding, recipe    2879:253

**LANGE, DORTHEA**

Photo story collage, making    2529:88

**LANTERNS**

Tin-can lantern, can, wire, making    2440:40-41

**LAOS—GAMES**

Jack sticks, how to play    2767:99

**LAOTIAN-AMERICANS—COOKERY**

Broiled chicken with Jaew som, recipe
    2879:167
Mien noodle soup, recipe    2879:168-169
Salad, recipe    2879:167-168

**LATIN AMERICA—CHRISTMAS—COOKERY**

Ponche Navideno (Christmas punch), recipe
    2671:57-58

**LATIN AMERICA—CHRISTMAS—
    DECORATIONS**

Christmas tree, paper, pattern, making
    2671:49-50
Three Kings silhouettes, cardstock, patterns,
    making    2671:51-53

**LATIN AMERICA—CHRISTMAS—GOD'S EYE**

Ojos de dios, toothpicks, yarns, making
    2671:54-56

**LATIN AMERICA—CHRISTMAS—LANTERNS**

Farolitos, lanterns, paper bags, sand, candles,
    making    2671:56-57

**LATIN AMERICA—COOKERY**

Aqua de Jamaica (hibiscus flower-flavored
    water), recipe    2671:64
Macaroni salad, recipe    2381:unp
Salsa, recipe    2671:65-66
Sweet tamales, recipe    2671:65

**LATIN AMERICA—FESTIVALS**

Carnival headdress, papier-mâché, beads, feath-
    ers, paints, making    2259:16-17

**LATIN AMERICA—NEW YEAR'S DAY—
    COOKERY**

Guacamole, recipe    2984:38

**LATIN AMERICA—PIÑATAS**

Paper bag piñata, paper bag, candies, making
    2671:59-60
Papier-mâché balloon piñata, making    2671:62

**LATVIA—GAMES**

Horns, horns, who has horns?, how to play
    2767:99-100

**LATVIAN-AMERICANS—COOKERY**

Caraway rolls, recipe   2879:170
Piragi (turnovers), recipe   2879:169-170

**LAWRENCE, JACOB**

Series drawing, how to do   2529:90

**LEBANON—CHRISTMAS—DECORATIONS**

seed sprouts, how to make   2403:34-35

**LEBANON—COOKERY**

Baked fish with tahini, recipe   2254:53
Baked kibbeh, lamb dish, recipe   2254:39
Bulgar pilaf, recipe   2254:56
Bulgar salad, recipe   2254:54
Bulgar salad, recipe   2271:38
Chard and yogurt soup, recipe   2254:34
Chickpea and tahini dip, recipe   2254:44
Eggplant dip, recipe   2254:45
Fish and rice stew, recipe   2254:40-41
Garlic chicken, recipe   2254:52
Ground lamb mixture, recipe   2254:37
Kabobs, recipe   2254:57
Kibbee (wheat and meat), recipe   2879:18
Kibbee balls (wheat and ground lamb), recipe
    2879:18
Lebanese menu   2254:28-29
Lebanese pizza, recipe   2254:46
Lemonade, recipe   2254:48
Meat loaf, recipe   2254:58-59
Mediterranean meatballs, recipe   2924:12-13
Peasant salad, recipe   2254:36
Pita toppers, recipe   2924:10-11
Rice pudding, recipe   2254:68
Stuffed pancakes, recipe   2396:68-69
Stuffed tomatoes, recipe   2254:32-33
Tabbouleh, recipe   2838:28-29
Tabouli salad, recipe   2879:18-19

**LEBANON—EASTER—COOKERY**

Eid Al-Fitr; nut filled pastries, recipe   2254:64
Lent; field bean stew, recipe   2254:67

**LEBANON—FESTIVALS—COOKERY**

Eid Al-Fitr; nut filled pastries, recipe   2254:64
Ramadan stuffed pancakes with syrup, recipe
    2888:144-146
Ramadan; lentil soup, recipe   2254:66
Ramadan; stuffed pancakes, recipe   2254:62-63

**LEBANON—GAMES**

Do you have fire?, how to play   2767:100

**LENAPE INDIANS—COOKERY**

Grape dumplings, recipe   2311:9-12

**LENT—COOKERY**

Pancakes, recipe   2985:29

**LESOTHO—FOLKLORE**

*Polo, the Snake-Girl,* story and activities
    2423:126-166

**LEWIS AND CLARK**

Lewis silhouette pattern, making   2739:14

**LEWIS AND CLARK—ARTIFACTS**

Artifact, making   2739:55-57, 59

**LEWIS AND CLARK—COOKERY**

Berry soup, recipe   2739:35
Fry bread, recipe   2739:35
Pemmican, recipe   2739:34-35
Salt, recipe   2739:48

**LEWIS AND CLARK—JOURNALS**

Personal journals, making   2739:22, 25, 26

**LEWIS AND CLARK EXPEDITION**

Beeswax candles, beeswax, wick, making
    2473:106
Sharp-tailed snake, how to do   2473:64

**LEWIS AND CLARK EXPEDITION—BOATS**

Bullboat model, papier-mâché, making
    2498:98-99
Keelboat model, balsa wood, patterns, making
    2498:17-22

**LEWIS AND CLARK EXPEDITION—CANOES**

Canoe, carve from balsa wood, making
    2498:64-65

**LEWIS AND CLARK EXPEDITION—
    COOKERY**

Fruit leather, recipe   2473:20

**LEWIS AND CLARK EXPEDITION—DANCES**

Whooping crane waltz, how to do   2473:64

**LEWIS AND CLARK EXPEDITION—
    FOOTWEAR**

Moccasins, felt, beads, patterns, making
    2473:76-77
Moccasins, leather, felt, or vinyl fabric, pattern,
    making   2498:74-75

**LEWIS AND CLARK EXPEDITION—INDIANS**

Arikara Indians, Great Plains stew, recipe
    2473:44
Basket; making a basket, twisted craft paper,
    making   2473:90
Drum, acetate cloth, embroidery hoop, feathers,
    ribbons, paints, making   2473:95
Hoop and pole game, how to play   2473:56
Plains Indians dance rattle, can, dried beans,
    paints, yarn, making   2473:36-37
Plains Indians tipi, muslin, bamboo poles, paints,
    making   2473:33-34

Plains Indians, speaking in signs, how to do 2473:85

Red face paint for Indians, recipe 2473:14

Sioux winter count, paper bag, paints, making 2473:32

Tracking animals, how to do 2473:50

Trail signs, how to do 2473:114

**LEWIS AND CLARK EXPEDITION—LAND SURVEYS**

Land survey, how to do 2498:30-31

Measuring distance; deall reckoning, how to do 2498:42-44

**LEWIS AND CLARK EXPEDITION—MASKS**

Buffalo mask, paper, pattern, making 2473:70-71

**LEWIS AND CLARK EXPEDITION—PLANTS**

Preserving plants, how to do 2473:17

**LEWIS AND CLARK EXPEDITION—SUPPLIES**

Supplies for trip, list 2739:16

**LEWIS AND CLARK EXPEDITION—SURVEY INSTRUMENTS**

Sextant; how to make and use a sextant 2739:13, 20

**LIBERIA—GAMES**

Jumping game, how to play 2767:101

**LIBERTY BELL**

Liberty Bell model, plastic cup, bell, string, making 2687:6-7

Liberty bell pattern 2475:74

**LIBYA—COOKERY**

Libyan fish soup, recipe 2871:39

Libyan potatoes with bzar, recipe 2871:53

**LIBYA—GAMES**

Hop tag, how to play 2767:101-102

**LICHTENSTEIN, ROY**

Comic dots, making 2529:102

**LIGHTHOUSES**

Assemble a lighthouse, plastic soda bottle, oatmeal box, markers, making 2934:118-119

**LIGHTHOUSES—PUPPETS**

Flashing lighthouse puppet, clear plastic bottle, paper, flashlight, making 2733:36-37

**LIMBOURG BROTHERS**

Book of days, making 2529:13

**LINCOLN, ABRAHAM (PRESIDENT)**

Abraham Lincoln, pattern 2754:44

Activities, puppets, patterns, making 2754:43-54

Personal time capsule, making 2263:58

Shadow box for Lincoln, making 2263:59

Silhouette of Abraham Lincoln pattern 2475:65

**LINCOLN, ABRAHAM (PRESIDENT)—BIRTHDAY**

Color Abraham Lincoln, pattern 2813:30

February 12, 1809, stories, music, games, activities, projects, patterns 2377:37-45

History of Abraham Lincoln's birthday 2813:28-29

Whole language thematic unit of activities in language, science, math, music and life skills 2797:19-31

**LINCOLN, ABRAHAM (PRESIDENT)—BIRTHDAY—GAMES**

Abraham Lincoln puzzle game 2813:31

Abraham Lincoln word search game 2813:32

**LINCOLN, ABRAHAM (PRESIDENT)—BIRTHDAY—PUPPETS**

Abraham Lincoln lunch bag puppet, pattern, making 2813:33

**LINCOLN, ABRAHAM (PRESIDENT)—COOKERY**

Lincoln's log cabin, recipe and activities 2576:97-100

**LINCOLN, ABRAHAM (PRESIDENT)—FICTION**

*Just Like Abraham Lincoln* by Bernard Waber, activities, crafts, patterns, games, masks, puppets, making 2329:82-86

**LINCOLN, ABRAHAM (PRESIDENT)—HANDICRAFTS**

Lincoln's cabin, paper model, pattern, making 2754:52

Log cabin pattern 2475:66

**LINCOLN, ABRAHAM (PRESIDENT)—HATS**

Lincoln's beard and hat, paper, pattern, making 2754:48

Stovepipe hat, patterns, making 2263:58

Top hat memo holder, making 2263:59

**LINCOLN, ABRAHAM (PRESIDENT)—PUPPETS**

Abraham Lincoln finger puppet, paper, patterns, making 2754:57

Abraham Lincoln puppet, yogurt container, yarn, fiberfill, making 2735:32-33

**LINCOLN, ABRAHAM (PRESIDENT)—SIZE**

Sizing up Abe, how to do 2667:9

**LINCOLN, MARY TODD (FIRST LADY)—COOKERY**
Chicken for company, recipe   2554:19
Chocolate dipped strawberries, recipe   2554:9
Coconut macaroons, recipe   2554:17
Spicy sour cream cookies and brown butter, recipe   2554:7

**LINDBERGH, CHARLES**
Spirit of St. Louis model, milk carton, cardboard, making   2686:16-17

**LINDBERGH, CHARLES—COOKERY**
Lindbergh's favorite Swedish party cakes, recipe   2977:23

**LINNAEUS, CARL**
Botanical illustrations, making   2529:30

**LITHUANIAN-AMERICANS—COOKERY**
Cookie slices, recipe   2879:172
Hot dish, recipe   2879:172
Potato casserole, recipe   2879:171

**LITTLE RED HEN**
Little red hen recipe holder, cardboard, clay, making   2729:18-19

**LITTLE RED RIDING HOOD**
Baskets, making   2423:3
Little Red pop-up, making   2423:7
Map to grandmother's house, making   2423:4
Pop-up wolf, making   2423:5-6

Wolf's envelope, making   2423:9
Wolf's letter, making   2423:8

**LOBEL, ARNOLD**
*Fables*, activities, literature, art, science, poetry, social studies, webbing   2435:1-24

**LOUISIANA—COOKERY**
Bread pudding with fruit, recipe   2359:41-42
Down-on-the-bayou gumbo, recipe   2534:34-35
King cake, recipe   2359:43-45
Shrimp and ham jambalaya, recipe   2359:39-40

**LOUISIANA, NEW ORLEANS—CARNAVAL**
Carnaval mystery masks, poster board, paints, decorations, making   2852:108-109

**LUMBEE INDIANS OF NORTH CAROLINA—COOKERY**
Blueberry sheet cake, recipe   2879:174-175
Ginger bread, recipe   2879:174
Sweet potato bread, recipe   2879:173-174

**LUXEMBOURG—GAMES**
Blind flight game, how to play   2525:179
Divisible snakes game, how to play   2525:24
Fir cone hide game, how to play   2525:102
Giischt game, how to play   2525:65
Hoop game, how to play   2767:102-103
One, two, three catch game, how to play   2525:114
Reaction ball game, how to play   2525:94
Twelve big eggs game, how to play   2525:97

# M

**MACEDONIAN-AMERICANS—COOKERY**
Bulgarian cucumber soup, recipe   2879:48
Bulgarian meatball soup, recipe   2879:48-49
Macedonian-style peppers, recipe   2879:46-47
Vlach cheese corn bread, recipe   2879:47

**MADAGASCAR—CLOTHING**
Lamba, fabric, making   2391:27

**MADAGASCAR—COOKERY**
Banana milk shake, recipe   2392:30-31
Lasary voatabia salad, recipe   2661:37

**MADAGASCAR—HANDICRAFTS**
Raffia coaster, colored raffia, making
2392:28-29

**MADAGASCAR—LANGUAGE**
Malagasy words for a few phrases   2661:21
Malagasy words for family members   2661:25

**MADISON, DOLLEY (FIRST LADY)—COOKERY**
Gingersnaps, recipe   2550:21
Hard-boiled eggs, recipe   2550:13
Peppermint ice cream, recipe   2550:8
Sardine tea toasts, recipe   2550:17

**MADISON, JAMES (PRESIDENT)**
Feathered headdress, patterns, making   2263:21
Heroine's scrapbook, making   2263:20
Montpelier bean mosaic, making   2263:20
Montpelier picture   2263:21
Patriotic parrot, patterns, making   2263:21

**MAGRITTE, RENÉ**
Giant tennis shoes, making   2529:77

**MAINE—COOKERY**
Blueberry pie, recipe   2635:25
Blueberry pie, recipe   2974:25
Hard-rock candy, recipe   2534:36-37

**MAINE—FICTION**
*Time of Wonder* by Robert McCloskey, activities, literature, science, poetry, social studies, webbing   2435:171-200

**MAKAH INDIANS—GAMES**
Shuttlecock, how to play   2767:169-170

**MALAGASY.** *See* **MADAGASCAR**

**MALAWI—COOKERY**
Peanut puffs, recipe   2396:33

**MALAWI—GAMES**
Chuchu, how to play   2767:103-104

**MALAWI—TOYS**
Galimoto, motorcar toy, sticks, old wires, making
2310:95-98

**MALAYSIA—BIRTHDAY CUSTOMS**
Malaysian birthday customs   2547:12-13

**MALAYSIA—COOKERY**
Begedil, potato cutlet, recipe   2638:123
Nasi lemak, coconut rice with anchovy or prawn side dish, recipe   2638:130
Satay citarasa, beef, squid and chicken barbequed, recipe   2638:131

**MALAYSIA—GAMES**
Main Chuta game, how to play   2767:104
Main Serembam game, how to play   2767:105
Ram, ram, rip game, how to play   2385:17

**MALAYSIA—LANGUAGE**
Simple phrases in Bahasa Malaysia   2638:82

**MALAYSIA—SKYSCRAPERS**
Petronas Towers model, how to build from milk cartons   2499:37

**MALI (AFRICAN PEOPLES)— FESTIVALS— HATS**
Chi Wara Festival; hats, cardboard, paints, raffia, patterns, making   2620:58-59

**MALI (AFRICAN PEOPLES)—GAMES**
Sey, how to play   2767:105-106

**MALI (AFRICAN PEOPLES)—MUD CLOTH**
Mud cloth, fabric, paints, embroidery floss, patterns, making   2620:22-23

**MALTA—EASTER—COOKERY**
Figolla, egg pastry, recipe   2677:14-15

**MALTA—GAMES**
Maltese Cross dominoes game, how to play
2548:16

**MANDAN INDIANS—BOATS**
Bullboat model, papier-mâché, making
2498:98-99

**MANDAN INDIANS—COOKERY**

Cornballs, recipe   2288:57

**MANDAN INDIANS—GAMES**

Hoop and pole game, how to play   2473:56

**MANDAN INDIANS—HOUSES**

Earth lodge model, indoors or out, making
2498:56

**MANDAN INDIANS—LANGUAGE**

Everyday words in Mandan language
2288:96-99

**MANET, EDOUARD**

Still-life in melted crayon, making   2529:38

**MAORIS—CLOTHING**

Maori grass skirt, raffia, ribbon, making
2934:135-136

**MAORIS—FOLKLORE**

*Maui and the Secret Fire,* story and activities   2423:71-78

**MAORIS—GAMES**

Hipitoi, how to play   2767:115

Polly put the kettle on jacks game, how to play
2330:84-85

**MAORIS—HAKA**

Maori haka chant, how to do   2458:27

**MAORIS—HOUSES**

Pare carving, design given, cardboard, paints,
making   2458:28-29

**MAORIS—TATTOOS**

How to tattoo your face like a Maori warrior
2458:26

**MAPS**

Antique map and case, how to make
2700:37-39

Deep map (below the surface map), how to
make   2700:54-57

Grid map, how to make   2700:41

How to make a map like a cartographer
2700:34-36

Mail map, how to make   2700:59

Neighborhood map, how to make   2700:42-43

**MARCH THEMES**

Thematic units, lessons, activities, art, poetry,
crafts, patterns, recipes   2320:185-219

**MARDI GRAS—COOKERY**

Bread pudding with fruit, recipe   2359:41-42

King cake, recipe   2359:43-45

King cake, recipe   2504:59-62

Shrimp and ham jambalaya, recipe   2359:39-40

**MARDI GRAS—DECORATIONS**

Carnival bead throws, beads, string, making
2504:57

**MARDI GRAS—MASKS**

Mardi Gras mask, paper, glitter, sequins, feathers, making   2542:42-43

Masquerade feather-work masks, cardboard,
feathers, string, making   2440:37-38

Paper plate masks, Mardi Gras design patterns,
making   2262:85-87

**MARDI GRAS—MUSICAL INSTRUMENTS**

Maracas, paper plates, Mardi Gras designs, rice,
patterns, making   2262:85-87

Tambourine, paper plates, dried beans and macaroni, beads, making   2784:6-7

**MARTIN, JAQUELINE BRIGGS**

*Snowflake Bentley* by Jaqueline Briggs Martin,
activities, literature, science, poetry, social
studies, webbing   2435:151-170

**MARYLAND—COOKERY**

Baked Anapolis seafood casserole, recipe
2502:63

Patty-cake crab cakes, recipe   2534:38

**MASACCIO, TOMMASSO**

Profile portrait, making   2529:17

**MASAI (AFRICAN PEOPLES)—JEWELRY**

Masai beaded necklace, paints, paper plate,
making   2686:67-68

Masai beaded women's collars, cardboard, paper
plates, markers, making   2620:42-43

Masai earrings, cardboard, string, markers,
making   2620:42-43

**MASKS**

Fantasy masks, making   2511:66

Language arts, poetry, hobby craft activities
2511:65-69

**MASSACHUSETTS—COOKERY**

Chocolate chip cookies, recipe   2567:62

Sugar-baked beans, recipe   2534:39

**MATISSE, HENRI**

Matisse collage, poster board, paper, patterns,
making   2326:12-13

Story color collage, making   2529:58

**MAY DAY**

Activities, crafts, plants, flowers, patterns
2759:35-54

**MAY DAY—DECORATIONS**

Fabric flower, making   2778:22-23

May baskets, paper, making   2407:55

**MAY DAY—MUSICAL INSTRUMENTS**

Flower drum, coffee can, flower patterns, making 2262:88-89

**MAY THEMES**

Thematic units, lessons, activities, art, poetry, crafts, patterns, recipes 2320:249-278

**MAYANS**

Ancient people of Mexico, history, activities 2759:72-75

**MAYANS—BATIK**

Batiker of Mayan Gods; careers in work, projects, stories, recipes, activities 2823:21-24

**MAYANS—CODEX**

Codex, cardboard, paints, making 2581:46-47

**MAYANS—COOKERY**

Tortillas, recipe 2365:89

**MAYANS—GAMES**

Bul game board, how to make and play 2365:88

Patolli board game, how to make and play 2581:56-57

**MAYANS—HOUSES**

Mayan house model, cardboard, plaster paste, balsa wood, paints, making 2581:20-21

**MAYANS—LANGUAGE**

Maya numbers used for secret number code, how to do 2353:41

Name, how to write using Maya syllabary 2353:44-45

Secret messages, how to write 2353:46-47

Stelae, make your own using Maya glyphs 2353:42-43

Words and phrases to use in the Yucatan 2365:43

**MAYANS—MATHEMATICS**

Figures zero through nineteen in Mayan; use numbers to do simple arithmetic 2571:8

**MAYANS—POTTERY**

Mayan clay pot, clay, paints, making 2581:36-37

**MAYANS—PRAYERS**

Prayer of rain forest people before cutting trees 2579:15

**MAYANS—PYRAMIDS**

Pyramid staircase, pattern, making 2759:74

**MAYANS—TEMPLES**

Pyramid temple, cardboard, balsa wood, paints, making 2581:52-53

**MAYANS—WEAVING**

Weaver; interview, projects, stories, recipes, activities 2823:151-153

**MAYFLOWER**

Mayflower, pattern, making 2760:90

Stained glass Mayflower, paper, tissue paper, making 2690:6-7

**MCCLOSKEY, ROBERT**

*Time of Wonder*, activities, literature, science, poetry, social studies, webbing 2435:171-200

**MCCULLY, EMILY ARNOLD**

*Mirette on the High Wire* by Emily Arnold McCully, activities, literature, art, science, poetry, social studies, webbing 2435:47-73

**MCDERMOTT, GERALD**

*Arrow to the Sun* by Gerald McDermott, literature, activities, art, curriculum 2436:1-13

**MCKINLEY, WILLIAM (PRESIDENT)**

Car Show 2000, making 2263:82

Red carnation sculptures, making 2263:82

**MELUNGEONS—COOKERY**

Chocolate gravy, recipe 2879:176-177

Stack cake, recipe 2879:177-178

Tomato gravy, recipe 2879:176-177

**MEMORIAL DAY**

History of Memorial Day 2877:50

**MEMORIAL DAY—COOKERY**

Cucumber, yogurt and mint salad, recipe 2877:52

Orange couscous, recipe 2877:53

Sweet and sour meatballs, recipe 2877:54

Veteran's vegetable kebabs, recipe 2877:55

Waldorf salad, recipe 2877:52

Wild rice pilaf, recipe 2877:53

**MEMORIAL DAY—DECORATIONS**

Cloud of witnesses Memorial Day mobile, making 2798:57-58

Memorial Day poppy, foil, red tissue, making 2735:14-15

**MENOMINEE INDIANS—COOKERY**

Wild rice, how to cook, recipe 2413:43

Wild rice, popped, how to cook, recipe 2413:44

**MERMAIDS**

Story times, activities, mermaid tubey pattern, craft instructions 2636:50-52

**MESOPOTAMIA—ARMIES**

Chariot model, cardboard, papier-mâché, dowel, cardboard tubes, paints, making 2654:42-43

## MESOPOTAMIA—BOATS

Boat, clay, dowel, paints, making    2654:34-35

## MESOPOTAMIA—BURIALS

Gold burial helmet, papier-mâché over balloon, old and black paint, making    2654:20-21

## MESOPOTAMIA—COOKERY

Booshala soup, recipe    2879:26-27

Flat egg and fresh herb pancakes, recipe 2879:26

Lettuce leaves with honey, vinegar and mint, recipe    2879:25

Zazich dip, recipe    2879:26

## MESOPOTAMIA—HOUSESHOLD ITEMS

Bronze and ivory mirror, silver cardboard, dowel, papier-mâché, paints, making 2654:46-47

Painted plate, papier-mâché over plate, paints, making    2654:32-33

Ram-headed drinking cups, papier-mâché over paper cup, paints, making    2654:30-31

## MESOPOTAMIA—JEWELRY

Necklace, clay, wire, paints, making 2654:28-29

## MESOPOTAMIA—KINGS—CLOTHING

Royal tunic, fabric, fabric paints, making 2654:50-51

## MESOPOTAMIA—KINGS—FLY WHISKS

Fly whisk, fabric, cardboard, paints, making 2654:52-53

## MESOPOTAMIA—KINGS—PARASOLS

Parasol, cardstock, string, paints, making 2654:40-41

## MESOPOTAMIA—MUSICAL INSTRUMENTS

Lyre, cardboard, dowel, papier-mâché, balsa wood, paints, making    2654:24-25

## MESOPOTAMIA—SEALS

Cylinder seal, clay, cardboard roll, making 2654:14-15

## MESOPOTAMIA—TEMPLES

Ziggurat temple model, cardboard, paints, making    2654:18-19

## MESOPOTAMIA—WEIGHTS

Set of lion weights, pebbles, clay, paints, making    2654:56-57

## MESOPOTAMIA—WRITING TABLETS

Clay tablet, cardboard, clay, paint, making 2654:12-13

## MEXICAN-AMERICANS (CHICANOS)—COOKERY

Chicken enchilada casserole, recipe    2879:182

Chicken pozole, recipe    2879:181

Chili beans, recipe    2879:180-181

Fried beans, recipe    2879:179-180

Grilled corn, recipe    2879:180

Migas (crumb and egg dish), recipe    2879:179

## MEXICAN-AMERICANS (CHICANOS)—FICTION

*Fiesta!* By June Behrens; activities, art, poetry, maps, crafts, foods, patterns    2642:90-93

## MEXICAN-AMERICANS (CHICANOS)—HANDICRAFTS

Yarn picture, poster board, yarn, making 2523:94-96

## MEXICAN-AMERICANS (CHICANOS)—PIÑATAS

Party piñata, papier-mâché, balloon, tissue paper, prizes, making    2523:98-101

## MEXICO

Mexican flag, pattern, making    2421:44

National symbol, eagle, pattern, making 2421:45-46

## MEXICO—BIRTHDAY CUSTOMS

Mexican birthday customs    2547:14-15

## MEXICO—BIRTHDAYS—GAMES

Game of colors, how to make and play 2957:32-33

## MEXICO—CHRISTMAS

Christmas story    2753:83

Feliz Navidad word search    2753:82

## MEXICO—CHRISTMAS—COOKERY

Apricot filled pastries, recipe    2718:68

Biscochitos, (anise seed Christmas cookies), recipe    2881:19

Bunuelos, pastry, recipe    2736:36-37

Bunuelos, recipe    2718:68-69

Candied pumpkin, recipe    2718:69

Capirotada (fruit, cheese and spice dish), recipe 2718:69

Chestnut cake, recipe    2718:68

Empanadas (meat filled pastries), recipe 2718:66-67

French toast, torrejas de coco, recipe    2718:67

Fried pastry, recipe    2348:64-65

Hot Mexican eggnog, recipe    2718:69

Nut cookies, recipe    2718:68

Ponche Navideno (Christmas punch), recipe 2671:57-58

Pozole soup, recipe    2718:66
Red snapper Vera Cruz style, recipe    2718:66
Sweet tamales, recipe    2718:67
Three Kings bread, recipe    2348:66

**MEXICO—CHRISTMAS—DECORATIONS**

Christmas tree, paper, pattern, making
2671:49-50
Las posadas candles, pattern, making    2753:84
Miniature piñata, pattern, making    2753:84
Nativity scene, pattern, making    2753:85
Piñata, papier-mâché, balloon, small treats,
making    2740:18-20
Poinsettia wreath, felt, pipe cleaners, florist tape,
patterns, making    2884:56-58
Star piñata, papier-mâché, tissue paper, foil,
making    2718:72-73
Three Kings box for gifts, shoebox, paints,
making    2403:36-37
Three Kings silhouettes, cardstock, patterns,
making    2671:51-53

**MEXICO—CHRISTMAS—GOD'S EYE**

Ojo de Dios, God's eye, ice cream sticks, yarn,
making    2718:71
Ojos de Dios, toothpicks, yarns, making
2671:54-56

**MEXICO—CHRISTMAS—HANDICRAFTS**

Wrapped yarn animals, yarn, glue, paper strips,
making    2718:70

**MEXICO—CHRISTMAS—LANTERNS**

Farolitos, lanterns, paper bags, sand, candles,
making    2671:56-57

**MEXICO—CLOTHING**

Man and woman traditional clothing, patterns
2642:56

**MEXICO—COAT OF ARMS**

Mexican coat of arms, paper, markers, pattern,
making    2671:28
Mexican coat of arms, pattern, making
2762:103

**MEXICO—COOKERY**

Aqua de Jamaica (hibiscus flower-flavored
water), recipe    2671:64
Arroz con leche (rice pudding), recipe
2850:36-37
Arroz Mexicano (Mexican rice), recipe
2850:26-27
Atole (corn drink), recipe    2850:10-11
Avocado dip (guacamole), recipe    2575:30-31
Avocado dip, recipe    2348:47
Bean and potato patties, recipe    2608:22-23
Beans and chips, recipe    2700:67

Beans cooked in a pot, recipe    2575:47
Caldito (beef and potato soup), recipe
2850:16-17
Caramel custard, recipe    2608:40-41
Cheese-filled enchiladas, recipe    2608:20-21
Chicken breasts in stock, recipe    2575:37
Chicken enchiladas, recipe    2269:9
Chicken in almond sauce, recipe    2575:52-54
Chicken stock, recipe    2575:20-21
Chilaquilles (tortillas and eggs), recipe
2850:8-9
Chili con carne, recipe    2608:26-27
Chocolate Mexicano (Mexican hot chocolate),
recipe    2850:12-13
Churritos (sweet tortilla fritters), recipe
2850:32-33
Cinnamon cookies, recipe    2396:53
Cinnamon oranges, recipe    2369:21
Cinnamon oranges, recipe    2608:38-39
Corn soup, recipe    2608:16-17
Crisp tortillas with beef, recipe    2348:59
Fajitas, recipe    2924:28-29
Fish burritos, recipe    2608:30-31
Flan (custard with caramel topping), rec-
ipe    2850:34-35
Flan dessert, recipe    2872:21
Fresh fruit cookers, recipe    2575:70
Frijoles (pinto beans with tomato and bacon),
recipe    2850:28-29
Fruit salad, recipe    2608:34-35
Green salsa, recipe    2575:25
Grilled corn on the cob with salsa, recipe
2608:18-19
Ground meat filling for tortillas, recipe
2575:38-39
Guacamole (avocado dip), recipe    2850:18-19
Guacamole, recipe    2276:30-31
Guacamole, recipe    2455:107
Guacamole, recipe    2517:29
Guacamole, recipe    2608:12-13
Hot chocolate, recipe    2276:26
Kidney bean salad, recipe    2348:58
Little pork, recipe    2575:40-41
Mango with cinnamon, recipe    2271:58
Mango with cinnamon, recipe    2348:44
Meatballs, recipe    2608:28-29
Mexican Celebration cookies, recipe
2575:68-69
Mexican chocolate, recipe    2742:51
Mexican hot chocolate, recipe    2348:32
Mexican hot chocolate, recipe    2517:29
Mexican hot chocolate, recipe    2575:71
Mexican hot chocolate, recipe    2608:42-43

Mexican menu    2348:28-29
Mexican rice, recipe    2348:49
Mexican rice, recipe    2608:32-33
Mexican sauce, recipe    2575:27
Nachos, recipe    2269:7
Nachos, recipe    2348:55
Nachos, recipe    2608:14-15
Nachos, recipe    2872:9
Picadillo, recipe    2608:24-25
Polvorones, recipe    2517:29
Red enchiladas, recipe    2575:58-59
Red snapper from Veracruz, recipe    2575:54-55
Red snapper with lime juice, recipe    2348:43
Refried beans, recipe    2348:41
Refried beans, recipe    2575:48-49
Rice pudding, recipe    2575:66-67
Rice pudding, recipe    2608:36-37
Rice with milk, recipe    2348:60
Salsa cruda, recipe    2348:55
Salsa pico de gallo (salsa sauce), recipe
    2850:20-21
Salsa, recipe    2269:17
Salsa, recipe    2671:65-66
Salsa, recipe    2809:24
Salsa, recipe    2872:15
Shredded chicken filling, recipe    2348:40
Shrimp in pumpkin seed sauce, recipe
    2575:56-57
Soft tacos, recipe    2872:13
Sopa de Arroz (rice soup), recipe    2269:15
Sopa de arroz (rice soup), recipe    2872:19
Sopa de tortilla (tortilla soup), recipe
    2850:14-15
Sweet tamales, recipe    2671:65
Sweet tamales, recipe    2881:31
Taco party, recipe    2575:34-36
Taco salad bowls, recipe    2684:74
Tacos, recipe    2348:54
Tacos, recipe    2517:28
Tacos, recipe    2845:32-33
Tacos, recipe    2850:30-31
Tamale pie, recipe    2575:60-63
Tortilla chips, recipe    2575:28-29
Tortilla soup, recipe    2575:23-24
Tortillas de harina (wheat flour tortillas),
    recipe    2850:24-25
Tortillas with chicken, recipe    2348:38-39
Tortillas, recipe    2608:10-11
Turkey mole, recipe    2348:69
Turkey mole, recipe    2481:49
Vermicelli soup, recipe    2348:36
White rice, recipe    2575:46
Zucchini and corn, recipe    2348:50

Zucchini with corn and tomatoes, recipe
    2575:45

**MEXICO—COSTUMES**
Boy and girl costumes, patterns, making
    2753:86-87

**MEXICO—DOLLS**
Hoopskirt doll, paper, paste, making    2407:70

**MEXICO—FESTIVALS**
Mexican Independence Day; activities, crafts,
    puppets, games, patterns    2762:101-108

**MEXICO—FESTIVALS—COOKERY**
Cinco de Mayo; nachos, recipe    2422:24
Cinco de Mayo; tacos and burritos, recipe
    2422:25
Day of the Dead; bread of the dead, recipe
    2850:22-23
Day of the Dead; bread, recipe    2888:185-186
Day of the Dead; chocolate skulls and bones,
    recipe    2846:32-33
Fiesta; arroz con leche (rice pudding), recipe
    2962:72
Fiesta; chicken enchiladas, recipe    2962:71
Fiesta; guacamole, recipe    2962:69
Fiesta; Mexican hot chocolate, recipe    2962:73
Fiesta; nachos, recipe    2962:70
Fiesta; refried beans, recipe    2962:70
Three Kings Day; hot chocolate, recipe
    2504:95

**MEXICO—FESTIVALS—DANCERS**
Festival of Our Lady of Guadalupe; dancers Az-
    tec shield, gold foil paper, yarn, paints,
    making    2276:28-29

**MEXICO—FESTIVALS—DECORATIONS**
Carnaval; cascarones, eggshells filled with con-
    fetti, making    2881:23
Carnaval; fiesta papal picado cut paper, making
    2881:37
Day of the Dead Festival; Calavera mask, paper,
    pattern, making    2671:38-39
Day of the Dead Festival; dough skull, making
    2671:40
Day of the Dead Festival; Papel picado, paper,
    patterns, making    2671:41-44

**MEXICO—FESTIVALS—FLAGS**
Fiesta flags, tissue paper, string, making
    2407:18

**MEXICO—FESTIVALS—HANDICRAFTS**
Cinco de Mayo; flowerpots, clay pots, paints,
    yarn, ribbons, making    2422:27
Cinco de Mayo; tissue paper flowers, pipe clean-
    ers, making    2422:26

**MEXICO—FESTIVALS—PIÑATAS**

Paper bag piñata, how to make   2369:25

Papier-mâché piñata, balloon, string, candy, making   2504:97-98

**MEXICO—FESTIVALS—PUPPETS**

Day of the Dead Festival; skeleton puppet, cardstock, paper fasteners, pattern, making 2671:44-47

**MEXICO—FICTION**

*Diego* by Jeanette Winter; activities, art, poetry, maps, crafts, foods, patterns   2642:17-19

*Hill of Fire* by Thomas P. Lewis; activities, art, poetry, maps, crafts, foods, patterns 2642:74-77

*Mother Goose on the Rio Grande* by Frances Alexander; activities, art, poetry, maps, crafts, foods, patterns   2642:110-111

**MEXICO—FLAGS**

Mexican flag, paper, markers, pattern, making 2671:28

Mexican flag, tissue papers, glue, making 2437:42-43

**MEXICO—FOLKLORE**

Activities, finger plays, songs, rhymes, crafts, patterns   2829:68-69

*Lady of Guadalupe* by Tomie dePaola; activities, art, poetry, maps, crafts, foods, patterns 2642:127-128

*Señor Coyote and the Tricked Trickster,* story and activities   2423:19-30

**MEXICO—GAMES**

Basta game, how to play   2369:17

Beanbag polo game, how to play   2525:108

Coin toss, how to play   2767:107

Coral tag game, how to play   2525:147

El bosque encantado game, how to play 2525:118

El Coyote game, how to play   2767:107-108

Gallo desplumado game, how to play   2525:139

Kickball, how to play   2310:55-59

Las Chivas (Beans), how to play   2767:106

Mexican maze, how to play   2847:32-33

Peleche, how to play   2767:108-110

Rubber band ball, how to make   2847:33

Run away kitten game, how to play   2525:50

Snake bridges to sea game, how to play   2525:32

Tin can toss game, how to play   2525:175

Ting, ting, ting game, how to play   2525:174

**MEXICO—GOD'S EYE**

God's eye, popsicle sticks, yarn, making 2440:107

Spider web Ojo de Dios, wool, yarn, beads, wire, making 2779:28-29

**MEXICO—HANDICRAFTS**

Armadillo, clay, poster paints, making 2784:20-21

Braided leather, leather strip, making 2440:91-92

Butterfly folded paper ornament, making 2407:36

Curlicue birds, paper, paints, paste, making 2407:71

Friendship bracelets, embroidery thread, acrylic yarn, making   2440:86-90

Seed spirits, paper, paints, making   2407:28

Tin or aluminum ornaments, tin, foil pans, making   2440:66-67

**MEXICO—HANDICRAFTS—PAPEL PICADO**

Diamonds, making   2424:30-32

Fan, making   2424:37-41

Flowers with leaves, making   2424:25-29

Flowers, making   2424:21-24

Four cardinal points, making   2424:12-16

Multiple tissue paper cutouts, making   2424:60

Papel picado, fancy cutout colored paper designs, making 2809:43

Sunburst project, making   2424:57-59

Tiles, making   2424:33-36

Twinkling stars, making   2424:17-20

Zigzag, making   2424:42-46

**MEXICO—LANGUAGE**

Spanish words for family members   2809:21

**MEXICO—MARKETPLACE**

Papel picado, tissue paper, yarn, making 2686:22-23

**MEXICO—MASKS**

Mexican mask, pattern, making   2761:77

**MEXICO—NEW YEAR**

Año Nuevo, eat twelve grapes, sound to twelve in Spanish   2402:38-39

**MEXICO—NUMBERS**

*Count Your Way through Mexico* by Jim Haskins; activities, art, poetry, maps, crafts, foods, patterns   2642:98-109

**MEXICO—PIÑATAS**

Paper bag piñata, paper bag, candies, making 2671:59-60

Papier-mâché balloon piñata, making   2671:62

Papier-mâché piñata, paper, paste, paints, making 2852:116-117

Piñata pattern   2762:106

Piñata, crepe paper, flowerpot, paints, candies, making 2794:48-49
Piñata, paper bag, crepe paper, candy, small toys, making 2407:89

**MEXICO—POTTERY**

Bowl, papier-mâché, beads, leather thong, paints, making 2259:18-19

**MEXICO—SONGS**

*La Cucaracha* song in Spanish and English 2276:27

**MICHELANGELO**

Fresco plaque, making 2529:24
Lie-down painting, making 2529:25

**MICHIGAN—COOKERY**

Cherry-apple crisp, recipe 2500:60
Creamy blueberry sherbet, recipe 2770:63
Snap, crackle, crunch snack, recipe 2534:40

**MICMAC INDIANS—CLOTHING**

Micmac woman's hood, paper, oil pastels, making 2621:51

**MICMAC INDIANS—CRADLEBOARD**

Micmac baby and cradleboard, clay, fabric, ribbons, paints, making 2350:22-23

**MIDDLE AGES—ARMOR**

Pattern for armor 2849:51

**MIDDLE AGES—BOOKS**

Book, cardboard, gift wrap, fabric, making 2324:116-117

**MIDDLE AGES—BOXES**

Golden gift box, paper, making 2324:145

**MIDDLE AGES—CANDLEMAKING**

Dip some candles, paraffin wax, making 2324:151-152

**MIDDLE AGES—CASTLES**

Cardboard model of castle, making 2849:61
Castle, cardboard box, plastic soda bottles, paints, making 2452:14
Castles for your pocket, paper, toothpicks, making 2324:169
Create a castle, large cans, paper tubes, cardboard, making 2324:167-168

**MIDDLE AGES—CATAPULTS**

Cardboard catapult model, making 2849:41

**MIDDLE AGES—CHRISTMAS—COOKERY**

Gingerbread, recipe 2964:28

**MIDDLE AGES—CLOTHING**

Cloak, paper bag, yarn, pattern, making 2324:23

Lady's looking glass, cardboard, foil, pattern, making 2324:18-19
Medieval outfit, old clothes, making 2324:7-10
Paper ruff, paper, pattern, making 2324:24
Pocket and almoner, felt, cord, pattern, making 2324:15-17
Princess hat, crepe paper, ribbons, pattern, making 2324:13-14
Robin Hood's cap, felt, feather, pattern, making 2324:12

**MIDDLE AGES—COAT OF ARMS**

Pattern for coat of arms 2849:25

**MIDDLE AGES—COINS**

Create coins, clay, foil, making 2324:157

**MIDDLE AGES—COMPASS**

Compass, cork, pin, magnet, making 2324:122

**MIDDLE AGES—COOKERY**

4 and 20 blackbird pie, recipe 2324:56-57
Butter; shake up some butter, recipe 2324:47
Cabbage stew and dumplings, recipe 2324:50-51
Curds and whey, recipe 2324:48
Gingerbread dolls, recipe 2324:59-60
Gingerbread, recipe 2324:61
Honey toasts with pine nuts, recipe 2452:17
Marzipan, recipe 2324:63-64
Mead, recipe 2324:62
Meat pies, recipe 2324:54
Pies and tarts, recipe 2324:52
Pocket pies, recipe 2324:53
Porridge, recipe 2324:49
Pretzels, recipe 2324:46
Raisin custard tarts, recipe 2324:55
Smothered bread, recipe 2324:45
Trencher; try a trencher, how to do 2324:44

**MIDDLE AGES—CROCHETING**

Crochet a bag, how to do 2324:137-139

**MIDDLE AGES—CROWNS**

Crowns, tiaras and garlands, plastic jug, glitter, flowers, making 2324:25-27

**MIDDLE AGES—DOLLS**

Doll house, cardboard boxes, fabric, pattern, making 2324:95
Sock doll, old socks, stuffing, yarn, paints, patterns, making 2324:93-94
Wooden dolls and soldiers, clothespins, fabric, foil, yarn, patterns, making 2324:90-91
Yarn doll, yarn, fabric scraps, making 2324:92

**MIDDLE AGES—DRAWING**

Perspective drawing, how to do 2324:144

114

**MIDDLE AGES—EMBROIDERY**

Embroider a bookmark, fabric, thread, making 2324:127-129

**MIDDLE AGES—FALCONRY**

Falconry, falcon model, paper, pattern, making 2324:159-160

**MIDDLE AGES—FESTIVALS**

Medieval Festival; how to plan 2849:67

**MIDDLE AGES—FESTIVALS—COOKERY**

Medieval Festival; bangers, sausages and onions on thick roll, recipe 2849:70

Medieval Festival; beef stew, recipe 2849:68

Medieval Festival; cheese and pancakes, recipe 2849:68

Medieval Festival; fruit platter, recipe 2849:69

Medieval Festival; salad, recipe 2849:69

Medieval Festival; scones, recipe 2849:70

Medieval Festival; Wassail punch, recipe 2849:70

Medieval Festival; Welsh rabbit, recipe 2849:68

Medieval Festival; Yorkshire pudding, recipe 2849:68

**MIDDLE AGES—FICTION**

*Catherine, Called Birdy* by Karen Cushman; activities, projects, reading, writing, science, social studies, food and art 2849:5-16

*Knight and the Dragon* by Tomie dePaola, activities, projects, patterns, art, crafts 2822:18-21

*Proud Taste for Scarlet and Miniver* by E. L. Konigsburg; activities, projects, reading, writing, science, social studies, food and art 2849:17-29

**MIDDLE AGES—FOOTWEAR**

Poulaines, paper, yarn, pattern, making 2324:22

Shoes, chamois, pattern, making 2324:20-21

**MIDDLE AGES—GAMES**

Alquerque games, how to make and play 2324:74-75

Blind man's bluff game, how to play 2849:63

Blind man's bluff, how to play 2324:85

Bone ace card game, how to play 2849:63

Checkerboard and pieces, how to make and play 2452:19

Draughts, how to make and play 2324:76-77

Fox and geese, how to make and play 2324:78

Gluckshaus, how to make and play 2324:83-84

Goose, how to make and play 2324:81

How many miles to London game, how to play 2849:63

Juggling, how to do 2324:97

Nine Men's Morris, how to make and play 2324:82

Nine Men's Morris board game, how to play 2849:64

Three throws, how to make and play 2324:79-80

Tom Tidler's ground game, how to play 2849:63

**MIDDLE AGES—GUILD SIGNS**

Guild sign, pattern, making 2849:60

**MIDDLE AGES—HAIRSTYLES**

Wig with braids, pantyhose, making 2324:11

**MIDDLE AGES—HANDICRAFTS**

Lady's pincushion, tuna can, fabric, ribbons, lace, making 2324:130

**MIDDLE AGES—HERALDRY**

Coat of arms, patterns, making 2324:66

Family names, making 2324:69

Family tree, chart, pattern, making 2324:70

Life mask, plaster bandages, paint, making 2324:71-72

Mini-banner, felt, yarn, patterns, making 2324:67-68

**MIDDLE AGES—HERBS**

Herb salts, herbs, making 2324:155

**MIDDLE AGES—HOUSEHOLD ITEMS**

Glorious goblet, tuna fish cans, can, making 2324:161

**MIDDLE AGES—HOUSES**

Cottage models, paper bags, patterns, making 2324:165-166

**MIDDLE AGES—JEWELRY**

Buttons and bracelets, string, buttons, making 2324:30

Twist some wire jewelry, thin wire, making 2324:126

**MIDDLE AGES—KNIGHTS**

Chest armor, plastic jug, fasteners, patterns, making 2324:35

Helmet, plastic jug, patterns, making 2324:32

Knight in armor picture, cardboard, foil, nuts, bolts, paints, pattern, making 2683:12-13

Lady's favors, lace, ribbons, flowers, making 2324:37

Shield, cardboard, paints, patterns, making 2324:33-34

**MIDDLE AGES—KNITTING**

Knit a scarf, how to do 2324:133-136

**MIDDLE AGES—MACE**

Royal mace, paper tube, colored paper, pattern, making 2324:28

**MIDDLE AGES—MAGIC TRICKS**

Coin catch, how to do 2324:100

Magic balloon, how to do 2324:102

Magic knot, how to do 2324:99

Magical money, how to do 2324:98

Magic wand, paper bag, foil, pattern, making 2324:29

Paper trick, how to do 2324:101

**MIDDLE AGES—MANUSCRIPTS**

Illuminations, how to make, paper, letter stencils, gold and silver pens, making 2849:57

**MIDDLE AGES—MAPS**

Medieval Europe map in 1360 2849:75

**MIDDLE AGES—MASKS**

Jolly jester mask, cardboard, gold bells, pipe cleaners, ribbons, making 2750:14-15

Knight and horse masks, silver cardboard, adhesive vinyl, plastic screening, making 2750:32-35

**MIDDLE AGES—MATHEMATICS**

Geometric shapes, how to make 2324:123-124

**MIDDLE AGES—MURALS**

Mural, paper, paints, making 2849:58

**MIDDLE AGES—MUSICAL INSTRUMENTS**

Shoebox psaltery, shoebox, rubber bands, making 2324:86

**MIDDLE AGES—PAINTS**

Pigments from Earth and nature, how to make 2331:24-25

**MIDDLE AGES—PAPER**

Marbled paper, paper, colored chalk, making 2324:115

**MIDDLE AGES—PARCHMENT**

Making parchment, paper, teabags 2849:56

**MIDDLE AGES—PERFUMES**

Mix some scent, glass jar, olive oil, flower petals, making 2324:153

Rose water, rose petals, glass jar, making 2324:154

**MIDDLE AGES—PICTURES**

Triptych, picture made in three sections, making 2324:132

**MIDDLE AGES—PRINTING**

Printed design, cardboard, string, making 2324:112

Printed words, cardboard, alphabet pasta, ink pad, making 2324:113

**MIDDLE AGES—PROVERBS**

List of proverbs 2324:162

**MIDDLE AGES—PUPPETS**

Blackbird pie puppet, paper, pie tin, popsicle stick, making 2324:58

Finger puppets, paper, crayons, patterns, making 2324:87-88

Marionette, fabric, stuffing, yarn, pattern, making 2324:89

**MIDDLE AGES—RELIGION**

Tin angel, aluminum pie tin, making 2324:146

**MIDDLE AGES—SCULPTURES**

Sculpt a statue, plaster of Paris, milk carton, making 2324:142-143

**MIDDLE AGES—SECRET MESSAGES**

Secret letters in invisible ink, making 2324:118

**MIDDLE AGES—SOAP**

Flowered soap, decorate a bar of soap, making 2324:156

**MIDDLE AGES—STAINED GLASS**

Stained glass paintings, paper, glue, paints, making 2324:131

Stained glass window, colored tissue paper, making 2849:59

**MIDDLE AGES—TIME**

Sand glass clock, bottles, salt, making 2324:148

Sundial, paper plates, making 2324:149-150

**MIDDLE AGES—TOYS**

Jumping Jacks, cardboard, patterns, making 2324:103-104

**MIDDLE AGES—WEAPONS**

Siege catapult, shoebox, plastic spoon, rubber band, paints, making 2452:28

**MIDDLE AGES—WEAVING**

Paper placemat, how to do 2324:140

Tapestry, cardboard, yarn, making 2324:141

**MIDDLE AGES—WEIGHTS AND MEASURES**

Weigh with a balance, wire coat hanger, string, making 2324:158

**MIDDLE AGES—WRITING**

Calligraphy, how to do 2324:108-109

Decorate some notepaper using calligraphy, how to do 2324:110-111

Scroll and carrier, towel tube, paper, yarn, making 2324:107

**MIDDLE EAST—CLOTHING**
Man and woman traditional clothing, patterns
2642:57
**MIDDLE EAST—COOKERY**
Chick-pea hummus, recipe 2684:50
**MIDDLE EAST—DESERT—CLOTHING**
Boy's outfit, fabric, making 2746:27-28
Girl's outfit, fabric, making 2746:24-26
**MIDDLE EAST—DESERT—COOKERY**
Lentil stew, recipe 2746:17-18
**MIDDLE EAST—DESERT—GAMES**
Sheep, goats, lions and bears game, how to
play 2746:21-22
**MIDDLE EAST—DESERT—HOUSES**
Sleeping mat, towels, fiberfill, making 2746:14
**MIDDLE EAST—DESERT—JEWELRY**
Anklet; decorate an anklet, pipe cleaners, but-
tons, making 2746:33
Necklace; design a necklace, pennies, index card,
making 2746:34
Ring; make a ring, pipe cleaners, buttons,
making 2746:33
**MIDDLE EAST—DESERT—RELIGION**
Memories display bowl, papier-mâché, making
2746:41-42
**MIDDLE EAST—DESERT—WEAVING**
Weaving with a loom, how to do 2746:29-31
**MIDDLE EAST—FESTIVALS—COOKERY**
Knishes or potato puffs, recipe 2983:21
**MIDDLE EAST—NUMBERS**
*Count Your Way through the Arab World* by Jim
Haskins; activities, art, poetry, maps, crafts,
foods, patterns 2642:98-109
**MIMBRENOS INDIANS**
Mimbrenos drawings of *Wild Brothers*, clay pots,
with drawing designs given, making
2349:16-19
**MINNESOTA—COOKERY**
Blueberry crumble, recipe 2467:44
Minne meatballs, recipe 2534:41
**MINOANS—SEALS**
Minoan seal, clay, glue, varnish, making
2816:10-11
**MISSISSIPPI—COOKERY**
Mississippi mud brownies, recipe 2699:63
Mississippi mud pie, recipe 2534:42
Fried corn pone, recipe 2935:101
Show-me cream 'n' homemade cones, recipe
2534:43-44

**MODELL, FRANK**
*One Zillion Valentines* by Frank Modell, activi-
ties, language arts, foods (recipes given),
science, arts and music 2446:18-27
**MOLAS—HANDICRAFTS**
Lizard mola book cover, felt, yarn, pattern,
making 2883:86-90
**MONDRIAN, PIET**
Straight line design, making 2529:61
**MONET, CLAUDE**
Bingo Monet game, how to play 2738:130
Dabble in paint, how to do 2529:39
Haystack and field, make and paint a haystack
like Monet did 2738:40
Make your own impressionist painting using
Monet's ideas 2738:21
Monet's garden, flowers in a flowerpot, how to
make 2738:35
Painting reflections like Monet, how to do
2738:30
Painting the shimmering sky like Monet, how to
do 2738:26
Water lily, paper, how to make 2738:43
**MONGOLIA—COOKERY**
Banch (steamed lamb dumplings), recipe
2409:30-31
**MONGOLIA—GAMES**
Mongolian chess set, note cards, clay, colored
pencils, making 2409:26-27
**MONGOLIA—HOUSES**
Ger, cardboard, fabric, making 2409:28-29
**MONROE, JAMES (PRESIDENT)**
Good feelings in America, patterns, making
2263:25
What's in James Monroe's desk? patterns,
making 2263:25
**MONTANA—COOKERY**
Huckleberry bars, recipe 2537:63
Huckleberry pudding, recipe 2865:59
Lamb kebobs, recipe 2426:107
Mountain man jerky, recipe 2534:45
**MONTENEGRIN-AMERICANS—COOKERY.**
*See* SERBIAN-AMERICANS—COOKERY
**MOORE, HENRY**
Carving stone, how to do 2529:67
**MORAVIANS—COOKERY**
Love feast buns, recipe 2879:183
Sugar cake, recipe 2879:183-184
**MORISOT, BERTHE**
Texture paints, making 2529:42

**MORMONS—COOKERY**

Honey butter, recipe    2879:185
Pancakes made in blender, recipe    2879:186
Potato salad, recipe    2879:185-186
Whole wheat waffles, recipe    2879:186-187

**MOROCCO—COOKERY**

Harira with lamb and chicken, recipe    2871:66
Mediterranean meatballs, recipe    2924:12-13
Moroccan date cake, recipe    2396:31
Moroccan orange and radish salad, recipe
2871:41

**MOROCCO—GAMES**

Higher and higher game, how to play    2385:37
Tabuaxrat, how to play    2767:110

**MOROCCO—PASSOVER—COOKERY**

Moroccan green soup, recipe    2737:132-133

**MOTHER'S DAY**

Activities, crafts, patterns    2759:55-66
Activities, finger plays, songs, rhymes, crafts,
patterns    2829:78-79
History of Mother's Day    2877:46
Mommy and me; activities, finger plays, songs,
rhymes, crafts, patterns    2828:80-81

**MOTHER'S DAY—COOKERY**

Chocolate-dipped strawberries, recipe    2877:49
Fluffy cinnamon French toast, recipe    2877:48
Mocha truffles, recipe    2877:48

**MOTHER'S DAY—DECORATIONS**

Card; box card, paper, making    2923:18-19
Grow in God's word Mother's Day bookmark,
making    2798:59
Mom plaque, cardboard, patterns, making
2262:89-92
Mother's Day bouquet, paper, crayons, pipe
cleaners, patterns, making    2811:44-46

**MOTHER'S DAY—FICTION**

*Mother's Day Mice* by Eve Bunting, activities,
art, games, songs, crafts, patterns
2812:62-69
*Mother's Day Mice* by Eve Bunting, activities,
crafts, patterns    2637:unp
*Mother's Day Mice* by Eve Bunting, activities,
crafts, patterns, games, masks, puppets,
making    2329:114-117

**MOTHER'S DAY—TEA PARTIES**

Moms and daughters tea party; invitations, decorations, foods, crafts, games, how to do
2386:44-51

**MOTHER'S DAY—TEA PARTIES—COOKERY**

Buttermilk scones, recipe    2386:46-47
Cambric tea, recipe    2386:48
Chocolate-dipped strawberries, recipe    2386:49
Mock Devonshire cream, recipe    2386:48

**MOZAMBIQUE—GAMES**

Umake (the coast), how to play    2767:110-111

**MUD**

Magic mud, recipe    2684:144

**MUNCH, EDVARD**

Clay facial expressions, making    2529:59

**MUSIC**

Language arts, poetry, hobby craft activities
2511:71-74

**MUSICAL INSTRUMENTS**

Hand bell, making    2511:72

**MUSLIMS—FESTIVALS—COOKERY**

Ramadam; stuffed dates, recipe    2590:19

**MYANMAR—GAMES**

Frog dance, how to play    2767:111-112
Guessing game, how to play    2767:112

# N

**NARRAGANSETT INDIANS—COOKERY**
Corn meal porridge, recipe   2879:188
Johnny cakes, recipe   2879:188
Quahog chowder, recipe   2879:187-188

**NATIONAL CHILDREN'S BOOK WEEK—FICTION**
*Just Open a Book* by P. K. Hallinan, activities, crafts, patterns, games, masks, puppets, making   2329:29-33

**NATIONAL LIBRARY WEEK**
Activities, projects, programs   2378:20-26

**NAVAHO INDIANS—BLANKETS**
Navajo designs for a blanket and a scrap doll, felt, fabric, paints, designs given, making   2349:32-35

**NAVAHO INDIANS—COOKERY**
Fry bread, recipe   2289:57
Fry bread, recipe   2879:189-190
Kneeldown bread, how to prepare from ears of corn and how to cook   2891:28-29
Kneeldown bread, recipe   2879:190-191
Mutton stew, recipe   2879:192
Powwow wow bread (fry bread), recipe   2534:15
Taco, recipe   2879:191-192

**NAVAHO INDIANS—FICTION**
*Annie and the Old One* by Miska Miles, activities and patterns   2325:22-35
*Goat in the Rug* by Charles L. Blood; activities, art, poetry, maps, crafts, foods, patterns   2642:60-63
*Goat in the Rug* by Charles L. Blood; activities, projects, patterns, art, crafts   2822:129-132
*Mystery of Navajo Moon* by Timothy Green; activities, art, poetry, maps, crafts, foods, patterns   2642:94-97

**NAVAHO INDIANS—HOUSES**
Hogan model, corrugated cardboard, pattern, making   2480:54-60

**NAVAHO INDIANS—JEWELRY**
Turquoise and silver jewelry, foil, Play-Doh, making   2644:12

**NAVAHO INDIANS—LANGUAGE**
Everyday words in Navajo language   2289:104-107

**NAVAHO INDIANS—MEDICINE MAN**
Career interview, projects, stories, recipes, activities   2823:111-112

**NAVAHO INDIANS—SAND PAINTING**
Sand painting, silver sand, poster paints, wooden picture frame, making   2781:12-13
Sky Mother and Sky Father sand paintings, sandpaper, paints, designs given, making   2349:36-37

**NAVAHO INDIANS—SECRET CODES**
Secret code, how to use Navajo words to write secret message   2891:25-27

**NAVAHO INDIANS—TRADING POSTS**
Shiprock Trading Post Clerk; interview, projects, stories, recipes, activities   2823:139-141

**NAVAHO INDIANS—WEAVING**
Navajo weaving, cardboard loom, yarn, making   2981:19-23
Rug, how to weave using shoebox loom, patterns, making   2642:61-63
Woven wall hanging, cardboard, yarn, making   2311:53-58

**NDEBELE (AFRICAN PEOPLES)—DOLLS**
Small tube doll, paper tube, fabric, making   2620:66-67

**NDEBELE (AFRICAN PEOPLES)—HOUSES**
Ndebele house front mural, paper, paints, making   2620:68-69

**NEBRASKA—COOKERY**
Cornbread muffins, recipe   2682:63
Cornhusker burger, recipe   2534:46-47

**NEPAL—GAMES**
Dhandi-biu, how to play   2767:113

**NESS, EVALINE**
*Sam, Bangs and Moonshine* by Evaline Ness, activities, literature, art, science, poetry, social studies, webbing   2435:137-150

**NETHERLANDS—BIRTHDAY CUSTOMS**
Netherlands birthday customs   2547:16-17

**NETHERLANDS—CHRISTMAS—COOKERY**

Sugar hearts, recipe    2406:30-31

**NETHERLANDS—CHRISTMAS—DECORATIONS**

Sinterklaas sack, burlap, paints, twine, making    2740:12-13

Windmill ornament, pattern, making    2753:102

Wooden shoe, pattern, making    2753:99

**NETHERLANDS—COOKERY**

Apple pancakes, recipe    2838:40-41

**NETHERLANDS—COSTUMES**

Boy and girl costumes, patterns, making    2753:100

**NETHERLANDS—EASTER—HANDICRAFTS**

Palmpaas tree, bamboo sticks, clay, tinsel, oranges, paints, making    2406:28-29

**NETHERLANDS—FOLKLORE**

*Flying Dutchman,* folktales, puppets, patterns, songs, food    2591:17-18

**NETHERLANDS—GAMES**

Bergen dominoes game, how to play    2548:18

Olika bolika game, how to play    2385:14

Water hopscotch, how to play    2767:113-114

**NETHERLANDS—NEW YEAR'S DAY—COOKERY**

Dutch doughnuts, recipe    2888:16-17

**NETHERLANDS—WINDMILLS**

Colored paper windmill, how to make    2406:27

Windmill model, round carton, paper, making    2686:94-95

**NEVADA—COOKERY**

Cowboy beans, recipe    2771:63

Gold nugget flan, recipe    2534:48-49

**NEVELSON, LOUISE**

Scrap box art, making    2529:95

**NEW CALEDONIA—GAMES**

Cup and saucer, string game, how to play    2310:47-52

**NEW HAMPSHIRE—COOKERY**

Baked apple pancake with pecans and maple syrup, recipe    2317:63

True blue soup, recipe    2534:50

Use-it-up, make-it-do, Franco-American toast, recipe    2763:57

**NEW JERSEY—COOKERY**

It's the berries cranberry muffins, recipe    2534:51

**NEW MEXICO—COOKERY**

Bizcochitos cookies, recipe    2389:63

Buenos dias tortillas, recipe    2534:52

**NEW MEXICO HISPANICS—COOKERY**

Bizcochitos (Christmas cookies), recipe    2879:193

Capirotada (bread pudding), recipe    2879:194

Quick chocolate, recipe    2879:194

Sopaipillas, recipe    2879:193

**NEW YEAR'S DAY**

Activities, patterns    2755:63-70

Activities, recipes, songs, games    2863:149-159

History of New Year's Day    2877:10

Thematic units, lessons, activities, art, poetry, crafts, patterns, recipes    2320:129-157

**NEW YEAR'S DAY—COOKERY**

Jack Frost's tropical punch, recipe    2877:12

New Year's slurpie, recipe and activities    2576:72-76

Potato crescent horns, recipe    2877:12-13

Quarterback quiche, recipe    2877:15

Three-bean chili and guacamole, recipe    2877:14

**NEW YEAR'S DAY—FICTION**

*Happy New Year* by Emily Kelley, activities, crafts, patterns, games, masks, puppets, making    2329:61-66

**NEW YEAR'S DAY—HANDICRAFTS**

Glitter fireworks dome, glass jam jar, clay, beads, glitter, making    2783:8-9

**NEW YEAR'S DAY—SOAP**

New Year's confetti soap, making    2936:38-39

**NEW YEAR'S EVE—DECORATIONS**

Confetti crackers, making    2857:25

New Year noisemakers, pipe cleaners, bell, making    2778:6-7

Prediction bowl of fortunes, making    2857:24

**NEW YORK CITY—COOKERY**

Delish deli duo, recipe    2534:53

**NEW YORK CITY—FICTION**

*Felita* by Nicholasa Mohr, activities for art, music, food, clothing and history    2478:4-37

*Molly's Pilgrim* by Barbara Cohen, activities for art, music, food, clothing and history    2478:38-72

**NEW ZEALAND—BIRDS**

Kiwi bird model, cardboard, Styrofoam tray, paints, making    2686:33-34

**NEW ZEALAND—BIRTHDAY CUSTOMS**

New Zealand birthday customs    2547:18-19

## NEW ZEALAND—COOKERY

Kiwi mango sorbet, recipe    2458:30-31

Oaty bars, recipe    2700:66

## NEW ZEALAND—GAMES

Animals game, how to play    2525:187

Balance challenge game, how to play    2525:160

Beanbag tag game, how to play    2525:96

Interceptor game, how to play    2525:181

Magic raygun game, how to play    2525:128

Open ball game, how to play    2525:39

Polly put the kettle on jacks game, how to
play    2330:84-85

Trick the guard game, how to play    2525:92

War game, how to play    2525:142

Warrior game, how to play    2882:12-13

## NEW ZEALAND—HAKA

Maori haka chant, how to do    2458:27

## NEW ZEALAND—HOUSES

Pare carving, design given, cardboard, paints,
making    2458:28-29

## NEW ZEALAND—TATTOOS

How to tattoo your face like a Maori warrior
2458:26

## NEW ZEALANDER-AMERICANS—COOKERY

Anzacs (cookies), recipe    2879:28

New Zealand bacon and egg pie, recipe
2879:28

Pikelets (grill cakes), recipe    2879:28-29

## NEZ PERCE INDIANS—CARRYING CASE

Isaaptakay (carrying case), poster board, yarn,
paints, making    2311:73-76

## NEZ PERCE INDIANS—COOKERY

Elk stew, recipe    2290:60-61

## NEZ PERCE INDIANS—LANGUAGE

Everyday words in Nez Perce language
2290:95-97

## NICARAGUA—COAT OF ARMS

Nicaraguan coat of arms, paper, markers, pattern,
making    2671:29

## NICARAGUA—COOKERY

Chocolate bananas, recipe    2947:53

Gallo pinto (speckled rooster) bean and rice dish,
recipe    2947:53

Picos cheese buns, recipe    2947:52

Pineapple and rice drink, recipe    2947:52

Three milks cake, recipe    2947:52

## NICARAGUA—FLAGS

Nicaraguan flag, paper, markers, pattern, making
2671:29

## NICARAGUA—FOLKLORE

*Uncle Nacho's Hat* by Harriet Rohmer; activities, art, poetry, maps, crafts, foods, patterns
2642:125-126

## NICARAGUA—GAMES

Jaguar game, how to play    2767:116

## NICARAGUA—LANGUAGE

Speak Spanish words, how to do    2705:23

## NICARAGUA—MURALS

Paint a mural, how to do    2705:22

## NICARAGUAN-AMERICANS—COOKERY

Gallo pinto (rice and beans), recipe    2879:195

Sopa de frijoles, recipe    2879:196

## NIGER—LANGUAGE

Common phrases in Hausa, Djerma, Tamasheq
and Fulfulde    2468: 86

## NIGERIA—CHRISTMAS—DECORATIONS

Palm leaf, green paper, glitter, making
2403:38-39

## NIGERIA—COOKERY

Fried plantain slices, recipe    2662:33

Groundnut balls, recipe    2628:38

## NIGERIA—FESTIVALS—COOKERY

Argungu Festival; ginger-fried fish, recipe
2628:66

Igbo New Yam Festival; fufu, yam dish, recipe
2504:77

Iri-Ji or Yam Festival; yams and squash, recipe
2628:68

Yoruba Naming Day Ceremony; ginger-fried
fish, recipe    2628:66

## NIGERIA—FESTIVALS—MUSICAL
INSTRUMENTS

Igbo Iriji, New Yam Festival; drum, coffee can,
twine, canvas sheet, decorative items,
making    2504:73-76

## NIGERIA—FOLKLORE

*Superman vs. the Forest Giant,* story and activities
2423:50-63

## NIGERIA—GAMES

Animals have horns game, how to play
2525:76

Ayo or mancala game, how to make board and
play    2662:43

Chiwewi, how to play    2767:116-117

Fire on the mountain game, how to play
2525:11

Hitting the snake game, how to play    2525:52

Lion and the lamb game, how to play    2820:22

Lion in the den game, how to play  2525:30
One-legged fight game, how to play  2525:139
Sand castle game, how to play  2439:38

**NIGERIA—LANGUAGE**

Few words in Hausa, Yoruba and Igbo languages  2716:28
Learn to speak Yoruban words  2820:23

**NIGERIA—NEW YEAR—MASKS**

New Year's mask, paper plate, tissue paper, making  2402:40-41

**NIGERIAN-AMERICANS—COOKERY**

A moi moi (tamale), recipe  2879:197
Akara (fried bean cake), recipe  2879:198-199
Black-eyed peas, recipe  2879:199
Pepper soup, recipe  2879:199

**NINETIES—COOKERY**

Fettuccine with porcini mushrooms and parmesan cheese, recipe  2359:159-160
Lemon blueberry muffins, recipe  2359:157-158
Roasted veggie pita rounds, recipe  2359:161-162

**NIXON, RICHARD (PRESIDENT)**

Giant gift from China, panda pattern, making  2263:117
Paper quilt for peace and goodwill, making  2263:117
Soda bottle bowling game, making  2263:116
Stars and stripes on the moon, making  2263:116

**NOOTKA INDIANS—GAMES**

Laughing Games, how to play  2767:170
Pin'an, how to play  2767:171

**NORTH CAROLINA—COOKERY**

Hush puppies, recipe  2253:53
Sweetie pie potatoes, recipe  2534:54

**NORTH CAROLINA—PASSOVER—COOKERY**

Charoset pyramid, recipe  2737:80-81

**NORTH DAKOTA—COOKERY**

Little Mac and big cheese, recipe  2534:55
Semolina pasta, recipe  2841:63

**NORTHWEST COAST INDIANS—BLANKETS**

Button blanket, cloth, buttons, making  2852:120-121

**NORTHWEST COAST INDIANS—FESTIVALS**

Button blanket dance robes, felt, buttons, making  2441:132-133

**NORTHWEST COAST INDIANS—GAMES**

Natural world memory game, how to make and play  2352:17

**NORTHWEST COAST INDIANS— HEADBANDS**

Eagle feathers and headbands, feathers, felt, paints, making  2352:18-19

**NORTHWEST COAST INDIANS—HOUSES**

Plank house model, shoebox, craft sticks, paints, making  2387:28-29

**NORTHWEST COAST INDIANS—SYMBOLS**

Plains and Plateau designs and symbols, designs given, making  2352:10-13

**NORTHWEST COAST INDIANS—TOTEM POLES**

Totem pole, cardboard tube, paper, paints, making  2840:20-21

**NORTHWEST COAST INDIANS.** *See also* **INDIANS OF THE NORTHWEST COAST**

**NORWAY—CHRISTMAS—COOKERY**

Christmas bread, recipe  2481:60-61
Christmas bread, recipe  2639:64-65
Gingerbread cookies, recipe  2639:66
Raspberry sauce, recipe  2639:68
Rice pudding, recipe  2639:69

**NORWAY—CHRISTMAS—DECORATIONS**

Clove ball, making  2530:39

**NORWAY—COOKERY**

Baked cod, recipe  2639:46
Beet patties, recipe  2639:52
Boiled potatoes, recipe  2639:45
Cucumber salad, recipe  2639:51
Flatbread, recipe  2639:38-39
Fruit soup, recipe  2639:55
Mashed rutabagas, recipe  2639:50
Meatcakes, recipe  2639:49
Norwegian menu  2639:28
Open-face sandwiches, recipe  2639:32-33
Poached salmon, recipe  2639:44
Potato soup, recipe  2639:34-35
Waffles, recipe  2639:40
Whipped cream cake, recipe  2639:56-57

**NORWAY—FESTIVALS—COOKERY**

Smoked salmon quiche, recipe  2639:60
Sour cream porridge, recipe  2639:63

**NORWAY—FOLKLORE**

*Kari Woodendress,* story and activities  2423:140-166
*Peter and the North Wind,* folktales, puppets, patterns, songs, food  2591:36-39
*Three Billy Goats Gruff,* folktales, puppets, patterns, songs, food  2591:49-52
*Why Bear Has a Short Tail,* folktales, puppets, patterns, songs, food  2591:63-66

**NORWAY—GAMES**

Thor's hammer, how to play    2767:117

**NORWAY—LANGUAGE**

Norwegian words for family members    2530:27

**NORWEGIAN-AMERICANS—COOKERY**

Kringles (cookies), recipe    2879:200-201

Lefse potato flatbread, recipe    2879:202

Microwave rommegrot, (porridge), recipe
2879:200

**NOVEMBER THEMES**

Thematic units, lessons, activities, art, poetry,
crafts, patterns, recipes    2320:69-96

**NURSERY RHYMES**

Three Blind Mice puppets, foam sheets, brass
brads, string, patterns, making    2884:59-61

**NURSERY RHYMES—HANDICRAFTS**

1, 2, 3, 4, 5 I Caught a Fish Alive key magnet,
old keys, paints, making    2730:46-47

Along came a spider car antenna friend, pantyhose, Styrofoam ball, making    2730:32-33

Egg-laying Hickity Pickity Black Hen, glove,
feathers, plastic egg, making    2730:26

Four and twenty blackbird pins, paper bowls,
foil, paints, making    2730:18-19

Hickory Dickory Dock clock and mouse costume, mitten, calendar page, yarn, making
2730:30-31

Horn blowing Little Boy Blue, paper plate,
paints, making    2730:20-21

Jack and Jill party hat, party hat, paints, yarn,
making    2730:12-13

Knave of Hearts tart-stealing knave, foil, beads,
deck of cards, making    2730:34-35

Mistress Mary's bouquet, photographs, bells,
plastic cap, making    2730:38-39

Old King Cole's crown, aluminum pie tin, craft
beads, making    2730:36-37

Old Mother Hubbard's dog, film canister, old
glove, yarn, making    2730:24-25

Old Woman's Shoe magnet, paper, marker, magnet, making    2730:10-11

Patty cake baby, fabric, net, yarn, making
2730:16-17

Peter's wife in a pumpkin shell, old computer
disks, yarn, making    2730:14-15

Pull out a plum from the pie, paper plates, paints,
making    2730:42-43

Roly-poly Humpty Dumpty, clay, plastic egg,
yarn, making    2730:22-23

Three Little Kittens, crying kitten soap dispenser,
pump bottles of soap, plastic bag, making
2730:40-41

Three Little Pigs squealing piggy, cups, sock,
yarn, making    2730:8-9

Wee Willie Winkie nightcap, tights, bell, making
2730:44-45

**NURSERY RHYMES—PUPPETS**

Little Bo Peep sleeve puppet, fabric, ribbons,
trims, making    2730:6-7

Runaway Dish and Spoon puppets, paper plates,
paints, pipe cleaners, making    2730:27-29

# O

## O'KEEFFE, GEORGIA
Close-up flower painting, making 2529:86

## OAXACA—CHRISTMAS—COOKERY
Fried pastry, recipe 2348:64-65

## OCCUPATIONS
Thematic units, lessons, activities, art, poetry, crafts, patterns, recipes 2320:249-278

## OCTOBER THEMES
Thematic units, lessons, activities, art, poetry, crafts, patterns, recipes 2320:41-68

## OHIO—COOKERY
Dogs in a blanket, recipe 2534:56

## OJIBWA INDIANS—COOKERY
Blueberry and wild rice breakfast, recipe 2291:57
Bread pudding, recipe 2879:204
Gagoonz (little porcupines, rice and meat dish), recipe 2879:203-204
Maple sugar taffy, recipe 2599:41
Popped wild rice, recipe 2826:15
Spinach-rice casserole, recipe 2879:203

## OJIBWA INDIANS—DREAMCATCHERS
Dreamcatcher, macrame ring, suede, lace, making 2598:unp

## OJIBWA INDIANS—GAMES
Moccasin game, how to make and play 2599:42

## OJIBWA INDIANS—LANGUAGE
Everyday words in Ojibwe language 2291:89-91

## OJIBWA INDIANS—PRAYERS
Ojibwa vision prayer in Ojibwe and English 2599:40

## OKINAWAN-AMERICANS—COOKERY
Chanpuru (stir-fry), recipe 2879:205
Fried somen (sardine and noodle dish), recipe 2879:206
Spareribs, recipe 2879:205

## OKLAHOMA—COOKERY
Cornbread, recipe 2538:63
Sooner sloppies, recipe 2534:57-58

## OLYMPICS
Awards, patterns 2764:118-120
Greek boy and girl costume, pattern 2752:116-117
Medals, patterns 2764:121
Olympic champion cards, patterns 2752:127
Olympic competition, activities 2664:41-57
Olympic competition, activities 2764:67-88
Olympic events, activities 2664:30-40
Olympic events, activities 2764:45-66
Olympic games and you, activities 2664:58-79
Olympic games and you, activities 2764:89-116
Olympic games bingo, pattern 2752:128
Olympic games on the playground, how to play 2752:118
Olympic head wreath, pattern 2752:121
Olympic history, activities 2664:8-12
Olympic history, activities 2764:12-18
Olympic logos, patterns 2764:128-134
Olympic medals, patterns 2752:119
Olympic motto, pattern, making 2764:27
Olympic rings, patterns 2764:124
Olympic rings, patterns 2752:123
Olympic rings color page, patterns 2752:130
Olympic sites, activities 2664:20-29
Olympic sites, activities, making 2764:32-44
Olympic sport symbols, patterns 2752:122
Olympic sports cards, patterns 2752:126
Olympic symbol, pattern, making 2764:24
Olympic torch, pattern 2764:125
Olympic traditions, activities 2664:13-19
Olympic traditions, activities 2764:19-31
Olympic T-shirt, pattern 2764:135
Olympic visor, pattern 2752:129
U.S. flag, pattern 2764:122
U.S. Olympic flag, pattern 2764:123
World map, pattern 2764:126-127

## OLYMPICS—GAMES
Curling game, how to play 2328:142-143

## OLYMPICS—PATTERNS
Olympic symbol, pattern 2664:15
Olympic torch, pattern 2664:17

## OMAHA INDIANS—GAMES
Dua, how to play 2767:170-171

**ONEIDA INDIANS—COOKERY**

Baked walleye, recipe   2615:42

Maple sugar cookies, recipe   2615:42

Oneida corn soup, recipe   2644:26

**ONEIDA INDIANS—CREATION STORY**

Creation story   2615:4-6

**ONEIDA INDIANS—FOLKLORE**

*Fox and the Mice*   2615:7

**ONEIDA INDIANS—PRAYERS**

Oneida prayer in Oneida and English   2615:41

**OPPENHEIM, MERET**

Wacky work of Dada, making   2529:75

**OREGON—COOKERY**

Hazelnut chocolate, recipe   2312:63

Very cherry and cream, recipe   2534:59

**OREGON TRAIL—COOKERY**

Johnny cake, recipe   2868:13

**OREGON TRAIL—GAMES**

Cheyenne throwing sticks game, how to play
2868:13

**ORIENT—HANDICRAFTS**

Caterpillar, paper, making   2407:62

**OSAGE INDIANS—FICTION**

*Ba-Nam* by Jeanne M. Lee; activities, art, poetry,
maps, crafts, foods, patterns   2642:44-46

**OSAGE INDIANS—GAMES**

Osage hand game, how to play   2706:22

**OSAGE INDIANS—WEAVING**

Finger-weaving belt, yarn, making   2311:37-42

# P

**PACIFIC ISLANDS—GAMES**

Cat's cradle, how to play 2441:112-116

**PAIK, NAM JUNE**

Robot people, making 2529:100-101

**PAINTING**

Language arts, poetry, hobby craft activities 2511:27-30

**PAINTS**

Bubble-print paint, recipe 2918:22

Crayon melt paint, recipe 2918:26-27

Frosting paint, recipe 2918:18

Marbled paint, recipe 2918:20-21

Poster paint, recipe 2918:17

Scratch 'n' sniff paint, recipe 2918:15

Shaving cream paint, recipe 2918:19

Shimmering crystal paint, recipe 2918:23

Shiny paint, recipe 2918:24

Soapy finger paint gel, recipe 2918:25

Washable window paint, recipe 2918:14

Watercolors paints, recipe 2918:16

**PAKISTAN—COOKERY**

Unday ka halva, egg pudding, recipe 2651:53

Vegetable curry, recipe 2924:8-9

**PAKISTAN—FESTIVALS—KITES**

Basant Festival; girdha kite, tissue paper, crepe paper, making 2985:21

**PAKISTAN—GAMES**

Mazdoori, how to play 2767:117-118

Oonch Neech, tag game, how to play 2310:60-63

Up and down game, how to play 2385:27

**PAKISTAN—LANGUAGE**

Urdu language, learn to speak a few words 2651:49

**PAKISTANI-AMERICANS—COOKERY**

Biryani (rice pilaf), recipe 2879:207

Carrot halva, recipe 2879:207-208

**PAMUNKEY INDIANS—GAMES**

Hide-and-switch, how to play 2767:171

**PANAMA—COOKERY**

Corn tortilla with farmer's cheese, recipe 2948:52

Garbanzos dish, recipe 2948:52

Hojaldres pancakes, recipe 2948:53

Lemon pie, recipe 2948:53

Papaya fruit drink, recipe 2948:53

Rice with quandu (pigeon or black-eyed peas), recipe 2948:52

**PANAMA—GAMES**

El Peregrino (The Pilgrim), how to play 2767:118-119

Usted es el mono, counting game, how to play 2652:22

**PANAMANIAN-AMERICANS—COOKERY**

Foo-foo, pork, okra, cornmeal dish, recipe 2879:209-210

Fried chicken, recipe 2879:208-209

Platanos ententacion (plantain dish), recipe 2879:209

**PAPER**

Basic paper, recipe 2918:82-84

Colored paper, recipe 2918:85-86

Fine paper clay, recipe 2918:94

Nature paper, recipe 2918:89-90

Paper pulp dough, recipe 2918:93

Papier-mâché, recipe 2918:91-92

Party paper, recipe 2918:87

Scented paper, recipe 2918:88

**PAPUA NEW GUINEA—GAMES**

Mailong sera, how to play 2767:119

Tomong gilang bogl tondip (singing tops), how to play 2767:120

**PARAGUAY—CHRISTMAS—COOKERY**

Chicken, recipe 2920:53

**PARAGUAY—COOKERY**

Beef and vegetable soup, recipe 2920:52

Cornbread, recipe 2920:52

Meat turnovers, recipe 2920:53

**PARAGUAY—FESTIVALS—COOKERY**

Independence Day Festival; Paraguayan corn bread, recipe 2670:68-69

**PARAGUAY—GAMES**

El pan quemado (burned bread), how to play 2767:121

**PARKS, ROSA**

*A Picture Book of Rosa Parks* by David Adler; readers theater booktalks with literature, poetry, music and creative writing activities 2681:41

**PARKS, ROSA—BIRTHDAY**

February 4, 1913, stories, music, games, activities, projects, patterns 2377:30-36

**PASSAMAQUODDY INDIANS—ART**

Passamaquoddy birch bark picture frame, cardboard, making 2621:43

Passamaquoddy round lidded box, cardboard, making 2621:43

**PASSOVER**

History of Passover 2877:38

**PASSOVER—COOKERY**

Almond cake, recipe 2737:136-137

Apple and walnut haroset, recipe 2876:11

Apple and walnut haroset, recipe 2877:42

Apple cake, recipe 2953:56

Apple crisp, recipe 2888:108

Applesauce, recipe 2953:32

Apricot chicken, recipe 2953:42

Ashkenazic recipe: knaidlach or matzo balls, recipe 2737:128-130

Baby Moses salad, recipe 2953:30

Banana pancakes, recipe 2953:23

Betzah (red eggs), recipe 2737:83-84

Brownies, recipe 2888:103

Butter cookies, recipe 2888:102

Carrot-raisin salad, recipe 2953:34

Charoset pyramid, recipe 2737:80-81

Charoset, greens, salt water, matzah, recipe 2953:11-12

Charoset, recipe 2695:17

Charoset, recipe 2737:77

Chicken shake, recipe 2953:43

Chicken soup for beginners, recipe 2953:16

Chicken soup for experts, recipe 2953:17

Chocolate cake, recipe 2888:99-100

Chocolate chip cookies, recipe 2953:52

Chocolate egg cream, recipe 2953:62

Chocolate macaroons, recipe 2695:13

Chocolate matzah, recipe 2953:59

Chocolate meringue, recipe 2888:109

Chocolate nut bark, recipe 2953:58

Chocolate nut-raisin clusters, recipe 2953:59

Chocolate-covered fruit, recipe 2953:60

Classic brisket, recipe 2877:44

Coconut pyramids, recipe 2697:20

Coolers, recipe 2953:63

Cottage cheese pancakes, recipe 2953:22

Cranberry Mandelbrot, recipe 2876:10

Cranberry relish, recipe 2953:33

Date and almond haroset, recipe 2876:11

Date and almond haroset, recipe 2877:42

Egg drop soup, recipe 2953:48

Eggplant parmesan, recipe 2953:38

Flourless chocolate cake, recipe 2877:45

Fondue, recipe 2953:50

French toast, recipe 2953:24

Frozen fruit yogurt popsicles, recipe 2953:55

Fruit compote, recipe 2953:33

Fruit kabobs, recipe 2953:31

Fruit shake, recipe 2953:62

Gefilte fish kabobs, recipe 2953:18

Glazed carrots, recipe 2953:34

Granola, recipe 2953:21

Grilled cheese sandwich, recipe 2953:28

Haroset balls, recipe 2305:53

Haroset, recipe 2346:61

Hawaiian matzah fry, recipe 2953:49

Horseradish sauce, recipe 2953:47

Hot dog kabobs, recipe 2953:40

Ice-box cookies, recipe 2953:53

Jam-filled muffins, recipe 2953:20

Lox and onion matzah brei, recipe 2953:25

Macaroons, quick recipe 2953:53

Matzah balls, recipe 2953:17

Matzah brei, recipe 2953:25

Matzah egg foo young, recipe 2953:48

Matzah meal latkes, recipe 2953:22

Matzah pizza, recipe 2953:46

Matzah, recipe 2697:16-17

Matzah, recipe 2737:96-97

Matzo brie, recipe 2695:11

Matzo layer cake, recipe 2481:59

Matzoh, how to make 2876:14

Meat loaf, recipe 2953:41

Meatballs, recipe 2953:41

Meringue kisses, recipe 2953:54

Orange and nut cake, recipe 2888:104-105

Oven-baked chicken, recipe 2953:42

Passover matzo layer cake, recipe 2271:67

Passover sandwich rolls, recipe 2953:26

Peach kugel, recipe 2953:37

Potato pancakes, blender recipe 2953:36

Potato pudding, recipe 2953:36

Raspberry jam cookies, recipe 2888:106-107

Roasted egg and bone, horseradish, recipe 2953:11

Salami latkes, recipe 2953:40

Sandwich fillings, recipe 2953:27

Sandwich spreads, recipe 2953:27

Scrambled eggs, recipe 2953:21

Seder plate, recipe    2877:40-41

Sephardic recipes, Italian rice soup and Moroccan green soup, recipes    2737:131-133

Setting the Seder table    2953:10

Spicy eggplant, recipe    2737:134-135

Spinach frittata, recipe    2697:18-19

Strawberry layer cake, recipe    2953:56

Strawberry mousse, recipe    2953:55

Sweet Israel chicken, recipe    2737:135-136

Sweet potato kugel, recipe    2695:21

Toffee squares, recipe    2953:57

Tostado, recipe    2953:47

Tsimmes, recipe    2953:35

TV munch, recipe    2953:58

"Unsandwiches," recipe    2953:28

Veal or chicken cutlets in tomato sauce, recipe    2953:44

Vegetarian matzoh ball soup, recipe    2877:43

Veggies and dips, recipe    2953:18

Waldorf salad, recipe    2953:30

Walnut and apple haroset, recipe    2888:101

## PASSOVER—DECORATIONS

Elijah's/Miriam's cups, cardboard, beads, gold trim, making    2876:28

Exodus mural, life-size, making    2737:8-9

Matzoh cover, fabric, markers, making    2876:15

Passover place cards, index cards, gold and silver markers, beads, making    2876:25

Passover scroll for front door or welcome wall hanging, tree branch, paper, paints, making    2876:7

Place mat of the Exodus from Egypt, paper, tea, paints, making    2876:20

Seder invitation, making    2737:55-56

Seder plate, tissue paper, clay, paints, making    2876:31

Seder table crafts, making    2953:13-14

## PASSOVER—GAMES

No yeast game, how to play    2746:59

## PASSOVER—HANDICRAFTS

Afikoman bag, making    2737:146-147

Chad Gadya glove from Portugal and Spain, making    2737:191

Elijah's cup, clay, making    2737:161

Ethiopian clay figures, making    2737:167

Four questions Kippah, making    2737:113

Freedom banner, making    2737:42-43

Illuminated page of a *Haggadah*, making    2737:66-67

Immigration bookmarks, making    2737:174

Immigration tiles, making    2737:167

Jerusalem puzzle, a papercut Mizrach, making    2737:180-187

Matzah cover; iron-on matzah cover, making    2737:95

Micrography picture, making    2737:122-123

Passover pocket to hide, felt, sequins, making    2778:14-15

Reclining pillow, fabric, felt, sequins, making    2876:27

Seder plate; stenciled Seder plate symbols tablecloth; a Hamsa Seder plate, making    2737:85-89

Ten plagues froggy critter, a plague of puppets, patterns, making    2737:20-23

Welcome blessing place mat, making    2737:161-162

## PASSOVER—MUSICAL INSTRUMENTS

Miriam's tambourine, making    2737:31

Miriam's timbrels, drum and tambourine, making    2876:29

## PASSOVER—PUPPETS

Finger puppets, muslin, markers, making    2876:26

Four children puppets, tongue depressors, pipe cleaners, making    2876:27

## PASSOVER—SONGS

*Mah Nishtanah, Dayenu, Chad Gadya* song    2876:43-47

## PASTES

Colored paste, recipe    2918:68

Paper paste, recipe    2918:65

Stiff-a-craft paste, recipe    2918:66-67

## PENDE (AFRICAN PEOPLES)—MASKS

Forehead mask, cardboard, paints, patterns, making    2620:48-49

## PENDE (AFRICAN PEOPLES)—PUPPETS

Ceremonial puppets, dowels, fabric, pictures, making    2620:64-65

## PENNSYLVANIA—COOKERY

Dutch-treat funnel cakes, recipe    2534:60-61

## PENNSYLVANIA DUTCH—COOKERY

Goose eggs, dyed, recipe    2879:211-212

Pickled eggs and red beets, recipe    2879:211

Rosina boy (raisin pie), recipe    2879:212-213

Shoo-fly pie, recipe    2979:212

## PENNSYLVANIA DUTCH—HANDICRAFTS

Ochter-foggel, paper folded bird, making    2407:34

**PENNSYLVANIA DUTCH—VALENTINE'S DAY—HANDICRAFTS**

Puzzle purse, folded paper, making    2407:44

**PENOBSCOT INDIANS—JEWELRY**

Bone or antler combs, cardboard, patterns, making    2621:45

Penobscot embroidered collar, patterns, paper, yarn, making    2621:45

Porcupine quilled earrings, toothpicks, felt, patterns, making    2621:45

Silver gorget, aluminum baking sheet, tie, making    2621:45

**PENS**

Quill pen, feather, making    2687:14-15

**PENTECOST—DECORATIONS**

Come, Holy Spirit paper dove, making    2798:55

Flames of the spirit tissue collage, making    2798:52

Tongues of fire framed drawing, pattern, making    2798:49-50

**PEQUOT INDIANS—JEWELRY**

Shell necklace, shells, string, making    2562:22

**PERSIA—COOKERY**

Fresh herb mezze, recipe    2566:63

Persian kebab, recipe    2566:63

Persian rice, recipe    2566:63

**PERSIAN-AMERICANS (IRANIANS)—COOKERY**

Chelo (rice and potatoes), recipe    2879:214-215

Gormeh sabzi (stew), recipe    2879:215

Persian cutlet, recipe    2879:213-214

Potato-tomato omelet, recipe    2879:214

**PERU—COOKERY**

Arroz con leche, recipe    2563:53

Beef stew, recipe    2670:33

**PERU—GAMES**

Arquitos game, how to play    2525:46

Carbonales game, how to play    2525:25

Columbola game, how to play    2525:113

El reloj (the clock), how to play    2767:122

Grasshopper game, how to play    2525:188

Lobo, ya estas?, (Mr. Wolf, are you ready?), how to play    2767:121-122

Magazine ball game, how to play    2525:89

Quechibola game, how to play    2525:95

Rabbit in the hole game, how to play    2525:4

Seven sins game, how to play    2525:36

Socorro game, how to play    2385:24

Wizard game, how to play    2525:136

**PERU—HANDICRAFTS**

Party favor, paper, clay, pipe cleaners, making    2407:92

**PERU—JEWELRY**

Paper beads, paper, glue, making    2671:8

**PERU—KNITTING**

Cat's-tail finger-knitting, yarn, making    2440:97-98

**PERU—LANGUAGE**

Learn a few words in Spanish    2563:50

**PERU—NAZCA DRAWINGS**

Nazca birds, corrugated cardboard, sandpaper, patterns, making    2326:8-9

**PERUVIAN-AMERICANS—COOKERY**

Causa limena (mashed potato salad), recipe    2879:216

Ceviche Peruano (raw fish), recipe    2879:217-218

Shrimp chowder, recipe    2879:217

**PETER PAN**

Flying Peter Pan, paper, paints, making    2729:30-31

Peter Pan hat, paper, making    2676:5

**PETS**

Dog soap, making    2936:24-25

Thematic units, lessons, activities, art, poetry, crafts, patterns, recipes    2320:11-40

**PHILIPPINES—BIRTHDAY CUSTOMS**

Philippines birthday customs    2547:20-21

**PHILIPPINES—CHRISTMAS—DECORATIONS**

Parol, star of Bethlehem, bamboo strips, wire strips, tinsel, colored paper, making    2619:28-29

Parol star, paper, crepe paper, ribbon, making    2407:90

Parol, bamboo sticks, tissue paper, yarn, making    2532:35

Star parol, balsa wood, tissue paper, ribbon, making    2740:36-39

Star parols, paper, sticks, ribbon, making    2403:40-41

**PHILIPPINES—CHRISTMAS—LANTERNS**

Paper lantern, making    2362:22

**PHILIPPINES—COOKERY**

Chicken adobo, recipe    2532:41

Coconut cookies, recipe    2532:11

Halo halo, sweet treat, recipe    2619:30-31

Polvoron, powdered milk candy, recipe
2749:35
Saba fritters, recipe    2532:41

**PHILIPPINES—DANCES**
Singkil dance, how to do    2619:26

**PHILIPPINES—GAMES**
Hep, how to play    2767:122-123
Sipa, how to play    2532:11
Tabis-tabis, how to play    2767:123-124

**PHILIPPINES—LANGUAGE**
Everyday words in Filipino    2362:23
Filipino words for members of the family
2749:17
Greetings in Filipino    2749:31

**PHILIPPINES—WEAVING**
Mat, paper, how to weave    2749:39

**PHILISTINES—ARCHITECTURE**
Hearth room model, shoebox, paints, making
2313:99

**PHILISTINES—BOWLS**
Bird-shaped bowl, foil, papier-mâché, making
2313:113

**PHILISTINES—CLOTHING**
Simple spinning, how to do    2313:106
Warrior's headdress, poster board, paints,
making    2313:103-104

**PHILISTINES—COOKERY**
Oil and water press, how to observe    2313:120
Philistine stew, recipe    2313:118

**PHILISTINES—RELIGION**
Lyre, box, rubber bands, making    2313:124
Model seashell horn, tiny bottle, foil, clay,
making    2313:125

**PHILISTINES—SCALES**
Merchant's scale, paper cups, paints, wood
pieces, making    2313:115

**PHILISTINES—WRITING**
Playing the name game, how to do    2313:110

**PHOENICIANS—ARCHITECTURE**
Model of Tyre, baking soda, cornstarch, foil, paper plates, making    2313:59-60

**PHOENICIANS—BOATS**
Boat, clay, dowel, paints, making    2654:34-35

**PHOENICIANS—BOWLS**
Decorated cup or bowl, Styrofoam cup, paints,
making    2313:76

**PHOENICIANS—CLOTHING**
Dyeing; becoming a master dyer, how to do
2313:68

Dyes; simple blackberry dye, recipe    2313:67
Long dress or tunic, t-shirt, fabric, making
2313:63
Man's soft cap, fabric, making    2313:64
Woman's headdress, poster board, old pillow-
case, making    2313:65-66

**PHOENICIANS—COOKERY**
Amphora wine shipping bottle model, plastic
bottle, papier-mâché, foil, paints, making
2313:83-84
Cucumbers in yogurt sauce, recipe    2313:82

**PHOENICIANS—RELIGION**
Phoenician mask, clay, making    2313:87

**PHOENICIANS—SHIPS**
Model trading ship, soda bottle, foil, paste,
making    2313:77-80

**PHOENICIANS. *See also* MESOPOTAMIA**

**PHOENIX BIRD—MASKS**
Punk bird, plastic beach bottle, cardboard, tissue
paper, paints, making    2750:26-28

**PICASSO, PABLO**
Fractured friend, making    2529:70-71
One color painting, how to do    2529:69
Picasso mirror, cardboard, paints, making
2258:26-27

**PICASSO, PABLO—BIOGRAPHY**
*Picasso* by Mike Venezia, activities, projects,
patterns, art, crafts    2822:12-14

**PICTS—WRITINGS IN STONE**
Ogham stone, clay, cardstock, white paint, making    2582:50-51

**PIERCE, FRANKLIN (PRESIDENT)**
Crystal Palace diorama, making    2263:51
Let me introduce myself, making    2263:51
Schoolhouse writing tablet, schoolhouse pattern,
making    2263:51

**PILGRIMS**
Activities, trips, laws, news, toy making, chores
and trades    2388:10-13
Mayflower, pattern, making    2760:90

**PILGRIMS—COOKERY**
Baked butternut squash, recipe    2411:9
Honey apples, recipe    2411:19
Maple-ginger tea, recipe    2411:21
New England mashed turnips, recipe    2411:19
Stewed pompion, recipe    2442:35

**PILGRIMS—COSTUMES**
Pilgrim bonnet and collar, patterns, making
2760:82
Pilgrim boy, pattern, making    2760:81

Pilgrim girl, pattern, making   2760:80
Pilgrim hat and Indian vest, patterns, making
     2760:83
Pilgrim man and woman pattern   2475:73

## PILGRIMS—DOLLS

Pilgrim corn dolly, corn husks, pipe cleaners,
     yarn, making   2504:89-90

## PILGRIMS—FICTION

*Landing of the Pilgrim Fathers* (poem) by Felicia
     Hemans; readers theater booktalks with lit-
     erature, poetry, music and creative writing
     activities   2681:6
*Molly's Pilgrim* by Barbara Cohen, activities for
     art, music, food, clothing and history
     2478:38-72
*Samuel Eaton's Day* by Kate Walters; readers
     theater booktalks with literature, poetry,
     music and creative writing activities
     2681:7

## PILGRIMS—HATS

Pilgrim hat, black poster board, felt, making
     2690:8-9

## PILGRIMS—ORNAMENTS

Pilgrim ornament, man and woman in Pilgrim
     clothes, making   2690:12-13

## PILGRIMS—PUPPETS

Pilgrim family finger puppets, glove, felt, yarn,
     eyes, making   2690:16-17

## PILGRIMS—THANKSGIVING—COOKERY

Baked apricot apples, recipe   2696:7
Corn pudding, recipe   2696:19
Cornmeal blueberry mush (sautauthig), recipe
     2359:20
Cranberry bread, recipe   2696:21
Golden harvest pumpkin bread, recipe
     2359:18-19
Roasted turkey breast, recipe   2359:21
Traditional cranberry sauce, recipe   2359:22-23
Turkey pot pie, recipe   2696:17

## PILGRIMS—THANSKGIVING— DECORATIONS

Mobile of images from first Thanksgiving din-
     ner, making   2690:20-21

## PIMA AND PAPAGO (TOHONO O'ODHAM) INDIANS—COOKERY

Papago Tepary bean soup, recipe   2879:219
Pima poshol soup, recipe   2879:219
Pima tortillas, recipe   2879:218

## PIMA INDIANS—GAMES

Gins (sticks), how to play   2767:171-173

Wee-ichida (racing game), how to play
     2767:173

## PIÑATAS

Piñata, paper bag, crepe paper, candy, small toys,
     making   2407:89
Piñata, papier-mâché, balloon, colored tissue pa-
     per, many small gifts, making   2908:unp

## PINOCCHIO—PUPPETS

Growing nose Pinocchio puppet, Styrofoam ball,
     paints, making   2729:32-33

## PIONEERS

Activities, wagons, diaries, food, quilts, making
     2388:22-29

## PIONEERS—COOKERY

Apple pie, recipe   2441:41-43
Beef jerky, recipe   2359:67
Buckwheat griddle cakes, recipe   2359:63-64
Butter, recipe   2388:25
Country scrambled eggs, recipe   2359:65-66
Crank ice cream, recipe   2441:34-35
Doughnuts, recipe   2441:36-37
Lemonade, recipe   2441:44

## PIONEERS—COWS

Milking a live cow or goat, how to do   2441:32
Milking practice without a cow, how to do
     2441:32

## PIONEERS—FICTION

*Ox-Cart Man* by Donald Hall, literature, activi-
     ties, art, curriculum   2436:121-132

## PIONEERS—GAMES

Marbles, how to play   2450:25
Rin taw, marble games, how to play   2436:131

## PIONEERS—PARTIES

Taffy pull party, taffy recipe and how to do the
     pulling   2450:29

## PIONEERS—QUILTING

Album quilt, paper, pattern, making   2388:29

## PIONEERS—TOYS

Snowstorm in a bottle, bottle, glitter, making
     2441:48-49
Yarn people, yarn or straw, making   2441:47

## PIONEERS—TRANSPORTATION

Prairie Schooner, pattern, decorate, making
     2618:34-35

## PIONEERS—WRITING SLATES

Writing slate, piece of wood, blackboard paint,
     making   2450:13

**PIPER, WATTY**

*Little Engine that Could* by Watty Piper, take the toys up the mountain, cardboard, zipper, paints, making   2729:10-11

**PIRATES—COSTUMES**

Pirate costume, paper, pattern, making 2757:127

**PIRATES—FACE PAINT**

Pirate face painting, how to do   2952:33

**PIRATES—GAMES**

Treasure hunt game and game board, patterns, making   2757:128-129

**PIRATES—HANDICRAFTS**

Hide the treasure, make a treasure map 2441:27-29

Ocean in a bottle, bottle, food coloring, oil, making   2441:22-23

Treasure, jewelry, coins, foils, making   2441:26

Treasure chest, container, foil, velvet, cloth, decorations, making   2441:24-25

**PIRATES—TREASURE CHESTS**

Treasure chest, pattern   2757:126

**PLAINS INDIANS**

Activities, games, buffalo use, sign language, pouches, patterns   2421:15-24

**PLAINS INDIANS—ALPHABET**

Native American decorative alphabet, letters given, making   2352:41

**PLAINS INDIANS—BUFFALO**

Buffalo hide painting, records important event, chamois cloth, fabric, paints, designs given, making   2352:22-25

Wild woolly buffalo model, clay, paints, making   2352:20-21

**PLAINS INDIANS—COOKERY**

Berry and corn bread, recipe   2352:42-43

**PLAINS INDIANS—DOLLS**

Rainbow corncob dolls, corncobs, fabric, decorations, patterns, making   2352:14-16

**PLAINS INDIANS—FOLKLORE**

*Coyote Sings to the Moon* handmade book, paper, string, makers, making   2352:34-35

Ghost hunter fringed shirt, sweatshirt, paints, designs given, making   2352:30-31

*Girl Who Loved Wild Horses* by Paul Goble, literature, activities, art, curriculum 2436:15-28

**PL AINS INDIANS—GAMES**

Natural world memory game, how to make and play   2352:17

**PLAINS INDIANS—HEADBANDS**

Eagle feathers and headbands, feathers, felt, paints, making   2352:18-19

**PLAINS INDIANS—HOUSES**

Tepee, old sheet, paints, making   2804:10-11

Tipis of the Plains, cardboard, paints, twigs, designs given, making   2352:36-39

**PLAINS INDIANS—PARFLECHE**

Comanche parfleche, oak tag, paints, designs given, making   2352:32

**PLAINS INDIANS—SIGN LANGUAGE**

Sign language communicating, hand signs given   2352:39-40

Speaking in signs, how to do   2473:85

**PLAINS INDIANS—SYMBOLS**

Plains and Plateau designs and symbols, designs given, making   2352:10-13

**PLAINS INDIANS—WRITINGS**

Native American writings, songs and poems, how to copy   2352:44-45

**PLANTATION LIFE—COOKERY**

Peaches and cream ice cream sundae with gingersnaps, recipe   2359:77-78

Plantation-baked corn bread, recipe   2359:75

Southern fried chicken wings, recipe 2359:73-74

Sweet potato pie, recipe   2359:76

**PLANTATION LIFE—SOUTHERN STATES—HISTORY—19TH CENTURY—CALLING CARDS**

Calling cards, index cards, silver paint, making 2893:34-37

**PLANTATION LIFE—SOUTHERN STATES—HISTORY—19TH CENTURY—COOKERY**

Hoppin' John, recipe   2893:24-25

**PLANTATION LIFE—SOUTHERN STATES—HISTORY—19TH CENTURY—COTTON**

Miniature cotton bale, paper tube, burlap, cotton balls, making   2893:38-41

**PLANTATION LIFE—SOUTHERN STATES—HISTORY—19TH CENTURY—GAMES**

Graces game for girls, how to make and play 2893:42-44

Marbles and ringtaw game, how to play
2893:28-31

**PLANTATION LIFE—SOUTHERN STATES—HISTORY—19TH CENTURY—HANDICRAFTS**

Yoke for carrying water, plastic tubs, dowel, yarn, making   2893:20-21

**PLANTATION LIFE—SOUTHERN STATES—HISTORY—19TH CENTURY—MEDICINE**

Cold remedy, recipe   2893:26-27

**PLANTATION LIFE—SOUTHERN STATES—HISTORY—19TH CENTURY—NOTEBOOKS**

Commonplace book, paper, markers, making
2893:16-19

**PLANTATION LIFE—SOUTHERN STATES—HISTORY—19TH CENTURY—SLAVES**

Slave cabin model, cardboard, fake dirt, paints, making   2893:12-15

**PLASTIC**

Plastic, recipe for making   2918:96-97

**POCAHONTAS**

Story times, activities, Pocahontas tubey pattern, craft instructions   2636:64-66

**POLAND—CHRISTMAS—COOKERY**

Bowties, recipe   2900:79
Christmas Eve borscht, recipe   2271:68
Christmas Eve borscht, recipe   2878:62
Herring paste on bread, recipe   2878:63
Honey cake, recipe   2878:67
Honey cookies, recipe   2900:79
Hunter's stew, recipe   2900:78
Kolacky (cookies), recipe   2900:78
Mushroom uszka, recipe   2900:77
Noodles with poppy seeds, recipe   2481:43
Noodles with poppy seeds, recipe   2878:64
Northern pike, Polish style, recipe   2900:78
Polish sausage with sauerkraut, recipe   2900:77
Sauerkraut filling for pierogi, recipe   2900:77
Twelve fruit compote, recipe   2900:79

**POLAND—CHRISTMAS—DECORATIONS**

Eggshell pitcher ornaments, egg, colored paper, making   2900:68-69
First star, cardboard, gold paint, making
2740:10-11
Geometric ornament, plastic drinking straws, yarn, patterns, making   2900:70-71
Porcupine ornaments, heavy duty foil, cardboard, patterns, making   2900:66-67

Spider decorations, paper, ribbon, wiggly eyes, making   2403:42-43

**POLAND—COOKERY**

Barley and vegetable soup, recipe   2838:18-19
Barley soup, recipe   2878:32
Berry bomb dessert, recipe   2602:29
Cabbage rolls, recipe   2878:54-55
Cauliflower with Polish sauce, recipe   2878:47
Eggs stuffed with ham, recipe   2878:40
Hunter's stew, recipe   2878:34-35
Mushrooms in vinegar, recipe   2878:33
Pierozki, recipe   2878:42-43
Plum and rhubarb soup, recipe   2878:52
Polish menu   2878:28
Roast stuffed fish, recipe   2878:48
Rutabagas and carrots, recipe   2878:44
Semi-short bread with plums, recipe
2878:56-57
Tomato and onion tier salad, recipe   2878:39
Vegetable bouquet, recipe   2878:58
Vegetable salad, recipe   2878:38

**POLAND—EASTER—COOKERY**

Royal mazurek (pastries), recipe   2878:68

**POLAND—GAMES**

An eye game, how to play   2525:115
Chocolate game, how to play   2525:118
Cymbergaj, how to play   2767:124
Initiator game, how to play   2525:78
Squares game, how to play   2525:53
Yo-yo game, how to play   2525:126

**POLAND—LANGUAGE**

Phrases in Polish   2375:23
Polish words for family members   2602:26

**POLAND—PAPER CUTTING**

Gwiazdy (stars) paper cut, making   2407:16
Ribands, paper, making   2407:30
Wycinanki paper designs, making   2375:22
Wycinanki, paper, making   2407:31

**POLISH-AMERICANS—COOKERY**

Chocolate babka, recipe   2981:25
Friendly Polish tea, recipe   2879:220
Hunter's stew, recipe   2879:222
Lazy pierogi (noodle stew), recipe
2879:222-223
Mazurek pastry, recipe   2879:224
Polish Kluski (potato dumplings), recipe
2879:223
Stuffed cabbage, recipe   2879:220-222

**POLISH-AMERICANS—PISANKI EGGS**

Pisanki egg decorating, eggs, beeswax, dyes, varnish, making   2981:9

133

**POLK, JAMES KNOX (PRESIDENT)**
Life in the original mobile home, log cabin, patterns, making 2263:44-45
White House Thanksgiving, picture, making 2263:46

**POLLACK, JACKSON**
Action splatter, how to do 2529:93

**POLO, MARCO**
Marco Polo travel journal, how to make 2700:30-31
Persian artist's mosaic, mosaic pieces, plaster of Paris, patterns, making 2474:22-23
Turkish wall hanging, how to weave, nails, yarn, cloth 2474:6-7
Turkish words, how to say 2474:3

**POLO, MARCO—KUBLAI KHAN**
Dragon mask, colored paper, buttons, glitter, ribbons, making 2474:58-59
Emperor's tomb soldiers made of kitchen terra cotta, recipe, how to make 2474:35
Fun with feng shui, how to do 2474:50-51
Modern version of an ancient art, making paper, paper, window screen 2474:54-55
Stage an opera Chinese style, how to do 2474:60-61
Tibetan monks mandala, sand paints, making 2474:69

**POLO, MARCO—LANTERN FESTIVAL**
Paper lantern, tissue paper, wire, floral stems, making 2474:82-83

**POLO, MARCO—MONGOLS**
Mongol words, how to say 2474:41
Yogurt, breakfast of warriors, recipe 2474:38

**POLO, MARCO—TIBET**
Mandarin language, how to say a few words 2474:74
Tibetan monk's mandala, sand paints, making 2474:69

**POLO, MARCO—TIBET—COOKERY**
Chinese stir-fry, recipe 2474:79
Moon cakes, recipe 2474:87

**POLO, MARCO—TIBET—GAMES**
Eagle and chicks, how to play 2474:86
Jug or "narrow-neck," how to play 2474:86
Stone paper scissors, how to play 2474:86

**POMO INDIANS—BASKETRY**
Pomo basket and decorated feathers, basket, feathers, paints, making 2349:10-11

**PONY EXPRESS**
Pony Express diorama, box, tissue paper, felt, making 2691:18-19
Pony Express envelopes, envelopes, labels, making 2691:8-9
Pony Express letter-sack magnets, paper, yarn, magnets, making 2691:16-17
Pony Express poster, poster board, markers, making 2691:12-13
Pony Express station-house, shoebox, egg carton, paints, making 2691:20-21

**PONY EXPRESS—MAP**
Map of the Pony Express route, poster board, U.S. wall map, making 2691:14-15

**PONY EXPRESS—PUPPETS**
Pony Express sock puppet, socks, felt, yarn, making 2691:10-11

**PONY EXPRESS—RIDERS**
Pony Express paper doll riders, cardboard, markers, making 2691:6-7

**POPCORN**
How to pop popcorn in a pan or in an electric popper 2543:26-27

**POPCORN—COOKERY**
Popcorn balls, recipe 2543:31
Super savory sprinkles, recipe 2543:30

**PORTUGAL—GAMES**
Jogo da pedra (stone game), how to play 2767:125

**PORTUGAL—HANDICRAFTS**
Flower spray, poster board, crepe paper, beads, making 2407:93

**PORTUGAL—PASSOVER—HANDICRAFTS**
Chad Gadya glove, making 2737:191

**PORTUGESE-AMERICANS—COOKERY**
Leaf cake, recipe 2879:225-226
Portugese soup (kale soup), recipe 2879:224-225
Vinha d'alhos (pork dish), recipe 2879:226

**POTATOES**
History of potatoes 2717:30-31

**POTATOES—FICTION**
*Thanksgiving at the Tappletons'* by Eileen Spinelli, activities, crafts, patterns, mathematics, art, music and science 2445:31-41

**POTAWATOMI INDIANS—COOKERY**
Baked corn, recipe 2879:227
Sweet potato biscuits, recipe 2879:227-228

**POTAWATOMI INDIANS—GAMES**

Woodpecker game, how to make and play 2432:22

**POTTER, BEATRIX—PUPPETS**

*Tale of Peter Rabbit* by Beatrix Potter, hide Peter in the watering can puppet, cup, foil, yarn, making 2729:23-25

**POTTERY**

Greenware pottery items, making 2511:76

Language arts, poetry, hobby craft activities 2511:75-78

**POWHATAN INDIANS—COOKERY**

Corn and bean stew, recipe 2292:59

**POWHATAN INDIANS—LANGUAGE**

Everyday words in Powhatan language 2292:97-99

**PREHISTORIC MAN—ROCK CARVINGS**

Rock carvings, rocks, paints, making 2331:10

**PREHISTORIC MAN—ROCK PAINTINGS**

Rock painting, how to make ancient rock and paint, paper, glue, sand, making 2331:11

**PRESIDENTS**

Engraved lockets, poster board, foil, yarn, making 2263:6

Great Seal of the United States, pattern, making 2263:141

Presidential monument, chip cans, paper portrait, making 2263:6

Presidential Seal, patterns 2263:141

Presidents Concentration game, how to make and play 2263:6

United States flags, first flag and current flags patterns, making 2263:140

White House picture 2263:139

**PRESIDENTS—NAMES**

The name's James, how to do 2667:7

**PRESIDENTS' DAY**

Story times, activities, Washington and Lincoln tubey patterns, craft instructions 2636:16-20

Thematic units, lessons, activities, art, poetry, crafts, patterns, recipes 2320:158-184

Whole language thematic unit of activities in language, science, math, music and life skills 2797:32-45

**PRINCESSES—FACE PAINT**

Princess face painting, how to do 2952:32

**PRINCESSES—MASKS**

Princess mask, papier-mâché, paints, template given, making 2978:98-99

**PRINCESSES—TEA PARTIES**

Invitations, decorations, foods, crafts, games, how to do 2386:18-25

**PRINCESSES—TEA PARTIES—COOKERY**

Jewel tea biscuits, recipe 2386:22

Strawberry tea punch, recipe 2386:21

Truffles, recipe 2386:23

**PRINCESSES—TEA PARTIES— DECORATIONS**

Princess crowns, paper, decorations, making 2386:24

**PRINCESSES—TEA PARTIES—GAMES**

Cinderella shoe hunt, how to play 2386:25

**PRINTING**

Printer's type, potatoes, inks, making 2935:10-11

Slate, cardboard, self adhesive paper, making 2935:18-19

**PROVENSEN, ALICE**

*Glorious Flight: Across the Channel with Louis Bleriot* by Alice Provensen, literature, activities, art, curriculum 2436:29-43

**PUEBLO INDIANS**

Pueblo village, clay, twigs, paints, making 2349:30-31

**PUEBLO INDIANS—COOKERY**

Corn pudding, recipe 2644:14

Fry bread, recipe 2644:14

Hamburger stew, recipe 2293:63

Laguna cake pudding, recipe 2399:17

Native American cornbread, recipe 2349:42-43

Pojoaque cream soup, recipe 2879:229

Spani and potatoes, recipe 2879:229-230

Wild sage bread, recipe 2879:229

**PUEBLO INDIANS—FICTION**

*Arrow to the Sun* by Gerald McDermott, activities, projects, patterns, art, crafts 2822:73-77

**PUEBLO INDIANS—FOLKLORE**

*Arrow to the Sun* by Gerald McDermott, literature, activities, art, curriculum 2436:1-13

**PUEBLO INDIANS—HOUSES**

Pueblo dwelling model, cardboard boxes, paints, making 2698:28-29

Pueblo home, tissue box, chopsticks, paint, cornmeal or sand, pipe cleaners, making 2891:10-12

**PUEBLO INDIANS—LANGUAGE**

Everyday words in Tewa language 2293:97-99

## PUEBLO INDIANS—POTTERY

Clay pots, making 2644:12

## PUEBLO INDIANS—ROCK PAINTINGS

Rock painting, flat rock, paints (recipe for paint), making 2891:13-15

## PUEBLO INDIANS—STORYTELLERS

Pueblo storytellers, clay, paints, designs given, making 2349:38-39

## PUERTO RICAN-AMERICANS—COOKERY

Kidney bean dish, recipe 2879:230
Roast pork shoulder, recipe 2879:232
Shrimp and rice stew, recipe 2879:231

## PUERTO RICAN-AMERICANS—FICTION

*Friday Night is Papa Night* by Ruth Sonneborn; activities, art, poetry, maps, crafts, foods, patterns 2642:30-32

## PUERTO RICO—CHRISTMAS—COOKERY

Annatto oil, recipe 2338:76
Candied plantains, recipe 2338:71
Chilled tropical salad, recipe 2338:72
Coconut pudding, recipe 2338:71
Pasteles (boiled meat-filled dough roll), recipe 2338:75
Rice fritters, recipe 2338:74
Spice cake, recipe 2338:72
Stewed shrimp, recipe 2338:73

## PUERTO RICO—CHRISTMAS— DECORATIONS

Coqui ornament, green foam sheet, pattern, making 2338:63
Nativity diorama, wood doll, head beads, clothespins, ribbons, straw, making 2338:64-65
Poinsettia centerpiece, ribbon, floral wire, Styrofoam brick, making 2338:66

## PUERTO RICO—CHRISTMAS—MUSICAL INSTRUMENTS

Maracas, balloons, papier-mâché, beans, paints, making 2338:66
Maracas, cans, dried beans, paints, making 2403:44-45

## PUERTO RICO—COOKERY

Asopao (chicken, rice and vegetable dish), recipe 2925:32-33
Besitos de coco cookies, coconut kisses, recipe 2412:30-31
Callaloo, recipe 2925:35
Chuleton pea soup, recipe 2380:unp
Green plantains, fried, recipe 2921:53
Mango smoothie, recipe 2623:31

Mofongo, green plantains and pork rinds dish, recipe 2921:53
Pepperpot stew, recipe 2925:36-37
Rice with chicken, recipe 2921:52
Rice with pigeon peas, recipe 2921:52

## PUERTO RICO—EPIPHANY—COOKERY

Cinnamon topped coconut rice pudding, recipe 2888:29

## PUERTO RICO—FESTIVALS—COOKERY

Three Kings Day; eggnog, recipe 2888:30

## PUERTO RICO—FESTIVALS—MASKS

Feast of Santiago Apostol mask, papier-mâché, paints, making 2412:28-29
Papier-mâché mask, paints, paste, making 2623:41

## PUERTO RICO—FICTION

Felita by Nicholasa Mohr, activities for art, music, food, clothing and history 2478:4-37

## PUERTO RICO—FOLKLORE

*Traveling Musicians,* story and activities 2423:106-119

## PUERTO RICO—GAMES

Here is a light, how to play 2767:179-180

## PUERTO RICO—LANGUAGE

Spanish words for family members 2623:23

## PUERTO RICO—MASKS

Puerto Rican vejigante masks, papier-mâché, paints, making 2817:40-45

## PUERTO RICO—MUSICAL INSTRUMENTS

Maracas, papier-mâché, balloon, stick, paints, making 2412:26

## PUMPKINS

Activities, finger plays, songs, rhymes, crafts, patterns 2828:24-25
Patty and Peter pumpkin figures, paper, crayons, patterns, making 2811:5-7
Teaching themes, activities, games, crafts, patterns, recipes 2410:30-40

## PUMPKINS—FICTION

*Biggest Pumpkin Ever* by Steven Kroll, activities, art, games, songs, crafts, patterns 2812:3-10

## PUPPETS

Language arts, poetry, hobby craft activities 2511:79-82
Puppet stage, making 2511:80

## PURIM—COOKERY

Almond macaroons, recipe 2888:93
Hamantaschen cookies, recipe 2414:30-31

Hamantaschen, recipe    2346:53
Peter rabbit's carrot pudding, recipe    2888:92
Poppy seed and almond cake with chocolate icing, recipe    2888:94-95
Poppy seed Hamantaschen with apricot-pineapple filling, recipe    2888:87-89
Queen Esther's Sephardic cookie rings, recipe    2888:91

Sour cream poppy seed cookies, recipe    2888:90

**PURIM—DECORATIONS**
Afikomen cover, cloth napkin, fabric scraps, making    2346:62
Grogger noisemaker can, paper, dried beans, making    2346:54

# Q

## QUILTING

Bowls; fabric mache bowls, balloons, fabric, papier-mâché, making    2883:91-93

Language arts, poetry, hobby craft activities    2511:89-93

Patchwork candy jar, glass jar, colored fabrics, paints, making    2258:16-17

Quilt patch, making    2511:90

## QUILTING—FICTION

*Sam Johnson and the Blue Ribbon Quilt* by Lisa Campbell, activities, projects, patterns, art, crafts    2822:121-123

# R

**RAGGEDY ANN—COOKERY**
Super-special stripey cake, recipe    2768:unp

**RAGGEDY ANN—GAMES**
Pin the tail on the donkey, how to play
     2768:unp
Spider web game, how to play    2768:unp

**RAILROADS**
Laying the tracks model, making    2497:32-33

**RAILROADS—FICTION**
*John Henry* by Ezra Jack Keats; readers theater
     booktalks with literature, poetry, music and
     creative writing activities    2681:32

**RAIN FOREST—BIRDS**
Balancing bird, cardboard, paints, making
     2579:19

**RAIN FOREST—GAMES**
Mancala game, how to build and play    2579:17

**RAIN FOREST—PRAYERS**
Prayer of rain forest people before cutting
     trees    2579:15

**RAMADAN—COOKERY**
Fig and date bread, recipe    2888:143
Fig layer cake, recipe    2888:141
Ground rice pudding, recipe    2888:147
Hazelnut baklava, recipe    2888:139-140
Semolina cookies, recipe    2888:142

**RANSOME, ARTHUR**
*Fool of the World and the Flying Ship* by Arthur
     Ransome, activities, literature, art, science,
     poetry, social studies, webbing
     2435:25-33

**RAPHAEL**
Mother and baby painting, making    2529:23

**RAUSCHENBERG, ROBERT**
Combines, making    2529:96

**REAGAN, RONALD (PRESIDENT)**
Butterflies for "Dutch," pattern, making
     2263:124
Soda bottle shuttle, pattern, making    2263:124

**REMBRANDT**
Making faces, how to do    2529:28
Shadowy faces, how to do    2529:29

**RENAISSANCE—PAPER MUSEUMS**
Paper museums to hold paper, drawings, interest-
     ing things, how to make    2367:88

**RENAISSANCE—PORTRAITS**
Paint a portrait, how to do    2367:89

**RENOIR, PIERRE AUGUSTE**
How to draw a face like Renoir    2738:50
Mixed media still life, making    2529:45

**RHODE ISLAND—COOKERY**
Apple crisp, recipe    2851:63
Little Rhody fried egg-in-a-hole, recipe
     2534:62-63

**RHODE ISLAND RED CHICKENS—HISTORY**
Little Rhody fried egg-in-a-hole, recipe
     2534:62-63

**RINGGOLD, FAITH**
Quilted work, making    2529:104

**RIVERA, DIEGO**
*Diego* by Jeanette Winter; activities, art, poetry,
     maps, crafts, foods, patterns    2642:17-19
Giant projector mural, making    2529:72

**ROARING TWENTIES—COOKERY**
Baby Ruth homerun bars, recipe    2359:103-104
Citrus sundae, recipe    2359:106-107
Fast and easy Caesar salad, recipe    2359:105

**ROBIN HOOD—CLOTHING**
Robin Hood's cap, felt, feather, pattern, making
     2324:12

**ROCKS**
Crystals, growing, how to do    2511:95-99
Language arts, poetry, hobby craft activities
     2511:95-99

**ROCKWELL, NORMAN**
Tell-a-story illustration, making    2529:85

**RODIN, AUGUSTE**
Carving clay, how to do    2529:50

**ROMANIA—COOKERY**
Layered sauerkraut, recipe    2867:121

**ROMANIA—EASTER—EGGS**
Decorated Easter eggs, making    2986:31

**ROMANIA—GAMES**
Conductor game, how to play    2525:133

Dangerous circle game, how to play 2525:106
Flying saucers game, how to play 2525:116
Jobs game, how to play 2525:73
Oina game, how to play 2525:48
Ringlet turns, how to play 2767:125
Truck and tractor game, how to play 2525:135

**ROMANIA—NEW YEAR'S DAY—
       DECORATIONS**
Peasant staffs, paper, making 2407:66

**ROMANIAN-AMERICANS—COOKERY**
Cheese grits, recipe 2879:233
Eggplant salad, recipe 2879:233
Fried cookies, recipe 2879:234

**ROME, ANCIENT—AMPHORA**
Amphora model (used to transport wine, oil or
      fish sauce), cardboard, paints, making
      2791:58-59

**ROME, ANCIENT—AQUEDUCTS**
Aqueduct bridge model, cardboard, clay, paints,
      making 2791:16-17
Aqueduct model, foil, cardboard tubes, making
      2323:155-156
Roman aqueduct, cereal box, cardboard, paper
      towel tube, making 2463:56-58

**ROME, ANCIENT—ARCHITECTURE**
Colosseum zoetrope model, coffee can, card-
      board, pictures, making 2509:30-31
Column frame, cardboard, tissue paper, paints,
      making 2332:18-19
Roman Ruins, build columns, pediments, capi-
      tals, using salt clay, recipe given, making
      2509:26-27

**ROME, ANCIENT—ARMOR**
Metal strip chest armor to wear, silver cardboard,
      cord, making 2791:56-57

**ROME, ANCIENT—ARMY**
Ciphers, codes, making 2323:136-137
Elephant; papier-mâché elephant, making
      2323:134-135
Roman army helmet, papier-mâché, making
      2323:130-131
Standard to lead army, paper plates, foil, ribbons,
      making 2323:128-129

**ROME, ANCIENT—ATHLETES**
Winner's wreath, cardboard, ribbon, imitation
      leaves, gold paint, making 2482:89-91

**ROME, ANCIENT—BASKETS**
Maximus basket, cardboard, making
      2323:161-162

Weave a mini basket, paper cup, yarn, making
      2323:160

**ROME, ANCIENT—BATHS**
Aromatherapy bath oil, making 2463:75

**ROME, ANCIENT—BRIDGES**
Aqueduct bridge model, cardboard, clay, paints,
      making 2791:16-17

**ROME, ANCIENT—BUILDINGS**
Forum Romanus, pizza box, making 2463:51

**ROME, ANCIENT—CHARIOT RACES**
Circus Maximus chariot and horses models, card-
      board, box, paints, making 2332:32-33

**ROME, ANCIENT—CLOCKS**
Mosaic clock, quartz clock movement, card-
      board, magazine pictures, making
      2332:16-17

**ROME, ANCIENT—CLOTHING**
Golden headdress tiara, cardboard, gold foil,
      beads, making 2791:28-29
Palla, fabric, making 2323:105
Stola, fabric, making 2323:104
Stola, woman's tunic, fabric or sheet, rope, pat-
      tern, making 2482:6-8
Toga, brooch and laurel crown, cardboard, gold
      paint, fabric, making 2509:14-15
Toga, sheet, making 2323:102-103
Toga, white sheet, pattern, purple ribbon, making
      2482:32-33
Toga, white sheet, t-shirt, ribbon, making
      2791:26-27
Tunic exterior, child or man's tunic, fabric or
      sheet, rope, making 2482:8-9

**ROME, ANCIENT—COINS**
Celebration coin, cardboard, clay, paints, making
      2332:28-29
Coin rubbings, how to do 2323:141
Coins, bottle caps, cardboard, making
      2482:92-93
Coins, clay, making 2323:140

**ROME, ANCIENT—COOKERY**
Artichokes, recipe 2323:118-119
Bean salad, recipe 2323:120
Bread in a bag, recipe 2323:125
Carrots in sweet-sour sauce, recipe 2930:31
Cinnamon raisin rolls, recipe 2323:123-124
Crustulum, garlic toast, recipe 2323:121
Gustum appetizer, vegetable and fruit dish,
      recipe 2482:99-101
Honey omelet, recipe 2463:76
Honeyed dates, recipe 2791:24-25
Olive rolls, recipe 2323:122

Prima mensa (main course of dinner), ham with sauce, recipe    2482:101

**ROME, ANCIENT—EMPERORS**

Imperial bust, corrugated paper, paints, making    2332:26-27

Portrait coins of Emperors, bottle caps, foil, paint, making    2509:34-35

**ROME, ANCIENT—FESTIVALS**

Martinmas; how to celebrate    2328:131-132

Saturnali; pilei hats, making    2328:114

Saturnali; sigillaria pottery dolls, foil, clay, making    2328:115

Saturnalia candle, candles, photo, making    2463:80

**ROME, ANCIENT—FOOTWEAR**

Sandals, chamois, patterns, making    2323:108-109

**ROME, ANCIENT—GAMES**

Dice game, clay, glass tiles, beads, how to make and play    2791:48-49

Dice game, how to make and play    2323:172

Jacks game, how to play    2323:171

Knuckle bones, how to make and play    2482:62-63

Micatio game, how to play    2323:169

Mosaic decorated board games, checkers and Ludo, making    2332:12-13

Odd or even game, how to play    2323:170

Trigon game, how to play    2323:173

**ROME, ANCIENT—GARDENS**

Garden stepping stones, cement, making    2463:52-53

**ROME, ANCIENT—GLADIATORS**

Gladiator sword fight, cardboard, paints, brads, making    2332:30-31

**ROME, ANCIENT—GODS**

Janus doorway, paper, foamcore board, pattern, making    2463:40

Lararium cupboard, for praying to gods, cereal box, paper, paints, making    2482:34-37

**ROME, ANCIENT—HOUSES**

Roman home model, cardboard, paints, making\    2791:18-19

Roman kitchen, cardboard, clay, balsa wood, paints, plaster of Paris, making    2791:22-23

**ROME, ANCIENT—JEWELRY**

Beaded bracelet, gold safety pins, beads, making    2323:110

Bracelet, poster board, gold cord, glass gems, making    2482:85-86

Bulla, child's gold pendant charm, clay, paints, string, making    2482:9-11

Earrings, beads, gold thread, making    2323:111

Earrings, gold cord, gold foil, golden beads, making    2482:29-31

Necklace, gold cord, gold buttons, making    2482:83-84

Tiara for women, poster board, gold metallic pipe cleaners, gold buttons, making    2482:81-82

**ROME, ANCIENT—LAMPS**

Candle lamp, clay, paints, candle, making    2332:24-25

Oil lamp, clay, paints, making    2482:96-98

**ROME, ANCIENT—LANGUAGE**

Phrases in Latin    2323:174

**ROME, ANCIENT—MASKS**

Actor's mask, clay, cardboard, beads, paints, making    2791:46-47

**ROME, ANCIENT—MATHEMATICS**

Abacus, how to use    2323:146-147

Roman numerals, how to understand and use    2571:10-11

**ROME, ANCIENT—MOSAICS**

Border designs and square designs on cardboard, designs on cardboard boxes, making    2332:10-11

Box; mosaic, papier-mâché, paints, making    2259:26-27

Floor mosaic, cardboard, beans, glue, making    2482:22-23

Grecian coaster, clay, paints, pattern, making    2683:20-21

Mosaic tile, pasta, beads, paints, making    2509:18-19

Mosaic trivet, clay, flat glass, pebbles, making    2463:74

Mosaic, cardboard, clay, plaster of Paris, paints, making    2791:38-39

Picture mosaic, colored papers, glue, making    2482:24-26

Roman mosaic, posterboard, foam sheets, making    2257:12-13

**ROME, ANCIENT—NAMES**

Roman boys and girls name games activity    2482:16-19

**ROME, ANCIENT—NUMERALS**

Roman numerals chart, how to make    2482:57-59

**ROME, ANCIENT—PAINTING**

Fresco painting, foil, plaster of Paris, gold paint, making   2509:38-39

**ROME, ANCIENT—POTTERY**

Amphora vessel, coiled clay pot, clay, paint, making   2509:42-43

**ROME, ANCIENT—ROADS**

Groma (used to measure right angles and to make sure roads were straight), cardboard, balsa wood pole, silver foil, string, paints, making   2791:60-61

Hodometer to measure distance, making 2323:148-149

Roman highway, soil, pebbles, sand, gravel, making   2463:54-55

**ROME, ANCIENT—RUINS**

Roman ruin desk organizer, cardboard boxes, straws, tissue paper, paints, making 2332:36-37

**ROME, ANCIENT—SCROLLS**

Papyrus scroll, cardboard, paints, ribbons, making   2332:14-15

**ROME, ANCIENT—SCULPTURES**

Plaster paperweight, clay, paints, making 2332:22-23

**ROME, ANCIENT—SHIPS**

Merchant ship model, paper, straws, patterns   , making   2323:157-159

**ROME, ANCIENT—SIGNS**

Wall sign for home, cardboard, marker, string, making   2482:14-16

**ROME, ANCIENT—SOAP**

Bath oil, recipe   2323:114

**ROME, ANCIENT—SOLDIERS**

Legion's standard (sign), poster board, duct tape, making   2482:46-47

Legionary's helmet, paint bucket, paper, duct tape, making   2482:48-51

Legionary's shield, corrugated cardboard, red and black and yellow paper, making 2482:41-45

**ROME, ANCIENT—SUNDIALS**

Horogium, sundial with Latin mottoes, foam board, black marker, making   2482:64-67

**ROME, ANCIENT—TEMPLES**

Temple gift box, cardboard boxes, cardboard tubes, paints, making   2332:20-21

Temple model, cardboard, straws, paints, making   2791:50-51

**ROME, ANCIENT—THEATER**

Pantomime mask, paper plate, markers, yarn, making   2482:79-81

**ROME, ANCIENT—TRIUMPHAL ARCH**

Triumphal arch plaque model, cardboard, clay, making   2482:72-74

**ROME, ANCIENT—TRIUMPHAL COLUMN**

Triumphal column model, paper towel roll, markers, making   2482:75-77

**ROME, ANCIENT—VOLCANOES**

Volcano model, paper cone, baking soda, vinegar, making   2323:179

**ROME, ANCIENT—WEAPONS**

Catapult, milk cartons, making   2323:132

Seige tower periscope, cardboard, mirrors, plastic lids, popsicle sticks, making 2332:34-35

Slingshot, rubber bands, tree branch, making 2323:133

**ROME, ANCIENT—WREATHS**

Vine wreaths, vines, making   2440:100-102

Wreaths or crowns, silk flowers, wire, making 2323:163-164

**ROME, ANCIENT—WRITING**

Scroll for permanent writing, paper bag, ribbon, making   2482:56-59

Wax tablet for writing, cardboard, clay, making 2482:54-55

Wax tablet, cardboard, clay, paints, making 2509:22-23

Wax tablets, crayons, paints, making 2323:165-167

Writing tablet, balsa wood, clay, paints, making 2791:30-31

Writing tablet, small box, clay, making   2930:30

**ROOSEVELT, EDITH (FIRST LADY)**

America's First Ladies Portrait Gallery, making 2263:84

**ROOSEVELT, EDITH (FIRST LADY)—COOKERY**

Currant-filled biscuits, recipe   2551:11

Lemon-flavored milk ice, recipe   2551:17

Senegalese soup, recipe   2551:21

Sugar wafers, recipe   2551:7

**ROOSEVELT, ELEANOR (FIRST LADY)**

Eleanor Roosevelt portrait, pattern   2758:77

**ROOSEVELT, FRANKLIN DELANO (PRESIDENT)**

Design your own coat of arms, making 2263:101

Royal picnic, making 2263:101
Stamp collecting – one President's hobby, making
    2263:101

**ROOSEVELT, THEODORE (PRESIDENT)**

Bears for Theodore, patterns, making 2263:85
Insect observatory, making 2263:86
White House menagerie, making 2263:86

**ROSH HASHANAH—COOKERY**

Apple and honey cake, recipe 2697:10-11
Apple cake, recipe 2888:165
Apple honey servers, recipe 2346:19
Apple noodle kugel, recipe 2888:175
Apple-pecan crisp, recipe 2888:167
Carrot tzimmes, recipe 2697:12
Challah, poppy seed-topped, recipe
    2888:172-174
Challah, recipe 2984:27
Chocolate rocks, recipe 2888:166
Honey cookies, recipe 2888:170-171
Lekakh, honey cake, recipe 2888:168-169
Raisin-farfel kugel, recipe 2888:176
Round challah, recipe 2697:8-9

**ROSS, BETSY—BIRTHDAY**

January 1, 1752, stories, music, games, activities,
    projects, patterns 2377:16-20

**ROSS, BETSY—HATS**

Betsy Ross's colonial hat, tissue paper, ribbon,
    making 2735:8-9

**ROUSSEAU, HENRI**

Jungle prints, making 2529:49

**RUBBER**

Rubber, recipe for making 2918:100-104
Special effects rubber, recipe 2918:128-129

**RUBENS, PETER PAUL**

Chalk light face, making 2529:27

**RUDOLPH, WILMA**

Wilma Rudolph portrait, pattern 2758:81

**RUSSELL, C. M.**

Western sunset, making 2529:56

**RUSSIA—BIRTHDAYS—DECORATIONS**

Party line of decorations and favors, making
    2957:36-37

**RUSSIA—CHRISTMAS—COOKERY**

Pirozhki (meat pastry), recipe 2481:46-47
Wheat porridge, recipe 2680:67

**RUSSIA—COOKERY**

Appetizers, recipe 2680:38
Apple strudel, recipe 2710:123
Azerbaijan stew, recipe 2835:34-35

Baked fish, recipe 2680:53
Baked potatoes with sour cream, recipe
    2835:28-29
Beef stroganoff, recipe 2680:46
Beef stroganoff, recipe 2835:30-31
Beet and cabbage soup, recipe 2380:unp
Beet salad, recipe 2680:43
Beet soup, recipe 2680:40
Blini (buckwheat pancakes), recipe 2835:12-13
Blini pancakes, recipe 2870:107
Blinis, recipe 2845:37
Boiled potatoes, recipe 2680:52
Borscht (beet soup), recipe 2835:10-11
Cheese pancakes, recipe 2680:56
Cherry kissel, recipe 2835:42-43
Cream cheese tarts, recipe 2835:36-37
Deviled eggs, recipe 2835:16-17
Fruit compote, recipe 2680:49
Galushki (Russian dumplings), recipe
    2835:32-33
Georgian-style chicken casserole, recipe
    2835:20-21
Honey cake, recipe 2396:45
Liver pate, recipe 2835:18-19
Pancakes, recipe 2680:52
Paska (cottage cheese cake), recipe 2835:38-39
Piroshki (vegetable pastries), recipe
    2835:24-25
Potato and sorrel soup, recipe 2835:14-15
Potatoes with dressing, recipe 2680:34
Raspberry kisel, recipe 2680:59
Russian menu 2680:28-29
Russian salad, recipe 2680:54-55
Rye bread, recipe 2271:30-31
Rye bread, recipe 2680:32-33
Sausage, recipe 2680:35
Shashlyk lamb kebabs, recipe 2835:26-27
Spring vegetable salad, recipe 2680:41
St. Petersburg-style apples recipe 2835:40-41
Stuffed pastries, recipe 2680:44-45
Stuffed pumpkin, recipe 2835:22-23
Sweet treats, recipe 2858:30-31
Tea, recipe 2680:48
Zakuska, appetizers, recipe 2810:25

**RUSSIA—DOLLS**

Babushka dolls, papier-mâché, paints, making
    2858:28-29
Matryoshka dolls, paper, markers, making
    2686:88-89
Matryoshka dolls, plastic soda bottle, yarn, felt,
    paints, making 2780:6-7

**RUSSIA—EASTER—COOKERY**

Sweetbread, recipe 2680:64-65

143

**RUSSIA—EASTER—DECORATIONS**

Easter rooster, paper, dyes, food colorings, making 2407:85

Easter tree with painted eggs, making 2846:36-37

**RUSSIA—EPIPHANY—COOKERY**

Blinchiki pancakes, recipe 2888:34

Walnut butter cookies, recipe 2888:35

**RUSSIA—FESTIVALS**

May Day; activities, Russian boy and girl patterns, making 2759:35-39

**RUSSIA—FESTIVALS—COOKERY**

Name Day Festival; twig cookies, recipe 2680:68-69

**RUSSIA—FICTION**

*Baboushka and the Three Kings* by Nicolas Sidjakow, activities, projects, patterns, art, crafts 2822:90-92

*Molly's Pilgrim* by Barbara Cohen, activities for art, music, food, clothing and history 2478:38-72

*Rechenka's Eggs* by Patricia Polacco, activities, crafts, patterns, games, masks, puppets, making 2329:94-96

**RUSSIA—FOLKLORE**

*Cock and the Hen,* story and activities 2423:40-45

*Fool of the World and the Flying Ship* by Arthur Ransom, activities, literature, art, science, poetry, social studies, webbing 2435:25-33

*Ox and His Animal Friends,* story and activities 2423:108-119

**RUSSIA—GAMES**

Bear game, how to make and play 2821:22

Czar and peasants, how to play 2767:126

Egg rolling, how to play 2767:126

Ermine, how to play 2767:126-127

Gorodki game, how to play 2525:78

Gymnastic headstand, how to do 2847:36-37

Log roller game, how to play 2525:108

Word games from Russia, how to play 2310:3-8

**RUSSIA—LANGUAGE**

Learn to speak a few Russian words 2821:23

Russian words for family members 2810:23

Words and numbers in Russian, how to say 2870:108

**RUSSIA—LANTERNS**

Paper lanterns, paper, glue, making 2845:36

**RUSSIA—PYSANKY EGGS**

Decorated eggs, paper plate, crayons, making 2686:86-87

**RUSSIA—TEA PARTIES—COOKERY**

Cheese blintzes, recipe 2643:58

How to plan and set the table 2643:56-57

Russian caravan tea, recipe 2643:58

**RUSSIA—TEA PARTIES—DANCES**

Kazatsky dance, how to do 2643:59

**RUSSIA—TOYS**

Dancing bear, red cardboard, crochet thread, pattern, making 2784:24-25

**RUSSIAN-AMERICANS—COOKERY**

Cooked vegetable salad, recipe 2879:236-237

Marinated mushrooms, recipe 2879:235-236

Medovnichki, honey cookies, recipe 2965:11

Pate, liver, recipe 2879:236

Pilaf (rice and beef), recipe 2879:235

**RUSSIAN-AMERICANS—EASTER—EGGS**

Dyeing eggs with onion skins, eggs, onion skins, making 2965:23

**RWANDA—GAMES**

Matha Kisana (jackstones), how to play 2767:127-128

# S

**SAAMI PEOPLES—CLOTHING**
Saami hat, felt, ribbons, cardstock, making   2456:46-47

**SABBATH—COOKERY**
Chicken noodle soup, recipe   2346:12-13

**SABBATH—DECORATIONS**
Sand candle holders, jars, sand, making   2346:13

**SACAJAWEA**
Sacajawea portrait, pattern   2758:79

**SAILING SHIPS**
Anchor; make a ship's anchor   2934:36-37
Bell, clay flowerpot, paints, making   2934:96
Figure head, modeling dough, paint, making   2934:180-181
Shadow box ship, bark, dowels, foam sheets, making   2934:3-5
Wharf, soda bottles, wood paint stirrers, crafts sticks, making   2934:170

**SAILORS**
Collect fresh rainwater, how to do   2934:34-35
Ditty box; box, papier-mâché, making   2934:48-49
Marlinspike; making sailor's knots   2934:127-128
Scrimshaw; soap, black ink, making   2934:80-81
Sea chest, box, paints, making   2934:32-33
Sewing palm; vinyl leather, metal button, making   2934:94-95
Tattoo, making   2934:26-27
Walking stick; PVC pipe, pattern, making   2934:82-83

**SAILORS—CARGO**
Barrel, cardboard container, paint, making   2934:172-173

**SAILORS—CARVING**
Carve a soapstone whale, foil, clay, making   2934:146-147

**SAILORS—COOKERY**
Bean soup, recipe   2934:44-45
Boston baked beans, recipe   2934:176
Chinese tea, recipe   2934:110

Dandyfunk, recipe   2934:13
Lobscouse, recipe   2934:97
New England fish chowder, recipe   2934:167-168
Plum duff, recipe   2934:73-74
Sweet bird's nest, recipe   2934:111
Wampanoag clam casserole, recipe   2934:182-183

**SAILORS—DANCES**
Hornpipe dance, how to do   2934:40-41

**SAILORS—GAMES**
Dominoes, how to play   2934:178-179
Drop jack straws, how to play   2934:182
Fox and geese, how to play   2934:174
Morse code signal game, how to play   2934:125-126
Old Maid, how to play   2934:184-185
Ropewalk game, how to play   2934:177

**SAILORS—HANDICRAFTS**
Hide the treasure, make a treasure map   2441:27-29
Make the treasure, jewelry, coins, foils, making   2441:26
Ocean in a bottle, bottle, food coloring, oil, making   2441:22-23
Pirate treasure chest, container, foil, velvet, cloth, decorations, making   2441:24-25

**SAILORS—MUSICAL INSTRUMENTS**
Squeezebox, poster board, music disk, making   2934:38-39

**SAILORS—PLAYS**
Play about King Neptune's visit, how to do   2934:52-54

**SAILORS—SAILS**
Furl a sail, nylon plastic yarn, pillow case, coat hanger, making   2934:169

**SAILORS—VALENTINE'S DAY**
Sailor's Valentine, cardboard, shells, yarn, making   2934:163

**SALTEN, FELIX—PUPPETS**
*Bambi* puppet, lunch bag, fiberfill, making   2729:42-43

**SALVADORIAN-AMERICANS—COOKERY**

Crab salad, recipe   2879:239

Guacamole, recipe   2879:238

Stuffed tortillas, recipe   2879:238-239

**SAMOAN-AMERICANS—COOKERY**

Banana desert, recipe   2879:240

Chop sui, recipe   2879:240-241

**SANDWICH DAY—FICTION**

*The Giant Jam Sandwich* by John Vernon Lord, activities, crafts, patterns, games, masks, puppets, making   2329:25-28

**SAUDI ARABIA—FESTIVALS—COOKERY**

Eid ul-Fitr; date-nut cookies, recipe   2504:44-45

Khoshaf, sweet dessert, recipe   2665:30-31

**SAUDI ARABIA—FESTIVALS—GREETING CARDS**

Eid el-Fitr; card, paper, paints, making   2665:28-29

Eid ul-Fitr; greeting cards, paper, mosque pattern, ribbon   2504:46-47

**SAUDI ARABIA—GAMES**

Chase in order game, how to play   2525:34

Marbles, how to play   2767:128

**SAUDI ARABIA—WEDDINGS**

Henna decorated hands, how to do   2665:26-27

**SAY, ALLEN**

*Grandfather's Journey* by Allen Say, literature, activities, art, curriculum   2436:45-52

**SCANDINAVIA—COOKERY**

Bagels and lox, lox roll-ups, recipe   2924:18-19

**SCANDINAVIA—FAMILY TREE**

Family tree, how to make   2977:27

**SCANDINAVIA—FLAGS**

Flags, paper, making   2977:19

**SCANDINAVIA—HANDICRAFTS**

Scandinavian hearts, wheat or wild grass, ribbon, making   2440:110

Straw goat, wheat or rye stalks, making   2440:113-114

Wheat figure, wheat or rye stalks, making   2440:112

Wheat wreaths, wheat or rye stalks, wire, yarn, ribbons, making   2440:109

**SCARECROWS**

Scarecrows for class crops, oak tag, craft sticks, making   2298:64

Soft-sculpture scarecrow, old clothes, straw, twine, fabric paint, making   2440:118-119

Traditional scarecrow, old clothes, straw, twine, fabric paint, making   2440:115-117

**SCHOOLS—FICTION**

*School Days* by B. G. Hennessey, activities, crafts, patterns, games, masks, puppets, making   2329:5-10

**SCOTCH-IRISH-AMERICANS—COOKERY**

Apple stack cake, recipe   2879:242-243

Potato soup with cornmeal, recipe   2879:242

Shortbread, recipe   2879:243-244

**SCOTLAND—CHRISTMAS—COOKERY**

Black bun, recipe   2339:75

Cock-a-leekie soup, recipe   2339:74

Dundee cake, recipe   2339:76

Haggis, liver dish, recipe   2339:73

Roast goose, recipe   2339:73

Steak and kidney pie, recipe   2339:74

Venison stew, recipe   2339:75

**SCOTLAND—CHRISTMAS—DECORATIONS**

Candle holder, clay, candle, holiday decorations, making   2339:70

Holly jingle berry wreath, Styrofoam wreath, felt, red jingle bells, red ribbon, making   2339:67

Holly jingle leaves, green felt, cotton balls, bells, patterns, making   2339:65-66

Lamb ornament, cotton balls, ribbon, sequins, glitters, making   2339:68-69

**SCOTLAND—COOKERY**

Athol brosse, oatmeal dish, recipe   2838:42-43

Scotch shortbread, recipe   2459:30-31

**SCOTLAND—FAMILY CREST**

Family crest, cardboard, paper, paints, making   2504:18-20

**SCOTLAND—GAMES**

Albert Adams ate an alligator, how to play   2767:148

Easa matessa game, how to play   2525:72

Goal game, how to play   2525:46

Help game, how to play   2525:130

Leapfrog game, how to play   2525:66

Throw, catch, run game, how to play   2525:87

**SCOTLAND—LOCH NESS MONSTER**

Loch Ness monster model, paper plate, paints, making   2686:98-99

**SCOTLAND—NEW YEAR—COOKERY**

Hogmanay scones, recipe   2504:15-16

**SCOTLAND—NEW YEAR—SONGS**

Hogmanay, sing Auld Lang Syne   2402:42-43

146

**SCOTLAND—NEW YEAR'S DAY—COOKERY**

Almond shortbread, recipe   2888:20

Scottish scones, recipe   2888:18-19

**SCOTLAND—TARTANS**

Design and make a tartan, how to do
2459:28-29

**SCOTTISH-AMERICANS—COOKERY**

Highlander's soup, recipe   2879:246-247

Oatcakes, recipe   2879:245

Pancakes, recipe   2879:246

Shortbread, recipe   2879:244-245

**SCRAPBOOKS**

Language arts, poetry, hobby craft activities
2511:101-105

Memory scrapbook, making   2511:102

**SCRIMSHAW**

Carve scrimshaw, soap, black ink, making
2934:80-81

**SEA**

Thematic units, lessons, activities, art, poetry,
crafts, patterns, recipes   2320:129-157

**SECRET CODES**

Send a secret code message, how to do   2571:12

**SECRET GARDEN—GARDENS**

Bird bath, making   2342:115

Create your own secret garden, how to do
2342:76-117

Flowerpot garden, making   2342:81-82

Indoor secret garden, making   2342:83-85

Key wind chimes, making   2342:93-94

Moss-covered flower urns, making   2342:91-92

Nest building station, making   2342:116-117

Plant labels, making   2342:90

Pressed flower scrapbook, making
2342:101-102

Pressed flowers, making   2342:99-100

Robin's picnic tea basket, making
2342:113-114

Rose bouquet, making   2342:103-104

Spring bulb garden, making   2342:78-80

Topiary flower arrangement, making
2342:105-106

Twig tool holder, making   2342:88-89

Twig trellis, making   2342:97-98

Watering can planter, making   2342:95-96

**SECRET GARDEN—HANDICRAFTS**

Mary's skipping rope, making, English skipping
rhymes included   2342:108-112

**SEDER—COOKERY**

Setting the Seder table   2953:10

**SEDER—DECORATIONS**

Seder table crafts, making   2953:13-14

**SEMINOLE AND MICCOSUKEE
INDIANS—CLOTHING**

Miccosukee patchwork clothing, paper, patchwork, making   2480:66-69

**SEMINOLE AND MICCOSUKEE
INDIANS—COOKERY**

Fried pumpkin bread, recipe   2879:248

Pumpkin bread, recipe   2879:248

Sofkee (hominy grits), recipe   2879:247-248

**SEMINOLE INDIANS—COOKERY**

Pumpkin soup, recipe   2294:49

**SEMINOLE INDIANS—DOLLS**

Seminole doll, fabric, beads, paints, patterns,
making   2350:28-29

**SEMINOLE INDIANS—PATCHWORK**

Patchwork coaster, fabric, fill, making
2311:21-25

Seminole patchwork, cardboard, patterns,
making   2350:34-35

**SENEGAL—COOKERY**

Casamance fish stew, recipe   2628:60

Chickpeas with sugar snap peas, recipe
2838:20-21

Senegalese soup, recipe   2551:21

**SENEGAL—FESTIVALS—COOKERY**

Eid-al-Fitr; chicken yassa, recipe   2481:54-55

**SENEGAL—GAMES**

Lagan Buri, how to play   2767:128-129

**SENSES**

Thematic units, lessons, activities, art, poetry,
crafts, patterns, recipes   2320:41-68

**SENUFO (AFRICAN PEOPLES)—PAINTINGS**

Senufo figures prints, paper, fabric, paints, patterns, making   2620:16-17

**SEPTEMBER THEMES**

Thematic units, lessons, activities, art, poetry,
crafts, patterns, recipes   2320:11-40

**SERBIA—CHRISTMAS—COOKERY**

Cesnia rolls, recipe   2403:46-47

**SERBIA—GAMES**

Mother, mother, tell me the time, how to play
2767:129

Shapza, Lapza, who is my friend?, how to play
2767:129

**SERBIAN-AMERICANS—COOKERY**

Cucumber salad, recipe   2879:249-250

Juvech (rice casserole), recipe   2879:250

147

**SEURAT, GEORGES**

Pointillist color cards, making  2529:54

Seurat sugar cookies, recipe  2738:123

**SHAKESPEARE, WILLIAM**

Julius Caesar; produce a scene from *Julius Caesar*, how to do  2251:102-105

**SHAKESPEARE, WILLIAM—BIRDFEEDERS**

Build a bird feeder or nesting shelf, plastic jug, wire, making  2251:27

Feed the birds, suet recipe and hummingbird nectar recipe  2251:28

**SHAKESPEARE, WILLIAM—COAT OF ARMS**

Design a Coat of Arms, poster board, making  2251:76-78

**SHAKESPEARE, WILLIAM—COOKERY**

Apple moye, sweet apple dish, recipe  2251:34

**SHAKESPEARE, WILLIAM—COSTUMES**

Slashed-shirt costume, t-shirt, colored tights, making  2251:95-96

**SHAKESPEARE, WILLIAM—FAMILY TREE**

Your own family tree, how to do  2251:21

**SHAKESPEARE, WILLIAM—GAMES**

Juggling; learn how to juggle  2251:17-19

Nine Men's Morris, how to make and play  2251:49-50

Teetotum game, how to make and play  2251:48-49

**SHAKESPEARE, WILLIAM—HANDICRAFTS**

Folio; bind your own folio, paper, yard, ribbons, making  2251:122-123

Gloves; decorate a pair of gloves, leather gloves, lace, making  2251:12-13

Pomander ball, orange, cloves, spices, ribbons, making  2251:8-9

**SHAKESPEARE, WILLIAM—HORNBOOK**

Hornbook, cardboard, paper, clear plastic, making  2251:31-32

**SHAKESPEARE, WILLIAM—PENS**

Quill pen, feather, ink, making  2251:67-68

**SHAKESPEARE, WILLIAM—PLAYS**

Goblet for a prop, foil, plastic cup, making  2251:87-89

Sound effects, how to make  2251:84

**SHAKESPEARE, WILLIAM—SONGS**

Compose a sonnet, how to do  2251:69-70

**SHAKESPEARE, WILLIAM—SWORD FIGHT**

Stage a sword fight, how to do  2251:99-100

**SHAKESPEARE, WILLIAM—WEAPONS**

Sword, cardboard tube, crepe paper, making  2251:97-98

**SHAVUOT—COOKERY**

Cheese blintzes, recipe  2697:24-25

Cheese cake, recipe  2982:25

Fruit compote, recipe  2346:73

Mini cheesecakes, recipe  2697:26-27

Sweet milk pudding, recipe  2697:28

**SHAVUOT—DECORATIONS**

Fruit centerpiece, making  2346:74

**SHAWNEE INDIANS—COOKERY**

Cheemee (sweet treat), recipe  2879:251

Fried corn soup, recipe  2879:252

**SHAWNEE INDIANS—GAMES**

Tetepaulalowaawaa (rolling game), how to play  2767:174

**SHAWNEE INDIANS—JEWELRY**

Beaded necklace, leather strip, beads, making  2596:22

**SHOSHONE INDIANS—BASKETS**

Basket, tag board, yarn, making  2597:22

**SHOSHONE INDIANS—COOKERY**

Buffalo stew, recipe  2295:57

Fry bread, recipe  2634:28

**SHOSHONE INDIANS—GOD'S EYE**

God's Eyes, string or yarn, craft sticks, making  2634:30

**SHOSHONE INDIANS—LANGUAGE**

Everyday words in Shoshone language  2295:92-95

**SHROVE TUESDAY—COOKERY**

Pancakes, recipe  2678:9

**SIERRA LEONE—COOKERY**

Okra soup, recipe  2628:52

**SIHASAPA INDIANS. *See* BLACKFEET INDIANS**

**SIKSIKA INDIANS—COOKERY**

Pemmican patties, recipe  2430:13

**SIKSIKA INDIANS—LANGUAGE**

Blackfeet words for some foods, utensils and community helpers  2556:22

**SIKSIKA INDIANS. *See also* BLACKFEET INDIANS**

**SIMCHAT TORAH—COOKERY**

Caramel apples, recipe  2346:35

**SIMCHAT TORAH—FLAGS**

Simchat Torah flag, paper, glitter, glue, wooden sticks, making   2346:34

**SINGAPORE—COOKERY**

Curry puffs, recipe   2564:116

**SINGAPORE—GAMES**

Five sacks jacks game, how to play   2330:106-108

Wall refuge game, how to play   2525:30

Yea string game, how to play   2525:76

**SINGAPORE—PASSOVER—COOKERY**

Charoset, recipe   2737:78-79

**SIOUX INDIANS—COOKERY**

Beans and bacon, recipe   2879:255-256

Boiled meat, recipe   2879:254

Corn balls, recipe   2879:255

Fry bread, recipe   2879:253

Indian popovers, recipe   2879:254

Stuffed pumpkin, recipe   2879:254-255

Wojapi pudding, recipe   2879:253

Wo-Jopee, Sioux blackberry dessert, recipe   2523:70-71

**SIOUX INDIANS—OWNER STICKS**

Owner stick, dowels, markers, feathers, making   2523:59-60

**SIXTIES—COOKERY**

Green beans almandine, recipe   2359:150-151

Mother Earth's zucchini bread, recipe   2359:146

Peace, love and crunch granola, recipe   2359:145

Swift 'n' savory spinach and onion quiche, recipe   2359:148-149

**SLOPPY JOES—COOKERY—HISTORY**

Sloppy Joes, recipe   2359:124-125

Sooner sloppies, recipe   2534:57-58

**SLOVAK-AMERICANS—COOKERY**

Baba (potato and barley dish), recipe   2879:258

Cabbage and noodle dish, recipe   2879:258

Nut candy, recipe   2879:257

Old fashioned hamburgers, recipe   2879:256-257

Slovak cookies, recipe   2879:257

**SLOVAK REPUBLIC—GAMES**

Trades, how to play   2767:130

**SLOVAKIA—DOLLS**

Gourd dolls, gourd, paints, making   2407:84

**SLOVENE-AMERICANS—COOKERY**

Kifles (nut horns cookies), recipe   2879:261

Potato salad, recipe   2879:259

Potica coffeecake, recipe   2879:259-260

**SLOVENIA—FOLKLORE**

*Bull and His Animal Friends,* story and activities   2423:111-119

**SMITH, DAVID**

Cubi structure, making   2529:91

**SNOW GLOBES**

Snow globe soap, making   2936:46-47

Snow globes, baby food jars, plastic animals, glitter, making   2328:90-91

**SNOWFLAKES**

Paper snowflakes, pattern, making   2328:18-19

Silver snowflakes, silver wire, making   2883:14-18

Snowflake pattern and how to cut into paper circle   2755:38

Snowflakes, paper, how to cut   2318:12-13

**SNOWFLAKES—FICTION**

*Snowflake Bentley* by Jacqueline Briggs Martin, activities, literature, science, poetry, social studies, webbing   2435:151-170

**SNOWMEN**

Frosty the snowman soap, making   2936:64-65

Snowmen soap, making   2936:45

Sock snowmen, socks, stuffing, googly eyes, making   2883:34-37

**SOAP**

April Fool's soap, making   2936:43

Bathtub soap jelly, recipe   2918:98

Dog soap, making   2936:24-25

Easter eggs soap, making   2936:42

Frosty the snowman soap, making   2936:64-65

Gross eyeballs soap, making   2936:48-49

Halloween treat's soap, making   2936:44

Hearts soap, making   2936:41

New Year's confetti soap, making   2936:38-39

Snow globe soap, making   2936:46-47

Snowmen soap, making   2936:45

Soap bracelet, making   2936:40

**SOMALIA—FESTIVALS—COOKERY**

Eid al-Fitr; lamb and rice, recipe   2627:66

**SOMALIA—GAMES**

Garir jacks game, how to play   2330:95-96

**SOMALIA—LANGUAGE**

Speak Somali words   2443:23

**SOMALIA—POETRY**

Write Somalia poem   2443:22

**SOUTH AFRICA—CHRISTMAS—DECORATIONS**

Crinkle-paper chain, crepe paper, making 2740:21

**SOUTH AFRICA—COOKERY**

Coconut barfi, recipe 2663:35

Fish fingers, recipe 2845:41

**SOUTH AFRICA—FESTIVALS—BEADWORK**

Zulu bead keychain, felt, beads, keychain loop, making 2846:40-41

**SOUTH AFRICA—GAMES**

Beanbag smash game, how to play 2525:167

Count and cover, how to play 2357:22

Diketo, how to play 2767:130-131

Dithwai, how to play 2767:131-132

Dithwai: cattle game, how to play 2310:14-17

Double tag game, how to play 2525:160

Frog, jump, and slide game, how to play 2525:177

Hog ball game, how to play 2525:148

Hop, skip, jump game, how to play 2525:88

Moraba-raba (mancala) game, how to make and play 2847:40-41

One-legged concentration game, how to play 2525:100

Running steps game, how to play 2525:9

Stinger game, how to play 2525:20

**SOUTH AFRICA—LANGUAGE**

Afrikaans words for family members 2663:27

Greeting in Afrikaans and Zulu languages 2663:24

Learn to speak Afrikaans, few words 2357:23

**SOUTH AFRICA—PASSOVER—COOKERY**

Almond cake, recipe 2737:136-137

**SOUTH AFRICA—SONGS**

Sesotho song 2663:41

**SOUTH AMERICA—ANIMALS**

Constrictor snake model, green paper, paints, making 2686:109-110

Emerald tree boa, making 2686:107-108

Giant armadillo model, paper plate, making 2686:117-118

**SOUTH AMERICA—COOKERY**

South American menu 2670:28-29

Turnovers, recipe 2670:62-63

**SOUTH CAROLINA—COOKERY**

Benne cookies, recipe 2416:63

Frogmore stew, recipe 2470:75

Good-for-the-soul grits, recipe 2534:64

Peach cobbler, recipe 2853:66

**SOUTH CAROLINA—FESTIVALS—COOKERY**

World Grits Festival; good-for-the-soul grits, recipe 2534:64

**SOUTH DAKOTA—COOKERY**

Flappin' jacks, recipe 2534:65-66

**SOUTH KOREA—GAMES**

Flower relay, relay race, how to play 2310:69-73

Go game, how to play 2926:20-23

Kong-Keui jacks game, how to play 2330:79-81

**SOUTH PACIFIC**

Activities, patterns 2757:119-132

Pacific Islands boy and girl costumes, patterns 2757:122-123

**SOUTHEAST ASIA—FICTION**

*Through Moon and Stars and Night Skies* by Ann Turner; activities, art, poetry, maps, crafts, foods, patterns 2642:33-38

**SOUTHERN STATES—COOKERY**

Corn chowder, recipe 2380:unp

**SOUTHERN STATES—HANDICRAFTS**

Sticks and staffs, decorated sticks, making 2441:58-59

**SOUTHERN STATES—JEWELRY**

African jewelry, sewing leftovers, decorations, making 2441:60-61

**SOUTHERN STATES—MUSICAL INSTRUMENTS**

African drums, oatmeal boxes, paints, making 2441:56

Mouth bow, stick, string, making 2441:52-53

Musical jugs, bottles, water, making 2441:54

**SOUTHERN STATES—TEA PARTIES—COOKERY**

Fiddleless fudge, recipe 2643:38

How to plan and set the table 2643:36-37

Lemon iced tea, recipe 2643:38

**SOUTHERN STATES—TEA PARTIES—HANDICRAFTS**

Hoopskirts, hoola-hoop, fabric, making 2643:39

**SOUTHERN STATES—TOYS**

Dolls, clothespins, corks, making 2441:65-66

Hobby horse, sock, stuffing, stick, making 2441:62-63

**SOUTHWEST COAST INDIANS—DEER**

Ancient split twig deer, twigs, string, making 2349:28

**SOUTHWEST COAST INDIANS—JEWELRY**

Southwestern jewelry, clay, paints, wire, beads, making   2349:40-41

**SOUTHWEST COAST INDIANS—PETROGLYPHS**

Kokopelli, the flute player on stones or note paper, designs given, making   2349:22-23

Shell and rock drawings, designs given, making   2349:20-21

**SOUTHWEST COAST INDIANS—POTTERY**

Pinch pots, clay, paints, recipe for clay, making   2349:14-15

**SOUTHWEST COAST INDIANS—WRITINGS**

Native American writings, poems and songs to copy, making   2349:44-45

**SOUTHWEST, NEW—CHRISTMAS—COOKERY**

Black bean soup, recipe   2901:76

Calabacitas (vegetable and cheese dish), recipe   2901:77

Grilled marinated pork tenderloin, recipe   2901:78

Pineapple and jicama salad, recipe   2901:79

Salsa, recipe   2901:76

Sopaipillas, recipe   2901:77

Texas pecan pie, recipe   2901:79

**SOUTHWEST, NEW—CHRISTMAS—DECORATIONS**

Adobe candle house, clay, paints, patterns, making   2901:72-73

Clay ornaments, clay, paints, making   2901:70-71

Poinsettia place mat, felt, patterns, making   2901:65-67

Sponge painting, patterns, how to do   2901:68-69

**SOUTHWEST, NEW—FESTIVALS—COOKERY**

Day of the Dead; sugar skulls, recipe   2441:102-103

**SOUTHWEST, NEW—MUSICAL INSTRUMENTS**

Mexican maracas and Native American rattles, making   2441:100-101

**SOUTHWEST, NEW—WEAVING**

Drop spindle, how to make a schoolyard drop spindle   2441:96

Spun yarn and woven cloth, making   2441:94

Using a drop spindle   2441:96-97

Weaving with a hanging loom, how to do   2441:98-99

Wool for weaving, how to prepare   2441:95

**SPACE**

Thematic units, lessons, activities, art, poetry, crafts, patterns, recipes   2320:249-278

**SPAIN—CHRISTMAS—COOKERY**

Jijona Nougat sweet, recipe   2336:62

Paella, recipe   2481:50-51

**SPAIN—CHRISTMAS—DECORATIONS**

Farol star, paper, crepe paper, ribbon, making   2407:90

**SPAIN—COOKERY**

Artichokes with garlic mayonnaise, recipe   2836:32-33

Asparagus with ham, recipe   2836:12-13

Chicken with rice, recipe   2336:48

Cod croquettes, recipe   2836:30-31

Coffee with milk, recipe   2336:36

Cold fresh vegetable soup, recipe   2336:58

Crema frita (fried custard), recipe   2612:30-31

Cucumber, tomato and green pepper snack, recipe   2336:54

Flan (caramel custard), recipe   2336:49

Fruit punch, recipe   2336:52

Gazpacho (cold tomato soup), recipe   2836:10-11

How to set a Spanish table   2336:31

Lentil soup Madrid style, recipe   2336:40

Magdalenas (olive oil cakes), recipe   2836:40-41

Nut sweets, recipe   2836:36-37

Paella (rice, chicken and shrimp), recipe   2836:20-21

Paella, recipe   2336:44-45

Pork fillet with almonds, recipe   2836:22-23

Potato and onion omelette, recipe   2836:24-25

Prawns in batter, recipe   2836:14-15

Red pepper salad, recipe   2836:34-35

Roasted vegetable salad, recipe   2836:26-27

Russian salad, recipe   2336:69

Salad, recipe   2336:43

Spanish meatballs, recipe   2336:53

Spanish menu   2336:32-33

Spanish omelette, recipe   2271:45

Spanish omelette, recipe   2336:59

Spicy potatoes, recipe   2836:16-17

Stewed vegetables, recipe   2336:46

Torrijas (sugary egg-fried bread), recipe   2836:38-39

Tortilla, recipe   2712:126

Walnut puffs, recipe   2836:42-43

White bean and pork stew, recipe   2836:28-29

Zucchini and eggplant fritters, recipe   2836:18-19

**SPAIN—EASTER—COOKERY**

Holy week doughnuts, recipe   2336:65

**SPAIN—EPIPHANY—COOKERY**

Roscon de reyes (Three Kings cake), recipe   2677:26-27

**SPAIN—FESTIVALS—COOKERY**

Andalusian Flamenco Festival; gazpacho, recipe   2962:77

Andalusian Flamenco Festival; roasted pimentos, recipe   2962:76

Andalusian Flamenco Festival; sangria fruit punch, recipe   2962:75

Andalusian Flamenco Festival; seafood paella, recipe   2962:78

Flamenco Festival; flan, recipe   2962:79

Ham fritters, recipe   2336:66

**SPAIN—FESTIVALS—MASKS**

Carnival; mask, papier-mâché, paints, making   2612:28-29

**SPAIN—GAMES**

Alquerque, how to play   2767:132-134

Crazy circle game, how to play   2525:29

Gypsy wrestling game, how to play   2525:77

Matador dominoes game, how to play   2491:22-24

Matador dominoes game, how to play   2548:20

Moon and the morning stars, how to play   2767:134

Petanca game, how to play   2526:117

**SPAIN—HANDICRAFTS**

Mosaics; paper mosaics, colored paper, making   2852:110-111

**SPAIN—LANGUAGE**

Common phrases in Spanish   2712:95

**SPAIN—MUSICAL INSTRUMENTS**

Castanets, cardboard, making   2686:80-81

Castanets, wooden disks, string, paints, making   2612:27

**SPAIN—PASSOVER—HANDICRAFTS**

Chad Gadya glove, making   2737:191

**SPANISH-AMERICANS—COOKERY**

Gaspacho, recipe   2879:262-263

Spanish eggs, recipe   2879:262

Spanish rice, recipe   2879:262

Spanish soup, recipe   2879:263-264

**SPORTS—PUPPETS**

Football finger puppets, gloves, patterns, making   2675:46-48

**SRI LANKA—COOKERY**

Pineapple curry, recipe   2838:36-37

**SRI LANKA—FESTIVALS—DECORATIONS**

Peacock plumes, paper, straws, making   2407:81

**SRI LANKA—GAMES**

Cheetah and goats, how to play   2767:134

Cows and leopards, how to make and play   2882:40-41

Cows and leopards, how to play   2767:134-136

Cross your hands game, how to play   2385:13

**SRI LANKA—HANDICRAFTS**

Snake demon, folded newspaper, papier-mâché, tissue paper, poster paints, making   2781:8-9

**ST. LUCIA—CHRISTMAS—COOKERY**

Sorrel drink, recipe   2925:64

**ST. PATRICK'S DAY**

Activities, finger plays, songs, rhymes, crafts, patterns   2828:64-65

Activities, recipes, songs, games   2863:90-102

History of St. Patrick's Day   2877:22

Story times, activities, leprechaun tubey pattern, craft instructions   2636:21-23

Teacher activities, crafts, patterns, foods   2417:all

Thematic units, lessons, activities, art, poetry, crafts, patterns, recipes   2320:185-219

**ST. PATRICK'S DAY—COOKERY**

Bread and butter pudding, recipe   2888:69-70

Brownies, recipe   2888:66

Cinnamon rolls, recipe   2888:72

Corned beef and cabbage, recipe   2877:27

Irish scones, recipe   2758:37

Irish soda bread, recipe   2877:25

Irish soda bread, recipe   2888:67

Lucky clover salad, recipe   2877:24

Magical shamrock potion, recipe and activities   2576:105-108

Oatmeal-apple crumble, recipe   2888:71

Peanut cakes, recipe   2888:63-64

Pot of gold dessert, recipe and activities   2576:109-112

Potato and barley soup, recipe   2877:26

Potato soup, recipe   2417:unp

Raisin oatmeal cookies, recipe   2888:68

Shamrock butter cookies with green icing, recipe   2888:73-74

Shamrock cake, recipe   2939:unp

White icing, recipe   2888:65

## ST. PATRICK'S DAY—DECORATIONS

Leprechaun figure, paper, crayons, fasteners,
making 2811:31-33

Leprechaun, movable, patterns 2758:43-45

Leprechaun, paper plate, making 2863:96

Leprechaun, pattern 2758:50-51

Leprechaun's pot of gold model, paper cups, paper, pebbles, ribbons, gold paint, making
2544:42-43

Pot of gold, pattern 2758:48

Potatoes; how to grow 2939:unp

Shamrock cat figure, paper, crayons, patterns,
making 2811:34-36

Shamrock pattern 2758:40

Shamrocks, patterned paper, making
2923:12-13

## ST. PATRICK'S DAY—FICTION

*Leprechauns Never Lie* by Lorna Balian, activities, art, games, songs, crafts, patterns 2812:70-77

*St. Patrick's Day in the Morning* by Eve Bunting, activities, crafts, patterns, games, masks, puppets, making 2329:87-92

## ST. PATRICK'S DAY—HANDICRAFTS

Clover ring, jewelry wire, green beads, making
2857:32-33

## ST. PATRICK'S DAY—MARIONETTES

Leprechaun marionette, paper towel tube, stiff
paper, pattern, making 2417:unp

## ST. PATRICK'S DAY—PUPPETS

Leprechaun finger puppets, gloves, patterns,
making 2675:29-30

## STAMP COLLECTING

Language arts, poetry, hobby craft activities 2511:111-114

## STATUE OF LIBERTY

Liberty's torch pattern 2475:48

Statue of Liberty by the numbers, how to do
2667:5

Statue of Liberty clay model, clay, box, cardboard, paints, making 2687:18-19

Statue of Liberty crown, paper plates, gold paint,
making 2735:28-29

Statue of Liberty torch, paper, foil, colored paper, making 2686:14

## STEAMBOATS

Paddleboat model, milk cartons, making
2497:37-39

## STELLA, JOSEPH

Mixed media lines, making 2529:64

## STONE AGE PEOPLES—BOW DRILL

Bow drill model to make fire, dowels, balsa
wood, making 2487:20-21

## STONE AGE PEOPLES—CANOES

Model canoe, clay, cardboard, chamois leather,
making 2487:46-47

## STONE AGE PEOPLES—CAVE PAINTINGS

Clay painting, clay, paints, making 2487:42-43

## STONE AGE PEOPLES—COOKERY

Stewed fruit, recipe 2487:22-23

## STONE AGE PEOPLES—DYES

Dyeing cloth, natural dyes, making 2487:38-39

## STONE AGE PEOPLES—GRAVES

Passage grave, clay, soil, green fabric, making
2487:54-55

## STONE AGE PEOPLES—HENGES

Wood henge (circle) structure, cardboard, dowels, clay, making 2487:52-53

## STONE AGE PEOPLES—HUNTERS—HOUSES

Mammoth-bone home, clay, paints, making
2487:18-19

## STONE AGE PEOPLES—JEWELRY

Necklace, clay, paints, chamois leather, making
2487:40-41

## STONE AGE PEOPLES—PAINTINGS

Hand art, clay, paints, making 2487:16-17

## STONE AGE PEOPLES—POTTERY

Clay pot, clay, making 2487:36-37

## STONE AGE PEOPLES—SCULPTURES

Figurine, board, clay, varnish, making
2487:58-59

## STONE AGE PEOPLES—TOOLS

Axe model, clay, paints, dowel, chamois leather,
making 2487:32-33

## STONE AGE PEOPLES—WEAPONS

Bow and arrow, clay, paint, dowels, making
2487:48-49

Harpoon model, wood, dowel, paints, leather
laces, making 2487:24-25

## STORYTELLING

Language arts, poetry, hobby craft activities
2511:127-133

Mini flannel board, patterns, making 2511:128

## SUDAN—GAMES

Dala, how to play 2767:136-137

Hyena chase game, how to make and play
2882:36-37

Leopard trap, how to play 2767:137

Tricket game, how to make and
play 2882:38-39

**SUDAN—MUSICAL INSTRUMENTS**

"Calabash" rattle; forked stick, cardboard, paints,
making 2620:60-61

Sanza or thumb piano, box, paints, craft sticks,
pattern, making 2620:60-61

**SUKBOT—DECORATIONS**

Sukkah decoration, coat hanger, leaves, flowers,
fruits, making 2982:23

Etrog ball, citron, spices, making 2346:31

Fruit, papier-mâché, making 2478:69

Hanging decorations, making 2346:30

Sukkah model, clay, craft sticks, twigs, leaves,
making 2346:31

**SUMERIANS—BURIALS**

Gold burial helmet, papier-mâché over balloon,
gold and black paint, making 2654:20-21

**SUMERIANS.** *See also* **MESOPOTAMIA**

**SURINAME—COOKERY**

Brown beans, recipe 2961:53

Cassava cake, recipe 2961:53

Peanut soup, recipe 2961:52

Rice chicken, recipe 2961:52

**SURVEY INSTRUMENTS**

Sextant; make and use a sextant 2739:13, 20

**SUTTER, JOHN AUGUSTUS**

John Sutter mask, poster board, yarn, making
2689:6-7

**SWEDEN—BIRTHDAY CUSTOMS**

Swedish birthday customs 2547:22-23

**SWEDEN—CHRISTMAS—COOKERY**

Pepparkakor cookies, recipe 2677:28

Santa Lucia sweet rolls, recipe 2753:112

**SWEDEN—CHRISTMAS—DECORATIONS**

Advent calendar, pattern, making 2753:113

Heart-shaped baskets for tree, paper, making
2395:22

Julgrans Karamell (Christmas tree candy) decorations, tissue paper, ribbons, making
2707:22

Santa Lucia hat, paper, making 2407:73

Santa Lucia head wreath, pattern, making
2753:109

**SWEDEN—CHRISTMAS—HANDICRAFTS**

Sunburst folded paper ornament, making
2407:35

**SWEDEN—COOKERY**

Swedish compote, recipe 2306:51

**SWEDEN—COSTUMES**

Boy and girl costumes, patterns, making
2753:110

**SWEDEN—EASTER—COOKERY**

Semlor, marzipan and cream rolls, recipe
2321:109

**SWEDEN—FESTIVALS—CANDLES**

Santa Lucia Day; beeswax candles, beeswax,
wicking, making 2328:117-118

**SWEDEN—FESTIVALS—COOKERY**

Midsummer Festival; strawberry torte, recipe
2396:66-67

Santa Lucia Day; gingersnaps, recipe
2328:119-120

**SWEDEN—GAMES**

Bildaren game, how to play 2525:191

Bokstarsboll game, how to play 2525:104

Katter game, how to play 2525:100

Numbers tag, how to play 2767:138

Snabbmal game, how to play 2525:168

Stick hunter game, how to play 2525:131

Tradhok game, how to play 2525:10

**SWEDEN—LANGUAGE**

How to speak a few words in Swedish 2306:49

Phrases in Swedish 2321:111

Rune alphabet 2321:99

Seven words in Swedish 2707:23

**SWEDISH-AMERICANS—COOKERY**

Apple pie, recipe 2879:266-267

Asta kaka (cheesecake), recipe 2879:266

Gingerbread cookies, recipe 2879:267

Lindbergh's favorite Swedish party cakes, recipe
2977:23

Oven pancakes, recipe 2879:265

Rice porridge, recipe 2879:265-266

Swedish meatballs, recipe 2879:264-265

**SWISS-AMERICANS—COOKERY**

Pork chops, recipe 2879:268

Swiss cheese pie, recipe 2879:268

Swiss tea, recipe 2879:269

**SWITZERLAND—COAT OF ARMS**

Coat of arms, paper, making 2407:32

**SWITZERLAND—COOKERY**

Bircher muesli cereal, recipe 2713:126

Cheese fondue, recipe 2838:32-33

Dumplings, spaetzli or knopfli, recipe 2444:22

Swiss fondue, recipe 2613:30-31

**SWITZERLAND—COWBELLS**

Cowbell model, paper cup, foil, small bell,
painted macaroni, making 2613:28-29

**SWITZERLAND—FESTIVALS—HANDICRAFTS**

Klause Festival headdress, cereal box, colored paper, paper tube, making 2407:94

Klausjagen miter, paper, crayons, making 2407:19

**SWITZERLAND—GAMES**

Countries of the world game, how to play 2525:50

Grandmother, what do you want game, how to play 2385:22

Hallihallo, how to play 2767:138-139

One, two, three game, how to play 2525:34

Snatcher game, how to play 2525:106

Tail of the rat game, how to play 2525:34

Wolf, wolf, where are you game, how to play 2385:10

**SWITZERLAND—HANDICRAFTS**

Flower motifs, paper, paints, making 2407:26

Scroll frame, paper, making 2407:14

**SWITZERLAND—HATS**

Appenzell herdsman hat, black hat, flowers, ribbons, making 2613:27

**SWITZERLAND—LANGUAGE**

German words for greetings 2444:23

**SYMMETRY**

Tessellation patterns from symmetry, making 2571:18-19

**SYRIA—COOKERY**

Kibbee (wheat and meat), recipe 2879:18

Kibbee balls (wheat and ground lamb), recipe 2879:18

Tabouli salad, recipe 2879:18-19

**SYRIA—GAMES**

Add a movement game, how to play 2525:35

Bounce and whirl around game, how to play 2385:18

Countries game, how to play 2525:53

Don't laugh, how to play 2767:138

# T

## TAFT, WILLIAM HOWARD (PRESIDENT)
Cherry blossom forest, making    2263:88
Put it right here baseball picture, making
    2263:89

## TANGRAMS—GAMES
Nine connected rings tangram game, how to
    play    2382:21-23

## TANZANIA—COOKERY
Chapatis, recipe    2627:33

## TANZANIA—FESTIVALS—COOKERY
Eid al-Fitr; plantain soup, recipe    2627:69

## TANZANIA—GAMES
Fire on the mountain game, how to play
    2385:22
Giant's house, how to play    2767:139-140
Mancala game, how to make and play    2641:22

## TANZANIA—JEWELRY
Masai beaded women's collars, cardboard, paper
    plates, markers, making    2620:42-43
Masai earrings, cardboard, string, markers,
    making    2620:42-43

## TANZANIA—LANGUAGE
Kiswahili words, how to speak    2641:23

## TARASCAN INDIANS—GAMES
El coyote, how to play    2767:107-108
Peleche, how to play    2767:108-110

## TAXICABS—PUPPETS
Yellow taxicabs finger puppets, gloves, patterns,
    making    2675:51-52

## TAYLOR, ZACHARY (PRESIDENT)
Natural resources collage, making    2263:47
"Rough and Ready" straw hat, patterns, making
    2263:47

## TEA
How to prepare hot and cold tea    2643:8-9
Story of tea; a tale that spans 5,000 years and the
    globe    2643:6-7

## TEA—FICTION
*May I Bring a Friend?* By Beatrice Schenk de
    Regniers, literature, activities, act, curricu-
    lum    2436:87-103

## TEA PARTIES
Classic tea party; invitations, decorations, foods,
    crafts, games, how to do    2386:8-17
Garden tea party; invitations, decorations, foods,
    crafts, games, how to do    2386:52-61
Literary tea party; invitations, decorations, foods,
    crafts, games, how to do    2386:62-69
Pajama breakfast tea party; invitations, decora-
    tions, foods, crafts, games, how to do
    2386:70-77

## TEA PARTIES—COOKERY
Cucumber sandwiches, recipe    2386:13
Grandma's sweet tea, recipe    2386:12
Tea-pot topped cake, recipe    2386:15

## TEA PARTIES—HANDICRAFTS
Decorated tea cups, making    2386:16

## TEDDY BEAR DAY—FICTION
*The Teddy Bear's Picnic* by Jimmy Kennedy, ac-
    tivities, crafts, patterns, games, masks, pup-
    pets, making    2329:34-37

## TEDDY BEARS
Language arts, poetry, hobby craft activities
    2511:135-140
Terry cloth Teddy bear, patterns, making
    2511:136-137
Thematic units, lessons, activities, art, poetry,
    crafts, patterns, recipes    2320:279-304

## TEDDY BEARS—TEA PARTIES
Invitations, decorations, foods, crafts, games,
    how to do    2386:36-43

## TEDDY BEARS—TEA PARTIES—COOKERY
Beary good sandwiches, recipe    2386:41
Brown bear cookies, recipe    2386:40
Cinnamon tea, recipe    2643:18
Hot cocoa, recipe    2386:39
How to plan and set the table    2643:16-17
Spiced Teddy-Bear cookies, recipe    2643:18

## TEDDY BEARS—TEA PARTIES— HANDICRAFTS
Bear pageant, how to do    2643:19

## TENNESSEE—COOKERY
Apple crisp, recipe    2854:63
Strawberry bread, recipe    2772:63

Super southern pecan pie, recipe    2534:67

**TESSELLATION ART**

Tessellation patterns from symmetry, making    2571:18-19

**TETON SIOUX INDIANS—GAMES**

Hoop and pole, how to play    2767:175-176

**TEXAS—COOKERY**

Lone star chili and Tex-mex crackers, recipe    2534:68-69

**TEXAS—FOLKLORE**

*Legend of the Bluebonnet* by Tomie dePaola; activities, art, poetry, maps, crafts, foods, patterns    2642:129-132

**TEXAS WENDS—COOKERY**

Oven stew, recipe    2879:269-270

Sauerbraten, recipe    2879:270

**THAI-AMERICANS—COOKERY**

Pork stuffed omelet, recipe    2879:272

Spicy beef with mint leaves, recipe    2879:271

**THAILAND—COOKERY**

Bananas in syrup, recipe    2462:60

Beef noodles, recipe    2462:38

Chicken soup, recipe    2837:14-15

Chicken with basil, recipe    2837:24-25

Chili pineapple rice, recipe    2837:26-27

Coconut and mango ice cream, recipe    2837:36-37

Coconut custard, recipe    2307:51

Coconut milk, recipe    2462:36

Coconut soup and noodles, recipe    2924:24-25

Coconut tapioca with mango, recipe    2837:34-35

Crab and green onion cakes, recipe    2837:30-31

Cucumber salad, recipe    2462:50

Cucumber sauce, recipe    2462:55

Fish with vegetables, recipe    2837:18-19

Fresh fruit platter, recipe    2837:40-41

Fried bananas, recipe    2837:38-39

Fruit juice cocktail, recipe    2837:42-43

Galloping horses snacks, recipe    2462:66

Green beans with coconut, recipe    2837:22-23

Grilled marinated chicken, recipe    2462:46

Holiday fruit platter, recipe    2462:68

Lemon chicken soup, recipe    2462:31

Mango on sticky rice, recipe    2396:38-39

Nam Pla Prig sauce, recipe    2462:54

Pad Thai (Thai fried noodles), recipe    2462:64-65

Panaeng beef curry, recipe    2462:32

Papaya salad, recipe    2837:28-29

Pineapple-fish noodles, recipe    2462:37

Rice noodles, recipe    2462:36

Rice pancakes with shrimp and vegetables, recipe    2837:12-13

Rice with shrimp and tofu, recipe    2837:32-33

Rice, recipe    2462:30

Satay (meat dish), recipe    2837:10-11

Satay, recipe    2462:45

Spinach salad with chicken, recipe    2462:51

Stir-fried meat with basil, recipe    2462:42

Stir-fried noodles with chicken, shrimp, pork and vegetables, recipe    2837:16-17

Stir-fried vegetables, recipe    2462:52

Stir-fried vegetables, recipe    2837:20-21

Sweet and sour sauce, recipe    2462:55

Thai coconut custard, recipe    2462:60

Thai fried rice, recipe    2462:43

Thai menu    2462:26-27

Thai spring rolls, recipe    2462:58-59

Tropical fruit dessert, recipe    2462:67

Watermelon slushes, recipe    2700:66

Watermelon slushes, recipe    2859:30-31

**THAILAND—FESTIVALS—DECORATIONS**

Loy Krathong Festival boat, folded paper, making    2407:45

Loy Krathong Festival; Krathong floating flowers and candle, making    2859:28-29

**THAILAND—FLOWERS**

Lotus flower, paper plate, egg carton, paints, making    2686:54-55

**THAILAND—GAMES**

Here I come game, how to play    2385:21

Takraw, how to play    2767:140

Wing kala game, how to play    2859:26-27

**THAILAND—LANGUAGE**

How to speak a few words in Thai    2307:49

**THAILAND—NEW YEAR'S EVE—COOKERY**

Thai egg rolls, recipe    2481:28-29

**THANKSGIVING**

Activities, crafts, puppets, patterns    2760:77-90

Activities, recipes, songs, games    2863:141-148

Corn activities    2445:49-52

Feast; activities, finger plays, songs, rhymes, crafts, patterns    2828:32-34

Feather activities    2445:53-54

History of Thanksgiving    2445:5-6

History of Thanksgiving    2877:78

Popcorn activities    2445:25-27

Potato activities    2445:39-41

Story times, activities, turkey tubey pattern, craft instructions    2636:67-68

157

Thematic units, lessons, activities, art, poetry, crafts, patterns, recipes   2320:69-96

**THANKSGIVING—BIRDFEEDERS**

Pinecone bird feeder, making   2846:44-45

**THANKSGIVING—COOKERY**

Chestnut stuffing, recipe   2877:81
Classic pumpkin pie, recipe   2888:198-199
Cranberry-orange relish, recipe   2877:80
Cream and fruit salad, recipe   2888:202-203
Creamy apple pie, recipe   2888:194-195
Meringue hands, recipe   2783:20-21
Mushroom gravy, recipe   2877:83
Pilgrim pumpkin pie, recipe   2877:84-85
Pumpkin cheese cake with cranberry glaze, recipe   2888:200-201
Pumpkin ice cream pie, recipe   2888:204
Pumpkin pie, recipe   2504:86-87
Pumpkin pie, recipe   2888:196-197
Pumpkin pie, recipe   2982:37
Roast turkey with potatoes and carrots, recipe 2877:82
Spiced Thanksgiving cider, recipe   2888:205
Tiny turkey candy treats, recipe   2857:15

**THANKSGIVING—DECORATIONS**

Give thanks Thanksgiving Day napkin holder, making   2798:63-64
Turkey decoration, paper, crayons, patterns, making   2811:16-18
Turkey tubes, paper tubes, paper, making 2778:30-31
Turkey; fruit and vegetable turkey, making 2923:26-27
Turkey seating cards, brown paper, markers, making   2971:44
Turkey-tail napkins, making   2857:14

**THANKSGIVING—DOLLS**

Pilgrim corn dolly, corn husks, pipe cleaners, yarn, making   2504:89-90
Scarecrow cornhusk dolls, making   2445:59

**THANKSGIVING—FICTION**

*It's Thanksgiving* by Jack Prelutsky, activities, art, games, songs, crafts, patterns   2812:17-21
*Oh, What a Thanksgiving!* by Steven Kroll, activities, crafts, patterns, games, masks, puppets, making   2329:38-42
*Silly Tilly's Thanksgiving Dinner* by Lillian Hoban, activities, crafts, patterns, mathematics, art, music and science   2445:22-30
*Sometimes it's Turkey-Sometimes it's Feathers,* by Lorna Balian, activities, art, games, songs, crafts, patterns   2812:22-27

*Thanksgiving at the Tappletons'* by Eileen Spinelli, activities, crafts, patterns, mathematics, art, music and science   2445:31-41
*A Turkey for Thanksgiving* by Eve Bunting, activities, crafts, patterns, mathematics, art, music and science   2445:7-21

**THREE BEARS**

*Three Bears* family, poster board, making 2729:28-29

**THREE KINGS DAY—COOKERY**

Three King's cake, recipe   2888:31-32

**TIBET—GAMES**

Wolf and sheep, how to play   2767:140-141

**TIBET—MANDALAS**

Tibetan monks colored sand mandalas, patterns, making   2331:7

**TIBET—MASKS**

Monk's mask, papier-mâché, making   2407:95

**TIE-DYE**

Tie-dyed socks, drink mix, vinegar, water, making   2684:142

**TIME CAPSULES**

Time capsule, how to make   2700:72-73

**TISHA-B'AV—HANDICRAFTS**

Kaleidoscope, mirrors, cardboard, clear acetate, tiny decorations, making   2346:77-78

*TITANIC*

*Titanic* activities, *Titanic* life-preserver pattern, making   2618:37

**TLINGIT INDIANS—BASKETS**

Tlinglit and Haida baskets for a potlatch, straw basket, paints, patterns, making 2351:18-19

**TLINGIT INDIANS—BLANKETS**

Button blanket, felt, buttons, making 2311:83-87

**TLINGIT INDIANS—COOKERY**

Fish chowder, recipe   2879:273
Fish perok pie, recipe   2879:274
Fish pie, recipe   2297:57

**TLINGIT INDIANS—LANGUAGE**

Everyday words in Tlingit language and how to pronounce them   2297:95-99

**TLINGIT INDIANS—MOCCASINS**

Tlingit style moccasins, fur or felt fabric, yarn, rawhide, beads, pattern, making   2440:78-81

**TLINGIT INDIANS—TOTEM POLES**

Totem pole, tin cans, paper bowl, poster paints, making   2781:24-25

**TOBAGO—COOKERY**

Pelau, meat, rice and vegetable dish, recipe 2911:50

**TOBAGO—FESTIVALS—COOKERY**

Carnaval; boiled corn, recipe 2925:62

**TOBAGO—GAMES**

Trier, how to play 2767:141-142

**TOBAGO—NEW YEAR—MUSICAL INSTRUMENTS**

Old Year's Day, steel drums, cans with lids, paints, making 2402:44-45

**TOGO—GAMES**

Awako (the hawk), how to play 2767:141

**TOHONO O'ODHAM INDIANS—BASKETS**

Basket, yarn, making 2311:63-68

**TOTEM POLES**

Totem pole, paper tube, cardboard, markers, making 2686:26-27

**TOULOUSE-LAUTREC, HENRI DE**

Event poster, making 2529:52-53

**TOYS**

Language arts, poetry, hobby craft activities 2511:141-145

**TRAINS**

Language arts, poetry, hobby craft activities 2511:147-151

Railroad tunnel, oatmeal box, making 2511:148

**TRANSCONTINENTAL RAILROAD—COOKERY**

Chop suey, recipe 2359:83-84

Coast to coast apple pie, recipe 2359:85-86

Coconut pudding, recipe 2359:87

**TRANSPORTATION**

Activities about cars, trains, blimps, hot air balloons, boats, lighthouses; costumes, maps, picture books, rhymes, patterns 2618:1-80

**TRINIDAD—COOKERY**

Callaloo vegetable soup, recipe 2393:30-31

Pelau, meat, rice and vegetable dish, recipe 2911:50

**TRINIDAD—FESTIVALS—COOKERY**

Carnaval; boiled corn, recipe 2925:62

**TRINIDAD—FESTIVALS—DECORATIONS**

Hosay Festival; paper crescent moon, paper, gold foil, making 2393:28-29

**TRINIDAD—GAMES**

Trier, how to play 2767:141-142

**TRINIDAD—NEW YEAR—MUSICAL INSTRUMENTS**

Old Year's Day, steel drums, cans with lids, paints, making 2402:44-45

**TRINIDAD-AMERICANS—COOKERY**

Curried chicken, recipe 2879:275

Potato bread, recipe 2879:275-276

**TRUMAN, HARRY S. (PRESIDENT)**

Chasing a frog, making 2263:104

Frog's tale, making 2263:104

Wreath for peace, making 2263:104

**TSIMSHIAN INDIANS—CRESTS**

Life crest, wood, paints, making 2311:92-95

**TSONGA (AFRICAN PEOPLES)—STAFFS**

Human figure with Tsongan helmet and leg and neck rings, cardboard, paints, making 2620:44-45

**TU B'SHEVAT—PLANTS**

Growing plants (sweet potato and parsley), how to do 2346:47

**TUAREG (AFRICAN PEOPLES)—HANDICRAFTS**

Tuareg containers, paper, yarn, colored markers, making 2620:14-15

**TUBMAN, HARRIET**

Harriet Tubman's route to freedom maze, box, straws, making 2731:12-13

**TUNISIA—COOKERY**

Tunisian cucumber salad, recipe 2871:43

**TURKEY—CHRISTMAS—COOKERY**

Butter cookies, recipe 2888:231

**TURKEY—COOKERY**

Almond cream, recipe 2904:58

Baklava, recipe 2904:54-55

Burnt rice pudding, recipe 2904:57

Chicken with rice, tomatoes, peppers and tarragon, recipe 2904:46-47

Dumplings with yogurt, recipe 2904:48

Eggplant with onion and tomatoes, recipe 2904:51

Green beans with minced meat, recipe 2904:42

Lamb kebabs with tomatoes, peppers and onions, recipe 2904:50

Meat pizza, recipe 2904:32-33

Mediterranean meatballs, recipe 2924:12-13

Olive, pomegranate and walnut salad, recipe 2838:24-25

Pumpkin dessert, recipe 2666:30-31

Red lentil soup, recipe 2904:40

Shredded wheat soup with tomatoes, recipe
2904:41
Spinach-filled Anatolian flat bread, recipe
2904:36-37
Turkish delight candy, recipe    2904:60-61
Turkish menu    2904:28-29
Zucchini fritters, recipe    2904:34

**TURKEY—FESTIVALS—COOKERY**
Baked meat and cheese pie, recipe    2904:68-69
Noah's dessert, recipe    2904:66
Ramazan; flat bread with nigella seeds, recipe
2904:64-65

**TURKEY—GAMES**
Fox and hen, how to play    2767:142-143
How do you like your neighbor?, how to play
2767:143
Pebbles game, how to play    2666:26

**TURKEY—WEAVING**
Kilim rug, cardboard, yarn, making    2666:28-29

**TURKEYS**
Activities, crafts, puppets, patterns
2760:91-102
Moveable turkey, pattern, making    2760:100
Turkey centerpiece, pattern, making    2760:94
Turkey feathers, pattern, making    2760:95

**TURKEYS—PUPPETS**
Turkey paper bag puppet, lunch bag, patterns,
making    2760:102

**TURKISH-AMERICANS—COOKERY**
Shepherd's salad, recipe    2879:277
Siskebab, recipe    2879:276-277
Spicy rice pilaf, recipe    2879:277-278

**TWAIN, MARK**
Lead line to measure depth of water for boats
(called "Mark Twain"), making
2935:62-63
Match fingerprints, how to do    2935:119
Scrapbook keeping, how to do    2935:99
Superstitions, how to collect    2935:97
Write maxims, how to do    2935:136

**TWAIN, MARK—COOKERY**
Fried corn pone, recipe    2935:101

**TYLER, JOHN (PRESIDENT)**
Animal lovers stamp poster, patterns, making
2263:41
Everybody polka, how to do    2263:40
Pets for President, pet house, patterns, making
2263:42-43
Texas necklace, making    2263:40

# U

**UGANDA—COOKERY**
>Chapatis, recipe  2627:33
>Choroko sauce, recipe  2627:46
>Fresh steamed fish, recipe  2627:54
>Greens with coconut milk, recipe  2627:41
>Meat on a stick, recipe  2627:34
>Vegetable casserole, recipe  2627:56

**UGANDA—GAMES**
>Inzama, how to play  2767:143-144

**UKRAINE—CHRISTMAS—COOKERY**
>Borsch with Vushka, meatless beet soup with mushroom dumplings, recipe  2902:75
>Dried fruit compote, recipe  2902:76
>Dumplings stuffed with potatoes and cheese, recipe  2902:76
>Honey balls, recipe  2902:77
>Honey cake, recipe  2902:77
>Mushroom dumplings (Vushka), recipe  2902:75
>Stuffed cabbage with mushroom filling, recipe  2902:78
>Walnut torte with coffee custard filling, recipe  2902:79

**UKRAINE—CHRISTMAS—COSTUMES**
>Costumes to wear while caroling, making  2264:26

**UKRAINE—CHRISTMAS—DECORATIONS**
>Silver webs and golden walnuts, silver pipe cleaners, walnuts, gold paint, making  2740:8-9

**UKRAINE—CHRISTMAS—HANDICRAFTS**
>Bookmarks, paper, patterns, making  2902:70-71
>Didukh, used to commemorate a family's ancestors, wheat stalks, wire, ribbon, dried flowers, making  2902:65
>Spider ornament, felt, paints, glitter, beads, sequins, making  2902:66-67
>Wreath ornament, dough, recipe for dough, ribbon, decorations, making  2902:68-69

**UKRAINE—COOKERY**
>Borsch beet soup, recipe  2533:119
>Strawberry kysil dessert, recipe  2264:30-31

**UKRAINE—EASTER—EGGS**
>Krashanka decorated eggs, food coloring, eggs, making  2264:28-29

**UKRAINE—FESTIVALS—DECORATIONS**
>Ivana Kupala Midsummer Festival; flower crowns, making  2264:27

**UKRAINE—FOLKLORE**
>*Mitten,* bursting mitten, cups, craft sticks, making  2729:44-45

**UKRAINE—GAMES**
>Are you awake, Mister Bear?, how to play  2767:144-145
>Rubber bands game, how to play  2533:123
>Ukrainian dominoes game, how to play  2548:22

**UKRAINE—LANGUAGE**
>Cyrillic alphabet  2533:89

**UKRAINE—PYSANKY EGGS**
>Pysanky eggs, dyes, wax, making  2440:60-65

**UKRANIAN-AMERICANS—COOKERY**
>Borsch, recipe  2879:279
>Easter svikly beef dish, recipe  2879:279
>Sauerkraut soup, recipe  2879:280

**UNCLE SAM**
>Newspaper Uncle Sam, paints, ribbons, making  2735:38-40
>Story times, activities, Uncle Sam tubey pattern, craft instructions  2636:45-47
>Uncle Sam figure pattern  2475:76
>Uncle Sam hat pattern  2475:52
>Uncle Sam lapel pin, wooden spoon, fiberfill, making  2735:35-36
>Uncle Sam mask, paper plates, fiberfill, colored paper, making  2733:18-19
>Uncle Sam tissue box, red and blue paper, pom-pom, making  2735:44-45

**UNCLE SAM—PUPPETS**
>Uncle Sam yardstick puppet, red, white and blue felt, cardboard, yardstick, making  2687:16-17

**UNITED NATIONS DAY**
>History of United Nations Day  2813:15

United Nations Day paper doll cut-outs, patterns, making 2813:16-18

**UNITED NATIONS DAY—GAMES**

United Nations Day puzzle game 2813:19

**UNITED STATES**

Activities, crafts, maps, patterns, making 2760:103-114

Happy Birthday America, stories, music, games, activities, projects, patterns 2377:7-15

**UNITED STATES—AIRPLANES**

Spirit of St. Louis model, milk carton, cardboard, making 2686:16-17

**UNITED STATES—BERRIES—COOKERY**

Blueberry pie, recipe 2428:unp

History of berries in the United States 2428:unp

Raspberry ice cream, recipe 2428:unp

Strawberry jam, recipe 2428:unp

**UNITED STATES—BIRTH CUSTOMS**

Mobile for a baby, wire hoops, ribbons, crepe paper, making 2963:32

**UNITED STATES—BIRTH CUSTOMS— COOKERY**

Ladybug birthday cake, recipe 2963:11

**UNITED STATES—BIRTH CUSTOMS— MAGIC TRICKS**

Mysterious disappearing leg trick, how to do 2957:44-45

**UNITED STATES—CHEERLEADING**

Pompoms, paper, making 2407:56

**UNITED STATES—CIRCUS—MASKS**

Clown mask, papier-mâché, making 2407:95

**UNITED STATES—COOKERY**

American foods and cooking timeline 2359:163-166

Aprinana cake, recipe 2260:14-15

Best-ever brownies, recipe 2260:44-45

Birthday cake, recipe 2260:26-27

Brunch, a fruity feast, recipe 2260:6-7

Burger bites, recipe 2260:32-33

Chunky chocolate cookies, recipe 2260:16-17

Cider, mulled apple cider, recipe 2486:27

Cute cookies, recipe 2260:24-25

Dippy chicken, recipe 2260:34-35

Fig pudding, recipe 2486:59

Fruity freezies, recipe 2260:18-19

Lemon cooler and super shakes, recipe 2260:20-21

Mini muffins, recipe 2260:10-11

Nacho nibbles, recipe 2260:40-41

Orange drink, recipe 2486:74

Pasta, recipe 2260:36-37

Peach cobbler, recipe 2486:36

Pecan pie, recipe 2838:38-39

Pizzas, recipe 2260:30-31

Rainbow snack sticks, recipe 2260:22-23

S'mores, recipe 2845:45

Sandwich stack, recipe 2260:12-13

Stuffed baked potatoes, recipe 2260:38-39

Sunshine breakfast, recipe 2260:8-9

Super sundaes, recipe 2260:42-43

Sweet dream treats, recipe 2260:28-29

Taffy pull, recipe 2511:120

Two minute treats, recipe 2260:46-47

**UNITED STATES—DOLLS**

Raggedy Ann invitations, making 2951:unp

Raggedy Ann tea party, how to do 2951:unp

**UNITED STATES—DOLLS—COOKERY**

Raggedy Ann's and Marcella's lemonade, recipe 2951:unp

Raggedy Ann's and Uncle Clem's scotch shortbread, recipe 2951:unp

Raggedy Ann's candy heart cookies, recipe 2951:unp

Raggedy Ann's easy chocolate cake with creamy pink and white icing, recipe 2951:unp

Raggedy Ann's tiny sandwiches, recipe 2951:unp

**UNITED STATES—FLAGS**

American flag place mats, red, white and blue felt, making 2687:10-11

Stars and stripes, how to do 2667:7-8

**UNITED STATES—FOLKLORE**

Alfred Bulltop Stormalong; activities, history, poetry, songs, games, recipes 2673:40-46

Annie Oakley; activities, history, poetry, songs, games, recipes 2673:66-72

*Bingo,* folktales, puppets, patterns, songs, food 2591:11-13

*Brer Possum and Brer Snake,* story and activities 2423:22-30

Davy Crockett; activities, history, poetry, songs, games, recipes 2673:20-25

Febold Feboldson; activities, history, poetry, songs, games, recipes 2673:47-53

*I Know an Old Lady Who Swallowed a Fly,* folktales, puppets, patterns, songs, food 2591:25-30

Joe Magarac; activities, history, poetry, songs, games, recipes 2673:60-65

John Henry; activities, history, poetry, songs, games, recipes 2673:54-59

John Henry; folktales, puppets, patterns, songs, food   2591:31-33

Johnny Appleseed; activities, history, poetry, songs, games, recipes   2673:7-13

Mike Fink and his daughter Sal; activities, history, poetry, songs, games, recipes   2673:14-19

Paul Bunyan; activities, history, poetry, songs, games, recipes   2673:26-32

Pecos Bill; activities, history, poetry, songs, games, recipes   2673:33-39

*Rabbit Tricks Snake,* folktales, puppets, patterns, songs, food   2591:40-42

*Teeny Tiny Woman,* folktales, puppets, patterns, songs, food   2591:45-48

## UNITED STATES—GAMES

A, my name is Alice, how to play   2767:149

Acka backa boo game, how to play   2385:14

Andy Mandy, sugar candy game, how to play   2385:37

Around the world jacks game, how to play   2330:125

Basic beanbag juggle, how to do   2494:15-20

Blind Hughie dominoes game, how to play   2548:24

Block dominoes, how to play   2491:18-19

Broomball game, broom, ball, how to play   2328:134-135

Categories hopscotch, how to play   2767:150-151

Categories, how to play   2767:149-150

Checkmate game, how to play   2525:113

Chick-ur-mur cravy crow, how to play   2767:151

Circle catch game, how to play   2525:164

Crack the eggs jacks game, how to play   2330:70-71

Crossover volleyball game, how to play   2525:182

Dodgeball game, how to play   2525:40

Double bounce jacks game, how to play   2330:52-53

Downcast jacks game, how to play   2330:120-121

Downhill racing jacks game, how to play   2330:86-87

Draw dominoes, how to play   2491:20-21

Ducks and ptarmigans, how to play   2767:167-168

Eggs in the basket jacks game, how to play   2330:57-58

A fistful of jacks game, how to play   2330:113-114

Five finger jacks game, how to play   2330:92-94

Fizz-buzz, how to play   2767:152

Fox and geese, how to play   2767:152-153

Gins (sticks), how to play   2767:171-173

Go for it game, how to play   2525:135

Grizzly bear, how to play   2767:166-167

Head of the class, how to play   2767:153

Hide-and-switch, how to play   2767:171

Higher and higher game, how to play   2385:37

Hoop and pole, how to play   2767:175-176

Hopscotch game, how to play   2525:65

Hopscotch game, how to play   2882:30-31

Horsie Jacks game, how to play   2330:61

Hot potato game, how to play   2385:26

Huckle, buckle, beanstalk game, how to play   2385:32

Jacks on the rooftop game   2330:97-99

Jacks, how to play   2767:153-155

Jackstones, how to play   2767:163-164

Jump rope games, how to play   2882:28-29

Jump rope, how to play   2767:155-156

Jumpin' jacks, how to play   2493:18-19

Laughing games, how to play   2767:170

Lemonade, how to play   2767:156

Limbo game, how to make and play   2882:20-21

Loop de loop jacks game, how to play   2330:90-91

Marbles, how to play   2767:156-158, 164-165, 174-175

Marbles, how to play   2847:44

"May I?" hopscotch, how to play   2767:158-159

Mexican train dominoes game, how to play   2548:26

Miss Mary Mack, how to play   2767:159-160

Moccasin game, how to play   2767:166

Mugging dominoes game, how to play   2548:28

No bounce jacks game, how to play   2330:54-55

No bouncing no way jacks game, how to play   2330:104-105

Onesies jacks game, how to play   2330:48-49

Over the back jacks game, how to play   2330:109-110

Peggy in the ring, how to play   2767:160-161

Pig in the pen jacks game, how to play   2330:62-63

Pigs over the fence jacks game, how to play   2330:64-65

Poker card game, how to play   2926:58-59

Potsy hopscotch, how to play   2492:16-19

Prince of Morocco, how to play    2767:161

Raven goes to his child, how to play    2767:168

Red rover game, how to play    2525:15

Ring and pin, how to play    2767:165-166

Ringtaw marbles, how to play    2495:20-21

Rounding up the horses jacks game, how to play    2330:82-83

Rummy card game, how to play    2926:44-45

Scatter Jacks game, how to play    2330:111-112

Scoop ball game, how to play    2525:92

Scratches and kisses jacks game, how to play    2330:118-119

Search for the name game, how to play    2525:72

Shuttlecock, how to play    2767:169-170

Skelly, how to play    2767:161-162

Soapbox soccer game, how to play    2525:171

Spades card game, how to play    2926:52-53

Spell and catch game, how to play    2525:101

Sweeps jacks game, how to play    2330:59-60

Toad in the hole jacks game, how to play    2330:129-130

Tossless and scatterfree jacks game, how to play    2330:77-78

Trust jacks game, how to play    2330:74-76

Twelve days of Christmas, how to play    2767:162-163

Twenty-one basketball game, how to play    2847:45

Twosies, threesies jacks game, how to play    2330:49-51

Ula maika game, how to play    2525:44

The whole kit and caboodle jacks game, how to play    2330:124

With my hands game, how to play    2385:18

**UNITED STATES—HANDICRAFTS**

Advertisement fan, 1900s, poster board, ice cream sticks, markers, making    2407:80

Ochter-foggel, paper folded bird, making    2407:34

Paper doll chains, making    2407:39

**UNITED STATES—HISTORY**

Activities, games, songs, book links    2667:3-32

Betsy Ross birthday, stories, music, games, activities, projects, patterns    2377:16-20

**UNITED STATES—HISTORY—19TH CENTURY—SCHOOL CLASSROOM GAMES**

Alphabet games; I love my love, the preachers cat, initials, how to play    2515:8-9

Alphabet geography, how to play    2515:18-19

Anagrams game, how to play    2515:12

Arithmetic games, how to play    2515:16-17

History games, how to play    2515:20-24

I spy game, how to play    2515:6

Rigamarole phrases game, how to play    2515:13

Word games; crambo, sentence relay, how to play    2515:10-11

**UNITED STATES—HISTORY—19TH CENTURY—TOYS**

Thaumatrope, cardboard, making    2515:25

**UNITED STATES—HISTORY—20TH CENTURY—CALLING CARDS**

Calling cards, magazines, glue, making    2744:16-17

**UNITED STATES—HISTORY—20TH CENTURY—COOKERY**

Blueberry muffins, recipe    2744:34-35

Brunch punch, recipe    2744:38-39

Cheesy omelet, recipe    2744:42-43

Chicken salad sandwiches, recipe    2744:24

Cream cheese and walnut sandwiches, recipe    2744:25

Gingerbread, recipe    2744:86-87

Ice cream snowballs, recipe    2744:80-81

Jelly biscuits, recipe    2744:20-21

Lemon ice, recipe    2744:26-27

Nut crunch apples, recipe    2744:72-73

Petits fours, recipe    2744:22-23

Saratoga potatoes, recipe    2744:36-37

Strawberries with cream, recipe    2744:41

Sunday ham, recipe    2744:40

**UNITED STATES—HISTORY—20TH CENTURY—DECORATIONS**

Flower basket, poster board, paints, lace, making    2744:30-31

Stand-up napkins, fabric, making    2744:32-33

**UNITED STATES—HISTORY—20TH CENTURY—FANS**

Fancy fan, sticks, ribbons, making    2744:18-19

**UNITED STATES—HISTORY—20TH CENTURY—GAMES**

Get shocked game, how to play    2744:89

Hopscotch, how to play    2744:75

I am a gold lock, how to play    2744:89

Plum pudding game, how to play    2744:75

Tableaux vivants (living pictures) game, how to play    2744:89

Twine the garland game, how to play    2744:88

**UNITED STATES—HISTORY—20TH CENTURY—HAIRBOWS**

Big hairbows, ribbons, barrette, making    2744:14

**UNITED STATES—HISTORY—20TH CENTURY—HANDICRAFTS**

Candy crystals, sugar, making   2744:84-85
Silhouettes, paper, chalk, making   2744:78-79
Tasseled toss billow, fabric, tassels, making 2744:82-83

**UNITED STATES—HISTORY—20TH CENTURY—VALENTINE'S DAY**

Glass paperweight, jar, felt, decorative items, making   2744:68-69
Pressed-flower bookmark, paper, paints, paper lace, making   2744:62-63
Seashell picture frame, shells, paints, making 2744:60-61

**UNITED STATES—HISTORY—CIVIL WAR—CANDLES**

Homemade candles, making   2447:26

**UNITED STATES—HISTORY—CIVIL WAR—COOKERY**

Herbal tea, recipe   2447:15

**UNITED STATES—HISTORY—CIVIL WAR—FICTION**

*Frank Thompson* by Byrna Stevens; readers theater booktalks with literature, poetry, music and creative writing activities   2681:29
*Now Let Me Fly* by Delores Johnson; readers theater booktalks with literature, poetry, music and creative writing activities   2681:27
*Turn Homeward, Annalee* by Patricia Beatty; readers theater booktalks with literature, poetry, music and creative writing activities 2681:30
*Who Comes with Cannons?* by Patricia Beatty; readers theater booktalks with literature, poetry, music and creative writing activities 2681:28

**UNITED STATES—HISTORY—CIVIL WAR—GAMES**

Hoops, how to play   2448:19

**UNITED STATES—HISTORY—CIVIL WAR—SONGS**

*Rally Round the Flag*   2448:25

**UNITED STATES—HISTORY—COLONIAL PERIOD**

Activities, crafts, hornbooks, quilts, trades, games, patterns   2388:14-20

**UNITED STATES—HISTORY—COLONIAL PERIOD—BANNERS**

Roger Williams banner, fabric squares, fabric paints, making   2621:67

**UNITED STATES—HISTORY—COLONIAL PERIOD—BOOKS**

Hornbook, pattern, making   2388:18

**UNITED STATES—HISTORY—COLONIAL PERIOD—CANDLEMAKING**

Candle making, paraffin, crayons, cotton twine, making   2314:19-21
Candles, how to dip and make   2388:44

**UNITED STATES—HISTORY—COLONIAL PERIOD—CANDLES**

Dipped candles, tin cans, wax, crayons, making   2441:17-19

**UNITED STATES—HISTORY—COLONIAL PERIOD—CHAP BOOKS**

Chap book of sandpaper prints, making 2621:61

**UNITED STATES—HISTORY—COLONIAL PERIOD—CLOTHING**

Carrying bag, fabric, flowering plants for printing fabric, making   2621:69
Sewing a pocket, fabric, felt, ribbon, making 2314:40-42

**UNITED STATES—HISTORY—COLONIAL PERIOD—COOKERY**

Apple cheddar muffins, recipe   2516:25
Baked apple crisp with dried fruits, recipe 2359:33-34
Corn chowder, recipe   2359:30
Cranberry apple crisp, recipe   2516:25
Creamy chicken on biscuits, recipe   2516:26
Hasty pudding, recipe   2516:19
Hearty soup, recipe   2516:27
Hot cider toddy, recipe   2823:90
Johnny cake, recipe   2684:26
Maple pumpkin pie, recipe   2516:28
Old-fashioned dried apple rings, recipe 2359:32
Pretzels, soft, recipe   2388:46
Sappawn (hasty pudding), recipe   2314:29
Shrewsbury cakes, recipe   2314:38-39
Spiced pears, recipe   2516:24
Virginia ham with cherry sauce, recipe   2359:31

**UNITED STATES—HISTORY—COLONIAL PERIOD—CURRENCY**

Money; pieces of eight, sculpey, foil, making 2314:44-45

**UNITED STATES—HISTORY—COLONIAL PERIOD—DOLLS**

Corn husk dolls, dried corn husks, twine, making 2621:65

**UNITED STATES—HISTORY—COLONIAL PERIOD—FICTION**

*Ox-Cart Man* by Barbara Cooney, activities, projects, patterns, art, crafts  2822:110-113

**UNITED STATES—HISTORY—COLONIAL PERIOD—FISHING**

Fishnet, jute, twine, making  2314:10-14

**UNITED STATES—HISTORY—COLONIAL PERIOD—FOODS**

Wreath of new world foods, salt dough, making  2621:63

**UNITED STATES—HISTORY—COLONIAL PERIOD—FURNITURE**

Cradle, box, cardboard, paints, making  2314:22-25

**UNITED STATES—HISTORY—COLONIAL PERIOD—GAMES**

Blind man's bluff game, how to play  2388:16
Hop, skip, jump game, how to play  2388:16
Hopscotch game, how to play  2388:16
Leapfrog game, how to play  2388:16
London bridge is falling down game, how to play  2388:16
Nine Men's Morris game, how to make and play  2366:88
Squat lap game, how to play  2388:16
Stone poison game, how to play  2388:16

**UNITED STATES—HISTORY—COLONIAL PERIOD—HANDICRAFTS**

Paper chains, paper, patterns, making  2621:73
Pomander balls, fruit, cloves, ribbon, making  2388:14
Shop sign, pattern, making  2388:19

**UNITED STATES—HISTORY—COLONIAL PERIOD—HOUSEHOLD ITEMS**

Chinese plate; plate, stencils, blue paint, making  2934:107-109

**UNITED STATES—HISTORY—COLONIAL PERIOD—INCOME**

Incomes of different professions  2366:27

**UNITED STATES—HISTORY—COLONIAL PERIOD—INKS**

Berry ink, recipe  2747:23

**UNITED STATES—HISTORY—COLONIAL PERIOD—LANTERNS**

Tin can lantern, cans, wire, making  2441:20-21

**UNITED STATES—HISTORY—COLONIAL PERIOD—PENS**

Quill pen, making  2747:23

**UNITED STATES—HISTORY—COLONIAL PERIOD—PEOPLES**

Stand-up people, manila folders, paints, patterns, making  2621:59

**UNITED STATES—HISTORY—COLONIAL PERIOD—QUILL PENS**

Writing with a quill pen, feather, ink, making  2314:34-35

**UNITED STATES—HISTORY—COLONIAL PERIOD—QUILTING**

Friendship quilt, paper, pattern, making  2388:20

**UNITED STATES—HISTORY—COLONIAL PERIOD—SCHOOLS**

Hornbook, cardboard, plastic, making  2314:15-17
Spelling bee, how to do  2747:29

**UNITED STATES—HISTORY—COLONIAL PERIOD—SIGNS**

Business sign, paper, how to make  2366:89

**UNITED STATES—HISTORY—COLONIAL PERIOD—THANKSGIVING— DECORATIONS**

Turkey and lobster salt dough models, making  2621:59

**UNITED STATES—HISTORY—COLONIAL PERIOD—WEATHER VANES**

Weather vane, aluminum baking sheets, patterns, making  2621:71

**UNITED STATES—HISTORY—COLONIAL PERIOD—WINDMILLS**

Model windmill, milk carton, small rocks, felt, making  2314:31-33

**UNITED STATES—HISTORY— DECLARATION OF INDEPENDENCE— DECORATIONS**

Liberty bell favor, corrugated cardboard, foil, making  2735:36-37

**UNITED STATES—HISTORY—FICTION**

*Coyote Places the Stars* by Harriet Peak Taylor; readers theater booktalks with literature, poetry, music and creative writing activities  2681:4-5
*First Strawberries: A Cherokee Story* by Joesph Bruchac; readers theater booktalks with literature, poetry, music and creative writing activities  2681:2
*Her Seven Brothers* by Paul Gobel; readers theater booktalks with literature, poetry, music and creative writing activities  2681:1

*Mud Pony* by Caron Lee Cohen; readers theater booktalks with literature, poetry, music and creative writing activities  2681:3

**UNITED STATES—HISTORY—LOUISIANA TERRITORY—COOKERY**

Bread pudding with fruit, recipe  2359:41-42

King cake, recipe  2359:43-45

Shrimp and ham jambalaya, recipe  2359:39-40

**UNITED STATES—HISTORY— REVOLUTIONARY WAR**

Soldiers patterns  2475:15

**UNITED STATES—HISTORY— REVOLUTIONARY WAR— CHRISTMAS—COOKERY**

Chewy Noels, recipe  2522:84

**UNITED STATES—HISTORY— REVOLUTIONARY WAR—CLOTHING**

Crewel embroidery pocket, fabric, embroidery floss, making  2522:69-72

Fringed hunting shirt, fabric, making  2471:75

Hunter's bag, chamois or felt, pattern, making  2522:7-9

**UNITED STATES—HISTORY— REVOLUTIONARY WAR—COOKERY**

Boston brown bread and churned butter, recipe  2471:24

Brew a batch of root beer, recipe  2471:5

Cream scones, recipe  2522:14-15

Independence Day shortcake, recipe  2522:40-41

Liberty tea punch, recipe  2471:12

New England Indian pudding, recipe  2522:16-17

Nut sweetmeats, recipe  2522:39

Patriot Tea Party; cinnamon tea toasties, recipe  2522:89-90

Patriot Tea Party; mulled cider, recipe  2522:89

Patriot Tea Party; tea, recipe  2522:88

Philadelphia pepper pot, recipe  2522:82-83

Spiced acorn squash, recipe  2522:54-55

**UNITED STATES—HISTORY— REVOLUTIONARY WAR—DANCES**

Dance a minuet, how to do  2471:39

**UNITED STATES—HISTORY— REVOLUTIONARY WAR— DECORATIONS**

Herbal hotplate, fabric, herbs, making  2522:86-87

Quilt pattern bookmark, making  2522:51-53

**UNITED STATES—HISTORY— REVOLUTIONARY WAR—DIORAMAS**

Diorama, shoebox, making  2522:46-48

**UNITED STATES—HISTORY— REVOLUTIONARY WAR—FICTION**

*Calico and Tin Horns* by Candace Christiansen; readers theater booktalks with literature, poetry, music and creative writing activities  2681:9

*George Washington's Mother* by Jean Fritz; readers theater booktalks with literature, poetry, music and creative writing activities  2681:10

*Johnny Tremain* by Esther Forbes; readers theater booktalks with literature, poetry, music and creative writing activities  2681:13

*Katie's Trunk* by Ann Turner; readers theater booktalks with literature, poetry, music and creative writing activities  2681:11

*This Time Tempe Wick* by Patricia Lee Gauch; readers theater booktalks with literature, poetry, music and creative writing activities  2681:12

**UNITED STATES—HISTORY— REVOLUTIONARY WAR—FLAGS**

Stars and stripes flag, felt, making  2522:29-30

**UNITED STATES—HISTORY— REVOLUTIONARY WAR—FOOTWEAR**

Moccasins, chamois, patterns, making  2522:78-80

**UNITED STATES—HISTORY— REVOLUTIONARY WAR—GAMES**

I sent a letter to my love, how to play  2471:23

Patriots and Redcoats, how to make and play  2522:19-21

Skin the snake, how to play  2471:23

Stool ball, how to play  2471:23

**UNITED STATES—HISTORY— REVOLUTIONARY WAR— HANDICRAFTS**

Almanac, colored paper, making  2471:28

Sampler, fabric, embroidery thread, making  2471:18

**UNITED STATES—HISTORY— REVOLUTIONARY WAR—HATS**

Three-cornered hat, felt, pattern, making  2522:10-12

Tricornered hat, paper, cardboard, black felt, making  2471:42

**UNITED STATES—HISTORY—
REVOLUTIONARY WAR—HOME
REMEDIES**

Home remedies, oatmeal scrub, toothpaste,
cough syrup, balm for chapped lips, recipes
2522:43-45

**UNITED STATES—HISTORY—
REVOLUTIONARY WAR—LANTERNS**

Pierced-tin lantern, tin can, patterns, making 2522:22-24

**UNITED STATES—HISTORY—
REVOLUTIONARY WAR—LIBERTY
BELL**

Model Liberty Bell, clay, making 2522:31-33

**UNITED STATES—HISTORY—
REVOLUTIONARY WAR—MUSICAL
INSTRUMENTS**

Ben Franklin's glass harmonica, making
2522:57-58

Spirit of '76 drum, cans, balloons, paper, making
2687:20-21

**UNITED STATES—HISTORY—
REVOLUTIONARY WAR—PAPER
CUTOUTS**

Papyrotamia, paper, making 2471:25

**UNITED STATES—HISTORY—
REVOLUTIONARY WAR—PICTURE
FRAMES**

Fabric-covered picture frame, fabric, cardboard,
making 2522:66-68

**UNITED STATES—HISTORY—
REVOLUTIONARY WAR—RUGS**

Stenciled floor cloth, cardboard, paints, making
2522:34-37

**UNITED STATES—HISTORY—
REVOLUTIONARY WAR—SCHOOLS**

School slate, masonite, blackboard paint, making
2522:25-26

**UNITED STATES—HISTORY—
REVOLUTIONARY WAR—TOYS**

Hand puppets, papier-mâché, making
2522:59-62

Tops, cardboard, making 2522:64-65

**UNITED STATES—HISTORY—
REVOLUTIONARY WAR—
VALENTINE'S DAY—GREETING
CARDS**

Pennsylvania Dutch Valentine, colored paper,
pattern, making 2522:91-92

**UNITED STATES—HISTORY—
REVOLUTIONARY WAR—WEAPONS**

Pouch, felt, making 2471:82

Powder horn, cardboard, papier-mâché, making
2471:82

**UNITED STATES—HISTORY—
REVOLUTIONARY WAR—
WOODWORKING**

Pegged-pine planter, pine shelving, patterns,
making 2522:75-77

**UNITED STATES—HISTORY—THE GREAT
DEPRESSION, 1929—COOKERY**

Ambrosia, recipe 2526:13

Apple kuchen, recipe 2526:36-37

Baked macaroni and cheese, recipe 2526:80-81

Banana cake, recipe 2526:84-85

Banana fritters, recipe 2526:18-19

Bread pudding, recipe 2526:48-49

Checkerboard sandwiches, recipe 2526:60

Cincinnati chili, recipe 2526:46-47

Club sandwiches, recipe 2526:34-35

Fruity freezer jam, recipe 2526:32-33

Glazed carrots, recipe 2526:78-79

Goldenrod eggs, recipe 2526:14-15

Iced fruit tea, recipe 2526:38-39

Oatmeal raisin cookies, recipe 2526:58-59

Oatmeal with peaches, recipe 2526:12

Roast beef hash, recipe 2526:82-83

Vanilla milk shake, recipe 2526:61

Waffles, recipe 2526:16-17

**UNITED STATES—HISTORY—THE GREAT
DEPRESSION, 1929—COOKERY. *See
also* GREAT DEPRESSION—COOKERY**

**UNITED STATES—HISTORY—THE GREAT
DEPRESSION, 1929—GAMES**

Alphabet traveling, how to play 2526:73

Barnyard confusion game, how to play 2526:41

Button race, how to play 2526:72

Checkerboard, craft board, paints, making
2526:86-87

Do this do that, how to play 2526:72

I stay stoop game, how to play 2526:41

Japanese fan race, how to play 2526:73

Jigsaw puzzle, making 2526:53

Marble maze game, how to make and play
2526:54-55

Roll ball game, how to play 2526:40

Tag and sing game, how to play 2526:41

Yo-yo, how to make 2526:52

**UNITED STATES—HISTORY—THE GREAT
DEPRESSION, 1929—HANDICRAFTS**

Clutch purse, felt, thread, making 2526:30-31

Flour-sack napkin, fabric, thread, making
2526:76-77
Mosaic tile trivet, making    2526:20-21
Scottie pillow, felt, stuffing, making
2526:62-63
Scrapbook, making    2526:28-29
Sew a patch, making    2526:22-23
Sun print greeting card, making    2526:26-27
Tommy-walkers, cans, paints, making
2526:66-67

**UNITED STATES—HISTORY—THE GREAT DEPRESSION, 1929—TOYS**

Tin can stompers, coffee cans, rope, making
2449:17

**UNITED STATES—HISTORY—WORLD WAR II—NAVAHO INDIANS**

Secret code, how to use Navajo words to write
secret message    2891:25-27

**UNITED STATES—JEWELRY**

Bracelet; stars and stripes bracelet, safety pin,
seed beads, making    2884:22-25

**UNITED STATES—MAY DAY—DECORATIONS**

May baskets, paper, making    2407:55

**UNITED STATES—NEW YEAR'S DAY—COOKERY**

Cream cheese pound cake, recipe    2888:23
Punch, recipe    2888:21

**UNITED STATES—NEW YEAR'S EVE—COOKERY**

Hoppin' John, cowpeas and rice, recipe
2504:31-32

**UNITED STATES—NEW YEAR'S EVE—DECORATIONS**

Noisemaker, papier-mâché, cardboard tube,
beans, paints, making    2504:29-30

**UNITED STATES—SCHOOLS**

Activities, crafts, puppets, games, patterns
2762:43-64

**UNITED STATES—SEALS**

Great seal model, poster board, dollar bill, green
and black markers, making    2687:8-9

**UNITED STATES—SONGS—HANDICRAFTS**

All the pretty horses, pretty horse, glove, felt,
yarn, making    2728:36-37
Bingo, there was a farmer who had a dog, bingo
marker can, brown bag, sticky magnets, bottle caps, coffee can, making    2728:46-47
Black sheep lapel pin, pipe cleaners, yarn, ribbon, making    2728:20-21

Eensy, weensy spider, washed out spider, cardboard tubes, pipe cleaners, yarn, tinsel,
making    2728:42-43
Farmer and friends in the dell, paper, markers,
making    2728:32-33
Farmer's wife chasing mice spinner, paper plate,
paper, pom-poms, paint, making    2728:7-9
Five little speckled frogs, bug-eating frog on a
log, cardboard tube, pom-poms, pipe cleaners, making    2728:38-39
I'm a little teapot, tippy teapot, old glove, wiggly
eyes, trims, making    2728:34-35
Jack-in-the-box pop-up, sliding matchbox, trims,
yarn, making    2728:22-23
Little Bo Peep, find Bo Peep's sheep wheel, paper plates, cotton balls, pipe cleaners,
paints, making    2728:44-45
Old MacDonald's barn, toilet paper tube, envelope, egg carton, making    2728:12-13
Pocket full of posies, old shirt pocket, trims,
flowers, making    2728:14-15
Rock-a-bye baby rocking baby toy, yarn, fabric
scraps, egg carton, old glove, making
2728:30-31
A tisket a tasket green and yellow basket necklace, pipe cleaners, fabric scraps, yarn,
making    2728:26-27
Wheels on the bus go round and round, people
on the bus going up and down, box, pasta
wheels, tape, foil, making    2728:40-41
*Wide Mouth Frog*, song, puppets, patterns,
songs, food    2591:74-78

**UNITED STATES—SONGS—PUPPETS**

Bear over the mountain puppet, paper plate, coffee grounds, making    2728:10-11
If you're happy and you know it changing face
cup puppet, plastic cups, markers, making
2728:24-25
Old man is snoring puppet, paper bowl, balloon,
paper, cotton balls, making    2728:16-17
Twinkle star puppet, CD disc, wiggly eyes,
making    2728:18-19
Where is thumbkin finger puppets of the whole
family, beads, pom-poms, trims, felt,
making    2728:28-29

**UNITED STATES—SYMBOLS**

American eagle magnet, brown bag, tissue paper,
pipe cleaner, making    2735:16-17
Bald eagle paper model, paper, black pen,
making    2687:12-13
Bald eagle, paper lunch bag, paper, markers,
making    2686:28-29

Eagle, paper bag, patterns, making   2760:140

**UNITED STATES—TOTEM POLES**

Totem pole, paper tube, cardboard, markers, making   2686:26-27

**UNITED STATES—TOYS**

Jumping jack toy, poster board, fabric scraps, string, pattern, making   2310:99-105

**UNITED STATES—TREES**

Giant Sequoia, colored paper, paper towel tube, making   2686:24-25

**UNITED STATES—WINDOW PICTURES**

Nightscape window pictures, paper, tissue paper, making   2407:9

**UR—BURIALS**

Gold burial helmet, papier-mâché over balloon, gold and black paint, making   2654:20-21

**UR—TEMPLES**

Ziggurat, boxes, paints, making   2746:11-12

**UR.** *See also* **MESOPOTAMIA**

**URUGUAY—COOKERY**

Ambrosia, recipe   2949:52
Celery and pea soup, recipe   2949:52
Pascualina pie, recipe   2949:53
Stewed lentils, recipe   2949:53
Uruguayan bean salad, recipe   2670:34

**URUGUAY—GAMES**

Man-tan-tiru-lira-la, how to play   2767:180-181

**UTAH—COOKERY**

Buzzy bee salad dressing, recipe   2534:70
Navajo fry bread, recipe   2773:63

**UTE INDIANS—HORSES**

Ute miniature horse, paper, felt, markers, making   2349:12-13

**UZBEKISTAN—HANDICRAFTS**

Floral mosaic, colored paper, making   2407:25

# V

**VALENTINE'S DAY**
Activities, finger plays, songs, rhymes, crafts, patterns   2828:56-57
Activities, language arts, foods (recipes given), science, arts and music   2446:3-79
Activities, puppets, patterns, making   2754:65-82
History of Valentine's Day   2877:16
Storytimes, activities, lovebird tubey pattern, craft instructions   2636:13-15
Thematic units, lessons, activities, art, poetry, crafts, patterns, recipes   2320:158-184

**VALENTINE'S DAY—CARDS**
Be My Valentine pop-up card, making   2778:10-11
Bear Valentine card, paper, yarn, paint, making   2923:10-11
Button nose Valentine, felt, ribbons, making   2720:4-5
Candy flower Valentine, lollipop, red paper, making   2720:30-31
Heart-in-hand Valentine, paper, making   2407:61
Hearts dog Valentine, paper, ribbon, making   2720:13-15
Love bug card, paper, glitter, wiggle eyes, making   2910:18-19
Plastic plate Valentine wreath, plate, flowers, making   2710:10-12
Pop-up Valentine's Day card, making   2715:unp
Victorian Valentines, paper, doilies, ribbon, making   2744:48

**VALENTINE'S DAY—COOKERY**
Chocolate butter icing, recipe   2888:48
Chocolate cream cheese frosting, recipe   2888:43
Chocolate lollipops, recipe   2782:28-29
Chocolate-lover's lollipops, recipe   2877:19
Cupid cupcakes with pink frosting, recipe   2877:20-21
Cupids cupcakes with pink frosting, recipe   2888:44-45
Dark chocolate truffle balls, recipe   2888:39
French chocolate custard, recipe   2888:47

Friendship hearts, recipe and activities   2576:93-96
Fruity chocolate fondue, recipe   2888:49
Heart cookies, recipe   2782:24-25
Heart pops, recipe   2857:30
Hearts aflutter sandwiches, recipe and activities   2576:89-92
Heart-shaped sugar cookies, recipe   2877:18
Hot chocolate sauce, recipe   2888:50
Hot cocoa with vanilla whipped cream, recipe   2888:40
Love bugs, recipe   2782:12-13
Milk chocolate three-layer cake, recipe   2888:41-42
Strawberry cheese cake, recipe   2888:46
Sugar cookies, recipe   2715:unp
Sweet heart cookies, recipe   2744:46-47
Sweet heart decorated cake, recipe   2583:8
Sweet surprise cupcakes, recipe and activities   2576:85-88

**VALENTINE'S DAY—CUPID**
Cupid wheel, pattern of cupid, making   2754:76, 78

**VALENTINE'S DAY—DECORATIONS**
Amore napkin rings, paper rolls, felt, making   2910:12-13
Bag of Valentine wishes, paper bag, glitter pens, craft sticks, making   2910:6-7
Bookmark; lacy bookmark, red paper, yarn, making   2910:16-17
Broken heart jigsaw puzzle, cardboard, matchbox, gold paper, felt, making   2782:20-21
Butterfly paper clip, tissue paper, clothespin, making   2910:22-23
Cat; Valentine cat, red paper, felt, glitter, making   2910:14-15
Changing message magnet, magnet, old greeting cards, making   2720:26-27
Doorknob nose heart, paper plate, ribbon, making   2720:20-21
Envelope corner heart basket, beads, sequins, making   2720:6-7
Fold-up Valentine surprise, red paper, toy, candy, making   2910:10-11

Garden of love Valentine holder, paper plate, ribbons, making   2720:24-25

Heart butterflies garland, ribbons, sequins, making   2720:8-9

Heart ornament, red paper, glitter pens, making   2910:20-21

Heart people, paper, hearts, making   2545:42-43

Heart wind chime, red plastic plates, jingle bells, beads, making   2720:32-33

Heart; stuffed heart, paper, yarn, patterns, making   2811:27-28

Heart; sun catcher heart, paper plate, tissue paper, ribbon, making   2910:24-25

Hearts and buttons flowers, buttons, yarn, making   2720:45-47

Hearts crown, paper, sequins, making   2720:22-23

Hearts; chain of hearts, paper, patterns, making   2811:29-30

Jesus loves you Valentine's Day plaque, making   2798:56

Kiss seal, shiny red paper, glitter pens, paints, making   2782:8-9

Lip smackers, cardboard, shiny red cardboard, making   2782:14-15

Love knot, pattern   2754:70

Lovebird, plastic bottle, plastic ball, felt, colored paper, making   2782:16-17

Message pad Valentine, sticky notes, wrapping paper, making   2720:36-37

Paper-and-pins hearts, paper, ribbon, making   2778:12-13

Party blower Valentine, party blower, stickers, making   2720:18-19

Penny wrapper heart basket, bead or macaroni letters, making   2720:40-41

Priority mail box Valentine's holder, tissue box, lunch bag, making   2720:42-43

Red rose, clay, florist's wire, paints, making   2782:18-19

Rubber band Valentine bracelets, paper, sequins, making   2720:28-29

Spinning Valentine, cardboard, red shiny paper, glitter pens, making   2782:6-7

Valentine bookmark, red cardboard, lace, making   2720:16-17

Valentine candy jewelry, Valentine candies, ribbon, making   2720:38-39

**VALENTINE'S DAY—FICTION**

*Best Valentine in the World* by Marjorie Weinman Sharmat, activities, art, games, songs, crafts, patterns   2812:41-50

*Four Valentines in a Rainstorm* by Felicia Bond, activities, crafts, patterns, games, masks, puppets, making   2329:79-81

*One Zillion Valentines* by Frank Modell, activities, language arts, foods (recipes given), science, arts and music   2446:18-27

*Valentine Bears* by Eve Bunting, activities, language arts, foods (recipes given), science, arts and music   2446:7-17

**VALENTINE'S DAY—GAMES**

Racing hearts game, paper, yarn, how to make and play   2720:34-35

**VALENTINE'S DAY—HANDICRAFTS**

CD case photo frame, making   2748:25-27

Coupon book, making   2748:21-24

Flower cage, cobweb cut paper, making   2407:52

Heart-shaped sachet, ribbons, lace, making   2744:50-51

Keepsakes fabric hearts, red felt, plastic gems, making   2782:26-27

Lavender heart, felt, velvet fabric, cotton wool, gold fabric pen, making   2782:22-23

Puzzle purse, folded paper, making   2407:44

Trinket box, box, paints, making   2744:52-53

**VALENTINE'S DAY—JEWELRY**

Charm bracelet and earrings, making   2748:18-21

Necklace; friendship necklace, cardboard, gift wrap, making   2910:8-9

**VALENTINE'S DAY—LANGUAGE**

"I love you" in 16 languages   2715:unp

**VALENTINE'S DAY—SOAP**

Hearts soap, making   2936:41

Soap bracelet, making   2936:40

**VAN ALLSBURG, CHRIS**

Glowing house, making   2529:106

*The Polar Express* by Chris Van Allsburg, activities, literature, art, science, poetry, social studies, webbing   2435:103-114

**VAN BUREN, MARTIN (PRESIDENT)**

Fishy potato paintings, making   2263:35

Mini potato patch, making   2263:37

Morse code message, Morse code symbols given   2263:35

Poster for the "Little Magician," making   2263:35

**VAN EYCK, JAN**

Triptych panel, making   2529:15

**VAN GOGH, VINCENT**
Impasto, making   2529:46
Starry night, making   2529:47

**VANILLA**
History of vanilla   2717:54

**VASARELY, VICTOR**
Dizzy op art, making   2529:92

**VENEZUELA—COOKERY**
Black beans and rice, recipe   2950:52
Corn pancakes, recipe   2922:51
Corn pancakes, recipe   2950:52
Flan, recipe   2396:56
Guasacaca, avocado dish, recipe   2950:53
Quesilla, custard, recipe   2950:53
Sweet corn, pepper, and pumpkin stew, recipe
2838:26-27

**VENEZUELA—GAMES**
Plant market, how to play   2767:181

**VENEZUELA—MUSICAL INSTRUMENTS**
Maraca, beans, cup, paints, making
2686:103-104

**VERMONT—COOKERY**
Maple oatmeal drops, recipe   2469:104
Nutty maple brittle, recipe   2534:71

**VERMONT—SNOWFLAKES**
*Snowflake Bentley* by Jaqueline Briggs Martin,
activities, literature, science, poetry, social
studies, webbing   2435:151-170

**VETERAN'S DAY—DECORATIONS**
Veteran's Day thank you card, paper, making
2546:42-43

**VICTORIAN AGE—COOKERY**
Lemon and poppy seed afternoon tea bread,
recipe   2359:93-94
Noodle kugel, recipe   2359:96-97
Old-fashioned root beer float, recipe   2359:95

**VIETNAM—COOKERY**
Banana and pineapple fritters, recipe
2839:38-39
Banana, mango and pineapple in coconut milk,
recipe   2839:42-43
Beef in coconut milk, recipe   2839:28-29
Beef pho, recipe   2839:24-25
Braised chicken, recipe   2646:56
Caramelized chicken wings, recipe   2839:22-23
Carrot salad, recipe   2646:34
Chicken and vegetables, recipe   2839:20-21
Crab and asparagus soup, recipe   2839:10-11
Fresh fruit salad, recipe   2646:68
Fried fish with lemongrass, recipe   2839:32-33
Fried pork with prawns and cucumber, recipe
2839:18-19
Fried rice, recipe   2646:46
Grilled lemon grass beef, recipe   2646:52
Lychee sorbet, recipe   2839:40-41
Mini fish cakes, recipe   2839:12-13
Nuoc cham, recipe   2646:33
Pork, crab and grapefruit salad, recipe
2839:34-35
Prawn fried rice, recipe   2839:26-27
Rice noodle salad, recipe   2646:42
Rice noodles, recipe   2646:32
Rice, recipe   2646:32
Shredded chicken-cabbage salad, recipe
2646:41
Shrimp cakes, recipe   2646:65
Shrimp salad, recipe   2646:39
Soda chanh drink, recipe   2655:19
Spare ribs with lemongrass and chili peppers,
recipe   2839:16-17
Spicy eggplant and tomatoes, recipe
2839:14-15
Spring rolls with peanut sauce, recipe   2381:unp
Spring rolls, recipe   2646:51
Steamed fish, recipe   2646:60
Steamed tofu, recipe   2271:50
Steamed tofu, recipe   2646:59
Sticky rice with corn and coconut, recipe
2646:57
Sticky rice with mango, recipe   2614:30-31
Stir-fried beef with green beans, recipe
2646:47
Stir-fried cauliflower, recipe   2646:48
Stir-fried noodles with bean sprouts, recipe
2839:30-31
Sweet and sour pork, recipe   2839:36-37
Sweet and sour soup, recipe   2646:38
Sweet potatoes with peanuts, recipe   2271:50
Sweet potatoes with peanuts, recipe   2646:59
Vietnamese menu   2646:28

**VIETNAM—FESTIVALS—COOKERY**
Tet Nguyen-dan; asparagus soup, recipe
2646:64

**VIETNAM—FESTIVALS—LANTERNS**
Tet Trung Thu; lantern, tissue paper, making
2982:14

**VIETNAM—FESTIVALS—MASKS**
Mid-Autumn Festival; mask, basket, yarn, paints,
making   2614:28-29

**VIETNAM—FOLKLORE**
*Cam and the Magic Fish,* story and activities
2423:151-166

*Why the Moon Does Not Shine in the Sky,* folktales, puppets, patterns, songs, food 2591:71-73

**VIETNAM—GAMES**

Biting the carp's tail, how to play 2767:181-182

O-lang game, how to make and play 2614:26-27

Truyen-Truyen jacks game, how to play 2330:115-117

Vietnamese dominoes game, how to play 2548:30

**VIETNAM—HATS**

Conical hat, paper, yarn, making 2686:52-53

**VIETNAM—LANGUAGE**

Vietnamese words for family members 2655:13

**VIETNAM—NEW YEAR—COOKERY**

Tet; New Year's cake, recipe 2646:66-67

**VIETNAM—NEW YEAR—DECORATIONS**

Tet; red paper banners with wishes written on them, making 2402:46-47

**VIETNAM—NEW YEAR'S DAY—COOKERY**

Asparagus soup, recipe 2481:34

**VIETNAMESE-AMERICANS—COOKERY**

Cabbage and grapefruit salad, recipe 2879:283

Chicken noodle soup, recipe 2879:281

Mixed vegetables, recipe 2879:282

Nuoc cham (dipping sauce), recipe 2879:283

Rice rolls, recipe 2879:283-284

**VIETNAMESE-AMERICANS—FICTION**

*Angel Child, Dragon Child* by Michele Maria Surat; activities, art, poetry, maps, crafts, foods, patterns 2642:50-52

**VIKINGS—AMULETS**

Lucky charm amulet, cardboard, clay, silver paint, making 2792:14-15

**VIKINGS—ART**

Scary face for a stone memorial, clay, paints, making 2792:52-53

**VIKINGS—BURIALS**

Silver vessel, plastic pot, tissue paper, split peas, paints, making 2333:22-23

**VIKINGS—CHIEFTAINS**

Viking chieftain boxes models, cardboard tubes, paints, making 2333:28-29

**VIKINGS—COINS**

Coin and die, clay, bronze and silver paint, making 2792:42-43

Die stamp and coins, clay, cardboard tube, metallic paints, felt, making 2333:20-21

Viking coins, clay, paints, making 2510:30-31

**VIKINGS—COOKERY**

Bread loaf, recipe 2792:32-33

**VIKINGS—FOSSILS**

Footprints, plaster of Paris, making 2464:28

**VIKINGS—GAMES**

Gambling game, birds from salt dough, fabric square, paints, making 2621:19

Hnefatafl board for the Hnefatafl game, making 2792:58-59

Hnefatafl board game, thick cardboard, cardboard tubes, pebbles, paints, making 2333:26-27

Hnefatafl game, how to make and play 2897:30-31

Viking game board, clay, paints, making 2510:42-43

**VIKINGS—GODS**

Odin's raven; easy small raven, paper, paints, pattern, making 2621:21

Odin's raven; flapping winged raven, black poster board, paper, pattern, making 2621:21

Thor's hammer-shaped amulet, cardboard, tissue paper, buttons, peas, gold paint, making 2333:24

**VIKINGS—HELMETS**

Helmet of foil with gold and brass trim, patterns, making 2621:77

Helmet with nose guard, silver wrapping paper, patterns, making 2621:13

Helmet, papier-mâché, bronze paint, making 2792:46-47

Helmet, papier-mâché, paints, making 2333:16-17

Paperbag helmet, patterns, making 2621:13

Viking helmet, cardboard, papier-mâché, making 2510:18-19

**VIKINGS—HOUSEHOLD ITEMS**

Drinking horn, thick paper, clay, paints, foil, making 2792:22-23

**VIKINGS—HOUSES**

Sod house model, florist foam blocks, craft sticks, reindeer moss, making 2464:72

Viking house, wood, cardboard, balsa wood, paints, making 2792:20-21

**VIKINGS—JEWELRY**

Arm rings, string, gold paint, making 2333:25

Brooch, clay, gold foil, bronze paint, making 2792:28-29

Gotland stone, plaster of Paris, paints, twine, making 2621:15

Hammer of Thor pendant, aluminum foil, lacing, making 2621:15

Necklaces, salt dough clay, silver paper, paints, recipe for dough, making 2621:15

Round brooch for fastening shawls and tunic straps, silver cardboard, silver paint, making 2621:15

Silver bracelet, clay, string, silver paint, making 2792:50-51

Viking jewelry, clay, paints, making 2510:34-35

## VIKINGS—LONGSHIPS

Dragon figurehead picture frame, cardboard, split peas, silver and black paint, making 2333:14-15

Longboat, paper, enlarged patterns, making 2621:17

Longship model, cardboard, balsa wood, making 2792:36-39

Longship model, cardboard, paints, making 2333:10-11

Viking longboat model, milk carton, paints, making 2510:14-15

## VIKINGS—NAVIGATORS

Sun compass, round box with lid, colored cardboard, paints, making 2333:12-13

## VIKINGS—RELIGION

Jelling stone model, sand clay (recipe given), paints, making 2510:38-39

## VIKINGS—RUNESTONES

Runestone bookends, plaster, poster paint, making 2333:9

Runestone, cardboard, clay, red paint, making 2792:54-55

## VIKINGS—SHIELDS

Shield, cardboard, foil, papier-mâché, paints, making 2792:48-49

Viking shield, pizza box, paints, making 2510:22-23

## VIKINGS—SHIPS

Knorr ship model, cardboard, foil, paints, making 2464:68-69

## VIKINGS—SLEDS

Sled model, cardboard, balsa wood, red paint, making 2792:34-35

## VIKINGS—TRADE

Trader's scales model, round cardboard boxes, paints, string, clay, making 2333:18-19

Trading scale model, paper towel roll, clay, paints, making 2510:26-27

## VIKINGS—WEATHER VANES

Weather vane, cardboard, brass hinges, gold paint, making 2792:40-41

## VIRGINIA—COOKERY

Peanut butter and apple cookies, recipe 2774:63

Peanut candy, recipe 2370:64

Saucy down-home country ham, recipe 2534:72

## VLACH (ARUMANIANS)-AMERICANS—COOKERY

Bulgarian cucumber soup, recipe 2879:48

Bulgarian meatball soup, recipe 2879:48-49

Macedonian-style peppers, recipe 2879:46-47

Vlach cheese corn bread, recipe 2879:47

## VUILLARD, EDOUARD

Artist's studio; making 2529:55

# W

**WAITRESSES**

Wacky waitress outfit, paper, doilies, making 2676:12-13

**WALES—COOKERY**

Bara Lawr, lava bread or caviar, recipe 2476:119

Lamb roast, recipe 2476:121

**WALES—GAMES**

Avoid the circle game, how to play 2525:112

Ball catch game, how to play 2525:89

How many fingers?, how to play 2767:148

Ice cream game, how to play 2525:17

Roll ball home game, how to play 2525:47

Rope-skipping game, how to play 2525:70

Surprise, surprise game, how to play 2525:97

**WALES—LANGUAGE**

Numbers one to ten in Welch language 2476:80

Welch words and phrases 2476:81

**WAMPANOAG INDIANS—COOKERY**

Bannock bread, recipe 2879:285-286

Cranberry sauce, recipe 2879:286-287

Nasaump, dried corn and fruits or clam broth dish, recipe 2442:34

Three sisters rice, recipe 2879:286

**WAMPANOAG INDIANS—JEWELRY**

Shell run tee pendant, making 2644:31

**WAMPANOAG INDIANS—WIGWAMS**

Wigwam model, pattern, making 2644:37

**WARHOL, ANDY**

Lots of me, making 2529:103

**WASHINGTON, D.C.—COOKERY**

Cherry lemonade, recipe 2503:63

Cornbread, recipe 2420:57

**WASHINGTON, GEORGE (PRESIDENT)**

Activities, puppet, patterns, making 2754:55-64

Farm friends' trunk, shoebox, paper, making 2263:7

Medallion fans, paper, ribbons, making 2263:9

Shoe box diorama, making 2263:7

Vernon picture, patterns of animals given, making 2263:8

**WASHINGTON, GEORGE (PRESIDENT)—BIRTHDAY**

Activities, recipes, songs, games 2863:120-130

Color George Washington, pattern 2813:36

February 22, 1732, stories, music, games, activities, projects, patterns 2377:53-59

George Washington cylinder, pattern, making 2813:41

George Washington puzzle, pattern 2813:40

History of George Washington's birthday 2813:34-35

Whole language thematic unit of activities in language, science, math, music and life skills 2797:32-45

**WASHINGTON, GEORGE (PRESIDENT)—BIRTHDAY—COOKERY**

Mini-cherry pies, recipe 2863:121

**WASHINGTON, GEORGE (PRESIDENT)—BIRTHDAY—GAMES**

George Washington word game 2813:37

Washington code game 2813:38

Washington trail game 2813:39

**WASHINGTON, GEORGE (PRESIDENT)—FICTION**

*George Washington's Breakfast* by Jean Fritz, activities, crafts, patterns, games, masks, puppets, making 2329:82-86

**WASHINGTON, GEORGE (PRESIDENT)—HATS**

Three-cornered hat, paper, pattern, making 2754:59

**WASHINGTON, GEORGE (PRESIDENT)—PUPPETS**

George Washington finger puppet, paper, patterns, making 2754:57

George Washington puppet, yogurt container, yarn, fiberfill, making 2735:32-33

**WASHINGTON, GEORGE (PRESIDENT)—SILHOUETTES**

George Washington silhouette, making 2863:127

Silhouette of George Washington pattern 2475:63

**WASHINGTON, MARTHA (FIRST LADY)—COOKERY**

Baked apples, recipe 2553:19
Cherry bread pudding, recipe 2553:9
Cornbread, recipe 2553:7
Lemonade, recipe 2553:13

**WASHINGTON (STATE)—COOKERY**

Juicy baked apple treat, recipe 2534:73

**WEAVING**

Belt and headband, loom and yarn, making 2440:94-96
Homemade loom, popsicle sticks, making 2440:93
Language arts, poetry, hobby craft activities 2511:153-159
Mug mat, making 2511:154-155

**WELSH-AMERICANS—COOKERY**

Raisin bread, recipe 2879:288
Tea cakes, recipe 2879:287

**WEST INDIES—FESTIVALS**

Carnival headdress, papier-mâché, beads, feathers, paints, making 2259:16-17

**WEST NIGERIA—HANDICRAFTS**

Adire tie and dye paper, making 2407:50

**WEST (U.S.)—HISTORY—BOATS**

Bullboat model, papier-mâché, making 2498:98-99
Keelboat model, balsa wood, patterns, making 2498:17-22

**WEST (U.S.)—HISTORY—CANALS**

Build a canal lock, milk cartons, tape, making 2497:28-29

**WEST (U.S.)—HISTORY—CANOES**

Canoe, carve from balsa wood, making 2498:64-65

**WEST (U.S.)—HISTORY—DISCOVERY AND EXPLORATION. *See* LEWIS AND CLARK**

**WEST (U.S.)—HISTORY—FICTION**

*Bonanza Girl* by Patricia Beatty; readers theater booktalks with literature, poetry, music and creative writing activities 2681:38
*Buffalo Skinners* (song); readers theater booktalks with literature, poetry, music and creative writing activities 2681:36
*Calamity Jane at Fort Sanders* by Ron Fontes; readers theater booktalks with literature, poetry, music and creative writing activities 2681:35

*Hats Off to John Stetson* by Mary Blount Christian; readers theater booktalks with literature, poetry, music and creative writing activities 2681:37
*Wagon Wheels* by Barbara Brenner, activities for art, music, food, clothing and history 2478:73-104
*Wagon Wheels* by Barbara Brenner; readers theater booktalks with literature, poetry, music and creative writing activities 2681:34

**WEST (U.S.)—HISTORY—FOOTWEAR**

Moccasins, leather, felt, or vinyl fabric, pattern, making 2498:74-75

**WEST (U.S.)—HISTORY—FORTS**

Fort Laramie model, popsicle sticks, dowels, making 2497:78-79

**WEST (U.S.)—HISTORY—HOUSES**

Flatboat house model, cardboard, felt, paints, making 2688:8-9
Log cabin model, snap-on building sticks, brown paper, making 2688:12-13

**WEST (U.S.)—HISTORY—INDIANS— HOUSES**

Earth lodge model, indoors or out, making 2498:56

**WEST (U.S.)—HISTORY—JOURNALS**

Twine trail journal, cardboard, paper, twine, making 2688:10-11

**WEST (U.S.)—HISTORY—LAND SURVEYS**

Land survey, how to do 2498:30-31
Measuring distance; deall reckoning, how to do 2498:42-44

**WEST (U.S.)—HISTORY—LANTERNS**

Tin can lantern, tin can, paints, wire handle, making 2688:18-19

**WEST (U.S.)—HISTORY—MUSICAL INSTRUMENTS**

Fiddle, cardboard model, twine, making 2688:20-21

**WEST (U.S.)—HISTORY—SCHOONERS**

Prairie schooner model, box, balsa wood, fabric, paints, making 2497:44-45

**WEST (U.S.)—HISTORY—TOOLS**

Ax; wooden pioneer ax, cardboard, balsa wood, foil, making 2688:14-15

**WEST (U.S.)—HISTORY—WAGONS**

Covered wagon model, cardboard, yarn, plastic horses, making 2688:6-7

**WEST VIRGINIA—COOKERY**

Mama Mia spaghetti, recipe 2534:74-75

**WHALING SHIPS**

Log book; keep a log book and make a whale stamp   2934:84-85

Shadow box ship; bark, dowels, foam sheets, making   2934:3-5

Whale boat and gear; foam sheet, aluminum tubes, paint, making   2934:68-70

**WHALING SHIPS—COOKERY**

Cabbage and Irish potatoes, recipe   2383:9

Holiday duff, boiled pudding, recipe   2383:27

Lobscouse, beef and ham, recipe   2383:16

New England clam chowder, recipe   2383:29

Pacific fruit plate, recipe   2383:25

Pumpkin soup, recipe   2383:23

Roast chicken, recipe   2383:13

Salt pork and beans, recipe   2383:21

**WHITE HOUSE**

Life-the-flap White House numbers, pattern, how to do   2667:10

**WILDER, LAURA INGALLS—CHRISTMAS—DECORATIONS**

Alanzo's jingle bells, making   2341:4

Carrie and Grace's Christmas candy bags, making   2341:3

Christmas tree paper streamers, making   2341:6-7

Plum Creek popcorn strings, making   2341:2

Red-and-white striped wrapping paper, making   2341:5

Star-edged shelf paper, making   2341:8

**WILDER, LAURA INGALLS—CHRISTMAS—HANDICRAFTS**

Aunt Eliza's needlebook, making   2341:10-13

Carrie's laced-edged handkerchief, making   2341:19-22

Laura and Mary's button string, making   2341:29-30

Laura's embroidered picture frame, making   2341:22-28

Ma's clove apple, making   2341:14

Mary's braided rug, making   2341:15-18

**WILDER, LAURA INGALLS—COOKERY**

Laura's heart-shaped cakes, recipe   2341:36-37

Molasses-on-snow candy, recipe   2341:40-41

Mother Wilder's Christmas mincemeat pie, recipe   2341:38-39

Pancake men, recipe   2341:32-33

Popcorn balls, recipe   2341:34-35

**WILSON, WOODROW (PRESIDENT)**

Animating "Arizona," patterns, making   2263:90

Handmade sketchbook, making   2263:90

Sheep on the lawn, making   2263:90

**WINNEBAGO INDIANS—GAMES**

Hahi'bidjikeeun (tree game), how to play   2767:176-177

**WINNEBAGO INDIANS—SHOULDER BAGS**

Winnebago shoulder bag, felt, patterns, making   2311:3-8

**WINTER—FESTIVALS**

Winter window, poster board, foam, polystyrene balls, making   2326:26-27

**WINTER SOLSTICE**

Find the sun's northernmost and southernmost points   2674:unp

Make a winter sunrise/sunset chart   2674:unp

Measure shadows on the shortest day of the year   2674:unp

Show how tilt of the earth makes the seasons   2674:unp

Winter Solstice party for the birds   2674:unp

Winter Solstice party, make sun cupcakes, recipe   2674:unp

Winter solstice starry sky, black plastic foam tray, making   2440:42-44

**WISCONSIN—COOKERY**

Moo soup, recipe   2534:76-77

Norwegian pancakes, recipe   2570:67

**WIZARD OF OZ**

Spinning house, milk carton, paper, making   2729:26-27

**WOMEN'S SUFFRAGE. See ANTHONY, SUSAN B.**

**WOODLAND INDIANS—ART**

Passamaquoddy birch bark picture frame, cardboard, making   2621:43

Passamaquoddy round lidded box, cardboard, making   2621:43

**WOODLAND INDIANS—BAGS**

Friendship bag, cloth, felt, string beads, rope, pattern, making   2350:30-31

**WOODLAND INDIANS—CANOES**

Birch bark canoes, paper, bark strips, yarn, making   2621:39

**WOODLAND INDIANS—CLOTHING**

Men's leather leggings, animal skin-looking paper, cloth, braid, making   2621:35

Micmac woman's hood, paper, oil pastels, making   2621:51

**WOODLAND INDIANS—COOKERY**

Hominy, recipe   2644:26

Oneida corn soup, recipe   2644:26
Sunflower seed snack, recipe   2350:43

**WOODLAND INDIANS—DESIGNS**
Northeast and Southeast designs and symbols   2350:10-13

**WOODLAND INDIANS—FLOWERS**
Chief sunflower, grow sunflower seeds, making   2350:41-42

**WOODLAND INDIANS—GAMES**
Deer buttons game, how to play   2644:28
Hide the stone game, how to play   2644:28
Peach pits game, how to play   2644:28
Which hand game, how to play   2644:28

**WOODLAND INDIANS—HAIRSTYLES**
Basic headpiece, paper, yarn, feathers, making   2621:27
Classic braids, yarn, paper, making   2621:27
Porcupine roach hair style, paper, feathers, making   2621:27

**WOODLAND INDIANS—HATS**
Feathers-in-front hat, quills, paper, paints, making   2621:53
Iroquois gestowah hat with draping feathers, paper, feathers, patterns, making   2621:53

**WOODLAND INDIANS—HOUSEHOLD ITEMS**
Birch bark bowl, making   2644:26

**WOODLAND INDIANS—JEWELRY**
Bone or antler combs, cardboard, patterns, making   2621:45
Penobscot embroidered collar, patterns, paper, yarn, making   2621:45
Porcupine quilled earrings, toothpicks, felt, patterns, making   2621:45
Silver gorget, aluminum baking sheet, tie, making   2621:45

**WOODLAND INDIANS—MASKS**
Corn husk masks, paper plates, raffia, paints, making   2621:29
Iroquois false face masks, paper, raffia, yarn, patterns, making   2621:41
Simple paper plate mask, raffia, paints, making   2621:29

**WOODLAND INDIANS—MUSICAL INSTRUMENTS**
Birch bark rattle, cardboard, felt strips, yarn, beads, patterns, making   2621:47
Dew claw ankle rattle, scrunchy, paper, patterns, making   2621:47
Gourd rattle, papier-mâché, stickers, feathers, beans, paints, patterns, making   2621:47

Turkey rattle, cardboard, paints, felt, dowel, feathers, making   2621:31

**WOODLAND INDIANS—POTTERY**
Collared pots, salt dough, making   2621:27

**WOODLAND INDIANS—POUCHES**
Iroquois thunderbird pouch, paper, ribbons, beads, yarn, making   2621:33
Woodland pouch, felt or heavy fabric, shoelace, making   2350:16-17

**WOODLAND INDIANS—QUILLWORK**
Porcupine quill box, box, beads, toothpicks, pattern, making   2350:39-40

**WOODLAND INDIANS—WAMPUM**
Wampum design belt and bookmark, fabric, patterns, making   2350:26-27
Wampum, graph paper, colored markers, making   2621:49

**WOODLAND INDIANS—WIGWAMS**
Wigwam model, pattern, making   2644:37

**WOODLAND INDIANS—WRITINGS**
Native American writings, make poem on decorated paper   2350:44-45

**WORLD CULTURES**
Clay bowl, clay, paints, making   2700:74-75
Story cloth, felt, fusible webbing, making   2700:78-79
World drum, cardboard canister, rubber glove, paints, making   2700:76-77

**WORLD WAR II—AIRPLANES**
Jet-powered flight test, how to do   2524:31-32
Paper airplane, making   2524:29-20

**WORLD WAR II—ALLIED SHIPS—GAMES**
Latitude/longitude tracking game for allied ships and submarines, how to play   2668:100-101

**WORLD WAR II—BIRDS**
Suet cakes, recipe   2524:85-86

**WORLD WAR II—CHRISTMAS—COOKERY**
Orange-cranberry sauce, recipe   2524:82-83
Sweet potato pie, recipe   2524:76-77

**WORLD WAR II—CHRISTMAS—DECORATIONS**
Holiday banner, making   2524:78-79
Paper snowflakes, making   2524:80-81

**WORLD WAR II—CLOTHING**
Patched jeans, how to do   2524:69-71

**WORLD WAR II—COASTAL DEFENSES**
Coastal defense, how to plan   2668:94-96

**WORLD WAR II—CODES**

Communicating in secret codes, how to do
2524:65-66

Deciphering secret codes, how to do
2524:63-64

**WORLD WAR II—COOKERY**

Chicken veggie noodle stew, recipe
2359:122-123

Coney Island sausage or hotdog in bread roll,
recipe    2524:37-38

Cooking with substitutes, mock whipping cream,
mock maple syrup, recipes    2524:60-61

Crunchy carrots, recipe    2359:126

Fondue, recipe    2524:58-59

M & M's cookies, recipe    2359:127

Make-do cake, recipe    2860:40-42

Philadelphia soft pretzels, recipe    2524:39-41

Sloppy Joes, recipe    2359:124-125

Victory salad, recipe    2524:7-9

**WORLD WAR II—FLASHLIGHTS**

Homemade flashlight, making    2524:12-13

**WORLD WAR II—FOOD RATIONING**

Butter extender, recipe    2668:54

**WORLD WAR II—GAMES**

Colored-cube puzzle, how to make and play
2524:23-24

Ludo, how to make and play    2524:21-22

Sea battle, how to make and play    2524:27-29

**WORLD WAR II—HANDICRAFTS**

Appliqued apron, how to make    2524:55-56

Glycerine leaves, how to make    2524:51-52

Pressed flower bookmark, how to make
2524:52-54

Refinished picture frame, how to do
2524:72-74

**WORLD WAR II—LANGUAGES**

Key phrases of soldier language in English,
French, German and Russian    2668:109

**WORLD WAR II—MILITARY LINGO**

Several phrases of military lingo    2668:145

**WORLD WAR II—MOBILES**

Found-object mobile, making    2524:18-19

**WORLD WAR II—RADIO**

Crystal radio, how to make    2524:43-46

Sound effects for radio shows, how to make
2524:47-48

**WORLD WAR II—SCRAP METAL
COLLECTION**

Scrap metal, how to collect    2668:58

**WORLD WAR II—SOLDIERS—RATION KITS**

Ration kit for a soldier, how to make    2668:77

**WORLD WAR II—SUBMARINES**

Periscope for a submarine, making    2524:33-36

**WORLD WAR II—VICTORY GARDENS**

Grow a Victory garden, seeds, how to do
2668:52

Victory garden, how to make    2524:9-11

**WORLD WAR II—V-MAIL**

Write your own V-mail, how to do    2668:79

**WORLD WAR II—WEATHER**

3-D cloud chart, how to make    2524:15-17

**WORLD WAR II—WEATHER VANES**

Wind vane, how to make    2524:87-89

**WRIGHT, FRANK LLOYD**

Box house architect, making    2529:82

**WYANDOT INDIANS—COOKERY**

Sagamite (cornmeal soup), recipe    2285:59

**WYETH, ANDREW**

First snow, making    2529:87

**WYOMING—COOKERY**

Cowboy state barbecue sauce, recipe    2912:63

Cowboy stew, recipe    2534:78

# Y

**YEMEN—GAMES**

Name tag, how to play    2767:182

**YOLEN, JANE**

*Owl Moon* by Jane Yolen, activities, literature, art, science, poetry, social studies, webbing    2435:75-102

**YOM HA'AZTMA'UT—COOKERY**

Hummus, recipe    2346:68

**YOM HA'AZTMA'UT—DECORATIONS**

Israeli flag, cardboard, paints, stick, making    2346:68-69

**YOM HA-SHOAH HOLOCAUST REMEMBRANCE DAY**

List of books to read    2346:65

**YOM KIPPUR—COOKERY**

Noodle kugel, recipe    2346:25

**YOM KIPPUR—FICTION**

*Minnie's Yom Kippur Birthday* by Marilyn Singer; activities, art, poetry, maps, crafts, foods, patterns    2642:64-65

**YOM KIPPUR—HANDICRAFTS**

Tzedakah box, coffee can, paper, foil, making    2346:26

Yom Kippur journal, journal, making    2346:24

**YORKINKS, ARTHUR**

*Hey, Al* by Arthur Yorkinks, literature, activities, art, curriculum    2436:53-64

**YORUBA (AFRICAN PEOPLES)—MUSICAL INSTRUMENTS**

Drum rattle, small can, paints, making    2620:50-51

Drum; talking drum, cups, string, making    2620:50-51

"Pod" rattle, ten small cups, string, beans, making    2620:50-51

**YOUNG, ED**

*Lon Po Po: A Red-Riding Hood Story from China* by Ed Young, activities, literature, art, science, poetry, social studies, webbing    2435:35-45

**YUPIK INDIANS—COOKERY**

Wild raspberry dessert, recipe    2311:106-108

**YUPIK INDIANS—GAMES**

Uhl-ta (ring around), how to play    2767:177

**YUPIK INDIANS—MASKS**

Yup'ik spirit mask, paper plate, feathers, markers, patterns, making    2351:27-28

**YUPIK INDIANS.** *See also* INUIT INDIANS

# Z

## ZAIRE—DOLLS

Tall tube doll (Zaire carved wooden doll), cardboard tubes, fabric, buttons, beads, making 2620:66-67

## ZAIRE—GAMES

Bokwele, how to play    2767:182-183

Match my feet game, how to play    2385:21

## ZAIRE—MASKS

Forehead mask, cardboard, paints, patterns, making    2620:48-49

Kuba beaded mask, railroad board, paints, puffed cereal, patterns, making    2620:32-33

Wild mask from Zaire, cardboard, raffia, patterns, making    2620:38-39

## ZAIRE—MUSICAL INSTRUMENTS

"Calabash" rattle; forked stick, cardboard, paints, making    2620:60-61

Sanza or thumb piano, box, paints, craft sticks, pattern, making    2620:60-61

## ZAIRE—PUPPETS

Ceremonial puppets, dowels, fabric, pictures, making    2620:64-65

## ZAMBIA—GAMES

Hand-clapping game, how to play    2767:183

## ZELINSKY, PAUL O.

*Rapunzel* by Paul O. Zelinsky, activities, literature, art, science, poetry, social studies, webbing    2435:115-135

## ZIMBABWE—COOKERY

Sadza etiquette    2711:121

## ZIMBABWE—GAMES

Double or nothing game, how to play    2525:104

Dragnet game, how to play    2525:123

Eagle eats game, how to play    2525:16

Give and take game, how to play    2525:182

Iguni jacks game, how to play    2330:102-103

Kanzhinge, how to play    2767:184

Twenty-five game, how to play    2525:48

Whistling race, how to play    2767:184

Without hands game, how to play    2525:130

## ZIMBABWE—LANGUAGE

Common words and phrases in Shona language    2711:132-133

## ZULU (AFRICAN PEOPLES)—FESTIVALS—BEADWORK

Zulu bead keychain, felt, beads, keychain loop, making    2846:40-41

## ZULU (AFRICAN PEOPLES)—GAMES

Shell game, how to make and play    2882:8-9

## ZULU (AFRICAN PEOPLES)—HOUSES

Beehive hut model, paper bag, making    2686:73-74

## ZULU (AFRICAN PEOPLES)—JEWELRY

Bead necklaces, beads, strings, making    2852:112-113

## ZULU (AFRICAN PEOPLES)—STAFFS

Horned staff made for a Zulu chief, cardboard, paints, making    2620:44-45

## ZUNI INDIANS—CARVINGS

Zuni animal figures, clay, paints, designs, making    2349:24-26

## ZUNI INDIANS—COOKERY

Posole stew, recipe    2879:288-289

Pumpkin and pumpkin seeds, recipe    2879:289

## ZUNI INDIANS—FOLKLORE

*Turkey Girl*, story and activities    2423:145-166

## ZUNI INDIANS—GAMES

Kolowis Awithlaknannai (fighting serpents), how to play    2767:177-178

Tsi-ko-na (ring toss), how to play    2767:179

Zuni ring-in-a-ring game, how to make and play    2523:26-28

## ZUNI INDIANS—GARDENS

Waffle garden model, clay, sand, cornmeal, dirt, toothpicks, paint, making    2891:42-45

## ZUNI INDIANS—HOUSES

Model pueblo, cardboard boxes, paints, cornmeal or sand, making    2523:29-30

## ZUNI INDIANS—JEWELRY

Zuni necklace, sculpey, beads, cord, making    2891:39-41

## ZUNI INDIANS—POTTERY

Water jar, clay, paints, making    2311:59-62

# Books Indexed by Number

See "Books Indexed by Author" for an alphabetical list of books by author.

2251. Aagesen, Colleen. *Shakespeare for Kids: His Life and Times: 21 Activities.* Chicago, Illinois: Chicago Review Press, 1999.

2252. Adams, McCrea. *Tipi.* Vero Beach, Florida: The Rourke Book Co., 2000.

2253. Alex, Nan. *North Carolina.* Danbury, Connecticut: Children's Press, 2001.

2254. Amari, Suad. *Cooking the Lebanese Way.* Minneapolis, Minnesota: Lerner Publications Co., 2003.

2255. Augustin, Byron. *Bolivia.* Danbury, Connecticut: Children's Press, 2001.

2256. Bacon, Josephine. *Cooking the Israeli Way.* Minneapolis, Minnesota: Lerner Publications Co., 2002.

2257. Balchin, Judy. *Collage.* Chicago, Illinois: Heinemann Library, 2002.

2258. Balchin, Judy. *Decorative Painting.* Chicago, Illinois: Heinemann Library, 2001.

2259. Balchin, Judy. *Papier Mache.* Chicago, Illinois: Heinemann Library, 2000.

2260. *Barbie Fun to Cook.* New York: Dorling Kindersley, 2001.

2261. Barlas, Bob. *Canada.* Milwaukee, Wisconsin: Gareth Stevens Publishing, 1997.

2262. Barr, Marilynn G. *Seasons and Weather: Fascinating Facts and Creative Crafts.* Palo Alto, California: Monday Morning Books, 2001.

2263. Barr, Marilynn G. *The American Presidents.* Palo Alto, California: Monday Morning Books, 2000.

2264. Bassis, Vladimir. *Ukraine.* Milwaukee, Wisconsin: Gareth Stevens Publishing, 1998.

2265. Beatty, Theresa M. *Food and Recipes of Africa.* New York: The Rosen Publishing Group, 1999.

2266. Beatty, Theresa M. *Food and Recipes of China.* New York: PowerKids Press, 1999.

2267. Beatty, Theresa M. *Food and Recipes of Greece.* New York: PowerKids Press, 1999.

2268. Beatty, Theresa M. *Food and Recipes of Japan.* New York: PowerKids Press, 1999.

2269. Beatty, Theresa M. *Food and Recipes of Mexico.* New York: PowerKids Press, 1999.

2270. Beatty, Theresa M. *Food and Recipes of the Caribbean.* New York: PowerKids Press, 1999.

2271. Behnke, Alison. *Vegetarian Cooking Around the World.* Minneapolis, Minnesota: Lerner Publications Co., 2002.

2272. Berg, Elizabeth. *Egypt.* Milwaukee, Wisconsin: Gareth Stevens Publishing, 1997.

2273. Berg, Elizabeth. *Ethiopia.* Milwaukee, Wisconsin: Gareth Stevens Publishing, 1999.

2274. Berg, Elizabeth. *Indonesia.* Milwaukee, Wisconsin: Gareth Stevens Publishing, 1997.

2275. Berg, Elizabeth. *Italy.* Milwaukee, Wisconsin: Gareth Stevens Publishing, 1997.

2276. Berg, Elizabeth. *Mexico.* Milwaukee, Wisconsin: Gareth Stevens Publishing, 1997.

2277. *Best Bible Crafts, Pack-O-Fun.* Des Plaines, Illinois: Clapper Publishing Family, 1998.

2278. Bial, Raymond. *The Apache.* Tarrytown, New York: Marshall Cavendish Corp., 2001.

2279. Bial, Raymond. *The Blackfeet.* Tarrytown, New York: Marshall Cavendish Corp., 2003.

2280. Bial, Raymond. *The Cherokee.* Tarrytown, New York: Marshall Cavendish Corp., 1999.

2281. Bial, Raymond. *The Cheyenne.* Tarrytown, New York: Marshall Cavendish Corp., 2001.

2282. Bial, Raymond. *The Choctaw.* Tarrytown, New York: Marshall Cavendish Corp., 2002.

2283. Bial, Raymond. *The Comanche.* Tarrytown, New York: Marshall Cavendish Corp., 2000.

2284. Bial, Raymond. *The Haida.* Tarrytown, New York: Marshall Cavendish Corp., 2001.

2285. Bial, Raymond. *The Huron.* Tarrytown, New York: Marshall Cavendish Corp., 2001.

2286. Bial, Raymond. *The Inuit.* Tarrytown, New York: Marshall Cavendish Corp., 2001.

2287. Bial, Raymond. *The Iroquois.* Tarrytown, New York: Marshall Cavendish Corp., 1999.

2288. Bial, Raymond. *The Mandan.* Tarrytown, New York: Marshall Cavendish Corp., 2003.

2289. Bial, Raymond. *The Navajo.* Tarrytown, New York: Marshall Cavendish Corp., 1999.

2290. Bial, Raymond. *The Nez Perce.* Tarrytown, New York: Marshall Cavendish Corp., 2002.

2291. Bial, Raymond. *The Ojibwe.* Tarrytown, New York: Marshall Cavendish Corp., 2002.

2292. Bial, Raymond. *The Powhatan.* Tarrytown, New York: Marshall Cavendish Corp., 2002.

2293. Bial, Raymond. *The Pueblo.* Tarrytown, New York: Marshall Cavendish Corp., 2000.

2294. Bial, Raymond. *The Seminole.* Tarrytown, New York: Marshall Cavendish Corp., 2000.

2295. Bial, Raymond. *The Shoshone.* Tarrytown, New York: Marshall Cavendish Corp., 2001.

2296. Bial, Raymond. *The Sioux.* Tarrytown, New York: Marshall Cavendish Corp., 1999.

2297. Bial, Raymond. *The Tlingit.* Tarrytown, New York: Marshall Cavendish Corp., 2002.

2298. Birchall, Lorrie L. *The Farm: Favorite Literature and Great Activities.* New York: Scholastic Professional Books, 1996.

2299. Bisignano, Alphonse. *Cooking the Italian Way.* Minneapolis, Minnesota: Lerner Publications Co., 2002.

2300. Boraas, Tracey. *Australia.* Mankato, Minnesota: Bridgestone Books, 2002.

2301. Boraas, Tracey. *Brazil.* Mankato, Minnesota: Bridgestone Books, 2002.

2302. Boraas, Tracey. *Canada.* Mankato, Minnesota: Bridgestone Books, 2002.

2303. Boraas, Tracey. *Colombia.* Mankato, Minnesota: Bridgestone Books, 2002.

2304. Boraas, Tracey. *Egypt.* Mankato, Minnesota: Bridgestone Books, 2002.

2305. Boraas, Tracey. *Israel.* Mankato, Minnesota: Bridgestone Books, 2003.

2306. Boraas, Tracey. *Sweden.* Mankato, Minnesota: Bridgestone Books, 2003.

2307. Boraas, Tracey. *Thailand.* Mankato, Minnesota: Bridgestone Books, 2003.

2308. Borenstein, Shery Koons. *Christian Crafts from Paper Bags.* Torrance, California: Shining Star Publications, 1994.

2309. Boyd, Heidi. *Fairy Crafts.* Cincinnati, Ohio: North Light Books, 2003.

2310. Braman, Arlette N. *Kids Around the World Play!: The Best Fun and Games from Many Lands.* New York: John Wiley & Sons, 2002.

2311. Braman, Arlette N. *Traditional Native American Arts and Activities.* New York: John Wiley & Sons, 2000.

2312. Bratvold, Gretchen. *Oregon.* Minneapolis, Minnesota: Lerner Publications Co., 2003.

2313. Broida, Marian. *Ancient Israelites and Their Neighbors: An Activity Guide.* Chicago, Illinois: Chicago Review Press, 2003.

2314. Broida, Marian. *Projects about Colonial Life.* Tarrytown, New York: Benchmark Books, 2004.

2315. Brown, Dottie. *Delaware.* Minneapolis, Minnesota: Lerner Publications Co., 2002.

2316. Brown, Dottie. *Kentucky.* Minneapolis, Minnesota: Lerner Publications Co., 2002.

2317. Brown, Dottie. *New Hampshire.* Minneapolis, Minnesota: Lerner Publications Co., 2002.

2318. Bull, Jane. *The Christmas Book.* New York: Dorling Kindersley Publishing, 2001.

2319. Bull, Jane. *The Halloween Book.* New York: Dorling Kindersley Publishing, 2000.

2320. Burda, Jan. *Year-Round Units for Early Childhood.* Westminster, California: Teacher Created Materials, 2000.

2321. Butler, Robbie. *Sweden.* New York: Raintree Steck-Vaughn Publishers, 2000.

2322. Capek, Michael. *Jamaica.* Minneapolis, Minnesota: Carolrhoda Books, 1999.

2323. Carlson, Laurie. *Classical Kids: An Activity Guide to Life in Ancient Greece and Rome.* Chicago, Illinois: Chicago Review Press, 1998.

2324. Carlson, Laurie. *Days of Knights and Damsels.* Chicago, Illinois: Chicago Review Press, 1998.

2325. Carratello, Patty. *Literature and Critical Thinking.* Huntington Beach, California: Teacher Created Materials, 1989.

2326. Carter, Tamsin. *Handmade Cards.* Chicago, Illinois: Heinemann Library, 2002.

2327. Cassidy, Picot. *Italy.* Austin, Texas: Steck-Vaughn Publishers, 2001.

2328. Castaldo, Nancy. *Winter Day Play: Activities, Crafts and Games for Indoor and Out.* Chicago, Illinois: Chicago Review Press, 2001.

2329. Cerbus, Deborah Plona. *Connecting Holidays and Literature.* Huntington Beach, California: Teacher Created Materials, 1992.

2330. Chabert, Sally. *The Jacks Book.* New York: Workman Publishing Co., 1999.

2331. Chapman, Gillian. *Art from Sand and Earth: With Projects Using Clay, Plaster and Natural Fibers.* Austin, Texas: Raintree Steck-Vaughn Publishers, 1997.

2332. Chapman, Gillian. *The Romans.* Des Plaines, Illinois: Heinemann Library, 1998.

2333. Chapman, Gillian. *The Vikings.* Chicago, Illinois: Heinemann Library, 2000.

2334. Cheong, Colin. *China.* Milwaukee, Wisconsin: Gareth Stevens Publishing, 1997.

2335. Cherkerzian, Diane. *Merry Things to Make: Christmas Fun and Crafts.* Honesdale, Pennsylvania: Boyds Mills Press, 1999.

2336. Christian, Rebecca. *Cooking the Spanish Way.* Minneapolis, Minnesota: Lerner Publications Co., 2002.

2337. *Christmas in Finland.* Chicago, Illinois: World Book, 1999.

2338. *Christmas in Puerto Rico.* Chicago, Illinois: World Book, 2004.

2339. *Christmas in Scotland.* Chicago, Illinois: World Book, 2001.

2340. Chung, Okwha. *Cooking the Korean Way.* Minneapolis, Minnesota: Lerner Publications Co., 2003.

2341. Collier, Mary. *My Little House Christmas Crafts Book: Christmas Decorations, Gifts and Recipes from the Little House Books.* New York: HarperCollins Publishers, 1997.

2342. Collins, Carolyn Strom. *Inside the Secret Garden: A Treasury of Crafts, Recipes and Activities.* New York: HarperCollins Publishers, 2001.

2343. Compestine, Ying Chang. *The Runaway Rice Cake*. New York: Simon & Schuster, 2001.

2344. Compestine, Ying Chang. *The Story of Chopsticks*. New York: Holiday House, 2001.

2345. Compestine, Ying Chang. *The Story of Noodles*. New York: Holiday House, 2002.

2346. Cooper, Ilene. *Jewish Holidays All Year Round: A Family Treasury*. New York: Harry N. Abrams, 2002.

2347. Cordoba, Yasmine A. *Igloo*. Vero Beach, Florida: Rourke Book Co., 2000.

2348. Coronado, Rosa. *Cooking the Mexican Way*. Minneapolis, Minnesota: Lerner Publication Co., 2002.

2349. Corwin, Judith Hoffman. *Native American Crafts of California, the Great Basin and the Southwest*. New York: Franklin Watts, 1999.

2350. Corwin, Judith Hoffman. *Native American Crafts of the Northeast and Southeast*. New York: Franklin Watts, 2002.

2351. Corwin, Judith Hoffman. *Native American Crafts of the Northwest Coast, the Arctic and the Subarctic*. New York: Franklin Watts, 2002.

2352. Corwin, Judith Hoffman. *Native American Crafts of the Plains and Plateau*. New York: Franklin Watts, 2002.

2353. Coulter, Laurie. *Secrets in Stone: All About Maya Hieroglyphs*. Boston, Massachusetts: Little Brown and Co., 2001.

2354. Currier, Mary. *Christian Crafts from Paper Plates*. Torrance, California: Shining Star Publications, 1989.

2355. Dahl, Michael. *France*. Mankato, Minnesota: Bridgestone Books, 1998.

2356. Dahl, Michael. *Germany*. Mankato, Minnesota: Bridgestone Books, 1997.

2357. Dahl, Michael. *South Africa*. Mankato, Minnesota: Bridgestone Books, 1998.

2358. Dalal, Anita. *Argentina*. Austin, Texas: Raintree Steck-Vaughn Publishers, 2000.

2359. D'Amico, Joan. *The U.S. History Cookbook: Delicious Recipes and Exciting Events from the Past*. New York: John Wiley & Sons, 2003.

2360. Darlington, Robert. *Australia*. Austin, Texas: Raintree Steck-Vaughn Publishers, 2001.

2361. Davis, Lucile. *Ghana*. Mankato, Minnesota: Bridgestone Books, 1999.

2362. Davis, Lucile. *The Philippines*. Mankato, Minnesota: Bridgestone Books, 1999.

2363. Day, Nancy. *Your Travel Guide to Ancient Egypt*. Minneapolis, Minnesota: Runestone Press, 2001.

2364. Day, Nancy. *Your Travel Guide to Ancient Greece*. Minneapolis, Minnesota: Runestone Press, 2001.

2365. Day, Nancy. *Your Travel Guide to Ancient Mayan Civilization*. Minneapolis, Minnesota: Runestone Press, 2001.

2366. Day, Nancy. *Your Travel Guide to Colonial America*. Minneapolis, Minnesota: Runestone Press, 2001.

2367. Day, Nancy. *Your Travel Guide to Renaissance Europe*. Minneapolis, Minnesota: Runestone Press, 2001.

2369. DeAngelis, Gina. *Mexico*. Mankato, Minnesota: Blue Earth Books, 2003.

2370. DeAngelis, Gina. *Virginia*. Danbury, Connecticut: Children's Press, 2001.

2371. Deady, Kathleen W. *Egypt*. Mankato, Minnesota: Bridgestone Books, 2001.

2372. Deady, Kathleen W. *England*. Mankato, Minnesota: Bridgestone Books, 2001.

2373. Dell'Oro, Suzanne Paul. *Argentina*. Minneapolis, Minnesota: Carolrhoda Books, 1998.

2374. Dell'Oro, Suzanne Paul. *Haiti*. Mankato, Minnesota: Bridgestone Books, 2002.

2375. Dell'Oro, Suzanne Paul. *Poland*. Mankato, Minnesota: Bridgestone Books, 2002.

2376.

2377. Dingwall, Cindy. *Happy Birthday, America!* Fort Atkinson, Wisconsin: Alleyside Press, 2000.

2378. Dingwall, Cindy. *Library Celebrations.* Fort Atkinson, Wisconsin: Alleyside Press, 1999.

2379. Donoughue, Carol. *The Mystery of the Hieroglyphs.* New York: Oxford University Press, 1999.

2380. Dooley, Norah. *Everybody Needs Soup.* Minneapolis, Minnesota: Carolrhoda Books, 2000.

2381. Dooley, Norah. *Everybody Brings Noodles.* Minneapolis, Minnesota: Carolrhoda Books, 2002.

2382. Dramer, Kim. *China.* Danbury, Connecticut: Children's Press, 1997.

2383. Draper, Charla L. *Cooking on Nineteenth-Century Whaling Ships.* Mankato, Minnesota: Blue Earth Books, 2001.

2384. Dubois, Muriel L. *Ethiopia.* Mankato, Minnesota: Bridgestone Books, 2001.

2385. Dunn, Opal. *Acka Backa Boo! Playground Games from Around the World.* New York: Henry Holt and Company, 2000.

2386. Dunnewind, Stephanie. *Come to Tea: Fun Tea Party Themes, Recipes, Crafts, Games, Etiquette and More.* New York: Sterling Publishing Co., 2002.

2387. Dyer, Dolores A. *Plank House.* Vero Beach, Florida: Rourke Book Co., 2000.

2388. *Early America.* Greensboro, North Carolina: The Education Center, 2002.

2389. Early, Theresa S. *New Mexico.* Minneapolis, Minnesota: Lerner Publications Co., 2003.

2390. *Earth Day Activities.* Westminster, California: Teacher Created Materials, 1996.

2391. Eder, Jeanne Oyawin. *The Dakota Sioux.* Austin, Texas: Raintree Steck-Vaughn, 2000.

2392. Ellis, Royston. *Madagascar.* Milwaukee, Wisconsin: Gareth Stevens Publishing, 1999.

2393. Ellis, Royston. *Trinidad.* Milwaukee, Wisconsin: Gareth Stevens Publishing, 1999.

2394. Enderlein, Cheryl. *Christmas in England.* New York: Hilltop Books, 1998.

2395. Enderlein, Cheryl. *Christmas in Sweden.* New York: Hilltop Books, 1998.

2396. Engfer, Lee. *Desserts Around the World.* Minneapolis, Minnesota: Lerner Publications Co., 2004.

2397. Englar, Mary. *Afghanistan.* Mankato, Minnesota: Capstone Press, 2004.

2398. Englar, Mary. *The Iroquois, the Six Nations Confederacy.* Mankato, Minnesota: Bridgestone Books, 2003.

2399. Englar, Mary. *Pueblos: Farmers of the Southwest.* Mankato, Minnesota: Bridgestone Books, 2003.

2400. Erlbach, Arlene. *Christmas: Celebrating Life, Giving and Kindness.* Berkeley Heights, New Jersey: Enslow Publishers, 2002.

2401. Erlbach, Arlene. *Hanukkah: Celebrating the Holiday of Lights.* Berkeley Heights, New Jersey: Enslow Publishers, 2001.

2402. Erlbach, Arlene. *Happy New Year, Everywhere!* Brookfield, Connecticut: The Millbrook Press, 2000.

2403. Erlbach, Arlene. *Merry Christmas Everywhere!* Brookfield, Connecticut: The Millbrook Press, 2002.

2404. *Father's Day Activities.* Huntington Beach, California: Teacher Created Materials, 1995.

2405. Feeney, Kathy. *Alabama.* Danbury, Connecticut: Children's Press, 2002.

2406. Fenema, Joyce Van. *Netherlands.* Milwaukee, Wisconsin: Gareth Stevens Publishing, 1998.

2407. Fiarotta, Phyllis. *Papercrafts Around the World.* New York: Sterling Publishing Co., 1996.

2408. Fisher, Frederick. *Costa Rica.* Milwaukee, Wisconsin: Gareth Stevens Publishing, 1999.

2409. Fisher, Frederick. *Mongolia.* Milwaukee, Wisconsin: Gareth Stevens Publishing, 1999.

2410. Flagg, Ann. *Apples, Pumpkins and Harvest.* New York: Scholastic Professional Books, 1998.

2411. Florence, Sarah. *Pilgrim Foods and Recipes.* New York: The Rosen Publishing Group, 2002.

2412. Foley, Erin. *Puerto Rico.* Milwaukee, Wisconsin: Gareth Stevens Publishing, 1997.

2413. Fowler, Verna. *The Menominee.* Austin, Texas: Steck-Vaughn Publishers, 2001.

2414. Foy, Don. *Israel.* Milwaukee, Wisconsin: Gareth Stevens Publishing, 1997.

2415. Fredeen, Charles. *Kansas.* Minneapolis, Minnesota: Lerner Publications Co., 2002.

2416. Fredeen, Charles. *South Carolina.* Minneapolis, Minnesota: Lerner Publications Co., 2002.

2417. Friedman, Pamela. *St. Patrick's Day Activities.* Westminster, California: Teacher Created Materials, 1999.

2418. Frost, Helen. *German Immigrants, 1820-1920.* Mankato, Minnesota: Blue Earth Books, 2002.

2419. Furlong, Arlene. *Argentina.* Milwaukee, Wisconsin: Gareth Stevens Publishing, 1999.

2420. Furman, Elina. *Washington D.C.* Danbury, Connecticut: Children's Press, 2002.

2421. Gabet, Marcia. *Fun with Social Studies: Mini Social Studies Units and Projects.* Huntington Beach, California: Teacher Created Materials, 1985.

2422. Garcia, James. *Cinco de Mayo: A Mexican Holiday About Unity and Pride.* Chanhassen, Minnesota: Child's World, 2002.

2423. Garrity, Linda K. *The Tale Spinner: Folktales, Themes and Activities.* Golden, Colorado: Fulcrum Publishing, 1999.

2424. Garza, Carmen Lomas. *Making Magic Windows: Creating Papel Picado/Cut-Paper Art.* San Francisco, California: Children's Book Press, 1999.

2425. Gelman, Amy. *Connecticut.* Minneapolis, Minnesota: Lerner Publications Co., 2002.

2426. George, Charles. *Montana.* Danbury, Connecticut: Children's Press, 2000.

2427. Germaine, Elizabeth. *Cooking the Australian Way.* Minneapolis, Minnesota: Lerner Publications Co., 2004.

2428. Gibbons, Gail. *The Berry Book.* New York: Holiday House, 2002.

2429. Gibson, Karen Bush. *The Arapaho: Hunters of the Great Plains.* Mankato, Minnesota: Bridgestone Books, 2003.

2430. Gibson, Karen Bush. *The Blackfeet: People of the Dark Moccasins.* Mankato, Minnesota: Bridgestone Books, 2003.

2431. Gibson, Karen Bush. *The Chickasaw Nation.* Mankato, Minnesota: Bridgestone Books, 2003.

2432. Gibson, Karen Bush. *The Potawatomi.* Mankato, Minnesota: Bridgestone Books, 2003.

2433. Gioffre, Rosalba. *The Young Chef's French Cookbook.* New York: Crabtree Publishing Co., 2001.

2434. Gioffre, Rosalba. *The Young Chef's Italian Cookbook.* New York: Crabtree Publishing Co., 2001.

2435. Glandon, Shan. *Caldecott Connections to Language Arts.* Englewood, Colorado: Libraries Unlimited, 2000.

2436. Glandon, Shan. *Caldecott Connections to Social Studies.* Englewood, Colorado: Libraries Unlimited, 2000.

2437. Gnojewski, Carol. *Cinco de Mayo: Celebrating Hispanic Pride.* Berkeley Heights, New Jersey: Enslow Publishers, 2002.

2438. Gnojewski, Carol. *Martin Luther King Day: Honoring a Man of Peace.* Berkeley Heights, New Jersey: Enslow Publishers, 2002.

2439. Golding, Vivien. *Traditions from Africa.* Austin, Texas: Steck-Vaughn Publishers, 1998.

2440. Gould, Roberta. *The Kids' Book of Incredible Fun Crafts.* Charlotte, Vermont: Williamson Publishing Co., 2003.

2441. Gould, Roberta. *Kidtopia: Round the Country and Back through Time in 60 Pro-

*jects.* Berkeley, California: Tricycle Press, 2000.

2442. Grace, Catherine O'Neill. *1621: A New Look at Thanksgiving.* Washington, D.C.: National Geographic Society, 2001.

2443. Graf, Mike. *Somalia.* Mankato, Minnesota: Bridgestone Books, 2002.

2444. Graf, Mike. *Switzerland.* Mankato, Minnesota: Bridgestone Books, 2002.

2445. Graube, Ireta Sitts. *Thanksgiving.* Westminster, California: Teacher Created Materials, 2000, reprint of 1992 ed.

2446. Graube, Ireta Sitts. *Valentine's Day.* Westminster, California: Teacher Created Materials, 1999.

2447. Graves, Kerry A. *Going to School during the Civil War: The Confederacy.* Mankato, Minnesota: Blue Earth Books, 2002.

2448. Graves, Kerry A. *Going to School during the Civil War: The Union.* Mankato, Minnesota: Blue Earth Books, 2002.

2449. Graves, Kerry A. *Going to School during the Great Depression.* Mankato, Minnesota: Blue Earth Books, 2002.

2450. Graves, Kerry A. *Going to School in Pioneer Times.* Mankato, Minnesota: Blue Earth Books, 2002.

2451. Graves, Kerry A. *Haiti.* Mankato, Minnesota: Bridgestone Books, 2002.

2452. Gravett, Christopher. *The Knights Handbook: How to Become a Champion in Shining Armor.* New York: Cobblehill Books, 1997.

2453. Green, Jen. *Israel.* Austin, Texas: Steck-Vaughn Publishers, 2001.

2454. Green, Jen. *Japan.* Austin, Texas: Raintree Steck-Vaughn Publishers, 2000.

2455. Green, Jen. *Mexico.* Austin, Texas: Raintree Steck-Vaughn Publishers, 2000.

2456. Green, Jen. *Step into the. . . Arctic World.* New York: Lorenz Books, 2000.

2457. Gresko, Marcia S. *Israel.* Minneapolis, Minnesota: Carolrhoda Books, 2000.

2458. Griffiths, Jonathan. *New Zealand.* Milwaukee, Wisconsin: Gareth Stevens Publishing, 1999.

2459. Griffiths, Jonathan. *Scotland.* Milwaukee, Wisconsin: Gareth Stevens Publishing, 1999.

2460. Hamilton, Janice. *Canada.* Minneapolis, Minnesota: Carolrhoda Books, 1999.

2461. Hargittai, Magdolna. *Cooking the Hungarian Way.* Minneapolis, Minnesota: Lerner Publications Co., 2003.

2462. Harrison, Supenn. *Cooking the Thai Way.* Minneapolis, Minnesota: Lerner Publications Co., 2003.

2463. Hart, Avery. *Ancient Rome: Exploring the Culture, People and Ideas of this Powerful Empire.* Charlotte, Vermont: Williamson Publishing Co., 2002.

2464. Hart, Avery. *Who Really Discovered America: Unraveling the Mystery and Solving the Puzzle.* Charlotte, Vermont: Williamson Publishing Co., 2001.

2465. Harvey, Miles. *Italy.* Danbury, Connecticut: Children's Press, 1996.

2466. Heinrichs, Ann. *Colorado.* Minneapolis, Minnesota: Compass Point Books, 2003.

2467. Heinrichs, Ann. *Minnesota.* Minneapolis, Minnesota: Compass Point Books, 2003.

2468. Heinrichs, Ann. *Niger.* Danbury, Connecticut: Children's Press, 2001.

2469. Heinrichs, Ann. *Vermont.* Danbury, Connecticut: Children's Press, 2001.

2470. Herbert, Jane. *South Carolina.* Tarrytown, New York: Marshall Cavendish Corp., 2001.

2471. Herbert, Janis. *The American Revolution for Kids.* Chicago, Illinois: Chicago Review Press, 2002.

2472. Herbert, Janis. *Leonardo da Vinci for Kids: His Life and Ideas: 21 Activities.* Chicago, Illinois: Chicago Review Press, 1998.

2473. Herbert, Janis. *Lewis and Clark for Kids: Their Journey of Discovery with 21 Activities.* Chicago, Illinois: Chicago Review Press, 2000.

2474. Herbert, Janis. *Marco Polo for Kids: His Marvelous Journey to China: 21 Activities.* Chicago, Illinois: Chicago Review Press, 2001.

2475. Herweck, Dona. *Patterns and Clip Art.* Huntington Beach, California: Teacher Created Materials, 1991.

2476. Hestler, Anna. *Wales.* Tarrytown, New York: Marshall Cavendish Corp., 2001.

2477. Hill, Barbara W. *Cooking the English Way.* Minneapolis, Minnesota: Lerner Publications Co., 2003.

2478. Hill, Linda Burrell. *Using Multicultural Literature: Journeys.* Huntington Beach, California: Teacher Created Materials, 1994.

2479. Hippely, Hillary Horder. *A Song for Lena.* New York: Simon & Schuster, 1996.

2480. Hirschfelder, Arlene. *Native Americans Today: Resources and Activities for Educators, Grades 4-8.* Englewood, Colorado: Teacher Ideas Press, 2000.

2481. *Holiday Cooking Around the World.* Minneapolis, Minnesota: Lerner Publications Co., 2002.

2482. Honan, Linda. *Spend the Day in Ancient Rome: Projects and Activities that Bring the Past to Life.* New York: John Wiley & Sons, 1998.

2483. Hopkinson, Deborah. *Fannie in the Kitchen!* New York: Atheneum Books for Young Readers, 1999.

2484. Howard, Dale E. *India.* Danbury, Connecticut: Children's Press, 1996.

2485. Hughes, Helga. *Cooking the Austrian Way.* Minneapolis, Minnesota: Lerner Publications Co., 2004.

2486. Hughes, Meredith Sayles. *Tall and Tasty: Fruit Trees.* Minneapolis, Minnesota: Lerner Publications Co., 2000.

2487. Hurdman, Charlotte. *Step into… the Stone Age.* New York: Lorenz Books, 1998.

2488. Ichord, Loretta Frances. *Skillet Bread, Sourdough, and Vinegar Pie: Cooking in Pioneer Days.* Brookfield, Connecticut: The Millbrook Press, 2003.

2489. Ingham, Richard. *France.* Austin, Texas: Raintree Steck-Vaughn Publishers, 2000.

2490. Innes, Brian. *United Kingdom.* Austin, Texas: Steck-Vaughn Publishers, 2001.

2491. Jaffe, Elizabeth Dana. *Dominoes.* Minneapolis, Minnesota: Compass Point Books, 2002.

2492. Jaffe, Elizabeth Dana. *Hopscotch.* Minneapolis, Minnesota: Compass Point Books, 2002.

2493. Jaffe, Elizabeth Dana. *Jacks.* Minneapolis, Minnesota: Compass Point Books, 2002.

2494. Jaffe, Elizabeth Dana. *Juggling.* Minneapolis, Minnesota: Compass Point Books, 2002.

2495. Jaffe, Elizabeth Dana. *Marbles.* Minneapolis, Minnesota: Compass Point Books, 2002.

2496. Jermyn, Leslie. *Belize.* Tarrytown, New York: Marshall Cavendish Corp., 2001.

2497. Johmann, Carol A. *Going West!: Journey on a Wagon Train to Settle a Frontier Town.* Charlotte, Vermont: Williamson Publishing Co., 2000.

2498. Johmann, Carol A. *The Lewis and Clark Expedition.* Charlotte, Vermont: Williamson Publishing Co., 2003.

2499. Johmann, Carol A. *Skyscrapers: Super Structures to Design and Build.* Charlotte, Vermont: Williamson Publishing Co., 2001.

2500. Johnson, Elizabeth M. *Michigan.* Danbury, Connecticut: Children's Press, 2002.

2501. Johnson, Ron M. E. *Leonardo da Vinci.* Irving, Texas: Nest Entertainment, 1996.

2502. Johnston, Joyce. *Maryland.* Minneapolis, Minnesota: Lerner Publications Co., 2003.

2503. Johnston, Joyce. *Washington, D.C.* Minneapolis, Minnesota: Lerner Publications Co., 2003.

2504. Jones, Lynda. *Kids Around the World Celebrate: The Best Feasts and Festivals from Many Lands.* New York: John Wiley & Sons, 2000.

2505. Jovinelly, Joann. *The Crafts and Culture of the Ancient Egyptians.* New York: The Rosen Publishing Group, 2002.

2506. Jovinelly, Joann. *The Crafts and Culture of the Ancient Greeks.* New York: The Rosen Publishing Group, 2002.

2507. Jovinelly, Joann. *The Crafts and Culture of the Ancient Hebrews.* New York: The Rosen Publishing Group, 2002.

2508. Jovinelly, Joann. *The Crafts and Culture of the Aztecs.* New York: The Rosen Publishing Group, 2002.

2509. Jovinelly, Joann. *The Crafts and Culture of the Romans.* New York: The Rosen Publishing Group, 2002.

2510. Jovinelly, Joann. *The Crafts and Culture of the Vikings.* New York: The Rosen Publishing Group, 2002.

2511. Jurenka, Nancy Allen. *Hobbies through Children's Books and Activities.* Englewood, Colorado: Teacher Ideas Press, 2001.

2512. Kagda, Falaq. *India.* Milwaukee, Wisconsin: Gareth Stevens Publishing, 1997.

2513. Kagda, Falaq. *Kenya.* Milwaukee, Wisconsin: Gareth Stevens Publishing, 1997.

2514. Kalman, Bobbie. *China, the Culture.* New York: Crabtree Publishing Co., 2001.

2515. Kalman, Bobbie. *Classroom Games.* New York: Crabtree Publishing Co., 2001.

2516. Kalman, Bobbie. *The Colonial Cook.* New York: Crabtree Publishing Co., 2002.

2517. Kalman, Bobbie. *Mexico, the Culture.* New York: Crabtree Publishing Co., 2002.

2518. Kalman, Bobbie. *Pioneer Recipes.* New York: Crabtree Publishing Co., 2001.

2519. Kalman, Bobbie. *Schoolyard Games.* New York: Crabtree Publishing Co., 2001.

2520. Kimble-Ellis, Sonya. *Traditional African American Arts and Activities.* New York: John Wiley & Sons, 2002.

2521. Kimmel, Eric A. *A Hanukkah Treasury.* New York: Henry Holt and Co., 1997.

2522. King, David C. *Revolutionary War Days: Discover the Past with Exciting Projects, Games, Activities and Recipes.* New York: John Wiley & Sons, 2001.

2523. King, David C. *Wild West Days: Discovering the Past with Fun Projects, Games, Activities and Recipes.* New York: John Wiley & Sons, 1998.

2524. King, David C. *World War II Days: Discover the Past with Exciting Projects, Games, Activities and Recipes.* New York: John Wiley & Sons, 2000.

2525. Kirchner, Glenn. *Children's Games from Around the World, 2nd ed.* Boston, Massachusetts: Allyn and Bacon, 2000.

2526. *Kit's Friendship Fun.* Middleton, Wisconsin: American Girl Publications, 2002.

2527. Knoell, Donna L. *France.* Mankato, Minnesota: Bridgestone Books, 2002.

2528. Koestler, Rachel A. *Going to School during the Civil Rights Movement.* Mankato, Minnesota: Blue Earth Books, 2002.

2529. Kohl, Mary Ann F. *Discovering Great Artists: Hands-on Art for Children in the Styles of the Great Masters.* Bellingham, Washington: Bright Ring Publishing, 1997.

2530. Kopka, Deborah. *Norway.* Minneapolis, Minnesota: Carolrhoda Books, 2001.

2531. Krasno, Rena. *Floating Lanterns and Golden Shrines: Celebrating Japanese Festivals.* Berkeley, California: Pacific View Press, 2000.

2532. Krasno, Rena. *Kneeling Carabao and Dancing Giants: Celebrating Filipino Festivals.* Berkeley, California: Pacific View Press, 1997.

2533. Kummer, Patricia K. *Ukraine.* Danbury, Connecticut: Children's Press, 2001.

2534. Kuntz, Lynn. *American Grub: Eats for Kids from all Fifty States.* New York: Scholastic, 1997.

2535. LaDoux, Rita C. *Georgia.* Minneapolis, Minnesota: Lerner Publications Co., 2002.

2536. LaDoux, Rita C. *Iowa.* Minneapolis, Minnesota: Lerner Publications Co., 2002.

2537. LaDoux, Rita C. *Montana.* Minneapolis, Minnesota: Lerner Publications Co., 2003.

2538. LaDoux, Rita C. *Oklahoma.* Minneapolis, Minnesota: Lerner Publications Co., 2003.

2539. Landau, Elaine. *Columbus Day: Celebrating a Famous Explorer.* Berkeley Heights, New Jersey: Enslow Publishers, 2002.

2540. Landau, Elaine. *Earth Day: Keeping our Planet Clean.* Berkeley Heights, New Jersey: Enslow Publishers, 2002.

2541. Landau, Elaine. *Independence Day: Birthday of the United States.* Berkeley Heights, New Jersey: Enslow Publishers, 2001.

2542. Landau, Elaine. *Mardi Gras: Parades, Costumes and Parties.* Berkeley Heights, New Jersey: Enslow Publishers, 2002.

2543. Landau, Elaine. *Popcorn.* Watertown, Massachusetts: Charlesbridge Publishing, 2003.

2544. Landau, Elaine. *St. Patrick's Day: Parades, Shamrocks and Leprechauns.* Berkeley Heights, New Jersey: Enslow Publishers, 2002.

2545. Landau, Elaine. *Valentine's Day: Candy, Love and Hearts.* Berkeley Heights, New Jersey: Enslow Publishers, 2002.

2546. Landau, Elaine. *Veteran's Day: Remembering Our War Heroes.* Berkeley Heights, New Jersey: Enslow Publishers, 2002.

2547. Lankford, Mary D. *Birthdays Around the World.* New York: HarperCollins Publishers, 2002.

2548. Lankford, Mary D. *Dominoes Around the World.* New York: William Morrow and Co., 1998.

2549. Larkin, Tanya. *What Was Cooking in Abigail Adams' White House?* New York: PowerKids Press, 2000.

2550. Larkin, Tanya. *What Was Cooking in Dolley Madison's White House?* New York: PowerKids Press, 2000.

2551. Larkin, Tanya. *What Was Cooking in Edith Roosevelt's White House?* New York: PowerKids Press, 2000.

2552. Larkin, Tanya. *What Was Cooking in Julia Grant's White House?* New York: PowerKids Press, 2001.

2553. Larkin, Tanya. *What Was Cooking in Martha Washington's Presidential Mansions?* New York: PowerKids Press, 2001.

2554. Larkin, Tanya. *What Was Cooking in Mary Todd Lincoln's White House?* New York: PowerKids Press, 2001.

2555. Lassieur, Allison. *The Arapaho Tribe.* Mankato, Minnesota: Bridgestone Books, 2002.

2556. Lassieur, Allison. *The Blackfeet Nation.* Mankato, Minnesota: Bridgestone Books, 2002.

2557. Lassieur, Allison. *The Cheyenne.* Mankato, Minnesota: Bridgestone Books, 2001.

2558. Lassieur, Allison. The *Choctaw Nation.* Mankato, Minnesota: Bridgestone Books, 2001.

2559. Lassieur, Allison. *The Creek Nation.* Mankato, Minnesota: Bridgestone Books, 2002.

2560. Lassieur, Allison. *The Delaware People.* Mankato, Minnesota: Bridgestone Books, 2002.

2561. Lassieur, Allison. *Ethiopia.* Mankato, Minnesota: Capstone Press, 2004.

2562. Lassieur, Allison. *The Pequot Tribe.* Mankato, Minnesota: Bridgestone Books, 2002.

2563. Lassieur, Allison. *Peru.* Mankato, Minnesota: Capstone Press, 2004.

2564. Layton, Lesley. *Singapore.* Tarrytown, New York: Marshall Cavendish Corp., 2002.

2565. Lee, Frances. *The Young Chef's Chinese Cookbook.* New York: Crabtree Publishing Co., 2001.

2566. Lehman-Wilzig, Tami. *Tasty Bible Stories: A Menu of Tales and Matching Recipes.* Minneapolis, Minnesota: Kar-Ben Publishing, 2003.

2567. Leotta, Joan. *Massachusetts.* Danbury, Connecticut: Children's Press, 2001.

2568. Lim, Robin. *Indonesia.* Minneapolis, Minnesota: Carolrhoda Books, 2001.

2569. Limberhand, Dennis. *The Cheyenne.* Austin, Texas: Raintree Steck-Vaughn Publishers, 2001.

2570. Ling, Bettina. *Wisconsin.* Danbury, Connecticut: Children's Press, 2002.

2571. Littlefield, Cynthia. *Real-World Math for Hands-On Fun!* Charlotte, Vermont: Williamson Publishing Co., 2001.

2572. Locricchio, Matthew. *The Cooking of China.* Tarrytown, New York: Benchmark Books, 2002.

2573. Locricchio, Matthew. *The Cooking of France.* Tarrytown, New York: Benchmark Books, 2002.

2574. Locricchio, Matthew. *The Cooking of Italy.* Tarrytown, New York: Benchmark Books, 2002.

2575. Locricchio, Matthew. *The Cooking of Mexico.* Tarrytown, New York: Benchmark Books, 2002.

2576. *Look 'N' Cook.* Greensboro, North Carolina: The Education Center, 2001.

2577. Lord, Richard. *Germany.* Milwaukee, Wisconsin: Gareth Stevens Publishing, 1997.

2578. Love, Ann. *Kids and Grandparents: An Activity Book.* Toronto, Ontario: KidsCan Press, 2000.

2579. Macdonald, Fiona. *Rain Forest.* New York: Franklin Watts, 2000.

2580. Macdonald, Fiona. *Step into Ancient Japan.* New York: Lorenz Books, 1999.

2581. Macdonald, Fiona. *Step into the…Aztec and Maya World.* New York: Lorenz Books, 1998.

2582. Macdonald, Fiona. *Step into the…Celtic World.* New York: Lorenz Books, 1999.

2583. MacLeod, Elizabeth. *Bake and Make Amazing Cakes.* Tonawanda, New York: KidsCan Press, 2001.

2584. Madavan, Vijay. *Cooking the Indian Way.* Minneapolis, Minnesota: Lerner Publications Co., 2002.

2585. Maher, Erin. *Chinese Foods and Recipes.* New York: The Rosen Publishing Group, 2002.

2586. Mamdani, Shelby. *Traditions from China.* Austin, Texas: Steck-Vaughn Publishers, 1998.

2587. Mamdani, Shelby. *Traditions from India.* Austin, Texas: Steck-Vaughn Publishers, 1999.

2588. Marchant, Kerena. *Hindu Festivals Cookbook.* Austin, Texas: Raintree Steck-Vaughn Publishers, 2001.

2589. Marchant, Kerena. *Hindu Festival Tales.* Austin, Texas: Raintree Steck-Vaughn Publishers, 2001.

2590. Marchant, Kerena. *Muslim Festival Tales.* Austin, Texas: Raintree Steck-Vaughn Publishers, 2001.

2591. Marsh, Valerie. *Puppet Tales.* Fort Atkinson, Wisconsin: Alleyside Press, 1998.

2592. *Martin Luther King, Jr. Day Activities.* Westminster, California: Teacher Created Materials, 1999 reprint.

2593. Master, Nancy Robinson. *Kansas.* Danbury, Connecticut: Children's Press, 1999.

2594. Mattern, Joanne. *India.* Mankato, Minnesota: Bridgestone Books, 2003.

2595. Mattern, Joanne. *Ireland.* Mankato, Minnesota: Bridgestone Books, 2003.

2596. Mattern, Joanne. *The Shawnee Indians.* Mankato, Minnesota: Bridgestone Books, 2001.

2597. Mattern, Joanne. *The Shoshone People.* Mankato, Minnesota: Bridgestone Books, 2001.

2598. McCain, Becky Ray. *Grandmother's Dreamcatcher.* Morton Grove, Illinois: Albert Whitman & Company, 1998.

2599. McCarthy, Cathy. *The Ojibwa.* Austin, Texas: Raintree Steck-Vaughn Publishers, 2001.

2600. McCollum, Sean. *Australia.* Minneapolis, Minnesota: Carolrhoda Books, 1999.

2601. McCollum, Sean. *Kenya.* Minneapolis, Minnesota: Carolrhoda Books, 1999.

2602. McCollum, Sean. *Poland.* Minneapolis, Minnesota: Carolrhoda Books, 1999.

2603. McCulloch, Julie. *The Caribbean.* Chicago, Illinois: Heinemann Library, 2001.

2604. McCulloch, Julie. *China.* Chicago, Illinois: Heinemann Library, 2001.

2605. McCulloch, Julie. *India.* Chicago, Illinois: Heinemann Library, 2001. -

2606. McCulloch, Julie. *Italy.* Chicago, Illinois: Heinemann Library, 2001.

2607. McCulloch, Julie. *Japan.* Chicago, Illinois: Heinemann Library, 2001.

2608. McCulloch, Julie. *Mexico.* Chicago, Illinois: Heinemann Library, 2001.

2609. McKay, Susan. *Brazil.* Milwaukee, Wisconsin: Gareth Stevens Publishing, 1997.

2610. McKay, Susan. *France.* Milwaukee, Wisconsin: Gareth Stevens Publishing, 1998.

2611. McKay, Susan. *Japan.* Milwaukee, Wisconsin: Gareth Stevens Publishing, 1997.

2612. McKay, Susan. *Spain.* Milwaukee, Wisconsin: Gareth Stevens Publishing, 1999.

2613. McKay, Susan. *Switzerland.* Milwaukee, Wisconsin: Gareth Stevens Publishing, 1999.

2614. McKay, Susan. *Vietnam.* Milwaukee, Wisconsin: Gareth Stevens Publishing, 1997.

2615. McLester, L. Gordon. *The Oneida.* Austin, Texas: Raintree Steck-Vaughn Publishers, 2001.

2616. McMillan, Mary. *Christian Crafts from Hand-Shaped Art.* Torrance, California: Shining Star Publications, 1991.

2618. McMorrow, Annalisa. *Terrific Transportation: Reading, Writing and Speaking about Transportation.* Palo Alto, California: Monday Morning Books, 2000.

2619. Mendoza, Lunita. *Philippines.* Milwaukee, Wisconsin: Gareth Stevens Publishing, 1999.

2620. Merrill, Yvonne Y. *Hands-On Africa: Art Activities for All Ages Featuring Sub-Saharan Africa.* Salt Lake City, Utah: Kits Publishing, 2000.

2621. Merrill, Yvonne Y. *Hands-On America, Volume 1: Art Activities about Vikings, Woodland Indians and Early Colonists.* Salt Lake City, Utah: Kits Publishing, 2001.

2622. Miescke, Lori. *Christian Crafts from Construction Paper.* Torrance, California: Shining Star Publications, 1992.

2623. Milivojevic, JoAnn. *Puerto Rico.* Minneapolis, Minnesota: Carolrhoda Books, 2000.

2624. Miller, Amy. *Colorado.* Danbury, Connecticut: Children's Press, 2002.

2625. Mirpuri, Gouri. *Indonesia.* Tarrytown, New York: Marshall Cavendish Corp., 2002.

2626. Mitchell, Kevin M. *Wickiup.* Vero Beach, Florida: Rourke Book Co., 2000.

2627. Montgomery, Bertha Vining. *Cooking the East African Way.* Minneapolis, Minnesota: Lerner Publications Co., 2002.

2628. Montgomery, Bertha Vining. *Cooking the West African Way.* Minneapolis, Minnesota: Lerner Publications Co., 2002.

2629. Moore, Sharon. *Native American Foods and Recipes.* New York: The Rosen Publishing Group, 2002.

2630. Morris, Ann. *Grandma Esther Remembers.* Brookfield, Connecticut: The Millbrook Press, 2002.

2631. Morris, Ann. *Grandma Francisca Remembers.* Brookfield, Connecticut: The Millbrook Press, 2002.

2632. Morris, Ann. *Grandma Lai Goon Remembers: A Chinese-American Family Story.* Brookfield, Connecticut: The Millbrook Press, 2002.

2633. Morris, Ann. *Grandma Lois Remembers: An African-American Family Story.* Brookfield, Connecticut: The Millbrook Press, 2002.

2634. Morris, Ann. *Grandma Maxine Remembers.* Brookfield, Connecticut: The Millbrook Press, 2002.

2635. Morris, Ann. *Grandma Susan Remembers.* Brookfield, Connecticut: The Millbrook Press, 2002.

2636. Morrow, Priscella. *Totally Tubeys: 24 Storytimes with Tube Crafts.* Fort Atkinson, Wisconsin: Upstart Books, 2003.

2637. *Mother's Day Activities.* Westminster, California: Teacher Created Materials, 1999 reprint.

2638. Munan, Heidi. *Malaysia.* Tarrytown, New York: Marshall Cavendish Corp., 2002.

2639. Munsen, Sylvia. *Cooking the Norwegian Way.* Minneapolis, Minnesota: Lerner Publications Co., 2002.

2640. Murphy, Patricia J. *Denmark.* Mankato, Minnesota: Bridgestone Books, 2003.

2641. Murphy, Patricia J. *Tanzania.* Mankato, Minnesota: Bridgestone Books, 2003.

2642. Nakajima, Caroline. *Connecting Cultures and Literature.* Huntington Beach, California: Teacher Created Materials, 1992.

2643. Napier, Tanya. *Totally Tea-rific Tea Party Book.* San Francisco, California: Orange Avenue Publishing, 2002.

2644. *Native Americans, Primary.* Greensboro, North Carolina: The Education Center, 2002.

2645. NgCheong-Lum, Roseline. *Haiti.* Milwaukee, Wisconsin: Gareth Stevens Publishing, 1998.

2646. Nguyen, Chi. *Cooking the Vietnamese Way.* Minneapolis, Minnesota: Lerner Publications Co., 2002.

2647. Nickles, Greg. *Argentina.* New York: Crabtree Publishing Co., 2001.

2648. Nickles, Greg. *Germany.* Austin, Texas: Raintree Steck-Vaughn Publishers, 2000.

2649. Nobleman, Marc Tyler. *Cambodia.* Mankato, Minnesota: Bridgestone Books, 2003.

2650. Nobleman, Marc Tyler. *Greece.* Mankato, Minnesota: Bridgestone Books, 2003.

2651. Nobleman, Marc Tyler. *Pakistan.* Mankato, Minnesota: Bridgestone Books, 2003.

2652. Nobleman, Marc Tyler. *Panama.* Mankato, Minnesota: Bridgestone Books, 2003.

2653. Nollen, Tim. *Czech Republic.* Milwaukee, Wisconsin: Gareth Stevens Publishing, 1999.

2654. Oakes, Lorna. *Step into... Mesopotamia.* New York: Lorenz Books, 2001.

2655. O'Connor, Karen. *Vietnam.* Minneapolis, Minnesota: Carolrhoda Books, 1999.

2656. O'Hara, Megan. *Irish Immigrants, 1840-1920.* Mankato, Minnesota: Blue Earth Books, 2002.

2657. O'Hare, Jeff. *Hanukkah, Festival of Lights.* Honesdale, Pennsylvania: Boyds Mills Press, 2000.

2658. Olson, Kay Melchisedech. *China.* Mankato, Minnesota: Blue Earth Books, 2003.

2659. Olson, Kay Melchisedech. *Chinese Immigrants, 1850-1900.* Mankato, Minnesota: Blue Earth Books, 2002.

2660. Olson, Kay Melchisedech. *England.* Mankato, Minnesota: Blue Earth Books, 2003.

2661. Oluonye, Mary N. *Madagascar.* Minneapolis, Minnesota: Carolrhoda Books, 2000.

2662. Oluonye, Mary N. *Nigeria.* Minneapolis, Minnesota: Carolrhoda Books, 1998.

2663. Oluonye, Mary N. *South Africa.* Minneapolis, Minnesota: Carolrhoda Books, 1999.

2664. *The Olympic Dream Primary Curriculum Guide to the Olympic Games.* Glendale, California: Griffin Publishing Group, 1997.

2665. O'Shea, Maria. *Saudi Arabia.* Milwaukee, Wisconsin: Gareth Stevens Publishing, 1999.

2666. O'Shea, Maria. *Turkey.* Milwaukee, Wisconsin: Gareth Stevens Publishing, 1999.

2667. *Our Country: Dozens of Instant and Irresistible Ideas and Activities to Teach About the Flag, the Pledge, the Presidents and More.* New York: Scholastic Professional Books, 2002.

2668. Panchyk, Richard. *World War II for Kids: A History with 21 Activities.* Chicago, Illinois: Chicago Review Press, 2002.

2669. Parnell, Helga. *Cooking the German Way.* Minneapolis, Minnesota: Lerner Publications Co., 2003.

2670. Parnell, Helga. *Cooking the South American Way.* Minneapolis, Minnesota: Lerner Publications Co., 2003.

2671. Pavon, Ana-Elba. *25 Latino Craft Projects.* Chicago, Illinois: American Library Association, 2003.

2672. Pelta, Kathy. *Idaho.* Minneapolis, Minnesota: Lerner Publications Co., 2002.

2673. Perry, Phyllis J. *Ten Tall Tales: Origins, Activities and More.* Fort Atkinson, Wisconsin: Upstart Books, 2002.

2674. Pfeffer, Wendy. *The Shortest Day: Celebrate the Winter Solstice.* New York: Dutton Children's Books, 2003.

2675. Phelps, Joan Hilyer. *Finger Tales.* Fort Atkinson, Wisconsin: Upstart Books, 2002.

2676. Pinol, Roser. *Creating Costumes.* Woodbridge, Connecticut: Blackbirch Press, 2000.

2677. Pirotta, Saviour. *Christian Festival Cookbook.* Austin, Texas: Raintree Steck-Vaughn Publishers, 2001.

2678. Pirotta, Saviour. *Christian Festival Tales.* Austin, Texas: Steck-Vaughn Publishers, 2001.

2679. Pirotta, Saviour. *Jewish Festival Tales.* Austin, Texas: Steck-Vaughn Publishers, 2001.

2680. Plokin, Gregory. *Cooking the Russian Way.* Minneapolis, Minnesota: Lerner Publications Co., 2003.

2681. Polette, Nancy. *U.S. History Readers Theatre: 200+ Years of History through Booktalks, Songs, Poetry and Creative Writing Activities.* O'Fallon, Missouri: Book Lures, 1994.

2682. Porter, A. P. *Nebraska.* Minneapolis, Minnesota: Lerner Publications Co., 2003.

2683. Powell, Michelle. *Mosaics.* Chicago, Illinois: Heinemann Library, 2001.

2684. Pratt, Diane. *Hey Kids! You're Cookin' Now: A Global Awareness Cooking Adventure.* Salisbury Cove, Maine: Harvest Hill Press, 1998.

2685. Press, Judy. *All Around Town: Exploring Your Community Through Craft Fun.* Charlotte, Vermont: Williamson Publishing Co., 2002.

2686. Press, Judy. *Around the World Art and Activities: Visiting the Continents through Craft Fun.* Charlotte, Vermont: Williamson Publishing Co., 2001.

2687. Quasha, Jennifer. *The Birth and Growth of a Nation: Hands-On Projects about Symbols of American Liberty.* New York: PowerKids Press, 2000.

2688. Quasha, Jennifer. *Covered Wagons: Hands-On Projects about America's Westward Expansion.* New York: PowerKids Press, 2001.

2689. Quasha, Jennifer. *Gold Rush: Hands-On Projects about Mining the Riches of California.* New York: PowerKids Press, 2001.

2690. Quasha, Jennifer. *Pilgrims and Native Americans: Hands-On Projects about Life in Colonial America.* New York: PowerKids Press, 2000.

2691. Quasha, Jennifer. *The Pony Express: Hands-On Projects about Early Communication.* New York: PowerKids Press, 2000.

2692. Raabe, Emily. *Christmas Holiday Cookbook.* New York: The Rosen Publishing Group, 2002.

2693. Raabe, Emily. *An Easter Holiday Cookbook.* New York: PowerKids Press, 2002.

2694. Raabe, Emily. *A Kwanzaa Holiday Cookbook.* New York: The Rosen Publishing Group, 2002.

2695. Raabe, Emily. *A Passover Holiday Cookbook.* New York: The Rosen Publishing Group, 2002.

2696. Raabe, Emily. *A Thanksgiving Holiday.* New York: The Rosen Publishing Group, 2002.

2697. Randall, Ronne. *Jewish Festival Cookbook.* Austin, Texas: Steck-Vaughn Publishers, 2001.

2698. Rasmussen, R. Kent. *Pueblo.* Vero Beach, Florida: Rourke Book Company, 2000.

2699. Ready, Anna. *Mississippi.* Minneapolis, Minnesota: Lerner Publications Co., 2003.

2700. Rhatigan, Joe. *Geography Crafts for Kids: 50 Cool Projects and Activities for Exploring the World.* New York: Lark Books, 2002.

2701. Riehecky, Janet. *China.* Minneapolis, Minnesota: Carolrhoda Books, 1999.

2702. Riehecky, Janet. *The Cree Tribe.* Minneapolis, Minnesota: Bridgestone Books, 2003.

2703. Riehecky, Janet. *Greece.* Mankato, Minnesota: Bridgestone Books, 2001.

2704. Riehecky, Janet. *Indonesia.* Mankato, Minnesota: Bridgestone Books, 2002.

2705. Riehecky, Janet. *Nicaragua.* Mankato, Minnesota: Bridgestone Books, 2002.

2706. Riehecky, Janet. *The Osage.* Mankato, Minnesota: Bridgestone Books, 2003.

2707. Riehecky, Janet. *Sweden.* Mankato, Minnesota: Bridgestone Books, 2001.

2708. Robinson, Fay. *Chinese New Year, a Time for Parades, Family and Friends.* Berkeley Heights, New Jersey: Enslow Publishers, 2001.

2709. Robinson, Fay. *Halloween: Costumes and Treats on All Hallow's Eve.* Berkeley Heights, New Jersey: Enslow Publishers, 2001.

2710. Rocklin, Joanne. *Strudel Stories.* New York: Delacorte Press, 1999.

2711. Rogers, Barbara Radcliffe. *Zimbabwe.* Danbury, Connecticut: Children's Press, 2002.

2712. Rogers, Lura. *Spain.* Danbury, Connecticut: Children's Press, 2001.

2713. Rogers, Lura. *Switzerland.* Danbury, Connecticut: Children's Press, 2001.

2714. Roop, Peter. *Let's Celebrate Earth Day.* Brookfield, Connecticut: The Millbrook Press, 2001.

2715. Roop, Peter. *Let's Celebrate Valentine's Day.* Brookfield, Connecticut: The Millbrook Press, 1999.

2716. Rosenberg, Anne. *Nigeria, the Culture.* New York: Crabtree Publishing Co., 2001.

2717. Rosin, Arielle. *Pizzas and Punk Potatoes.* New York: Ticknor & Fields, 1994.

2718. Ross, Corinne. *Christmas in Mexico.* Lincolnwood, Illinois: Passport Books, 1991.

2719. Ross, Kathy. *All New Crafts for Halloween.* Brookfield, Connecticut: The Millbrook Press, 2003.

2720. Ross, Kathy. *All New Crafts for Valentine's Day.* Brookfield, Connecticut: The Millbrook Press, 2002.

2721. Ross, Kathy. *Christian Crafts for Christmastime.* Brookfield, Connecticut: The Millbrook Press, 2001.

2722. Ross, Kathy. *Christmas Decorations Kids Can Make.* Brookfield, Connecticut: The Millbrook Press, 1999.

2723. Ross, Kathy. *Christmas Ornaments Kids Can Make.* Brookfield, Connecticut: The Millbrook Press, 1998.

2724. Ross, Kathy. *Christmas Presents Kids Can Make.* Brookfield, Connecticut: The Millbrook Press, 2001.

2725. Ross, Kathy. *Crafts for Christian Values.* Brookfield, Connecticut: The Millbrook Press, 2000.

2726. Ross, Kathy. *Crafts for Easter.* Brookfield, Connecticut: The Millbrook Press, 1995.

2727. Ross, Kathy. *Crafts for Hanukkah.* Brookfield, Connecticut: The Millbrook Press, 1996.

2728. Ross, Kathy. *Crafts from Your Favorite Children's Songs.* Brookfield, Connecticut: The Millbrook Press, 2001.

2729. Ross, Kathy. *Crafts from Your Favorite Children's Stories.* Brookfield, Connecticut: The Millbrook Press, 2001.

2730. Ross, Kathy. *Crafts from Your Favorite Nursery Rhymes.* Brookfield, Connecticut: The Millbrook Press, 2002.

2731. Ross, Kathy. *Crafts That Celebrate Black History.* Brookfield, Connecticut: The Millbrook Press, 2002.

2732. Ross, Kathy. *Crafts to Celebrate God's Creation.* Brookfield, Connecticut: The Millbrook Press, 2001.

2733. Ross, Kathy. *Crafts to Make in the Summer.* Brookfield, Connecticut: The Millbrook Press, 1998.

2734. Ross, Kathy. *Make Yourself a Monster.* Brookfield, Connecticut: The Millbrook Press, 1999.

2735. Ross, Kathy. *Star-Spangled Crafts.* Brookfield, Connecticut: The Millbrook Press, 2003.

2736. Ross, Michael Elsohn. *A Mexican Christmas.* Minneapolis, Minnesota: Carolrhoda Books, 2002.

2737. Rush, Barbara. *The Kids' Catalog of Passover: A World Wide Celebration.* Philadelphia, Pennsylvania: Jewish Publication Society, 1999.

2738. Sabbeth, Carol. *Monet and the Impressionists for Kids: Their Lives and Ideas, 21 Activities.* Chicago, Illinois: Chicago Review Press, 2002.

2739. Sachatello-Sawyer, Bonnie. *Lewis and Clark: Background Information, Activities.* New York: Scholastic Professional Books, 1997.

2740. Sadler, Judy Ann. *Christmas Crafts from Around the World.* Tonawanda, New York: KidsCan Press, 2003.

2741. Saffer, Barbara. *Kenya.* Mankato, Minnesota: Bridgestone Books, 2000.

2742. Saffer, Barbara. *Mexico.* Mankato, Minnesota: Bridgestone Books, 2002.

2743. Salas, Laura P. *China.* Mankato, Minnesota: Bridgestone Books, 2002.

2744. *Samantha's Fun.* Middleton, Wisconsin: Pleasant Company Publications, 2002.

2745. Sanders, Nancy I. *A Kid's Guide to African American History: More than 70 Activities.* Chicago, Illinois: Chicago Review Press, 2000.

2746. Sanders, Nancy I. *Old Testament Days: An Activity Guide.* Chicago, Illinois: Chicago Review Press, 1999.

2747. Sateren, Shelley Swanson. *Going to School in Colonial America.* Mankato, Minnesota: Blue Earth Books, 2002.

2748. Scheffler, Carol. *Family Crafting: Fun Projects to Do Together.* New York: Sterling Publishing Co., 2000.

2749. Schraff, Anne. *Philippines.* Minneapolis, Minnesota: Carolrhoda Books, 2001.

2750. Schwarz, Renee. *Making Masks.* Tonawanda, New York: KidsCan Press, 2001.

2751. Senterfitt, Marilyn. *Christian Crafts from Egg Cartons.* Torrance, California: Shining Star Publications, 1991.

2752. Sevaly, Karen. *April: A Creative Idea Book for the Elementary Teacher.* Riverside, California: Teacher's Friend Publications, 1998.

2753. Sevaly, Karen. *December: A Creative Idea Book for the Elementary Teacher.* Riverside, California: Teacher's Friend Publications, 1997.

2754. Sevaly, Karen. *February: A Creative Idea Book for the Elementary Teacher.* Riverside, California: Teacher's Friend Publications, 1997.

2755. Sevaly, Karen. *January: A Creative Idea Book for the Elementary Teacher.* Riverside, California: Teacher's Friend Publications, 1997.

2756. Sevaly, Karen. *July/August: A Creative Idea Book for the Elementary Teacher.* Riverside, California: Teacher's Friend Publications, 1998.

2757. Sevaly, Karen. *June: A Creative Idea Book for the Elementary Teacher.* Riverside, California: Teacher's Friend Publications, 1998.

2758. Sevaly, Karen. *March: A Creative Idea Book for the Elementary Teacher.* Riverside, California: Teacher's Friend Publications, 1998.

2759. Sevaly, Karen. *May: A Creative Idea Book for the Elementary Teacher.* Riverside, California: Teacher's Friend Publications, 1997.

2760. Sevaly, Karen. *November: A Creative Idea Book for the Elementary Teacher.* Riverside, California: Teacher's Friend Publications, 1997.

2761. Sevaly, Karen. *October: A Creative Idea Book for the Elementary Teacher.* Riverside, California: Teacher's Friend Publications, 1997.

2762. Sevaly, Karen. *September: A Creative Idea Book for the Elementary Teacher.* Riverside, California: Teacher's Friend Publications, 1997.

2763. Shannon, Terry Miller. *New Hampshire.* Danbury, Connecticut: Children's Press, 2002.

2764. *Share the Olympic Dream Vol. II: Curriculum Guide to the Olympic Games.* Glendale, California: Griffin Publishing Group, 1995.

2765. Shelley, Rex. *Japan.* Tarrytown, New York: Marshall Cavendish Corp., 2002.

2766. Shipman, Doug. *Christian Crafts: Paper Plate Animals.* Torrance, California: Shining Star Publications, 1993.

2767. Sierra, Judy. *Children's Traditional Games: Games from 137 Countries and Cultures.* Phoenix, Arizona: Oryx Press, 1995.

2768. Silbaugh, Elizabeth. *Raggedy Ann's Birthday Party Book.* New York: Simon & Schuster, 2001.

2769. Simonds, Nina. *Moonbeams, Dumplings and Dragon Boats: A Treasury of Chinese Holiday Tales, Activities and Recipes.* New York: Gulliver Books, 2002.

2770. Sirvaitis, Karen. *Michigan.* Minneapolis, Minnesota: Lerner Publications Co., 2002.

2771. Sirvaitis, Karen. *Nevada.* Minneapolis, Minnesota: Lerner Publications Co., 2003.

2772. Sirvaitis, Karen. *Tennessee.* Minneapolis, Minnesota: Lerner Publications, Co., 2003.

2773. Sirvaitis, Karen. *Utah.* Minneapolis, Minnesota: Lerner Publications Co., 2002.

2774. Sirvaitis, Karen. *Virginia.* Minneapolis, Minnesota: Lerner Publications Co., 2002.

2775. Somerville, Barbara A. *Alaska.* Danbury, Connecticut: Children's Press, 2001.

2776. Somerville, Barbara A. *Florida.* Danbury, Connecticut: Children's Press, 2001.

2777. Somerville, Barbara A. *Illinois.* Danbury, Connecticut: Children's Press, 2001.

2778. Souter, Gillian. *Holiday Handiwork.* Milwaukee, Wisconsin: Gareth Stevens Publishing, 2002.

2779. Speechley, Greta. *Bead Book.* Danbury, Connecticut: Grolier Educational, 2003.

2780. Speechley, Greta. *Dolls and Bears.* Danbury, Connecticut: Grolier Educational, 2003.

2781. Speechley, Greta. *Myths and Tales Book.* Danbury, Connecticut: Grolier Educational, 2003.

2782. Speechley, Greta. *Valentine Book.* Danbury, Connecticut: Grolier Educational, 2003.

2783. Speechley, Greta. *Winter Holiday Book.* Danbury, Connecticut: Grolier Educational, 2003.

2784. Speechley, Greta. *World Book.* Danbury, Connecticut: Grolier Educational, 2003.

2785. Srinivasan, Radhika. *India.* Tarrytown, New York: Marshall Cavendish Corp., 2002.

2786. Standard, Carole K. *Arizona.* Danbury, Connecticut: Children's Press, 2002.

2787. Stechschulte, Pattie. *Georgia.* Danbury, Connecticut: Children's Press, 2001.

2788. Steele, Philip. *Step into... Ancient Egypt.* New York: Lorenz Books, 2001.

2789. Steele, Philip. *Step into the... Chinese Empire.* New York: Lorenz Books, 1998.

2790. Steele, Philip. *Step into the... Inca World.* New York: Lorenz Books, 2000.

2791. Steele, Philip. *Step into...the Roman Empire.* New York: Lorenz Books, 1998.

2792. Steele, Philip. *Step into... the Viking World.* New York: Lorenz Books, 1998.

2793. Stegenga, Susan J. *Christian Crafts: Paper Bag Puppets.* Torrance, California: Shining Star Publications, 1990.

2794. Stein, R. Conrad. *Mexico.* Chicago, Illinois: Children's Press, 1995.

2795. Stepanchuk, Carol. *Exploring Chinatown: A Children's Guide to Chinatown.* Berkeley, California: Pacific View Press, 2001.

2796. Stepanchuk, Carol. *Red Eggs and Dragon Boats: Celebrating Chinese Festivals.* Berkeley, California: Pacific View Press, 1994.

2797. Sterling, Mary Ellen. *Presidents' Day and Martin Luther King, Jr. Day.* Westminster, California: Teacher Created Materials, 1992.

2798. Stohs, Anita Reith. *Christian Crafts for Holidays: Hand-Shaped Art.* Torrance, California: Shining Star Publications, 1994.

2799. Stohs, Anita Reith. *Christian Crafts from Cardboard Tubes.* Torrance, California: Shining Star Publications, 1992.

2800. Stohs, Anita Reith. *Christian Crafts from Folded Paper.* Torrance, California: Shining Star Publications, 1994.

2801. Stohs, Anita Reith. *Christian Crafts from Nature's Gifts.* Torrance, California: Shining Star Publications, 1994.

2802. Stohs, Anita Reith. *Christian Crafts from Tissue Paper.* Torrance, California: Shining Star Publications, 1993.

2803. Stohs, Anita Reith. *Christian Crafts: Yarn Art.* Torrance, California: Shining Star Publications, 1992.

2804. Stotter, Michael. *Step into...the World of North American Indians.* New York: Lorenz Books, 1999.

2805. Streissguth, Thomas. *Egypt.* Minneapolis, Minnesota: Carolrhoda Books, 1999.

2806. Streissguth, Thomas. *France.* Minneapolis, Minnesota: Carolrhoda Books, 1997.

2807. Streissguth, Thomas. *India.* Minneapolis, Minnesota: Carolrhoda Books, 1999.

2808. Streissguth, Thomas. *Japan.* Minneapolis, Minnesota: Carolrhoda Books, 1997.

2809. Streissguth, Thomas. *Mexico.* Minneapolis, Minnesota: Carolrhoda Books, 1997.

2810. Streissguth, Thomas. *Russia.* Minneapolis, Minnesota: Carolrhoda Books, 1997.

2811. Sullivan, Dianna J. *Holiday Art.* Huntington Beach, California: Teacher Created Materials, 1985.

2812. Sullivan, Dianna. *Literature Activities for Children.* Huntington Beach, California: Teacher Created Materials, 1990.

2813. Sullivan, Dianna. *Patriotic Holidays.* Huntington Beach, California: Teacher Created Materials, 1985.

2814. Swain, Gwenyth. *Indiana.* Minneapolis, Minnesota: Lerner Publications Co., 2002.

2815. Swain, Ruth Freeman. *How Sweet It Is (And Was): The History of Candy.* New York: Holiday House, 2003.

2816. Tames, Richard. *Step into... Ancient Greece.* New York: Lorenz Books, 1999.

2817. Temko, Florence. *Traditional Crafts from the Caribbean.* Minneapolis, Minnesota: Lerner Publications Co., 2001.

2818. Temko, Florence. *Traditional Crafts from China.* Minneapolis, Minnesota: Lerner Publications Co., 2001.

2819. Temko, Florence. *Traditional Crafts from Japan.* Minneapolis, Minnesota: Lerner Publications Co., 2001.

2820. Thoennes, Kristin. *Nigeria.* Mankato, Minnesota: Bridgestone Books, 1999.

2821. Thoennes, Kristin. *Russia.* Mankato, Minnesota: Bridgestone Books, 1999.

2822. Thomas, Jennifer. *Connecting Art and Literature.* Huntington Beach, California: Teacher Created Materials, 1992.

2823. Thompson, Susan Conklin. *Celebrating the World of Work: Interviews and Activities.* Englewood, Colorado: Teacher Ideas Press, 2001.

2824. Thompson, Stuart. *Chinese Festivals Cookbook.* Austin, Texas: Raintree Steck-Vaughn Publishers, 2001.

2825. Todd, Anne M. *Italian Immigrants, 1880-1920.* Mankato, Minnesota: Blue Earth Books, 2002.

2826. Todd, Anne M. *The Ojibway.* Mankato, Minnesota: Bridgestone Books, 2003.

2827. Todd, Anne M. *The Sioux: People of the Great Plains*. Mankato, Minnesota: Bridgestone Books, 2003.

2828. Totten, Kathryn. *Seasonal Storytime Crafts*. Fort Atkinson, Wisconsin: Upstart Books, 2002.

2829. Totten, Kathryn. *Storytime Crafts*. Fort Atkinson, Wisconsin: Alleyside Press, 1998.

2830. Townsend, Sue. *Egypt*. Chicago, Illinois: Heinemann Library, 2003.

2831. Townsend, Sue. *France*. Chicago, Illinois: Heinemann Library, 2002.

2832. Townsend, Sue. *Germany*. Chicago, Illinois: Heinemann Library, 2002.

2833. Townsend, Sue. *Greece*. Chicago, Illinois: Heinemann Library, 2002.

2834. Townsend, Sue. *Indonesia*. Chicago, Illinois: Heinemann Library, 2003.

2835. Townsend, Sue. *Russia*. Chicago, Illinois: Heinemann Library, 2003.

2836. Townsend, Sue. *Spain*. Chicago, Illinois: Heinemann Library, 2003.

2837. Townsend, Sue. *Thailand*. Chicago, Illinois: Heinemann Library, 2002.

2838. Townsend, Sue. *Vegetarian Recipes from Around the World*. Chicago, Illinois: Heinemann Library, 2003.

2839. Townsend, Sue. *Vietnam*. Chicago, Illinois: Heinemann Library, 2003.

2840. Trottier, Maxine. *Native Crafts: Inspired by North America's First Peoples*. Niagara Falls, New York: KidsCan Press, 2000.

2841. Verba, Joan Marie. *North Dakota*. Minneapolis, Minnesota: Lerner Publications Co., 2003.

2842. Villios, Lynne W. *Cooking the Greek Way*. Minneapolis, Minnesota: Lerner Publications Co., 2002.

2843. Waldee, Lynne Marie. *Cooking the French Way*. Minneapolis, Minnesota: Lerner Publications Co., 2002.

2844. Wallace, Mary. *Make Your Own Inuksuk*. Toronto, Ontario: Greey de Pencier Books, 2001.

2845. Wallace, Paula S. *The World of Food*. Milwaukee, Wisconsin: Gareth Stevens Publishing, 2003.

2846. Wallace, Paula S. *The World of Holidays*. Milwaukee, Wisconsin: Gareth Stevens Publishing, 2003.

2847. Wallace, Paula S. *The World of Sports*. Milwaukee, Wisconsin: Gareth Stevens Publishing, 2003.

2848. Wallner, Rosemary. *Japanese Immigrants, 1850-1950*. Mankato, Minnesota: Blue Earth Books, 2002.

2849. Walters, Scott T. *Knights and Castles*. Westminster, California: Teacher Created Materials, 2000.

2850. Ward, Karen. *The Young Chef's Mexican Cookbook*. New York: Crabtree Publishing Co., 2001.

2851. Warner, J. F. *Rhode Island*. Minneapolis, Minnesota: Lerner Publications Co., 2003.

2852. Warshaw, Hallie. *Zany Rainy Days: Indoor Ideas for Active Kids*. New York: Sterling Publishing Co., 2000.

2853. Weatherly, Myra S. *South Carolina*. Danbury, Connecticut: Children's Press, 2002.

2854. Weatherly, Myra S. *Tennessee*. Danbury, Connecticut: Children's Press, 2001.

2855. Weitzman, Elizabeth. *Brazil*. Minneapolis, Minnesota: Carolrhoda Books, 1998.

2856. Weston, Reiko. *Cooking the Japanese Way*. Minneapolis, Minnesota: Lerner Publications Co., 2002.

2857. Whitney, Brooks. *Celebrate: Four Seasons of Holiday Fun*. Middleton, Wisconsin: Pleasant Company Publications, 1998.

2858. Whyte, Harlinah. *Russia*. Milwaukee, Wisconsin: Gareth Stevens Publishing, 1997.

2859. Whyte, Harlinah. *Thailand*. Milwaukee, Wisconsin: Gareth Stevens Publishing, 1998.

2860. Whitman, Sylvia. *Children of the World War II Home Front*. Minneapolis, Minnesota: Carolrhoda Books, 2001.

2861. Whyte, Harlinah. *England*. Milwaukee, Wisconsin: Gareth Stevens Publishing, 1997.

2863. Wiland, Adrienne. *Cook and Learn: Recipes, Songs and Activities for Children*. Westminster, California: Teacher Created Materials, 2000.

2864. Wilkes, Angela. *The Children's Step-by-Step Cookbook*. New York: Dorling Kindersley, 1994.

2865. Williams, Judith M. *Montana*. Danbury, Connecticut: Children's Press, 2002.

2866. Williams, Suzanne M. *Kentucky*. Danbury, Connecticut: Children's Press, 2001.

2867. Willis, Terry. *Romania*. Danbury, Connecticut: Children's Press, 2001.

2868. Wilson, Laura. *How I Survived the Oregon Trail: The Journal of Jesse Adams*. New York: Beech Tree Books, 1999.

2869. Wilson, Neil. *Egypt*. Austin, Texas: Raintree Steck-Vaughn Publishers, 2000.

2870. Wilson, Neil. *Russia*. Austin, Texas: Raintree Steck-Vaughn Publishers, 2001.

2871. Winget, Mary. *Cooking the North African Way*. Minneapolis, Minnesota: Lerner Publications Co., 2004.

2872. Wood, Ira. *A Mexican Feast*. New York: The Rosen Publishing Group, 2003.

2873. Yee, Ling. *Cooking the Chinese Way*. Minneapolis, Minnesota: Lerner Publications Co., 2002.

2874. Yin, Saw Myat. *Myanmar*. Tarrytown, New York: Marshall Cavendish Corp., 2002.

2875. Zalben, Jane Breskin. *Pearl's Eight Days of Chanukah*. New York: Simon & Schuster, 1998.

2876. Zalben, Jane Breskin. *Pearl's Passover: A Family Celebration through Recipes, Crafts and Songs*. New York: Simon & Schuster, 2002.

2877. Zalben, Jane Breskin. *To Every Season: A Family Holiday Cookbook*. New York: Simon & Schuster, 1999.

2878. Zamojska-Hutchins, Danuta. *Cooking the Polish Way*. Minneapolis, Minnesota: Lerner Publications Co., 2002.

2879. Zanger, Mark H. *The American Ethnic Cookbook for Students*. Phoenix, Arizona: Oryx Press, 2001.

2880. Zimmerman, Susan A. *Quilts*. Westminster, California: Teacher Created Materials, 1999.

2881. Zoe, Harris. *Pinatas and Smiling Skeletons: Celebrating Mexican Festivals*. Berkeley, California: Pacific View Press, 1998.

2882. Adams, Susan. *The Great Games Book*. New York: Dorling Kindersley Publishing, 1997.

2883. Alder, Holly. *Storytime Crafts for Kids, Volume 1: Projects Based on Your Children's Favorite Books*. Cincinnati, Ohio: North Light Books, 2000.

2884. Alder, Holly. *Storytime Crafts for Kids, Volume 2: Projects Based on Your Children's Favorite Books*. Cincinnati, Ohio: North Light Books, 2000.

2885. Behnke, Alison. *Cooking the Brazilian Way*. Minneapolis, Minnesota: Lerner Publications Co., 2004.

2886. Behnke, Alison. *Cooking the Cuban Way*. Minneapolis, Minnesota: Lerner Publications Co., 2004.

2887. Beres, Cynthia Breslin. *Longhouse*. Vero Beach, Florida: Rourke Book Company, 2000.

2888. Black, Rosemary. *The Kids' Holiday Baking Book: 150 Favorite Dessert Recipes from Around the World*. New York: St. Martin's Press, 2003.

2889. Bledsoe, Karen E. *Hanukkah Crafts*. Berkeley Heights, New Jersey: Enslow Publishers, 2004.

2890. Boraas, Tracey. *The Creek: Farmers of the Southeast*. Mankato, Minnesota: Bridgestone Books, 2003.

2891. Broida, Marian. *Projects about American Indians of the Southwest*. Tarrytown, New York: Benchmark Books, 2004.

2893. Broida, Marian. *Projects about Plantation Life*. Tarrytown, New York: Benchmark Books, 2003.

2894. Broida, Marian. *Projects about the Plains Indians.* Tarrytown, New York: Benchmark Books, 2004.

2895. Broida, Marian. *Projects about Westward Expansion.* Tarrytown, New York: Benchmark Books, 2004.

2896. Bruchac, James. *Native American Games and Stories.* Golden, Colorado: Fulcrum Resources, 2000.

2897. Chrisp, Peter. *The Vikings.* Chicago, Illinois: Raintree, 2003.

2898. *Christmas in Australia.* Chicago, Illinois: World Book, 1998.

2899. *Christmas in Belgium.* Chicago, Illinois: World Book, 2002.

2900. *Christmas in Poland.* Chicago, Illinois: World Book, 1989.

2901. *Christmas in the American Southwest.* Chicago, Illinois: World Book, 1996.

2902. *Christmas in the Ukraine.* Chicago, Illinois: World Book, 1997.

2903. Cornell, Kari. *Cooking the Indonesian Way.* Minneapolis, Minnesota: Lerner Publications Co., 2004.

2904. Cornell, Kari. *Cooking the Turkish Way.* Minneapolis, Minnesota: Lerner Publications Co., 2004.

2905. DeAngelis, Gina. *Greece.* Mankato, Minnesota: Blue Earth Books, 2004.

2906. DeAngelis, Gina. *Japan.* Mankato, Minnesota: Blue Earth Books, 2003.

2907. Delzio, Suzanne. *Ethiopia.* Mankato, Minnesota: Blue Earth Books, 2004.

2908. Emberley, Rebecca. *Pinata.* New York: Little, Brown & Company, 2004 in Spanish and English.

2909. Englar, Mary. *The Comanche: Nomads of the Southern Plains.* Mankato, Minnesota: Capstone Press, 2004.

2910. Erlbach, Arlene. *Valentine's Day Crafts.* Berkeley Heights, New Jersey: Enslow Publishers, 2004.

2911. Fernandez, Romel. *Caribbean Islands: Facts and Figures.* Philadelphia, Pennsylvania: Mason Crest Publishers, 2003.

2912. Frisch, Carlienne. *Wyoming.* Minneapolis, Minnesota: Lerner Publications Co., 2003.

2913. Gelletly, LeeAnne. *Bolivia.* Philadelphia, Pennsylvania: Mason Crest Publishers, 2003.

2914. Gelletly, LeeAnne. *Colombia.* Philadelphia, Pennsylvania: Mason Crest Publishers, 2003.

2915. Gibson, Karen Bush. *The Chumash Indians: Seafarers of the Pacific Coast.* Mankato, Minnesota: Capstone Press, 2004.

2916. Gnojewski, Carol. *Kwanzaa Crafts.* Berkeley Heights, New Jersey: Enslow Publishers, 2004.

2917. Gnojewski, Carol. *Kwanzaa: Seven Days of African-American Pride.* Berkeley Heights, New Jersey: Enslow Publishers, 2003.

2918. Hannah, Sue. *Crafty Concoctions.* Minnetonka, Minnesota: Meadowbrook Press, 2003.

2919. Herman, Debbie. *Eight Lights for Eight Nights.* Hauppauge, New York: Barron's Educational Series, 2003.

2920. Hernandez, Roger E. *Paraguay.* Philadelphia, Pennsylvania: Mason Crest Publishers, 2004.

2921. Hernandez, Romel. *Puerto Rico.* Philadelphia, Pennsylvania: Mason Crest Publishers, 2004.

2922. Hernandez, Roger E. *South America: Facts and Figures.* Philadelphia, Pennsylvania: Mason Crest Publishers, 2003.

2923. *Holiday and Everyday Projects: Festivals and Fun Creations.* Columbus, Ohio: Waterbird Books, 2003.

2924. Kalman, Bobbie. *Multicultural Meals.* New York: Crabtree Publishing Co., 2003.

2925. Kaufman, Cheryl Davidson. *Cooking the Caribbean Way.* Minneapolis, Minnesota: Lerner Publications Co., 2002.

2926. King, Daniel. *Games: Learn to Play, Play to Win.* Boston, Massachusetts: Kingfisher, 2003.

2927. Knox, Barbara. *Afghanistan.* Mankato, Minnesota: Blue Earth Books, 2004.

2928. Macdonald, Fiona. *The Aztecs.* Chicago, Illinois: Raintree, 2003.

2929. Macdonald, Fiona. *The Greeks.* Chicago, Illinois: Raintree, 2003.

2930. Macdonald, Fiona. *The Romans.* Chicago, Illinois: Raintree, 2003.

2931. Olson, Kay Melchisedech. *Ireland.* Mankato, Minnesota: Blue Earth Books, 2004.

2932. Orr, Tamra. *Barbados.* Philadelphia, Pennsylvania: Mason Crest Publishers, 2003.

2933. Parker-Rock, Michelle. *Diwali: The Hindu Festival of Lights, Feasts and Family.* Berkeley Heights, New Jersey: Enslow Publishers, 2003.

2934. Petrillo, Valerie. *Sailors, Whalers, Fantastic Sea Voyages: An Activity Guide to North American Sailing Life.* Chicago, Illinois: Chicago Review Press, 2003.

2935. Rasmussen, R. Kent. *Mark Twain for Kids: His Life and Times: 21 Activities.* Chicago, Illinois: Chicago Review Press, 2004.

2936. Rhatigan, Joe. *Soapmaking: 50 Fun and Fabulous Soaps to Melt and Pour.* New York: Lark Books, 2003.

2937. Robinson, Fay. *Christmas Crafts.* Berkeley Heights, New Jersey: Enslow Publishers, 2003.

2938. Robinson, Fay. *Halloween Crafts.* Berkeley Heights, New Jersey: Enslow Publishers, 2003.

2939. Roop, Peter. *Let's Celebrate St. Patrick's Day.* Brookfield, Connecticut: The Millbrook Press, 2003.

2940. Roy, Jennifer Rozines. *Israel.* Tarrytown, New York: Benchmark Books, 2003.

2941. Shields, Charles J. *Belize.* Philadelphia, Pennsylvania: Mason Crest Publishers, 2003.

2942. Shields, Charles J. *Brazil.* Philadelphia, Pennsylvania: Mason Crest Publishers, 2003.

2943. Shields, Charles J. *Chile.* Philadelphia, Pennsylvania: Mason Crest Publishers, 2003.

2944. Shields, Charles J. *Costa Rica.* Philadelphia, Pennsylvania: Mason Crest Publishers, 2003.

2945. Shields, Charles J. *El Salvador.* Philadelphia, Pennsylvania: Mason Crest Publishers, 2003.

2946. Shields, Charles J. *Guatemala.* Philadelphia, Pennsylvania: Mason Crest Publishers, 2003.

2947. Shields, Charles J. *Nicaragua.* Philadelphia, Pennsylvania: Mason Crest Publishers, 2003.

2948. Shields, Charles J. *Panama.* Philadelphia, Pennsylvania: Mason Crest Publishers, 2003.

2949. Shields, Charles J. *Uruguay.* Philadelphia, Pennsylvania: Mason Crest Publishers, 2003.

2950. Shields, Charles J. *Venezuela.* Philadelphia, Pennsylvania: Mason Crest Publishers, 2003.

2951. Silbaugh, Elizabeth. *Raggedy Ann's Tea Party Book.* New York: Simon & Schuster, 1999.

2952. Silver, Patricia. *Face Painting.* Tonawanda, New York: KidsCan Press, 2000.

2953. Tabs, Judy. *Matzah Meals: A Passover Cookbook for Kids.* Minneapolis, Minnesota: Kar-Ben Publishing, 2004.

2954. Temple, Bob. *Dominican Republic.* Philadelphia, Pennsylvania: Mason Crest Publishers, 2003.

2955. Temple, Bob. *Haiti.* Philadelphia, Pennsylvania: Mason Crest Publishers, 2004.

2956. Turck, Mary C. *The Civil Rights Movement for Kids: A History with 21 Activities.* Chicago, Illinois: Chicago Review Press, 2000.

2957. Wallace, Paula S. *The World of Birthdays.* Milwaukee, Wisconsin: Gareth Stevens Publishing, 2003.

2958. Wellington, Monica. *Crepes by Suzette.* New York: Dutton Children's Books, 2004.

2959. Williams, Colleen Madonna Flood. *Ecuador.* Philadelphia, Pennsylvania: Mason Crest Publishers, 2003.

2960. Williams, Colleen Madonna Flood. *Jamaica.* Philadelphia, Pennsylvania: Mason Crest Publishers, 2003.

2961. Williams, Colleen Madonna Flood. *Suriname.* Philadelphia, Pennsylvania: Mason Crest Publishers, 2004.

2962. Bart, Kathleen. *Global Gourmet.* Cumberland, Maryland: Reverie Publishing Company, 2003.

2963. *Birth and Growing Up Celebrations.* Chicago, Illinois: World Book, 2003.

2964. Elliott, Lynne. *Children and Games in the Middle Ages.* New York: Crabtree Publishing Company, 2004.

2965. Frost, Helen. *Russian Immigrants, 1860-1915.* Mankato, Minnesota: Blue Earth Books, 2003.

2966. Gordon, Sharon. *Cuba.* Tarrytown, New York: Benchmark Books, 2003.

2967. Haberle, Susan E. *Jewish Immigrants, 1880-1924.* Mankato, Minnesota: Blue Earth Books, 2003.

2968. Hintz, Martin. *Croatia.* Danbury, Connecticut: Children's Press, 2004.

2969. Kummer, Patricia K. *Cameroon.* Danbury, Connecticut: Children's Press, 2004.

2970. Kummer, Patricia K. *Korea.* Danbury, Connecticut: Children's Press, 2004.

2971. Landau, Elaine. *Thanksgiving Day: A Time to Be Thankful.* Berkeley Heights, New Jersey: Enslow Publishers, 2001.

2972. McMillan, Dana. *Construction Site.* Carthage, Illinois: Teaching and Learning Company, 2000.

2973. Milivojevic, JoAnn. *Czech Republic.* Danbury, Connecticut: Children's Press, 2004.

2975. Olson, Kay Melchisedech. *Africans in America, 1619-1865.* Mankato, Minnesota: Blue Earth Books, 2003.

2976. Olson, Kay Melchisedech. *French Immigrants, 1840-1940.* Mankato, Minnesota: Blue Earth Books, 2003.

2977. Olson, Kay Melchisedech. *Norwegian, Swedish and Danish Immigrants, 1820-1920.* Mankato, Minnesota: Blue Earth Books, 2002.

2978. Rhatigan, Joe. *Paper Fantastic: 50 Creative Projects to Fold, Cut, Glue, Paint and Weave.* New York: Lark Books, 2004.

2979. Sloat, Teri. *Berry Magic.* Portland, Oregon: Alaska Northwest Books, 2004.

2980. Wallner, Rosemary. *Greek Immigrants, 1890-1920.* Mankato, Minnesota: Blue Earth Books, 2002.

2981. Wallner, Rosemary. *Polish Immigrants, 1890-1920.* Mankato, Minnesota: Blue Earth Books, 2003.

2982. *Harvest Celebrations.* Chicago, Illinois: World Book, 2003.

2983. *National Celebrations.* Chicago, Illinois: World Book, 2003.

2984. *New Year's Celebrations.* Chicago, Illinois: World Book, 2003.

2985. *Spring Celebrations.* Chicago, Illinois: World Book, 2003.

# Books Indexed by Author

The bold number indicates the book number.
See "Books Indexed by Number" for a numerical list of books.

Aagesen, Colleen. *Shakespeare for Kids: His Life and Times: 21 Activities.* Chicago, Illinois: Chicago Review Press, 1999. **2251**

Adams, McCrea. *Tipi.* Vero Beach, Florida: The Rourke Book Co., 2000. **2252**

Adams, Susan. *The Great Games Book.* New York: Dorling Kindersley Publishing, 1997. **2882**

Alder, Holly. *Storytime Crafts for Kids, Volume 1: Projects Based on Your Children's Favorite Books.* Cincinnati, Ohio: North Light Books, 2000. **2883**

Alder, Holly. *Storytime Crafts for Kids, Volume 2: Projects Based on Your Children's Favorite Books.* Cincinnati, Ohio: North Light Books, 2000. **2884**

Alex, Nan. *North Carolina.* Danbury, Connecticut: Children's Press, 2001. **2253**

Amari, Suad. *Cooking the Lebanese Way.* Minneapolis, Minnesota: Lerner Publications Co., 2003. **2254**

Augustin, Byron. *Bolivia.* Danbury, Connecticut: Children's Press, 2001. **2255**

Bacon, Josephine. *Cooking the Israeli Way.* Minneapolis, Minnesota: Lerner Publications Co., 2002. **2256**

Balchin, Judy. *Collage.* Chicago, Illinois: Heinemann Library, 2002. **2257**

Balchin, Judy. *Decorative Painting.* Chicago, Illinois: Heinemann Library, 2001. **2258**

Balchin, Judy. *Papier Mache.* Chicago, Illinois: Heinemann Library, 2000. **2259**

*Barbie Fun to Cook.* New York: Dorling Kindersley, 2001. **2260**

Barlas, Bob. *Canada.* Milwaukee, Wisconsin: Gareth Stevens Publishing, 1997. **2261**

Barr, Marilynn G. *The American Presidents.* Palo Alto, California: Monday Morning Books, 2000. **2263**

Barr, Marilynn G. *Seasons and Weather: Fascinating Facts and Creative Crafts.* Palo Alto, California: Monday Morning Books, 2001. **2262**

Bart, Kathleen. *Global Gourmet.* Cumberland, Maryland: Reverie Publishing Company, 2003. **2962**

Bassis, Vladimir. *Ukraine.* Milwaukee, Wisconsin: Gareth Stevens Publishing, 1998. **2264**

Beatty, Theresa M. *Food and Recipes of Africa.* New York: The Rosen Publishing Group, 1999. **2265**

Beatty, Theresa M. *Food and Recipes of China.* New York: PowerKids Press, 1999. **2266**

Beatty, Theresa M. *Food and Recipes of Greece.* New York: PowerKids Press, 1999. **2267**

Beatty, Theresa M. *Food and Recipes of Japan.* New York: The Rosen Publishing Group, 1999. **2268**

Beatty, Theresa M. *Food and Recipes of Mexico.* New York: PowerKids Press, 1999. **2269**

Beatty, Theresa M. *Food and Recipes of the Caribbean.* New York: PowerKids Press, 1999. **2270**

Behnke, Alison. *Cooking the Brazilian Way.* Minneapolis, Minnesota: Lerner Publications Co., 2004. **2885**

Behnke, Alison. *Cooking the Cuban Way.* Minneapolis, Minnesota: Lerner Publications Co., 2004. **2886**

Behnke, Alison. *Vegetarian Cooking Around the World.* Minneapolis, Minnesota: Lerner Publications Co., 2002. **2271**

Beres, Cynthia Breslin. *Longhouse.* Vero Beach, Florida: Rourke Book Company, 2000. **2887**

Berg, Elizabeth. *Egypt.* Milwaukee, Wisconsin: Gareth Stevens Publishing, 1997. **2272**

Berg, Elizabeth. *Ethiopia.* Milwaukee, Wisconsin: Gareth Stevens Publishing, 1999. **2273**

Berg, Elizabeth. *Indonesia.* Milwaukee, Wisconsin: Gareth Stevens Publishing, 1997. **2274**

Berg, Elizabeth. *Italy.* Milwaukee, Wisconsin: Gareth Stevens Publishing, 1997. **2275**

Berg, Elizabeth. *Mexico.* Milwaukee, Wisconsin: Gareth Stevens Publishing, 1997. **2276**

*Best Bible Crafts, Pack-O-Fun.* Des Plaines, Illinois: Clapper Publishing Family, 1998. **2277**

Bial, Raymond. *The Apache.* Tarrytown, New York: Marshall Cavendish Corp., 2001. **2278**

Bial, Raymond. *The Blackfeet.* Tarrytown, New York: Marshall Cavendish Corp., 2003. **2279**

Bial, Raymond. *The Cherokee.* Tarrytown, New York: Marshall Cavendish Corp., 1999. **2280**

Bial, Raymond. *The Cheyenne.* Tarrytown, New York: Marshall Cavendish Corp., 2001. **2281**

Bial, Raymond. *The Choctaw.* Tarrytown, New York: Marshall Cavendish Corp., 2002. **2282**

Bial, Raymond. *The Comanche.* Tarrytown, New York: Marshall Cavendish Corp., 2000. **2283**

Bial, Raymond. *The Haida.* Tarrytown, New York: Marshall Cavendish Corp., 2001. **2284**

Bial, Raymond. *The Huron.* Tarrytown, New York: Marshall Cavendish Corp., 2001. **2285**

Bial, Raymond. *The Inuit.* Tarrytown, New York: Marshall Cavendish Corp., 2001. **2286**

Bial, Raymond. *The Iroquois.* Tarrytown, New York: Marshall Cavendish Corp., 1999. **2287**

Bial, Raymond. *The Mandan.* Tarrytown, New York: Marshall Cavendish Corp., 2003. **2288**

Bial, Raymond. *The Navajo.* Tarrytown, New York: Marshall Cavendish Corp., 1999. **2289**

Bial, Raymond. *The Nez Perce.* Tarrytown, New York: Marshall Cavendish Corp., 2002. **2290**

Bial, Raymond. *The Ojibwe.* Tarrytown, New York: Marshall Cavendish Corp., 2002. **2291**

Bial, Raymond. *The Powhatan.* Tarrytown, New York: Marshall Cavendish Corp., 2002. **2292**

Bial, Raymond. *The Pueblo.* Tarrytown, New York: Marshall Cavendish Corp., 2000. **2293**

Bial, Raymond. *The Seminole.* Tarrytown, New York: Marshall Cavendish Corp., 2000. **2294**

Bial, Raymond. *The Shoshone.* Tarrytown, New York: Marshall Cavendish Corp., 2001. **2295**

Bial, Raymond. *The Sioux.* Tarrytown, New York: Marshall Cavendish Corp., 1999. **2296**

Bial, Raymond. *The Tlingit.* Tarrytown, New York: Marshall Cavendish Corp., 2002. **2297**

Birchall, Lorrie L. *The Farm: Favorite Literature and Great Activities.* New York: Scholastic Professional Books, 1996. **2298**

*Birth and Growing Up Celebrations.* Chicago, Illinois: World Book, 2003. **2963**

Bisignano, Alphonse. *Cooking the Italian Way.* Minneapolis, Minnesota: Lerner Publications Co., 2002. **2299**

Black, Rosemary. *The Kids' Holiday Baking Book: 150 Favorite Dessert Recipes from Around the World.* New York: St. Martin's Press, 2003. **2888**

Bledsoe, Karen E. *Hanukkah Crafts.* Berkeley Heights, New Jersey: Enslow Publishers, 2004. **2889**

Boraas, Tracey. *Australia.* Mankato, Minnesota: Bridgestone Books, 2002. **2300**

Boraas, Tracey. *Brazil.* Mankato, Minnesota: Bridgestone Books, 2002. **2301**

Boraas, Tracey. *Canada.* Mankato, Minnesota: Bridgestone Books, 2002. **2302**

Boraas, Tracey. *Colombia.* Mankato, Minnesota: Bridgestone Books, 2002. **2303**

Boraas, Tracey. *Egypt.* Mankato, Minnesota: Bridgestone Books, 2002. **2304**

Boraas, Tracey. *Israel.* Mankato, Minnesota: Bridgestone Books, 2003. **2305**

Boraas, Tracey. *Sweden.* Mankato, Minnesota: Bridgestone Books, 2003. **2306**

Boraas, Tracey. *Thailand.* Mankato, Minnesota: Bridgestone Books, 2003. **2307**

Boraas, Tracey. *The Creek: Farmers of the Southeast.* Mankato, Minnesota: Bridgestone Books, 2003. **2890**

Borenstein, Shery Koons. *Christian Crafts from Paper Bags.* Torrance, California: Shining Star Publications, 1994. **2308**

Boyd, Heidi. *Fairy Crafts.* Cincinnati, Ohio: North Light Books, 2003. **2309**

Braman, Arlette N. *Kids Around the World Play!: The Best Fun and Games from Many Lands.* New York: John Wiley & Sons, 2002. **2310**

Braman, Arlette N. *Traditional Native American Arts and Activities.* New York: John Wiley & Sons, 2000. **2311**

Bratvold, Gretchen. *Oregon.* Minneapolis, Minnesota: Lerner Publications Co., 2003. **2312**

Broida, Marian. *Ancient Israelites and Their Neighbors: An Activity Guide.* Chicago, Illinois: Chicago Review Press, 2003. **2313**

Broida, Marian. *Projects about American Indians of the Southwest.* Tarrytown, New York: Benchmark Books, 2004. **2891**

Broida, Marian. *Projects about Colonial Life.* Tarrytown, New York: Benchmark Books?, 2004. **2314**

Broida, Marian. *Projects about Plantation Life.* Tarrytown, New York: Benchmark Books, 2003. **2893**

Broida, Marian. *Projects about the Plains Indians.* Tarrytown, New York: Benchmark Books, 2004. **2894**

Broida, Marian. *Projects about Westward Expansion.* Tarrytown, New York: Benchmark Books, 2004. **2895**

Brown, Dottie. *Delaware.* Minneapolis, Minnesota: Lerner Publications Co., 2002. **2315**

Brown, Dottie. *Kentucky.* Minneapolis, Minnesota: Lerner Publications Co., 2002. **2316**

Brown, Dottie. *New Hampshire.* Minneapolis, Minnesota: Lerner Publications Co., 2002. **2317**

Bruchac, James. *Native American Games and Stories.* Golden, Colorado: Fulcrum Resources, 2000. **2896**

Bull, Jane. *The Christmas Book.* New York: Dorling Kindersley Publishing, 2001. **2318**

Bull, Jane. *The Halloween Book.* New York: Dorling Kindersley Publishing, 2000. **2319**

Burda, Jan. *Year-Round Units for Early Childhood.* Westminster, California: Teacher Created Materials, 2000. **2320**

Butler, Robbie. *Sweden.* New York: Raintree Steck-Vaughn Publishers, 2000. **2321**

Capek, Michael. *Jamaica.* Minneapolis, Minnesota: Carolrhoda Books, 1999. **2322**

Carlson, Laurie. *Classical Kids: An Activity Guide to Life in Ancient Greece and Rome.* Chicago, Illinois: Chicago Review Press, 1998. **2323**

Carlson, Laurie. *Days of Knights and Damsels.* Chicago, Illinois: Chicago Review Press, 1998. **2324**

Carratello, Patty. *Literature and Critical Thinking.* Huntington Beach, California: Teacher Created Materials, 1989. **2325**

Carter, Tamsin. *Handmade Cards.* Chicago, Illinois: Heinemann Library, 2002. **2326**

Cassidy, Picot. *Italy.* Austin, Texas: Steck-Vaughn Publishers, 2001. **2327**

Castaldo, Nancy. *Winter Day Play: Activities, Crafts and Games for Indoor and Out.* Chicago, Illinois: Chicago Review Press, 2001. **2328**

Cerbus, Deborah Plona. *Connecting Holidays and Literature.* Huntington Beach, California: Teacher Created Materials, 1992. **2329**

Chabert, Sally. *The Jacks Book?.* New York: Workman Publishing Co., 1999. **2330**

Chapman, Gillian. *Art from Sand and Earth: With Projects Using Clay, Plaster and Natural Fibers.* Austin, Texas: Raintree Steck-Vaughn Publishers, 1997. **2331**

Chapman, Gillian. *The Romans.* Des Plaines, Illinois: Heinemann Library, 1998. **2332**

Chapman, Gillian. *The Vikings.* Chicago, Illinois: Heinemann Library, 2000. **2333**

Cheong, Colin. *China.* Milwaukee, Wisconsin: Gareth Stevens Publishing, 1997. **2334**

Cherkerzian, Diane. *Merry Things to Make: Christmas Fun and Crafts.* Honesdale, Pennsylvania: Boyds Mills Press, 1999. **2335**

Chrisp, Peter. *The Vikings.* Chicago, Illinois: Raintree, 2003. **2897**

Christian, Rebecca. *Cooking the Spanish Way.* Minneapolis, Minnesota: Lerner Publications Co., 2002. **2336**

*Christmas in Australia.* Chicago, Illinois: World Book, 1998. **2898**

*Christmas in Belgium.* Chicago, Illinois: World Book, 2002. **2899**

*Christmas in Finland.* Chicago, Illinois: World Book, 1999. **2337**

*Christmas in Poland.* Chicago, Illinois: World Book, 1989. **2900**

*Christmas in Puerto Rico.* Chicago, Illinois: World Book, 2004. **2338**

*Christmas in Scotland.* Chicago, Illinois: World Book, 2001. **2339**

*Christmas in the American Southwest.* Chicago, Illinois: World Book, 1996. **2901**

*Christmas in the Ukraine.* Chicago, Illinois: World Book, 1997. **2902**

Chung, Okwha. *Cooking the Korean Way.* Minneapolis, Minnesota: Lerner Publications Co., 2003. **2340**

Collier, Mary. *My Little House Christmas Crafts Book: Christmas Decorations, Gifts and Recipes from the Little House Books.* New York: HarperCollins Publishers, 1997. **2341**

Collins, Carolyn Strom. *Inside the Secret Garden: A Treasury of Crafts, Recipes and Activities.* New York: HarperCollins Publishers, 2001. **2342**

Compestine, Ying Chang. *The Runaway Rice Cake.* New York: Simon & Schuster, 2001. **2343**

Compestine, Ying Chang. *The Story of Chopsticks.* New York: Holiday House, 2001. **2344**

Compestine, Ying Chang. *The Story of Noodles.* New York: Holiday House, 2002. **2345**

Cooper, Ilene. *Jewish Holidays All Year Round: A Family Treasury.* New York: Harry N. Abrams, 2002. **2346**

Cordoba, Yasmine A. *Igloo.* Vero Beach, Florida: Rourke Book Co., 2000. **2347**

Cornell, Kari. *Cooking the Indonesian Way.* Minneapolis, Minnesota: Lerner Publications Co., 2004. **2903**

Cornell, Kari. *Cooking the Turkish Way.* Minneapolis, Minnesota: Lerner Publications Co., 2004. **2904**

Coronado, Rosa. *Cooking the Mexican Way.* Minneapolis, Minnesota: Lerner Publication Co., 2002. **2348**

Corwin, Judith Hoffman. *Native American Crafts of California, the Great Basin and the*

*Southwest.* New York: Franklin Watts, 1999. **2349**

Corwin, Judith Hoffman. *Native American Crafts of the Northeast and Southeast.* New York: Franklin Watts, 2002. **2350**

Corwin, Judith Hoffman. *Native American Crafts of the Northwest Coast, the Arctic and the Subarctic.* New York: Franklin Watts, 2002. **2351**

Corwin, Judith Hoffman. *Native American Crafts of the Plains and Plateau.* New York: Franklin Watts, 2002. **2352**

Coulter, Laurie. *Secrets in Stone: All About Maya Hieroglyphs.* Boston, Massachusetts: Little Brown and Co., 2001. **2353**

Currier, Mary. *Christian Crafts from Paper Plates.* Torrance, California: Shining Star Publications, 1989. **2354**

D'Amico, Joan. *The U.S. History Cookbook: Delicious Recipes and Exciting Events from the Past.* New York: John Wiley & Sons, 2003. **2359**

Dahl, Michael. *France.* Mankato, Minnesota: Bridgestone Books, 1998. **2355**

Dahl, Michael. *Germany.* Mankato, Minnesota: Bridgestone Books, 1997. **2356**

Dahl, Michael. *South Africa.* Mankato, Minnesota: Bridgestone Books, 1998. **2357**

Dalal, Anita. *Argentina.* Austin, Texas: Raintree Steck-Vaughn Publishers, 2000. **2358**

Darlington, Robert. *Australia.* Austin, Texas: Raintree Steck-Vaughn Publishers, 2001. **2360**

Davis, Lucile. *Ghana.* Mankato, Minnesota: Bridgestone Books, 1999. **2361**

Davis, Lucile. *The Philippines.* Mankato, Minnesota: Bridgestone Books, 1999. **2362**

Day, Nancy. *Your Travel Guide to Ancient Egypt.* Minneapolis, Minnesota: Runestone Press, 2001. **2363**

Day, Nancy. *Your Travel Guide to Ancient Greece.* Minneapolis, Minnesota: Runestone Press, 2001. **2364**

Day, Nancy. *Your Travel Guide to Ancient Mayan Civilization.* Minneapolis, Minnesota: Runestone Press, 2001. **2365**

Day, Nancy. *Your Travel Guide to Colonial America.* Minneapolis, Minnesota: Runestone Press, 2001. **2366**

Day, Nancy. *Your Travel Guide to Renaissance Europe.* Minneapolis, Minnesota: Runestone Press, 2001. **2367**

Deady, Kathleen W. *Egypt.* Mankato, Minnesota: Bridgestone Books, 2001. **2371**

Deady, Kathleen W. *England.* Mankato, Minnesota: Bridgestone Books, 2001. **2372**

DeAngelis, Gina. *Greece.* Mankato, Minnesota: Blue Earth Books, 2004. **2905**

DeAngelis, Gina. *Japan.* Mankato, Minnesota: Blue Earth Books, 2003. **2906**

DeAngelis, Gina. *Mexico.* Mankato, Minnesota: Blue Earth Books, ?2003. **2369**

DeAngelis, Gina. *Virginia.* Danbury, Connecticut: Children's Press, 2001. **2370**

Dell'Oro, Suzanne Paul. *Argentina.* Minneapolis, Minnesota: Carolrhoda Books, 1998. **2373**

Dell'Oro, Suzanne Paul. *Haiti.* Mankato, Minnesota: Bridgestone Books, 2002. **2374**

Dell'Oro, Suzanne Paul. *Poland.* Mankato, Minnesota: Bridgestone Books, 2002. **2375**

Delzio, Suzanne. *Ethiopia.* Mankato, Minnesota: Blue Earth Books, 2004. **2907**

Dingwall, Cindy. *Happy Birthday, America!* Fort Atkinson, Wisconsin: Alleyside Press, 2000. **2377**

Dingwall, Cindy. *Library Celebrations.* Fort Atkinson, Wisconsin: Alleyside Press, 1999. **2378**

Donoughue, Carol. *The Mystery of the Hieroglyphs.* New York: Oxford University Press, 1999. **2379**

Dooley, Norah. *Everybody Brings Noodles.* Minneapolis, Minnesota: Carolrhoda Books, 2002. **2381**

Dooley, Norah. *Everybody Needs Soup.* Minneapolis, Minnesota: Carolrhoda Books, 2000. **2380**

Dramer, Kim. *China.* Danbury, Connecticut: Children's Press, 1997. **2382**

Draper, Charla L. *Cooking on Nineteenth-Century Whaling Ships.* Mankato, Minnesota: Blue Earth Books, 2001. **2383**

Dubois, Muriel L. *Ethiopia.* Mankato, Minnesota: Bridgestone Books, 2001. **2384**

Dunn, Opal. *Acka Backa Boo! Playground Games from Around the World.* New York: Henry Holt and Company, 2000. **2385**

Dunnewind, Stephanie. *Come to Tea: Fun Tea Party Themes, Recipes, Crafts, Games, Etiquette and More.* New York: Sterling Publishing Co., 2002. **2386**

Dyer, Dolores A. *Plank House.* Vero Beach, Florida: Rourke Book Co., 2000. **2387**

*Early America.* Greensboro, North Carolina: The Education Center, 2002. **2388**

Early, Theresa S. *New Mexico.* Minneapolis, Minnesota: Lerner Publications Co., 2003. **2389**

*Earth Day Activities.* Westminster, California: Teacher Created Materials, 1996. **2390**

Eder, Jeanne Oyawin. *The Dakota Sioux.* Austin, Texas: Raintree Steck-Vaughn, 2000. **2391**

Elliott, Lynne. *Children and Games in the Middle Ages.* New York: Crabtree Publishing Company, 2004. **2964**

Ellis, Royston. *Madagascar.* Milwaukee, Wisconsin: Gareth Stevens Publishing, 1999. **2392**

Ellis, Royston. *Trinidad.* Milwaukee, Wisconsin: Gareth Stevens Publishing, 1999. **2393**

Emberley, Rebecca. *Piñata.* New York: Little, Brown & Company, 2004 in Spanish and English. **2908**

Enderlein, Cheryl. *Christmas in England.* New York: Hilltop Books, 1998. **2394**

Enderlein, Cheryl. *Christmas in Sweden.* New York: Hilltop Books, 1998. **2395**

Engfer, Lee. *Desserts Around the World.* Minneapolis, Minnesota: Lerner Publications Co., 2004. **2396**

Englar, Mary. *Afghanistan.* Mankato, Minnesota: Capstone Press, 2004. **2397**

Englar, Mary. *Pueblos: Farmers of the Southwest.* Mankato, Minnesota: Bridgestone Books, 2003. **2399**

Englar, Mary. *The Comanche: Nomads of the Southern Plains.* Mankato, Minnesota: Capstone Press, 2004. **2909**

Englar, Mary. *The Iroquois, the Six Nations Confederacy.* Mankato, Minnesota: Bridgestone Books, 2003. **2398**

Erlbach, Arlene. *Christmas: Celebrating Life, Giving and Kindness.* Berkeley Heights, New Jersey: Enslow Publishers, 2002. **2400**

Erlbach, Arlene. *Hanukkah: Celebrating the Holiday of Lights.* Berkeley Heights, New Jersey: Enslow Publishers, 2001. **2401**

Erlbach, Arlene. *Happy New Year, Everywhere!* Brookfield, Connecticut: The Millbrook Press, 2000. **2402**

Erlbach, Arlene. *Merry Christmas Everywhere!* Brookfield, Connecticut: The Millbrook Press, 2002. **2403**

Erlbach, Arlene. *Valentine's Day Crafts.* Berkeley Heights, New Jersey: Enslow Publishers, 2004. **2910**

*Father's Day Activities.* Huntington Beach, California: Teacher Created Materials, 1995. **2404**

Feeney, Kathy. *Alabama.* Danbury, Connecticut: Children's Press, 2002. **2405**

Fenema, Joyce Van. *Netherlands.* Milwaukee, Wisconsin: Gareth Stevens Publishing, 1998. **2406**

Fernandez, Romel. *Caribbean Islands: Facts and Figures.* Philadelphia, Pennsylvania: Mason Crest Publishers, 2003. **2911**

Fiarotta, Phyllis. *Papercrafts Around the World.* New York: Sterling Publishing Co., 1996. **2407**

Fisher, Frederick. *Costa Rica.* Milwaukee, Wisconsin: Gareth Stevens Publishing, 1999. **2408**

Fisher, Frederick. *Mongolia.* Milwaukee, Wisconsin: Gareth Stevens Publishing, 1999. **2409**

Flagg, Ann. *Apples, Pumpkins and Harvest.* New York: Scholastic Professional Books, 1998. **2410**

Florence, Sarah. *Pilgrim Foods and Recipes.* New York: The Rosen Publishing Group, 2002. **2411**

Foley, Erin. *Puerto Rico.* Milwaukee, Wisconsin: Gareth Stevens Publishing, 1997. **2412**

Fowler, Verna. *The Menominee.* Austin, Texas: Steck-Vaughn Publishers, 2001. **2413**

Foy, Don. *Israel.* Milwaukee, Wisconsin: Gareth Stevens Publishing, 1997. **2414**

Fredeen, Charles. *Kansas.* Minneapolis, Minnesota: Lerner Publications Co., 2002. **2415**

Fredeen, Charles. *South Carolina.* Minneapolis, Minnesota: Lerner Publications Co., 2002. **2416**

Friedman, Pamela. *St. Patrick's Day Activities.* Westminster, California: Teacher Created Materials, 1999. **2417**

Frisch, Carlienne. *Wyoming.* Minneapolis, Minnesota: Lerner Publications Co., 2003. **2912**

Frost, Helen. *German Immigrants, 1820-1920.* Mankato, Minnesota: Blue Earth Books, 2002. **2418**

Frost, Helen. *Russian Immigrants, 1860-1915.* Mankato, Minnesota: Blue Earth Books, 2003. **2965**

Furlong, Arlene. *Argentina.* Milwaukee, Wisconsin: Gareth Stevens Publishing, 1999. **2419**

Furman, Elina. *Washington D.C.* Danbury, Connecticut: Children's Press, 2002. **2420**

Gabet, Marcia. *Fun with Social Studies: Mini Social Studies Units and Projects.* Huntington Beach, California: Teacher Created Materials, 1985. **2421**

Garcia, James. *Cinco de Mayo: A Mexican Holiday About Unity and Pride.* Chanhassen, Minnesota: Child's World, 2002. **2422**

Garrity, Linda K. *The Tale Spinner: Folktales, Themes and Activities.* Golden, Colorado: Fulcrum Publishing, 1999. **2423**

Garza, Carmen Lomas. *Making Magic Windows: Creating Papel Picado/Cut-Paper Art.* San Francisco, California: Children's Book Press, 1999. **2424**

Gelletly, LeeAnne. *Bolivia.* Philadelphia, Pennsylvania: Mason Crest Publishers, 2003. **2913**

Gelletly, LeeAnne. *Colombia.* Philadelphia, Pennsylvania: Mason Crest Publishers, 2003. **2914**

Gelman, Amy. *Connecticut.* Minneapolis, Minnesota: Lerner Publications Co., 2002. **2425**

George, Charles. *Montana.* Danbury, Connecticut: Children's Press, 2000. **2426**

Germaine, Elizabeth. *Cooking the Australian Way.* Minneapolis, Minnesota: Lerner Publications Co., 2004. **2427**

Gibbons, Gail. *The Berry Book.* New York: Holiday House, 2002. **2428**

Gibson, Karen Bush. *The Arapaho: Hunters of the Great Plains.* Mankato, Minnesota: Bridgestone Books, 2003. **2429**

Gibson, Karen Bush. *The Blackfeet: People of the Dark Moccasins.* Mankato, Minnesota: Bridgestone Books, 2003. **2430**

Gibson, Karen Bush. *The Chickasaw Nation.* Mankato, Minnesota: Bridgestone Books, 2003. **2431**

Gibson, Karen Bush. *The Chumash Indians: Seafarers of the Pacific Coast.* Mankato, Minnesota: Capstone Press, 2004. **2915**

Gibson, Karen Bush. *The Potawatomi.* Mankato, Minnesota: Bridgestone Books, 2003. **2432**Gioffre, Rosalba. *The Young Chef's French Cookbook.* New York: Crabtree Publishing Co., 2001. **2432**

Gioffre, Rosalba. *The Young Chef's Italian Cookbook.* New York: Crabtree Publishing Co., 2001. **2434**

Glandon, Shan. *Caldecott Connections to Language Arts.* Englewood, Colorado: Libraries Unlimited, 2000. **2435**

Glandon, Shan. *Caldecott Connections to Social Studies.* Englewood, Colorado: Libraries Unlimited, 2000. **2436**

Gnojewski, Carol. *Cinco de Mayo: Celebrating Hispanic Pride.* Berkeley Heights, New Jersey: Enslow Publishers, 2002. **2437**

Gnojewski, Carol. *Kwanzaa Crafts.* Berkeley Heights, New Jersey: Enslow Publishers, 2004. **2916**

Gnojewski, Carol. *Kwanzaa: Seven Days of African-American Pride.* Berkeley Heights, New Jersey: Enslow Publishers, 2003. **2917**

Gnojewski, Carol. *Martin Luther King Day: Honoring a Man of Peace.* Berkeley Heights, New Jersey: Enslow Publishers, 2002. **2438**

Golding, Vivien. *Traditions from Africa.* Austin, Texas: Steck-Vaughn Publishers, 1998. **2439**

Gordon, Sharon. *Cuba.* Tarrytown, New York: Benchmark Books, 2003. **2966**

Gould, Roberta. *Kidtopia: Round the Country and Back through Time in 60 Projects.* Berkeley, California: Tricycle Press, 2000. **2441**

Gould, Roberta. *The Kids' Book of Incredible Fun Crafts.* Charlotte, Vermont: Williamson Publishing Co., 2003. **2440**

Grace, Catherine O'Neill. *1621: A New Look at Thanksgiving.* Washington, D.C.: National Geographic Society, 2001. **2442**

Graf, Mike. *Somalia.* Mankato, Minnesota: Bridgestone Books, 2002. **2443**

Graf, Mike. *Switzerland.* Mankato, Minnesota: Bridgestone Books, 2002. **2444**

Graube, Ireta Sitts. *Thanksgiving.* Westminster, California: Teacher Created Materials, 2000, reprint of 1992 ed. **2445**

Graube, Ireta Sitts. *Valentine's Day.* Westminster, California: Teacher Created Materials, 1999. **2446**

Graves, Kerry A. *Going to School during the Civil War: The Confederacy.* Mankato, Minnesota: Blue Earth Books, 2002. **2447**

Graves, Kerry A. *Going to School during the Civil War: The Union.* Mankato, Minnesota: Blue Earth Books, 2002. **2448**

Graves, Kerry A. *Going to School during the Great Depression.* Mankato, Minnesota: Blue Earth Books, 2002. **2449**

Graves, Kerry A. *Going to School in Pioneer Times.* Mankato, Minnesota: Blue Earth Books, 2002. **2450**

Graves, Kerry A. *Haiti.* Mankato, Minnesota: Bridgestone Books, 2002. **2451**

Gravett, Christopher. *The Knights Handbook: How to Become a Champion in Shining Armor.* New York: Cobblehill Books, 1997. **2452**

Green, Jen. *Israel.* Austin, Texas: Steck-Vaughn Publishers, 2001. **2453**

Green, Jen. *Japan.* Austin, Texas: Raintree Steck-Vaughn Publishers, 2000. **2454**

Green, Jen. *Mexico.* Austin, Texas: Raintree Steck-Vaughn Publishers, 2000. **2455**

Green, Jen. *Step into the. . . Arctic World.* New York: Lorenz Books, 2000. **2456**

Gresko, Marcia S. *Israel.* Minneapolis, Minnesota: Carolrhoda Books, 2000. **2457**

Griffiths, Jonathan. *New Zealand.* Milwaukee, Wisconsin: Gareth Stevens Publishing, 1999. **2458**

Griffiths, Jonathan. *Scotland.* Milwaukee, Wisconsin: Gareth Stevens Publishing, 1999. **2459**

Haberle, Susan E. *Jewish Immigrants, 1880-1924.* Mankato, Minnesota: Blue Earth Books, 2003. **2967**

Hamilton, Janice. *Canada.* Minneapolis, Minnesota: Carolrhoda Books, 1999. **2460**

Hannah, Sue. *Crafty Concoctions.* Minnetonka, Minnesota: Meadowbrook Press, 2003. **2918**

Hargittai, Magdolna. *Cooking the Hungarian Way.* Minneapolis, Minnesota: Lerner Publications Co., 2003. **2461**

Harrison, Supenn. *Cooking the Thai Way.* Minneapolis, Minnesota: Lerner Publications Co., 2003. **2462**

Hart, Avery. *Ancient Rome: Exploring the Culture, People and Ideas of this Powerful Empire.* Charlotte, Vermont: Williamson Publishing Co., 2002. **2463**

Hart, Avery. *Who Really Discovered America: Unraveling the Mystery and Solving the Puzzle.* Charlotte, Vermont: Williamson Publishing Co., 2001. **2464**

*Harvest Celebrations.* Chicago, Illinois: World Book, 2003. **2982**

Harvey, Miles. *Italy.* Danbury, Connecticut: Children's Press, 1996. **2465**

Heinrichs, Ann. *Colorado.* Minneapolis, Minnesota: Compass Point Books, 2003. **2466**

Heinrichs, Ann. *Minnesota.* Minneapolis, Minnesota: Compass Point Books, 2003. **2467**

Heinrichs, Ann. *Niger.* Danbury, Connecticut: Children's Press, 2001. **2468**

Heinrichs, Ann. *Vermont.* Danbury, Connecticut: Children's Press, 2001. **2469**

Herbert, Jane. *South Carolina.* Tarrytown, New York: Marshall Cavendish Corp., 2001. **2470**

Herbert, Janis. *Leonardo da Vinci for Kids: His Life and Ideas: 21 Activities.* Chicago, Illinois: Chicago Review Press, 1998. **2472**

Herbert, Janis. *Lewis and Clark for Kids: Their Journey of Discovery with 21 Activities.* Chicago, Illinois: Chicago Review Press, 2000. **2473**

Herbert, Janis. *Marco Polo for Kids: His Marvelous Journey to China: 21 Activities.* Chicago, Illinois: Chicago Review Press, 2001. **2474**

Herbert, Janis. *The American Revolution for Kids.* Chicago, Illinois: Chicago Review Press, 2002. **2471**

Herman, Debbie. *Eight Lights for Eight Nights.* Hauppauge, New York: Barron's Educational Series, 2003. **2919**

Hernandez, Roger E. *Paraguay.* Philadelphia, Pennsylvania: Mason Crest Publishers, 2004. **2920**

Hernandez, Roger E. *South America: Facts and Figures.* Philadelphia, Pennsylvania: Mason Crest Publishers, 2003. **2922**

Hernandez, Romel. *Puerto Rico.* Philadelphia, Pennsylvania: Mason Crest Publishers, 2004. **2921**

Herweck, Dona. *Patterns and Clip Art.* Huntington Beach, California: Teacher Created Materials, 1991. **2475**

Hestler, Anna. *Wales.* Tarrytown, New York: Marshall Cavendish Corp., 2001. **2476**

Hill, Barbara W. *Cooking the English Way.* Minneapolis, Minnesota: Lerner Publications Co., 2003. **2477**

Hill, Linda Burrell. *Using Multicultural Literature: Journeys.* Huntington Beach, California: Teacher Created Materials, 1994. **2478**

Hintz, Martin. *Croatia.* Danbury, Connecticut: Children's Press, 2004. **2968**

Hippely, Hillary Horder. *A Song for Lena.* New York: Simon & Schuster, 1996. **2479**

Hirschfelder, Arlene. *Native Americans Today: Resources and Activities for Educators, Grades 4-8.* Englewood, Colorado: Teacher Ideas Press, 2000. **2480**

*Holiday and Everyday Projects: Festivals and Fun Creations.* Columbus, Ohio: Waterbird Books, 2003. **2923**

*Holiday Cooking Around the World.* Minneapolis, Minnesota: Lerner Publications Co., 2002. **2481**

Honan, Linda. *Spend the Day in Ancient Rome: Projects and Activities that Bring the Past to Life.* New York: John Wiley & Sons, 1998. **2482**

Hopkinson, Deborah. *Fannie in the Kitchen!* New York: Atheneum Books for Young Readers, 1999. **2483**

Howard, Dale E. *India.* Danbury, Connecticut: Children's Press, 1996. **2485**

Hughes, Helga. *Cooking the Austrian Way.* Minneapolis, Minnesota: Lerner Publications Co., 2004. **2485**

Hughes, Meredith Sayles. *Tall and Tasty: Fruit Trees.* Minneapolis, Minnesota: Lerner Publications Co., 2000. **2486**

Hurdman, Charlotte. *Step into... the Stone Age.* New York: Lorenz Books, 1998. **2487**

Ichord, Loretta Frances. *Skillet Bread, Sourdough, and Vinegar Pie: Cooking in Pioneer Days.* Brookfield, Connecticut: The Millbrook Press, 2003. **2488**

Ingham, Richard. *France.* Austin, Texas: Raintree Steck-Vaughn Publishers, 2000. **2489**

Innes, Brian. *United Kingdom.* Austin, Texas: Steck-Vaughn Publishers, 2001. **2490**

Jaffe, Elizabeth Dana. *Dominoes.* Minneapolis, Minnesota: Compass Point Books, 2002. **2491**

Jaffe, Elizabeth Dana. *Hopscotch.* Minneapolis, Minnesota: Compass Point Books, 2002. **2492**

Jaffe, Elizabeth Dana. *Jacks.* Minneapolis, Minnesota: Compass Point Books, 2002. **2493**

Jaffe, Elizabeth Dana. *Juggling.* Minneapolis, Minnesota: Compass Point Books, 2002. **2494**

Jaffe, Elizabeth Dana. *Marbles.* Minneapolis, Minnesota: Compass Point Books, 2002. **2495**

Jermyn, Leslie. *Belize.* Tarrytown, New York: Marshall Cavendish Corp., 2001. **2496**

Johmann, Carol A. *Going West!: Journey on a Wagon Train to Settle a Frontier Town.* Charlotte, Vermont: Williamson Publishing Co., 2000. **2497**

Johmann, Carol A. *The Lewis and Clark Expedition.* Charlotte, Vermont: Williamson Publishing Co., 2003. **2498**

Johmann, Carol A. *Skyscrapers: Super Structures to Design and Build.* Charlotte, Vermont: Williamson Publishing Co., 2001. **2499**

Johnson, Elizabeth M. *Michigan.* Danbury, Connecticut: Children's Press, 2002. **2500**

Johnson, Ron M. E. *Leonardo da Vinci.* Irving, Texas: Nest Entertainment, 1996. **2501**

Johnston, Joyce. *Maryland.* Minneapolis, Minnesota: Lerner Publications Co., 2003. **2502**

Johnston, Joyce. *Washington, D.C.* Minneapolis, Minnesota: Lerner Publications Co., 2003. **2503**

Jones, Lynda. *Kids Around the World Celebrate: The Best Feasts and Festivals from Many Lands.* New York: John Wiley & Sons, 2000. **2504**

Jovinelly, Joann. *The Crafts and Culture of the Ancient Egyptians.* New York: The Rosen Publishing Group, 2002. **2505**

Jovinelly, Joann. *The Crafts and Culture of the Ancient Greeks.* New York: The Rosen Publishing Group, 2002. **2506**

Jovinelly, Joann. *The Crafts and Culture of the Ancient Hebrews.* New York: The Rosen Publishing Group, 2002. **2507**

Jovinelly, Joann. *The Crafts and Culture of the Aztecs.* New York: The Rosen Publishing Group, 2002. **2508**

Jovinelly, Joann. *The Crafts and Culture of the Romans.* New York: The Rosen Publishing Group, 2002. **2509**

Jovinelly, Joann. *The Crafts and Culture of the Vikings.* New York: The Rosen Publishing Group, 2002. **2510**

Jurenka, Nancy Allen. *Hobbies through Children's Books and Activities.* Englewood, Colorado: Teacher Ideas Press, 2001. **2511**

Kagda, Falaq. *India.* Milwaukee, Wisconsin: Gareth Stevens Publishing, 1997. **2512**

Kagda, Falaq. *Kenya.* Milwaukee, Wisconsin: Gareth Stevens Publishing, 1997. **2513**

Kalman, Bobbie. *China, the Culture.* New York: Crabtree Publishing Co., 2001. **2514**

Kalman, Bobbie. *Classroom Games.* New York: Crabtree Publishing Co., 2001. **2515**

Kalman, Bobbie. *Mexico, the Culture.* New York: Crabtree Publishing Co., 2002. **2517**

Kalman, Bobbie. *Multicultural Meals.* New York: Crabtree Publishing Co., 2003. **2924**

Kalman, Bobbie. *Pioneer Recipes.* New York: Crabtree Publishing Co., 2001. **2518**

Kalman, Bobbie. *Schoolyard Games.* New York: Crabtree Publishing Co., 2001. **2519**

Kalman, Bobbie. *The Colonial Cook.* New York: Crabtree Publishing Co., 2002. **2516**

Kaufman, Cheryl Davidson. *Cooking the Caribbean Way.* Minneapolis, Minnesota: Lerner Publications Co., 2002. **2925**

Kimble-Ellis, Sonya. *Traditional African American Arts and Activities.* New York: John Wiley & Sons, 2002. **2520**

Kimmel, Eric A. *A Hanukkah Treasury.* New York: Henry Holt and Co., 1997. **2521**

King, Daniel. *Games: Learn to Play, Play to Win.* Boston, Massachusetts: Kingfisher, 2003. **2926**

King, David C. *Revolutionary War Days: Discover the Past with Exciting Projects, Games, Activities and Recipes.* New York: John Wiley & Sons, 2001. **2522**

King, David C. *Wild West Days: Discovering the Past with Fun Projects, Games, Activities and Recipes.* New York: John Wiley & Sons, 1998. **2523**

King, David C. *World War II Days: Discover the Past with Exciting Projects, Games, Activities and Recipes.* New York: John Wiley & Sons, 2000. **2524**

Kirchner, Glenn. *Children's Games from Around the World, 2nd ed.* Boston, Massachusetts: Allyn and Bacon, 2000. **2525**

*Kit's Friendship Fun.* Middleton, Wisconsin: American Girl Publications, 2002. **2526**

Knoell, Donna L. *France.* Mankato, Minnesota: Bridgestone Books, 2002. **2527**

Knox, Barbara. *Afghanistan.* Mankato, Minnesota: Blue Earth Books, 2004. **2926**

Koestler, Rachel A. *Going to School during the Civil Rights Movement.* Mankato, Minnesota: Blue Earth Books, 2002. **2528**

Kohl, Mary Ann F. *Discovering Great Artists: Hands-on Art for Children in the Styles of the Great Masters.* Bellingham, Washington: Bright Ring Publishing, 1997. **2529**

Kopka, Deborah. *Norway.* Minneapolis, Minnesota: Carolrhoda Books, 2001. **2530**

Krasno, Rena. *Floating Lanterns and Golden Shrines: Celebrating Japanese Festivals.* Berkeley, California: Pacific View Press, 2000. **2531**

Krasno, Rena. *Kneeling Carabao and Dancing Giants: Celebrating Filipino Festivals.* Berkeley, California: Pacific View Press, 1997. **2532**

Kummer, Patricia K. *Cameroon.* Danbury, Connecticut: Children's Press, 2004. **2969**

Kummer, Patricia K. *Korea.* Danbury, Connecticut: Children's Press, 2004. **2970**

Kummer, Patricia K. *Ukraine.* Danbury, Connecticut: Children's Press, 2001. **2533**

Kuntz, Lynn. *American Grub: Eats for Kids from all Fifty States.* New York: Scholastic, 1997. **2534**

LaDoux, Rita C. *Georgia.* Minneapolis, Minnesota: Lerner Publications Co., 2002. **2535**

LaDoux, Rita C. *Iowa.* Minneapolis, Minnesota: Lerner Publications Co., 2002. **2536**

LaDoux, Rita C. *Montana.* Minneapolis, Minnesota: Lerner Publications Co., 2003. **2537**

LaDoux, Rita C. *Oklahoma.* Minneapolis, Minnesota: Lerner Publications Co., 2003. **2538**

Landau, Elaine. *Columbus Day: Celebrating a Famous Explorer.* Berkeley Heights, New Jersey: Enslow Publishers, 2002. **2539**

Landau, Elaine. *Earth Day: Keeping our Planet Clean.* Berkeley Heights, New Jersey: Enslow Publishers, 2002. **2540**

Landau, Elaine. *Independence Day: Birthday of the United States.* Berkeley Heights, New Jersey: Enslow Publishers, 2001. **2541**

Landau, Elaine. *Mardi Gras: Parades, Costumes and Parties.* Berkeley Heights, New Jersey: Enslow Publishers, 2002. **2542**

Landau, Elaine. *Popcorn.* Watertown, Massachusetts: Charlesbridge Publishing, 2003. **2543**

Landau, Elaine. *St. Patrick's Day: Parades, Shamrocks and Leprechauns.* Berkeley Heights, New Jersey: Enslow Publishers, 2002. **2544**

Landau, Elaine. *Thanksgiving Day: A Time to Be Thankful.* Berkeley Heights, New Jersey: Enslow Publishers, 2001. **2971**

Landau, Elaine. *Valentine's Day: Candy, Love and Hearts.* Berkeley Heights, New Jersey: Enslow Publishers, 2002. **2545**

Landau, Elaine. *Veteran's Day: Remembering Our War Heroes.* Berkeley Heights, New Jersey: Enslow Publishers, 2002. **2546**

Lankford, Mary D. *Birthdays Around the World.* New York: HarperCollins Publishers, 2002. **2547**

Lankford, Mary D. *Dominoes Around the World.* New York: William Morrow and Co., 1998. **2548**

Larkin, Tanya. *What Was Cooking in Abigail Adam's White House?* New York: PowerKids Press, 2000. **2549**

Larkin, Tanya. *What Was Cooking in Dolley Madison's White House?* New York: PowerKids Press, 2000. **2550**

Larkin, Tanya. *What Was Cooking in Edith Roosevelt's White House?* New York: PowerKids Press, 2000. **2551**

Larkin, Tanya. *What Was Cooking in Julia Grant's White House?* New York: PowerKids Press, 2001. **2552**

Larkin, Tanya. *What Was Cooking in Martha Washington's Presidential Mansions?* New York: PowerKids Press, 2001. **2553**

Larkin, Tanya. *What Was Cooking in Mary Todd Lincoln's White House?* New York: PowerKids Press, 2001. **2554**

Lassieur, Allison. *Ethiopia.* Mankato, Minnesota: Capstone Press, 2004. **2561**

Lassieur, Allison. *Peru.* Mankato, Minnesota: Capstone Press, 2004. **2563**

Lassieur, Allison. *The Arapaho Tribe.* Mankato, Minnesota: Bridgestone Books, 2002. **2555**

Lassieur, Allison. *The Blackfeet Nation.* Mankato, Minnesota: Bridgestone Books, 2002. **2556**

Lassieur, Allison. *The Cheyenne.* Mankato, Minnesota: Bridgestone Books, 2001. **2557**

Lassieur, Allison. The *Choctaw Nation.* Mankato, Minnesota: Bridgestone Books, 2001. **2558**

Lassieur, Allison. *The Creek Nation.* Mankato, Minnesota: Bridgestone Books, 2002. **2559**

Lassieur, Allison. *The Delaware People.* Mankato, Minnesota: Bridgestone Books, 2002. **2560**

Lassieur, Allison. *The Pequot Tribe.* Mankato, Minnesota: Bridgestone Books, 2002. **2562**

Layton, Lesley. *Singapore.* Tarrytown, New York: Marshall Cavendish Corp., 2002. **2564**

Lee, Frances. *The Young Chef's Chinese Cookbook.* New York: Crabtree Publishing Co., 2001. **2565**

Lehman-Wilzig, Tami. *Tasty Bible Stories: A Menu of Tales and Matching Recipes.* Minneapolis, Minnesota: Kar-Ben Publishing, 2003. **2566**

Leotta, Joan. *Massachusetts.* Danbury, Connecticut: Children's Press, 2001. **2567**

Lim, Robin. *Indonesia.* Minneapolis, Minnesota: Carolrhoda Books, 2001. **2568**

Limberhand, Dennis. *The Cheyenne.* Austin, Texas: Raintree Steck-Vaughn Publishers, 2001. **2569**

Ling, Bettina. *Wisconsin.* Danbury, Connecticut: Children's Press, 2002. **2570**

Littlefield, Cynthia. *Real-World Math for Hands-On Fun!* Charlotte, Vermont: Williamson Publishing Co., 2001. **2571**

Locricchio, Matthew. *The Cooking of China.* Tarrytown, New York: Benchmark Books, 2002. **2572**

Locricchio, Matthew. *The Cooking of France.* Tarrytown, New York: Benchmark Books, 2002. **2573**

Locricchio, Matthew. *The Cooking of Italy.* Tarrytown, New York: Benchmark Books, 2002. **2574**

Locricchio, Matthew. *The Cooking of Mexico.* Tarrytown, New York: Benchmark Books, 2002. **2575**

*Look 'N' Cook.* Greensboro, North Carolina: The Education Center, 2001. **2576**

Lord, Richard. *Germany.* Milwaukee, Wisconsin: Gareth Stevens Publishing, 1997. **2577**

Love, Ann. *Kids and Grandparents: An Activity Book.* Toronto, Ontario: KidsCan Press, 2000. **2578**

Macdonald, Fiona. *Rain Forest.* New York: Franklin Watts, 2000. **2579**

Macdonald, Fiona. *Step into Ancient Japan.* New York: Lorenz Books, 1999. **2580**

Macdonald, Fiona. *Step into the...Aztec and Maya World.* New York: Lorenz Books, 1998. **2581**

Macdonald, Fiona. *Step into the...Celtic World.* New York: Lorenz Books, 1999. **2582**

Macdonald, Fiona. *The Aztecs.* Chicago, Illinois: Raintree, 2003. **2928**

Macdonald,. Fiona. *The Greeks.* Chicago, Illinois: Raintree, 2003. **2929**

Macdonald, Fiona. *The Romans.* Chicago, Illinois: Raintree, 2003. **2930**

MacLeod, Elizabeth. *Bake and Make Amazing Cakes.* Tonawanda, New York: KidsCan Press, 2001. **2583**

Madavan, Vijay. *Cooking the Indian Way.* Minneapolis, Minnesota: Lerner Publications Co., 2002. **2584**

Maher, Erin. *Chinese Foods and Recipes.* New York: The Rosen Publishing Group, 2002. **2585**

Mamdani, Shelby. *Traditions from China.* Austin, Texas: Steck-Vaughn Publishers, 1998. **2586**

Mamdani, Shelby. *Traditions from India.* Austin, Texas: Steck-Vaughn Publishers, 1999. **2587**

Marchant, Kerena. *Hindu Festival Tales.* Austin, Texas: Raintree Steck-Vaughn Publishers, 2001. **2589**

Marchant, Kerena. *Hindu Festivals Cookbook.* Austin, Texas: Raintree Steck-Vaughn Publishers, 2001. **2588**

Marchant, Kerena. *Muslim Festival Tales.* Austin, Texas: Raintree Steck-Vaughn Publishers, 2001. **2590**

Marsh, Valerie. *Puppet Tales.* Fort Atkinson, Wisconsin: Alleyside Press, 1998. **2591**

*Martin Luther King, Jr. Day Activities.* Westminster, California: Teacher Created Materials, 1999 reprint. **2592**

Master, Nancy Robinson. *Kansas.* Danbury, Connecticut: Children's Press, 1999. **2593**

Mattern, Joanne. *India.* Mankato, Minnesota: Bridgestone Books, 2003. **2594**

Mattern, Joanne. *Ireland.* Mankato, Minnesota: Bridgestone Books, 2003. **2595**

Mattern, Joanne. *The Shawnee Indians.* Mankato, Minnesota: Bridgestone Books, 2001. **2596**

Mattern, Joanne. *The Shoshone People.* Mankato, Minnesota: Bridgestone Books, 2001. **2597**

McCain, Becky Ray. *Grandmother's Dreamcatcher.* Morton Grove, Illinois: Albert Whitman & Company, 1998. **2598**

McCarthy, Cathy. *The Ojibwa.* Austin, Texas: Raintree Steck-Vaughn Publishers, 2001. **2599**

McCollum, Sean. *Australia.* Minneapolis, Minnesota: Carolrhoda Books, 1999. **2600**

McCollum, Sean. *Kenya.* Minneapolis, Minnesota: Carolrhoda Books, 1999. **2601**

McCollum, Sean. *Poland.* Minneapolis, Minnesota: Carolrhoda Books, 1999. **2602**

McCulloch, Julie. *China.* Chicago, Illinois: Heinemann Library, 2001. **2604**

McCulloch, Julie. *India.* Chicago, Illinois: Heinemann Library, 2001. **2605**

McCulloch, Julie. *Italy.* Chicago, Illinois: Heinemann Library, 2001. **2606**

McCulloch, Julie. *Japan.* Chicago, Illinois: Heinemann Library, 2001. **2607**

McCulloch, Julie. *Mexico.* Chicago, Illinois: Heinemann Library, 2001. **2608**

McCulloch, Julie. *The Caribbean.* Chicago, Illinois: Heinemann Library, 2001. **2603**

McKay, Susan. *Brazil.* Milwaukee, Wisconsin: Gareth Stevens Publishing, 1997. **2609**

McKay, Susan. *France.* Milwaukee, Wisconsin: Gareth Stevens Publishing, 1998. **2610**

McKay, Susan. *Japan.* Milwaukee, Wisconsin: Gareth Stevens Publishing, 1997. **2611**

McKay, Susan. *Spain.* Milwaukee, Wisconsin: Gareth Stevens Publishing, 1999. **2612**

McKay, Susan. *Switzerland.* Milwaukee, Wisconsin: Gareth Stevens Publishing, 1999. **2613**

McKay, Susan. *Vietnam.* Milwaukee, Wisconsin: Gareth Stevens Publishing, 1997. **2614**

McLester, L. Gordon. *The Oneida.* Austin, Texas: Raintree Steck-Vaughn Publishers, 2001. **2615**

McMillan, Dana. *Construction Site.* Carthage, Illinois: Teaching and Learning Company, 2000. **2972**

McMillan, Mary. *Christian Crafts from Hand-Shaped Art.* Torrance, California: Shining Star Publications, 1991. **2616**

McMorrow, Annalisa. *Terrific Transportation: Reading, Writing and Speaking about Transportation.* Palo Alto, California: Monday Morning Books, 2000. **2618**

Mendoza, Lunita. *Philippines.* Milwaukee, Wisconsin: Gareth Stevens Publishing, 1999. **2619**

Merrill, Yvonne Y. *Hands-On Africa: Art Activities for All Ages featuring Sub-Saharan Africa.* Salt Lake City, Utah: Kits Publishing, 2000. **2620**

Merrill, Yvonne Y. *Hands-On America, Volume 1: Art Activities about Vikings, Woodland Indians and Early Colonists.* Salt Lake City, Utah: Kits Publishing, 2001. **2621**

Miescke, Lori. *Christian Crafts from Construction Paper.* Torrance, California: Shining Star Publications, 1992. **2622**

Milivojevic, JoAnn. *Czech Republic.* Danbury, Connecticut: Children's Press, 2004. **2973**

Milivojevic, JoAnn. *Puerto Rico.* Minneapolis, Minnesota: Carolrhoda Books, 2000. **2623**

Miller, Amy. *Colorado.* Danbury, Connecticut: Children's Press, 2002. **2624**

Mirpuri, Gouri. *Indonesia.* Tarrytown, New York: Marshall Cavendish Corp., 2002. **2625**

Mitchell, Kevin M. *Wickiup.* Vero Beach, Florida: Rourke Book Co., 2000. **2626**

Montgomery, Bertha Vining. *Cooking the East African Way.* Minneapolis, Minnesota: Lerner Publications Co., 2002. **2627**

Montgomery, Bertha Vining. *Cooking the West African Way.* Minneapolis, Minnesota: Lerner Publications Co., 2002. **2628**

Moore, Sharon. *Native American Foods and Recipes.* New York: The Rosen Publishing Group, 2002. **2629**

Morris, Ann. *Grandma Francisca Remembers.* Brookfield, Connecticut: The Millbrook Press, 2002. **2631**

Morris, Ann. *Grandma Lai Goon Remembers: A Chinese-American Family Story.* Brookfield, Connecticut: The Millbrook Press, 2002. **2632**

Morris, Ann. *Grandma Lois Remembers: An African-American Family Story.* Brookfield, Connecticut: The Millbrook Press, 2002. **2633**

Morris, Ann. *Grandma Maxine Remembers.* Brookfield, Connecticut: The Millbrook Press, 2002. **2634**

Morris, Ann. *Grandma Susan Remembers.* Brookfield, Connecticut: The Millbrook Press, 2002. **2635**

Morris, Ann. *Grandma Susan Remembers: A British-American Family Story.* Brookfield, Connecticut: The Millbrook Press, 2002. **2974 <<dup entry?>>**

Morrow, Priscella. *Totally Tubeys: 24 Storytimes with Tube Crafts.* Fort Atkinson, Wisconsin: Upstart Books, 2003. **2636**

*Mother's Day Activities.* Westminster, California: Teacher Created Materials, 1999 reprint. **2637**

Munan, Heidi. *Malaysia.* Tarrytown, New York: Marshall Cavendish Corp., 2002. **2638**

Munsen, Sylvia. *Cooking the Norwegian Way.* Minneapolis, Minnesota: Lerner Publications Co., 2002. **2639**

Murphy, Patricia J. *Denmark.* Mankato, Minnesota: Bridgestone Books, 2003. **2640**

Murphy, Patricia J. *Tanzania.* Mankato, Minnesota: Bridgestone Books, 2003. **2641**

Nakajima, Caroline. *Connecting Cultures and Literature.* Huntington Beach, California: Teacher Created Materials, 1992. **2642**

Napier, Tanya. *Totally Tea-rific Tea Party Book.* San Francisco, California: Orange Avenue Publishing, 2002. **2643**

*National Celebrations.* Chicago, Illinois: World Book, 2003. **2983**

*Native Americans, Primary.* Greensboro, North Carolina: The Education Center, 2002. **2644**

*New Year's Celebrations.* Chicago, Illinois: World Book, 2003. **2984**

NgCheong-Lum, Roseline. *Haiti.* Milwaukee, Wisconsin: Gareth Stevens Publishing, 1998. **2645**

Nguyen, Chi. *Cooking the Vietnamese Way.* Minneapolis, Minnesota: Lerner Publications Co., 2002. **2646**

Nickles, Greg. *Argentina.* New York: Crabtree Publishing Co., 2001. **2647**

Nickles, Greg. *Germany.* Austin, Texas: Raintree Steck-Vaughn Publishers, 2000. **2648**

Nobleman, Marc Tyler. *Cambodia.* Mankato, Minnesota: Bridgestone Books, 2003. **2649**

Nobleman, Marc Tyler. *Greece.* Mankato, Minnesota: Bridgestone Books, 2003. **2650**

Nobleman, Marc Tyler. *Panama.* Mankato, Minnesota: Bridgestone Books, 2003. **2652**

Nobleman, Marc Tyler. *Pakistan.* Mankato, Minnesota: Bridgestone Books, 2003. **2651**

Nollen, Tim. *Czech Republic.* Milwaukee, Wisconsin: Gareth Stevens Publishing, 1999. **2653**

O'Connor, Karen. *Vietnam.* Minneapolis, Minnesota: Carolrhoda Books, 1999. **2655**

O'Hara, Megan. *Irish Immigrants, 1840-1920.* Mankato, Minnesota: Blue Earth Books, 2002. **2656**

O'Hare, Jeff. *Hanukkah, Festival of Lights.* Honesdale, Pennsylvania: Boyds Mills Press, 2000. **2657**

O'Shea, Maria. *Saudi Arabia.* Milwaukee, Wisconsin: Gareth Stevens Publishing, 1999. **2665**

O'Shea, Maria. *Turkey.* Milwaukee, Wisconsin: Gareth Stevens Publishing, 1999. **2666**

Oakes, Lorna. *Step into... Mesopotamia.* New York: Lorenz Books, 2001. **2654**

Olson, Kay Melchisedech. *Africans in America, 1619-1865.* Mankato, Minnesota: Blue Earth Books, 2003. **2975**

Olson, Kay Melchisedech. *China.* Mankato, Minnesota: Blue Earth Books, 2003. **2658**

Olson, Kay Melchisedech. *Chinese Immigrants, 1850-1900.* Mankato, Minnesota: Blue Earth Books, 2002. **2659**

Olson, Kay Melchisedech. *England.* Mankato, Minnesota: Blue Earth Books, ?, 2003. **2660**

Olson, Kay Melchisedech. *French Immigrants, 1840-1940.* Mankato, Minnesota: Blue Earth Books, 2003. **2976**

Olson, Kay Melchisedech. *Ireland.* Mankato, Minnesota: Blue Earth Books, 2004. **2931**

Olson, Kay Melchisedech. *Norwegian, Swedish and Danish Immigrants, 1820-1920.* Mankato, Minnesota: Blue Earth Books, 2002. **2977**

Oluonye, Mary N. *Madagascar.* Minneapolis, Minnesota: Carolrhoda Books, 2000. **2661**

Oluonye, Mary N. *Nigeria.* Minneapolis, Minnesota: Carolrhoda Books, 1998. **2662**

Oluonye, Mary N. *South Africa.* Minneapolis, Minnesota: Carolrhoda Books, 1999. **2663**

Orr, Tamra. *Barbados.* Philadelphia, Pennsylvania: Mason Crest Publishers, 2003. **2932**

*Our Country: Dozens of Instant and Irresistible Ideas and Activities to Teach About the Flag, the Pledge, the Presidents and More.* New York: Scholastic Professional Books, 2002. **2667**

Panchyk, Richard. *World War II for Kids: A History with 21 Activities*. Chicago, Illinois: Chicago Review Press, 2002. **2668**

Parker-Rock, Michelle. *Diwali: The Hindu Festival of Lights, Feasts and Family*. Berkeley Heights, New Jersey: Enslow Publishers, 2003. **2933**

Parnell, Helga. *Cooking the German Way*. Minneapolis, Minnesota: Lerner Publications Co., 2003. **2669**

Parnell, Helga. *Cooking the South American Way*. Minneapolis, Minnesota: Lerner Publications Co., 2003. **2670**

Pavon, Ana-Elba. *25 Latino Craft Projects*. Chicago, Illinois: American Library Association, 2003. **2671**

Pelta, Kathy. *Idaho*. Minneapolis, Minnesota: Lerner Publications Co., 2002. **2672**

Perry, Phyllis J. *Ten Tall Tales: Origins, Activities and More*. Fort Atkinson, Wisconsin: Upstart Books, 2002. **2673**

Petrillo, Valerie. *Sailors, Whalers, Fantastic Sea Voyages: An Activity Guide to North American Sailing Life*. Chicago, Illinois: Chicago Review Press, 2003. **2934**

Pfeffer, Wendy. *The Shortest Day: Celebrate the Winter Solstice*. New York: Dutton Children's Books, 2003. **2674**

Phelps, Joan Hilyer. *Finger Tales*. Fort Atkinson, Wisconsin: Upstart Books, 2002. **2675**

Pinol, Roser. *Creating Costumes*. Woodbridge, Connecticut: Blackbirch Press, 2000. **2676**

Pirotta, Saviour. *Christian Festival Cookbook*. Austin, Texas: Raintree Steck-Vaughn Publishers, 2001. **2677**

Pirotta, Saviour. *Christian Festival Tales*. Austin, Texas: Steck-Vaughn Publishers, 2001. **2678**

Pirotta, Saviour. *Jewish Festival Tales*. Austin, Texas: Steck-Vaughn Publishers, 2001. **2679**

Plokin, Gregory. *Cooking the Russian Way*. Minneapolis, Minnesota: Lerner Publications Co., 2003. **2680**

Polette, Nancy. *U.S. History Readers Theatre: 200+ Years of History through Booktalks, Songs, Poetry and Creative Writing Activities*. O'Fallon, Missouri: Book Lures, 1994. **2681**

Porter, A. P. *Nebraska*. Minneapolis, Minnesota: Lerner Publications Co., 2003. **2682**

Powell, Michelle. *Mosaics*. Chicago, Illinois: Heinemann Library, 2001. **2683**

Pratt, Diane. *Hey Kids! You're Cookin' Now: A Global Awareness Cooking Adventure*. Salisbury Cove, Maine: Harvest Hill Press, 1998. **2684**

Press, Judy. *All Around Town: Exploring Your Community Through Craft Fun*. Charlotte, Vermont: Williamson Publishing Co., 2002. **2685**

Press, Judy. *Around the World Art and Activities: Visiting the Continents through Craft Fun*. Charlotte, Vermont: Williamson Publishing Co., 2001. **2686**

Quasha, Jennifer. *Covered Wagons: Hands-On Projects about America's Westward Expansion*. New York: PowerKids Press, 2001. **2688**

Quasha, Jennifer. *Gold Rush: Hands-On Projects about Mining the Riches of California*. New York: PowerKids Press, 2001. **2689**

Quasha, Jennifer. *Pilgrims and Native Americans: Hands-On Projects about Life in Colonial America*. New York: PowerKids Press, 2000. **2690**

Quasha, Jennifer. *The Birth and Growth of a Nation: Hands-On Projects about Symbols of American Liberty*. New York: PowerKids Press, 2000. **2687**

Quasha, Jennifer. *The Pony Express: Hands-On Projects about Early Communication*. New York: PowerKids Press, 2000. **2691**

Raabe, Emily. *A Kwanzaa Holiday Cookbook*. New York: The Rosen Publishing Group, 2002. **2694**

Raabe, Emily. *A Passover Holiday Cookbook*. New York: The Rosen Publishing Group, 2002. **2695**

Raabe, Emily. *A Thanksgiving Holiday.* New York: The Rosen Publishing Group, 2002. **2696**

Raabe, Emily. *An Easter Holiday Cookbook.* New York: PowerKids Press, 2002. **2693**

Raabe, Emily. *Christmas Holiday Cookbook.* New York: The Rosen Publishing Group, 2002. **2692**

Randall, Ronne. *Jewish Festival Cookbook.* Austin, Texas: Steck-Vaughn Publishers, 2001. **2697**

Rasmussen, R. Kent. *Mark Twain for Kids: His Life and Times: 21 Activities.* Chicago, Illinois: Chicago Review Press, 2004. **2935**

Rasmussen, R. Kent. *Pueblo.* Vero Beach, Florida: Rourke Book Company, 2000. **2698**

Ready, Anna. *Mississippi.* Minneapolis, Minnesota: Lerner Publications Co., 2003. **2699**

Rhatigan, Joe. *Geography Crafts for Kids: 50 Cool Projects and Activities for Exploring the World.* New York: Lark Books, 2002. **2700**

Rhatigan, Joe. *Paper Fantastic: 50 Creative Projects to Fold, Cut, Glue, Paint and Weave.* New York: Lark Books, 2004. **2978**

Rhatigan, Joe. *Soapmaking: 50 Fun and Fabulous Soaps to Melt and Pour.* New York: Lark Books, 2003. **2936**

Riehecky, Janet. *China.* Minneapolis, Minnesota: Carolrhoda Books, 1999. **2701**

Riehecky, Janet. *Greece.* Mankato, Minnesota: Bridgestone Books, 2001. **2703**

Riehecky, Janet. *Indonesia.* Mankato, Minnesota: Bridgestone Books, 2002. **2704**

Riehecky, Janet. *Nicaragua.* Mankato, Minnesota: Bridgestone Books, 2002. **2705**

Riehecky, Janet. *Sweden.* Mankato, Minnesota: Bridgestone Books, 2001. **2707**

Riehecky, Janet. *The Cree Tribe.* Minneapolis, Minnesota: Bridgestone Books, 2003. **2702**

Riehecky, Janet. *The Osage.* Mankato, Minnesota: Bridgestone Books, 2003. **2706**

Robinson, Fay. *Chinese New Year, a Time for Parades, Family and Friends.* Berkeley Heights, New Jersey: Enslow Publishers, 2001. **2708**

Robinson, Fay. *Christmas Crafts.* Berkeley Heights, New Jersey: Enslow Publishers, 2003. **2937**

Robinson, Fay. *Halloween: Costumes and Treats on All Hallow's Eve.* Berkeley Heights, New Jersey: Enslow Publishers, 2001. **2709**

Robinson, Fay. *Halloween Crafts.* Berkeley Heights, New Jersey: Enslow Publishers, 2003. **2938**

Rocklin, Joanne. *Strudel Stories.* New York: Delacorte Press, 1999. **2710**

Rogers, Barbara Radcliffe. *Zimbabwe.* Danbury, Connecticut: Children's Press, 2002. **2711**

Rogers, Lura. *Spain.* Danbury, Connecticut: Children's Press, 2001. **2712**

Rogers, Lura. *Switzerland.* Danbury, Connecticut: Children's Press, 2001. **2713**

Roop, Peter. *Let's Celebrate Earth Day.* Brookfield, Connecticut: The Millbrook Press, 2001. **2714**

Roop, Peter. *Let's Celebrate St. Patrick's Day.* Brookfield, Connecticut: The Millbrook Press, 2003. **2939**

Roop, Peter. *Let's Celebrate Valentine's Day.* Brookfield, Connecticut: The Millbrook Press, 1999. **2715**

Rosenberg, Anne. *Nigeria, the Culture.* New York: Crabtree Publishing Co., 2001. **2716**

Rosin, Arielle. *Pizzas and Punk Potatoes.* New York: Ticknor & Fields, 1994. **2717**

Ross, Corinne. *Christmas in Mexico.* Lincolnwood, Illinois: Passport Books, 1991. **2718**

Ross, Kathy. *All New Crafts for Halloween.* Brookfield, Connecticut: The Millbrook Press, 2003. **2719**

Ross, Kathy. *All New Crafts for Valentine's Day.* Brookfield, Connecticut: The Millbrook Press, 2002. **2720**

Ross, Kathy. *Christian Crafts for Christmastime.* Brookfield, Connecticut: The Millbrook Press, 2001. **2721**

Ross, Kathy. *Christmas Decorations Kids Can Make.* Brookfield, Connecticut: The Millbrook Press, 1999. **2722**

Ross, Kathy. *Christmas Ornaments Kids Can Make.* Brookfield, Connecticut: The Millbrook Press, 1998. **2723**

Ross, Kathy. *Christmas Presents Kids Can Make.* Brookfield, Connecticut: The Millbrook Press, 2001. **2724**

Ross, Kathy. *Crafts for Christian Values.* Brookfield, Connecticut: The Millbrook Press, 2000. **2725**

Ross, Kathy. *Crafts for Easter.* Brookfield, Connecticut: The Millbrook Press, 1995. **2726**

Ross, Kathy. *Crafts for Hanukkah.* Brookfield, Connecticut: The Millbrook Press, 1996. **2727**

Ross, Kathy. *Crafts from Your Favorite Children's Songs.* Brookfield, Connecticut: The Millbrook Press, 2001. **2728**

Ross, Kathy. *Crafts from Your Favorite Children's Stories.* Brookfield, Connecticut: The Millbrook Press, 2001. **2729**

Ross, Kathy. *Crafts from Your Favorite Nursery Rhymes.* Brookfield, Connecticut: The Millbrook Press, 2002. **2730**

Ross, Kathy. *Crafts That Celebrate Black History.* Brookfield, Connecticut: The Millbrook Press, 2002. **2731**

Ross, Kathy. *Crafts to Celebrate God's Creation.* Brookfield, Connecticut: The Millbrook Press, 2001. **2732**

Ross, Kathy. *Crafts to Make in the Summer.* Brookfield, Connecticut: The Millbrook Press, 1998. **2733**

Ross, Kathy. *Make Yourself a Monster.* Brookfield, Connecticut: The Millbrook Press, 1999. **2734**

Ross, Kathy. *Star-Spangled Crafts.* Brookfield, Connecticut: The Millbrook Press, 2003. **2735**

Ross, Michael Elsohn. *A Mexican Christmas.* Minneapolis, Minnesota: Carolrhoda Books, 2002. **2736**

Roy, Jennifer Rozines. *Israel.* Tarrytown, New York: Benchmark Books, 2003. **2940**

Rush, Barbara. *The Kids' Catalog of Passover: A World Wide Celebration.* Philadelphia, Pennsylvania: Jewish Publication Society, 1999. **2737**

Sabbeth, Carol. *Monet and the Impressionists for Kids: Their Lives and Ideas, 21 Activities.* Chicago, Illinois: Chicago Review Press, 2002. **2738**

Sachatello-Sawyer, Bonnie. *Lewis and Clark: Background Information, Activities.* New York: Scholastic Professional Books, 1997. **2739**

Sadler, Judy Ann. *Christmas Crafts from Around the World.* Tonawanda, New York: KidsCan Press, 2003. **2740**

Saffer, Barbara. *Kenya.* Mankato, Minnesota: Bridgestone Books, 2000. **2741**

Saffer, Barbara. *Mexico.* Mankato, Minnesota: Bridgestone Books, 2002. **2742**

Salas, Laura P. *China.* Mankato, Minnesota: Bridgestone Books, 2002. **2743**

*Samantha's Fun.* Middleton, Wisconsin: Pleasant Company Publications, 2002. **2744**

Sanders, Nancy I. *A Kid's Guide to African American History: More than 70 Activities.* Chicago, Illinois: Chicago Review Press, 2000. **2745**

Sanders, Nancy I. *Old Testament Days: An Activity Guide.* Chicago, Illinois: Chicago Review Press, 1999. **2746**

Sateren, Shelley Swanson. *Going to School in Colonial America.* Mankato, Minnesota: Blue Earth Books, 2002. **2747**

Scheffler, Carol. *Family Crafting: Fun Projects to Do Together.* New York: Sterling Publishing Co., 2000. **2748**

Schraff, Anne. *Philippines.* Minneapolis, Minnesota: Carolrhoda Books, 2001. **2749**

Schwarz, Renee. *Making Masks.* Tonawanda, New York: KidsCan Press, 2001. **2750**

Senterfitt, Marilyn. *Christian Crafts from Egg Cartons.* Torrance, California: Shining Star Publications, 1991. **2751**

Sevaly, Karen. *April: A Creative Idea Book for the Elementary Teacher.* Riverside, California: Teacher's Friend Publications, 1998. **2752**

Sevaly, Karen. *December: A Creative Idea Book for the Elementary Teacher.* Riverside, California: Teacher's Friend Publications, 1997. **2753**

Sevaly, Karen. *February: A Creative Idea Book for the Elementary Teacher.* Riverside, California: Teacher's Friend Publications, 1997. **2754**

Sevaly, Karen. *January: A Creative Idea Book for the Elementary Teacher.* Riverside, California: Teacher's Friend Publications, 1997. **2755**

Sevaly, Karen. *July/August: A Creative Idea Book for the Elementary Teacher.* Riverside, California: Teacher's Friend Publications, 1998. **2756**

Sevaly, Karen. *June: A Creative Idea Book for the Elementary Teacher.* Riverside, California: Teacher's Friend Publications, 1998. **2757**

Sevaly, Karen. *March: A Creative Idea Book for the Elementary Teacher.* Riverside, California: Teacher's Friend Publications, 1998. **2758**

Sevaly, Karen. *May: A Creative Idea Book for the Elementary Teacher.* Riverside, California: Teacher's Friend Publications, 1997. **2759**

Sevaly, Karen. *November: A Creative Idea Book for the Elementary Teacher.* Riverside, California: Teacher's Friend Publications, 1997. **2760**

Sevaly, Karen. *October: A Creative Idea Book for the Elementary Teacher.* Riverside, California: Teacher's Friend Publications, 1997. **2761**

Sevaly, Karen. *September: A Creative Idea Book for the Elementary Teacher.* Riverside, California: Teacher's Friend Publications, 1997. **2762**

Shannon, Terry Miller. *New Hampshire.* Danbury, Connecticut: Children's Press, 2002. **2763**

*Share the Olympic Dream Vol. II: Curriculum Guide to the Olympic Games.* Glendale, California: Griffin Publishing Group, 1995. **2764**

Shelley, Rex. *Japan.* Tarrytown, New York: Marshall Cavendish Corp., 2002. **2765**

Shields, Charles J. *Belize.* Philadelphia, Pennsylvania: Mason Crest Publishers, 2003. **2941**

Shields, Charles J. *Brazil.* Philadelphia, Pennsylvania: Mason Crest Publishers, 2003. **2942**

Shields, Charles J. *Chile.* Philadelphia, Pennsylvania: Mason Crest Publishers, 2003. **2943**

Shields, Charles J. *Costa Rica.* Philadelphia, Pennsylvania: Mason Crest Publishers, 2003. **2944**

Shields, Charles J. *El Salvador.* Philadelphia, Pennsylvania: Mason Crest Publishers, 2003. **2945**

Shields, Charles J. *Guatemala.* Philadelphia, Pennsylvania: Mason Crest Publishers, 2003. **2946**

Shields, Charles J. *Nicaragua.* Philadelphia, Pennsylvania: Mason Crest Publishers, 2003. **2947**

Shields, Charles J. *Panama.* Philadelphia, Pennsylvania: Mason Crest Publishers, 2003. **2948**

Shields, Charles J. *Uruguay.* Philadelphia, Pennsylvania: Mason Crest Publishers, 2003. **2949**

Shields, Charles J. *Venezuela.* Philadelphia, Pennsylvania: Mason Crest Publishers, 2003. **2950**

Shipman, Doug. *Christian Crafts: Paper Plate Animals.* Torrance, California: Shining Star Publications, 1993. **2766**

Sierra, Judy. *Children's Traditional Games: Games from 137 Countries and Cultures.* Phoenix, Arizona: Oryx Press, 1995. **2767**

Silbaugh, Elizabeth. *Raggedy Ann's Birthday Party Book.* New York: Simon & Schuster, 2001. **2768**

Silbaugh, Elizabeth. *Raggedy Ann's Tea Party Book.* New York: Simon & Schuster, 1999. **2951**

Silver, Patricia. *Face Painting.* Tonawanda, New York: KidsCan Press, 2000. **2952**

Simonds, Nina. *Moonbeams, Dumplings and Dragon Boats: A Treasury of Chinese Holi-*

*day Tales, Activities and Recipes.* New York: Gulliver Books, 2002. **2769**

Sirvaitis, Karen. *Michigan.* Minneapolis, Minnesota: Lerner Publications Co., 2002. **2770**

Sirvaitis, Karen. *Nevada.* Minneapolis, Minnesota: Lerner Publications Co., 2003. **2771**

Sirvaitis, Karen. *Tennessee.* Minneapolis, Minnesota: Lerner Publications, Co., 2003. **2772**

Sirvaitis, Karen. *Utah.* Minneapolis, Minnesota: Lerner Publications Co., 2002. **2773**

Sirvaitis, Karen. *Virginia.* Minneapolis, Minnesota: Lerner Publications Co., 2002. **2774**

Sloat, Teri. *Berry Magic.* Portland, Oregon: Alaska Northwest Books, 2004. **2979**

Somerville, Barbara A. *Alaska.* Danbury, Connecticut: Children's Press, 2001. **2775**

Somerville, Barbara A. *Florida.* Danbury, Connecticut: Children's Press, 2001. **2776**

Somerville, Barbara A. *Illinois.* Danbury, Connecticut: Children's Press, 2001. **2777**

Souter, Gillian. *Holiday Handiwork.* Milwaukee, Wisconsin: Gareth Stevens Publishing, 2002. **2778**

Speechley, Greta. *Bead Book.* Danbury, Connecticut: Grolier Educational, 2003. **2779**

Speechley, Greta. *Dolls and Bears.* Danbury, Connecticut: Grolier Educational, 2003. **2780**

Speechley, Greta. *Myths and Tales Book.* Danbury, Connecticut: Grolier Educational, 2003. **2781**

Speechley, Greta. *Valentine Book.* Danbury, Connecticut: Grolier Educational, 2003. **2782**

Speechley, Greta. *Winter Holiday Book.* Danbury, Connecticut: Grolier Educational, 2003. **2783**

Speechley, Greta. *World Book.* Danbury, Connecticut: Grolier Educational, 2003. **2784**

*Spring Celebrations.* Chicago, Illinois: World Book, 2003. **2985**

Srinivasan, Radhika. *India.* Tarrytown, New York: Marshall Cavendish Corp., 2002. **2785**

Standard, Carole K. *Arizona.* Danbury, Connecticut: Children's Press, 2002. **2786**

Stechschulte, Pattie. *Georgia.* Danbury, Connecticut: Children's Press, 2001. **2787**

Steele, Philip. *Step into the... Chinese Empire.* New York: Lorenz Books, 1998. **2789**

Steele, Philip. *Step into the... Inca World.* New York: Lorenz Books, 2000. **2790**

Steele, Philip. *Step into... Ancient Egypt.* New York: Lorenz Books, 2001. **2788**

Steele, Philip. *Step into... the Viking World.* New York: Lorenz Books, 1998. **2792**

Steele, Philip. *Step into...the Roman Empire.* New York: Lorenz Books, 1998. **2791**

Stegenga, Susan J. *Christian Crafts: Paper Bag Puppets.* Torrance, California: Shining Star Publications, 1990. **2793**

Stein, R. Conrad. *Mexico.* Chicago, Illinois: Children's Press, 1995. **2794**

Stepanchuk, Carol. *Exploring Chinatown: A Children's Guide to Chinatown.* Berkeley, California: Pacific View Press, 2001. **2795**

Stepanchuk, Carol. *Red Eggs and Dragon Boats: Celebrating Chinese Festivals.* Berkeley, California: Pacific View Press, 1994. **2796**

Sterling, Mary Ellen. *Presidents' Day and Martin Luther King, Jr. Day.* Westminster, California: Teacher Created Materials, 1992. **2797**

Stohs, Anita Reith. *Christian Crafts for Holidays: Hand-Shaped Art.* Torrance, California: Shining Star Publications, 1994. **2798**

Stohs, Anita Reith. *Christian Crafts from Cardboard Tubes.* Torrance, California: Shining Star Publications, 1992. **2799**

Stohs, Anita Reith. *Christian Crafts from Folded Paper.* Torrance, California: Shining Star Publications, 1994. **2800**

Stohs, Anita Reith. *Christian Crafts from Nature's Gifts.* Torrance, California: Shining Star Publications, 1994. **2801**

Stohs, Anita Reith. *Christian Crafts from Tissue Paper*. Torrance, California: Shining Star Publications, 1993. **2802**

Stohs, Anita Reith. *Christian Crafts: Yarn Art*. Torrance, California: Shining Star Publications, 1992. **2803**

Stotter, Michael. *Step into...the World of North American Indians*. New York: Lorenz Books, 1999. **2804**

Streissguth, Thomas. *Egypt*. Minneapolis, Minnesota: Carolrhoda Books, 1999. **2805**

Streissguth, Thomas. *France*. Minneapolis, Minnesota: Carolrhoda Books, 1997. **2806**

Streissguth, Thomas. *India*. Minneapolis, Minnesota: Carolrhoda Books, 1999. **2807**

Streissguth, Thomas. *Japan*. Minneapolis, Minnesota: Carolrhoda Books, 1997. **2808**

Streissguth, Thomas. *Mexico*. Minneapolis, Minnesota: Carolrhoda Books, 1997. **2809**

Streissguth, Thomas. *Russia*. Minneapolis, Minnesota: Carolrhoda Books, 1997. **2810**

Sullivan, Dianna. *Holiday Art*. Huntington Beach, California: Teacher Created Materials, 1985. **2811**

Sullivan, Dianna. *Literature Activities for Children*. Huntington Beach, California: Teacher Created Materials, 1990. **2812**

Sullivan, Dianna. *Patriotic Holidays*. Huntington Beach, California: Teacher Created Materials, 1985. **2813**

Swain, Gwenyth. *Indiana*. Minneapolis, Minnesota: Lerner Publications Co., 2002. **2814**

Swain, Ruth Freeman. *How Sweet It Is (And Was): The History of Candy*. New York: Holiday House, 2003. **2815**

Tabs, Judy. *Matzah Meals: A Passover Cookbook for Kids*. Minneapolis, Minnesota: Kar-Ben Publishing, 2004. **2953**

Tames, Richard. *Step into... Ancient Greece*. New York: Lorenz Books, 1999. **2816**

Temko, Florence. *Traditional Crafts from China*. Minneapolis, Minnesota: Lerner Publications Co., 2001. **2818**

Temko, Florence. *Traditional Crafts from Japan*. Minneapolis, Minnesota: Lerner Publications Co., 2001. **2819**

Temko, Florence. *Traditional Crafts from the Caribbean*. Minneapolis, Minnesota: Lerner Publications Co., 2001. **2817**

Temple, Bob. *Dominican Republic*. Philadelphia, Pennsylvania: Mason Crest Publishers, 2003. **2954**

Temple, Bob. *Haiti*. Philadelphia, Pennsylvania: Mason Crest Publishers, 2004. **2955**

*The Olympic Dream Primary Curriculum Guide to the Olympic Games*. Glendale, California: Griffin Publishing Group, 1997. **2664**

Thoennes, Kristin. *Nigeria*. Mankato, Minnesota: Bridgestone Books, 1999. **2820**

Thoennes, Kristin. *Russia*. Mankato, Minnesota: Bridgestone Books, 1999. **2821**

Thomas, Jennifer. *Connecting Art and Literature*. Huntington Beach, California: Teacher Created Materials, 1992. **2822**

Thompson, Stuart. *Chinese Festivals Cookbook*. Austin, Texas: Raintree Steck-Vaughn Publishers, 2001. **2824**

Thompson, Susan Conklin. *Celebrating the World of Work: Interviews and Activities*. Englewood, Colorado: Teacher Ideas Press, 2001. **2823**

Todd, Anne M. *Italian Immigrants, 1880-1920*. Mankato, Minnesota: Blue Earth Books, 2002. **2825**

Todd, Anne M. *The Ojibway*. Mankato, Minnesota: Bridgestone Books, 2003. **2826**

Todd, Anne M. *The Sioux: People of the Great Plains*. Mankato, Minnesota: Bridgestone Books, 2003. **2827**

Totten, Kathryn. *Seasonal Storytime Crafts*. Fort Atkinson, Wisconsin: Upstart Books, 2002. **2828**

Totten, Kathryn. *Storytime Crafts*. Fort Atkinson, Wisconsin: Alleyside Press, 1998. **2829**

Townsend, Sue. *Egypt*. Chicago, Illinois: Heinemann Library, 2003. **2830**

Townsend, Sue. *France.* Chicago, Illinois: Heinemann Library, 2002. **2831**

Townsend, Sue. *Germany.* Chicago, Illinois: Heinemann Library, 2002. **2832**

Townsend, Sue. *Greece.* Chicago, Illinois: Heinemann Library, 2002. **2833**

Townsend, Sue. *Indonesia.* Chicago, Illinois: Heinemann Library, 2003. **2834**

Townsend, Sue. *Russia.* Chicago, Illinois: Heinemann Library, 2003. **2835**

Townsend, Sue. *Spain.* Chicago, Illinois: Heinemann Library, 2003. **2836**

Townsend, Sue. *Thailand.* Chicago, Illinois: Heinemann Library, 2002. **2837**

Townsend, Sue. *Vegetarian Recipes from Around the World.* Chicago, Illinois: Heinemann Library, 2003. **2838**

Townsend, Sue. *Vietnam.* Chicago, Illinois: Heinemann Library, 2003. **2839**

Trottier, Maxine. *Native Crafts: Inspired by North America's First Peoples.* Niagara Falls, New York: KidsCan Press, 2000. **2840**

Turck, Mary C. *The Civil Rights Movement for Kids: A History with 21 Activities.* Chicago, Illinois: Chicago Review Press, 2000. **2956**

Verba, Joan Marie. *North Dakota.* Minneapolis, Minnesota: Lerner Publications Co., 2003. **2841**

Villios, Lynne W. *Cooking the Greek Way.* Minneapolis, Minnesota: Lerner Publications Co., 2002. **2842**

Waldee, Lynne Marie. *Cooking the French Way.* Minneapolis, Minnesota: Lerner Publications Co., 2002. **2843**

Wallace, Mary. *Make Your Own Inuksuk.* Toronto, Ontario: Greey de Pencier Books, 2001. **2844**

Wallace, Paula S. *The World of Food.* Milwaukee, Wisconsin: Gareth Stevens Publishing, 2003. **2845**

Wallace, Paula S. *The World of Holidays.* Milwaukee, Wisconsin: Gareth Stevens Publishing, 2003. **2846**

Wallace, Paula S. *The World of Birthdays.* Milwaukee, Wisconsin: Gareth Stevens Publishing, 2003. **2957**

Wallace, Paula S. *The World of Sports.* Milwaukee, Wisconsin: Gareth Stevens Publishing, 2003. **2847**

Wallner, Rosemary. *Greek Immigrants, 1890-1920.* Mankato, Minnesota: Blue Earth Books, 2002. **2980**

Wallner, Rosemary. *Japanese Immigrants, 1850-1950.* Mankato, Minnesota: Blue Earth Books, 2002. **2847**

Wallner, Rosemary. *Polish Immigrants, 1890-1920.* Mankato, Minnesota: Blue Earth Books, 2003. **2981**

Walters, Scott T. *Knights and Castles.* Westminster, California: Teacher Created Materials, 2000. **2849**

Ward, Karen. *The Young Chef's Mexican Cookbook.* New York: Crabtree Publishing Co., 2001. **2850**

Warner, J. F. *Rhode Island.* Minneapolis, Minnesota: Lerner Publications Co., 2003. **2851**

Warshaw, Hallie. *Zany Rainy Days: Indoor Ideas for Active Kids.* New York: Sterling Publishing Co., 2000. **2852**

Weatherly, Myra S. *South Carolina.* Danbury, Connecticut: Children's Press, 2002. **2853**

Weatherly, Myra S. *Tennessee.* Danbury, Connecticut: Children's Press, 2001. **2854**

Weitzman, Elizabeth. *Brazil.* Minneapolis, Minnesota: Carolrhoda Books, 1998. **2855**

Wellington, Monica. *Crepes by Suzette.* New York: Dutton Children's Books, 2004. **2958**

Weston, Reiko. *Cooking the Japanese Way.* Minneapolis, Minnesota: Lerner Publications Co., 2002. **2856**

Whitman, Sylvia. *Children of the World War II Home Front.* Minneapolis, Minnesota: Carolrhoda Books, 2001. **2860**

Whitney, Brooks. *Celebrate: Four Seasons of Holiday Fun.* Middleton, Wisconsin: Pleasant Company Publications, 1998. **2857**

Whyte, Harlinah. *England.* Milwaukee, Wisconsin: Gareth Stevens Publishing, 1997. **2861**

Whyte, Harlinah. *Russia.* Milwaukee, Wisconsin: Gareth Stevens Publishing, 1997. **2858**

Whyte, Harlinah. *Thailand.* Milwaukee, Wisconsin: Gareth Stevens Publishing, 1998. **2859**

Wiland, Adrienne. *Cook and Learn: Recipes, Songs and Activities for Children.* Westminster, California: Teacher Created Materials, 2000. **2863**

Wilkes, Angela. *The Children's Step-by-Step Cookbook.* New York: Dorling Kindersley, 1994. **2864**

Williams, Colleen Madonna Flood. *Ecuador.* Philadelphia, Pennsylvania: Mason Crest Publishers, 2003. **2959**

Williams, Colleen Madonna Flood. *Jamaica.* Philadelphia, Pennsylvania: Mason Crest Publishers, 2003. **2960**

Williams, Colleen Madonna Flood. *Suriname.* Philadelphia, Pennsylvania: Mason Crest Publishers, 2004. **2961**

Williams, Judith M. *Montana.* Danbury, Connecticut: Children's Press, 2002. **2865**

Williams, Suzanne M. *Kentucky.* Danbury, Connecticut: Children's Press, 2001. **2866**

Willis, Terry. *Romania.* Danbury, Connecticut: Children's Press, 2001. **2867**

Wilson, Laura. *How I Survived the Oregon Trail: The Journal of Jesse Adams.* New York: Beech Tree Books, 1999. **2868**

Wilson, Neil. *Egypt.* Austin, Texas: Raintree Steck-Vaughn Publishers, 2000. **2869**

Wilson, Neil. *Russia.* Austin, Texas: Raintree Steck-Vaughn Publishers, 2001. **2870**

Winget, Mary. *Cooking the North African Way.* Minneapolis, Minnesota: Lerner Publications Co., 2004. **2871**

Wood, Ira. *A Mexican Feast.* New York: The Rosen Publishing Group, 2003. **2872**

Yee, Ling. *Cooking the Chinese Way.* Minneapolis, Minnesota: Lerner Publications Co., 2002. **2873**

Yin, Saw Myat. *Myanmar.* Tarrytown, New York: Marshall Cavendish Corp., 2002. **2874**

Zalben, Jane Breskin. *Pearl's Eight Days of Chanukah.* New York: Simon & Schuster, 1998. **2875**

Zalben, Jane Breskin. *Pearl's Passover: A Family Celebration through Recipes, Crafts and Songs.* New York: Simon & Schuster, 2002. **2876**

Zalben, Jane Breskin. *To Every Season: A Family Holiday Cookbook.* New York: Simon & Schuster, 1999. **2877**

Zamojska-Hutchins, Danuta. *Cooking the Polish Way.* Minneapolis, Minnesota: Lerner Publications Co., 2002. **2878**

Zanger, Mark H. *The American Ethnic Cookbook for Students.* Phoenix, Arizona: Oryx Press, 2001. **2879**

Zimmerman, Susan A. *Quilts.* Westminster, California: Teacher Created Materials, 1999. **2880**

Zoe, Harris. *Pinatas and Smiling Skeletons: Celebrating Mexican Festivals.* Berkeley, California: Pacific View Press, 1998. **2881**

# About the Author

MARY ANNE PILGER is the author of previous editions of this book and several editions of *Science Experiments Index for Young People*, all from Libraries Unlimited. She lives in New York.

WITHDRAWN